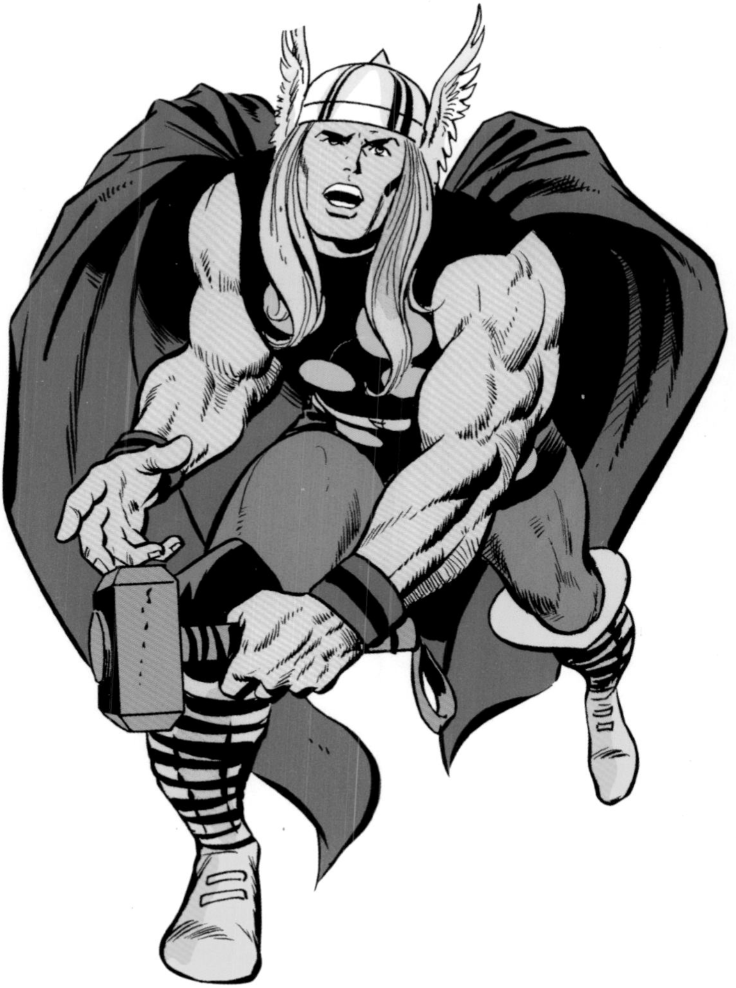

THE MIGHTY THOR

IN THE SHADO... 3

STA...

POCKET BOOK The Mighty Thor: In The Shadow Of Mangog

The Mighty Thor: In The Shadow Of Mangog. Marvel Pocketbook Vol. 2. Contains material originally published in magazine form as The Mighty Thor #189-198. First printing 2014. Published by Panini Publishing, a division of Panini UK Limited. Mike Riddell, Managing Director. Alan O'Keefe, Managing Editor. Mark Irvine, Production Manager. Marco M. Lupoi, Publishing Director Europe. Samuel Taylor, Editorial Assistant. Angela Hart & Alex Foot, Designers. Office of publication: Brockbourne House, 77 Mount Ephraim, Tunbridge Wells, Kent TN4 8BS. Licensed by Marvel Characters B.V. www.marvel. com. All rights reserved. No similarity between any of the names, characters, persons and/or institutions in this edition with those of any living or dead person or institution is intended, and any such similarity which may exist is purely coincidental. This publication may not be sold, except by authorised dealers, and is sold subject to the condition that it shall not be sold or distributed with any part of its cover or markings removed, nor in a mutilated condition.

Printed in the UK.

ISBN: 978-1-84653-191-0

MARVEL
marvel.com
© 2014 MARVEL

FSC

MIX
Paper from
responsible sources
FSC® C002386

THE MIGHTY THOR

IN THE SHADOW OF MANGOG

CONTENTS

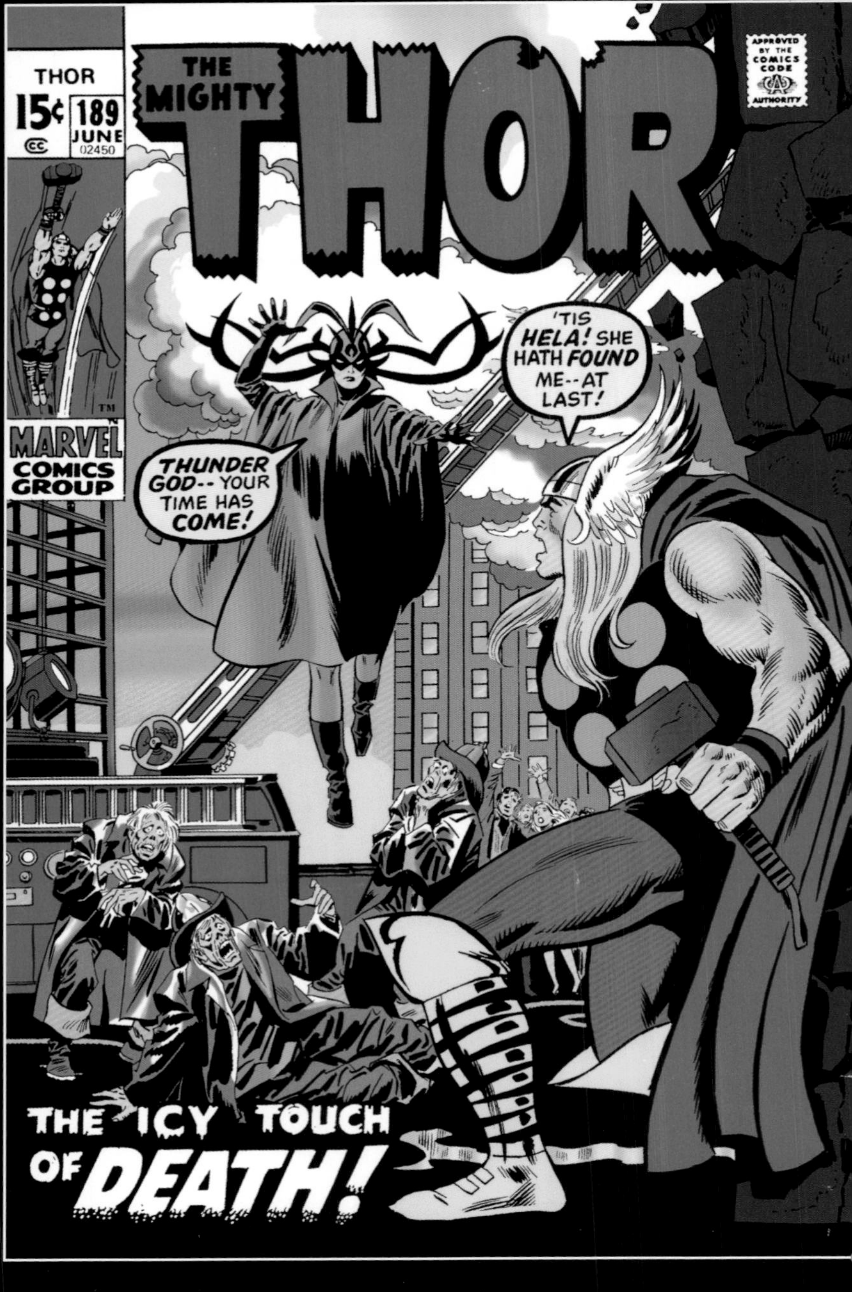
THOR
15¢
189
JUNE
02450
THE MIGHTY THOR
APPROVED BY THE COMICS CODE AUTHORITY
MARVEL COMICS GROUP
'TIS HELA! SHE HATH FOUND ME--AT LAST!
THUNDER GOD-- YOUR TIME HAS COME!
THE ICY TOUCH OF DEATH!

THE MIGHTY THOR!™
THE ICY TOUCH OF DEATH!
HELA, THE MERCILESS, ETERNAL GODDESS OF DEATH, HAS BEEN DEFEATED IN HER PLAN TO PUT AN END TO ALL LIVING THINGS! NOW, THE DEEPEST GLOOM SETTLES OVER ASGARD-- FOR, ALL KNOW FULL WELL--HELA SHALL SEEK REVENGE!
HELA HATH FAILED TO CONQUER ODIN--
THUS, SHE SHALL STRIKE AT THE ONE NEAREST AND DEAREST TO ME.
SHE SHALL SEEK TO SLAY --THE MIGHTY THOR!
NOW STAND WE HERE-- HELPLESS
OUR WEAPONS ARE USELESS 'GAINST THE POWER OF HELA
MY PRINCE--MY LORD-- MY TRUE AND CONSTANT LOVE--
I'LL PRAY FOR THEE! I'LL FIGHT FOR THEE! AND HAPPILY WOULD I DIE FOR THEE! FOR, THOU ART ALL TO ME
I BEG THEE-- HUSH, MY LADY! THY LOVING WORDS DO BUT TEAR MY HEART ANEW
THE THUNDER GOD IS DOOMED!
SO BE IT
SCRIPTED IN SPARKLING SPLENDOR, BY: STAN LEE
DRAWN IN DAZZLING DRAMA, BY: JOHN BUSCEMA
EMBELLISHED WITH EXOTIC ELAN, BY: JOE SINNOTT
LETTERED WITH A SCRATCHY PENPOINT, BY: SAM ROSEN
607 Z

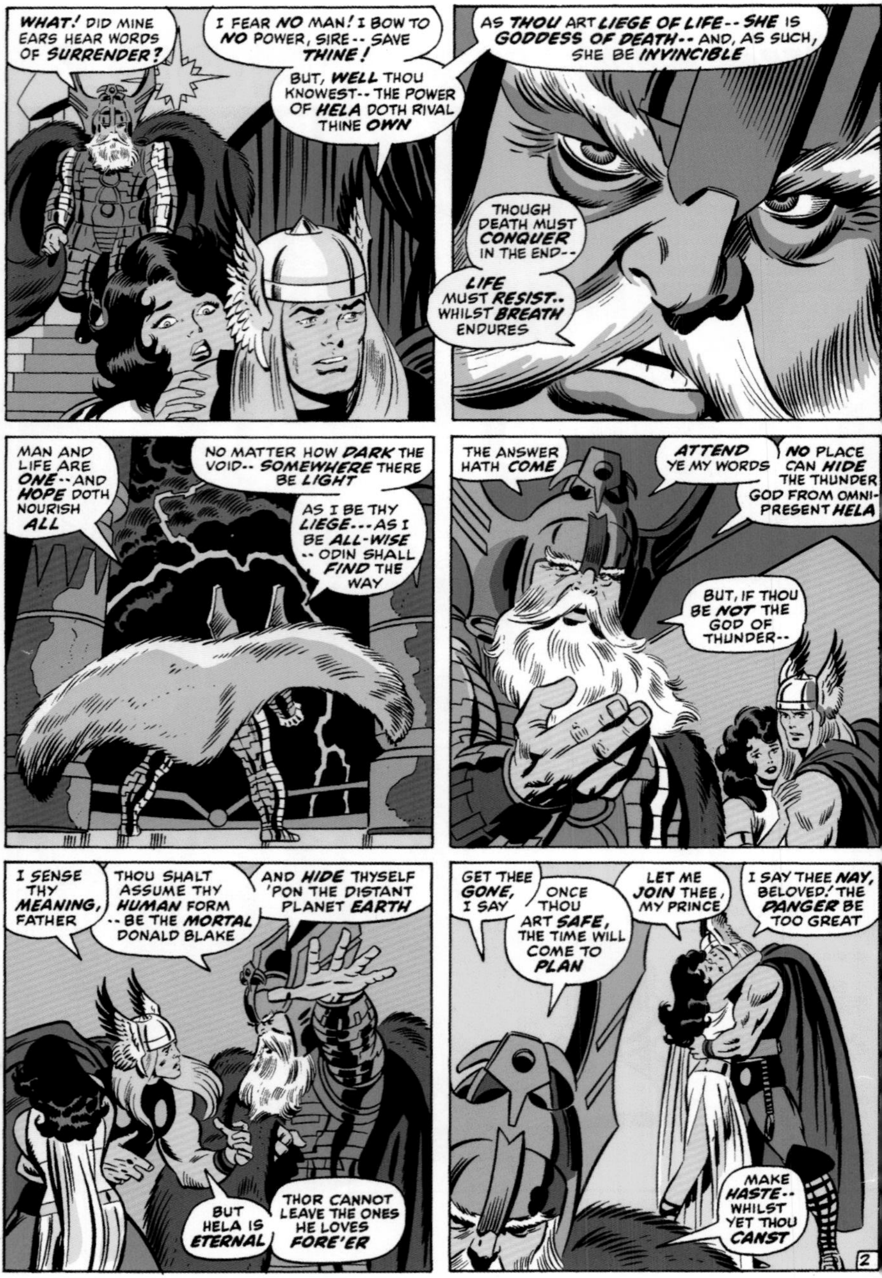
WHAT! DID MINE EARS HEAR WORDS OF SURRENDER?
I FEAR NO MAN! I BOW TO NO POWER, SIRE -- SAVE THINE!
BUT, WELL THOU KNOWEST -- THE POWER OF HELA DOTH RIVAL THINE OWN
AS THOU ART LIEGE OF LIFE -- SHE IS GODDESS OF DEATH -- AND, AS SUCH, SHE BE INVINCIBLE
THOUGH DEATH MUST CONQUER IN THE END --
LIFE MUST RESIST.. WHILST BREATH ENDURES
MAN AND LIFE ARE ONE -- AND HOPE DOTH NOURISH ALL
NO MATTER HOW DARK THE VOID -- SOMEWHERE THERE BE LIGHT
AS I BE THY LIEGE --- AS I BE ALL-WISE -- ODIN SHALL FIND THE WAY
THE ANSWER HATH COME
ATTEND YE MY WORDS
NO PLACE CAN HIDE THE THUNDER GOD FROM OMNI-PRESENT HELA
BUT, IF THOU BE NOT THE GOD OF THUNDER --
I SENSE THY MEANING, FATHER
THOU SHALT ASSUME THY HUMAN FORM -- BE THE MORTAL DONALD BLAKE
AND HIDE THYSELF 'PON THE DISTANT PLANET EARTH
BUT HELA IS ETERNAL
THOR CANNOT LEAVE THE ONES HE LOVES FORE'ER
GET THEE GONE, I SAY
ONCE THOU ART SAFE, THE TIME WILL COME TO PLAN
LET ME JOIN THEE, MY PRINCE
I SAY THEE NAY, BELOVED! THE DANGER BE TOO GREAT
MAKE HASTE -- WHILST YET THOU CANST
2

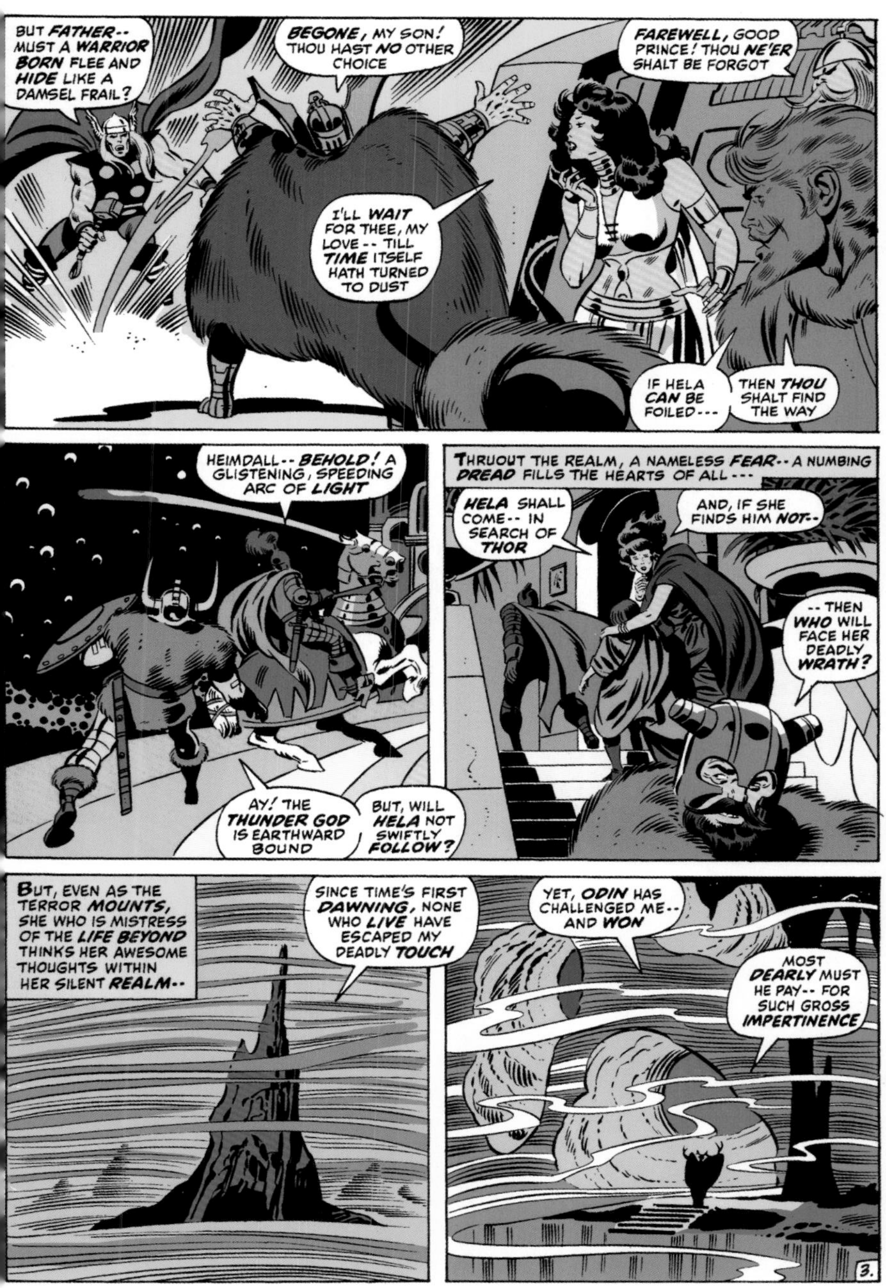

BUT FATHER-- MUST A WARRIOR BORN FLEE AND HIDE LIKE A DAMSEL FRAIL?
BEGONE, MY SON! THOU HAST NO OTHER CHOICE
FAREWELL, GOOD PRINCE! THOU NE'ER SHALT BE FORGOT
I'LL WAIT FOR THEE, MY LOVE -- TILL TIME ITSELF HATH TURNED TO DUST
IF HELA CAN BE FOILED---
THEN THOU SHALT FIND THE WAY
HEIMDALL-- BEHOLD! A GLISTENING, SPEEDING ARC OF LIGHT
AY! THE THUNDER GOD IS EARTHWARD BOUND
BUT, WILL HELA NOT SWIFTLY FOLLOW?
THRUOUT THE REALM, A NAMELESS FEAR-- A NUMBING DREAD FILLS THE HEARTS OF ALL---
HELA SHALL COME-- IN SEARCH OF THOR
AND, IF SHE FINDS HIM NOT--
-- THEN WHO WILL FACE HER DEADLY WRATH?
BUT, EVEN AS THE TERROR MOUNTS, SHE WHO IS MISTRESS OF THE LIFE BEYOND THINKS HER AWESOME THOUGHTS WITHIN HER SILENT REALM--
SINCE TIME'S FIRST DAWNING, NONE WHO LIVE HAVE ESCAPED MY DEADLY TOUCH
YET, ODIN HAS CHALLENGED ME-- AND WON
MOST DEARLY MUST HE PAY-- FOR SUCH GROSS IMPERTINENCE
3.

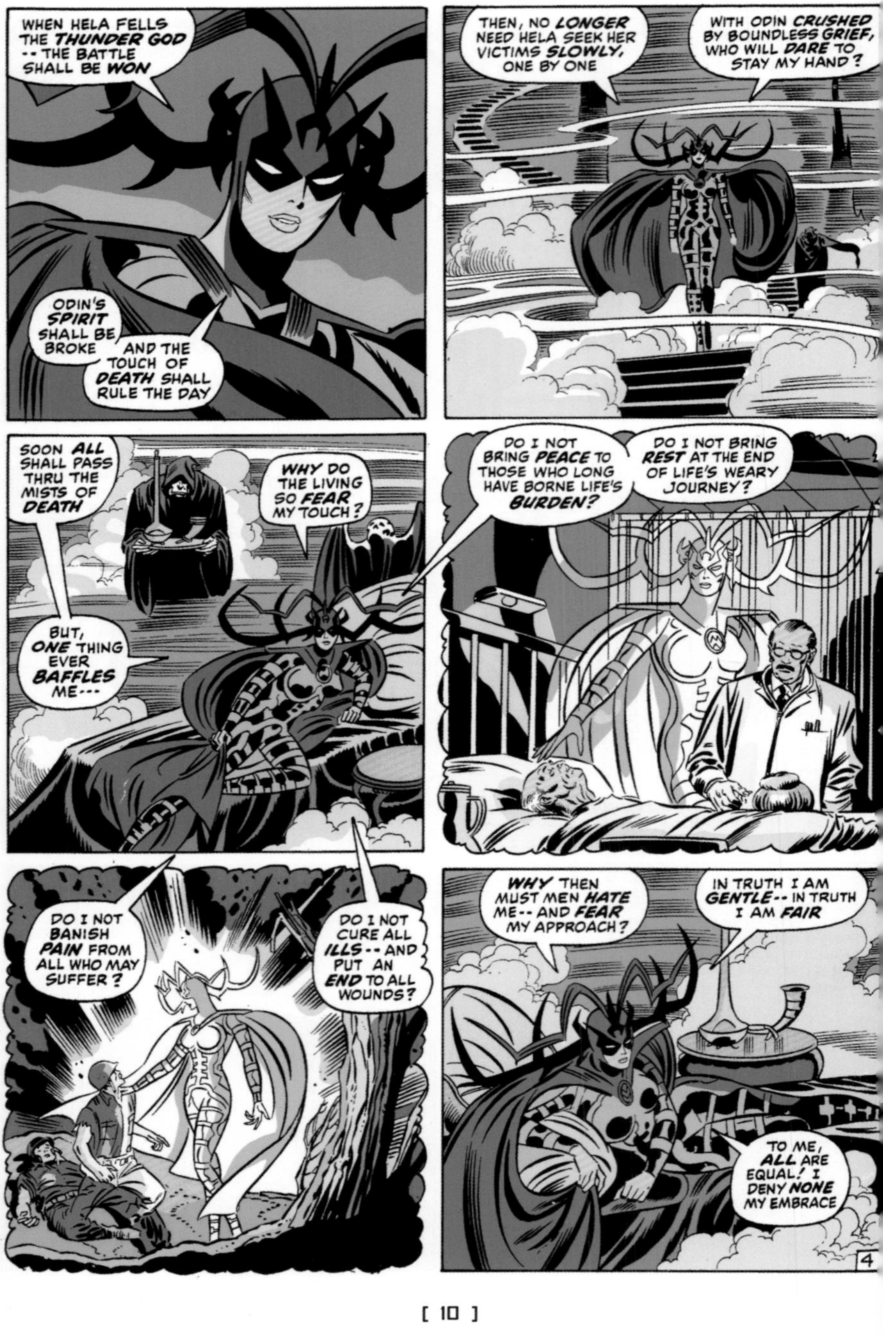
WHEN HELA FELLS THE THUNDER GOD -- THE BATTLE SHALL BE WON
ODIN'S SPIRIT SHALL BE BROKE
AND THE TOUCH OF DEATH SHALL RULE THE DAY
THEN, NO LONGER NEED HELA SEEK HER VICTIMS SLOWLY, ONE BY ONE
WITH ODIN CRUSHED BY BOUNDLESS GRIEF, WHO WILL DARE TO STAY MY HAND?
SOON ALL SHALL PASS THRU THE MISTS OF DEATH
BUT, ONE THING EVER BAFFLES ME---
WHY DO THE LIVING SO FEAR MY TOUCH?
DO I NOT BRING PEACE TO THOSE WHO LONG HAVE BORNE LIFE'S BURDEN?
DO I NOT BRING REST AT THE END OF LIFE'S WEARY JOURNEY?
DO I NOT BANISH PAIN FROM ALL WHO MAY SUFFER?
DO I NOT CURE ALL ILLS -- AND PUT AN END TO ALL WOUNDS?
WHY THEN MUST MEN HATE ME -- AND FEAR MY APPROACH?
IN TRUTH I AM GENTLE -- IN TRUTH I AM FAIR
TO ME, ALL ARE EQUAL! I DENY NONE MY EMBRACE
4

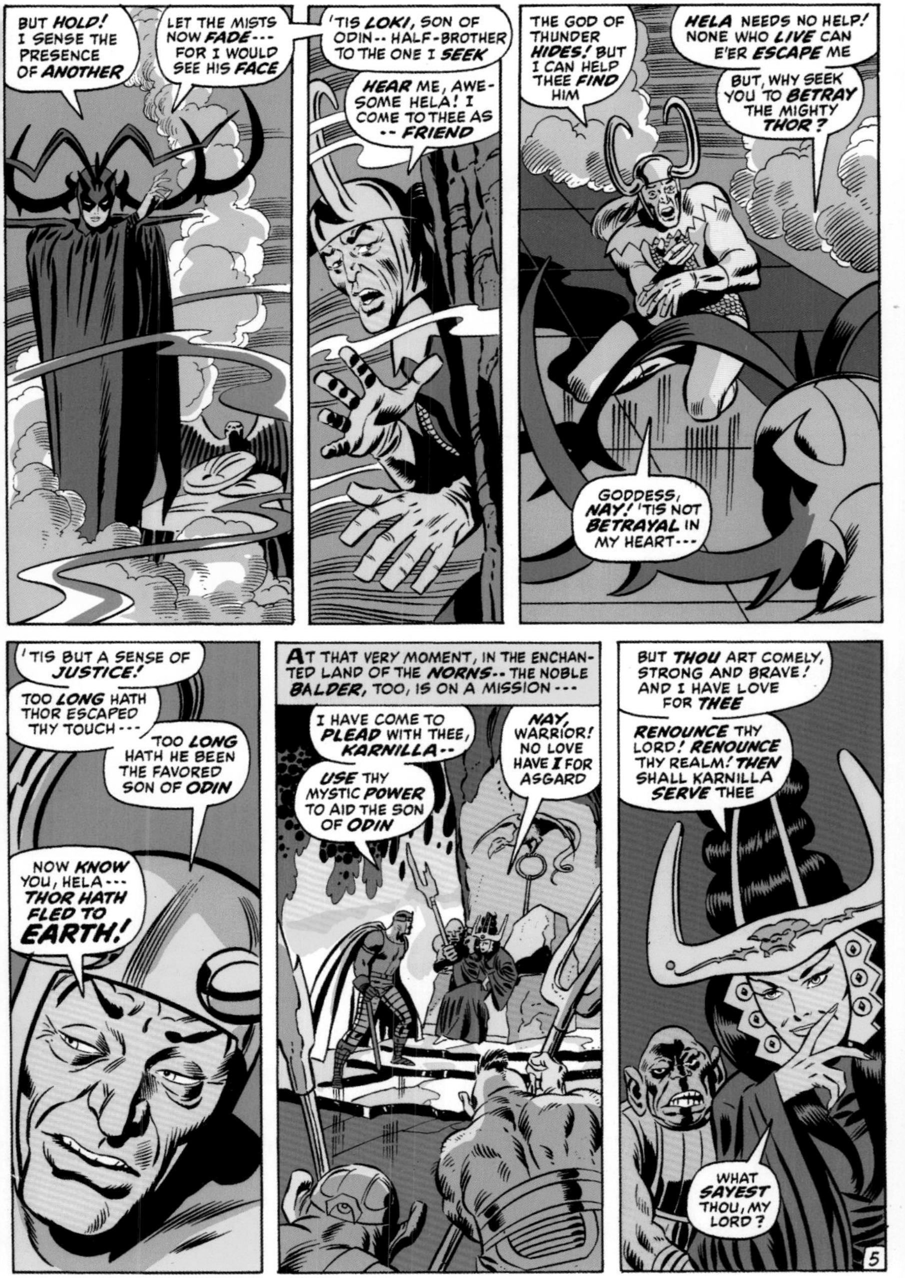
BUT HOLD! I SENSE THE PRESENCE OF ANOTHER
LET THE MISTS NOW FADE--- FOR I WOULD SEE HIS FACE
'TIS LOKI, SON OF ODIN -- HALF-BROTHER TO THE ONE I SEEK
HEAR ME, AWESOME HELA! I COME TO THEE AS -- FRIEND
THE GOD OF THUNDER HIDES! BUT I CAN HELP THEE FIND HIM
HELA NEEDS NO HELP! NONE WHO LIVE CAN E'ER ESCAPE ME
BUT, WHY SEEK YOU TO BETRAY THE MIGHTY THOR?
GODDESS, NAY! 'TIS NOT BETRAYAL IN MY HEART---
'TIS BUT A SENSE OF JUSTICE!
TOO LONG HATH THOR ESCAPED THY TOUCH---
TOO LONG HATH HE BEEN THE FAVORED SON OF ODIN
NOW KNOW YOU, HELA--- THOR HATH FLED TO EARTH!
AT THAT VERY MOMENT, IN THE ENCHANTED LAND OF THE NORNS-- THE NOBLE BALDER, TOO, IS ON A MISSION---
I HAVE COME TO PLEAD WITH THEE, KARNILLA--
USE THY MYSTIC POWER TO AID THE SON OF ODIN
NAY, WARRIOR! NO LOVE HAVE I FOR ASGARD
BUT THOU ART COMELY, STRONG AND BRAVE! AND I HAVE LOVE FOR THEE
RENOUNCE THY LORD! RENOUNCE THY REALM! THEN SHALL KARNILLA SERVE THEE
WHAT SAYEST THOU, MY LORD?
5

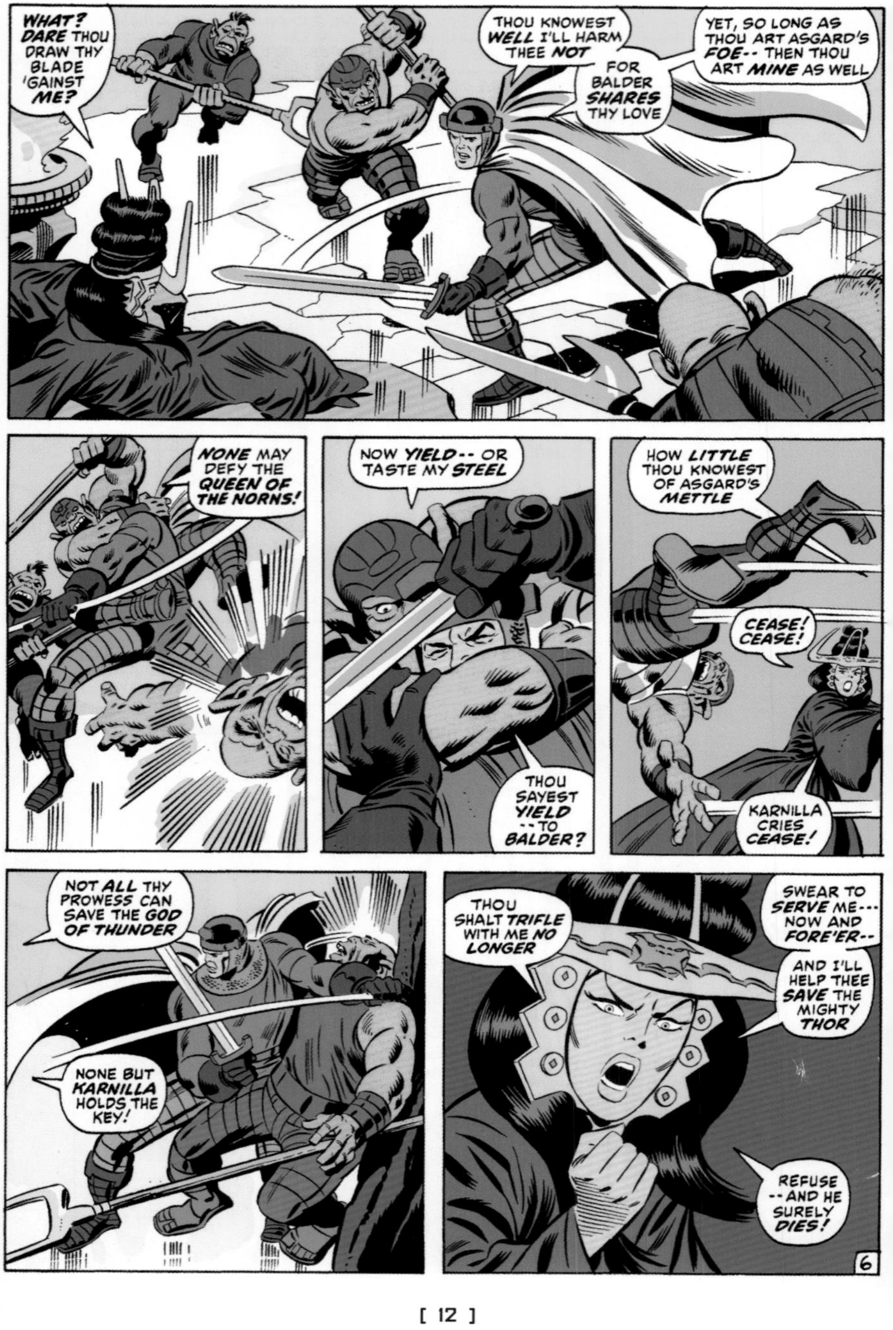
WHAT? DARE THOU DRAW THY BLADE 'GAINST ME?
THOU KNOWEST WELL I'LL HARM THEE NOT
FOR BALDER SHARES THY LOVE
YET, SO LONG AS THOU ART ASGARD'S FOE-- THEN THOU ART MINE AS WELL
NONE MAY DEFY THE QUEEN OF THE NORNS!
NOW YIELD-- OR TASTE MY STEEL
THOU SAYEST YIELD --TO BALDER?
HOW LITTLE THOU KNOWEST OF ASGARD'S METTLE
CEASE! CEASE!
KARNILLA CRIES CEASE!
NOT ALL THY PROWESS CAN SAVE THE GOD OF THUNDER
NONE BUT KARNILLA HOLDS THE KEY!
THOU SHALT TRIFLE WITH ME NO LONGER
SWEAR TO SERVE ME--- NOW AND FORE'ER--
AND I'LL HELP THEE SAVE THE MIGHTY THOR
REFUSE --AND HE SURELY DIES!
6

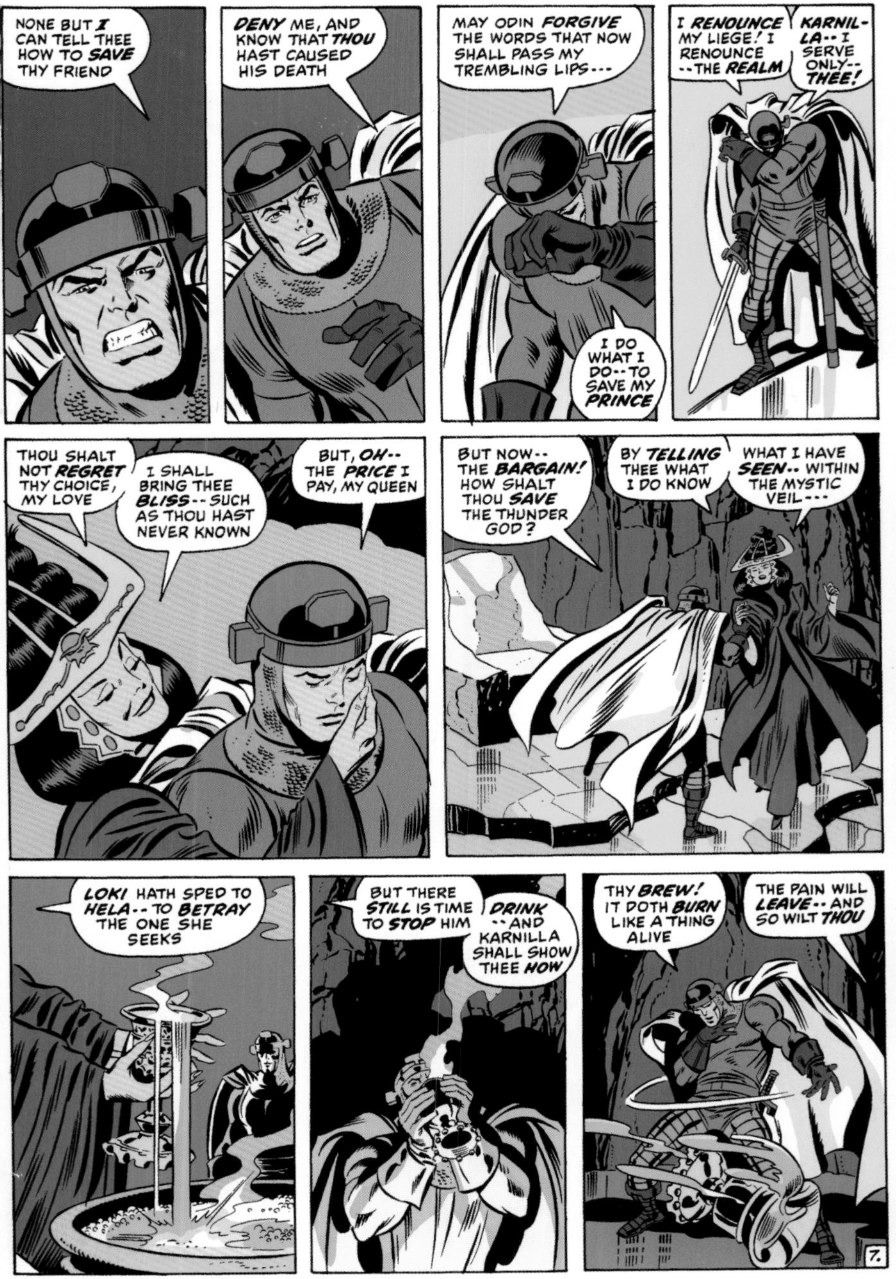
NONE BUT I CAN TELL THEE HOW TO SAVE THY FRIEND
DENY ME, AND KNOW THAT THOU HAST CAUSED HIS DEATH
MAY ODIN FORGIVE THE WORDS THAT NOW SHALL PASS MY TREMBLING LIPS---
I DO WHAT I DO--TO SAVE MY PRINCE
I RENOUNCE MY LIEGE! I RENOUNCE --THE REALM
KARNIL-LA--I SERVE ONLY--THEE!
THOU SHALT NOT REGRET THY CHOICE, MY LOVE
I SHALL BRING THEE BLISS--SUCH AS THOU HAST NEVER KNOWN
BUT, OH--THE PRICE I PAY, MY QUEEN
BUT NOW--THE BARGAIN! HOW SHALT THOU SAVE THE THUNDER GOD?
BY TELLING THEE WHAT I DO KNOW
WHAT I HAVE SEEN--WITHIN THE MYSTIC VEIL---
LOKI HATH SPED TO HELA--TO BETRAY THE ONE SHE SEEKS
BUT THERE STILL IS TIME TO STOP HIM
DRINK --AND KARNILLA SHALL SHOW THEE HOW
THY BREW! IT DOTH BURN LIKE A THING ALIVE
THE PAIN WILL LEAVE--AND SO WILT THOU
7.

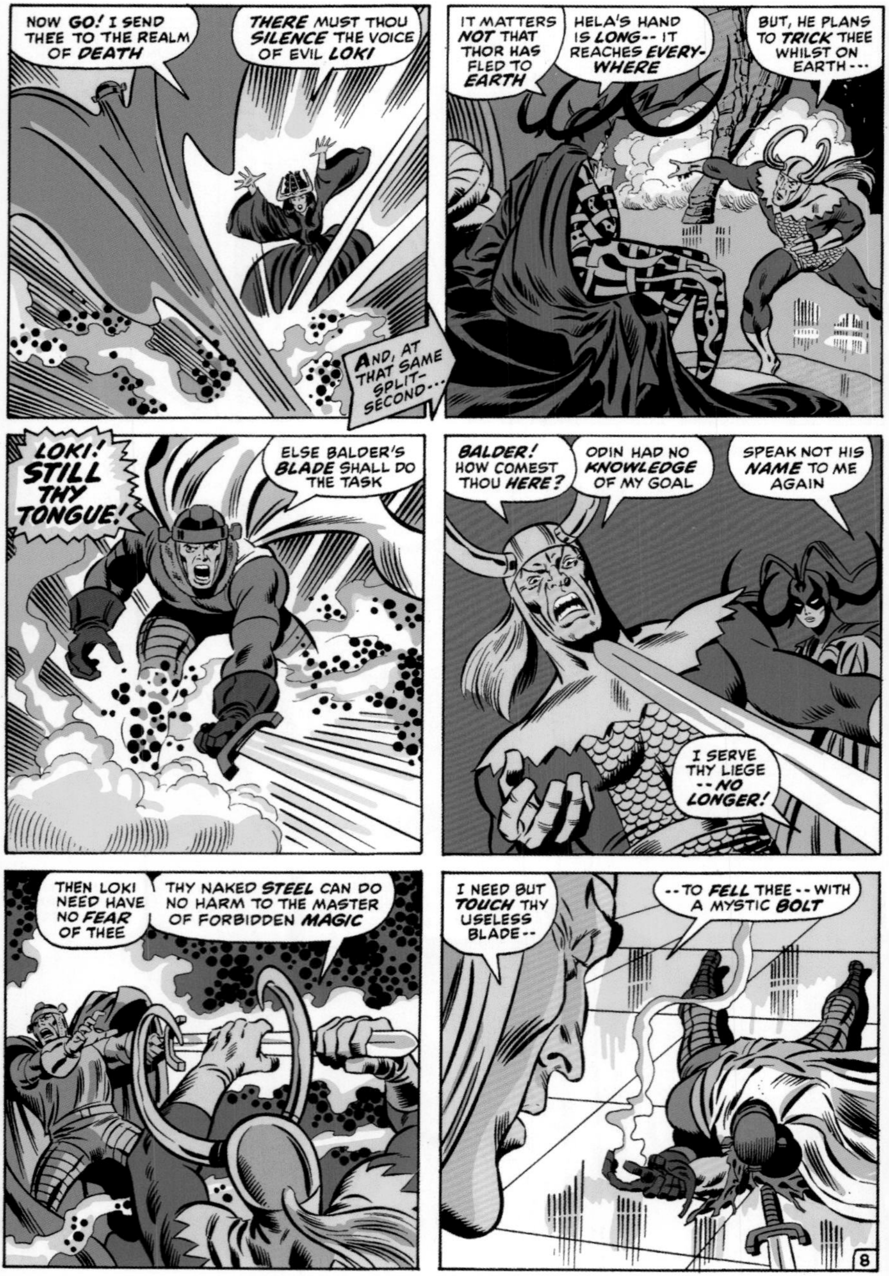
NOW GO! I SEND THEE TO THE REALM OF DEATH
THERE MUST THOU SILENCE THE VOICE OF EVIL LOKI
AND, AT THAT SAME SPLIT-SECOND...
IT MATTERS NOT THAT THOR HAS FLED TO EARTH
HELA'S HAND IS LONG-- IT REACHES EVERY-WHERE
BUT, HE PLANS TO TRICK THEE WHILST ON EARTH---
LOKI! STILL THY TONGUE!
ELSE BALDER'S BLADE SHALL DO THE TASK
BALDER! HOW COMEST THOU HERE?
ODIN HAD NO KNOWLEDGE OF MY GOAL
SPEAK NOT HIS NAME TO ME AGAIN
I SERVE THY LIEGE --NO LONGER!
THEN LOKI NEED HAVE NO FEAR OF THEE
THY NAKED STEEL CAN DO NO HARM TO THE MASTER OF FORBIDDEN MAGIC
I NEED BUT TOUCH THY USELESS BLADE--
--TO FELL THEE--WITH A MYSTIC BOLT
8

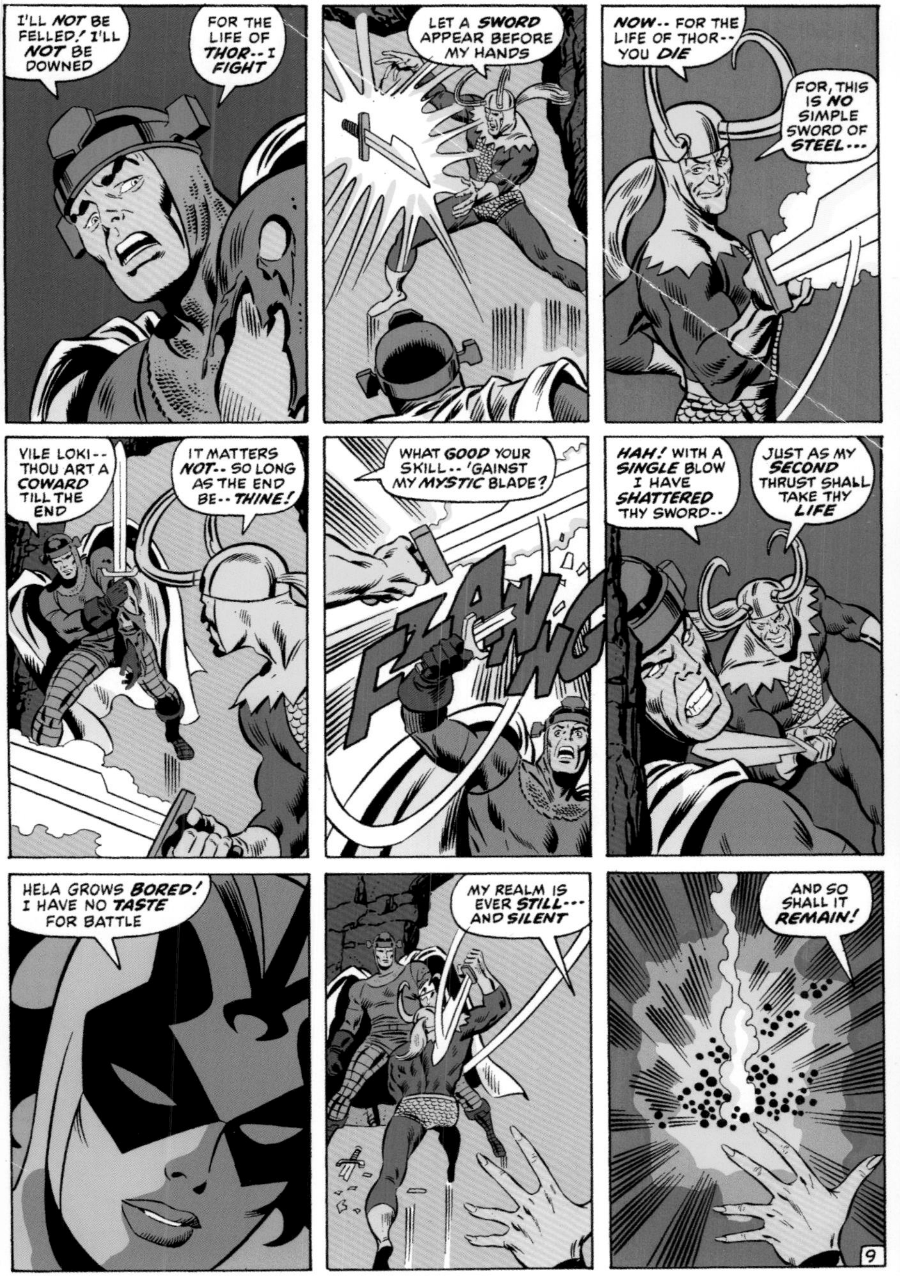
I'LL NOT BE FELLED! I'LL NOT BE DOWNED
FOR THE LIFE OF THOR-- I FIGHT
LET A SWORD APPEAR BEFORE MY HANDS
NOW-- FOR THE LIFE OF THOR-- YOU DIE
FOR, THIS IS NO SIMPLE SWORD OF STEEL---
VILE LOKI-- THOU ART A COWARD TILL THE END
IT MATTERS NOT-- SO LONG AS THE END BE-- THINE!
WHAT GOOD YOUR SKILL-- 'GAINST MY MYSTIC BLADE?
FZANNG
HAH! WITH A SINGLE BLOW I HAVE SHATTERED THY SWORD--
JUST AS MY SECOND THRUST SHALL TAKE THY LIFE
HELA GROWS BORED! I HAVE NO TASTE FOR BATTLE
MY REALM IS EVER STILL--- AND SILENT
AND SO SHALL IT REMAIN!
9

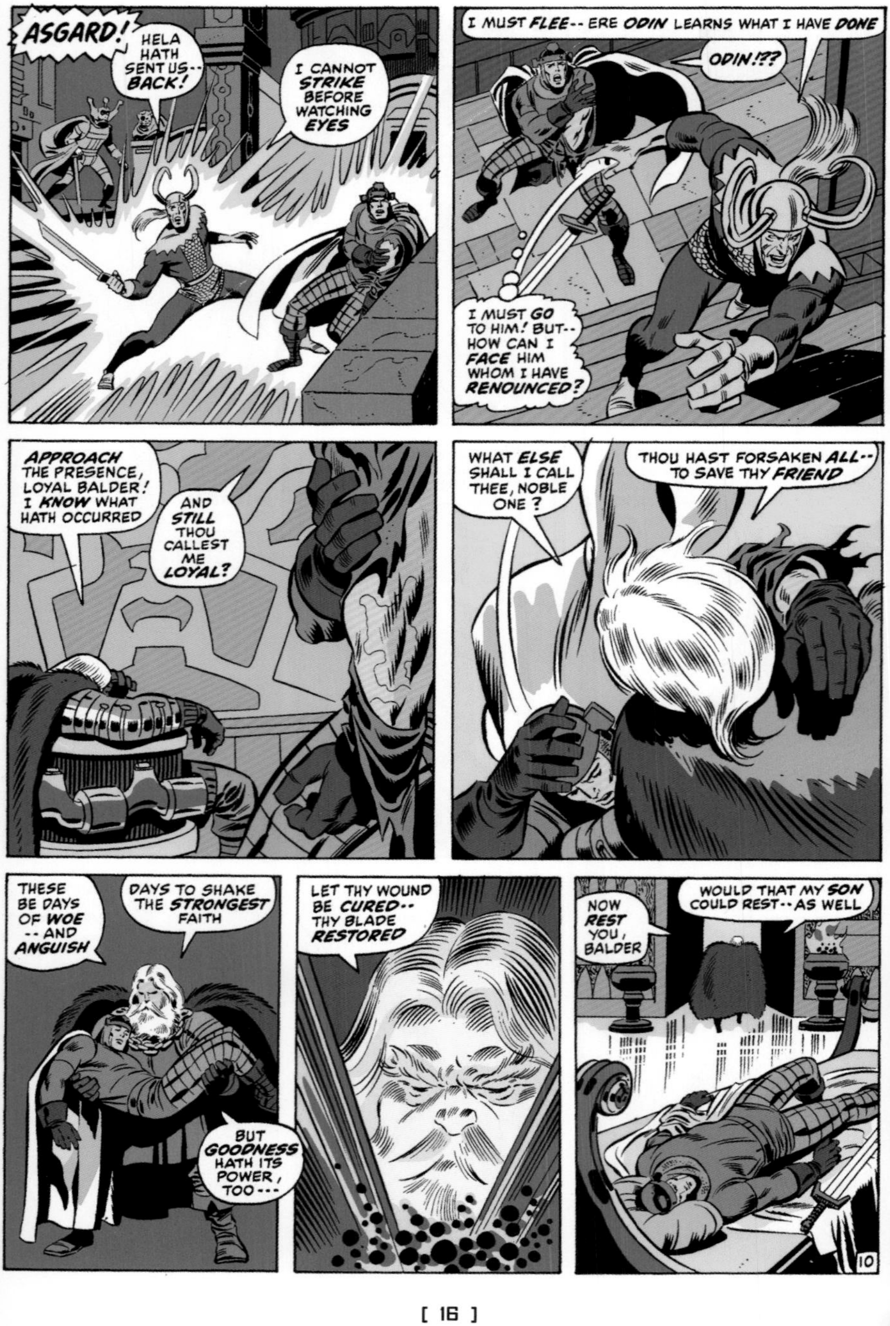

ASGARD!
HELA HATH SENT US-- BACK!
I CANNOT STRIKE BEFORE WATCHING EYES
I MUST FLEE-- ERE ODIN LEARNS WHAT I HAVE DONE
ODIN!??
I MUST GO TO HIM! BUT-- HOW CAN I FACE HIM WHOM I HAVE RENOUNCED?
APPROACH THE PRESENCE, LOYAL BALDER! I KNOW WHAT HATH OCCURRED
AND STILL THOU CALLEST ME LOYAL?
WHAT ELSE SHALL I CALL THEE, NOBLE ONE?
THOU HAST FORSAKEN ALL-- TO SAVE THY FRIEND
THESE BE DAYS OF WOE -- AND ANGUISH
DAYS TO SHAKE THE STRONGEST FAITH
BUT GOODNESS HATH ITS POWER, TOO---
LET THY WOUND BE CURED-- THY BLADE RESTORED
NOW REST YOU, BALDER
WOULD THAT MY SON COULD REST-- AS WELL
10

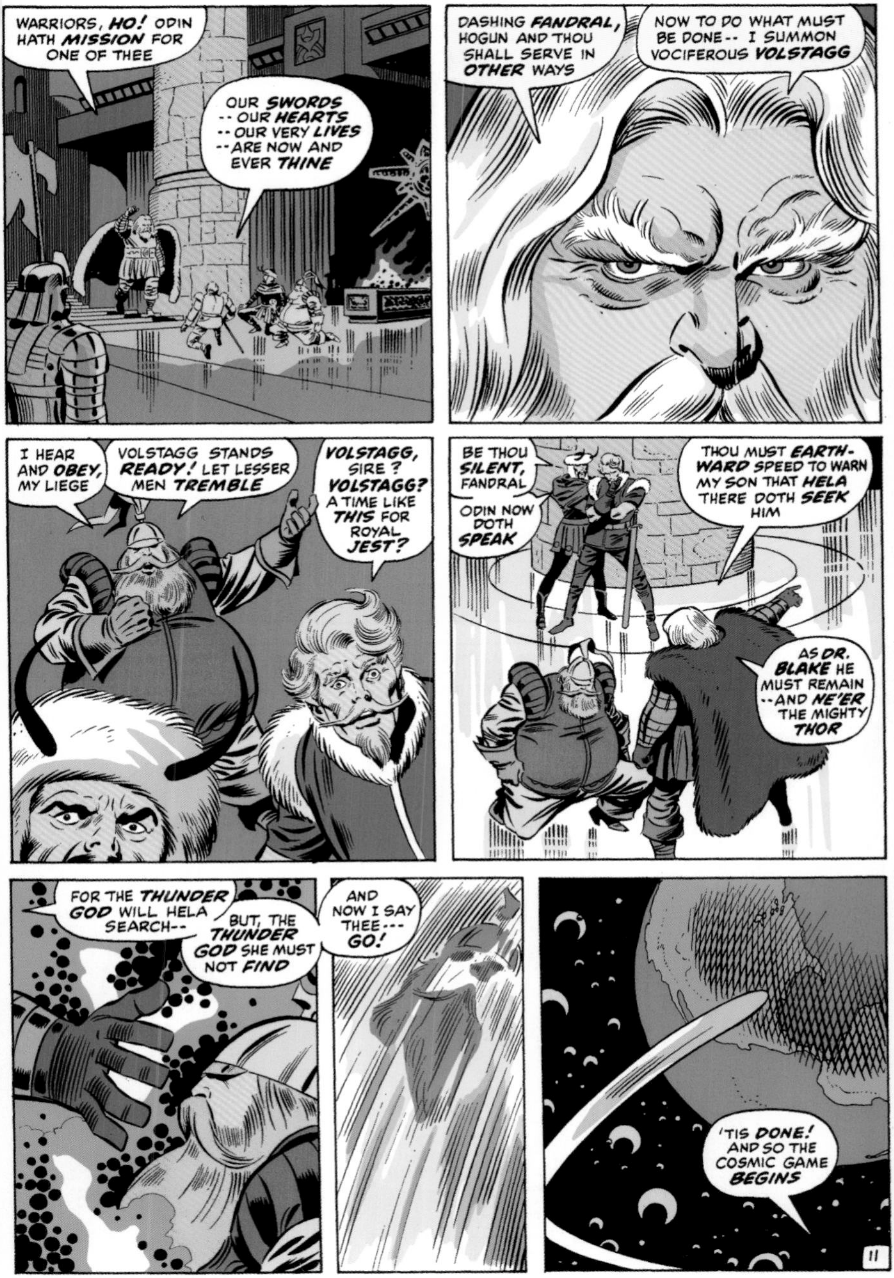
WARRIORS, HO! ODIN HATH MISSION FOR ONE OF THEE
OUR SWORDS -- OUR HEARTS -- OUR VERY LIVES --ARE NOW AND EVER THINE
DASHING FANDRAL, HOGUN AND THOU SHALL SERVE IN OTHER WAYS
NOW TO DO WHAT MUST BE DONE -- I SUMMON VOCIFEROUS VOLSTAGG
I HEAR AND OBEY, MY LIEGE
VOLSTAGG STANDS READY! LET LESSER MEN TREMBLE
VOLSTAGG, SIRE? VOLSTAGG? A TIME LIKE THIS FOR ROYAL JEST?
BE THOU SILENT, FANDRAL
ODIN NOW DOTH SPEAK
THOU MUST EARTH-WARD SPEED TO WARN MY SON THAT HELA THERE DOTH SEEK HIM
AS DR. BLAKE HE MUST REMAIN --AND NE'ER THE MIGHTY THOR
FOR THE THUNDER GOD WILL HELA SEARCH--
BUT, THE THUNDER GOD SHE MUST NOT FIND
AND NOW I SAY THEE--- GO!
'TIS DONE! AND SO THE COSMIC GAME BEGINS
11

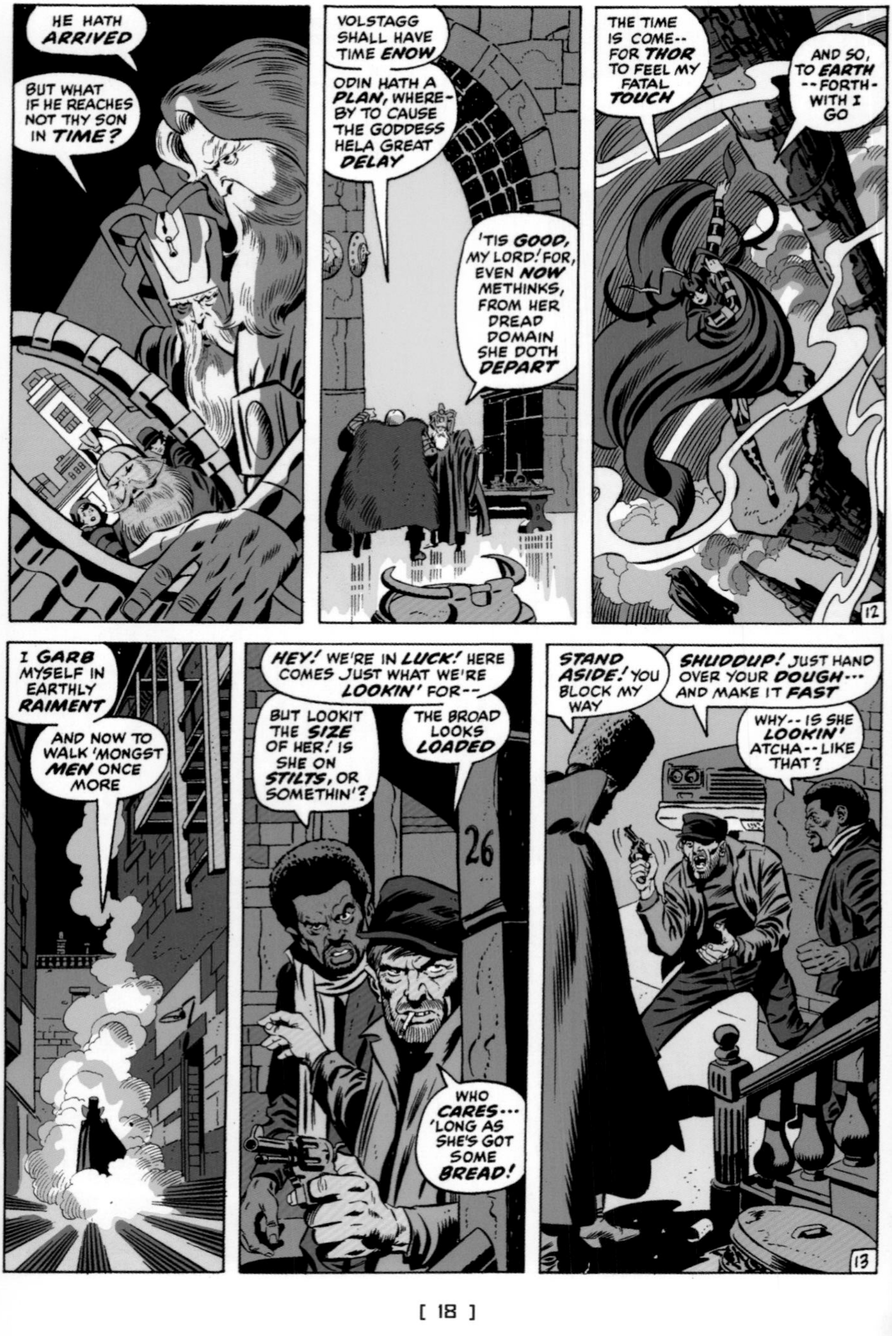
HE HATH ARRIVED
BUT WHAT IF HE REACHES NOT THY SON IN TIME?
VOLSTAGG SHALL HAVE TIME ENOW
ODIN HATH A PLAN, WHEREBY TO CAUSE THE GODDESS HELA GREAT DELAY
'TIS GOOD, MY LORD! FOR, EVEN NOW METHINKS, FROM HER DREAD DOMAIN SHE DOTH DEPART
THE TIME IS COME-- FOR THOR TO FEEL MY FATAL TOUCH
AND SO, TO EARTH --FORTH-WITH I GO
12
I GARB MYSELF IN EARTHLY RAIMENT
AND NOW TO WALK 'MONGST MEN ONCE MORE
HEY! WE'RE IN LUCK! HERE COMES JUST WHAT WE'RE LOOKIN' FOR--
BUT LOOKIT THE SIZE OF HER! IS SHE ON STILTS, OR SOMETHIN'?
THE BROAD LOOKS LOADED
26
WHO CARES... 'LONG AS SHE'S GOT SOME BREAD!
STAND ASIDE! YOU BLOCK MY WAY
SHUDDUP! JUST HAND OVER YOUR DOUGH--- AND MAKE IT FAST
WHY-- IS SHE LOOKIN' ATCHA-- LIKE THAT?
13

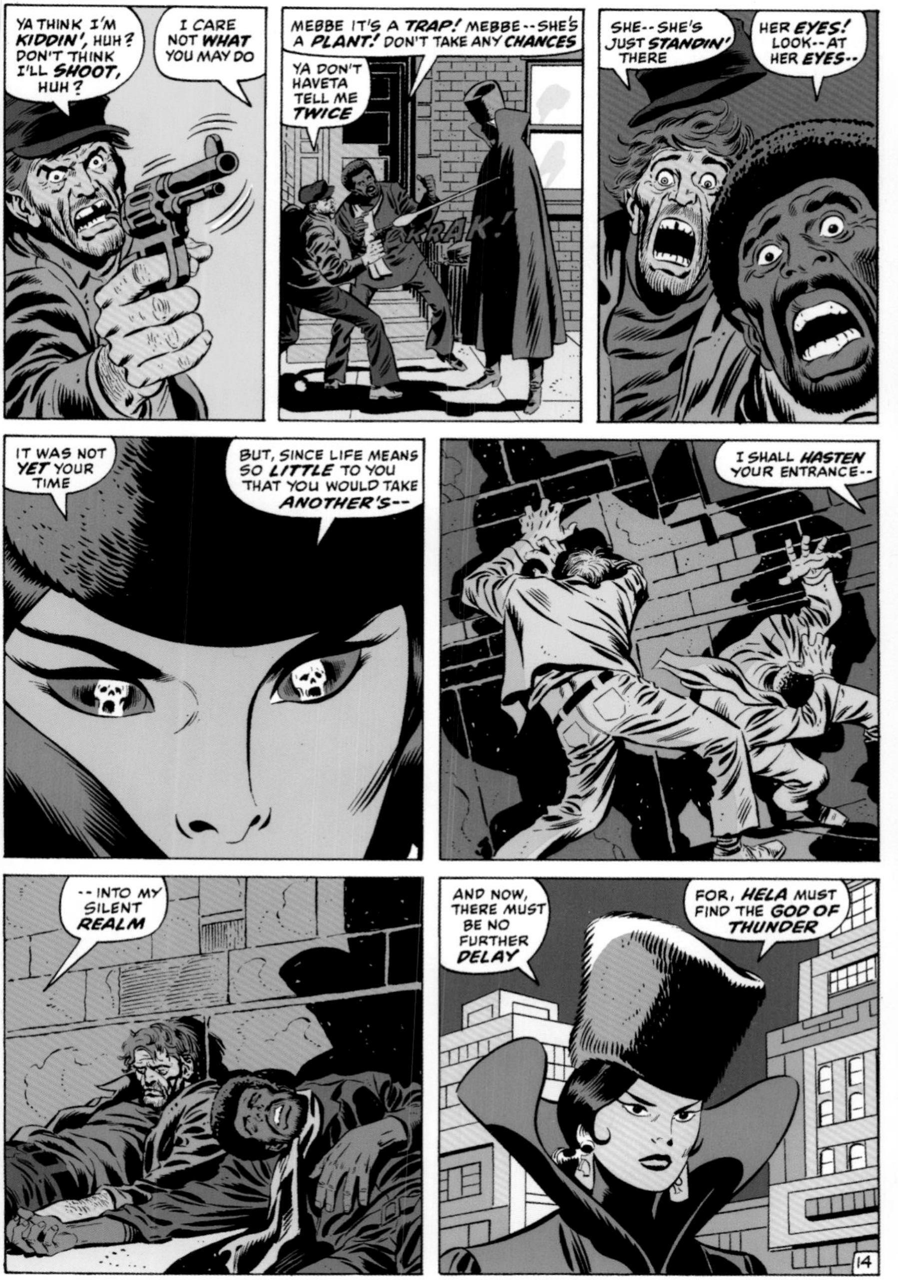
YA THINK I'M KIDDIN', HUH? DON'T THINK I'LL SHOOT, HUH?
I CARE NOT WHAT YOU MAY DO
MEBBE IT'S A TRAP! MEBBE--SHE'S A PLANT! DON'T TAKE ANY CHANCES
YA DON'T HAVETA TELL ME TWICE
KRAK!
SHE--SHE'S JUST STANDIN' THERE
HER EYES! LOOK--AT HER EYES--
IT WAS NOT YET YOUR TIME
BUT, SINCE LIFE MEANS SO LITTLE TO YOU THAT YOU WOULD TAKE ANOTHER'S--
I SHALL HASTEN YOUR ENTRANCE--
--INTO MY SILENT REALM
AND NOW, THERE MUST BE NO FURTHER DELAY
FOR, HELA MUST FIND THE GOD OF THUNDER
14

EVEN THE MOST HUMBLE BEAST *TREMBLES* AT MY PRESENCE

AT *HELA,* WHO IS THE FINAL *FRIEND* OF ALL WHO LIVE

HE IS IN A FAR *DISTANT* PART OF THIS TINY PLANET

BUT *HOLD!* AT LAST I *SENSE* THE ONE I SEEK

BUT, TIME AND SPACE MEAN *NAUGHT* TO ME

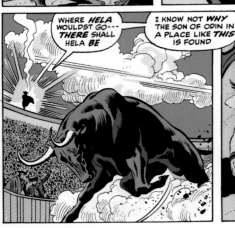

WHERE *HELA* WOULDST GO--- *THERE* SHALL HELA *BE*

I KNOW NOT *WHY* THE SON OF ODIN IN A PLACE LIKE *THIS* IS FOUND

BUT NOT FOR *ME* IS WHY OR WHERE- FORE---

DEATH NO QUESTIONS ASKS-- NOR *ANSWERS* GIVES

15

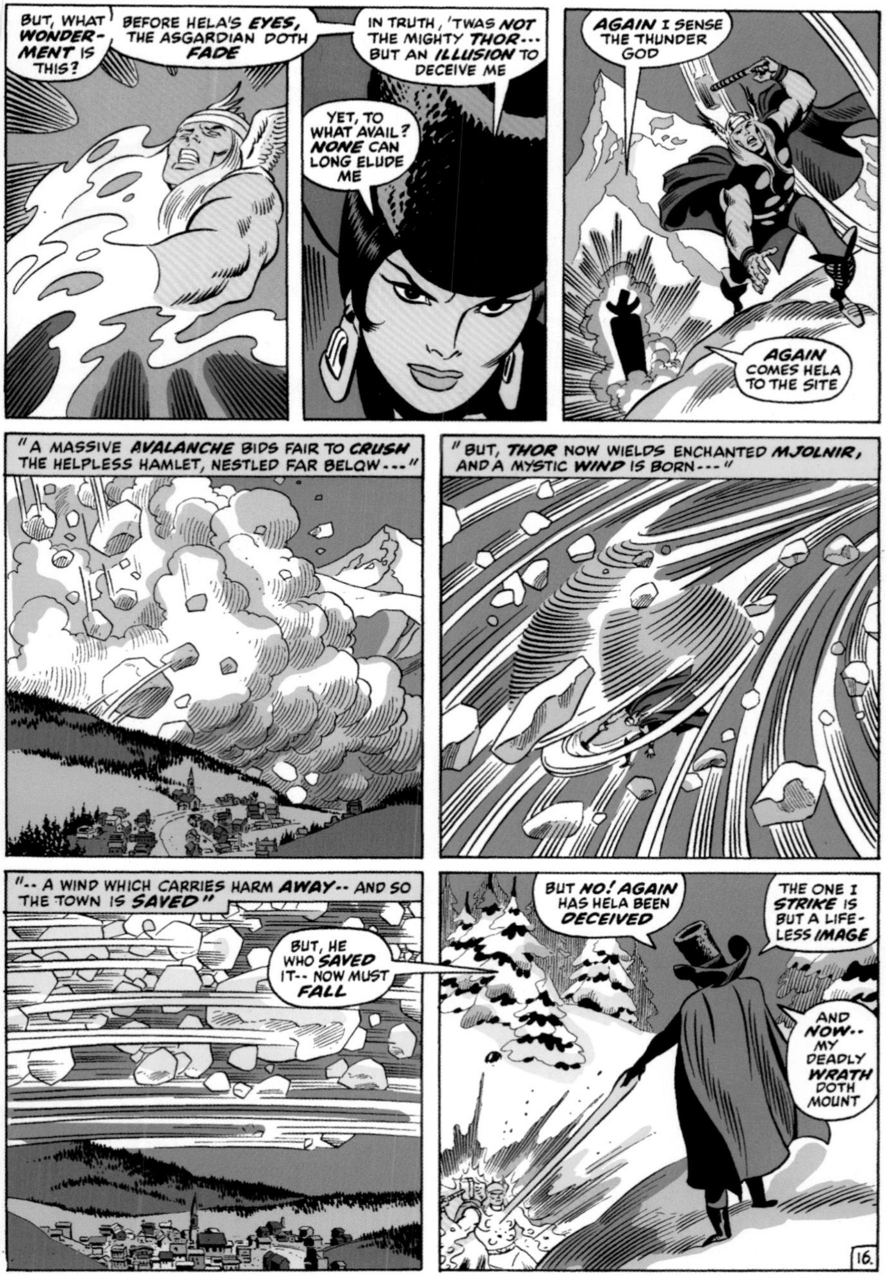
BUT, WHAT WONDER-MENT IS THIS?
BEFORE HELA'S EYES, THE ASGARDIAN DOTH FADE
IN TRUTH, 'TWAS NOT THE MIGHTY THOR--- BUT AN ILLUSION TO DECEIVE ME
YET, TO WHAT AVAIL? NONE CAN LONG ELUDE ME
AGAIN I SENSE THE THUNDER GOD
AGAIN COMES HELA TO THE SITE
"A MASSIVE AVALANCHE BIDS FAIR TO CRUSH THE HELPLESS HAMLET, NESTLED FAR BELOW---"
"BUT, THOR NOW WIELDS ENCHANTED MJOLNIR, AND A MYSTIC WIND IS BORN---"
"-- A WIND WHICH CARRIES HARM AWAY-- AND SO THE TOWN IS SAVED"
BUT, HE WHO SAVED IT-- NOW MUST FALL
BUT NO! AGAIN HAS HELA BEEN DECEIVED
THE ONE I STRIKE IS BUT A LIFE-LESS IMAGE
AND NOW-- MY DEADLY WRATH DOTH MOUNT
16.

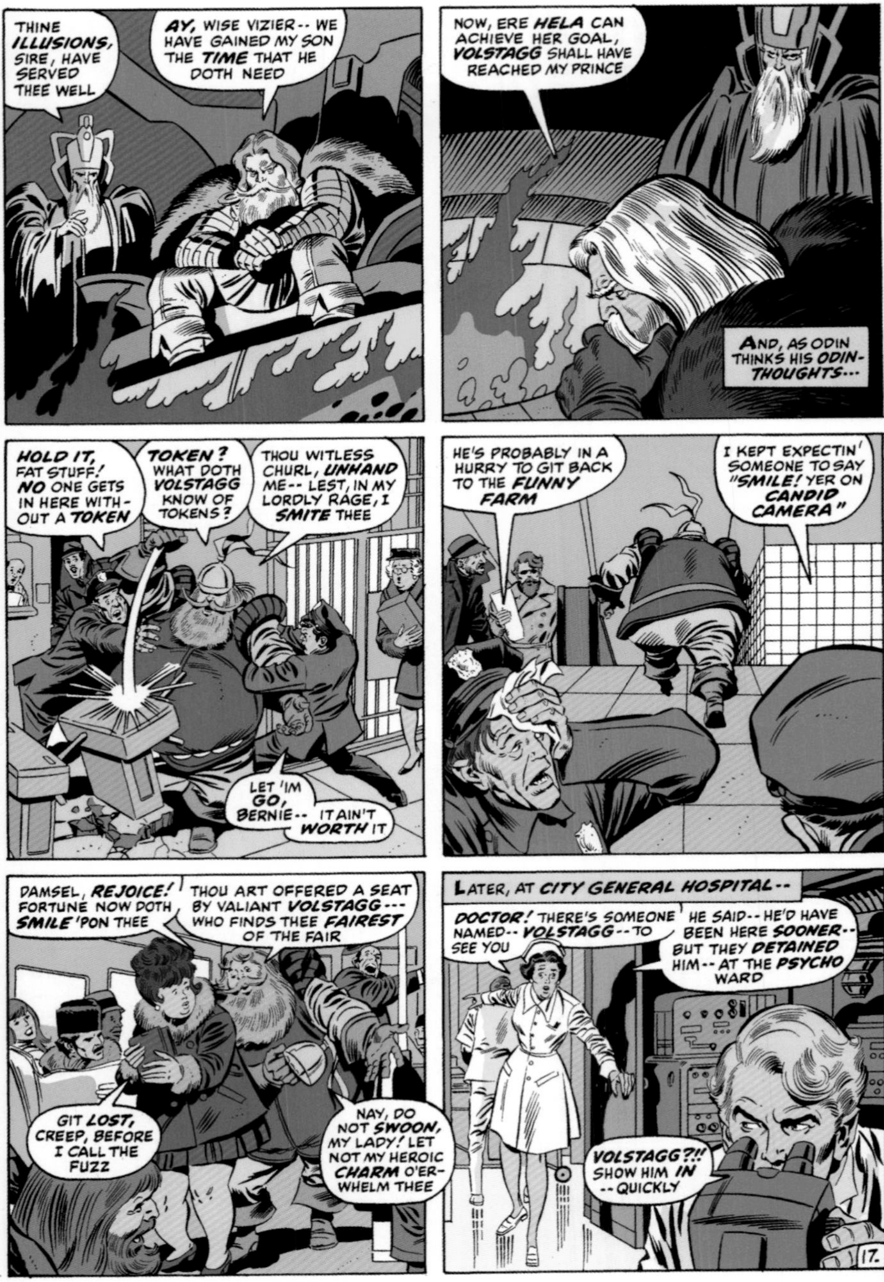
THINE ILLUSIONS, SIRE, HAVE SERVED THEE WELL
AY, WISE VIZIER-- WE HAVE GAINED MY SON THE TIME THAT HE DOTH NEED
NOW, ERE HELA CAN ACHIEVE HER GOAL, VOLSTAGG SHALL HAVE REACHED MY PRINCE
AND, AS ODIN THINKS HIS ODIN-THOUGHTS...
HOLD IT, FAT STUFF! NO ONE GETS IN HERE WITH-OUT A TOKEN
TOKEN? WHAT DOTH VOLSTAGG KNOW OF TOKENS?
THOU WITLESS CHURL, UNHAND ME-- LEST, IN MY LORDLY RAGE, I SMITE THEE
LET 'IM GO, BERNIE-- IT AIN'T WORTH IT
HE'S PROBABLY IN A HURRY TO GIT BACK TO THE FUNNY FARM
I KEPT EXPECTIN' SOMEONE TO SAY "SMILE! YER ON CANDID CAMERA"
DAMSEL, REJOICE! FORTUNE NOW DOTH SMILE 'PON THEE
THOU ART OFFERED A SEAT BY VALIANT VOLSTAGG--- WHO FINDS THEE FAIREST OF THE FAIR
GIT LOST, CREEP, BEFORE I CALL THE FUZZ
NAY, DO NOT SWOON, MY LADY! LET NOT MY HEROIC CHARM O'ER-WHELM THEE
LATER, AT CITY GENERAL HOSPITAL--
DOCTOR! THERE'S SOMEONE NAMED-- VOLSTAGG-- TO SEE YOU
HE SAID-- HE'D HAVE BEEN HERE SOONER-- BUT THEY DETAINED HIM-- AT THE PSYCHO WARD
VOLSTAGG?!! SHOW HIM IN --QUICKLY
17.

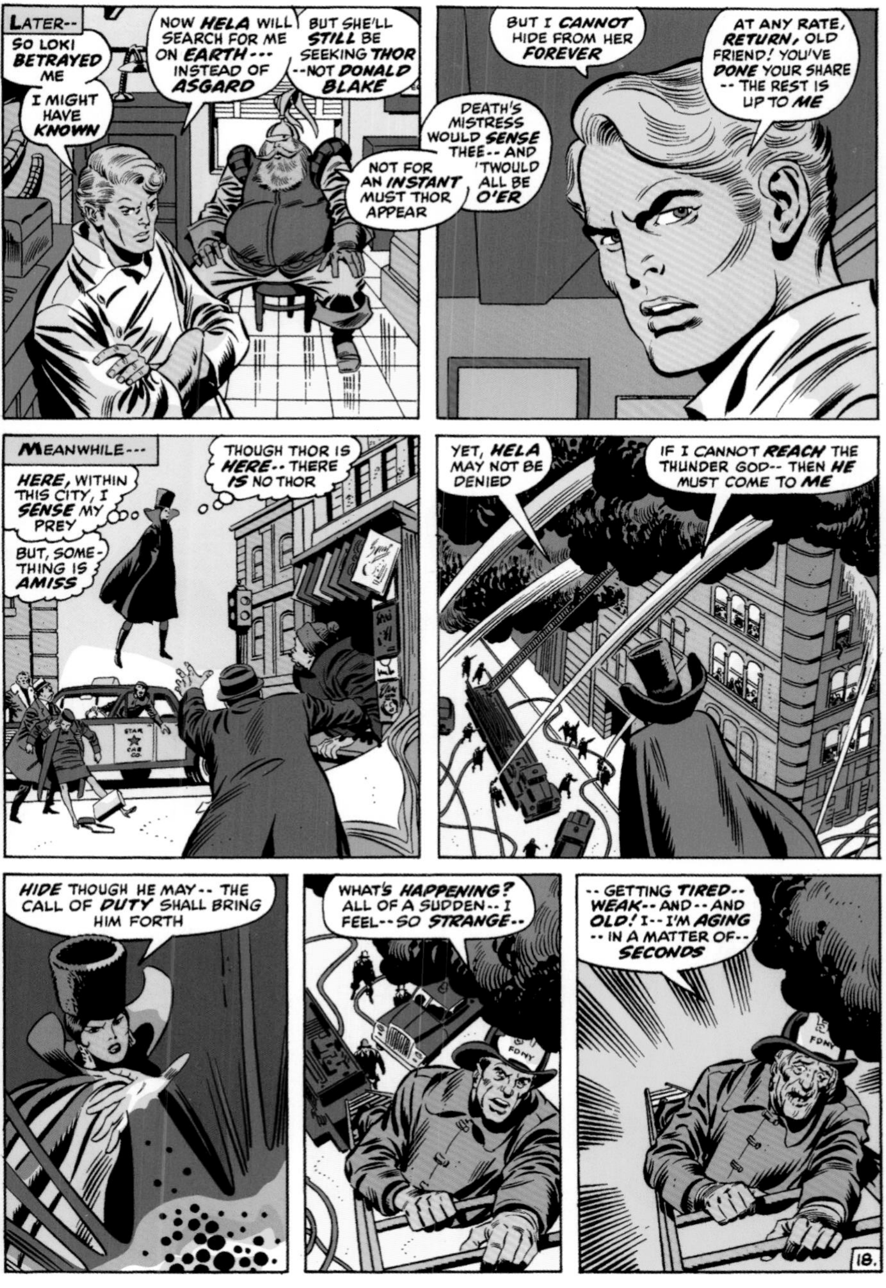
LATER--
SO LOKI BETRAYED ME
I MIGHT HAVE KNOWN
NOW HELA WILL SEARCH FOR ME ON EARTH--- INSTEAD OF ASGARD
BUT SHE'LL STILL BE SEEKING THOR --NOT DONALD BLAKE
DEATH'S MISTRESS WOULD SENSE THEE-- AND 'TWOULD ALL BE O'ER
NOT FOR AN INSTANT MUST THOR APPEAR
BUT I CANNOT HIDE FROM HER FOREVER
AT ANY RATE, RETURN, OLD FRIEND! YOU'VE DONE YOUR SHARE -- THE REST IS UP TO ME
MEANWHILE---
HERE, WITHIN THIS CITY, I SENSE MY PREY
BUT, SOMETHING IS AMISS
THOUGH THOR IS HERE-- THERE IS NO THOR
STAR CAB CO.
YET, HELA MAY NOT BE DENIED
IF I CANNOT REACH THE THUNDER GOD-- THEN HE MUST COME TO ME
HIDE THOUGH HE MAY-- THE CALL OF DUTY SHALL BRING HIM FORTH
WHAT'S HAPPENING? ALL OF A SUDDEN-- I FEEL--SO STRANGE--
FDNY
--GETTING TIRED-- WEAK-- AND-- AND OLD! I-- I'M AGING -- IN A MATTER OF-- SECONDS
FDNY
18.

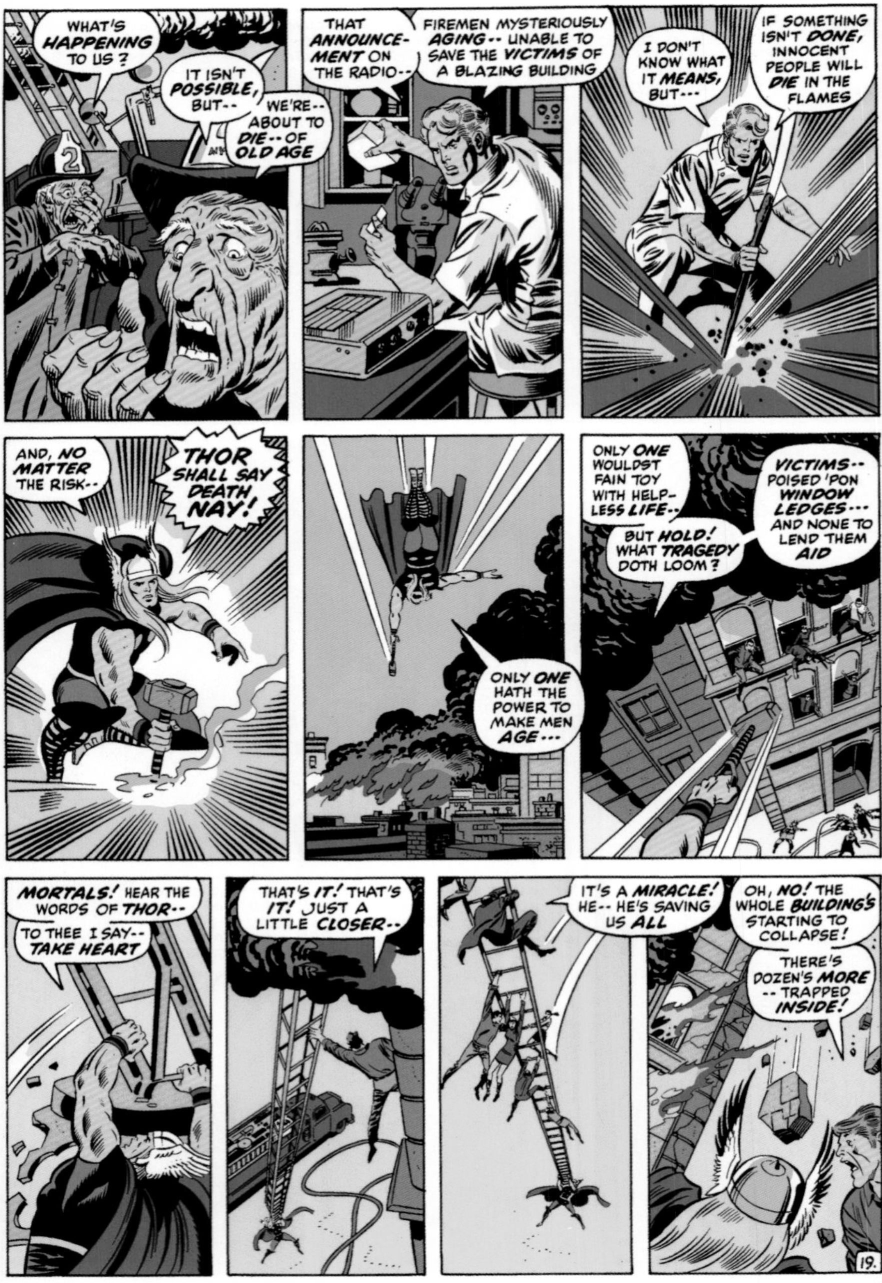

WHAT'S HAPPENING TO US?
IT ISN'T POSSIBLE, BUT--
WE'RE-- ABOUT TO DIE-- OF OLD AGE
THAT ANNOUNCEMENT ON THE RADIO--
FIREMEN MYSTERIOUSLY AGING-- UNABLE TO SAVE THE VICTIMS OF A BLAZING BUILDING
I DON'T KNOW WHAT IT MEANS, BUT---
IF SOMETHING ISN'T DONE, INNOCENT PEOPLE WILL DIE IN THE FLAMES
AND, NO MATTER THE RISK--
THOR SHALL SAY DEATH NAY!
ONLY ONE HATH THE POWER TO MAKE MEN AGE---
ONLY ONE WOULDST FAIN TOY WITH HELPLESS LIFE--
BUT HOLD! WHAT TRAGEDY DOTH LOOM?
VICTIMS-- POISED 'PON WINDOW LEDGES--- AND NONE TO LEND THEM AID
MORTALS! HEAR THE WORDS OF THOR--
TO THEE I SAY-- TAKE HEART
THAT'S IT! THAT'S IT! JUST A LITTLE CLOSER--
IT'S A MIRACLE! HE-- HE'S SAVING US ALL
OH, NO! THE WHOLE BUILDING'S STARTING TO COLLAPSE!
THERE'S DOZEN'S MORE -- TRAPPED INSIDE!
19.

LOOK! HE'S STOPPING IT FROM *FALLING*-- BY THE *STRENGTH* OF HIS OWN BODY

BUT THE *FIRE!* IT-- IT'S STILL *RAGING*

AS I BE *GOD* OF *THUNDER*-- I SUMMON FORTH THE *RAIN*

THE FLAMES SHALL RAGE *NO MORE*

WELL DONE, SON OF ODIN! YOUR *FINAL* DEED HAS BEEN -- MOST *NOBLE*

HELA! I KNEW I WOULDST *FIND* THEE HERE

BUT, AS THOR WAS BATTLE *BORN*-- SO SHALL HE *DIE!*

RAISE *NOT* YOUR HAMMER--

DEFY ME, AND THE HAPLESS MORTALS *FALL*

YIELD-- AND I TAKE *NO* LIVES-- BUT *THINE*

I-- CANNOT CAUSE-- THE DEATH OF *OTHERS*

THE GOD OF THUNDER --YIELDS

THEN *NELA* HAS WON-- AT LAST

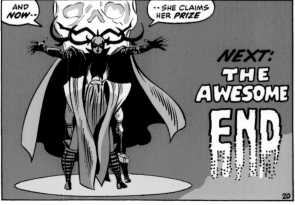

AND *NOW*--

-- SHE CLAIMS HER *PRIZE*

NEXT:
THE
AWESOME
END

20

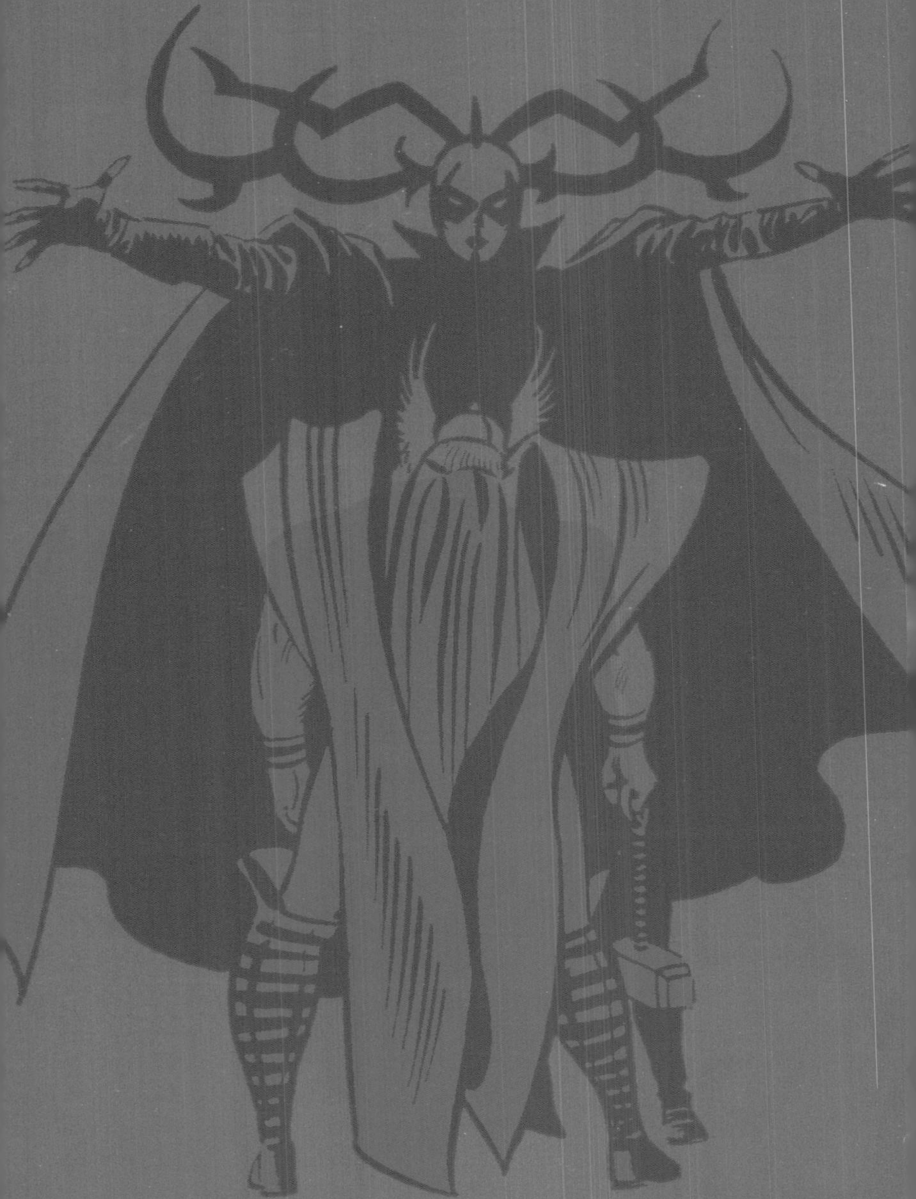

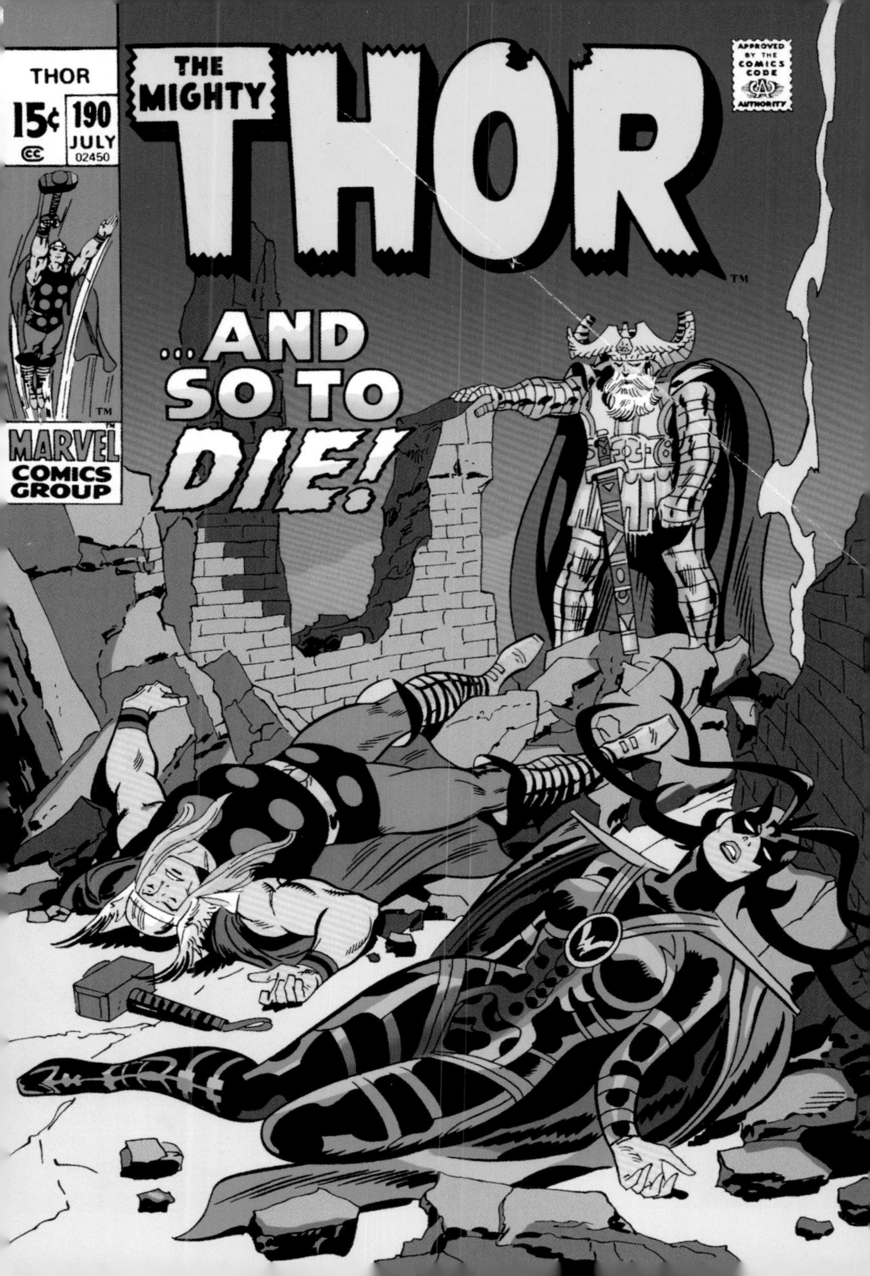
THOR
15¢
190
JULY
02450
MARVEL COMICS GROUP
APPROVED BY THE COMICS CODE AUTHORITY
THE MIGHTY THOR
...AND SO TO DIE!

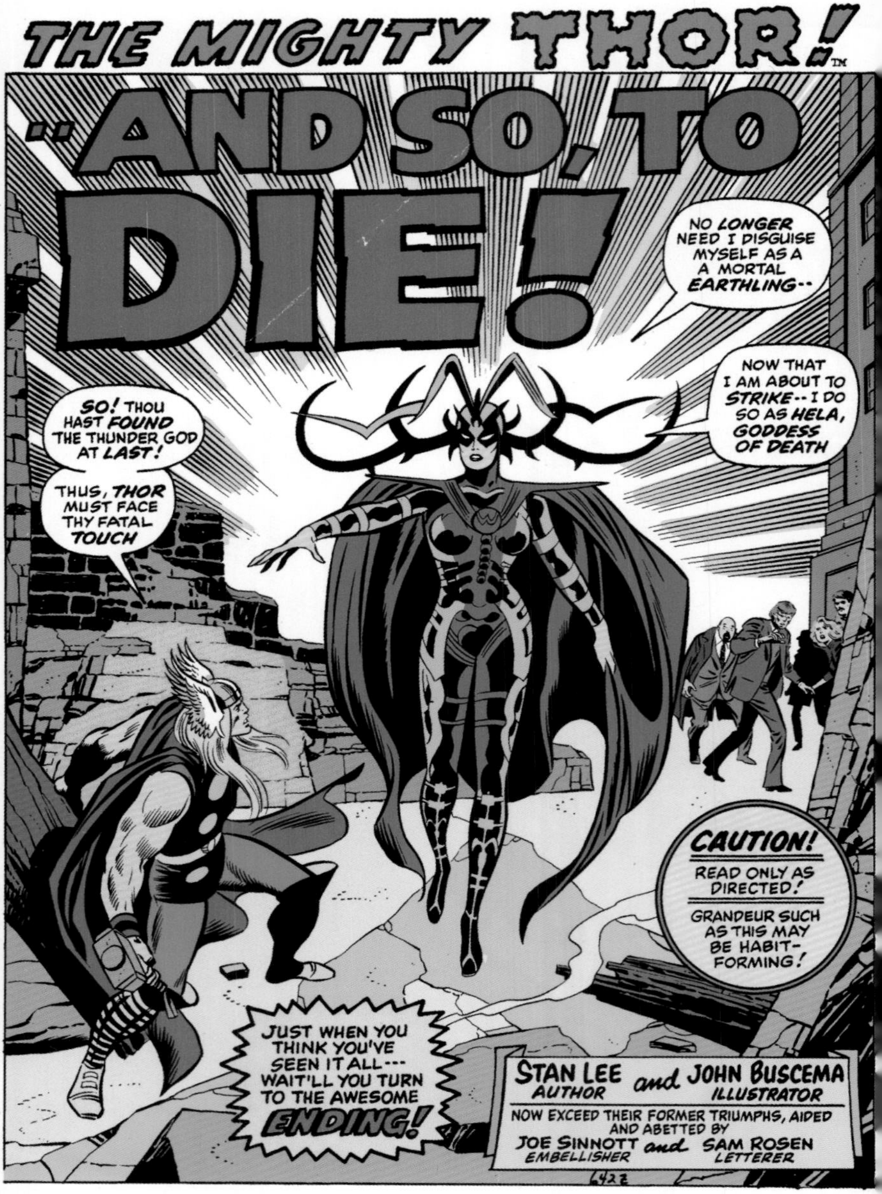
THE MIGHTY THOR!
..AND SO, TO DIE!
NO LONGER NEED I DISGUISE MYSELF AS A A MORTAL EARTHLING--
NOW THAT I AM ABOUT TO STRIKE-- I DO SO AS HELA, GODDESS OF DEATH
SO! THOU HAST FOUND THE THUNDER GOD AT LAST!
THUS, THOR MUST FACE THY FATAL TOUCH
CAUTION! READ ONLY AS DIRECTED! GRANDEUR SUCH AS THIS MAY BE HABIT-FORMING!
JUST WHEN YOU THINK YOU'VE SEEN IT ALL--- WAIT'LL YOU TURN TO THE AWESOME ENDING!
STAN LEE AUTHOR and JOHN BUSCEMA ILLUSTRATOR
NOW EXCEED THEIR FORMER TRIUMPHS, AIDED AND ABETTED BY
JOE SINNOTT EMBELLISHER and SAM ROSEN LETTERER

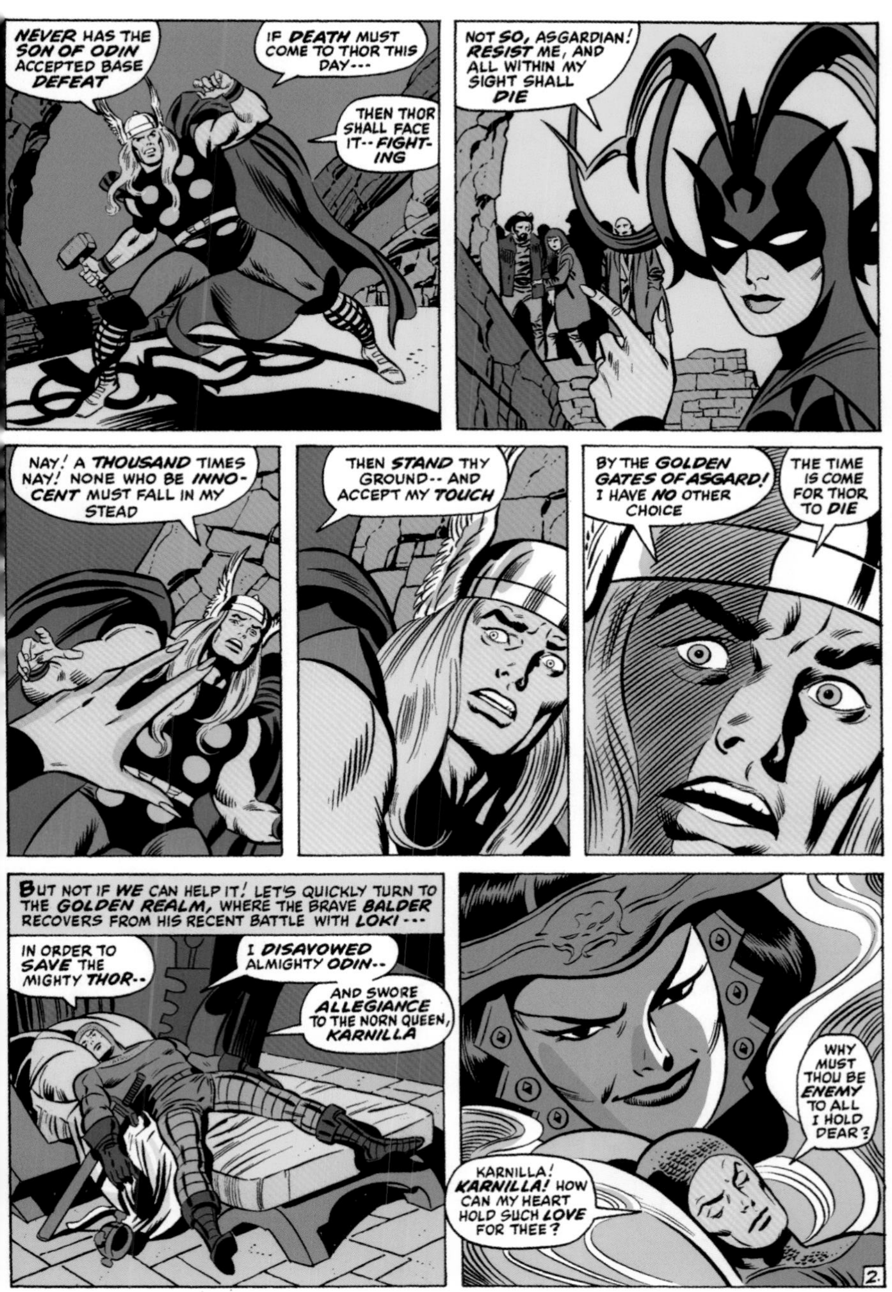
NEVER HAS THE SON OF ODIN ACCEPTED BASE DEFEAT
IF DEATH MUST COME TO THOR THIS DAY---
THEN THOR SHALL FACE IT-- FIGHTING
NOT SO, ASGARDIAN! RESIST ME, AND ALL WITHIN MY SIGHT SHALL DIE
NAY! A THOUSAND TIMES NAY! NONE WHO BE INNOCENT MUST FALL IN MY STEAD
THEN STAND THY GROUND-- AND ACCEPT MY TOUCH
BY THE GOLDEN GATES OF ASGARD! I HAVE NO OTHER CHOICE
THE TIME IS COME FOR THOR TO DIE
BUT NOT IF WE CAN HELP IT! LET'S QUICKLY TURN TO THE GOLDEN REALM, WHERE THE BRAVE BALDER RECOVERS FROM HIS RECENT BATTLE WITH LOKI ---
IN ORDER TO SAVE THE MIGHTY THOR--
I DISAVOWED ALMIGHTY ODIN--
AND SWORE ALLEGIANCE TO THE NORN QUEEN, KARNILLA
WHY MUST THOU BE ENEMY TO ALL I HOLD DEAR?
KARNILLA! KARNILLA! HOW CAN MY HEART HOLD SUCH LOVE FOR THEE?
2.

I AM *NOT* AS MUCH ENEMY AS YOU MAY *THINK,* BELOVED

ONCE *AGAIN* THE QUEEN OF THE NORNS DOTH COME TO GIVE THEE *AID*

BEGONE, ENCHANTRESS! HAUNT NOT BALDER'S *DREAMS*

AM I *NE'ER* TO BE FREE OF THY TAUNTS -- OF THY *SPELLS?*

AWAKE, MY LORD

IN TRUTH -- THIS IS *NO* DREAM

KARNILLA! THOU HAST *CONJURED* THYSELF TO BALDER'S SIDE

BUT NOW I ASK THEE -- *WHY?*

TO WARN THEE *AGAIN* OF THE THUNDER GOD'S *PLIGHT*

BUT IS HE NOT SAFELY *HID* -- UPON THE PLANET *EARTH?*

NOT *SO,* MY BRAVE ONE! *HELA* HATH FOUND HIM OUT

BEHOLD! THY QUEEN SHALL *SHOW* THEE --

SCANT *SECONDS* REMAIN 'ERE THOR SHALL *FALL* --- FOREVER

NAY! NOT WHILST *BALDER* STILL DOTH LIVE

NOT WHILST *ODIN* CAN BE WARNED

BUT REMEMBER *WELL* -- THINE *ALLEGIANCE* IS PLEDGED TO *ME*

3.

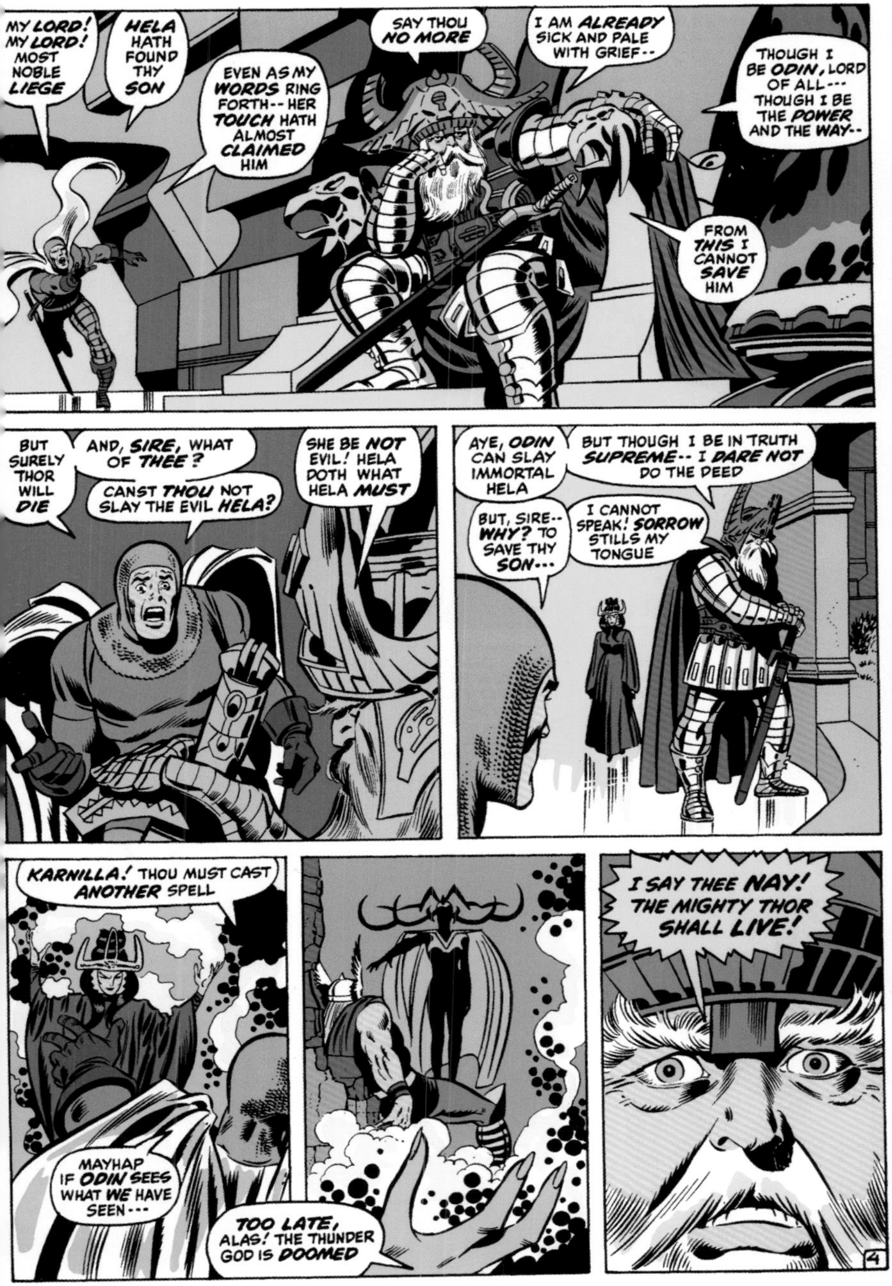
MY LORD! MY LORD! MOST NOBLE LIEGE
HELA HATH FOUND THY SON
EVEN AS MY WORDS RING FORTH-- HER TOUCH HATH ALMOST CLAIMED HIM
SAY THOU NO MORE
I AM ALREADY SICK AND PALE WITH GRIEF--
THOUGH I BE ODIN, LORD OF ALL--- THOUGH I BE THE POWER AND THE WAY--
FROM THIS I CANNOT SAVE HIM
BUT SURELY THOR WILL DIE
AND, SIRE, WHAT OF THEE?
CANST THOU NOT SLAY THE EVIL HELA?
SHE BE NOT EVIL! HELA DOTH WHAT HELA MUST
AYE, ODIN CAN SLAY IMMORTAL HELA
BUT THOUGH I BE IN TRUTH SUPREME-- I DARE NOT DO THE DEED
BUT, SIRE-- WHY? TO SAVE THY SON---
I CANNOT SPEAK! SORROW STILLS MY TONGUE
KARNILLA! THOU MUST CAST ANOTHER SPELL
MAYHAP IF ODIN SEES WHAT WE HAVE SEEN---
TOO LATE, ALAS! THE THUNDER GOD IS DOOMED
I SAY THEE NAY! THE MIGHTY THOR SHALL LIVE!
4

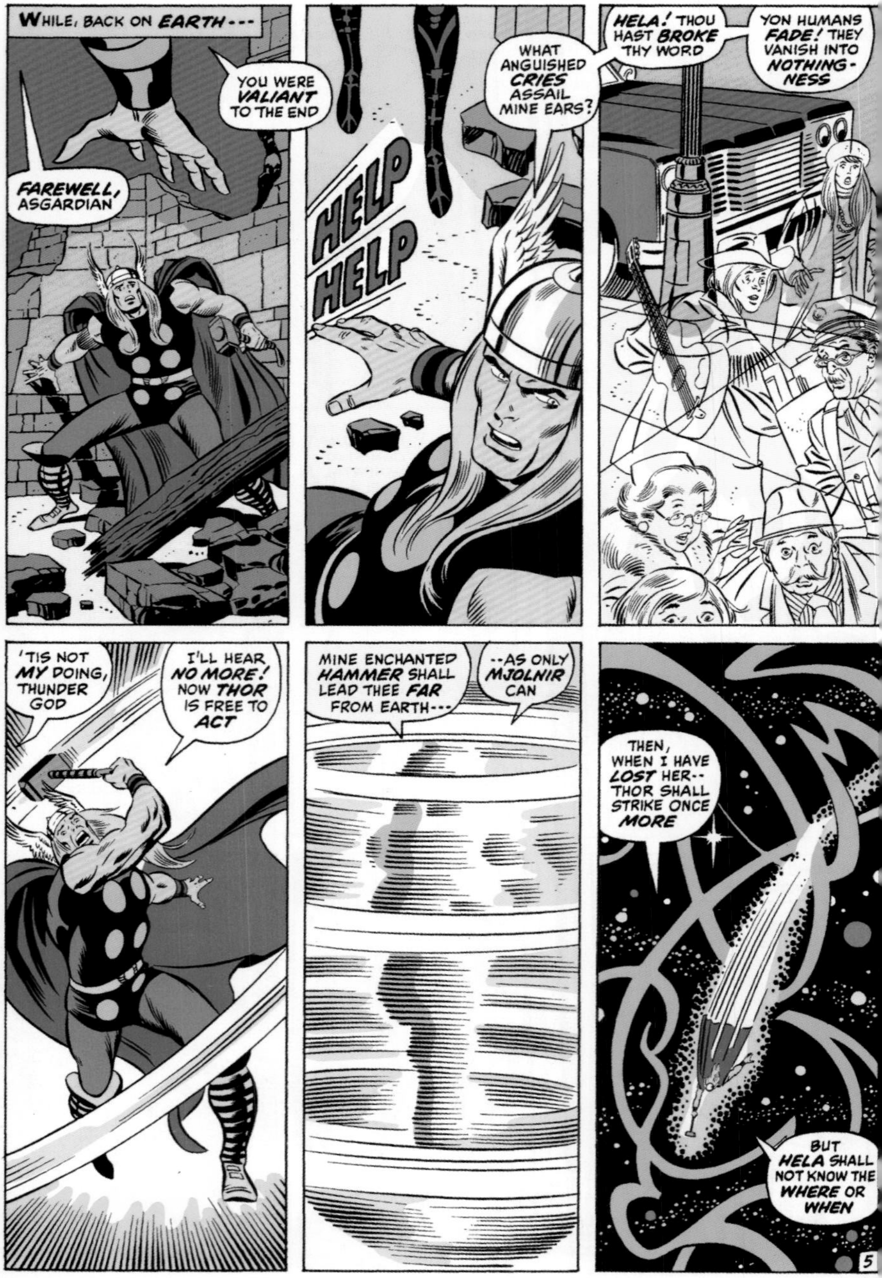
WHILE, BACK ON EARTH---
YOU WERE VALIANT TO THE END
FAREWELL, ASGARDIAN
HELP HELP
WHAT ANGUISHED CRIES ASSAIL MINE EARS?
HELA! THOU HAST BROKE THY WORD
YON HUMANS FADE! THEY VANISH INTO NOTHING-NESS
'TIS NOT MY DOING, THUNDER GOD
I'LL HEAR NO MORE! NOW THOR IS FREE TO ACT
MINE ENCHANTED HAMMER SHALL LEAD THEE FAR FROM EARTH---
--AS ONLY MJOLNIR CAN
THEN, WHEN I HAVE LOST HER-- THOR SHALL STRIKE ONCE MORE
BUT HELA SHALL NOT KNOW THE WHERE OR WHEN
5

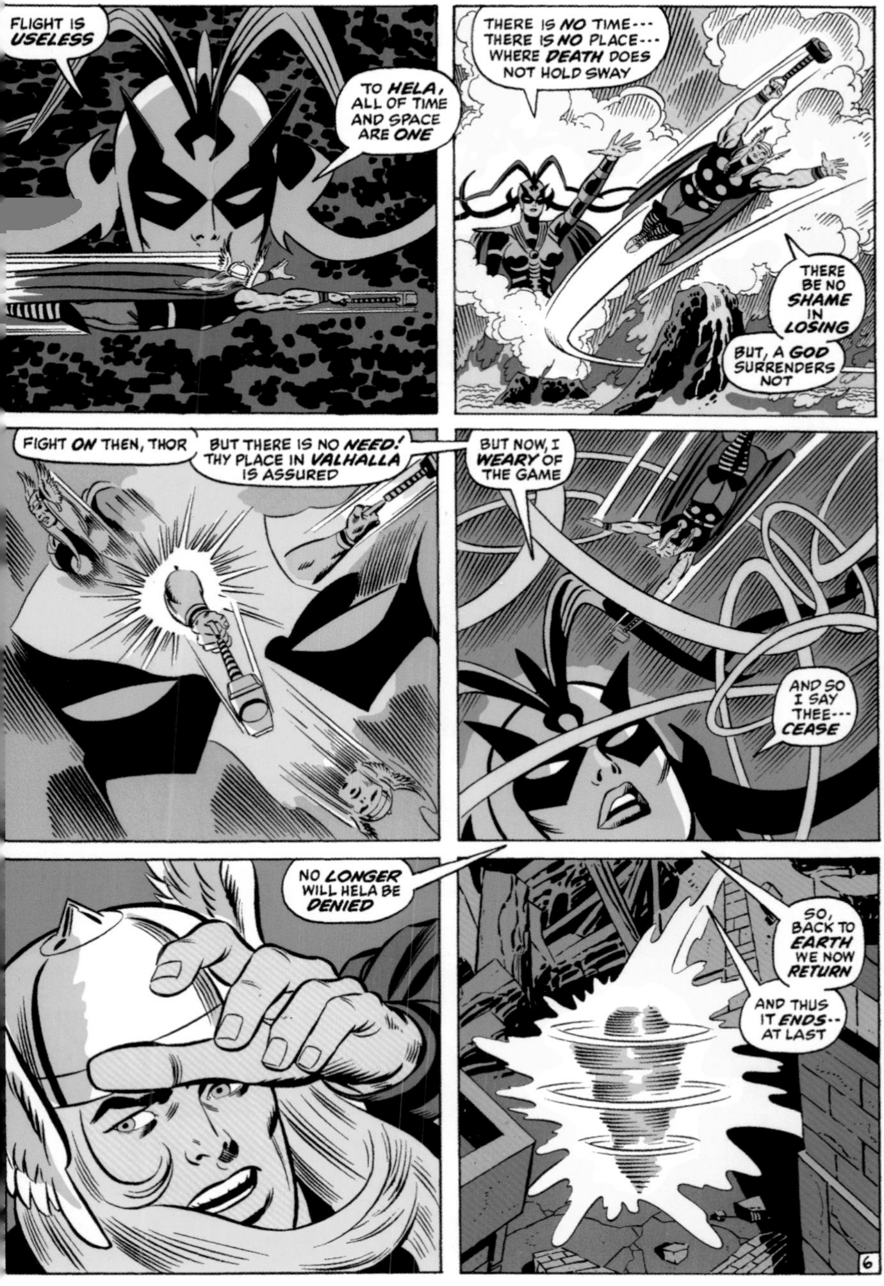
FLIGHT IS USELESS
TO HELA, ALL OF TIME AND SPACE ARE ONE
THERE IS NO TIME--- THERE IS NO PLACE--- WHERE DEATH DOES NOT HOLD SWAY
THERE BE NO SHAME IN LOSING
BUT, A GOD SURRENDERS NOT
FIGHT ON THEN, THOR
BUT THERE IS NO NEED! THY PLACE IN VALHALLA IS ASSURED
BUT NOW, I WEARY OF THE GAME
AND SO I SAY THEE--- CEASE
NO LONGER WILL HELA BE DENIED
SO, BACK TO EARTH WE NOW RETURN
AND THUS IT ENDS-- AT LAST
6

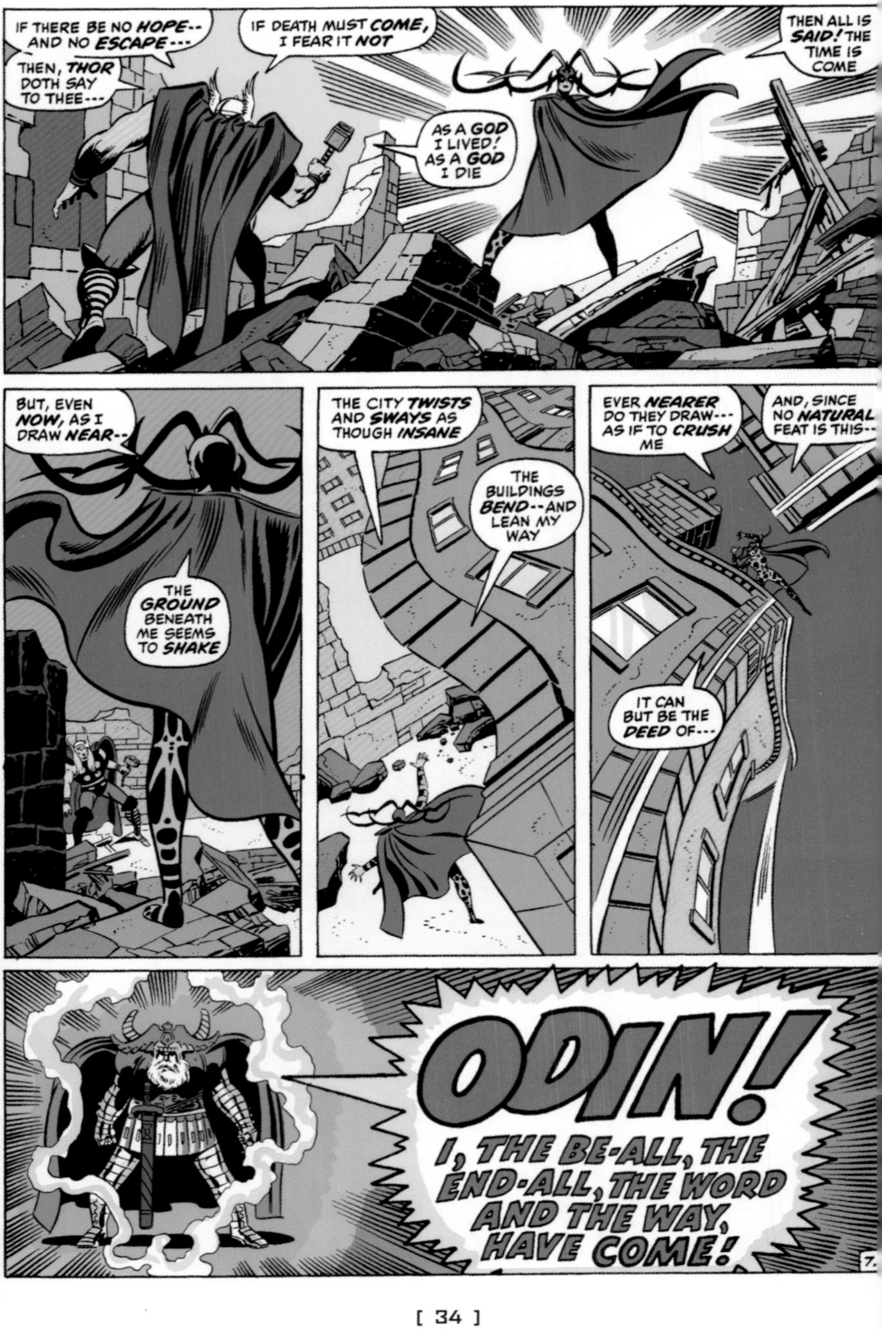
IF THERE BE NO HOPE-- AND NO ESCAPE---
THEN, THOR DOTH SAY TO THEE---
IF DEATH MUST COME, I FEAR IT NOT
AS A GOD I LIVED! AS A GOD I DIE
THEN ALL IS SAID! THE TIME IS COME
BUT, EVEN NOW, AS I DRAW NEAR--
THE GROUND BENEATH ME SEEMS TO SHAKE
THE CITY TWISTS AND SWAYS AS THOUGH INSANE
THE BUILDINGS BEND--AND LEAN MY WAY
EVER NEARER DO THEY DRAW--- AS IF TO CRUSH ME
AND, SINCE NO NATURAL FEAT IS THIS--
IT CAN BUT BE THE DEED OF---
ODIN!
I, THE BE-ALL, THE END-ALL, THE WORD AND THE WAY, HAVE COME!
7.

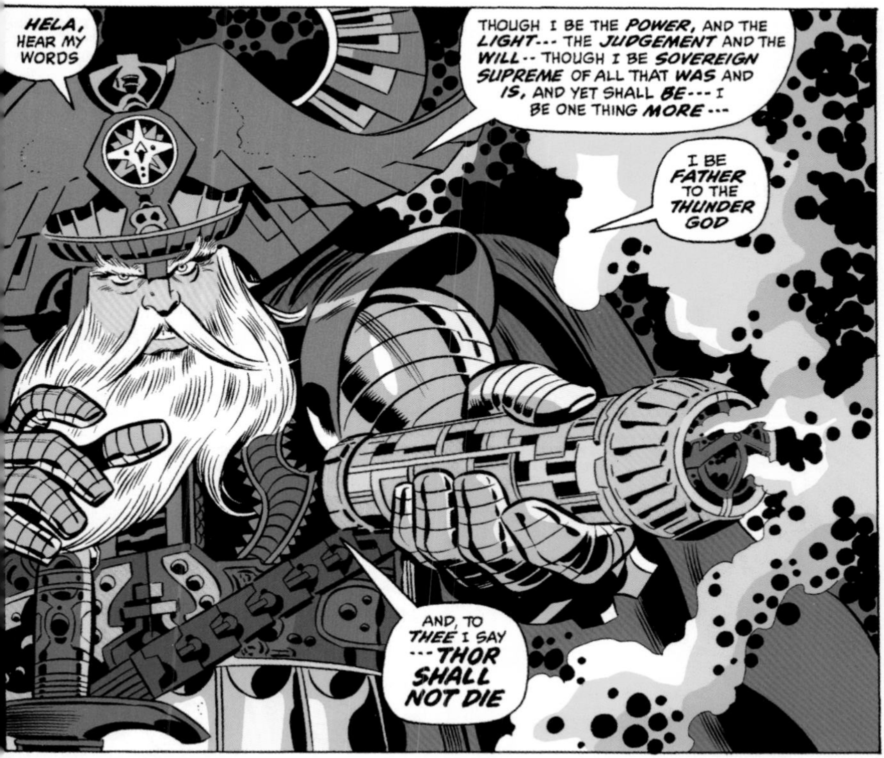
HELA, HEAR MY WORDS
THOUGH I BE THE POWER, AND THE LIGHT--- THE JUDGEMENT AND THE WILL -- THOUGH I BE SOVEREIGN SUPREME OF ALL THAT WAS AND IS, AND YET SHALL BE--- I BE ONE THING MORE ---
I BE FATHER TO THE THUNDER GOD
AND, TO THEE I SAY --- THOR SHALL NOT DIE

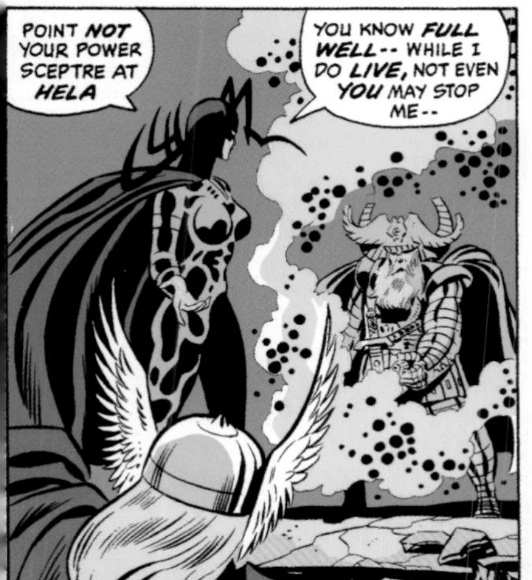
POINT NOT YOUR POWER SCEPTRE AT HELA
YOU KNOW FULL WELL -- WHILE I DO LIVE, NOT EVEN YOU MAY STOP ME --

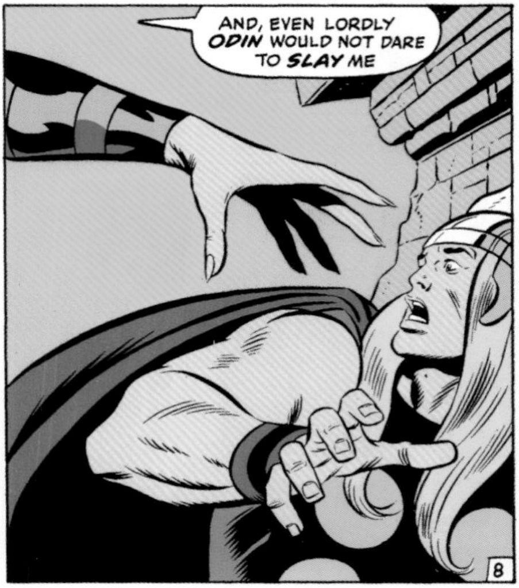
AND, EVEN LORDLY ODIN WOULD NOT DARE TO SLAY ME
8

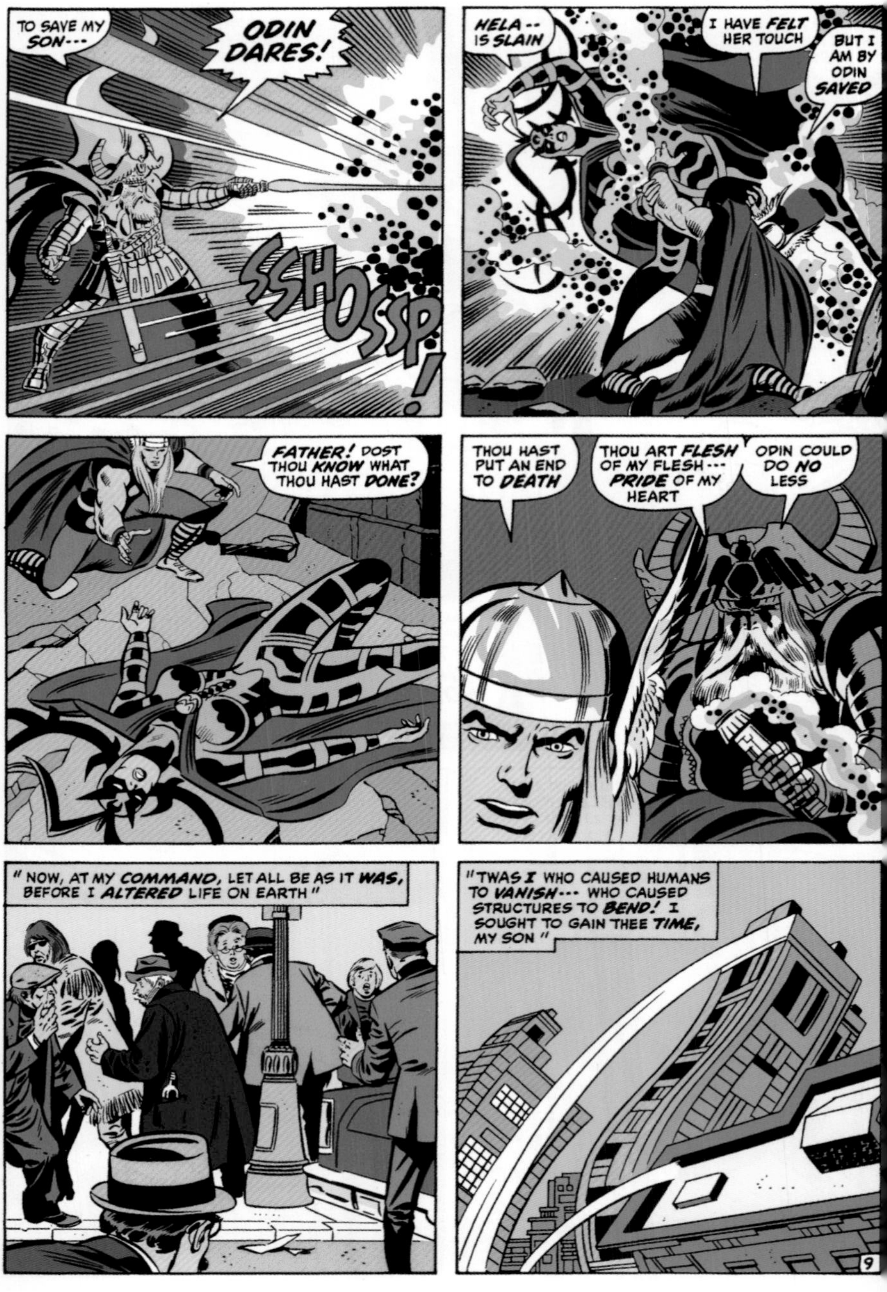
TO SAVE MY SON---
ODIN DARES!
SSHOSSP!
HELA -- IS SLAIN
I HAVE FELT HER TOUCH
BUT I AM BY ODIN SAVED
FATHER! DOST THOU KNOW WHAT THOU HAST DONE?
THOU HAST PUT AN END TO DEATH
THOU ART FLESH OF MY FLESH --- PRIDE OF MY HEART
ODIN COULD DO NO LESS
"NOW, AT MY COMMAND, LET ALL BE AS IT WAS, BEFORE I ALTERED LIFE ON EARTH"
"TWAS I WHO CAUSED HUMANS TO VANISH--- WHO CAUSED STRUCTURES TO BEND! I SOUGHT TO GAIN THEE TIME, MY SON"
9

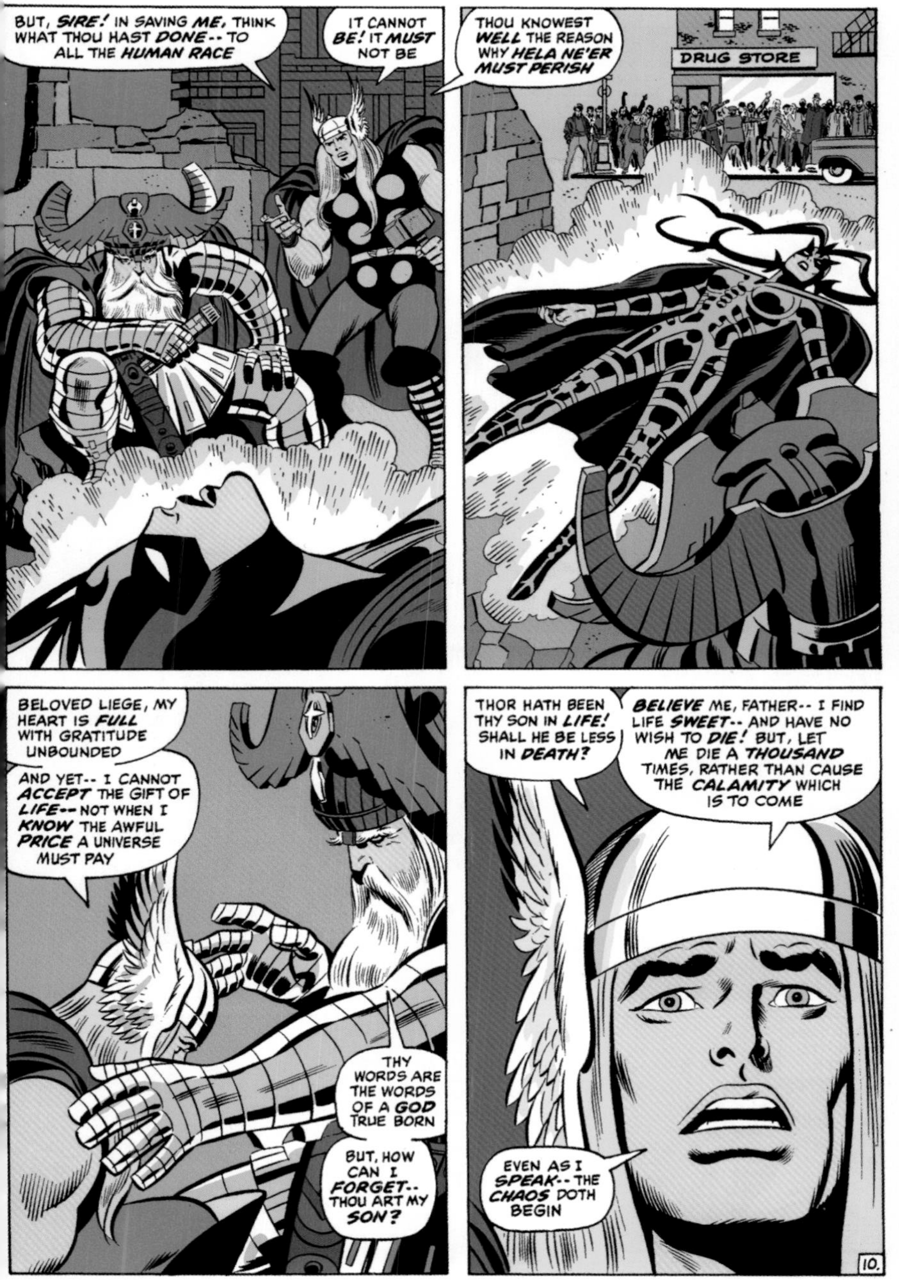
BUT, SIRE! IN SAVING ME, THINK WHAT THOU HAST DONE-- TO ALL THE HUMAN RACE
IT CANNOT BE! IT MUST NOT BE
THOU KNOWEST WELL THE REASON WHY HELA NE'ER MUST PERISH
DRUG STORE
BELOVED LIEGE, MY HEART IS FULL WITH GRATITUDE UNBOUNDED
AND YET-- I CANNOT ACCEPT THE GIFT OF LIFE-- NOT WHEN I KNOW THE AWFUL PRICE A UNIVERSE MUST PAY
THY WORDS ARE THE WORDS OF A GOD TRUE BORN
BUT, HOW CAN I FORGET.. THOU ART MY SON?
THOR HATH BEEN THY SON IN LIFE! SHALL HE BE LESS IN DEATH?
BELIEVE ME, FATHER-- I FIND LIFE SWEET-- AND HAVE NO WISH TO DIE! BUT, LET ME DIE A THOUSAND TIMES, RATHER THAN CAUSE THE CALAMITY WHICH IS TO COME
EVEN AS I SPEAK-- THE CHAOS DOTH BEGIN
10.

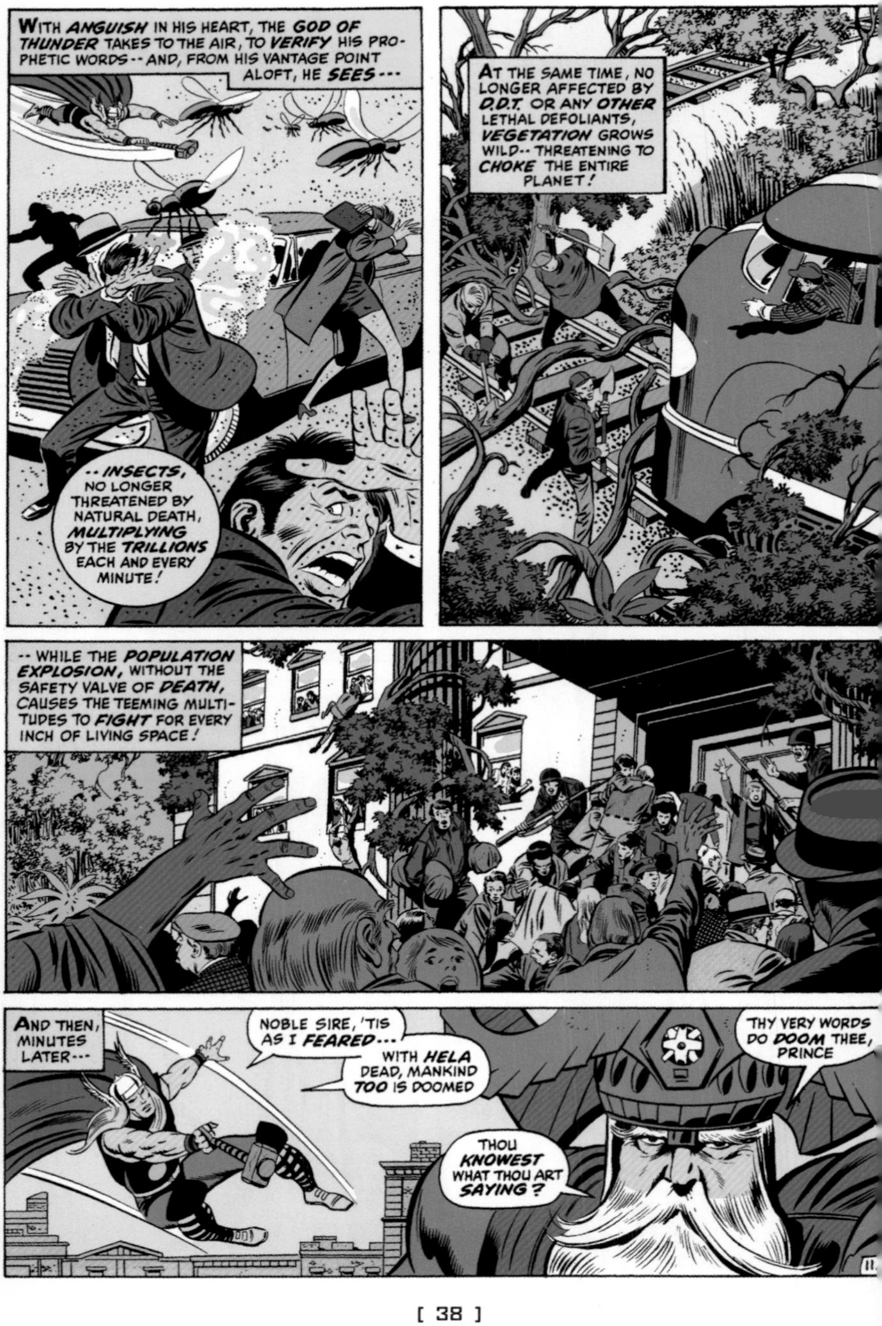
WITH ANGUISH IN HIS HEART, THE GOD OF THUNDER TAKES TO THE AIR, TO VERIFY HIS PROPHETIC WORDS-- AND, FROM HIS VANTAGE POINT ALOFT, HE SEES---
--INSECTS, NO LONGER THREATENED BY NATURAL DEATH, MULTIPLYING BY THE TRILLIONS EACH AND EVERY MINUTE!
AT THE SAME TIME, NO LONGER AFFECTED BY D.D.T. OR ANY OTHER LETHAL DEFOLIANTS, VEGETATION GROWS WILD-- THREATENING TO CHOKE THE ENTIRE PLANET!
-- WHILE THE POPULATION EXPLOSION, WITHOUT THE SAFETY VALVE OF DEATH, CAUSES THE TEEMING MULTITUDES TO FIGHT FOR EVERY INCH OF LIVING SPACE!
AND THEN, MINUTES LATER---
NOBLE SIRE, 'TIS AS I FEARED---
WITH HELA DEAD, MANKIND TOO IS DOOMED
THOU KNOWEST WHAT THOU ART SAYING?
THY VERY WORDS DO DOOM THEE, PRINCE
11

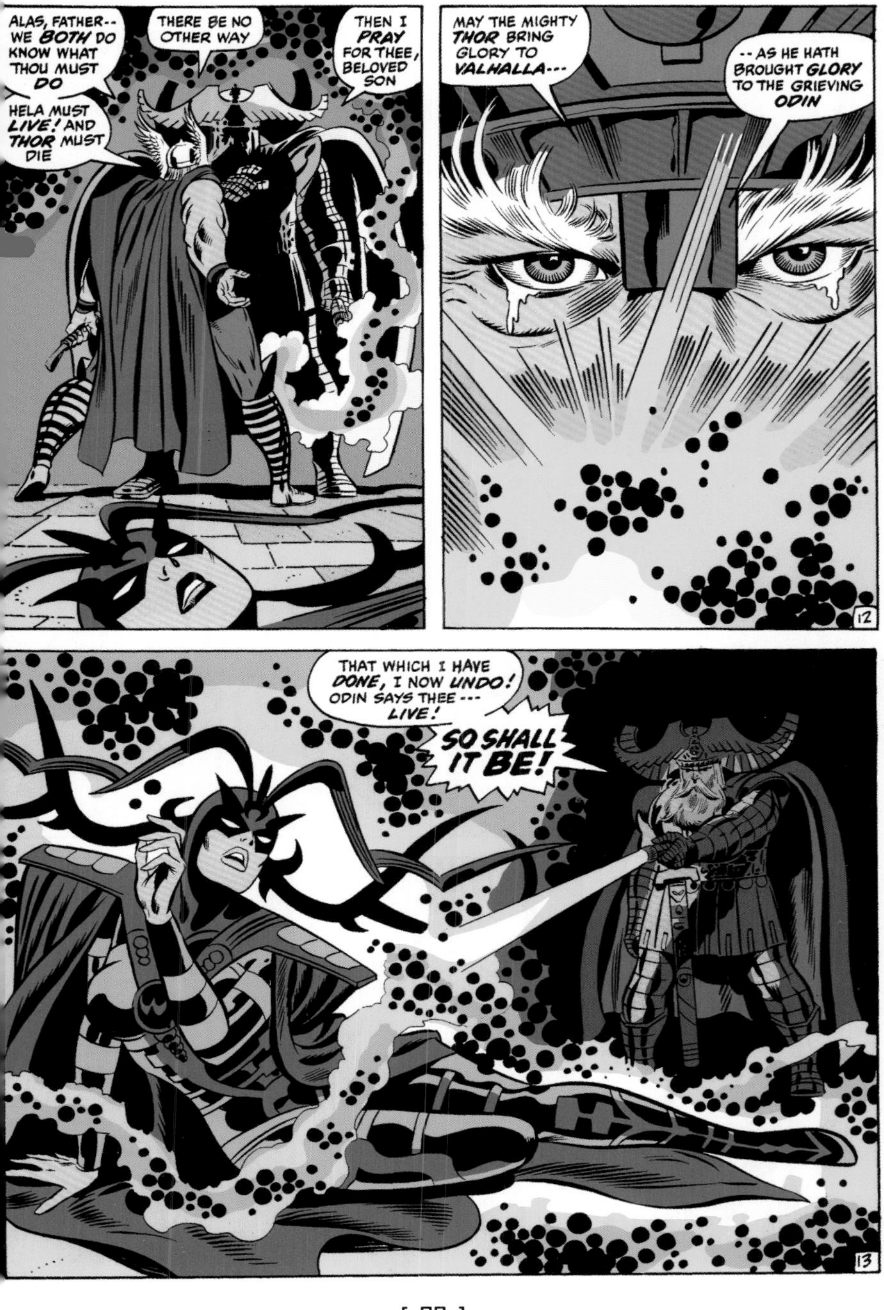
ALAS, FATHER-- WE BOTH DO KNOW WHAT THOU MUST DO
HELA MUST LIVE! AND THOR MUST DIE
THERE BE NO OTHER WAY
THEN I PRAY FOR THEE, BELOVED SON
MAY THE MIGHTY THOR BRING GLORY TO VALHALLA---
-- AS HE HATH BROUGHT GLORY TO THE GRIEVING ODIN
12
THAT WHICH I HAVE DONE, I NOW UNDO! ODIN SAYS THEE --- LIVE!
SO SHALL IT BE!
13

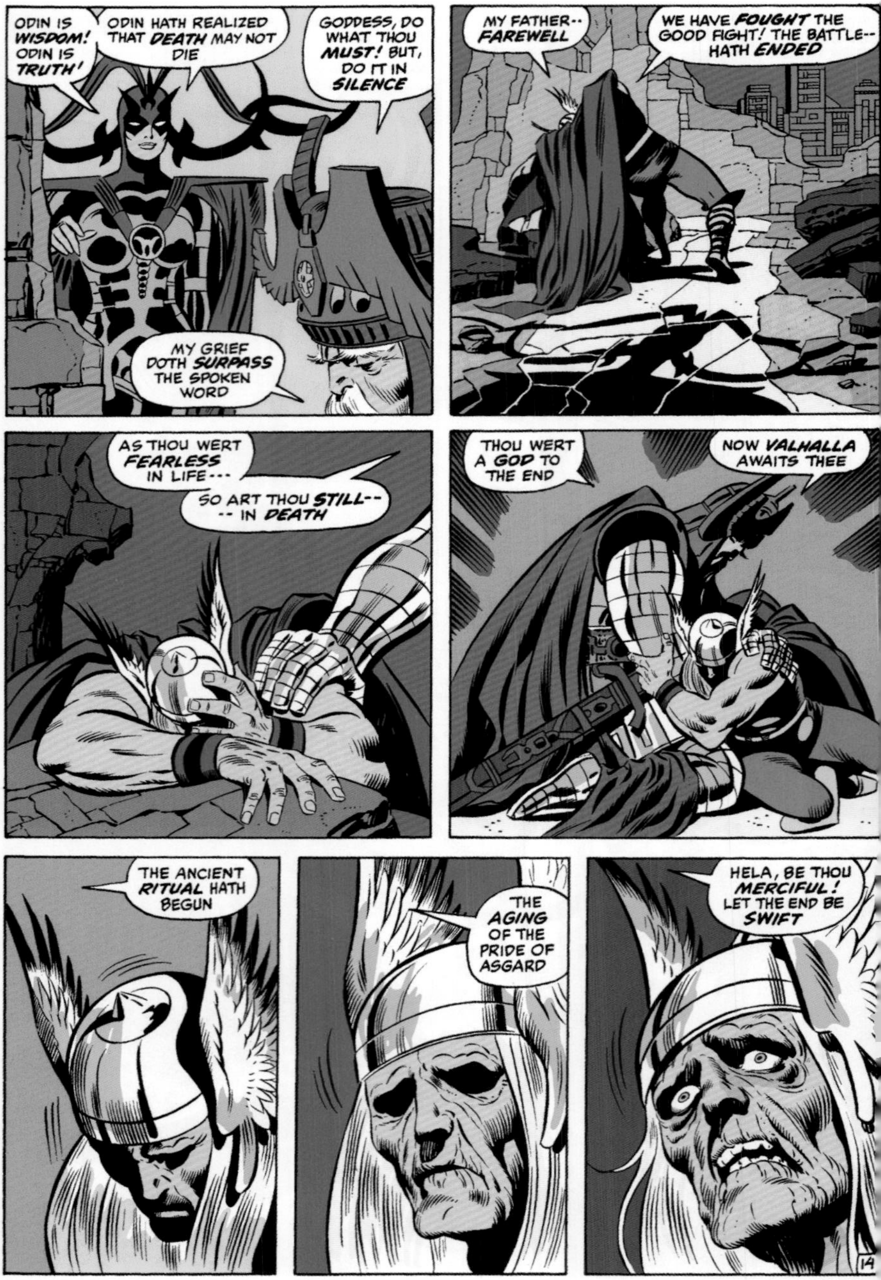
ODIN IS WISDOM! ODIN IS TRUTH!
ODIN HATH REALIZED THAT DEATH MAY NOT DIE
GODDESS, DO WHAT THOU MUST! BUT, DO IT IN SILENCE
MY GRIEF DOTH SURPASS THE SPOKEN WORD
MY FATHER-- FAREWELL
WE HAVE FOUGHT THE GOOD FIGHT! THE BATTLE-- HATH ENDED
AS THOU WERT FEARLESS IN LIFE---
SO ART THOU STILL-- -- IN DEATH
THOU WERT A GOD TO THE END
NOW VALHALLA AWAITS THEE
THE ANCIENT RITUAL HATH BEGUN
THE AGING OF THE PRIDE OF ASGARD
HELA, BE THOU MERCIFUL! LET THE END BE SWIFT
14

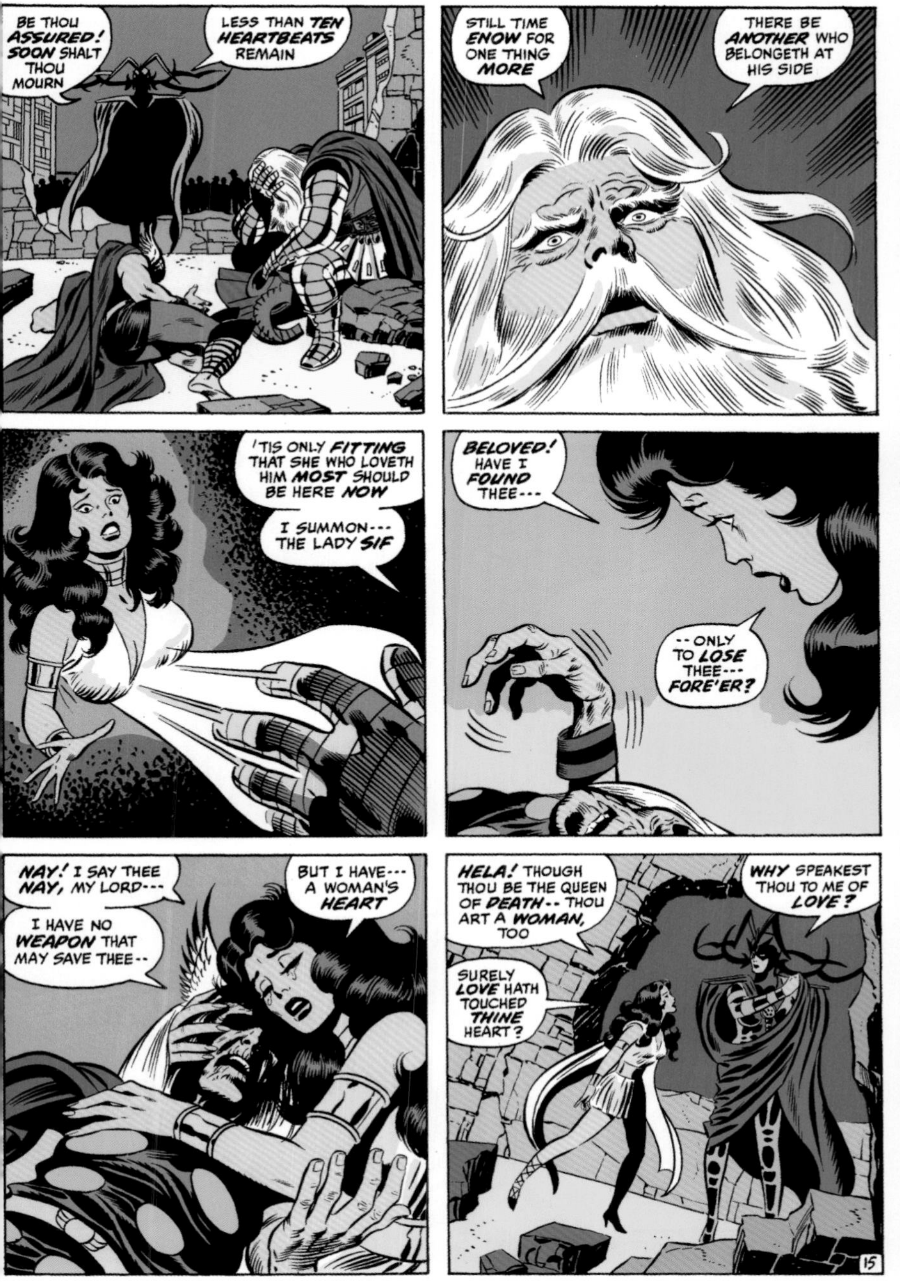
BE THOU ASSURED! SOON SHALT THOU MOURN
LESS THAN TEN HEARTBEATS REMAIN
STILL TIME ENOW FOR ONE THING MORE
THERE BE ANOTHER WHO BELONGETH AT HIS SIDE
'TIS ONLY FITTING THAT SHE WHO LOVETH HIM MOST SHOULD BE HERE NOW
I SUMMON--- THE LADY SIF
BELOVED! HAVE I FOUND THEE---
--ONLY TO LOSE THEE--- FORE'ER?
NAY! I SAY THEE NAY, MY LORD---
I HAVE NO WEAPON THAT MAY SAVE THEE--
BUT I HAVE--- A WOMAN'S HEART
HELA! THOUGH THOU BE THE QUEEN OF DEATH-- THOU ART A WOMAN, TOO
SURELY LOVE HATH TOUCHED THINE HEART?
WHY SPEAKEST THOU TO ME OF LOVE?
15

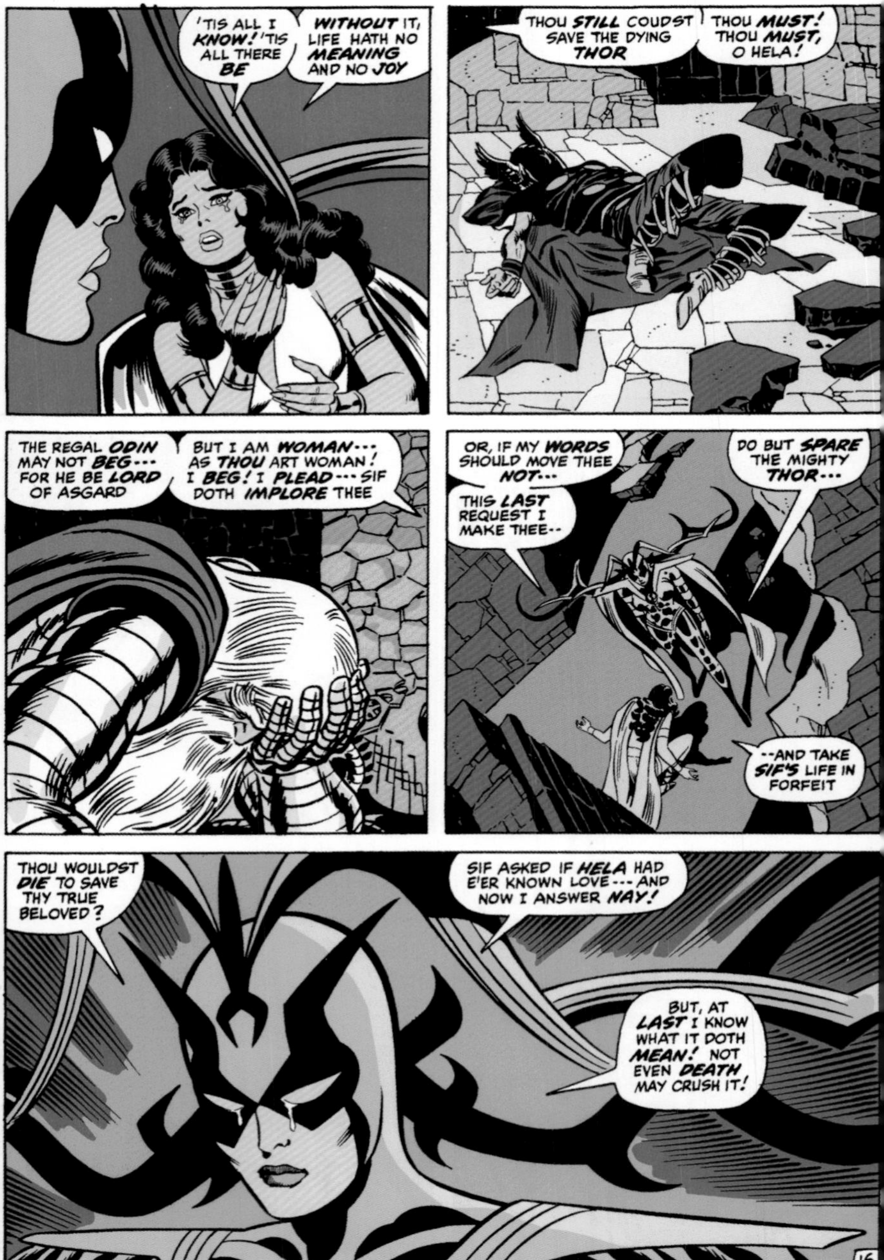
'TIS ALL I KNOW! 'TIS ALL THERE BE
WITHOUT IT, LIFE HATH NO MEANING AND NO JOY
THOU STILL COUDST SAVE THE DYING THOR
THOU MUST! THOU MUST, O HELA!
THE REGAL ODIN MAY NOT BEG--- FOR HE BE LORD OF ASGARD
BUT I AM WOMAN--- AS THOU ART WOMAN! I BEG! I PLEAD--- SIF DOTH IMPLORE THEE
OR, IF MY WORDS SHOULD MOVE THEE NOT---
THIS LAST REQUEST I MAKE THEE--
DO BUT SPARE THE MIGHTY THOR---
--AND TAKE SIF'S LIFE IN FORFEIT
THOU WOULDST DIE TO SAVE THY TRUE BELOVED?
SIF ASKED IF HELA HAD E'ER KNOWN LOVE--- AND NOW I ANSWER NAY!
BUT, AT LAST I KNOW WHAT IT DOTH MEAN! NOT EVEN DEATH MAY CRUSH IT!
16

THEN *TAKE* THY LORD, THE *WARRIOR GOD*

I *GIVE* THEE MIGHTY *THOR*

YEA, JUST THIS *ONCE*, BECAUSE OF *SIF*--

-- HELA HATH *LEARNED* WHAT IT MEANS TO BE -- *WOMAN*

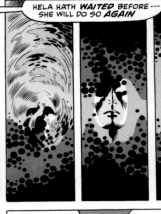

'TWAS NOT HIS *TIME* TO MEET HIS DEATH

HELA HATH *WAITED* BEFORE --- SHE WILL DO SO *AGAIN*

MY *LOVE!* MY *LORD!* BELOVED *PRINCE!* THOR DOTH *LIVE* AGAIN

BECAUSE OF *THEE*, MY LADY

I OWE MY *LIFE* TO THE TENDER *SIF*

ASGARDIANS --- *FAREWELL*

WHEN *NEXT* I COME, NOT ALL THY *TEARS* --- NOT ALL THY *PLEAS* --- SHALL *STAY* ME

-- TILL THEN, *REJOICE!* YE HAVE EACH *OTHER* -- WHILE *HELA* ENDURES -- *ALONE!*

17.

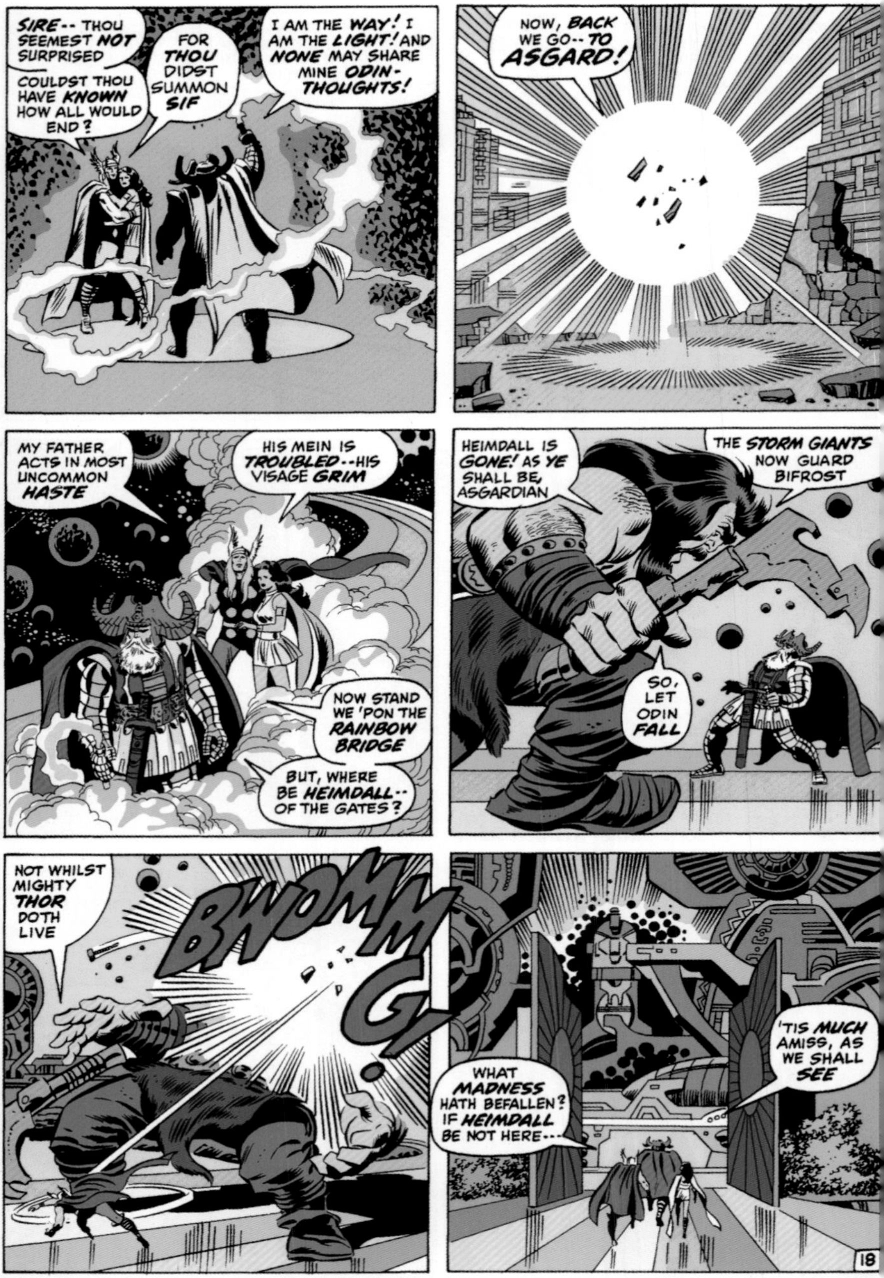

SIRE-- THOU SEEMEST NOT SURPRISED
COULDST THOU HAVE KNOWN HOW ALL WOULD END?
FOR THOU DIDST SUMMON SIF
I AM THE WAY! I AM THE LIGHT! AND NONE MAY SHARE MINE ODIN-THOUGHTS!
NOW, BACK WE GO-- TO ASGARD!
MY FATHER ACTS IN MOST UNCOMMON HASTE
HIS MEIN IS TROUBLED--HIS VISAGE GRIM
NOW STAND WE 'PON THE RAINBOW BRIDGE
BUT, WHERE BE HEIMDALL-- OF THE GATES?
HEIMDALL IS GONE! AS YE SHALL BE, ASGARDIAN
THE STORM GIANTS NOW GUARD BIFROST
SO, LET ODIN FALL
NOT WHILST MIGHTY THOR DOTH LIVE
BWOMMM
G
WHAT MADNESS HATH BEFALLEN? IF HEIMDALL BE NOT HERE---
'TIS MUCH AMISS, AS WE SHALL SEE
18

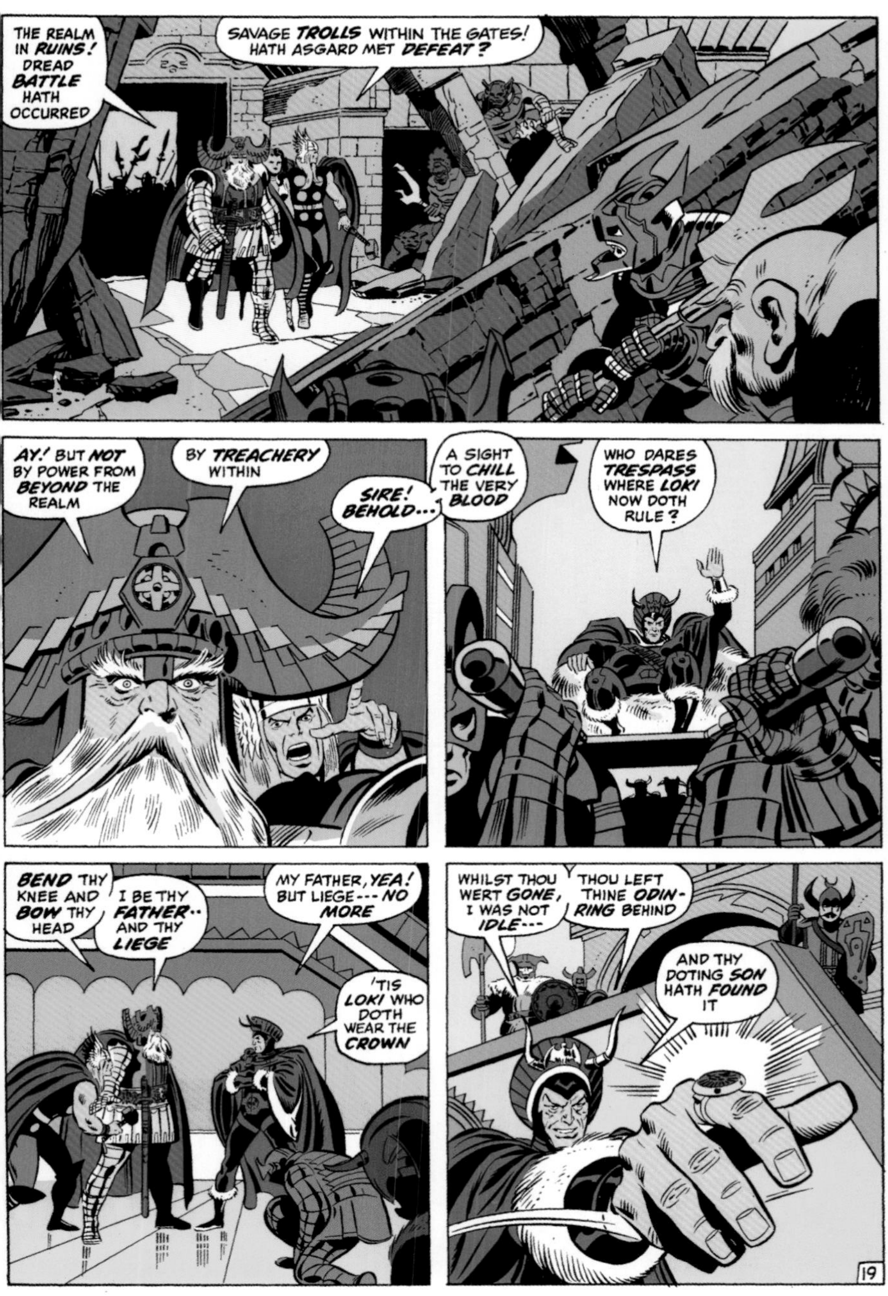
THE REALM IN RUINS! DREAD BATTLE HATH OCCURRED
SAVAGE TROLLS WITHIN THE GATES! HATH ASGARD MET DEFEAT?
AY! BUT NOT BY POWER FROM BEYOND THE REALM
BY TREACHERY WITHIN
SIRE! BEHOLD...
A SIGHT TO CHILL THE VERY BLOOD
WHO DARES TRESPASS WHERE LOKI NOW DOTH RULE?
BEND THY KNEE AND BOW THY HEAD
I BE THY FATHER.. AND THY LIEGE
MY FATHER, YEA! BUT LIEGE--- NO MORE
'TIS LOKI WHO DOTH WEAR THE CROWN
WHILST THOU WERT GONE, I WAS NOT IDLE---
THOU LEFT THINE ODIN-RING BEHIND
AND THY DOTING SON HATH FOUND IT
19

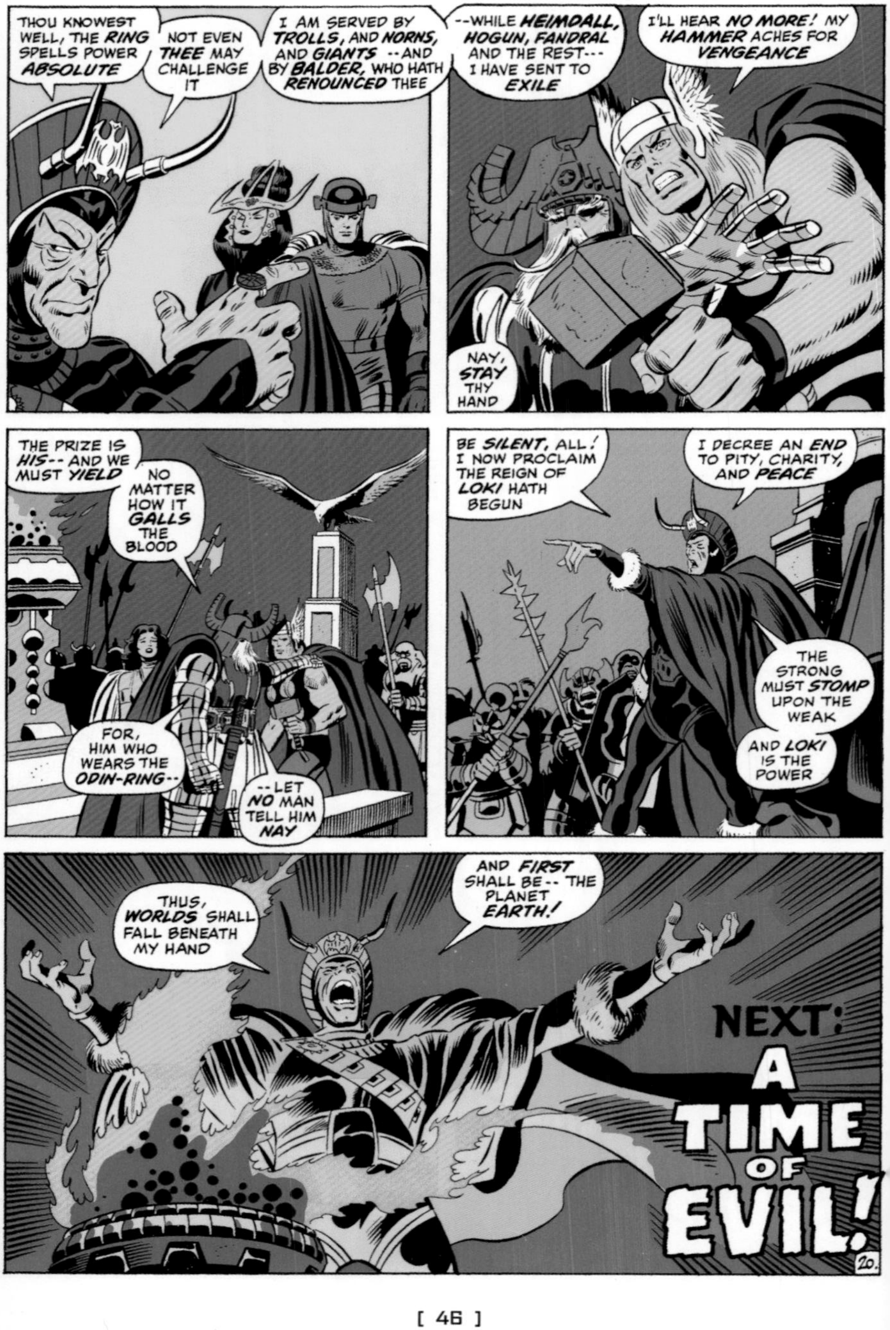

THOU KNOWEST WELL, THE RING SPELLS POWER ABSOLUTE
NOT EVEN THEE MAY CHALLENGE IT
I AM SERVED BY TROLLS, AND NORNS, AND GIANTS --AND BY BALDER, WHO HATH RENOUNCED THEE
--WHILE HEIMDALL, HOGUN, FANDRAL AND THE REST--- I HAVE SENT TO EXILE
I'LL HEAR NO MORE! MY HAMMER ACHES FOR VENGEANCE
NAY, STAY THY HAND
THE PRIZE IS HIS-- AND WE MUST YIELD
NO MATTER HOW IT GALLS THE BLOOD
FOR, HIM WHO WEARS THE ODIN-RING--
--LET NO MAN TELL HIM NAY
BE SILENT, ALL! I NOW PROCLAIM THE REIGN OF LOKI HATH BEGUN
I DECREE AN END TO PITY, CHARITY, AND PEACE
THE STRONG MUST STOMP UPON THE WEAK
AND LOKI IS THE POWER
THUS, WORLDS SHALL FALL BENEATH MY HAND
AND FIRST SHALL BE-- THE PLANET EARTH!
NEXT:
A TIME OF EVIL!
20.

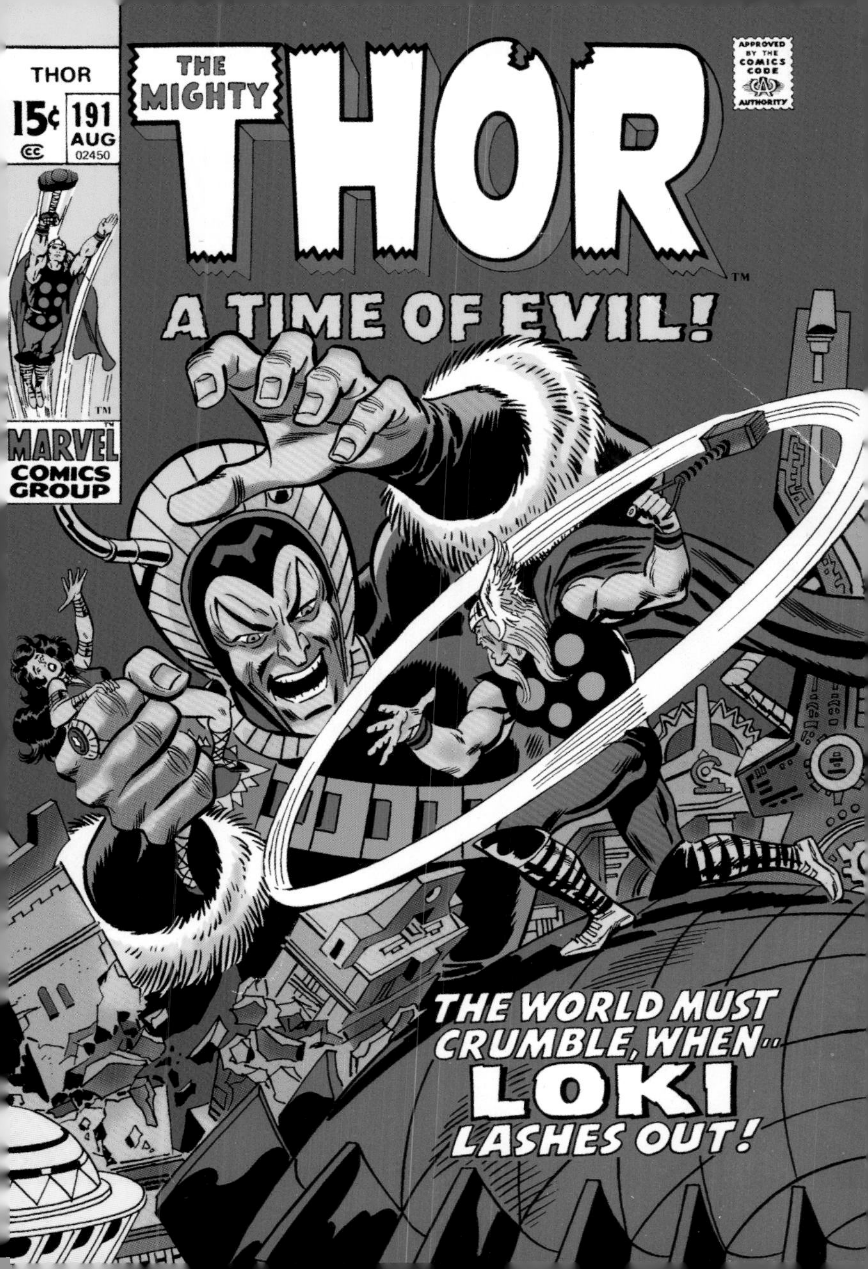
THOR
15¢ 191 AUG
02450
MARVEL COMICS GROUP
THE MIGHTY THOR
APPROVED BY THE COMICS CODE AUTHORITY
A TIME OF EVIL!
THE WORLD MUST CRUMBLE, WHEN..
LOKI
LASHES OUT!

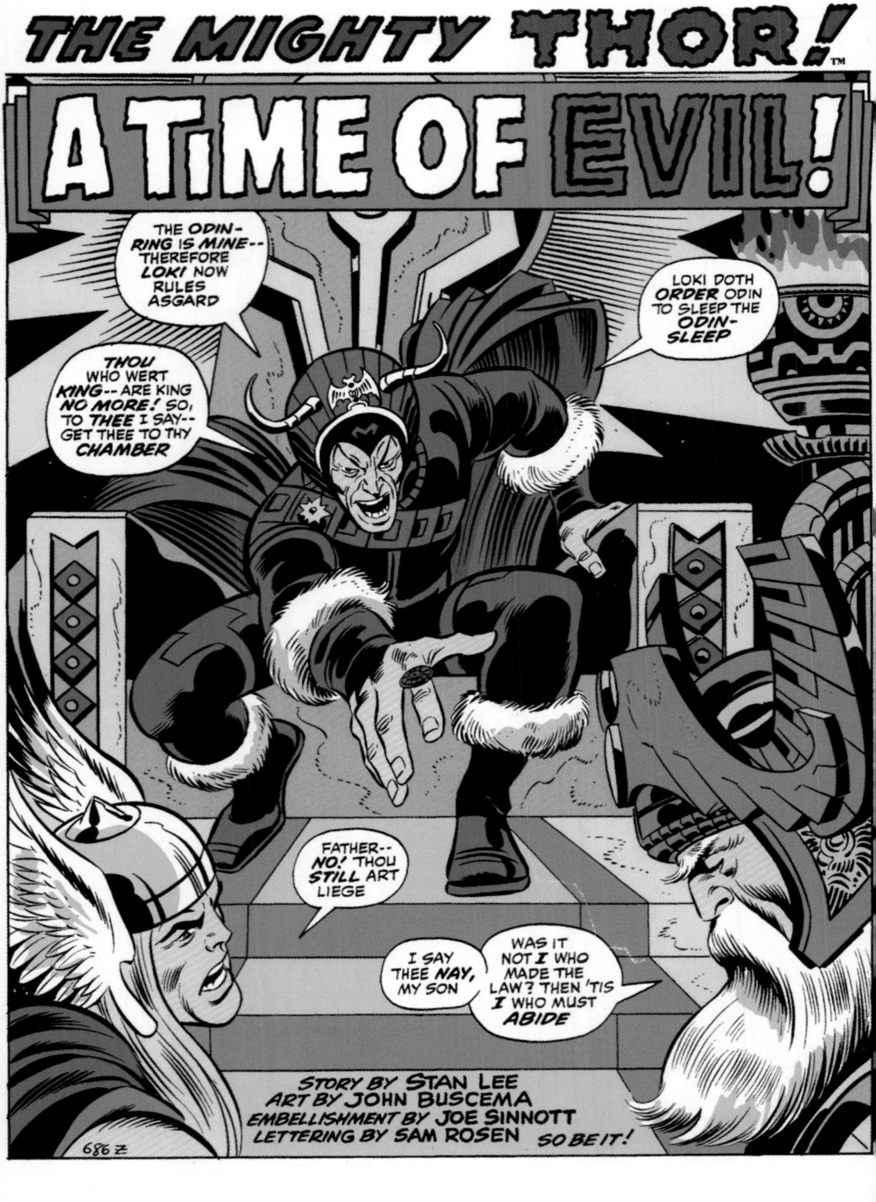
THE MIGHTY THOR!
A TIME OF EVIL!
THE ODIN-RING IS MINE-- THEREFORE LOKI NOW RULES ASGARD
THOU WHO WERT KING-- ARE KING NO MORE! SO, TO THEE I SAY-- GET THEE TO THY CHAMBER
LOKI DOTH ORDER ODIN TO SLEEP THE ODIN-SLEEP
FATHER-- NO! THOU STILL ART LIEGE
I SAY THEE NAY, MY SON
WAS IT NOT I WHO MADE THE LAW? THEN 'TIS I WHO MUST ABIDE
STORY BY STAN LEE
ART BY JOHN BUSCEMA
EMBELLISHMENT BY JOE SINNOTT
LETTERING BY SAM ROSEN SO BE IT!
686 Z

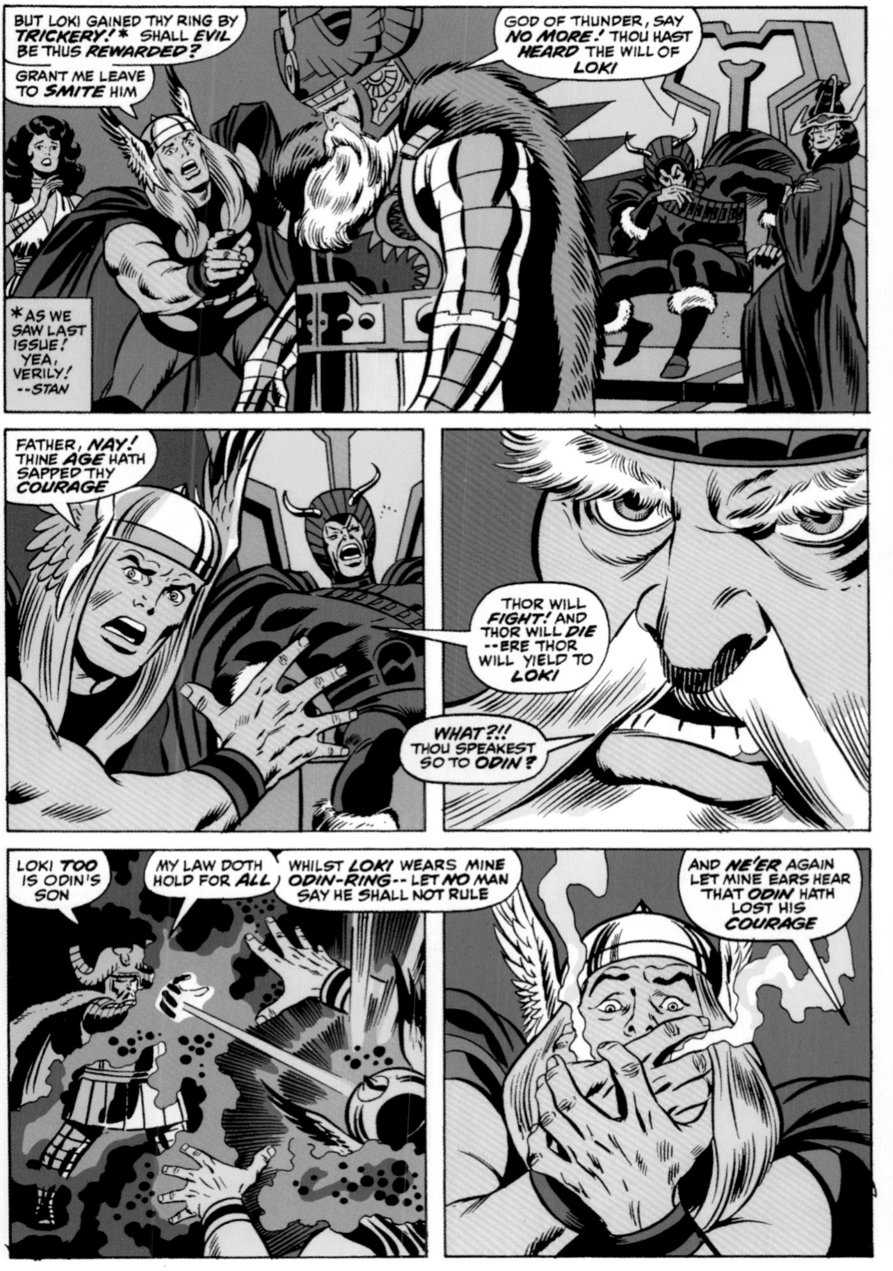

BUT LOKI GAINED THY RING BY TRICKERY!* SHALL EVIL BE THUS REWARDED?
GRANT ME LEAVE TO SMITE HIM
GOD OF THUNDER, SAY NO MORE! THOU HAST HEARD THE WILL OF LOKI
*AS WE SAW LAST ISSUE! YEA, VERILY! --STAN
FATHER, NAY! THINE AGE HATH SAPPED THY COURAGE
THOR WILL FIGHT! AND THOR WILL DIE --ERE THOR WILL YIELD TO LOKI
WHAT?!! THOU SPEAKEST SO TO ODIN?
LOKI TOO IS ODIN'S SON
MY LAW DOTH HOLD FOR ALL
WHILST LOKI WEARS MINE ODIN-RING-- LET NO MAN SAY HE SHALL NOT RULE
AND NE'ER AGAIN LET MINE EARS HEAR THAT ODIN HATH LOST HIS COURAGE

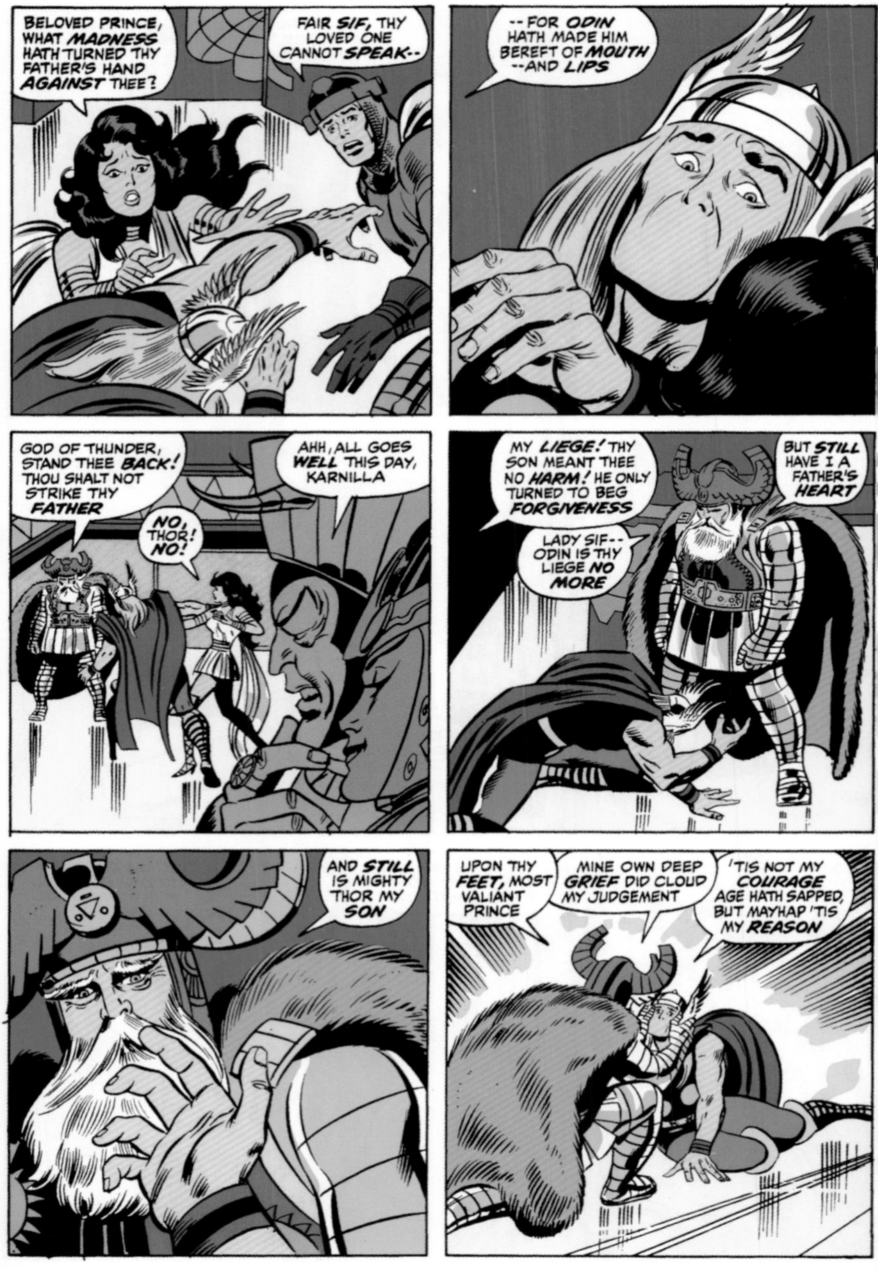
BELOVED PRINCE, WHAT MADNESS HATH TURNED THY FATHER'S HAND AGAINST THEE?
FAIR SIF, THY LOVED ONE CANNOT SPEAK--
--FOR ODIN HATH MADE HIM BEREFT OF MOUTH --AND LIPS
GOD OF THUNDER, STAND THEE BACK! THOU SHALT NOT STRIKE THY FATHER
NO, THOR! NO!
AHH, ALL GOES WELL THIS DAY, KARNILLA
MY LIEGE! THY SON MEANT THEE NO HARM! HE ONLY TURNED TO BEG FORGIVENESS
LADY SIF-- ODIN IS THY LIEGE NO MORE
BUT STILL HAVE I A FATHER'S HEART
AND STILL IS MIGHTY THOR MY SON
UPON THY FEET, MOST VALIANT PRINCE
MINE OWN DEEP GRIEF DID CLOUD MY JUDGEMENT
'TIS NOT MY COURAGE AGE HATH SAPPED, BUT MAYHAP 'TIS MY REASON

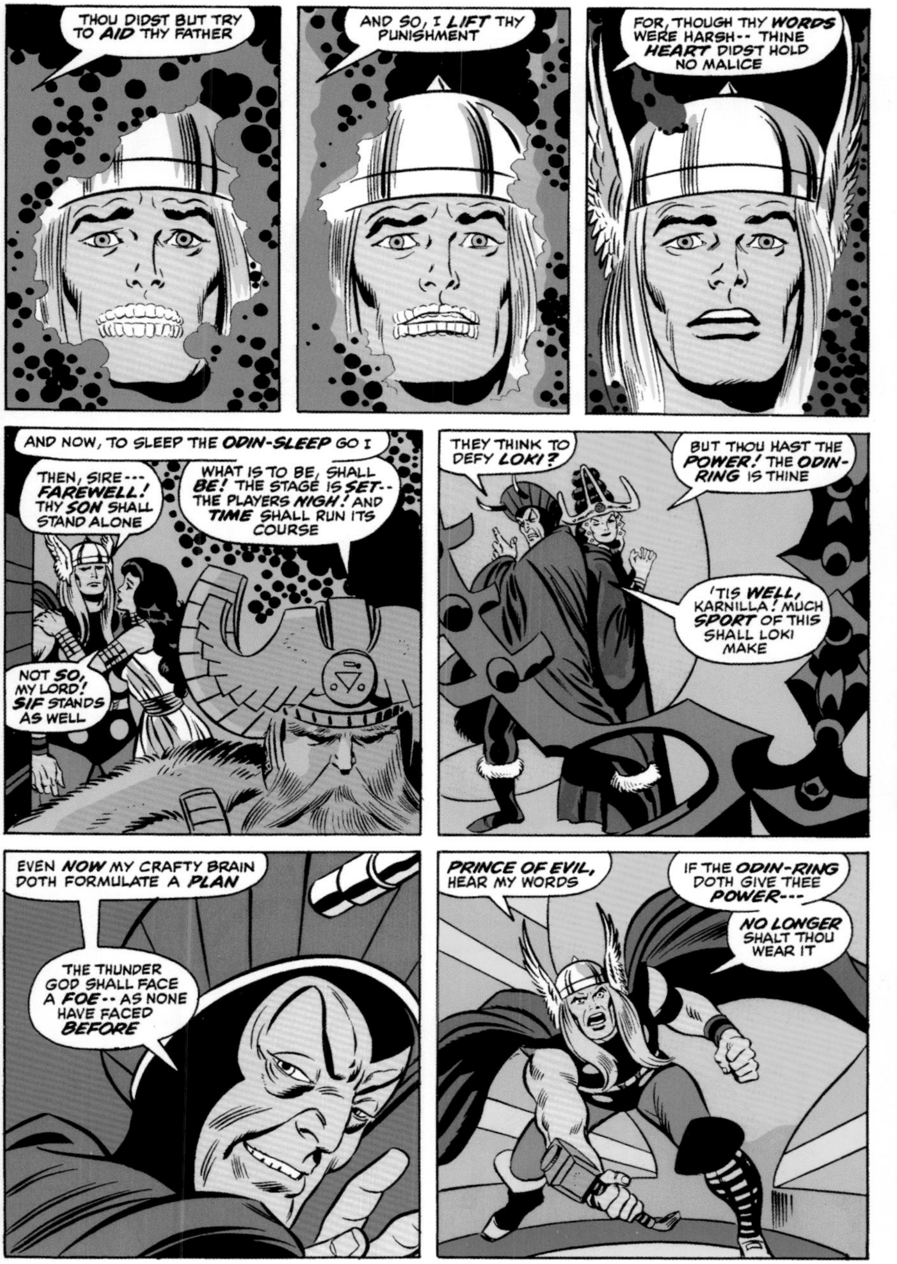
THOU DIDST BUT TRY TO AID THY FATHER
AND SO, I LIFT THY PUNISHMENT
FOR, THOUGH THY WORDS WERE HARSH-- THINE HEART DIDST HOLD NO MALICE
AND NOW, TO SLEEP THE ODIN-SLEEP GO I
THEN, SIRE--- FAREWELL! THY SON SHALL STAND ALONE
WHAT IS TO BE, SHALL BE! THE STAGE IS SET-- THE PLAYERS NIGH! AND TIME SHALL RUN ITS COURSE
NOT SO, MY LORD! SIF STANDS AS WELL
THEY THINK TO DEFY LOKI?
BUT THOU HAST THE POWER! THE ODIN-RING IS THINE
'TIS WELL, KARNILLA! MUCH SPORT OF THIS SHALL LOKI MAKE
EVEN NOW MY CRAFTY BRAIN DOTH FORMULATE A PLAN
THE THUNDER GOD SHALL FACE A FOE-- AS NONE HAVE FACED BEFORE
PRINCE OF EVIL, HEAR MY WORDS
IF THE ODIN-RING DOTH GIVE THEE POWER---
NO LONGER SHALT THOU WEAR IT

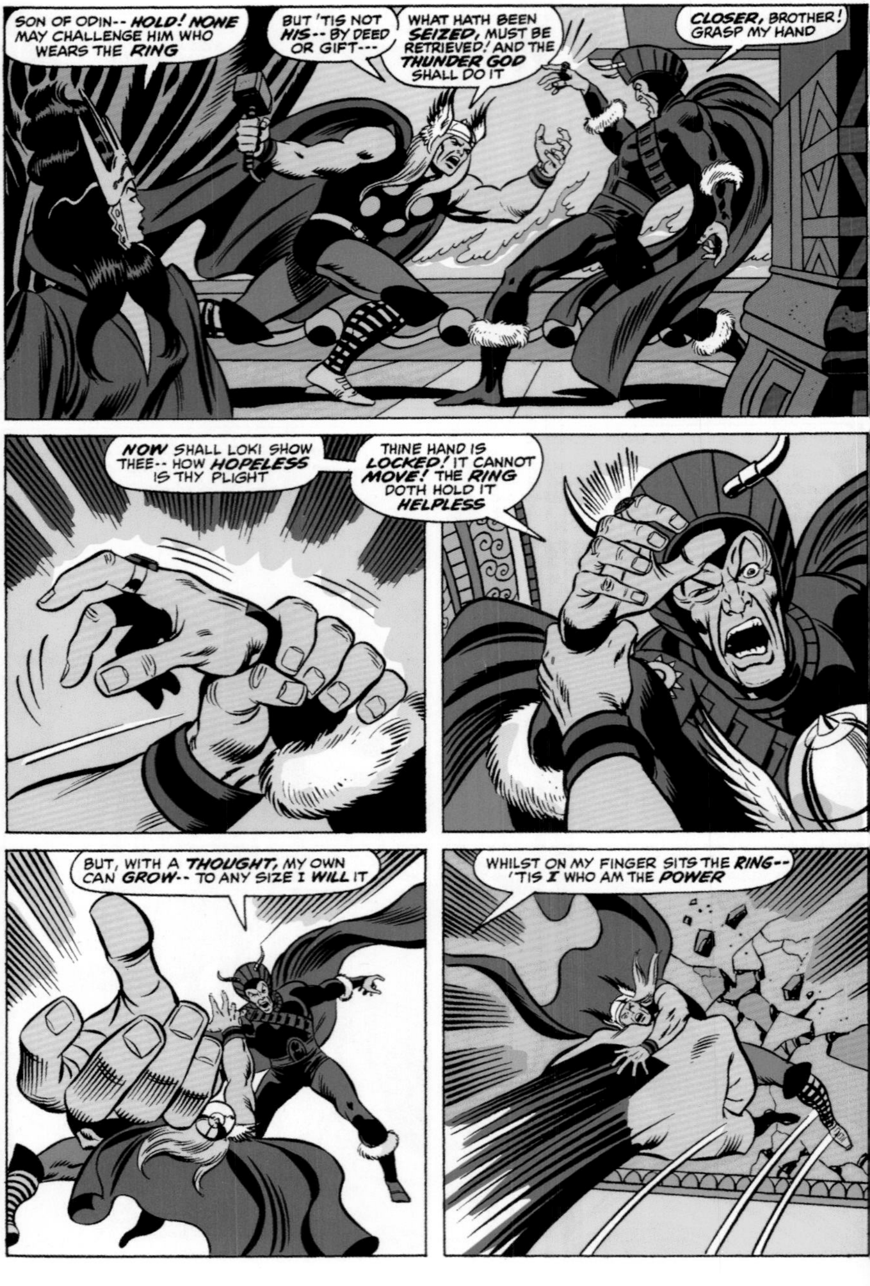
SON OF ODIN-- HOLD! NONE MAY CHALLENGE HIM WHO WEARS THE RING
BUT 'TIS NOT HIS-- BY DEED OR GIFT---
WHAT HATH BEEN SEIZED, MUST BE RETRIEVED! AND THE THUNDER GOD SHALL DO IT
CLOSER, BROTHER! GRASP MY HAND
NOW SHALL LOKI SHOW THEE-- HOW HOPELESS IS THY PLIGHT
THINE HAND IS LOCKED! IT CANNOT MOVE! THE RING DOTH HOLD IT HELPLESS
BUT, WITH A THOUGHT, MY OWN CAN GROW-- TO ANY SIZE I WILL IT
WHILST ON MY FINGER SITS THE RING-- 'TIS I WHO AM THE POWER

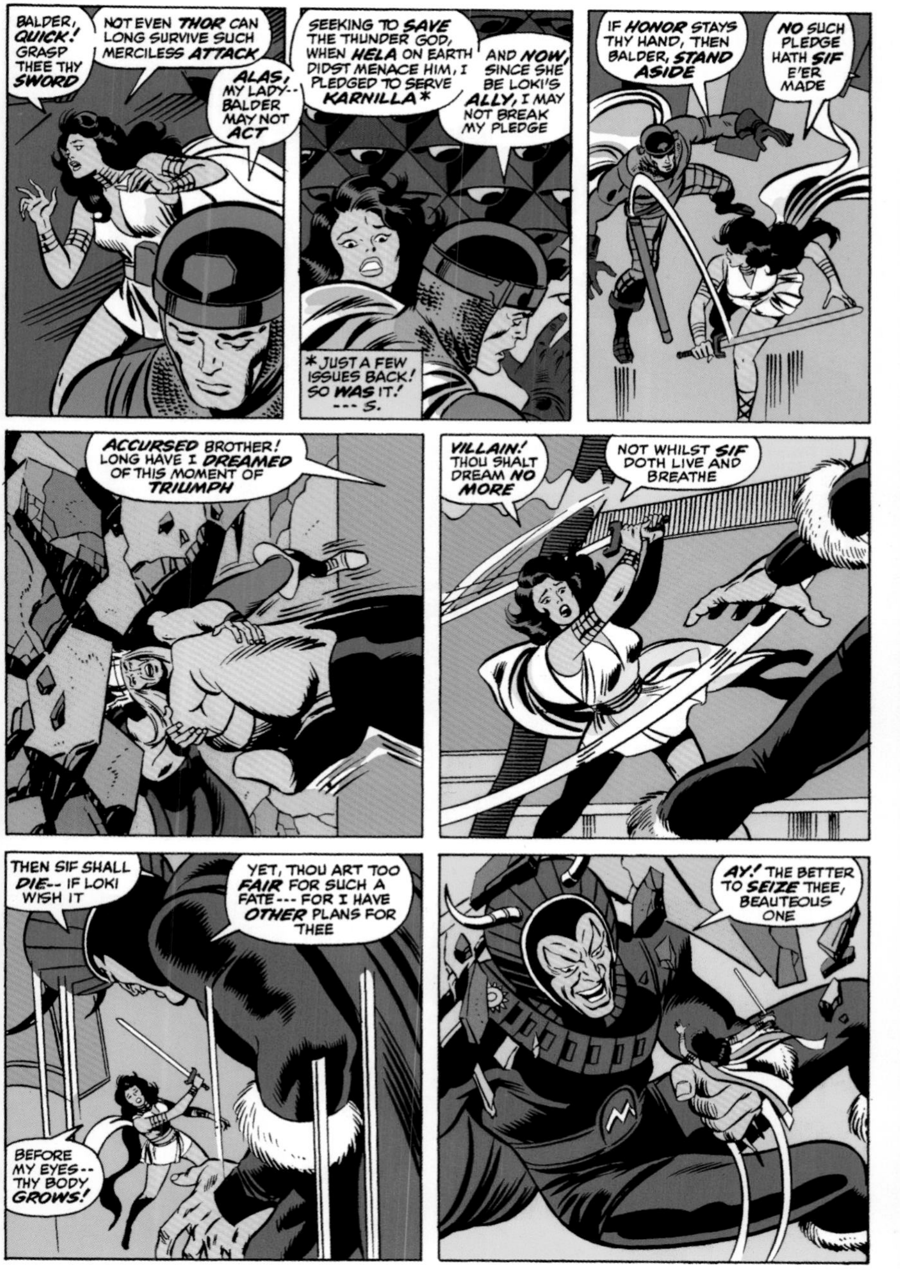
BALDER, QUICK! GRASP THEE THY SWORD
NOT EVEN THOR CAN LONG SURVIVE SUCH MERCILESS ATTACK
ALAS, MY LADY-- BALDER MAY NOT ACT
SEEKING TO SAVE THE THUNDER GOD, WHEN HELA ON EARTH DIDST MENACE HIM, I PLEDGED TO SERVE KARNILLA*
AND NOW, SINCE SHE BE LOKI'S ALLY, I MAY NOT BREAK MY PLEDGE
*JUST A FEW ISSUES BACK! SO WAS IT.' --- S.
IF HONOR STAYS THY HAND, THEN BALDER, STAND ASIDE
NO SUCH PLEDGE HATH SIF E'ER MADE
ACCURSED BROTHER! LONG HAVE I DREAMED OF THIS MOMENT OF TRIUMPH
VILLAIN! THOU SHALT DREAM NO MORE
NOT WHILST SIF DOTH LIVE AND BREATHE
THEN SIF SHALL DIE-- IF LOKI WISH IT
YET, THOU ART TOO FAIR FOR SUCH A FATE--- FOR I HAVE OTHER PLANS FOR THEE
BEFORE MY EYES-- THY BODY GROWS!
AY! THE BETTER TO SEIZE THEE, BEAUTEOUS ONE

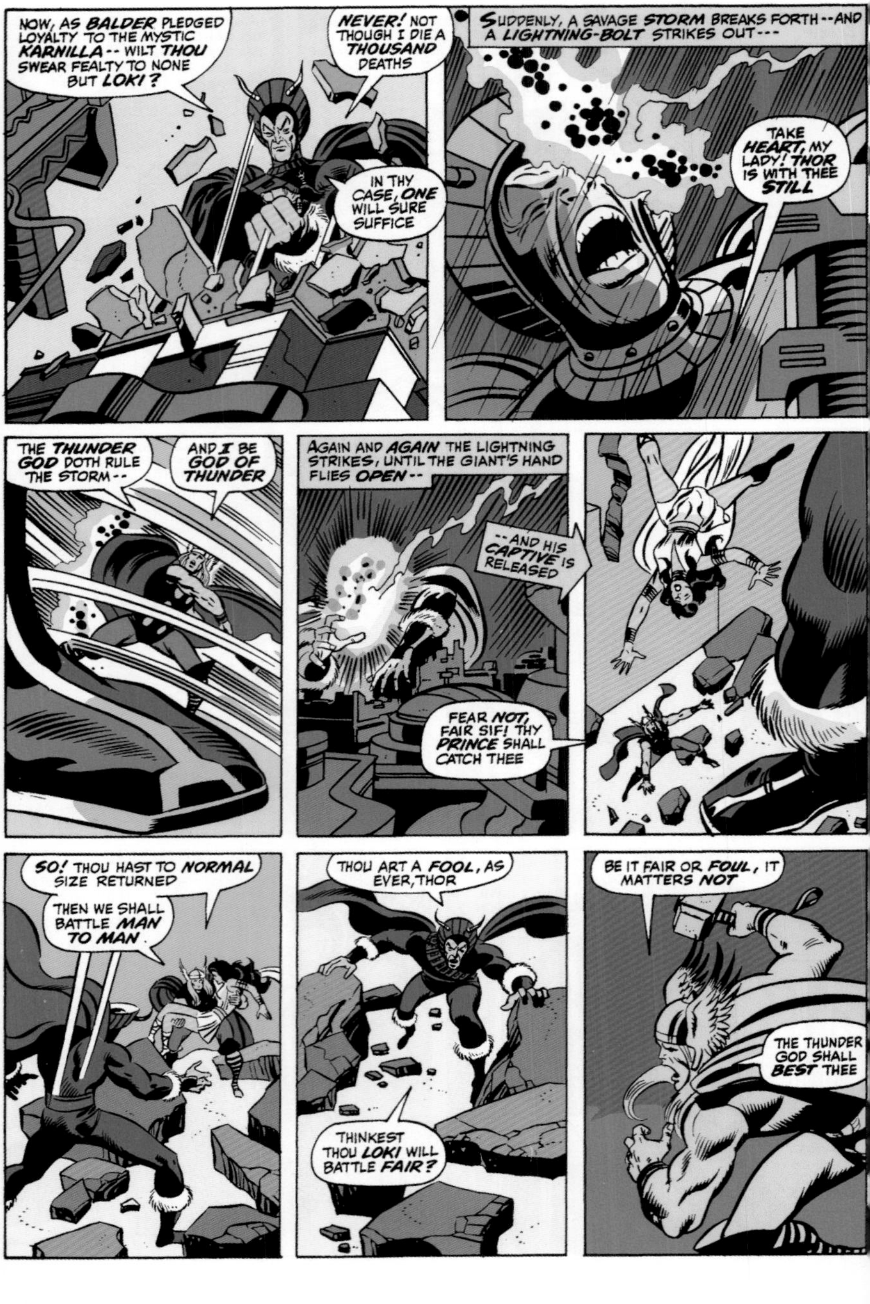
NOW, AS BALDER PLEDGED LOYALTY TO THE MYSTIC KARNILLA -- WILT THOU SWEAR FEALTY TO NONE BUT LOKI?
NEVER! NOT THOUGH I DIE A THOUSAND DEATHS
IN THY CASE, ONE WILL SURE SUFFICE
SUDDENLY, A SAVAGE STORM BREAKS FORTH -- AND A LIGHTNING-BOLT STRIKES OUT---
TAKE HEART, MY LADY! THOR IS WITH THEE STILL
THE THUNDER GOD DOTH RULE THE STORM --
AND I BE GOD OF THUNDER
AGAIN AND AGAIN THE LIGHTNING STRIKES, UNTIL THE GIANT'S HAND FLIES OPEN --
-- AND HIS CAPTIVE IS RELEASED
FEAR NOT, FAIR SIF! THY PRINCE SHALL CATCH THEE
SO! THOU HAST TO NORMAL SIZE RETURNED
THEN WE SHALL BATTLE MAN TO MAN
THOU ART A FOOL, AS EVER, THOR
THINKEST THOU LOKI WILL BATTLE FAIR?
BE IT FAIR OR FOUL, IT MATTERS NOT
THE THUNDER GOD SHALL BEST THEE

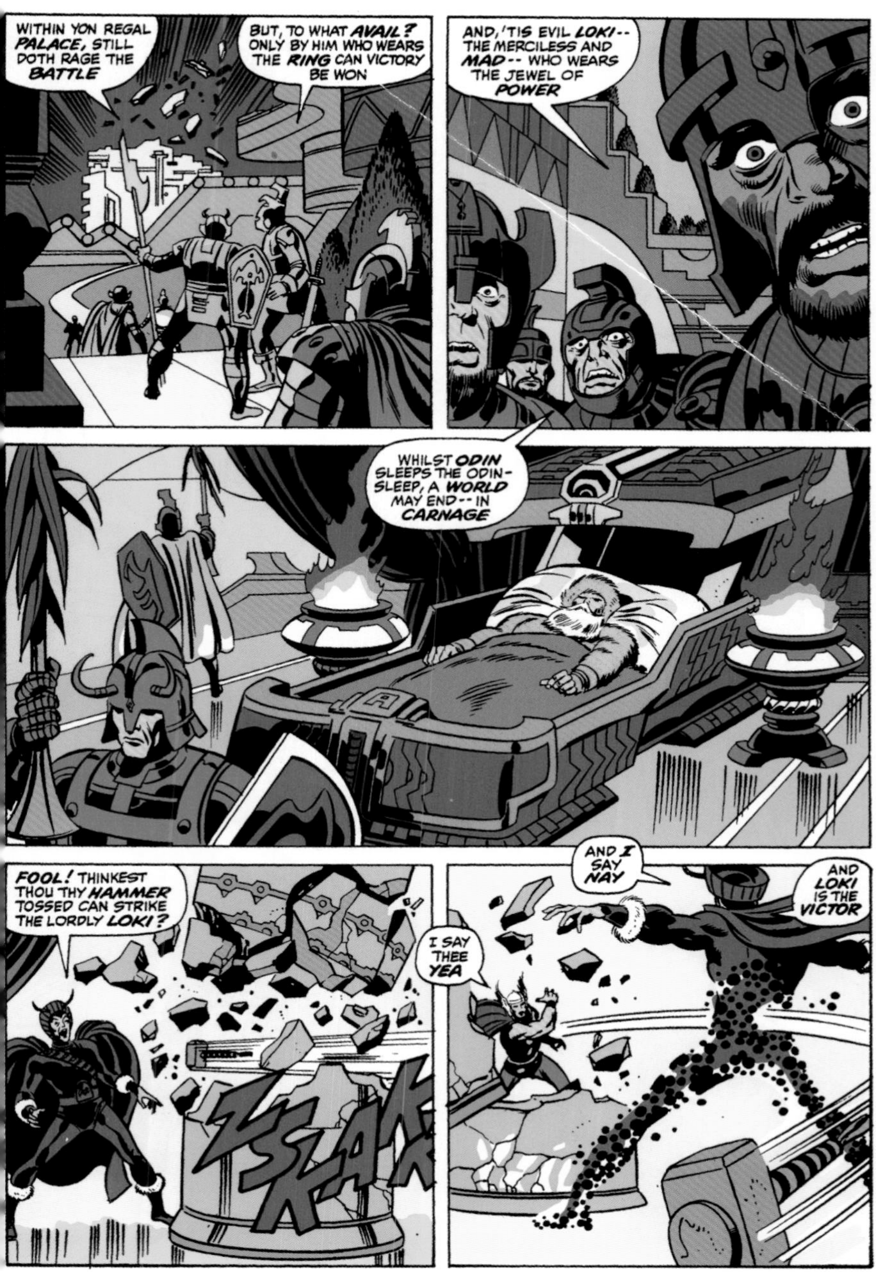
WITHIN YON REGAL PALACE, STILL DOTH RAGE THE BATTLE
BUT, TO WHAT AVAIL? ONLY BY HIM WHO WEARS THE RING CAN VICTORY BE WON
AND, 'TIS EVIL LOKI-- THE MERCILESS AND MAD-- WHO WEARS THE JEWEL OF POWER
WHILST ODIN SLEEPS THE ODIN-SLEEP, A WORLD MAY END--IN CARNAGE
FOOL! THINKEST THOU THY HAMMER TOSSED CAN STRIKE THE LORDLY LOKI?
AND I SAY NAY
I SAY THEE YEA
AND LOKI IS THE VICTOR

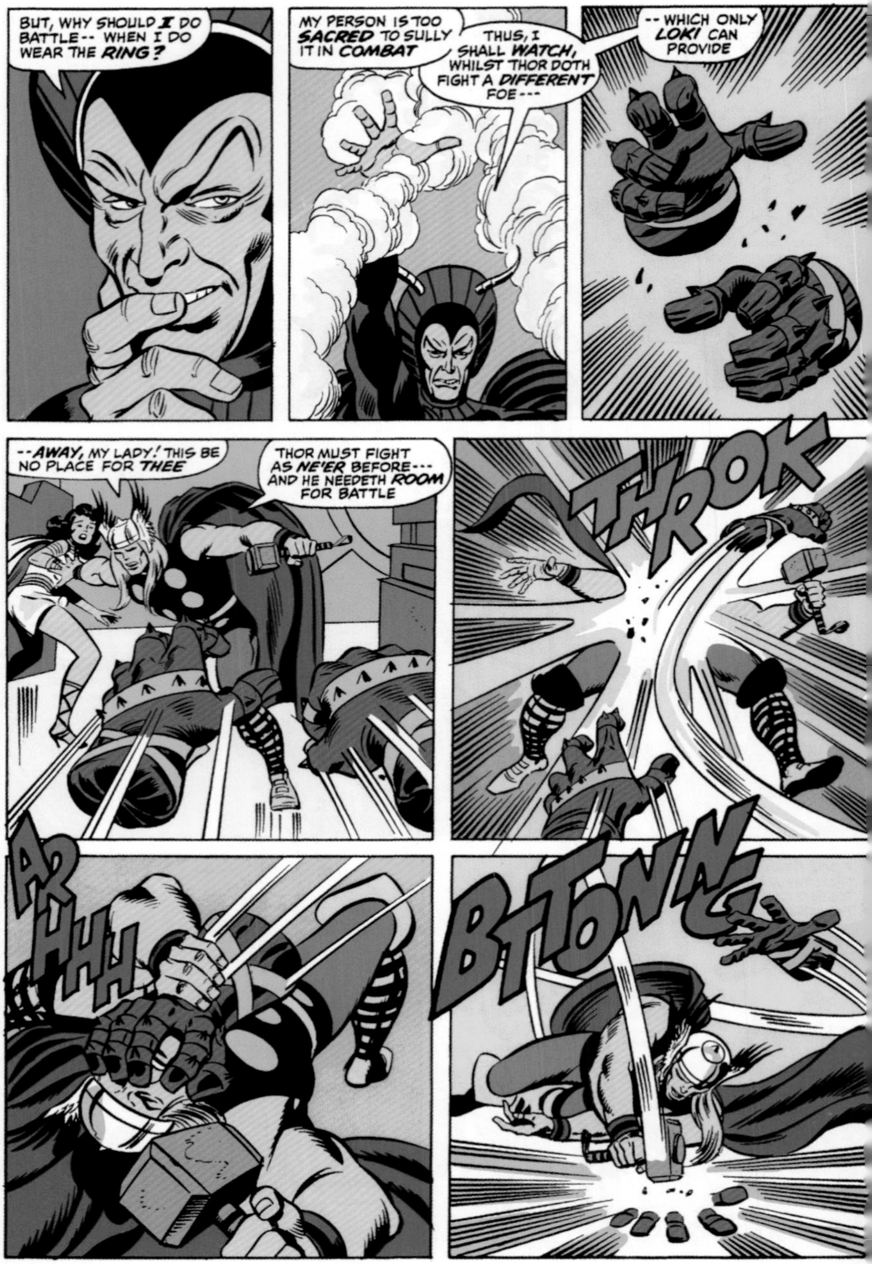
BUT, WHY SHOULD I DO BATTLE-- WHEN I DO WEAR THE RING?
MY PERSON IS TOO SACRED TO SULLY IT IN COMBAT
THUS, I SHALL WATCH, WHILST THOR DOTH FIGHT A DIFFERENT FOE---
--WHICH ONLY LOKI CAN PROVIDE
--AWAY, MY LADY! THIS BE NO PLACE FOR THEE
THOR MUST FIGHT AS NE'ER BEFORE--- AND HE NEEDETH ROOM FOR BATTLE
THROK
ARHHH
BTONNG

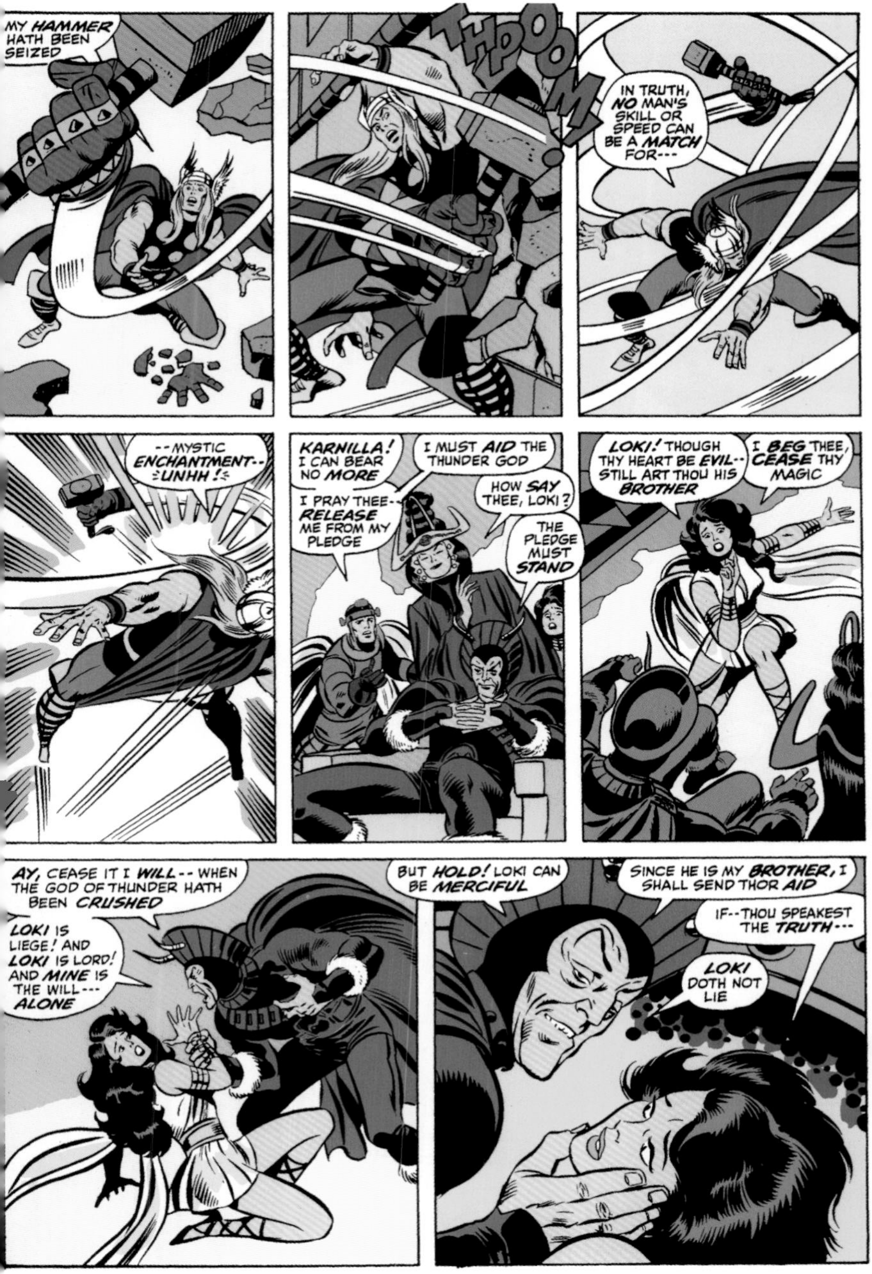
MY HAMMER HATH BEEN SEIZED
THHPOOOM!
IN TRUTH, NO MAN'S SKILL OR SPEED CAN BE A MATCH FOR---
--MYSTIC ENCHANTMENT-- UNHH!
KARNILLA! I CAN BEAR NO MORE
I PRAY THEE-- RELEASE ME FROM MY PLEDGE
I MUST AID THE THUNDER GOD
HOW SAY THEE, LOKI?
THE PLEDGE MUST STAND
LOKI! THOUGH THY HEART BE EVIL-- STILL ART THOU HIS BROTHER
I BEG THEE, CEASE THY MAGIC
AY, CEASE IT I WILL-- WHEN THE GOD OF THUNDER HATH BEEN CRUSHED
LOKI IS LIEGE! AND LOKI IS LORD! AND MINE IS THE WILL--- ALONE
BUT HOLD! LOKI CAN BE MERCIFUL
SINCE HE IS MY BROTHER, I SHALL SEND THOR AID
IF--THOU SPEAKEST THE TRUTH---
LOKI DOTH NOT LIE

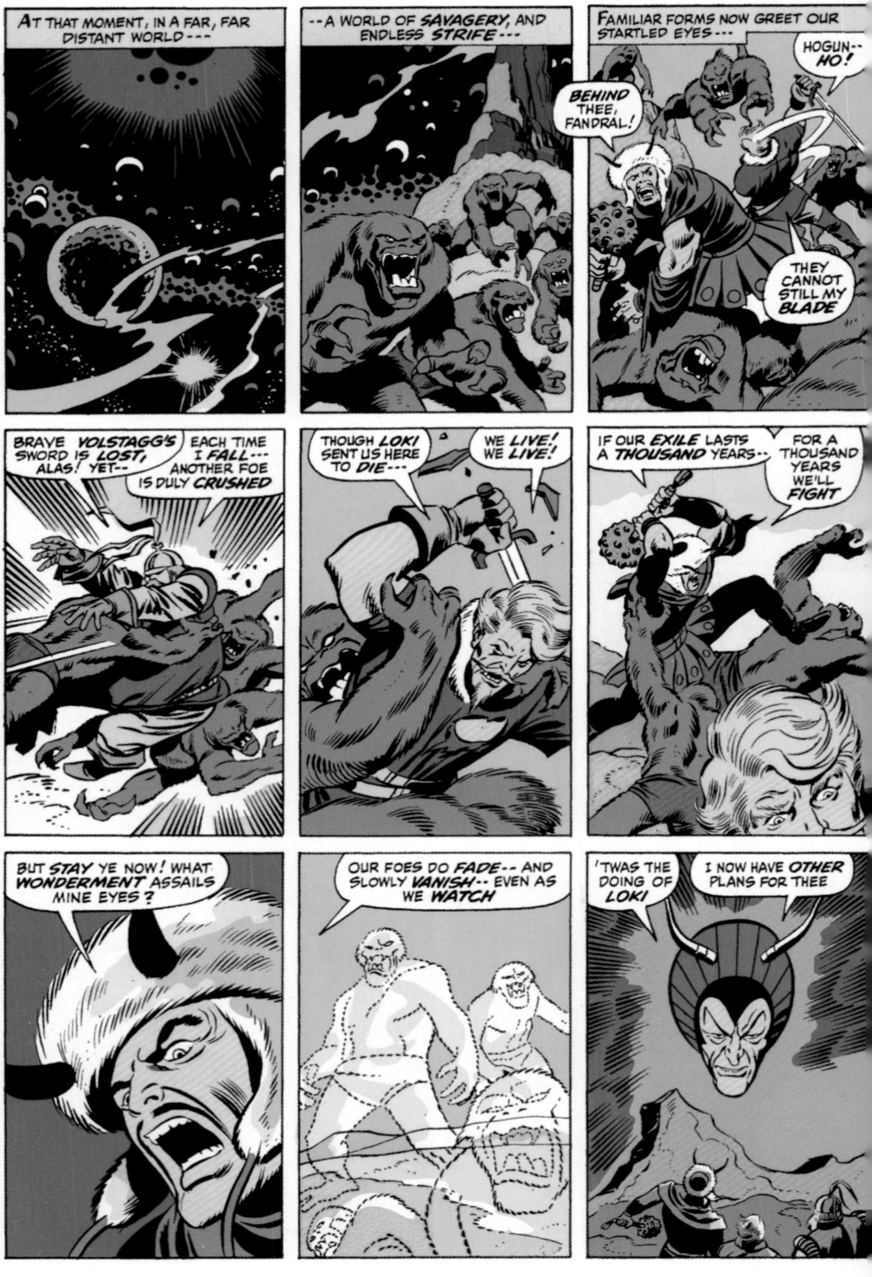
AT THAT MOMENT, IN A FAR, FAR DISTANT WORLD---
--A WORLD OF SAVAGERY, AND ENDLESS STRIFE---
FAMILIAR FORMS NOW GREET OUR STARTLED EYES---
HOGUN--HO!
BEHIND THEE, FANDRAL!
THEY CANNOT STILL MY BLADE
BRAVE VOLSTAGG'S SWORD IS LOST, ALAS! YET--
EACH TIME I FALL--- ANOTHER FOE IS DULY CRUSHED
THOUGH LOKI SENT US HERE TO DIE---
WE LIVE! WE LIVE!
IF OUR EXILE LASTS A THOUSAND YEARS--
FOR A THOUSAND YEARS WE'LL FIGHT
BUT STAY YE NOW! WHAT WONDERMENT ASSAILS MINE EYES?
OUR FOES DO FADE-- AND SLOWLY VANISH-- EVEN AS WE WATCH
'TWAS THE DOING OF LOKI
I NOW HAVE OTHER PLANS FOR THEE

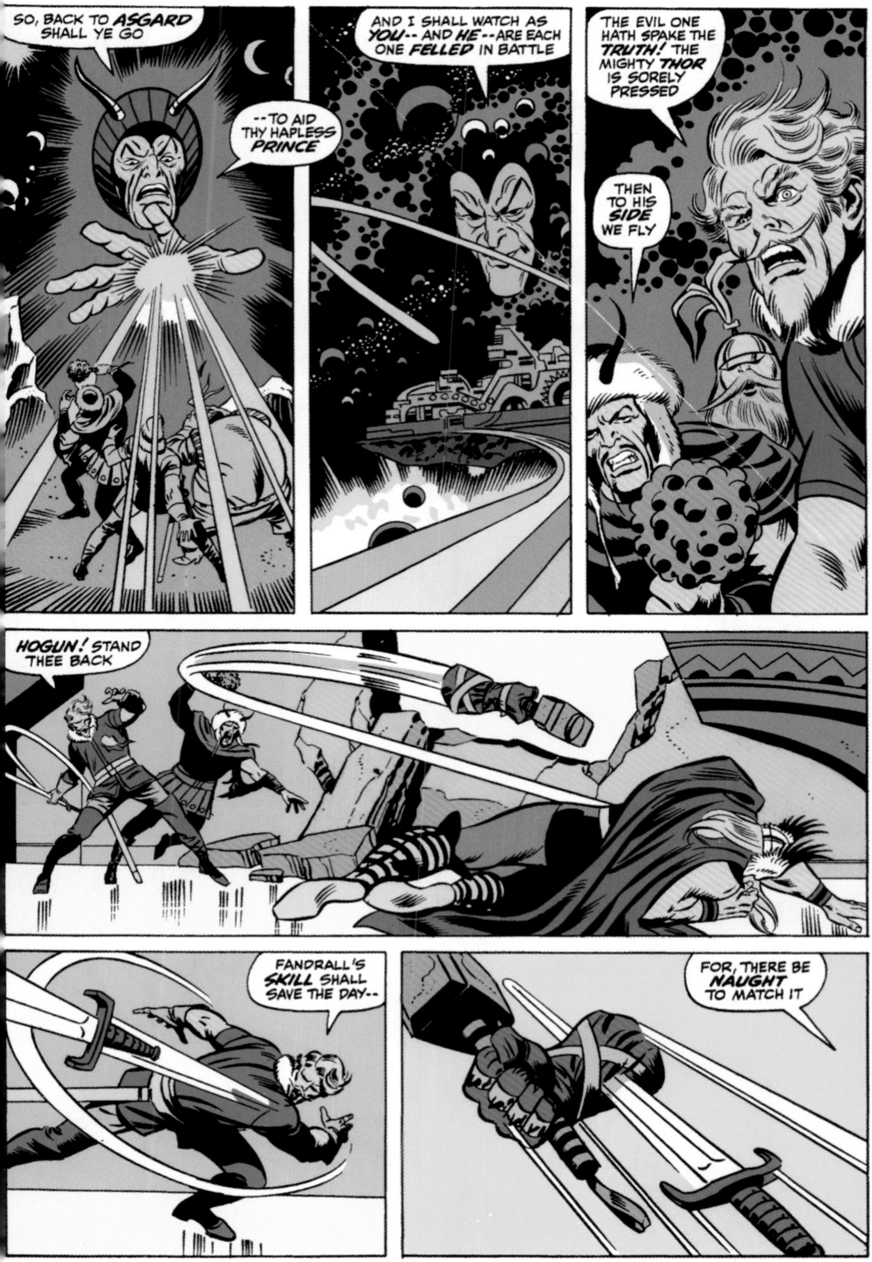
SO, BACK TO ASGARD SHALL YE GO
--TO AID THY HAPLESS PRINCE
AND I SHALL WATCH AS YOU-- AND HE--ARE EACH ONE FELLED IN BATTLE
THE EVIL ONE HATH SPAKE THE TRUTH! THE MIGHTY THOR IS SORELY PRESSED
THEN TO HIS SIDE WE FLY
HOGUN! STAND THEE BACK
FANDRALL'S SKILL SHALL SAVE THE DAY--
FOR, THERE BE NAUGHT TO MATCH IT

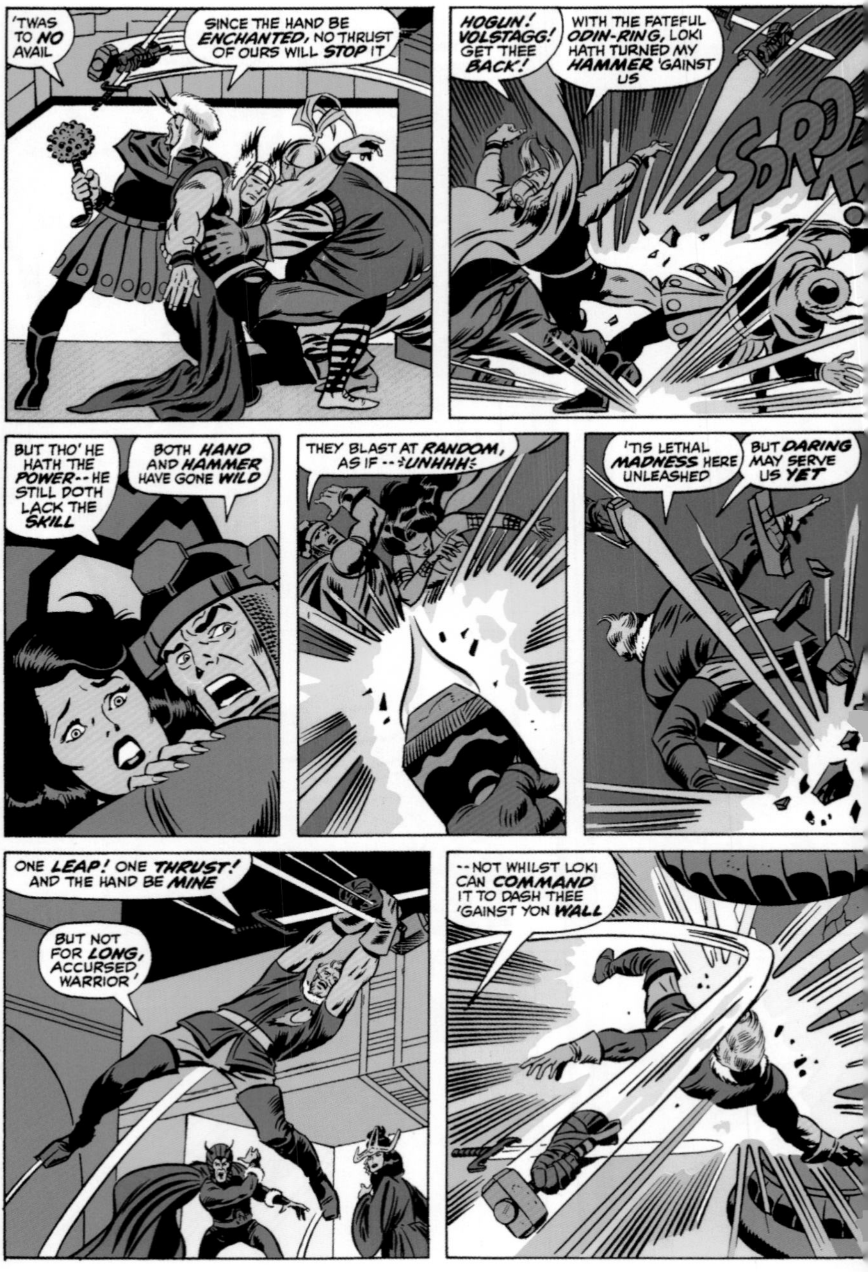
'TWAS TO NO AVAIL
SINCE THE HAND BE ENCHANTED, NO THRUST OF OURS WILL STOP IT
HOGUN! VOLSTAGG! GET THEE BACK!
WITH THE FATEFUL ODIN-RING, LOKI HATH TURNED MY HAMMER 'GAINST US
BUT THO' HE HATH THE POWER-- HE STILL DOTH LACK THE SKILL
BOTH HAND AND HAMMER HAVE GONE WILD
THEY BLAST AT RANDOM, AS IF -- UNHHH!
'TIS LETHAL MADNESS HERE UNLEASHED
BUT DARING MAY SERVE US YET
ONE LEAP! ONE THRUST! AND THE HAND BE MINE
BUT NOT FOR LONG, ACCURSED WARRIOR!
-- NOT WHILST LOKI CAN COMMAND IT TO DASH THEE 'GAINST YON WALL

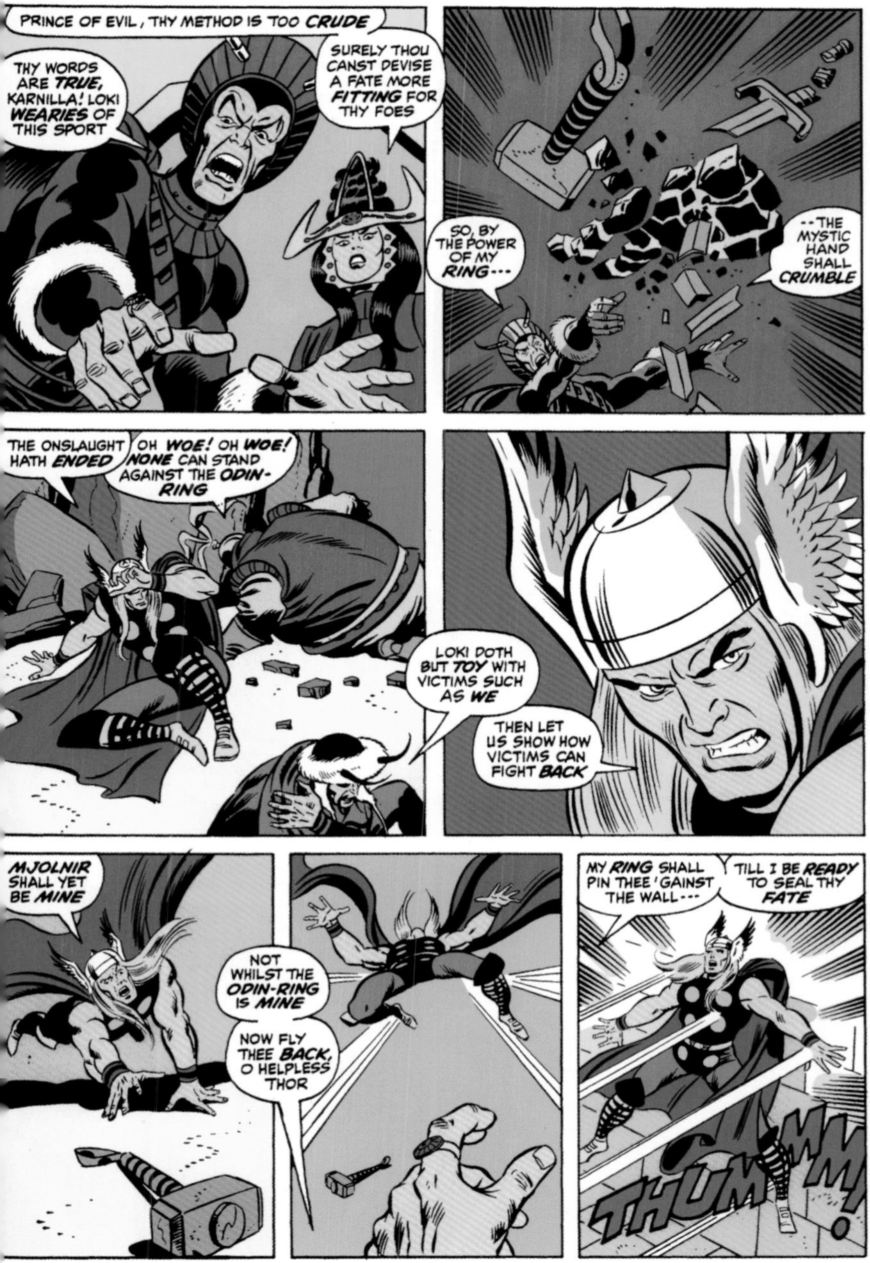
PRINCE OF EVIL, THY METHOD IS TOO CRUDE
THY WORDS ARE TRUE, KARNILLA! LOKI WEARIES OF THIS SPORT
SURELY THOU CANST DEVISE A FATE MORE FITTING FOR THY FOES
SO, BY THE POWER OF MY RING---
--THE MYSTIC HAND SHALL CRUMBLE
THE ONSLAUGHT HATH ENDED
OH WOE! OH WOE! NONE CAN STAND AGAINST THE ODIN-RING
LOKI DOTH BUT TOY WITH VICTIMS SUCH AS WE
THEN LET US SHOW HOW VICTIMS CAN FIGHT BACK
MJOLNIR SHALL YET BE MINE
NOT WHILST THE ODIN-RING IS MINE
NOW FLY THEE BACK, O HELPLESS THOR
MY RING SHALL PIN THEE 'GAINST THE WALL---
TILL I BE READY TO SEAL THY FATE
THUMMMM!

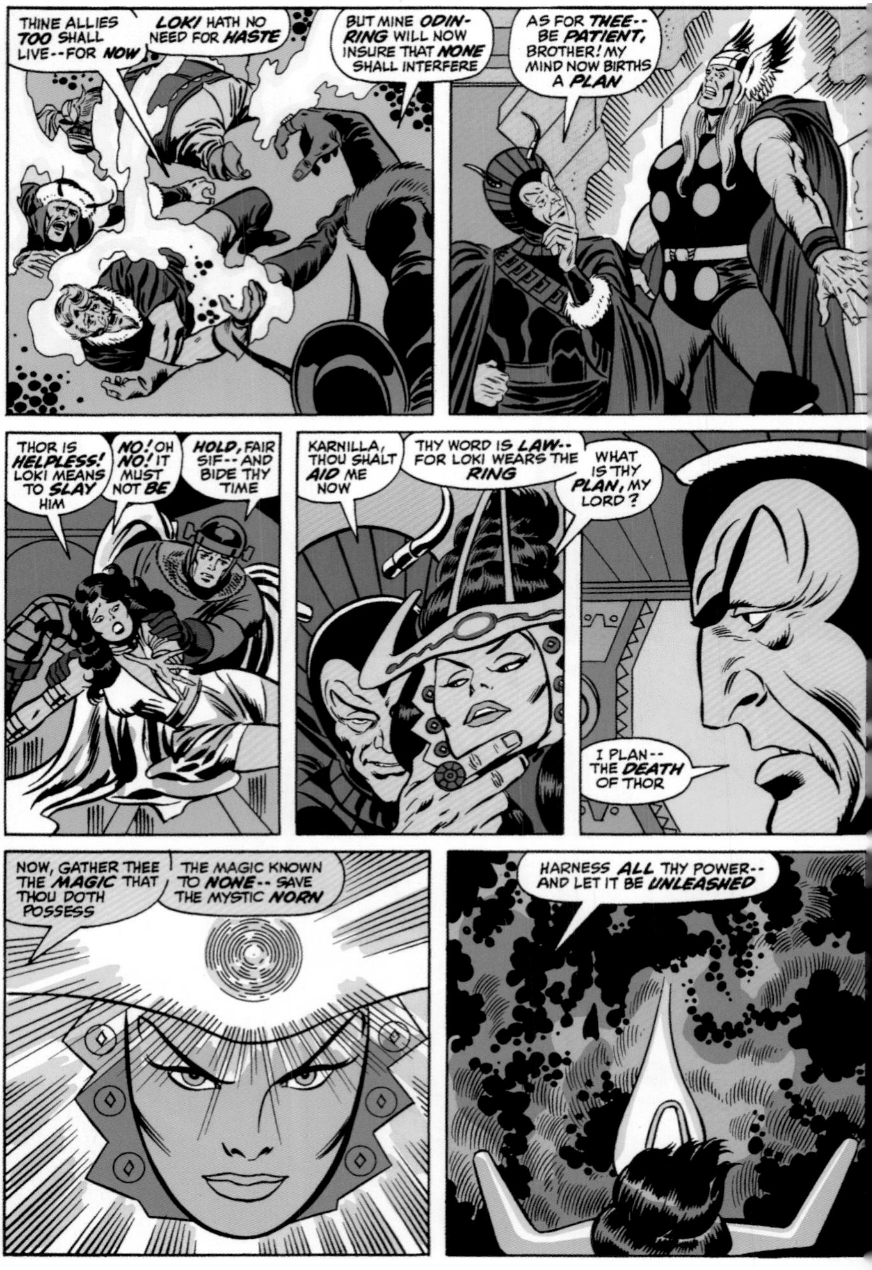
THINE ALLIES TOO SHALL LIVE--FOR NOW
LOKI! HATH NO NEED FOR HASTE
BUT MINE ODIN-RING WILL NOW INSURE THAT NONE SHALL INTERFERE
AS FOR THEE--BE PATIENT, BROTHER! MY MIND NOW BIRTHS A PLAN
THOR IS HELPLESS! LOKI MEANS TO SLAY HIM
NO! OH NO! IT MUST NOT BE
HOLD, FAIR SIF--AND BIDE THY TIME
KARNILLA, THOU SHALT AID ME NOW
THY WORD IS LAW--FOR LOKI WEARS THE RING
WHAT IS THY PLAN, MY LORD?
I PLAN--THE DEATH OF THOR
NOW, GATHER THEE THE MAGIC THAT THOU DOTH POSSESS
THE MAGIC KNOWN TO NONE--SAVE THE MYSTIC NORN
HARNESS ALL THY POWER--AND LET IT BE UNLEASHED

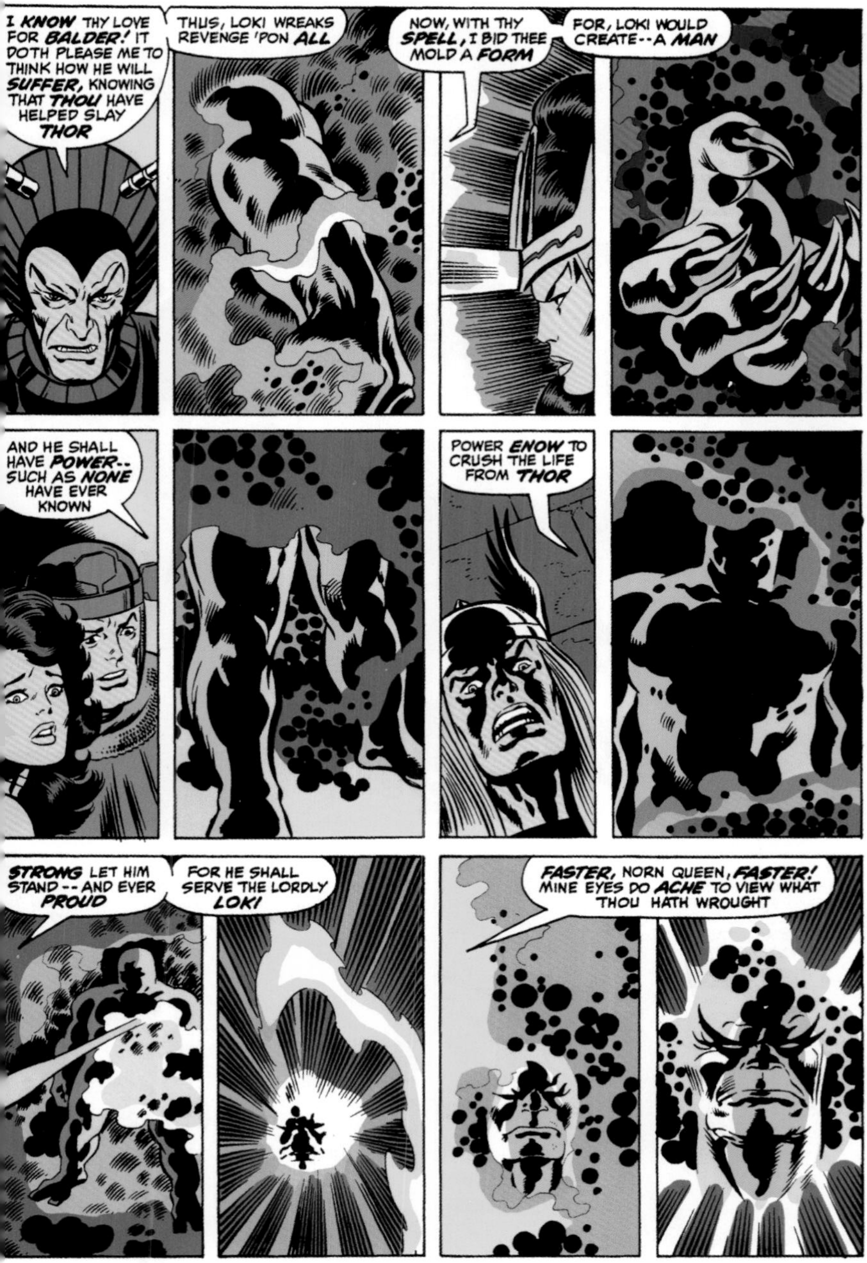
I KNOW THY LOVE FOR BALDER! IT DOTH PLEASE ME TO THINK HOW HE WILL SUFFER, KNOWING THAT THOU HAVE HELPED SLAY THOR
THUS, LOKI WREAKS REVENGE 'PON ALL
NOW, WITH THY SPELL, I BID THEE MOLD A FORM
FOR, LOKI WOULD CREATE--A MAN
AND HE SHALL HAVE POWER-- SUCH AS NONE HAVE EVER KNOWN
POWER ENOW TO CRUSH THE LIFE FROM THOR
STRONG LET HIM STAND -- AND EVER PROUD
FOR HE SHALL SERVE THE LORDLY LOKI
FASTER, NORN QUEEN, FASTER! MINE EYES DO ACHE TO VIEW WHAT THOU HATH WROUGHT

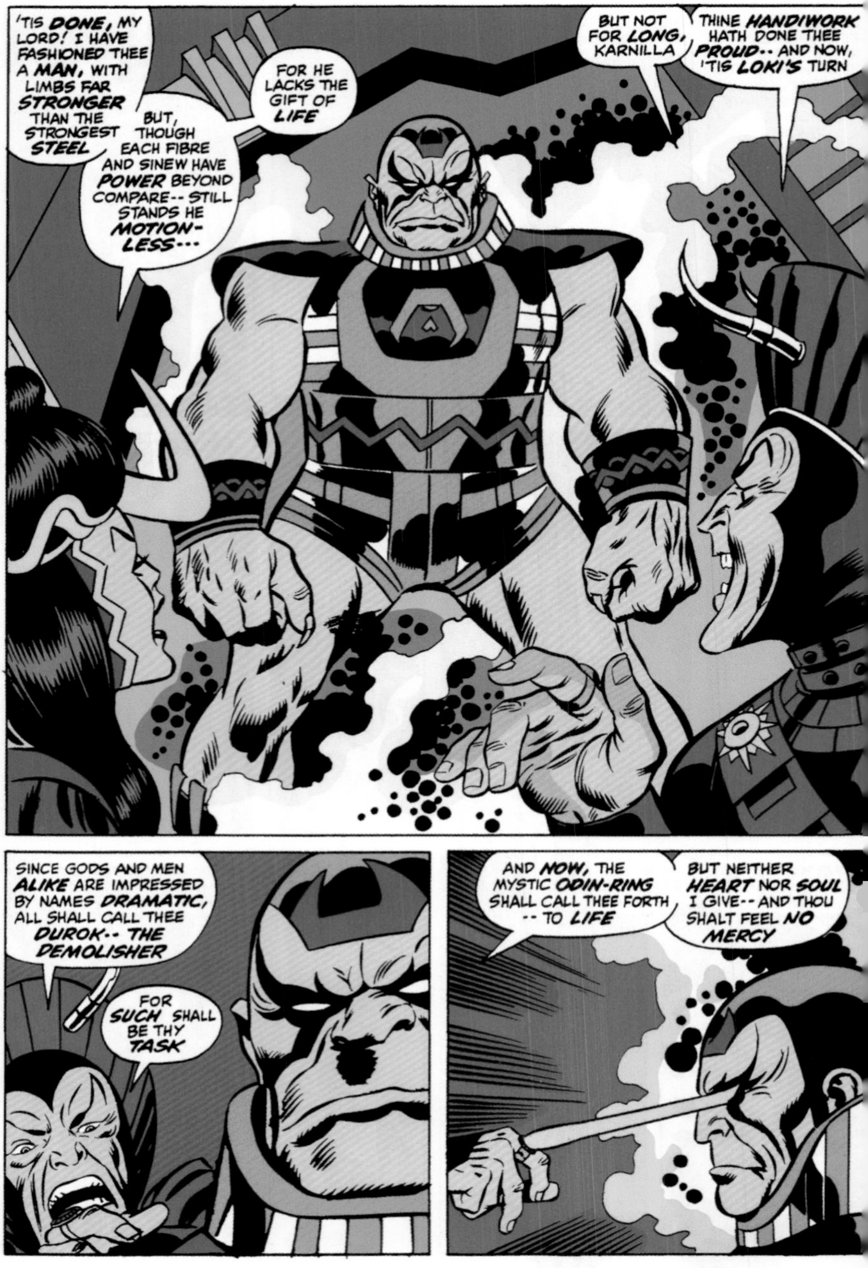
'TIS DONE, MY LORD! I HAVE FASHIONED THEE A MAN, WITH LIMBS FAR STRONGER THAN THE STRONGEST STEEL
BUT, THOUGH EACH FIBRE AND SINEW HAVE POWER BEYOND COMPARE-- STILL STANDS HE MOTION-LESS...
FOR HE LACKS THE GIFT OF LIFE
BUT NOT FOR LONG, KARNILLA
THINE HANDIWORK HATH DONE THEE PROUD-- AND NOW, 'TIS LOKI'S TURN
SINCE GODS AND MEN ALIKE ARE IMPRESSED BY NAMES DRAMATIC, ALL SHALL CALL THEE DUROK-- THE DEMOLISHER
FOR SUCH SHALL BE THY TASK
AND NOW, THE MYSTIC ODIN-RING SHALL CALL THEE FORTH -- TO LIFE
BUT NEITHER HEART NOR SOUL I GIVE-- AND THOU SHALT FEEL NO MERCY

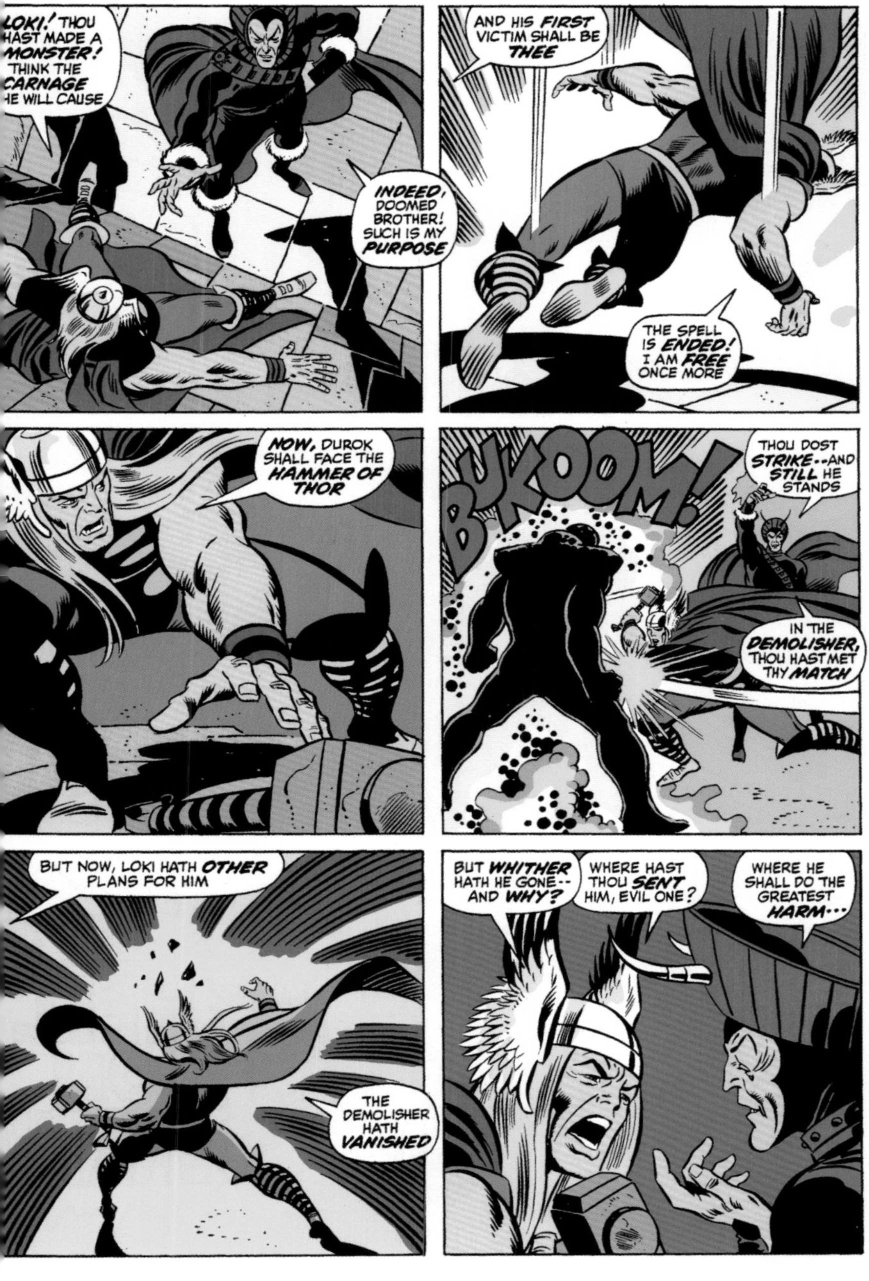
LOKI! THOU HAST MADE A MONSTER! THINK THE CARNAGE HE WILL CAUSE
INDEED, DOOMED BROTHER! SUCH IS MY PURPOSE
AND HIS FIRST VICTIM SHALL BE THEE
THE SPELL IS ENDED! I AM FREE ONCE MORE
NOW, DUROK SHALL FACE THE HAMMER OF THOR
BUKOOM!
THOU DOST STRIKE--AND STILL HE STANDS
IN THE DEMOLISHER, THOU HAST MET THY MATCH
BUT NOW, LOKI HATH OTHER PLANS FOR HIM
THE DEMOLISHER HATH VANISHED
BUT WHITHER HATH HE GONE--AND WHY?
WHERE HAST THOU SENT HIM, EVIL ONE?
WHERE HE SHALL DO THE GREATEST HARM...

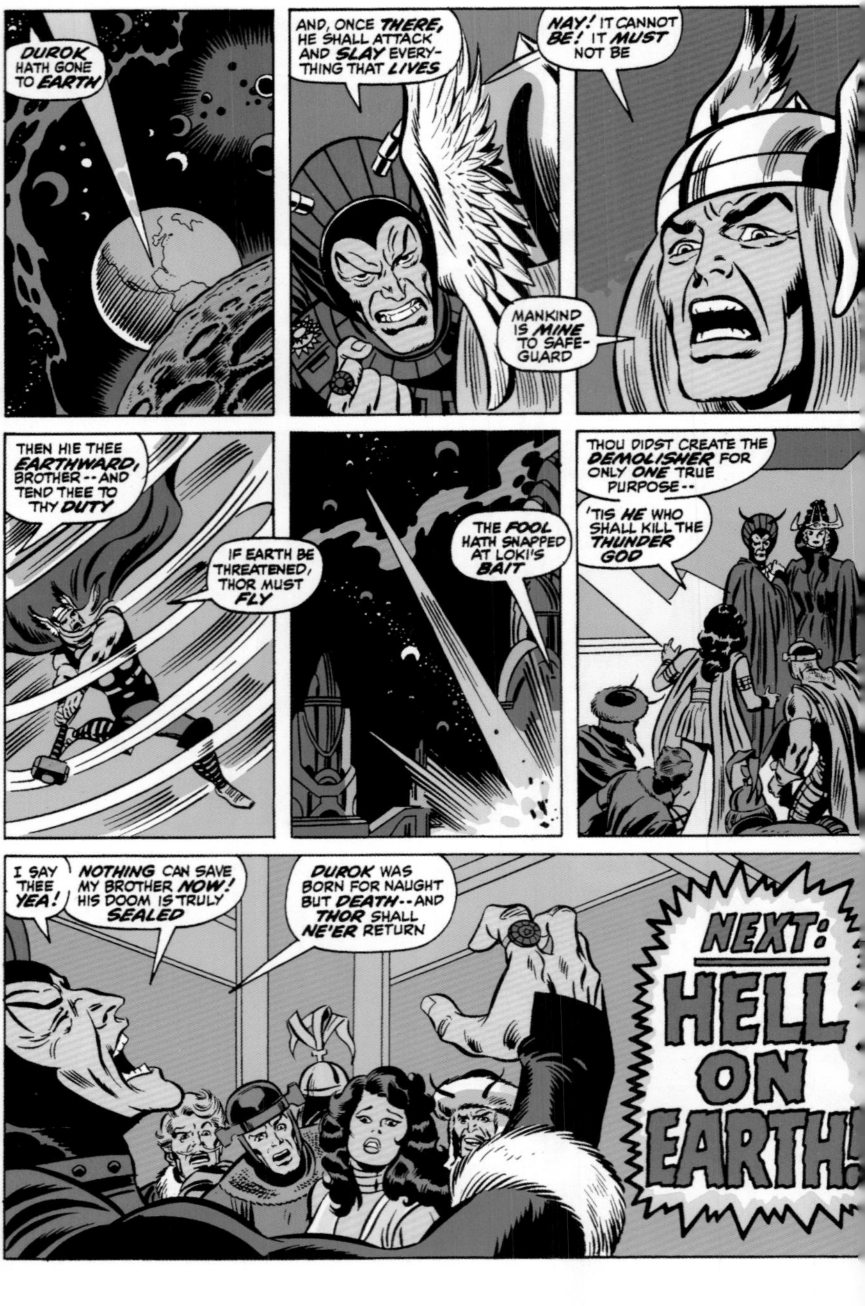
DUROK HATH GONE TO EARTH
AND, ONCE THERE, HE SHALL ATTACK AND SLAY EVERY-THING THAT LIVES
NAY! IT CANNOT BE! IT MUST NOT BE
MANKIND IS MINE TO SAFE-GUARD
THEN HIE THEE EARTHWARD, BROTHER -- AND TEND THEE TO THY DUTY
IF EARTH BE THREATENED, THOR MUST FLY
THE FOOL HATH SNAPPED AT LOKI'S BAIT
THOU DIDST CREATE THE DEMOLISHER FOR ONLY ONE TRUE PURPOSE --
'TIS HE WHO SHALL KILL THE THUNDER GOD
I SAY THEE YEA!
NOTHING CAN SAVE MY BROTHER NOW! HIS DOOM IS TRULY SEALED
DUROK WAS BORN FOR NAUGHT BUT DEATH -- AND THOR SHALL NE'ER RETURN
NEXT: HELL ON EARTH!

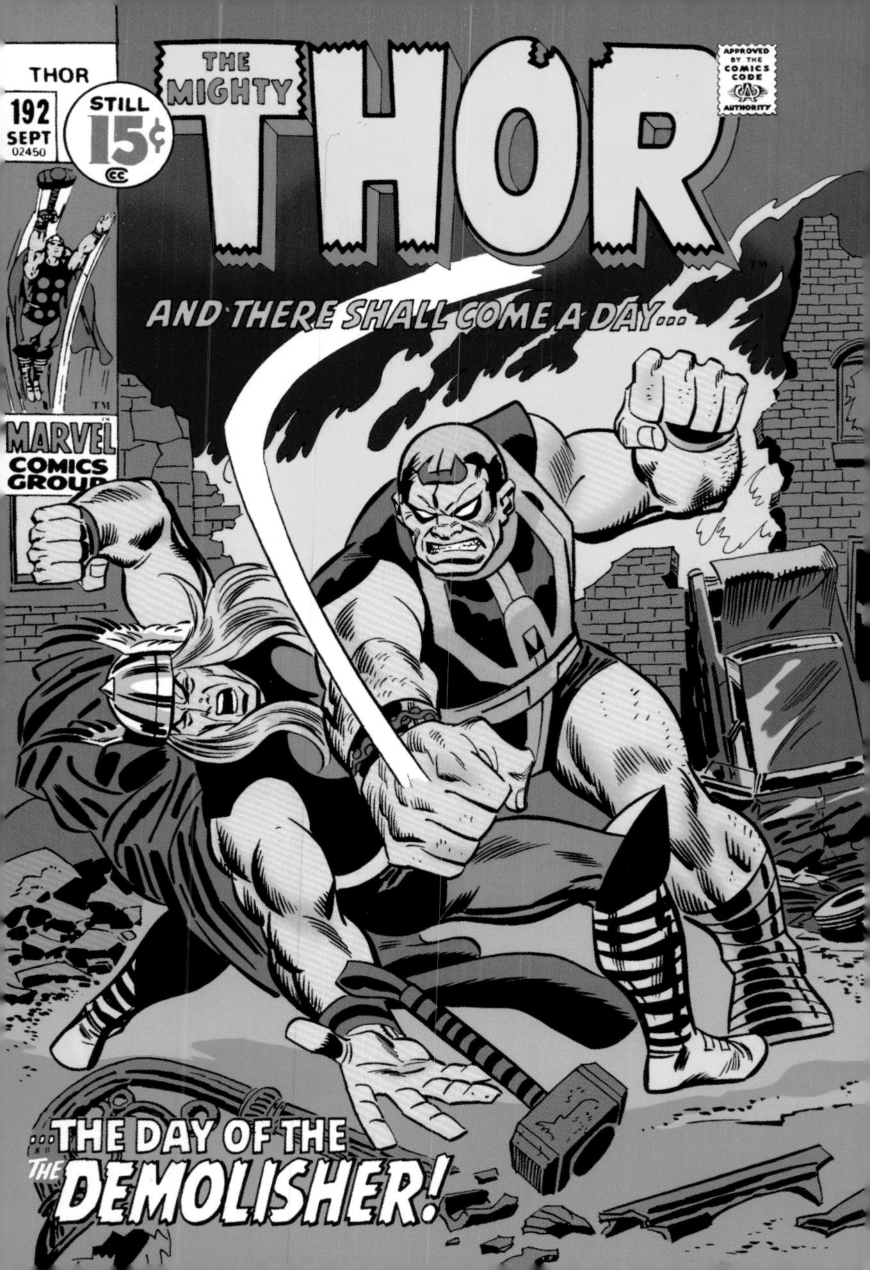
THOR
192
SEPT
02450
STILL 15¢
CC
MARVEL COMICS GROUP
APPROVED BY THE COMICS CODE AUTHORITY
THE MIGHTY THOR
AND THERE SHALL COME A DAY...
...THE DAY OF THE
THE DEMOLISHER!

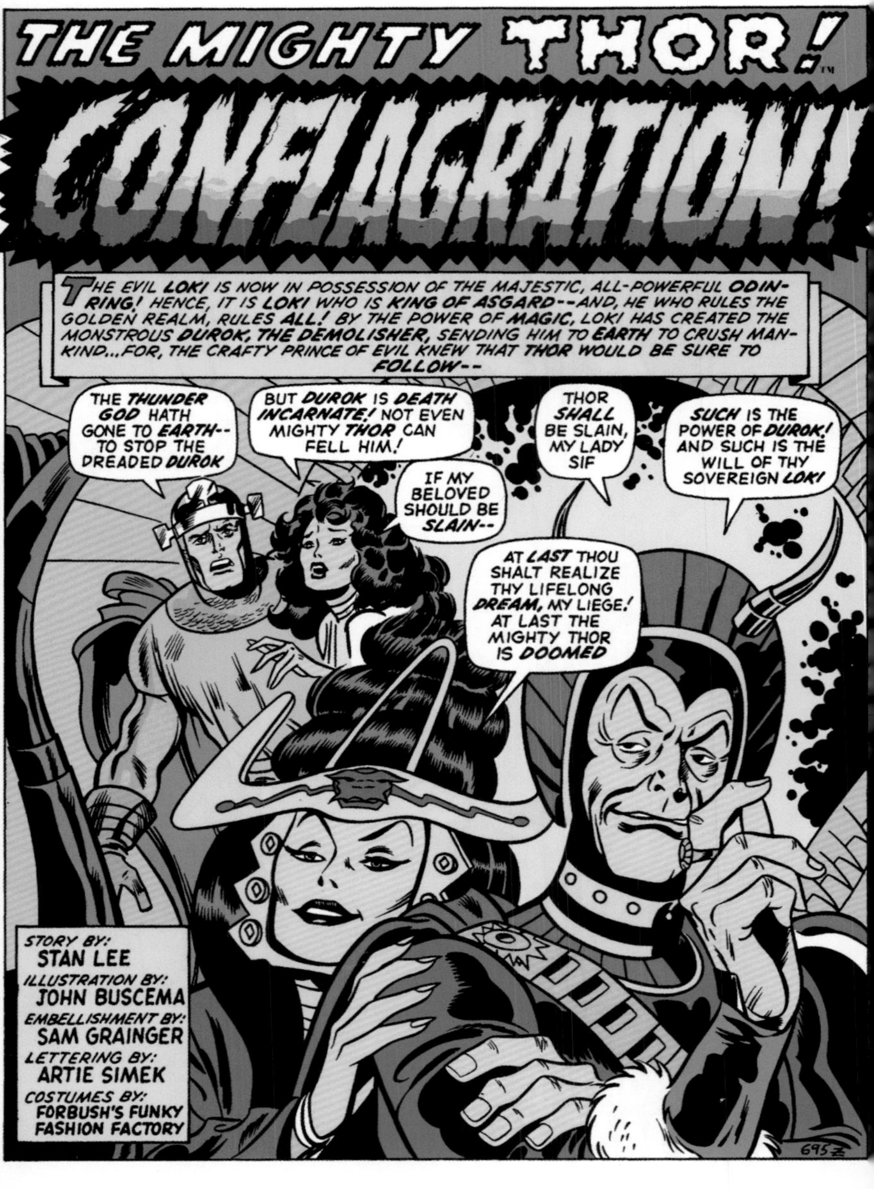
THE MIGHTY THOR!
CONFLAGRATION!
THE EVIL LOKI IS NOW IN POSSESSION OF THE MAJESTIC, ALL-POWERFUL ODIN-RING! HENCE, IT IS LOKI WHO IS KING OF ASGARD--AND, HE WHO RULES THE GOLDEN REALM, RULES ALL! BY THE POWER OF MAGIC, LOKI HAS CREATED THE MONSTROUS DUROK, THE DEMOLISHER, SENDING HIM TO EARTH TO CRUSH MANKIND...FOR, THE CRAFTY PRINCE OF EVIL KNEW THAT THOR WOULD BE SURE TO FOLLOW--
THE THUNDER GOD HATH GONE TO EARTH--TO STOP THE DREADED DUROK
BUT DUROK IS DEATH INCARNATE! NOT EVEN MIGHTY THOR CAN FELL HIM!
IF MY BELOVED SHOULD BE SLAIN--
THOR SHALL BE SLAIN, MY LADY SIF
SUCH IS THE POWER OF DUROK! AND SUCH IS THE WILL OF THY SOVEREIGN LOKI!
AT LAST THOU SHALT REALIZE THY LIFELONG DREAM, MY LIEGE! AT LAST THE MIGHTY THOR IS DOOMED
STORY BY: STAN LEE
ILLUSTRATION BY: JOHN BUSCEMA
EMBELLISHMENT BY: SAM GRAINGER
LETTERING BY: ARTIE SIMEK
COSTUMES BY: FORBUSH'S FUNKY FASHION FACTORY
695Z

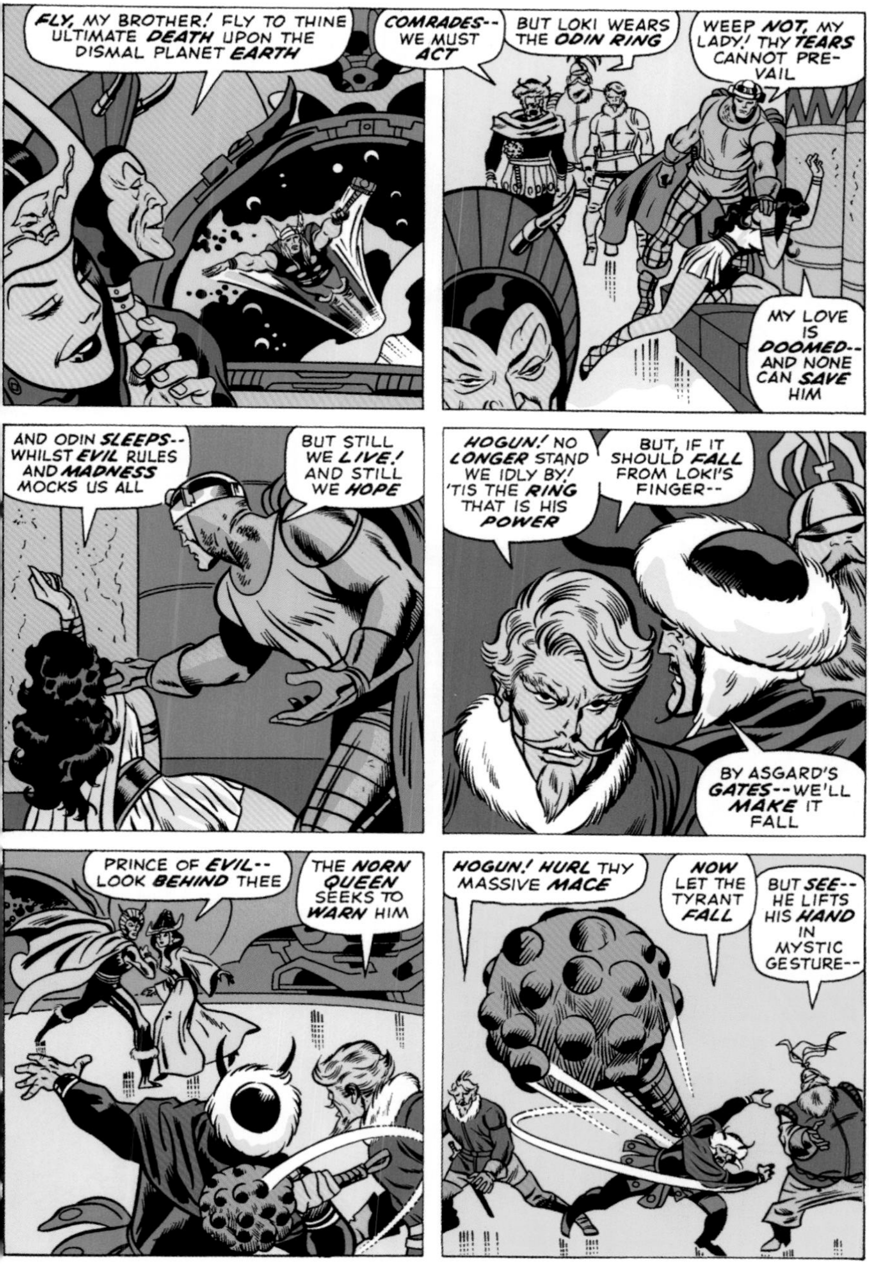
FLY, MY BROTHER! FLY TO THINE ULTIMATE DEATH UPON THE DISMAL PLANET EARTH
COMRADES-- WE MUST ACT
BUT LOKI WEARS THE ODIN RING
WEEP NOT, MY LADY! THY TEARS CANNOT PRE-VAIL
MY LOVE IS DOOMED-- AND NONE CAN SAVE HIM
AND ODIN SLEEPS-- WHILST EVIL RULES AND MADNESS MOCKS US ALL
BUT STILL THINE WE LIVE! AND STILL WE HOPE
HOGUN! NO LONGER STAND WE IDLY BY! 'TIS THE RING THAT IS HIS POWER
BUT, IF IT SHOULD FALL FROM LOKI'S FINGER--
BY ASGARD'S GATES--WE'LL MAKE IT FALL
PRINCE OF EVIL-- LOOK BEHIND THEE
THE NORN QUEEN SEEKS TO WARN HIM
HOGUN! HURL THY MASSIVE MACE
NOW LET THE TYRANT FALL
BUT SEE-- HE LIFTS HIS HAND IN MYSTIC GESTURE--

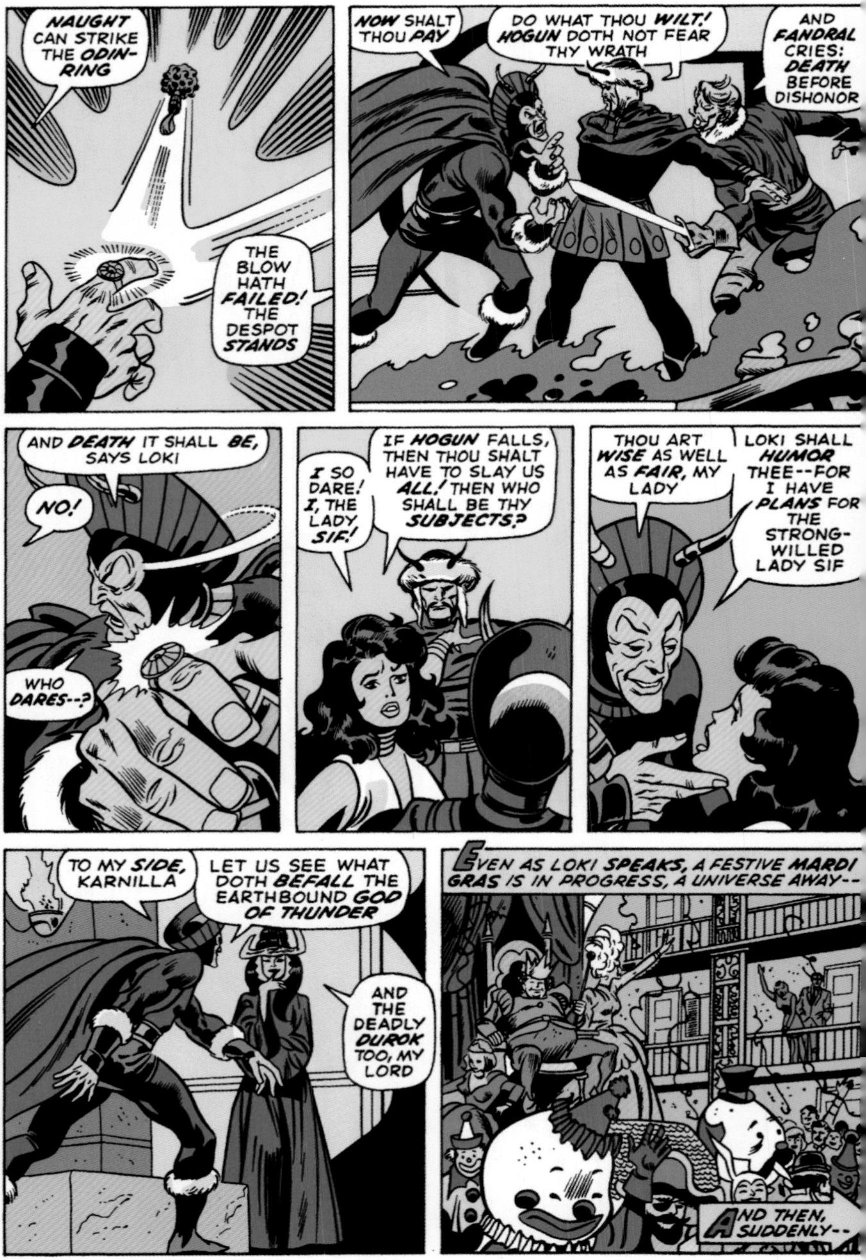
NAUGHT CAN STRIKE THE ODIN-RING
THE BLOW HATH FAILED! THE DESPOT STANDS
NOW SHALT THOU PAY
DO WHAT THOU WILT! HOGUN DOTH NOT FEAR THY WRATH
AND FANDRAL CRIES: DEATH BEFORE DISHONOR
AND DEATH IT SHALL BE, SAYS LOKI
NO!
WHO DARES--?
I SO DARE! I, THE LADY SIF!
IF HOGUN FALLS, THEN THOU SHALT HAVE TO SLAY US ALL! THEN WHO SHALL BE THY SUBJECTS?
THOU ART WISE AS WELL AS FAIR, MY LADY
LOKI SHALL HUMOR THEE--FOR I HAVE PLANS FOR THE STRONG-WILLED LADY SIF
TO MY SIDE, KARNILLA
LET US SEE WHAT DOTH BEFALL THE EARTHBOUND GOD OF THUNDER
AND THE DEADLY DUROK TOO, MY LORD
EVEN AS LOKI SPEAKS, A FESTIVE MARDI GRAS IS IN PROGRESS, A UNIVERSE AWAY--
AND THEN, SUDDENLY--

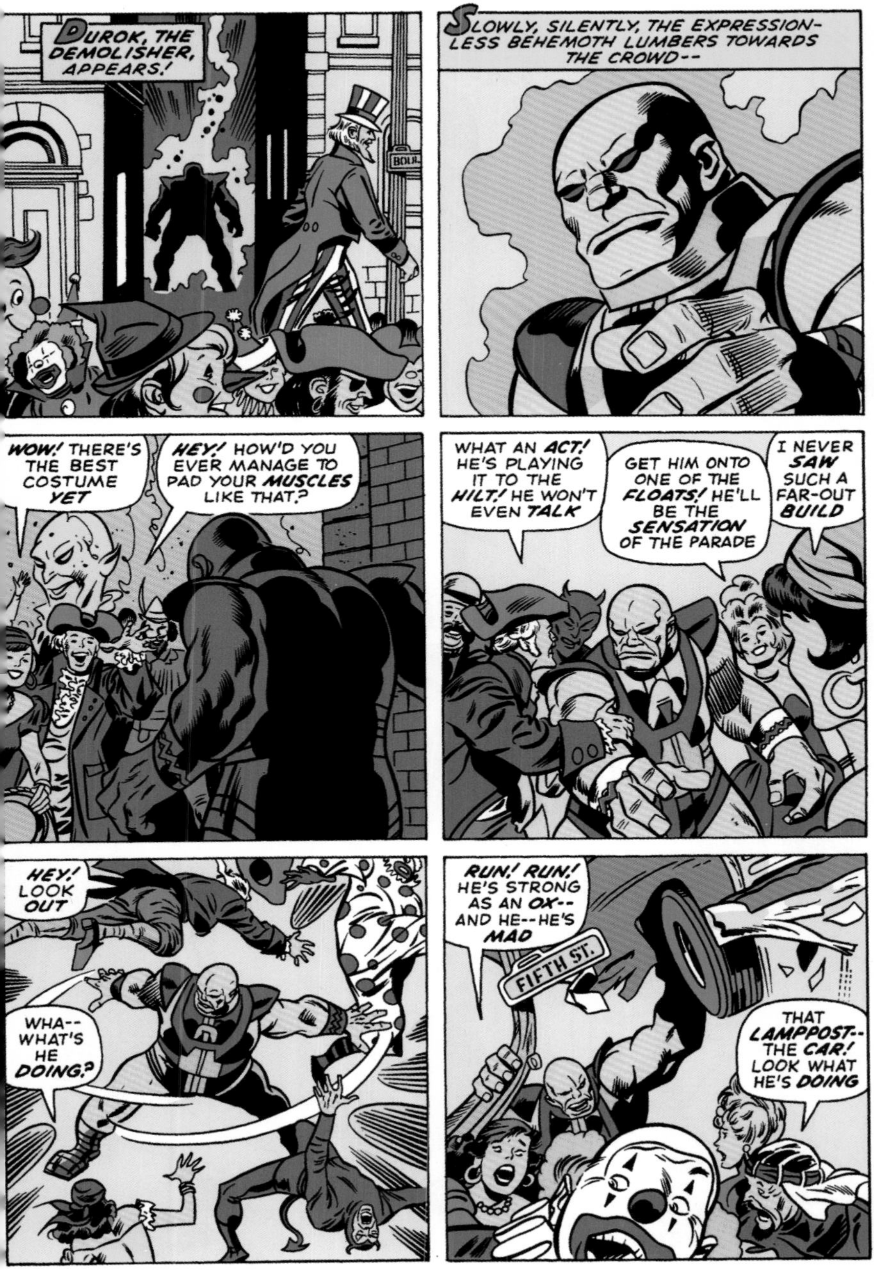
DUROK, THE DEMOLISHER, APPEARS!
BOUL
SLOWLY, SILENTLY, THE EXPRESSIONLESS BEHEMOTH LUMBERS TOWARDS THE CROWD--
WOW! THERE'S THE BEST COSTUME YET
HEY! HOW'D YOU EVER MANAGE TO PAD YOUR MUSCLES LIKE THAT?
WHAT AN ACT! HE'S PLAYING IT TO THE HILT! HE WON'T EVEN TALK
GET HIM ONTO ONE OF THE FLOATS! HE'LL BE THE SENSATION OF THE PARADE
I NEVER SAW SUCH A FAR-OUT BUILD
HEY! LOOK OUT
WHA-- WHAT'S HE DOING?
RUN! RUN! HE'S STRONG AS AN OX-- AND HE--HE'S MAD
FIFTH ST.
THAT LAMPPOST-- THE CAR! LOOK WHAT HE'S DOING

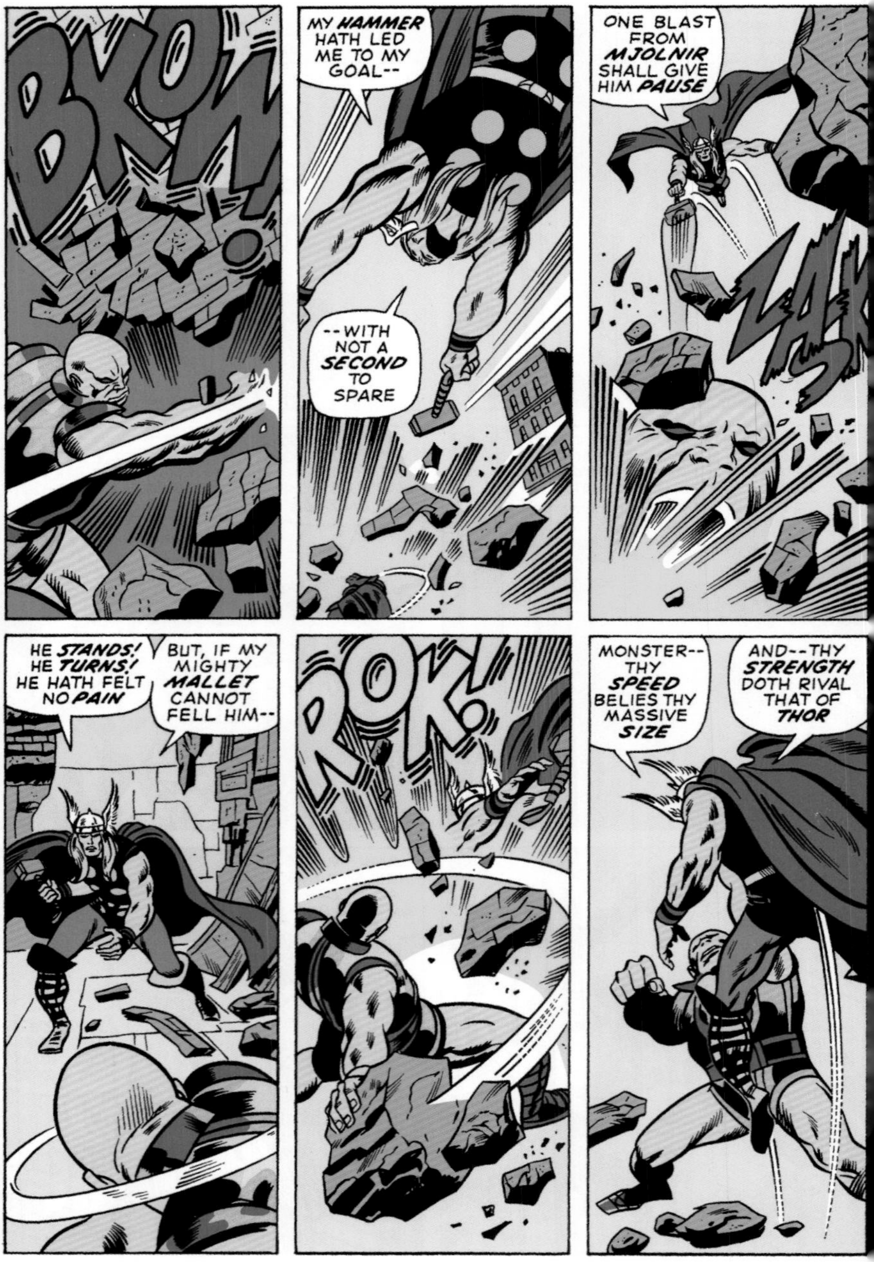
BKOW
MY HAMMER HATH LED ME TO MY GOAL--
--WITH NOT A SECOND TO SPARE
ONE BLAST FROM MJOLNIR SHALL GIVE HIM PAUSE
HE STANDS! HE TURNS! HE HATH FELT NO PAIN
BUT, IF MY MIGHTY MALLET CANNOT FELL HIM--
ROK!
MONSTER--THY SPEED BELIES THY MASSIVE SIZE
AND--THY STRENGTH DOTH RIVAL THAT OF THOR

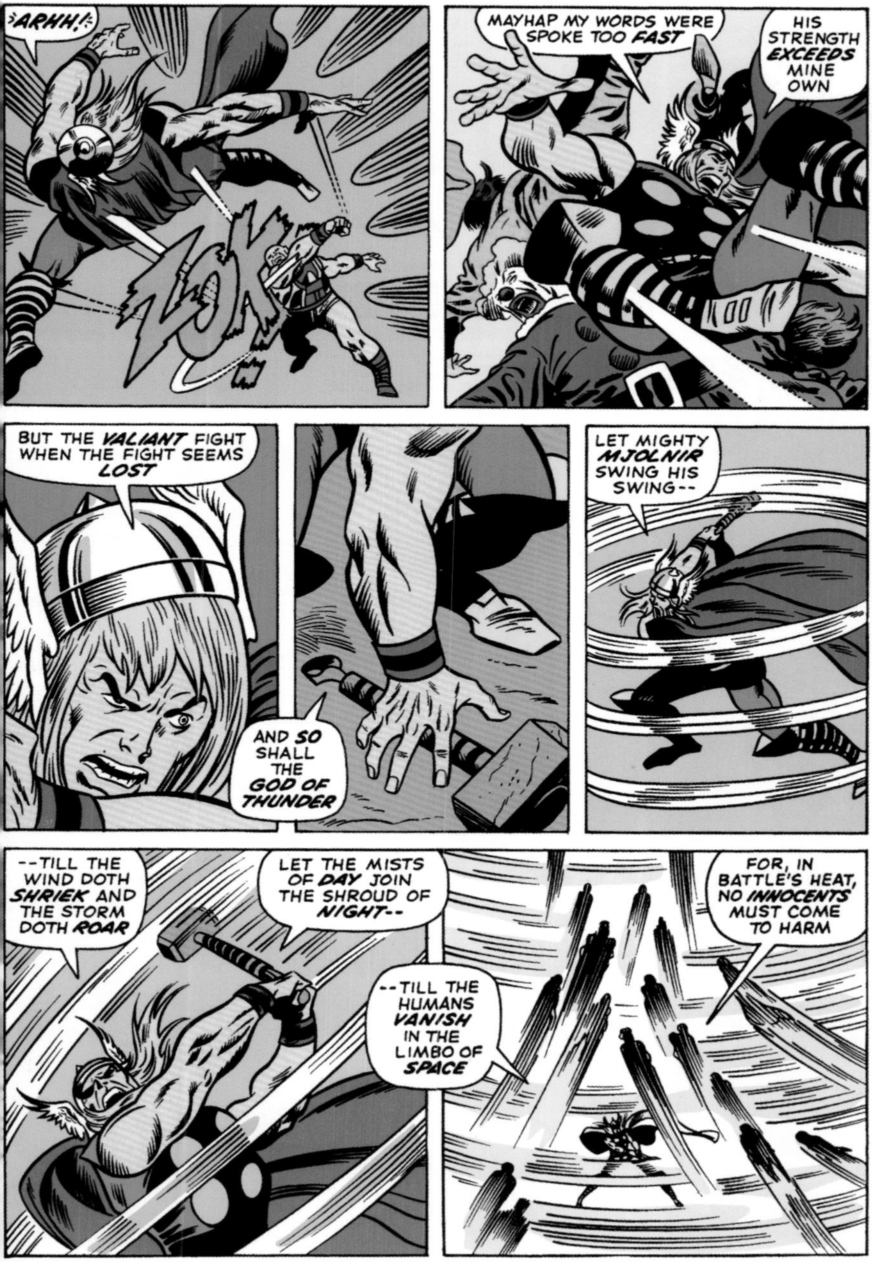
ARHH!
ZOK
MAYHAP MY WORDS WERE SPOKE TOO FAST
HIS STRENGTH EXCEEDS MINE OWN
BUT THE VALIANT FIGHT WHEN THE FIGHT SEEMS LOST
AND SO SHALL THE GOD OF THUNDER
LET MIGHTY MJOLNIR SWING HIS SWING--
--TILL THE WIND DOTH SHRIEK AND THE STORM DOTH ROAR
LET THE MISTS OF DAY JOIN THE SHROUD OF NIGHT--
--TILL THE HUMANS VANISH IN THE LIMBO OF SPACE
FOR, IN BATTLE'S HEAT, NO INNOCENTS MUST COME TO HARM

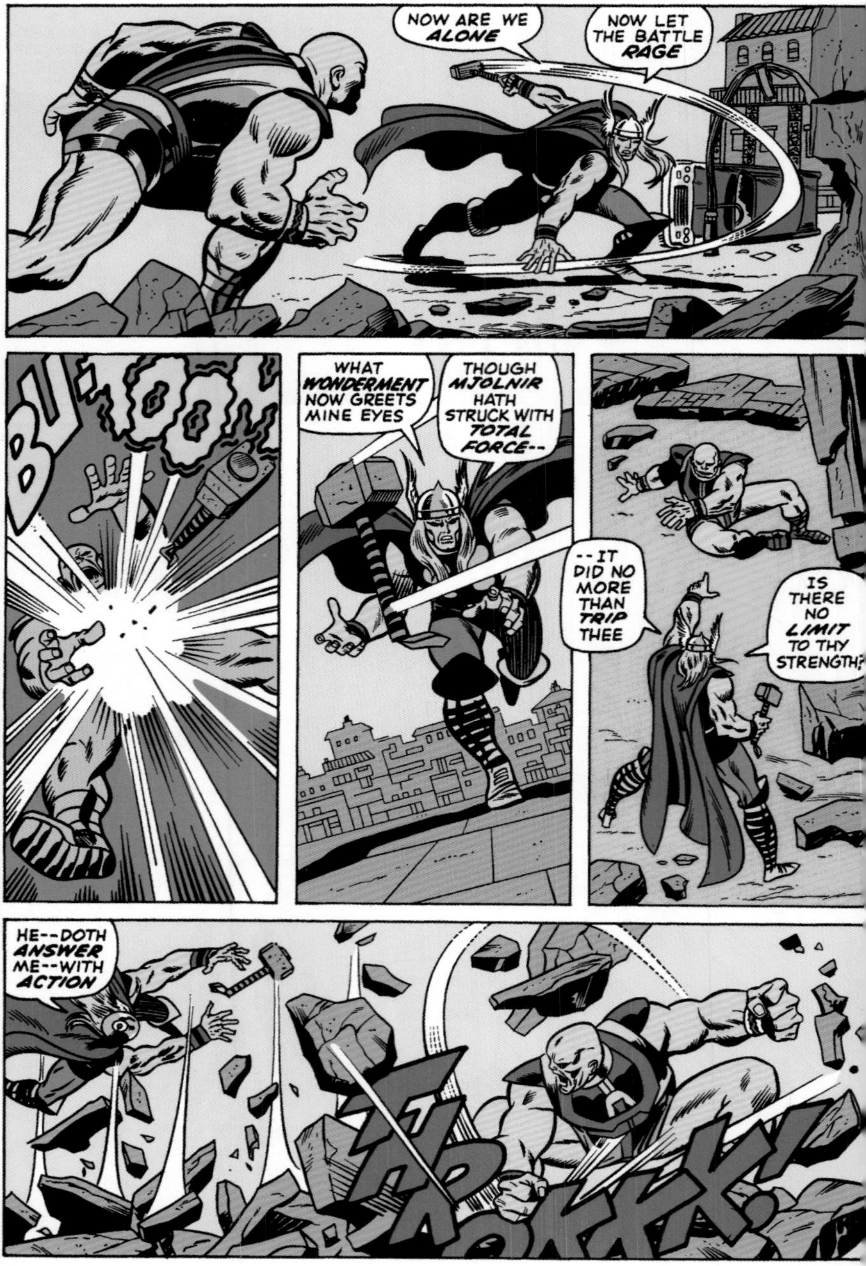
NOW ARE WE ALONE
NOW LET THE BATTLE RAGE
WHAT WONDERMENT NOW GREETS MINE EYES
THOUGH MJOLNIR HATH STRUCK WITH TOTAL FORCE--
--IT DID NO MORE THAN TRIP THEE
IS THERE NO LIMIT TO THY STRENGTH?
HE--DOTH ANSWER ME--WITH ACTION

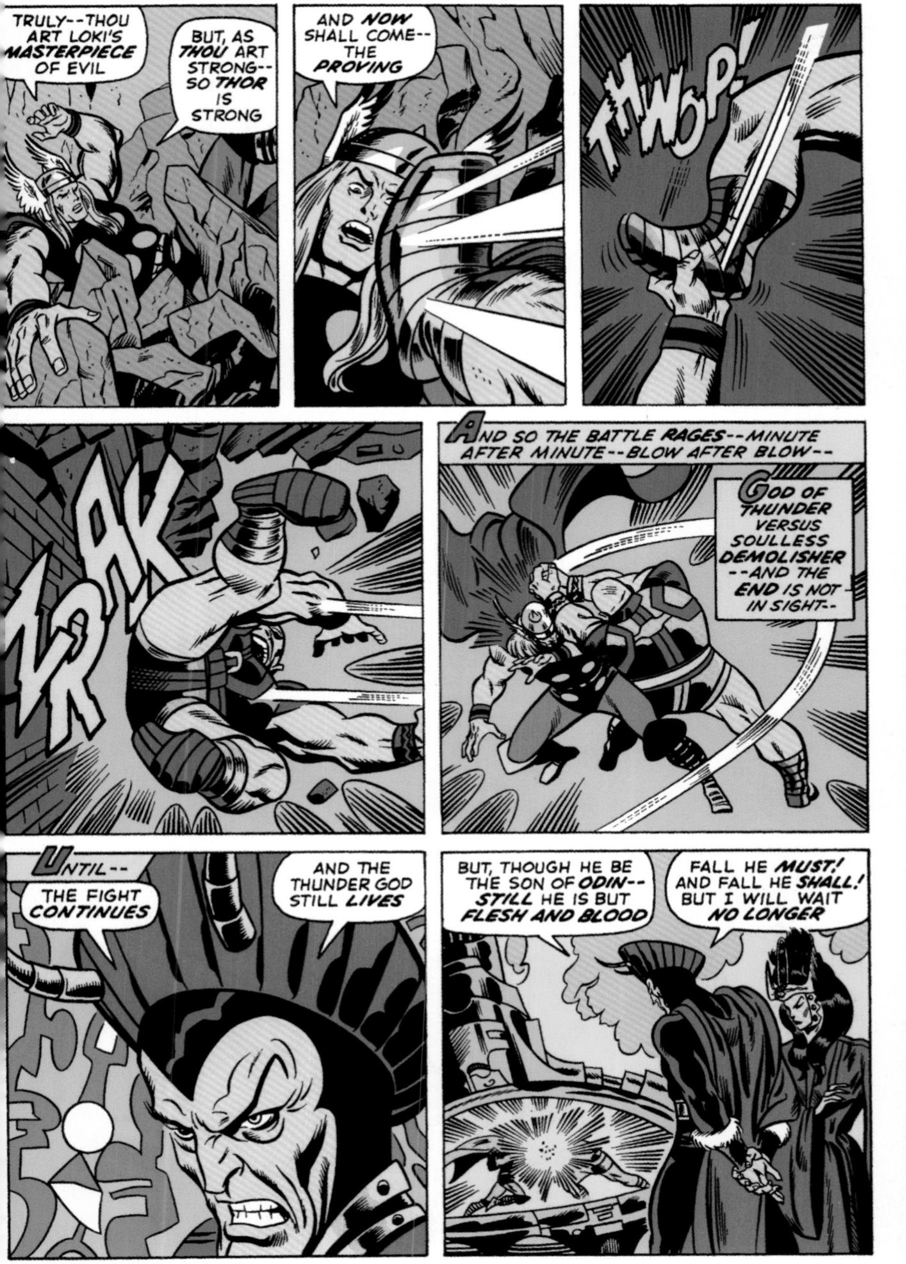
TRULY--THOU ART LOKI'S MASTERPIECE OF EVIL
BUT, AS THOU ART STRONG--SO THOR IS STRONG
AND NOW SHALL COME--THE PROVING
THWOP!
ZRAK
AND SO THE BATTLE RAGES--MINUTE AFTER MINUTE--BLOW AFTER BLOW--
GOD OF THUNDER VERSUS SOULLESS DEMOLISHER--AND THE END IS NOT IN SIGHT--
UNTIL--
THE FIGHT CONTINUES
AND THE THUNDER GOD STILL LIVES
BUT, THOUGH HE BE THE SON OF ODIN--STILL HE IS BUT FLESH AND BLOOD
FALL HE MUST! AND FALL HE SHALL! BUT I WILL WAIT NO LONGER

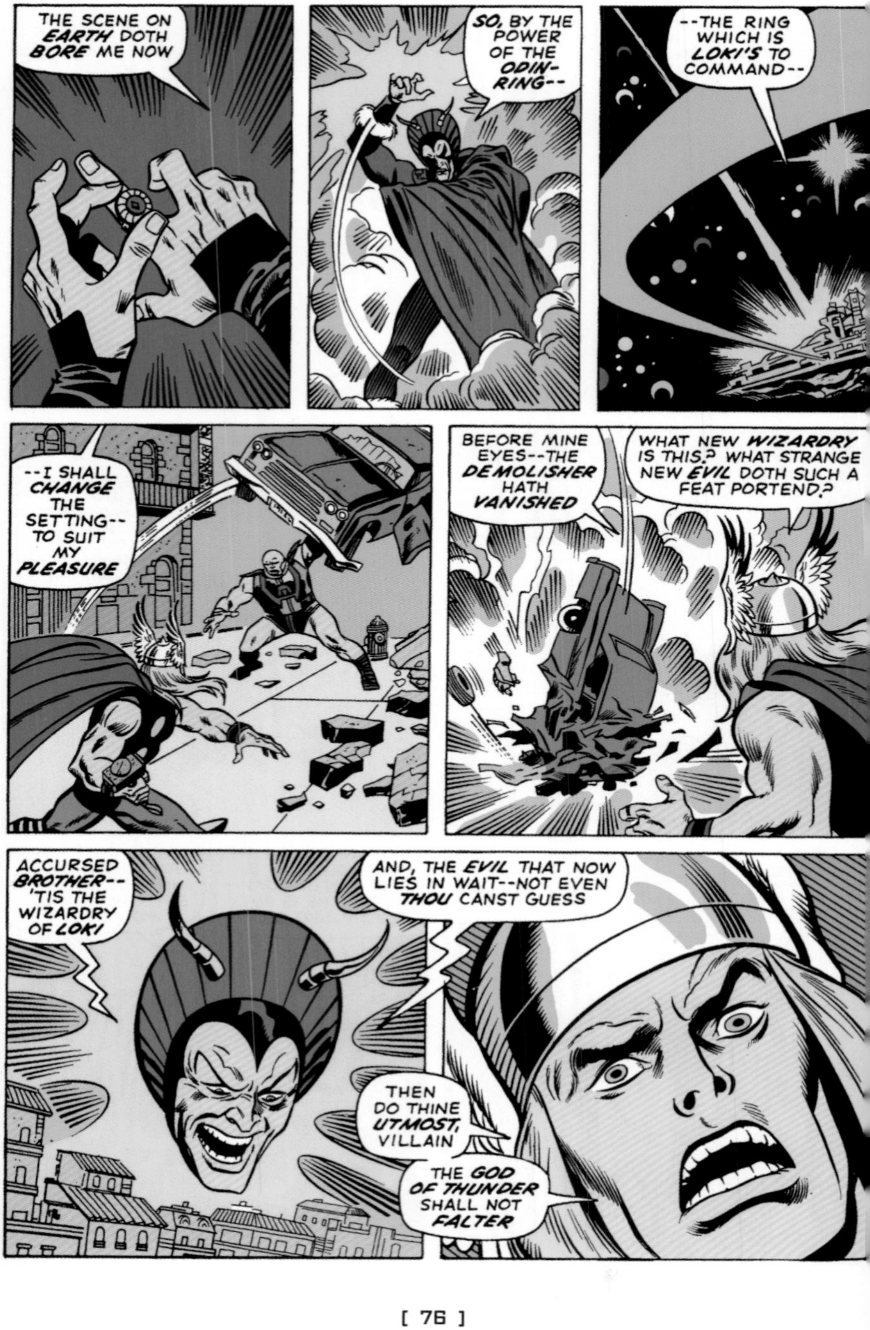
THE SCENE ON EARTH DOTH BORE ME NOW
SO, BY THE POWER OF THE ODIN-RING--
--THE RING WHICH IS LOKI'S TO COMMAND--
--I SHALL CHANGE THE SETTING-- TO SUIT MY PLEASURE
BEFORE MINE EYES--THE DEMOLISHER HATH VANISHED
WHAT NEW WIZARDRY IS THIS? WHAT STRANGE NEW EVIL DOTH SUCH A FEAT PORTEND?
ACCURSED BROTHER-- 'TIS THE WIZARDRY OF LOKI!
AND, THE EVIL THAT NOW LIES IN WAIT--NOT EVEN THOU CANST GUESS
THEN DO THINE UTMOST, VILLAIN
THE GOD OF THUNDER SHALL NOT FALTER

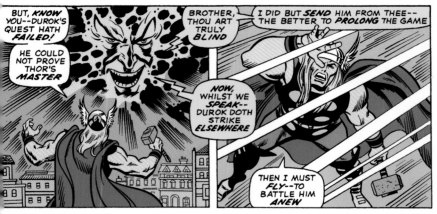

BUT, *KNOW* YOU--DUROK'S QUEST HATH *FAILED!*

HE COULD NOT PROVE THOR'S *MASTER*

BROTHER, THOU ART TRULY *BLIND*

I DID BUT *SEND* HIM FROM THEE-- THE BETTER TO *PROLONG* THE GAME

NOW, WHILST WE *SPEAK*-- DUROK DOTH STRIKE *ELSEWHERE*

THEN I MUST *FLY*--TO BATTLE HIM *ANEW*

BUT *FIRST*-- THERE BE A *TASK* TO DO--

AND ONLY *THOR* CAN *DO* IT

LET ALL *RETURN* FROM WHENCE THEY WERE --WITH *MEMORIES* ERASED

'TIS *DONE!* NOW, *LEAVE* I MUST.! BUT *HOLD*--THERE BE *NO* WAY

YON PRESSING *CROWD* AFFORDS NO *ROOM* FOR THOR TO SWING HIS *HAMMER*

LOOK! LOOK!

IT CAN'T *BE!* HE--HE'S MOVING THE *BUILDING*

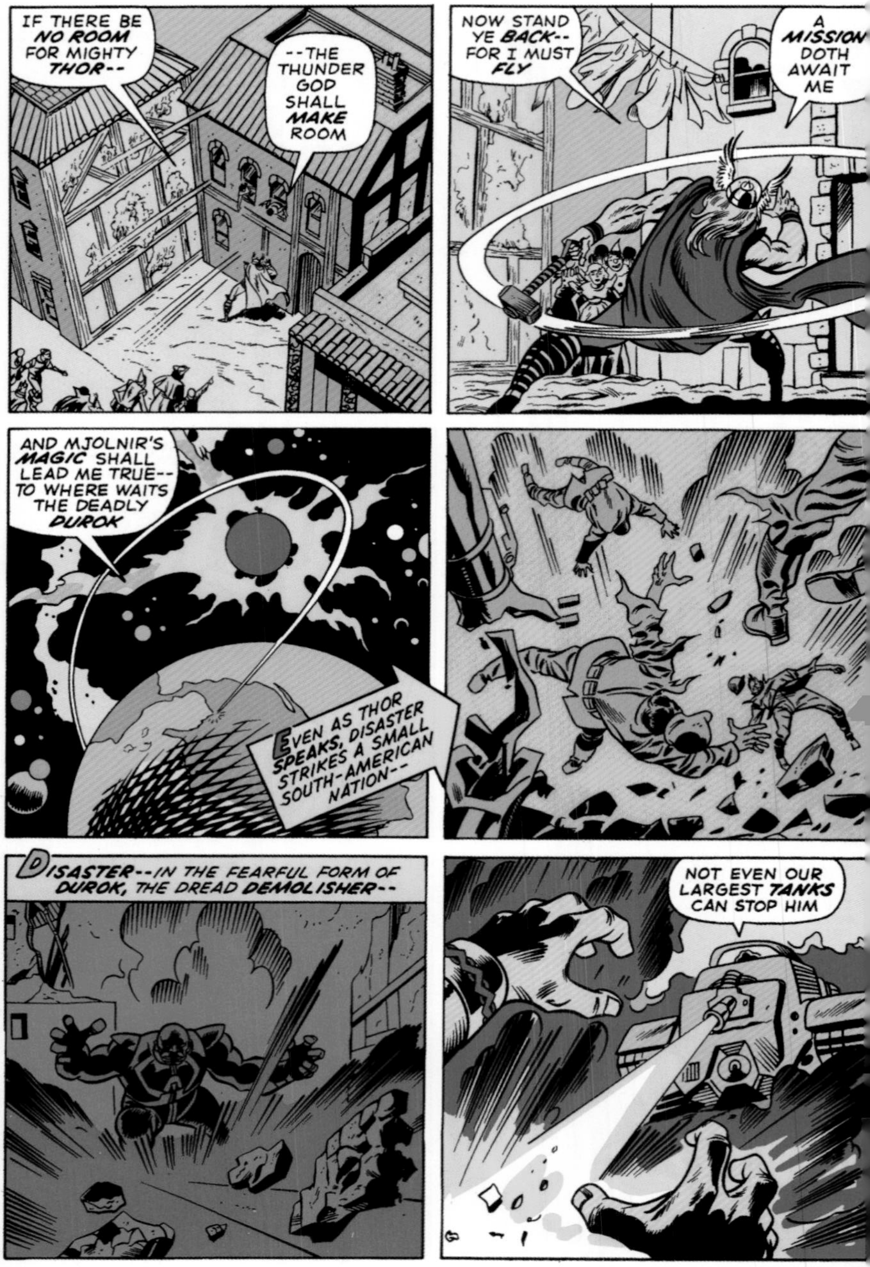
IF THERE BE NO ROOM FOR MIGHTY THOR--
--THE THUNDER GOD SHALL MAKE ROOM
NOW STAND YE BACK-- FOR I MUST FLY
A MISSION DOTH AWAIT ME
AND MJOLNIR'S MAGIC SHALL LEAD ME TRUE-- TO WHERE WAITS THE DEADLY DUROK
EVEN AS THOR SPEAKS, DISASTER STRIKES A SMALL SOUTH-AMERICAN NATION--
DISASTER--IN THE FEARFUL FORM OF DUROK, THE DREAD DEMOLISHER--
NOT EVEN OUR LARGEST TANKS CAN STOP HIM

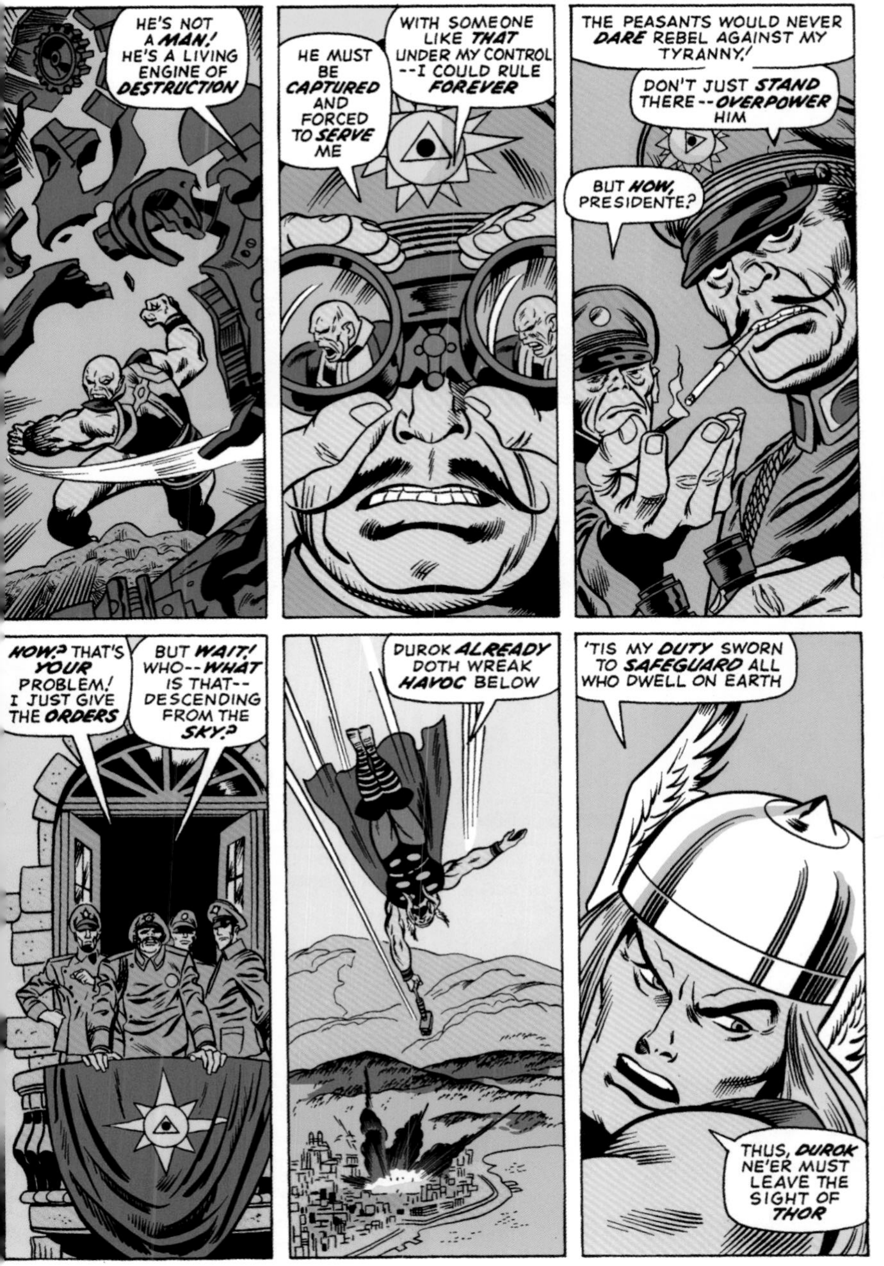
HE'S NOT A MAN! HE'S A LIVING ENGINE OF DESTRUCTION
HE MUST BE CAPTURED AND FORCED TO SERVE ME
WITH SOMEONE LIKE THAT UNDER MY CONTROL --I COULD RULE FOREVER
THE PEASANTS WOULD NEVER DARE REBEL AGAINST MY TYRANNY!
DON'T JUST STAND THERE --OVERPOWER HIM
BUT HOW, PRESIDENTE?
HOW? THAT'S YOUR PROBLEM! I JUST GIVE THE ORDERS
BUT WAIT! WHO--WHAT IS THAT-- DESCENDING FROM THE SKY?
DUROK ALREADY DOTH WREAK HAVOC BELOW
'TIS MY DUTY SWORN TO SAFEGUARD ALL WHO DWELL ON EARTH
THUS, DUROK NE'ER MUST LEAVE THE SIGHT OF THOR

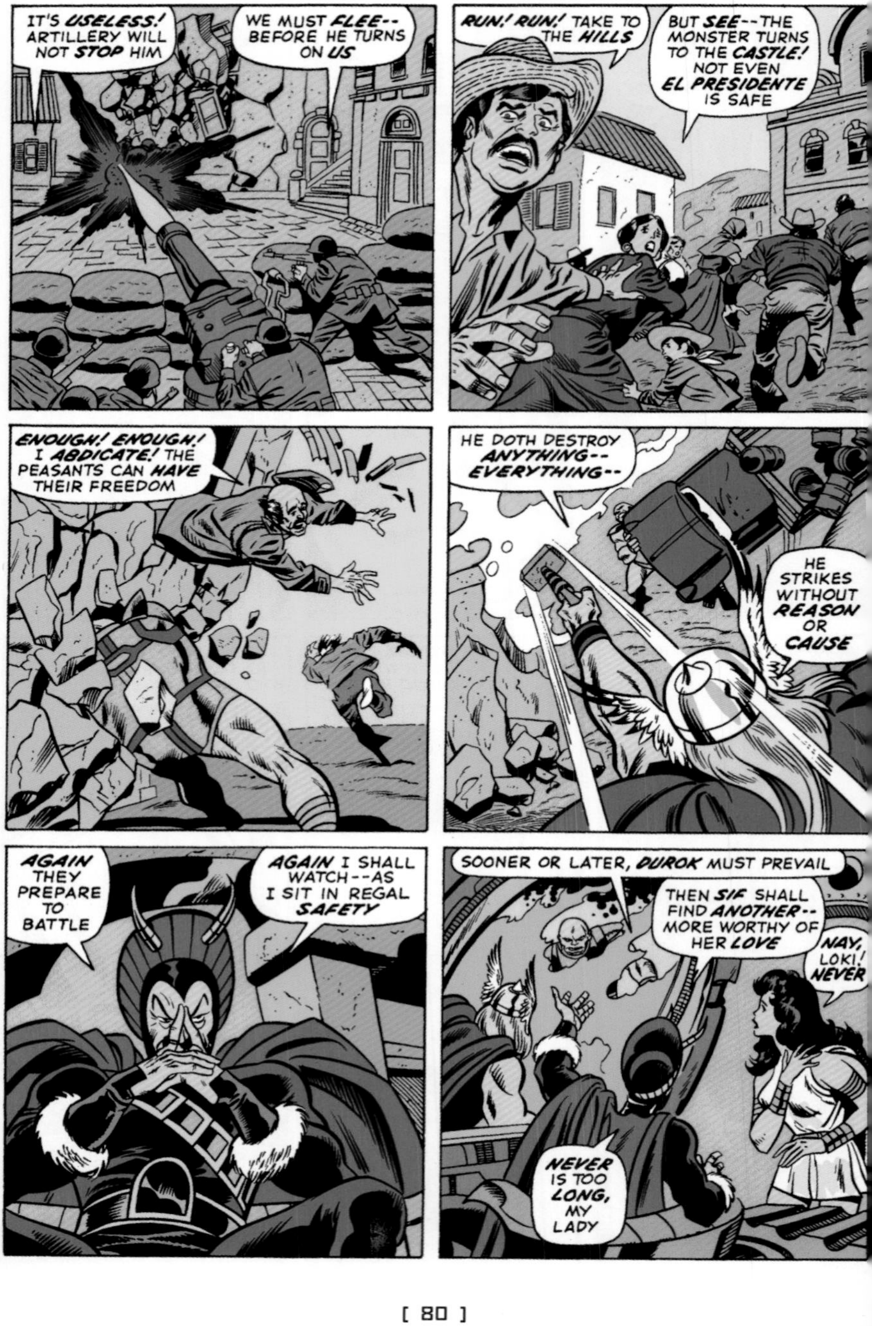

IT'S USELESS! ARTILLERY WILL NOT STOP HIM
WE MUST FLEE-- BEFORE HE TURNS ON US
RUN! RUN! TAKE TO THE HILLS
BUT SEE--THE MONSTER TURNS TO THE CASTLE! NOT EVEN EL PRESIDENTE IS SAFE
ENOUGH! ENOUGH! I ABDICATE! THE PEASANTS CAN HAVE THEIR FREEDOM
HE DOTH DESTROY ANYTHING-- EVERYTHING--
HE STRIKES WITHOUT REASON OR CAUSE
AGAIN THEY PREPARE TO BATTLE
AGAIN I SHALL WATCH--AS I SIT IN REGAL SAFETY
SOONER OR LATER, DUROK MUST PREVAIL
THEN SIF SHALL FIND ANOTHER-- MORE WORTHY OF HER LOVE
NAY, LOKI! NEVER
NEVER IS TOO LONG, MY LADY

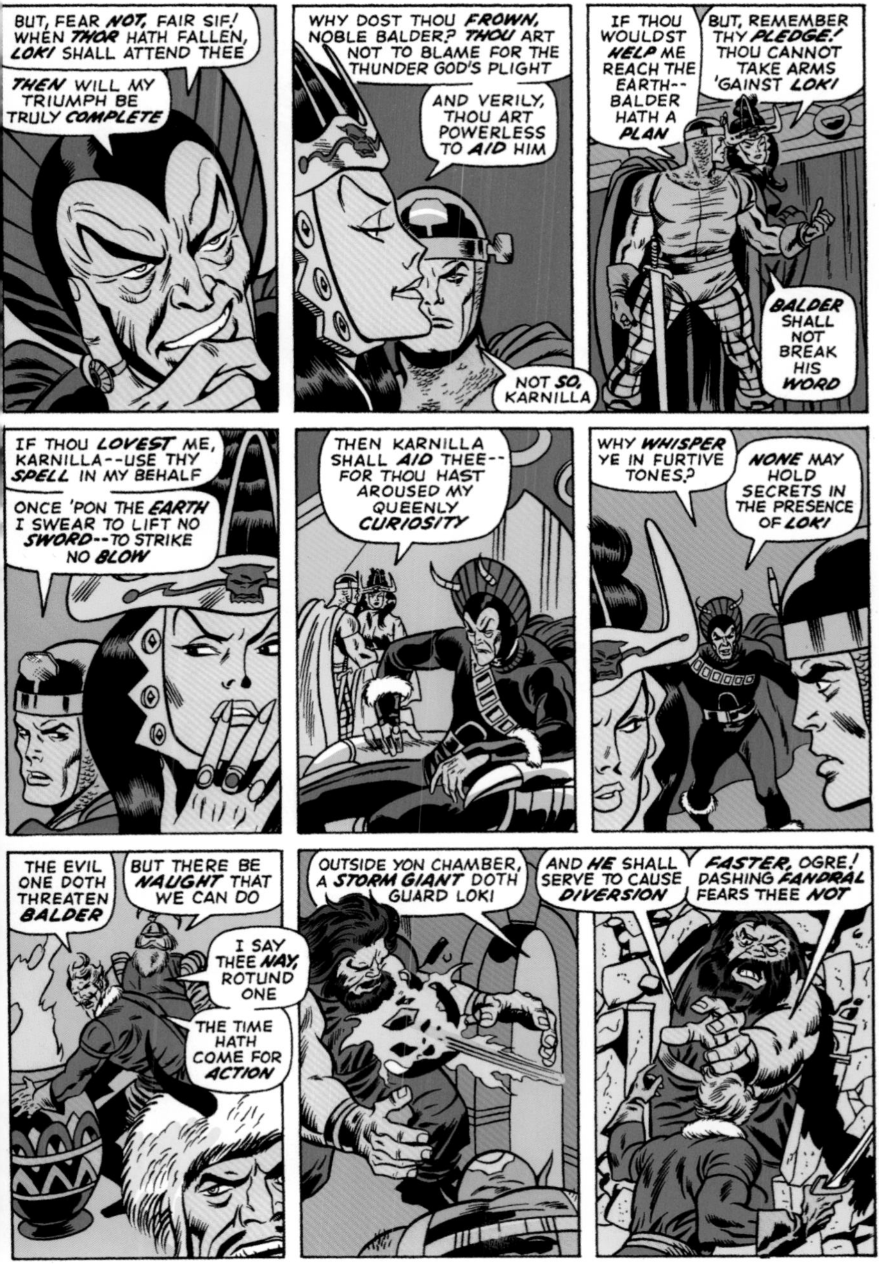
BUT, FEAR NOT, FAIR SIF! WHEN THOR HATH FALLEN, LOKI SHALL ATTEND THEE
THEN WILL MY TRIUMPH BE TRULY COMPLETE
WHY DOST THOU FROWN, NOBLE BALDER? THOU ART NOT TO BLAME FOR THE THUNDER GOD'S PLIGHT
AND VERILY, THOU ART POWERLESS TO AID HIM
NOT SO, KARNILLA
IF THOU WOULDST HELP ME REACH THE EARTH-- BALDER HATH A PLAN
BUT, REMEMBER THY PLEDGE! THOU CANNOT TAKE ARMS 'GAINST LOKI
BALDER SHALL NOT BREAK HIS WORD
IF THOU LOVEST ME, KARNILLA--USE THY SPELL IN MY BEHALF
ONCE 'PON THE EARTH I SWEAR TO LIFT NO SWORD--TO STRIKE NO BLOW
THEN KARNILLA SHALL AID THEE-- FOR THOU HAST AROUSED MY QUEENLY CURIOSITY
WHY WHISPER YE IN FURTIVE TONES?
NONE MAY HOLD SECRETS IN THE PRESENCE OF LOKI
THE EVIL ONE DOTH THREATEN BALDER
BUT THERE BE NAUGHT THAT WE CAN DO
I SAY THEE NAY, ROTUND ONE
THE TIME HATH COME FOR ACTION
OUTSIDE YON CHAMBER, A STORM GIANT DOTH GUARD LOKI
AND HE SHALL SERVE TO CAUSE DIVERSION
FASTER, OGRE! DASHING FANDRAL FEARS THEE NOT

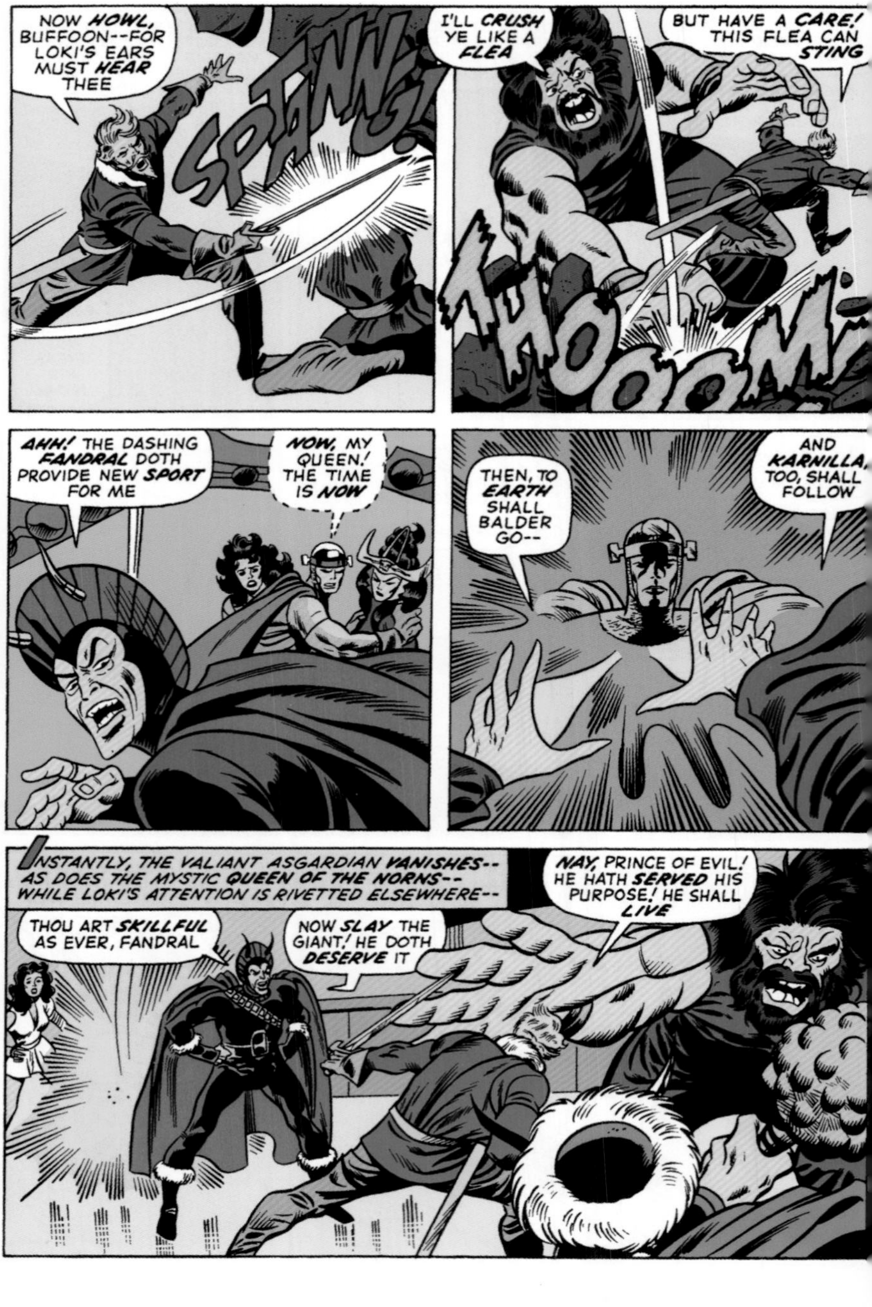
NOW HOWL, BUFFOON--FOR LOKI'S EARS MUST HEAR THEE
SPTANNG!
I'LL CRUSH YE LIKE A FLEA
BUT HAVE A CARE! THIS FLEA CAN STING
THHOOOM!
AHH! THE DASHING FANDRAL DOTH PROVIDE NEW SPORT FOR ME
NOW, MY QUEEN! THE TIME IS NOW
THEN, TO EARTH SHALL BALDER GO--
AND KARNILLA, TOO, SHALL FOLLOW
INSTANTLY, THE VALIANT ASGARDIAN VANISHES--AS DOES THE MYSTIC QUEEN OF THE NORNS--WHILE LOKI'S ATTENTION IS RIVETTED ELSEWHERE--
THOU ART SKILLFUL AS EVER, FANDRAL
NOW SLAY THE GIANT! HE DOTH DESERVE IT
NAY, PRINCE OF EVIL! HE HATH SERVED HIS PURPOSE! HE SHALL LIVE

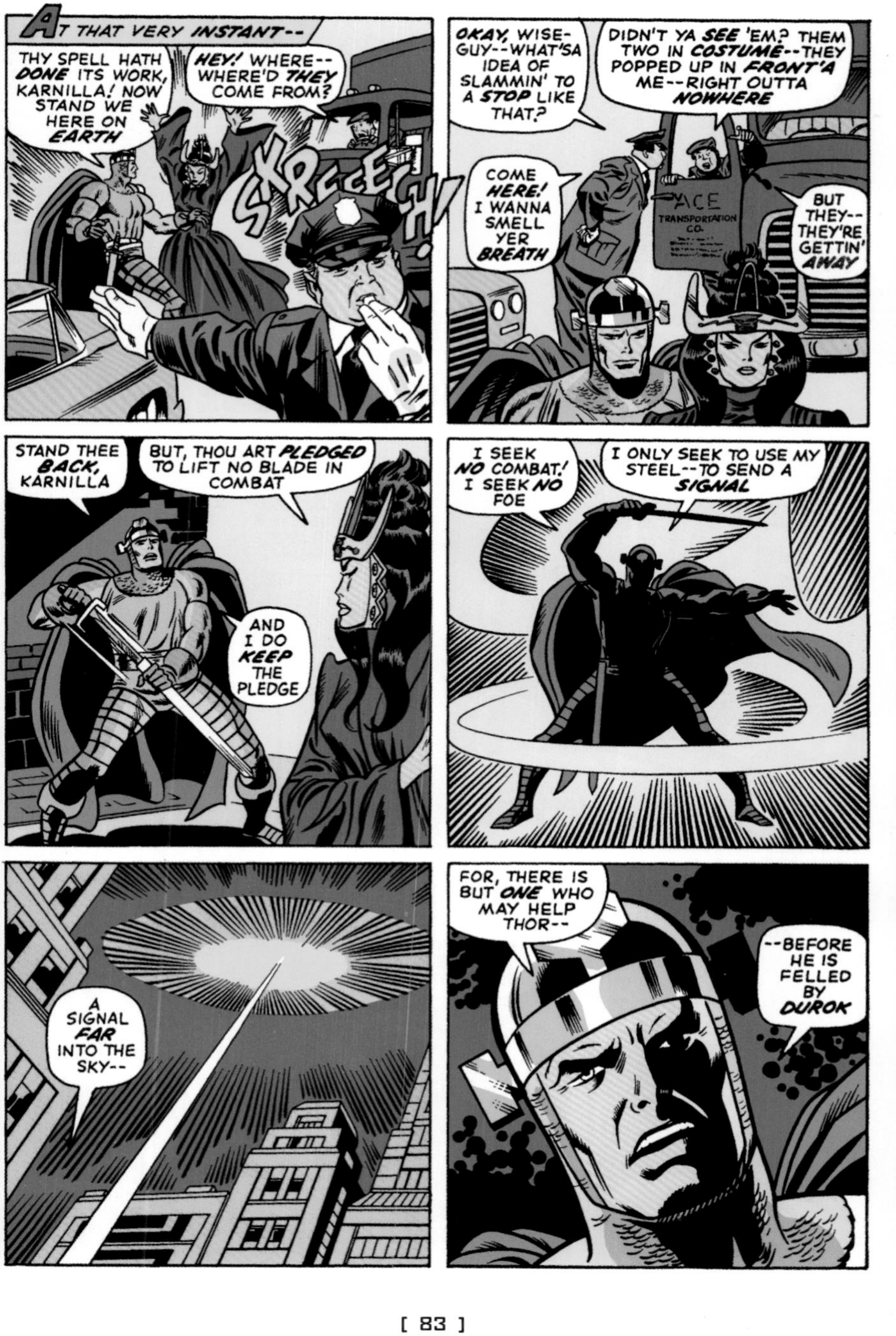
AT THAT VERY INSTANT--
THY SPELL HATH DONE ITS WORK, KARNILLA! NOW STAND WE HERE ON EARTH
HEY! WHERE-- WHERE'D THEY COME FROM?
SKREEECH!
OKAY, WISE-GUY--WHAT'SA IDEA OF SLAMMIN' TO A STOP LIKE THAT?
DIDN'T YA SEE 'EM? THEM TWO IN COSTUME--THEY POPPED UP IN FRONT'A ME--RIGHT OUTTA NOWHERE
COME HERE! I WANNA SMELL YER BREATH
ACE TRANSPORTATION CO.
BUT THEY-- THEY'RE GETTIN' AWAY
STAND THEE BACK, KARNILLA
BUT, THOU ART PLEDGED TO LIFT NO BLADE IN COMBAT
AND I DO KEEP THE PLEDGE
I SEEK NO COMBAT! I SEEK NO FOE
I ONLY SEEK TO USE MY STEEL--TO SEND A SIGNAL
A SIGNAL FAR INTO THE SKY--
FOR, THERE IS BUT ONE WHO MAY HELP THOR--
--BEFORE HE IS FELLED BY DUROK

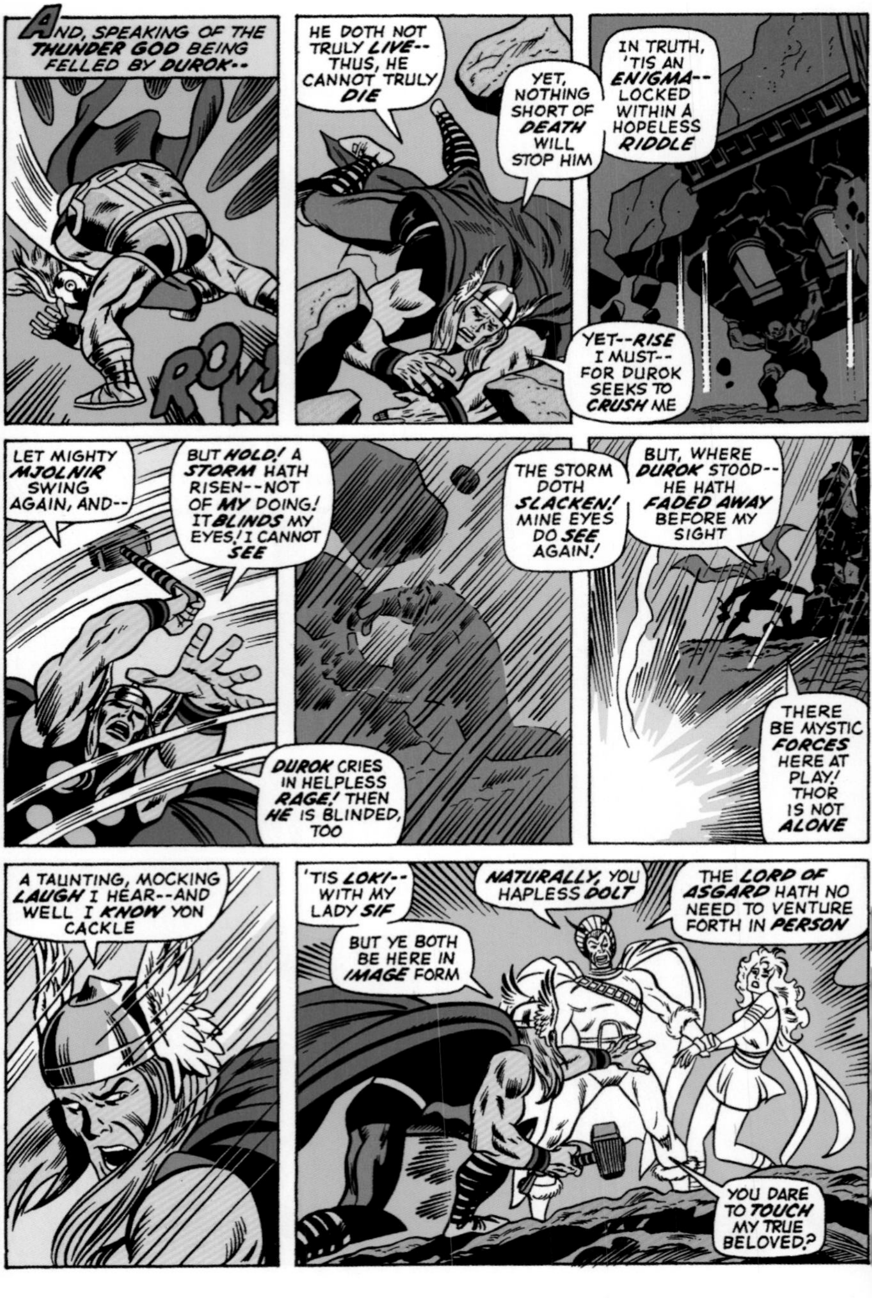
AND, SPEAKING OF THE THUNDER GOD BEING FELLED BY DUROK--
ROK!
HE DOTH NOT TRULY LIVE--THUS, HE CANNOT TRULY DIE
YET, NOTHING SHORT OF DEATH WILL STOP HIM
IN TRUTH, 'TIS AN ENIGMA--LOCKED WITHIN A HOPELESS RIDDLE
YET--RISE I MUST--FOR DUROK SEEKS TO CRUSH ME
LET MIGHTY MJOLNIR SWING AGAIN, AND--
BUT HOLD! A STORM HATH RISEN--NOT OF MY DOING! IT BLINDS MY EYES! I CANNOT SEE
DUROK CRIES IN HELPLESS RAGE! THEN HE IS BLINDED, TOO
THE STORM DOTH SLACKEN! MINE EYES DO SEE AGAIN!
BUT, WHERE DUROK STOOD--HE HATH FADED AWAY BEFORE MY SIGHT
THERE BE MYSTIC FORCES HERE AT PLAY! THOR IS NOT ALONE
A TAUNTING, MOCKING LAUGH I HEAR--AND WELL I KNOW YON CACKLE
'TIS LOKI--WITH MY LADY SIF
BUT YE BOTH BE HERE IN IMAGE FORM
NATURALLY, YOU HAPLESS DOLT
THE LORD OF ASGARD HATH NO NEED TO VENTURE FORTH IN PERSON
YOU DARE TO TOUCH MY TRUE BELOVED?

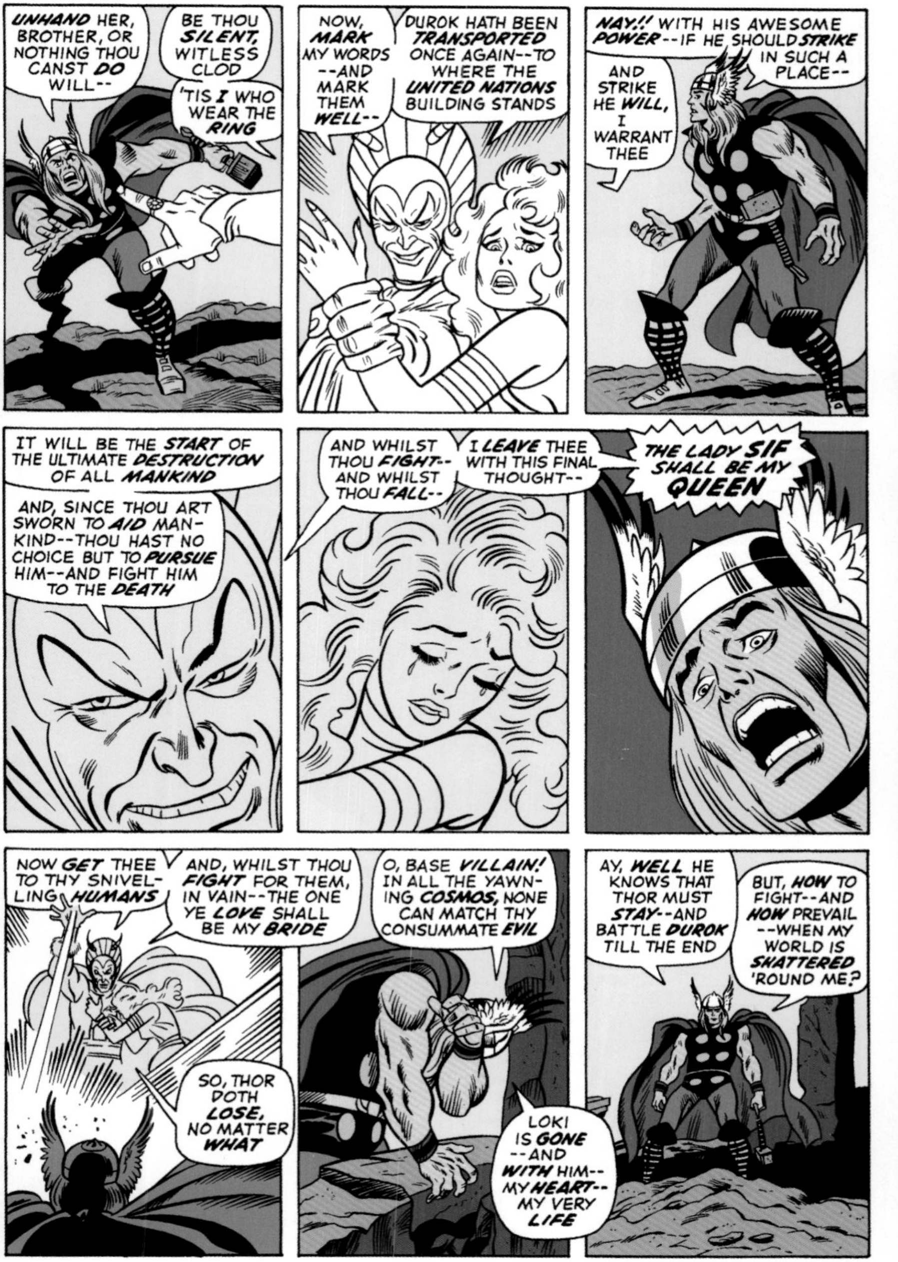

UNHAND HER, BROTHER, OR NOTHING THOU CANST DO WILL--
BE THOU SILENT, WITLESS CLOD
'TIS I WHO WEAR THE RING
NOW, MARK MY WORDS --AND MARK THEM WELL--
DUROK HATH BEEN TRANSPORTED ONCE AGAIN--TO WHERE THE UNITED NATIONS BUILDING STANDS
NAY!! WITH HIS AWESOME POWER--IF HE SHOULD STRIKE IN SUCH A PLACE--
AND STRIKE HE WILL, I WARRANT THEE
IT WILL BE THE START OF THE ULTIMATE DESTRUCTION OF ALL MANKIND
AND, SINCE THOU ART SWORN TO AID MANKIND--THOU HAST NO CHOICE BUT TO PURSUE HIM--AND FIGHT HIM TO THE DEATH
AND WHILST THOU FIGHT--AND WHILST THOU FALL--
I LEAVE THEE WITH THIS FINAL THOUGHT--
THE LADY SIF SHALL BE MY QUEEN
NOW GET THEE TO THY SNIVELLING HUMANS
AND, WHILST THOU FIGHT FOR THEM, IN VAIN--THE ONE YE LOVE SHALL BE MY BRIDE
SO, THOR DOTH LOSE, NO MATTER WHAT
O, BASE VILLAIN! IN ALL THE YAWNING COSMOS, NONE CAN MATCH THY CONSUMMATE EVIL
LOKI IS GONE --AND WITH HIM--MY HEART--MY VERY LIFE
AY, WELL HE KNOWS THAT THOR MUST STAY--AND BATTLE DUROK TILL THE END
BUT, HOW TO FIGHT--AND HOW PREVAIL--WHEN MY WORLD IS SHATTERED 'ROUND ME?

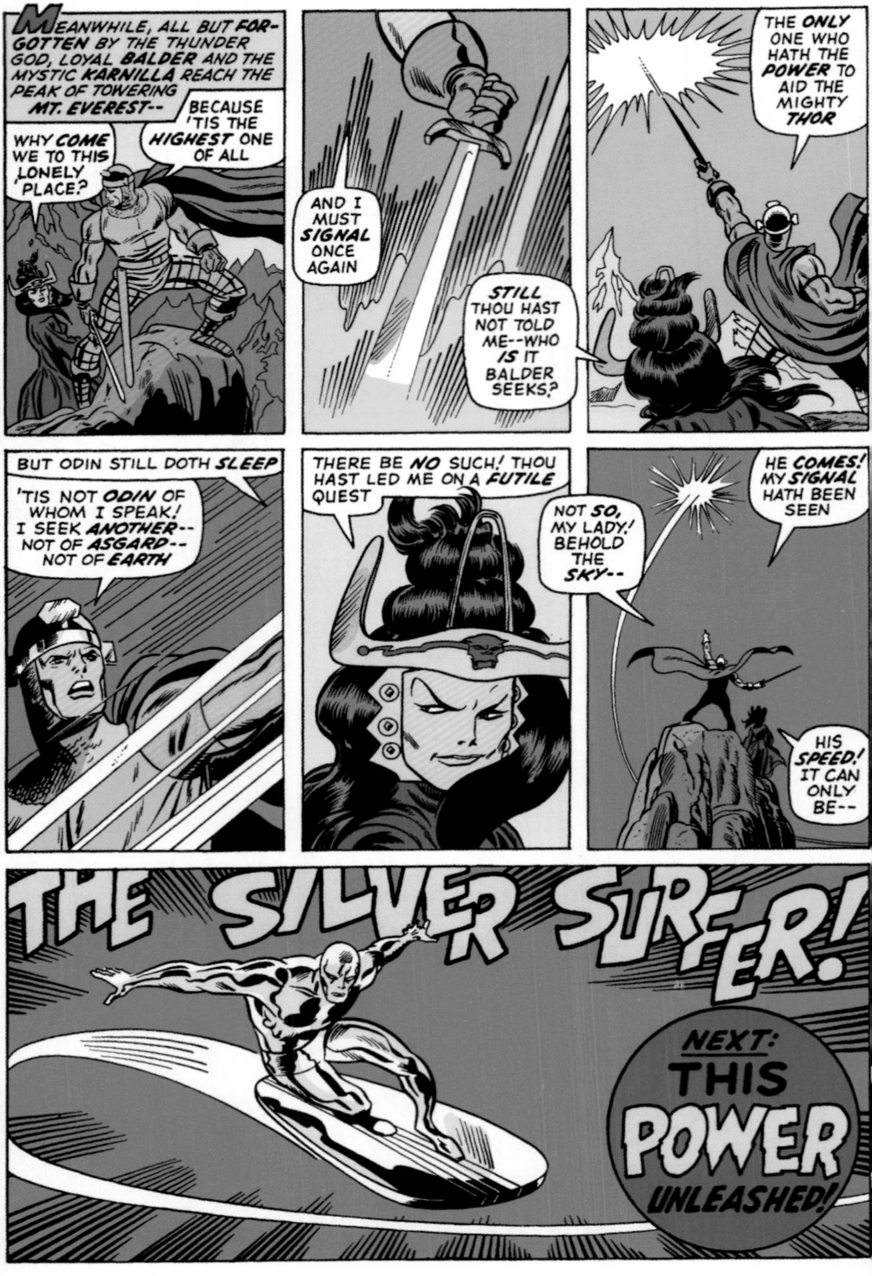
MEANWHILE, ALL BUT FORGOTTEN BY THE THUNDER GOD, LOYAL BALDER AND THE MYSTIC KARNILLA REACH THE PEAK OF TOWERING MT. EVEREST--
WHY COME WE TO THIS LONELY PLACE?
BECAUSE 'TIS THE HIGHEST ONE OF ALL
AND I MUST SIGNAL ONCE AGAIN
STILL THOU HAST NOT TOLD ME--WHO IS IT BALDER SEEKS?
THE ONLY ONE WHO HATH THE POWER TO AID THE MIGHTY THOR
BUT ODIN STILL DOTH SLEEP
'TIS NOT ODIN OF WHOM I SPEAK! I SEEK ANOTHER-- NOT OF ASGARD-- NOT OF EARTH
THERE BE NO SUCH! THOU HAST LED ME ON A FUTILE QUEST
NOT SO, MY LADY! BEHOLD THE SKY--
HE COMES! MY SIGNAL HATH BEEN SEEN
HIS SPEED! IT CAN ONLY BE--
THE SILVER SURFER!
NEXT: THIS POWER UNLEASHED!

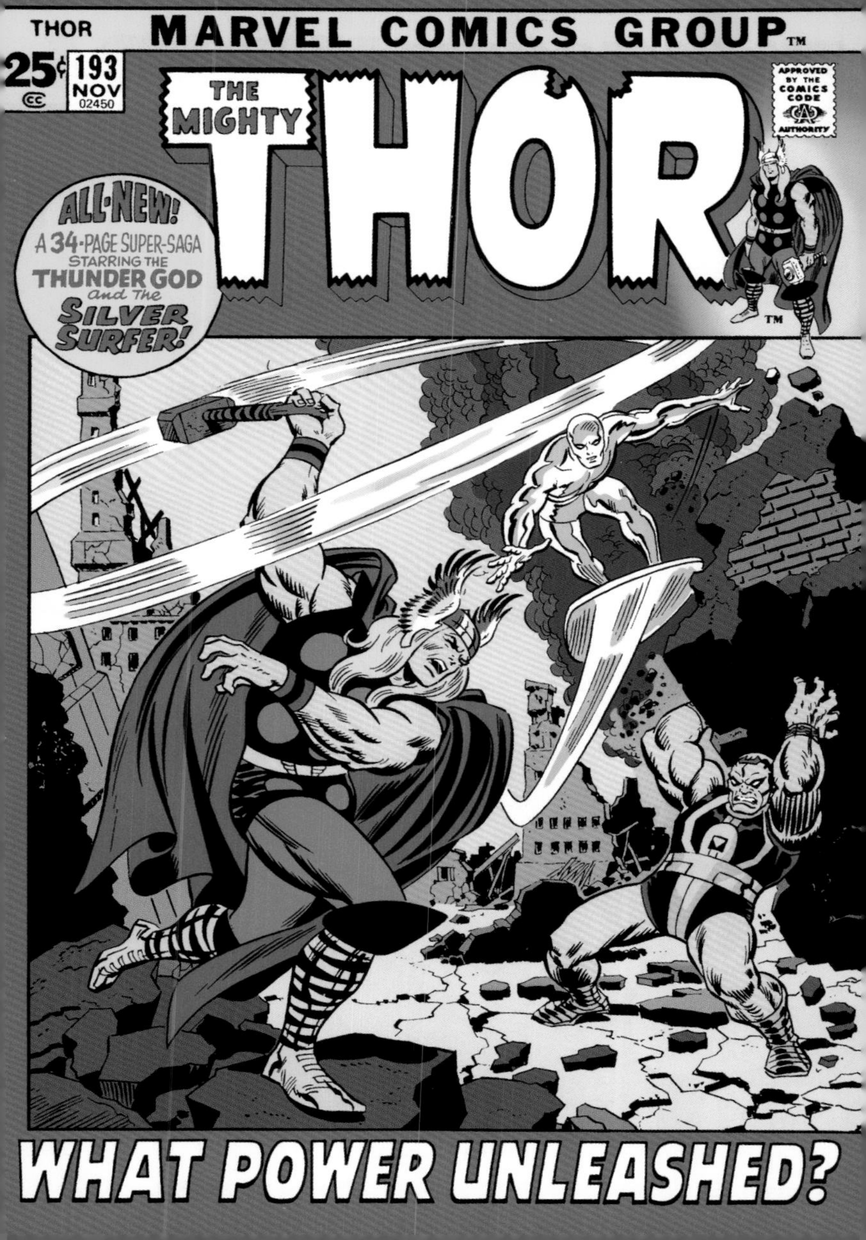

THOR
MARVEL COMICS GROUP™
25¢
CC
193
NOV
02450
THE MIGHTY
THOR
APPROVED BY THE COMICS CODE AUTHORITY
ALL-NEW!
A 34-PAGE SUPER-SAGA STARRING THE THUNDER GOD and the SILVER SURFER!
™
WHAT POWER UNLEASHED?

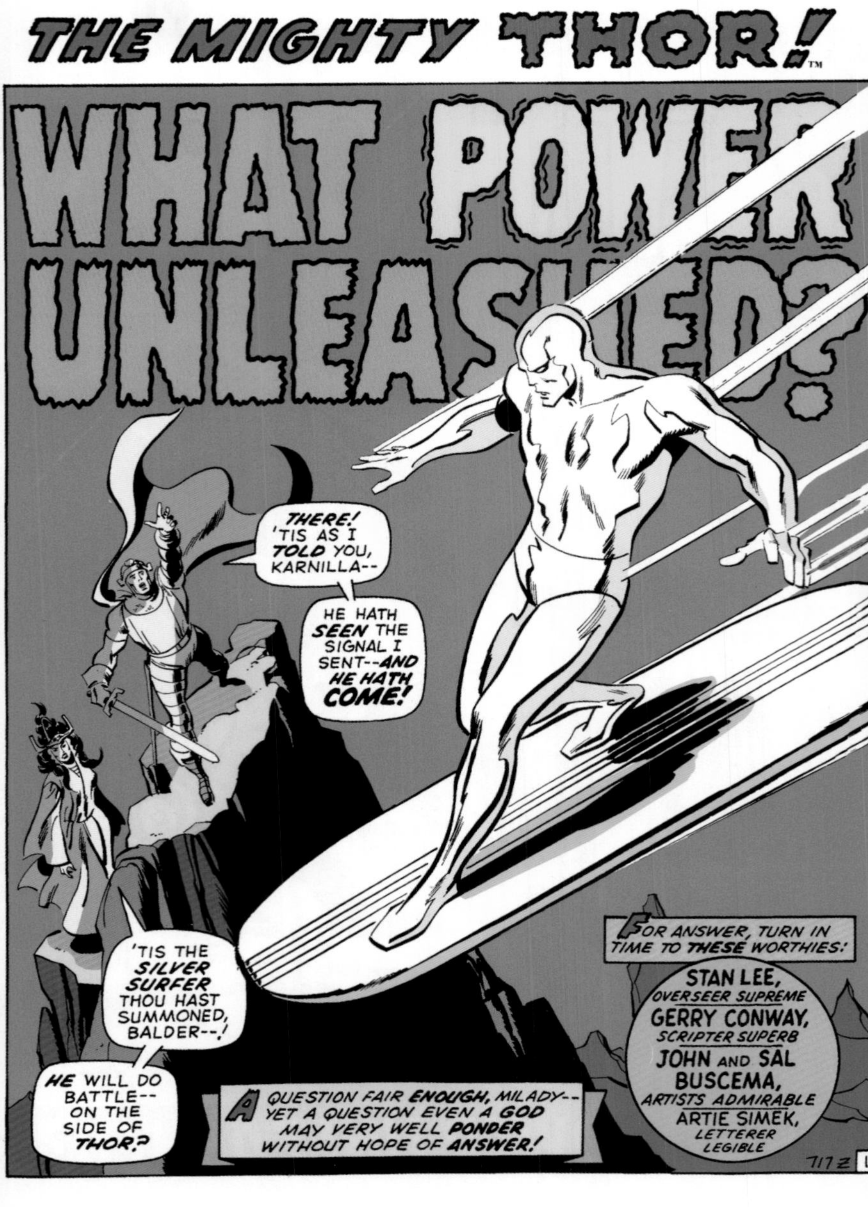

THE MIGHTY THOR!
WHAT POWER UNLEASHED?
THERE! 'TIS AS I TOLD YOU, KARNILLA--
HE HATH SEEN THE SIGNAL I SENT--AND HE HATH COME!
'TIS THE SILVER SURFER THOU HAST SUMMONED, BALDER--.!
HE WILL DO BATTLE-- ON THE SIDE OF THOR?
A QUESTION FAIR ENOUGH, MILADY-- YET A QUESTION EVEN A GOD MAY VERY WELL PONDER WITHOUT HOPE OF ANSWER!
FOR ANSWER, TURN IN TIME TO THESE WORTHIES!
STAN LEE, OVERSEER SUPREME
GERRY CONWAY, SCRIPTER SUPERB
JOHN AND SAL BUSCEMA, ARTISTS ADMIRABLE
ARTIE SIMEK, LETTERER LEGIBLE
717Z 1

UPON THAT WIND-SWEPT *PEAK*--

TWO HUMAN *FORMS*... ARE *THEY* THE ONES WHO CALLED ME FROM THE COSMIC PATH?

NO--THE HUMANS ARE TOO *WEAK*--

AND YET...I SENSE SOMETHING *OTHER* THAN A *HUMAN* SPIRIT HEREIN PRESENT.

PERHAPS I JUDGED THEM TOO-- *RASHLY*.

PERHAPS... THERE IS SOMETHING THE SILVER SURFER MAY *YET* LEARN--

--MAY YET *DISCOVER*-- UPON THIS TEAR-WASHED *GLOBE*.

WHAT *NAME* HAVE YOU WHO SUMMONED ME.?

I AM CALLED BALDER... THE *BRAVE*.

PRESUMPTUOUS ENOUGH-- FOR A *HUMAN*.

NO HUMANS WE--BUT *GODS*.

AND THIS DAY...THE *GODS* NEED THINE *AID*!

MY AID.?

I'VE SWORN TO AID YOUR DECEITFUL KIND-- *NEVERMORE*.

FORGET THIS USELESS PLOY, BALDER--!

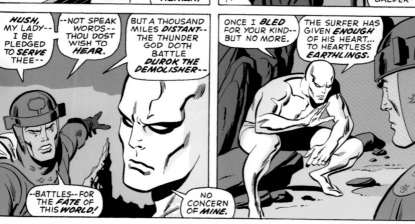

HUSH, MY LADY-- I BE PLEDGED TO *SERVE* THEE--

--NOT SPEAK WORDS-- THOU DOST WISH TO *HEAR*.

BUT A THOUSAND MILES *DISTANT*-- THE THUNDER GOD DOTH BATTLE *DUROK THE DEMOLISHER*--

--BATTLES-- FOR THE *FATE* OF THIS *WORLD*!

ONCE I *BLED* FOR YOUR KIND-- BUT NO MORE.

THE SURFER HAS GIVEN *ENOUGH* OF HIS HEART... TO HEARTLESS *EARTHLINGS*.

NO CONCERN OF *MINE*.

2

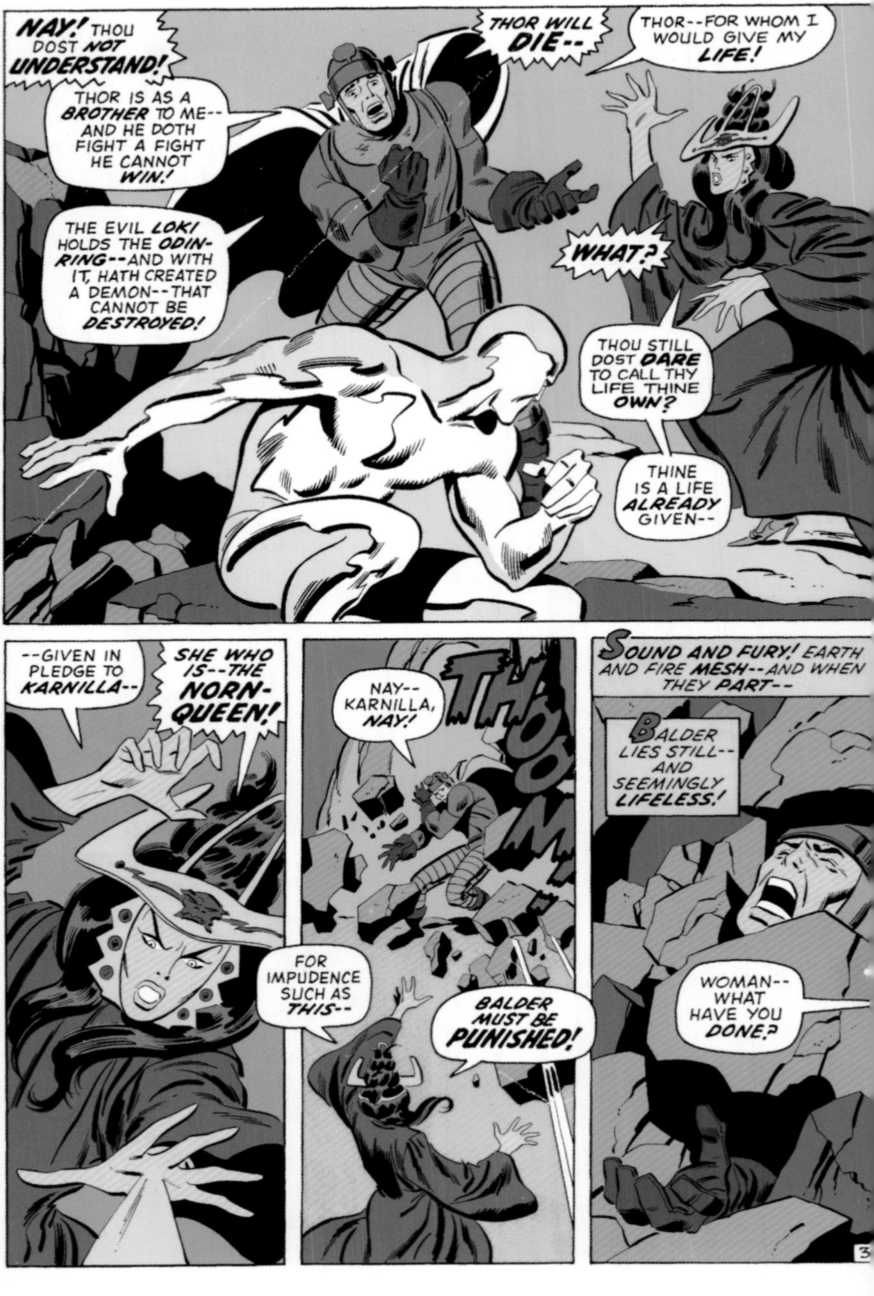
NAY! THOU DOST NOT UNDERSTAND!
THOR IS AS A BROTHER TO ME--AND HE DOTH FIGHT A FIGHT HE CANNOT WIN!
THE EVIL LOKI HOLDS THE ODIN-RING--AND WITH IT, HATH CREATED A DEMON--THAT CANNOT BE DESTROYED!
THOR WILL DIE--
THOR--FOR WHOM I WOULD GIVE MY LIFE!
WHAT?
THOU STILL DOST DARE TO CALL THY LIFE THINE OWN?
THINE IS A LIFE ALREADY GIVEN--
--GIVEN IN PLEDGE TO KARNILLA--
SHE WHO IS--THE NORN-QUEEN!
NAY--KARNILLA, NAY!
THOOOM!
FOR IMPUDENCE SUCH AS THIS--
BALDER MUST BE PUNISHED!
SOUND AND FURY! EARTH AND FIRE MESH--AND WHEN THEY PART--
BALDER LIES STILL--AND SEEMINGLY LIFELESS!
WOMAN--WHAT HAVE YOU DONE?
3

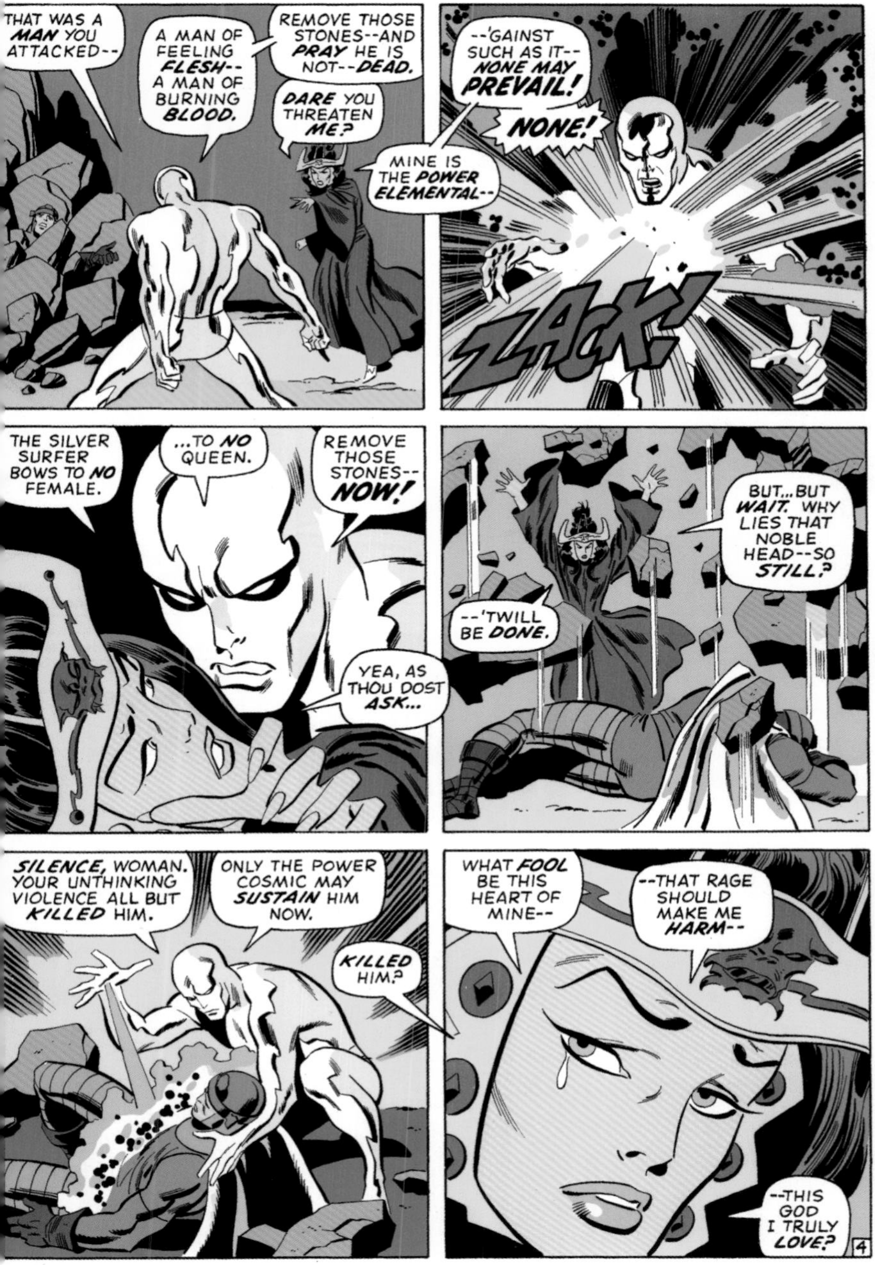
THAT WAS A MAN YOU ATTACKED--
A MAN OF FEELING FLESH-- A MAN OF BURNING BLOOD.
REMOVE THOSE STONES--AND PRAY HE IS NOT--DEAD.
DARE YOU THREATEN ME?
MINE IS THE POWER ELEMENTAL--
--'GAINST SUCH AS IT-- NONE MAY PREVAIL!
NONE!
ZACK!
THE SILVER SURFER BOWS TO NO FEMALE.
...TO NO QUEEN.
REMOVE THOSE STONES-- NOW!
YEA, AS THOU DOST ASK...
--'TWILL BE DONE.
BUT...BUT WAIT. WHY LIES THAT NOBLE HEAD--SO STILL?
SILENCE, WOMAN. YOUR UNTHINKING VIOLENCE ALL BUT KILLED HIM.
ONLY THE POWER COSMIC MAY SUSTAIN HIM NOW.
KILLED HIM?
WHAT FOOL BE THIS HEART OF MINE--
--THAT RAGE SHOULD MAKE ME HARM--
--THIS GOD I TRULY LOVE?
4

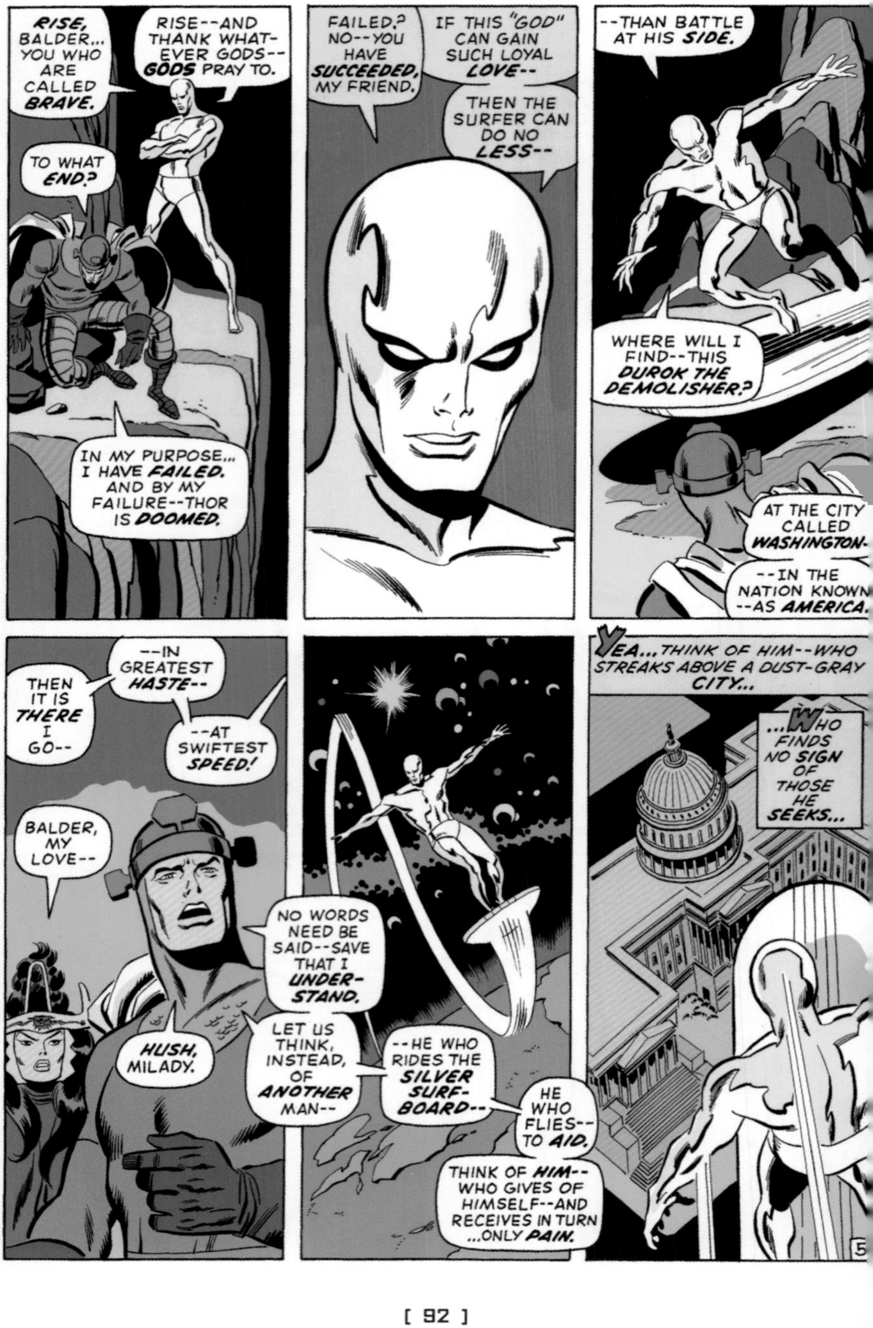
RISE, BALDER... YOU WHO ARE CALLED BRAVE.
RISE--AND THANK WHAT-EVER GODS--GODS PRAY TO.
TO WHAT END?
IN MY PURPOSE... I HAVE FAILED. AND BY MY FAILURE--THOR IS DOOMED.
FAILED? NO--YOU HAVE SUCCEEDED, MY FRIEND.
IF THIS "GOD" CAN GAIN SUCH LOYAL LOVE--
THEN THE SURFER CAN DO NO LESS--
--THAN BATTLE AT HIS SIDE.
WHERE WILL I FIND--THIS DUROK THE DEMOLISHER?
AT THE CITY CALLED WASHINGTON-
--IN THE NATION KNOWN --AS AMERICA.
THEN IT IS THERE I GO--
--IN GREATEST HASTE--
--AT SWIFTEST SPEED!
BALDER, MY LOVE--
NO WORDS NEED BE SAID--SAVE THAT I UNDER-STAND.
HUSH, MILADY.
LET US THINK, INSTEAD, OF ANOTHER MAN--
--HE WHO RIDES THE SILVER SURF-BOARD--
HE WHO FLIES--TO AID.
THINK OF HIM--WHO GIVES OF HIMSELF--AND RECEIVES IN TURN ...ONLY PAIN.
YEA... THINK OF HIM--WHO STREAKS ABOVE A DUST-GRAY CITY...
...WHO FINDS NO SIGN OF THOSE HE SEEKS...
5

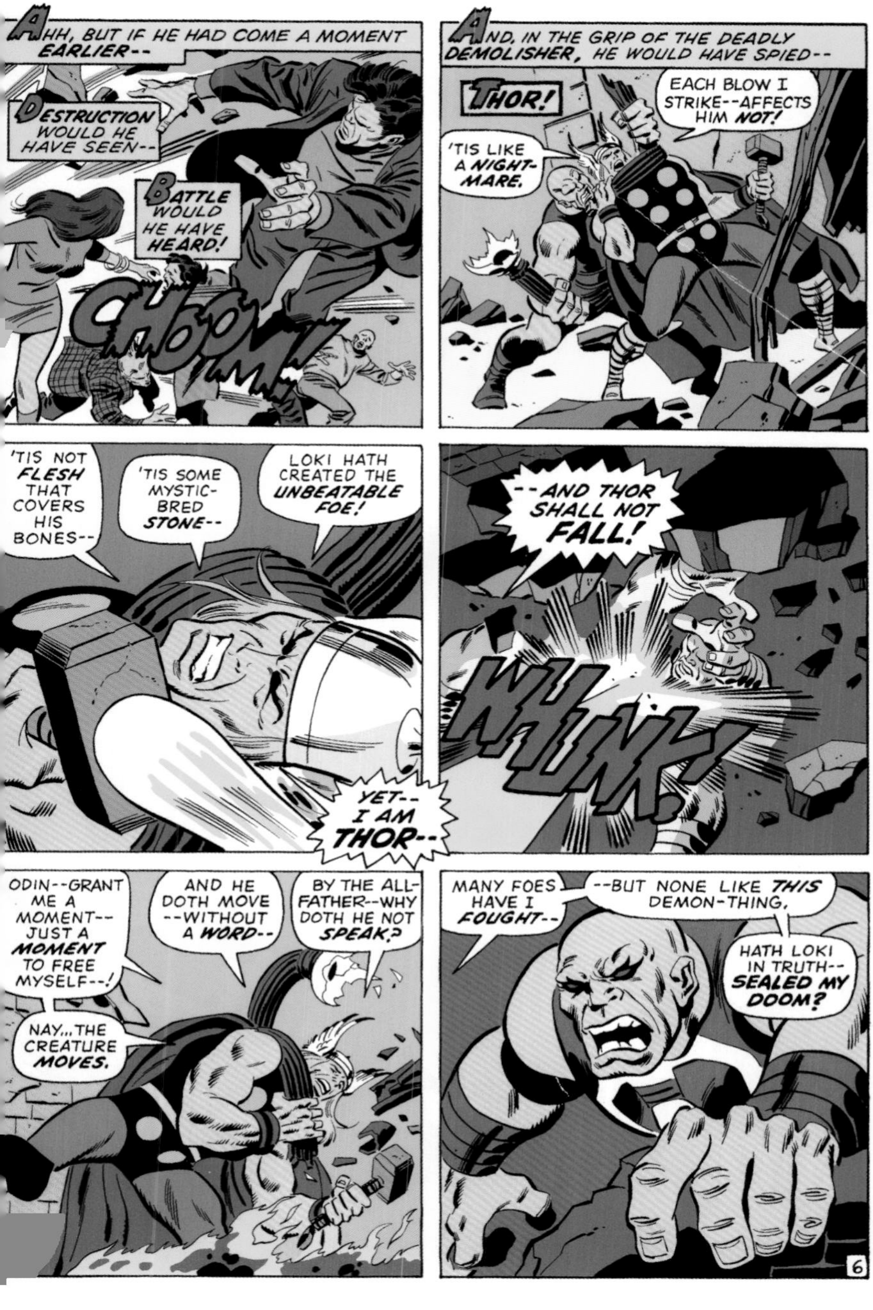
AHH, BUT IF HE HAD COME A MOMENT EARLIER--
DESTRUCTION WOULD HE HAVE SEEN--
BATTLE WOULD HE HAVE HEARD!
CHOOM!
AND, IN THE GRIP OF THE DEADLY DEMOLISHER, HE WOULD HAVE SPIED--
THOR!
EACH BLOW I STRIKE--AFFECTS HIM NOT!
'TIS LIKE A NIGHT-MARE.
'TIS NOT FLESH THAT COVERS HIS BONES--
'TIS SOME MYSTIC-BRED STONE--
LOKI HATH CREATED THE UNBEATABLE FOE!
YET-- I AM THOR--
--AND THOR SHALL NOT FALL!
WHUNK!
ODIN--GRANT ME A MOMENT-- JUST A MOMENT TO FREE MYSELF--!
NAY... THE CREATURE MOVES.
AND HE DOTH MOVE --WITHOUT A WORD--
BY THE ALL-FATHER--WHY DOTH HE NOT SPEAK?
MANY FOES HAVE I FOUGHT--
--BUT NONE LIKE THIS DEMON-THING.
HATH LOKI IN TRUTH-- SEALED MY DOOM?
6

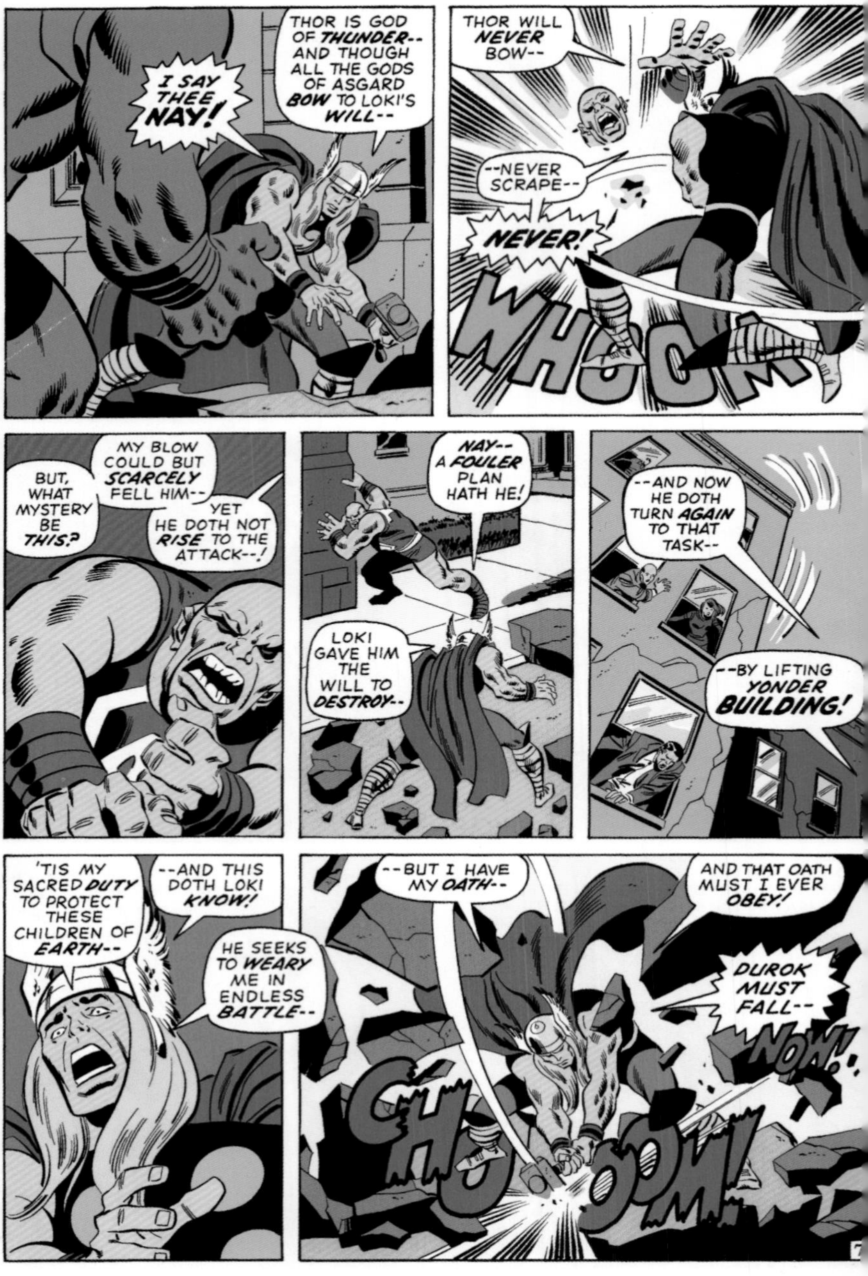
I SAY THEE NAY!
THOR IS GOD OF THUNDER-- AND THOUGH ALL THE GODS OF ASGARD BOW TO LOKI'S WILL--
THOR WILL NEVER BOW--
--NEVER SCRAPE--
NEVER!
WHOOM
MY BLOW COULD BUT SCARCELY FELL HIM--
BUT, WHAT MYSTERY BE THIS?
YET HE DOTH NOT RISE TO THE ATTACK--!
NAY-- A FOULER PLAN HATH HE!
LOKI GAVE HIM THE WILL TO DESTROY--
--AND NOW HE DOTH TURN AGAIN TO THAT TASK--
--BY LIFTING YONDER BUILDING!
'TIS MY SACRED DUTY TO PROTECT THESE CHILDREN OF EARTH--
--AND THIS DOTH LOKI KNOW!
HE SEEKS TO WEARY ME IN ENDLESS BATTLE--
--BUT I HAVE MY OATH--
AND THAT OATH MUST I EVER OBEY!
DUROK MUST FALL--
NOW!
CHOOOM!
7

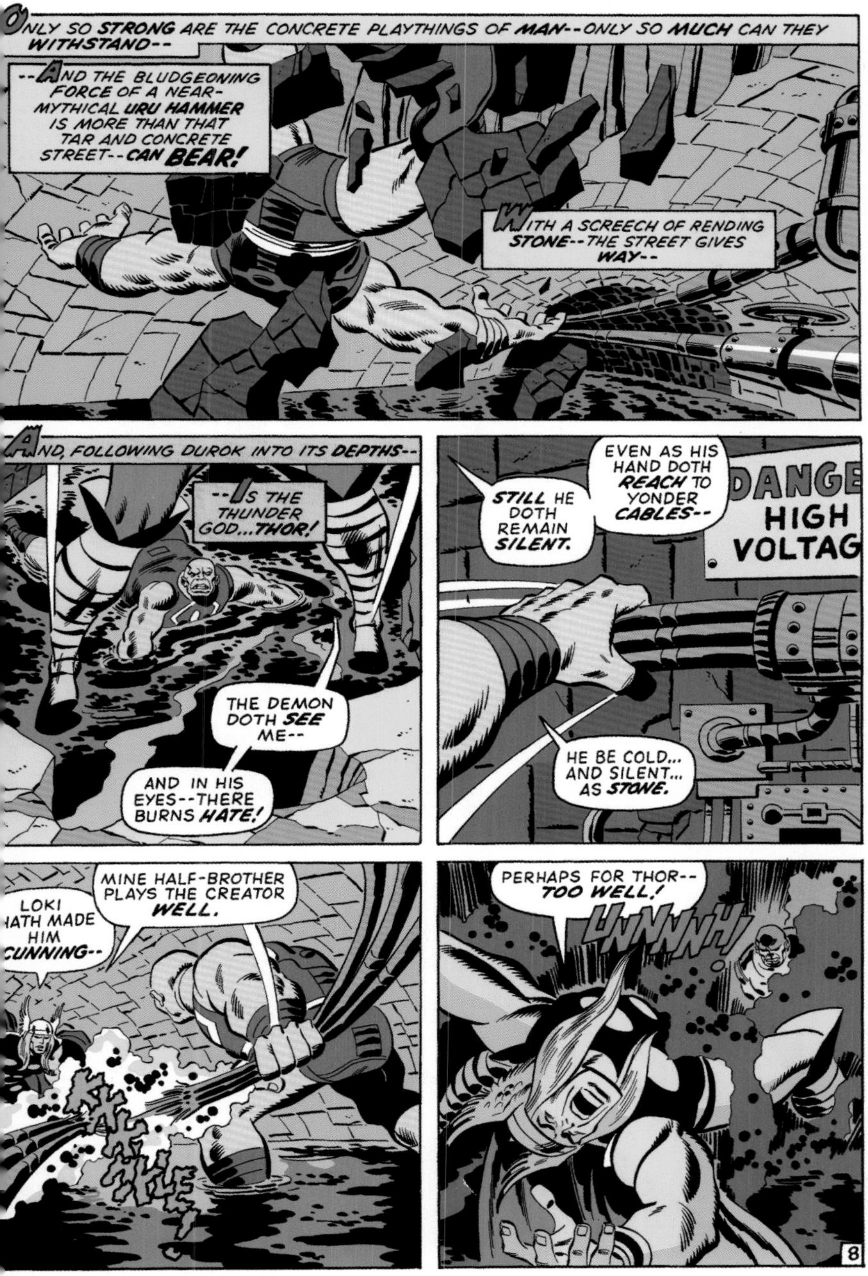
ONLY SO STRONG ARE THE CONCRETE PLAYTHINGS OF MAN--ONLY SO MUCH CAN THEY WITHSTAND--
--AND THE BLUDGEONING FORCE OF A NEAR-MYTHICAL URU HAMMER IS MORE THAN THAT TAR AND CONCRETE STREET--CAN BEAR!
WITH A SCREECH OF RENDING STONE--THE STREET GIVES WAY--
AND, FOLLOWING DUROK INTO ITS DEPTHS--
--IS THE THUNDER GOD...THOR!
THE DEMON DOTH SEE ME--
AND IN HIS EYES--THERE BURNS HATE!
STILL HE DOTH REMAIN SILENT.
EVEN AS HIS HAND DOTH REACH TO YONDER CABLES--
DANGE
HIGH
VOLTAG
HE BE COLD... AND SILENT... AS STONE.
LOKI HATH MADE HIM CUNNING--
MINE HALF-BROTHER PLAYS THE CREATOR WELL.
PERHAPS FOR THOR--TOO WELL!
UNNNH!
8

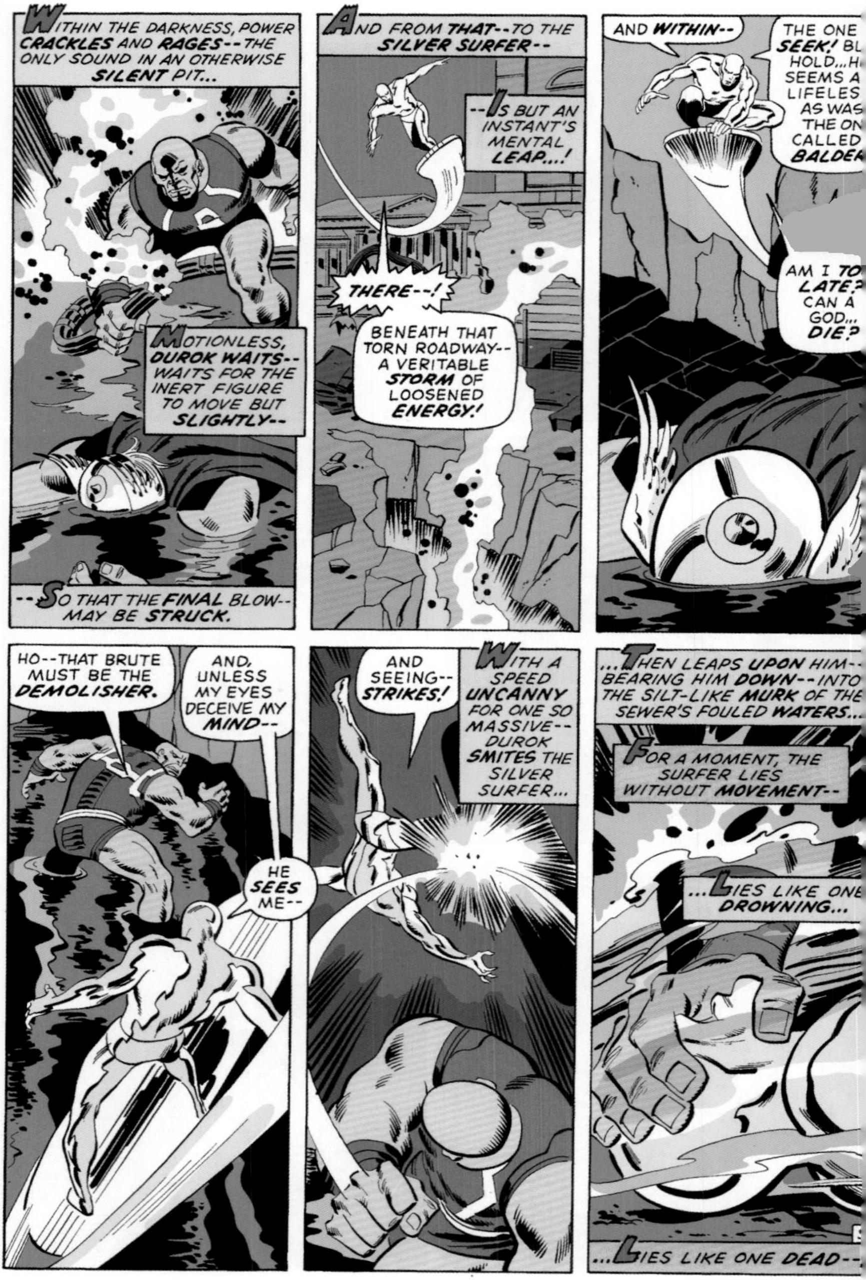

WITHIN THE DARKNESS, POWER CRACKLES AND RAGES--THE ONLY SOUND IN AN OTHERWISE SILENT PIT...
MOTIONLESS, DUROK WAITS--WAITS FOR THE INERT FIGURE TO MOVE BUT SLIGHTLY--
--SO THAT THE FINAL BLOW--MAY BE STRUCK.
AND FROM THAT--TO THE SILVER SURFER--
--IS BUT AN INSTANT'S MENTAL LEAP...!
THERE--!
BENEATH THAT TORN ROADWAY--A VERITABLE STORM OF LOOSENED ENERGY!
AND WITHIN--
THE ONE SEEK! BL HOLD...H SEEMS A LIFELES AS WAS THE ON CALLED BALDER
AM I TO LATE? CAN A GOD... DIE?
HO--THAT BRUTE MUST BE THE DEMOLISHER.
AND, UNLESS MY EYES DECEIVE MY MIND--
HE SEES ME--
AND SEEING--STRIKES!
WITH A SPEED UNCANNY FOR ONE SO MASSIVE--DUROK SMITES THE SILVER SURFER...
...THEN LEAPS UPON HIM--BEARING HIM DOWN--INTO THE SILT-LIKE MURK OF THE SEWER'S FOULED WATERS...
FOR A MOMENT, THE SURFER LIES WITHOUT MOVEMENT--
...LIES LIKE ONE DROWNING...
...LIES LIKE ONE DEAD--

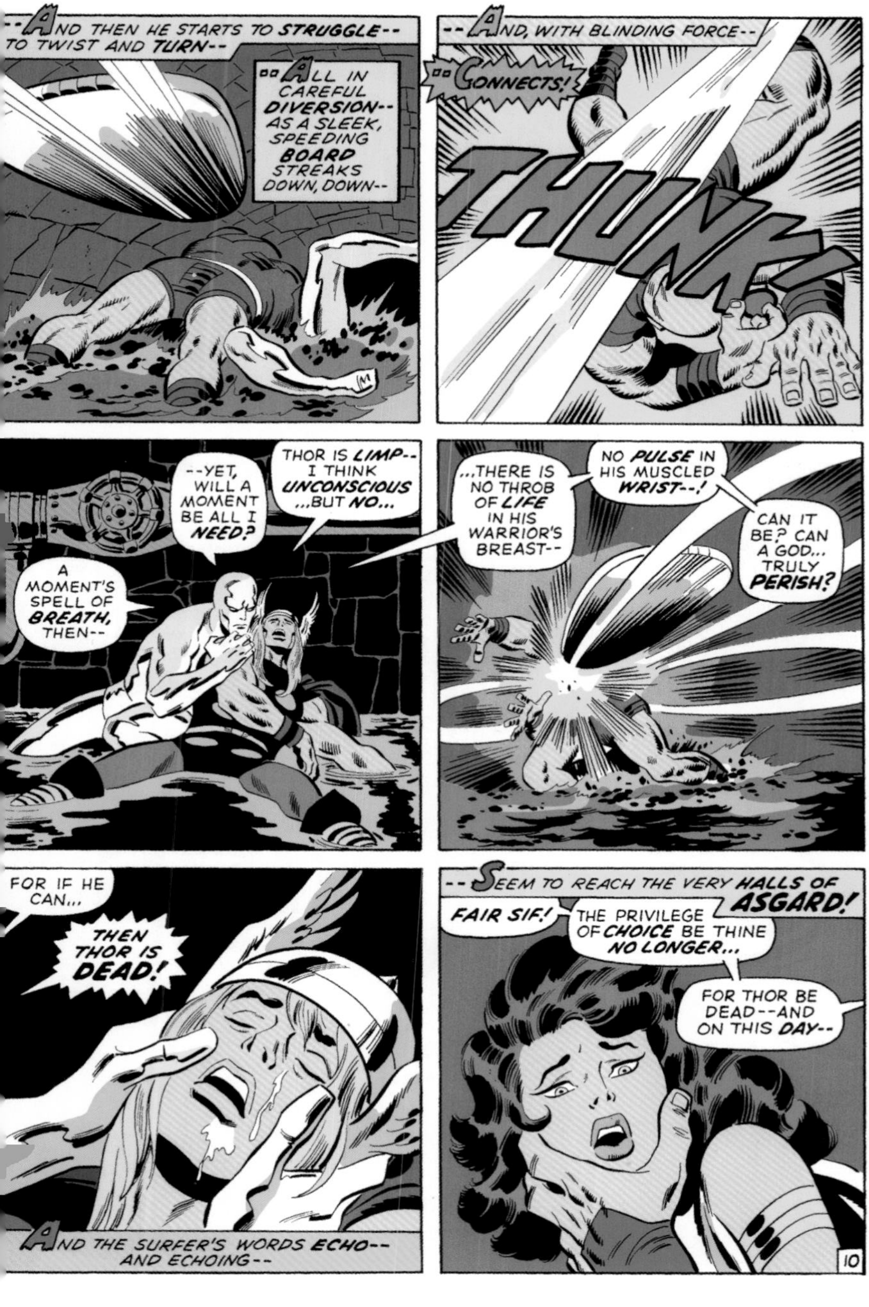
--AND THEN HE STARTS TO STRUGGLE--
TO TWIST AND TURN--
--ALL IN CAREFUL DIVERSION--AS A SLEEK, SPEEDING BOARD STREAKS DOWN, DOWN--
--AND, WITH BLINDING FORCE--
--CONNECTS!
THUNK!
--YET, WILL A MOMENT BE ALL I NEED?
THOR IS LIMP--I THINK UNCONSCIOUS ...BUT NO...
A MOMENT'S SPELL OF BREATH, THEN--
...THERE IS NO THROB OF LIFE IN HIS WARRIOR'S BREAST--
NO PULSE IN HIS MUSCLED WRIST--!
CAN IT BE? CAN A GOD... TRULY PERISH?
FOR IF HE CAN...
THEN THOR IS DEAD!
AND THE SURFER'S WORDS ECHO--AND ECHOING--
--SEEM TO REACH THE VERY HALLS OF ASGARD!
FAIR SIF!
THE PRIVILEGE OF CHOICE BE THINE NO LONGER...
FOR THOR BE DEAD--AND ON THIS DAY--
10

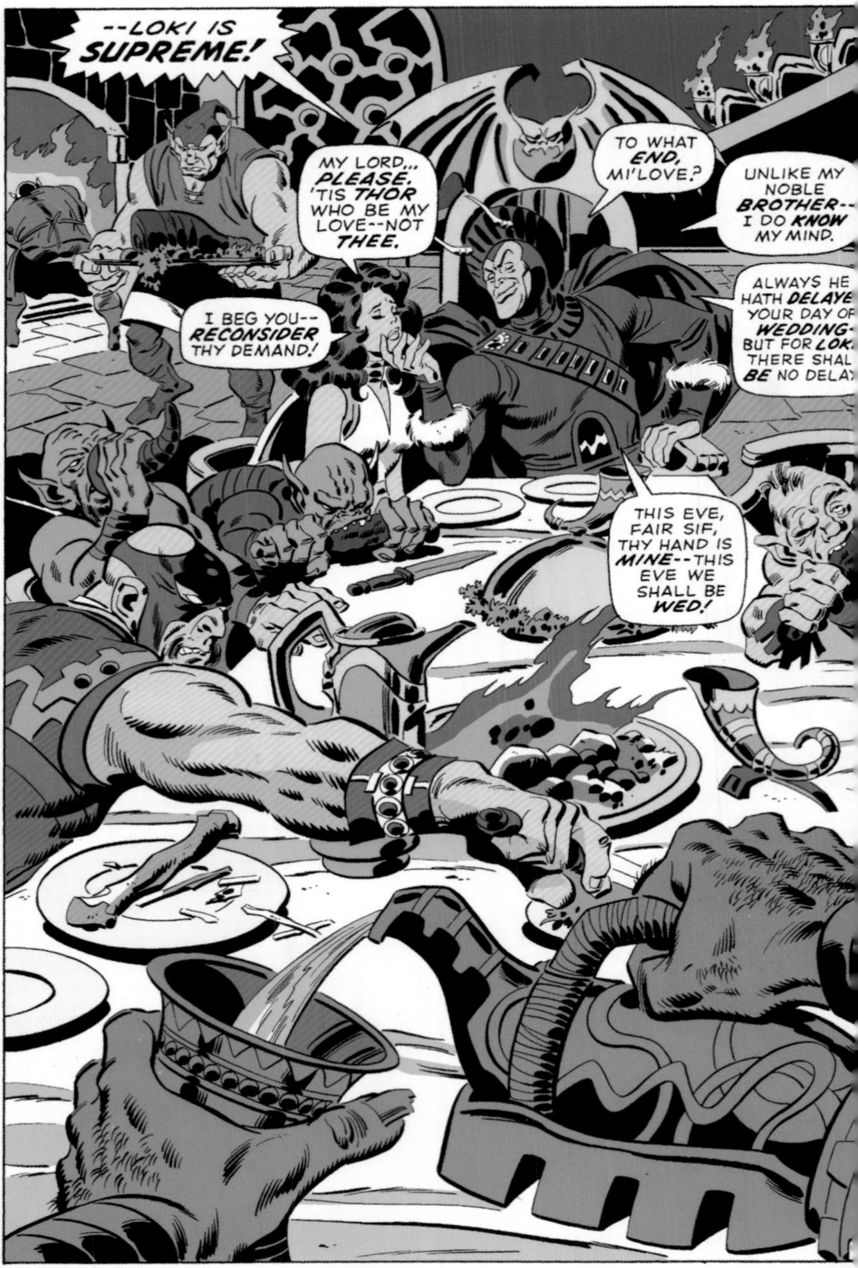
--LOKI IS SUPREME!
MY LORD... PLEASE. 'TIS THOR WHO BE MY LOVE--NOT THEE.
TO WHAT END, MI'LOVE?
UNLIKE MY NOBLE BROTHER-- I DO KNOW MY MIND.
I BEG YOU-- RECONSIDER THY DEMAND!
THIS EVE, FAIR SIF, THY HAND IS MINE--THIS EVE WE SHALL BE WED!

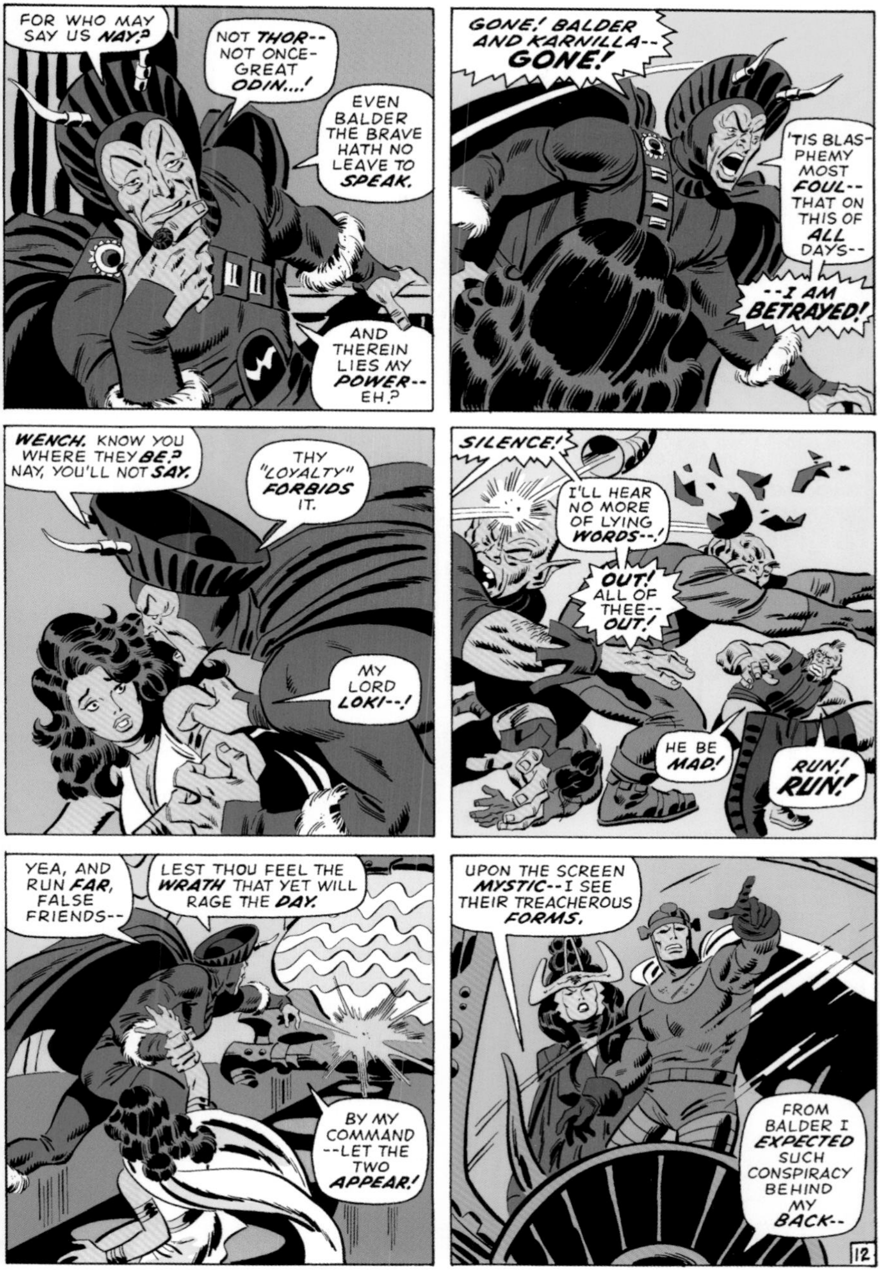
FOR WHO MAY SAY US NAY?
NOT THOR-- NOT ONCE-GREAT ODIN....!
EVEN BALDER THE BRAVE HATH NO LEAVE TO SPEAK.
AND THEREIN LIES MY POWER-- EH?
GONE! BALDER AND KARNILLA-- GONE!
'TIS BLASPHEMY MOST FOUL-- THAT ON THIS OF ALL DAYS--
--I AM BETRAYED!
WENCH. KNOW YOU WHERE THEY BE? NAY, YOU'LL NOT SAY.
THY "LOYALTY" FORBIDS IT.
MY LORD LOKI--!
SILENCE!
I'LL HEAR NO MORE OF LYING WORDS--!
OUT! ALL OF THEE-- OUT!
HE BE MAD!
RUN! RUN!
YEA, AND RUN FAR, FALSE FRIENDS--
LEST THOU FEEL THE WRATH THAT YET WILL RAGE THE DAY.
BY MY COMMAND --LET THE TWO APPEAR!
UPON THE SCREEN MYSTIC--I SEE THEIR TREACHEROUS FORMS.
FROM BALDER I EXPECTED SUCH CONSPIRACY BEHIND MY BACK--
12

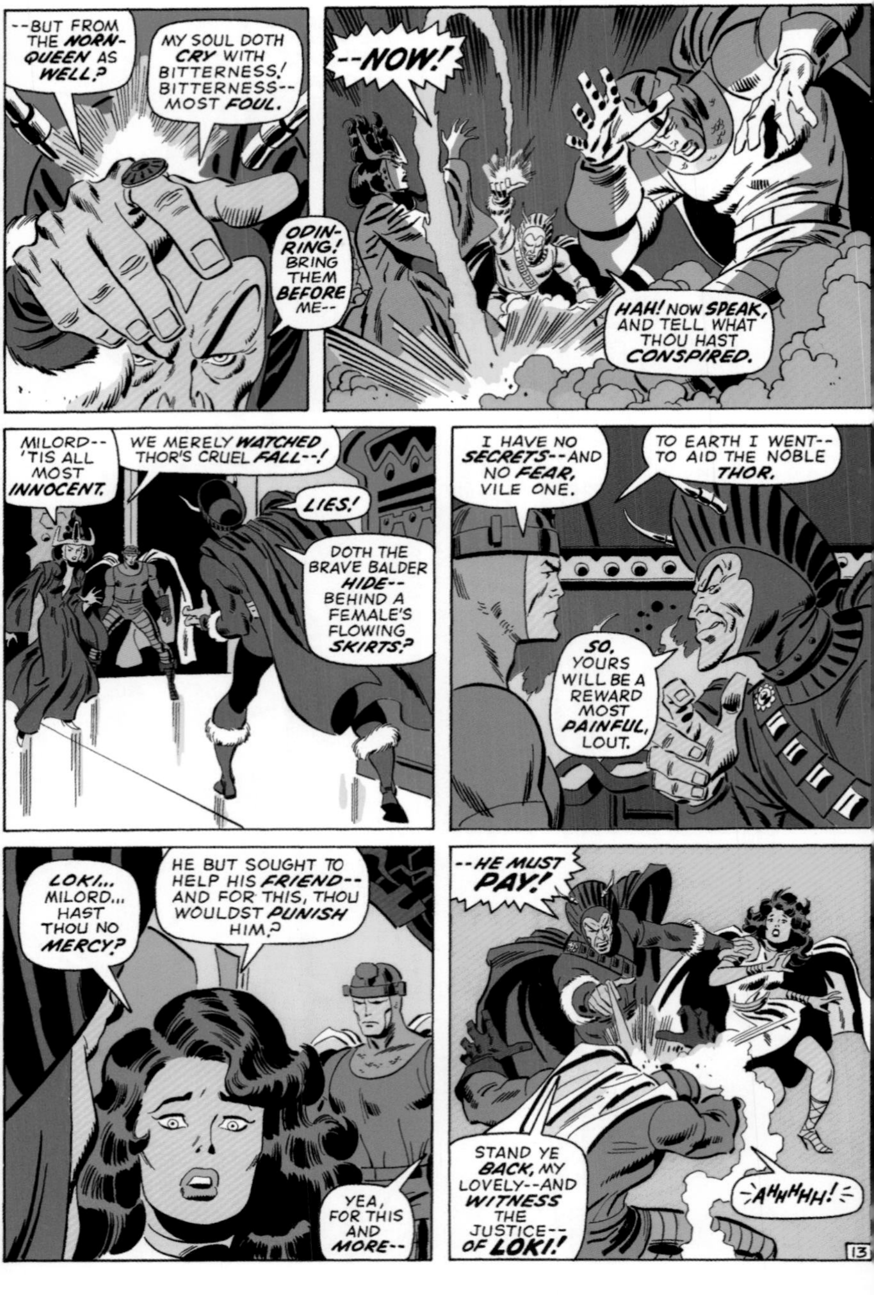
--BUT FROM THE NORN-QUEEN AS WELL?
MY SOUL DOTH CRY WITH BITTERNESS! BITTERNESS--MOST FOUL.
ODIN-RING! BRING THEM BEFORE ME--
--NOW!
HAH! NOW SPEAK, AND TELL WHAT THOU HAST CONSPIRED.
MILORD--'TIS ALL MOST INNOCENT.
WE MERELY WATCHED THOR'S CRUEL FALL--!
LIES!
DOTH THE BRAVE BALDER HIDE--BEHIND A FEMALE'S FLOWING SKIRTS?
I HAVE NO SECRETS--AND NO FEAR, VILE ONE.
TO EARTH I WENT--TO AID THE NOBLE THOR.
SO, YOURS WILL BE A REWARD MOST PAINFUL, LOUT.
LOKI... MILORD... HAST THOU NO MERCY?
HE BUT SOUGHT TO HELP HIS FRIEND--AND FOR THIS, THOU WOULDST PUNISH HIM?
YEA, FOR THIS AND MORE--
--HE MUST PAY!
STAND YE BACK, MY LOVELY--AND WITNESS THE JUSTICE--OF LOKI!
AHHHHH!
13

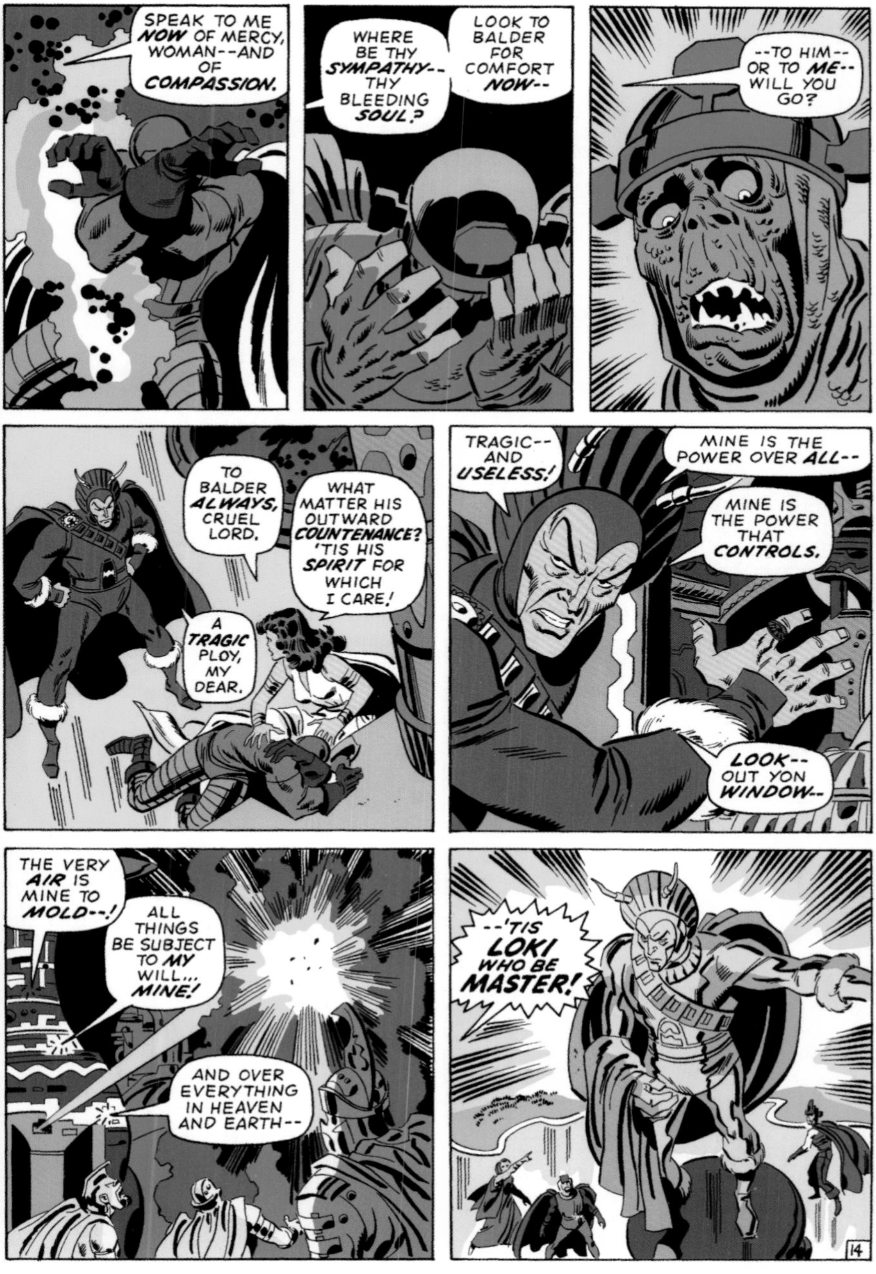
SPEAK TO ME NOW OF MERCY, WOMAN--AND OF COMPASSION.
WHERE BE THY SYMPATHY-- THY BLEEDING SOUL?
LOOK TO BALDER FOR COMFORT NOW--
--TO HIM-- OR TO ME-- WILL YOU GO?
TO BALDER ALWAYS, CRUEL LORD.
WHAT MATTER HIS OUTWARD COUNTENANCE? 'TIS HIS SPIRIT FOR WHICH I CARE!
A TRAGIC PLOY, MY DEAR.
TRAGIC-- AND USELESS!
MINE IS THE POWER OVER ALL--
MINE IS THE POWER THAT CONTROLS.
LOOK-- OUT YON WINDOW--
THE VERY AIR IS MINE TO MOLD--!
ALL THINGS BE SUBJECT TO MY WILL... MINE!
AND OVER EVERYTHING IN HEAVEN AND EARTH--
--'TIS LOKI WHO BE MASTER!
14

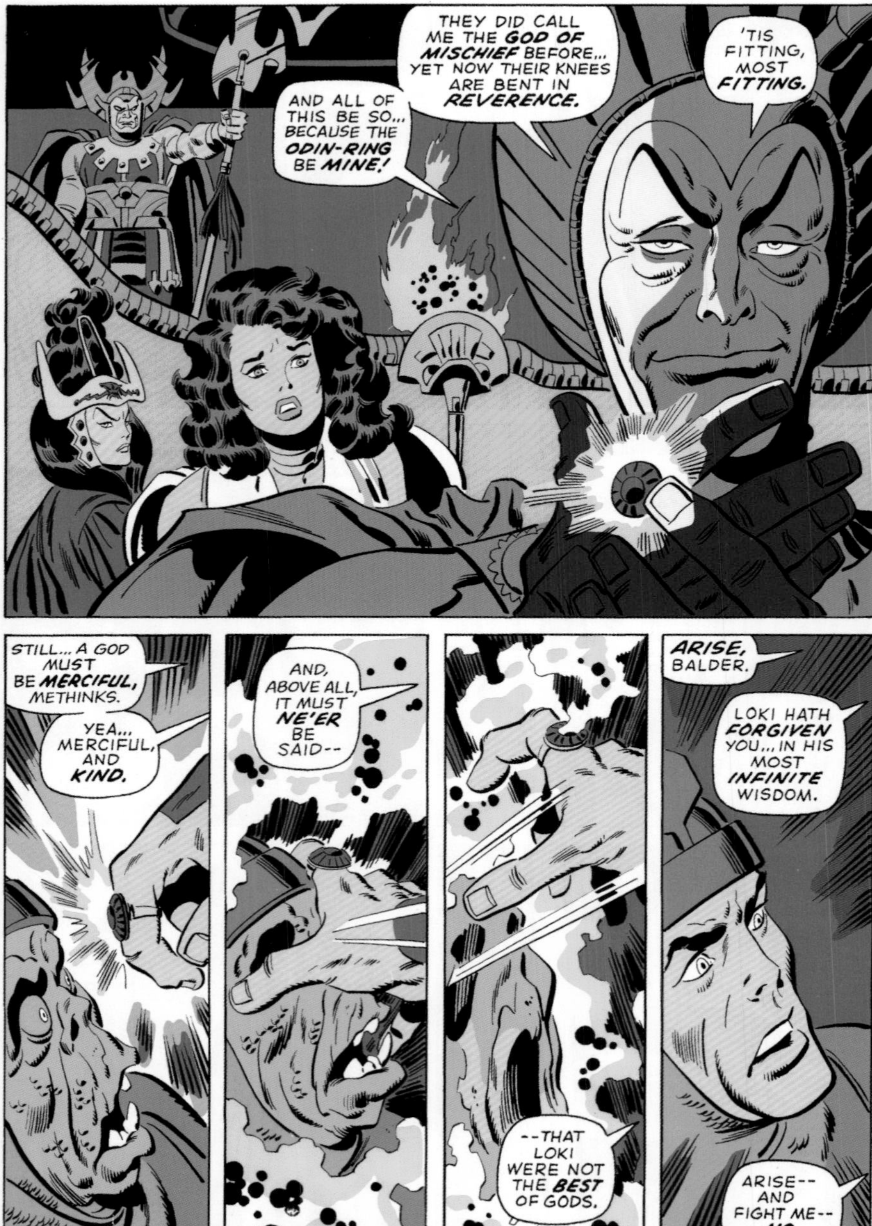
AND ALL OF THIS BE SO... BECAUSE THE ODIN-RING BE MINE!
THEY DID CALL ME THE GOD OF MISCHIEF BEFORE... YET NOW THEIR KNEES ARE BENT IN REVERENCE.
'TIS FITTING, MOST FITTING.
STILL... A GOD MUST BE MERCIFUL, METHINKS.
YEA... MERCIFUL, AND KIND.
AND, ABOVE ALL, IT MUST NE'ER BE SAID--
--THAT LOKI WERE NOT THE BEST OF GODS.
ARISE, BALDER.
LOKI HATH FORGIVEN YOU... IN HIS MOST INFINITE WISDOM.
ARISE-- AND FIGHT ME-- NO MORE.
15

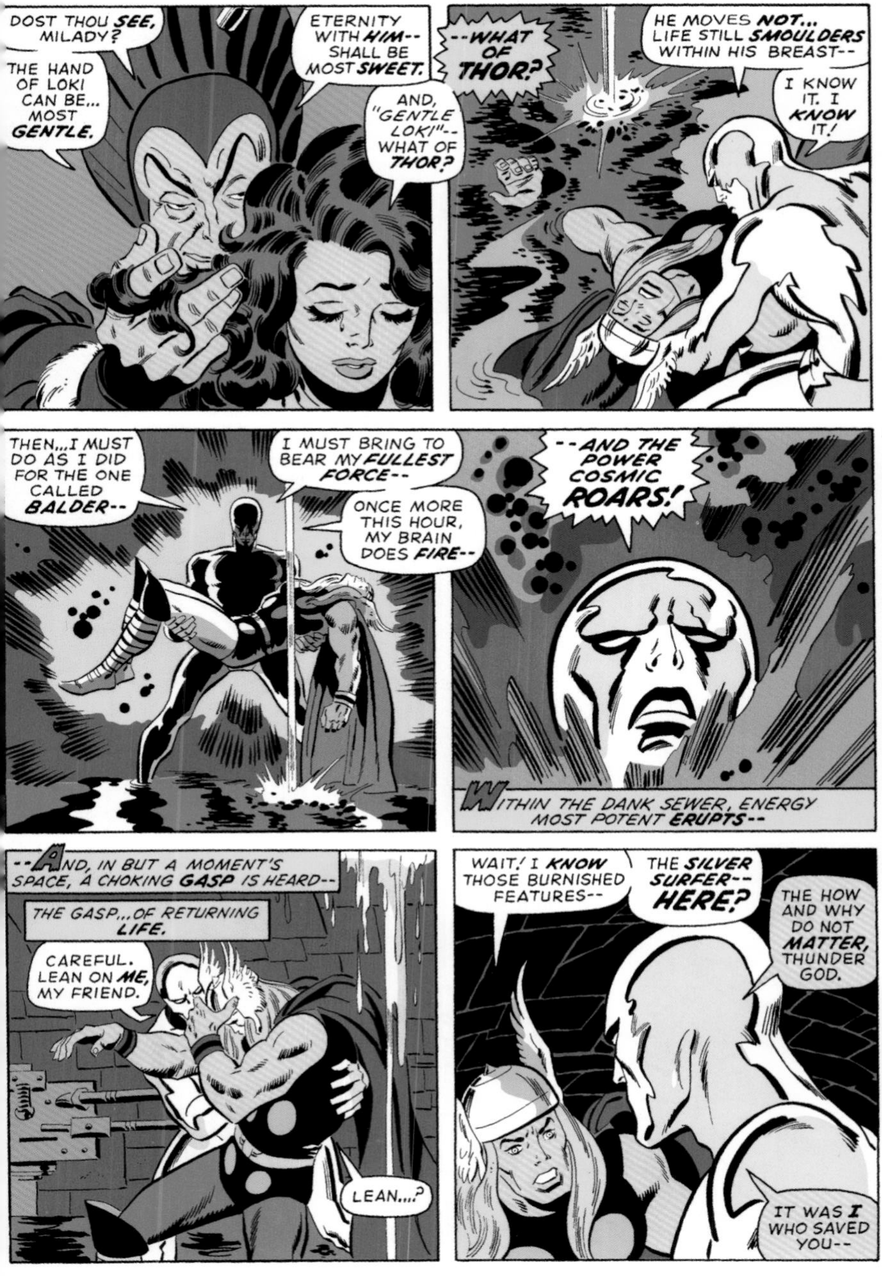
DOST THOU SEE, MILADY?
THE HAND OF LOKI CAN BE... MOST GENTLE.
ETERNITY WITH HIM-- SHALL BE MOST SWEET.
AND, "GENTLE LOKI"-- WHAT OF THOR?
--WHAT OF THOR?
HE MOVES NOT... LIFE STILL SMOULDERS WITHIN HIS BREAST--
I KNOW IT. I KNOW IT!
THEN...I MUST DO AS I DID FOR THE ONE CALLED BALDER--
I MUST BRING TO BEAR MY FULLEST FORCE--
ONCE MORE THIS HOUR, MY BRAIN DOES FIRE--
--AND THE POWER COSMIC ROARS!
WITHIN THE DANK SEWER, ENERGY MOST POTENT ERUPTS--
--AND, IN BUT A MOMENT'S SPACE, A CHOKING GASP IS HEARD--
THE GASP...OF RETURNING LIFE.
CAREFUL. LEAN ON ME, MY FRIEND.
LEAN...?
WAIT! I KNOW THOSE BURNISHED FEATURES--
THE SILVER SURFER-- HERE?
THE HOW AND WHY DO NOT MATTER, THUNDER GOD.
IT WAS I WHO SAVED YOU--

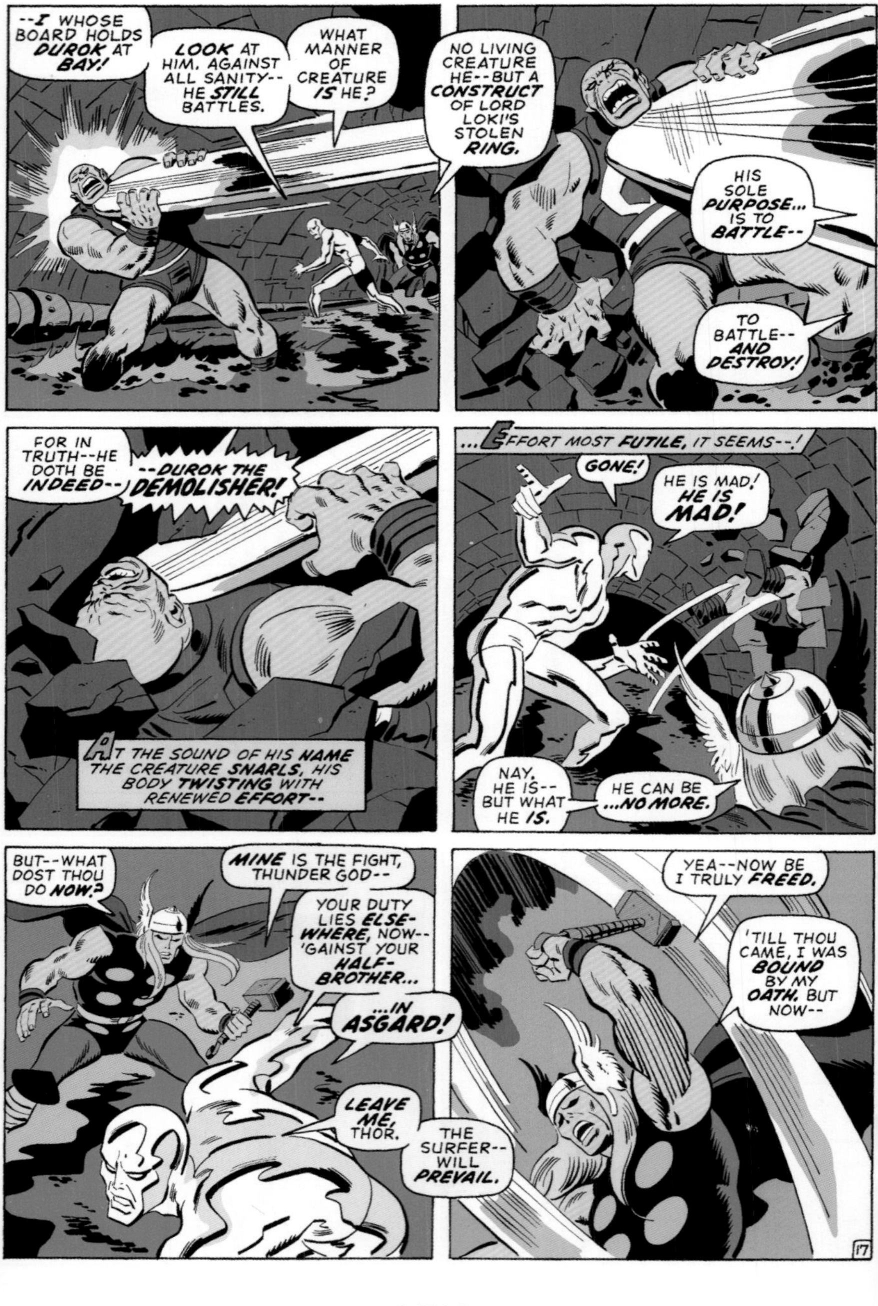
--I WHOSE BOARD HOLDS DUROK AT BAY!
LOOK AT HIM. AGAINST ALL SANITY-- HE STILL BATTLES.
WHAT MANNER OF CREATURE IS HE?
NO LIVING CREATURE HE--BUT A CONSTRUCT OF LORD LOKI'S STOLEN RING.
HIS SOLE PURPOSE... IS TO BATTLE--
TO BATTLE-- AND DESTROY!
FOR IN TRUTH--HE DOTH BE INDEED--
--DUROK THE DEMOLISHER!
AT THE SOUND OF HIS NAME THE CREATURE SNARLS, HIS BODY TWISTING WITH RENEWED EFFORT--
...EFFORT MOST FUTILE, IT SEEMS--!
GONE!
HE IS MAD! HE IS MAD!
NAY, HE IS-- BUT WHAT HE IS.
HE CAN BE ...NO MORE.
BUT--WHAT DOST THOU DO NOW?
MINE IS THE FIGHT, THUNDER GOD--
YOUR DUTY LIES ELSE-WHERE, NOW-- 'GAINST YOUR HALF-BROTHER...
...IN ASGARD!
LEAVE ME, THOR.
THE SURFER-- WILL PREVAIL.
YEA--NOW BE I TRULY FREED.
'TILL THOU CAME, I WAS BOUND BY MY OATH. BUT NOW--
17

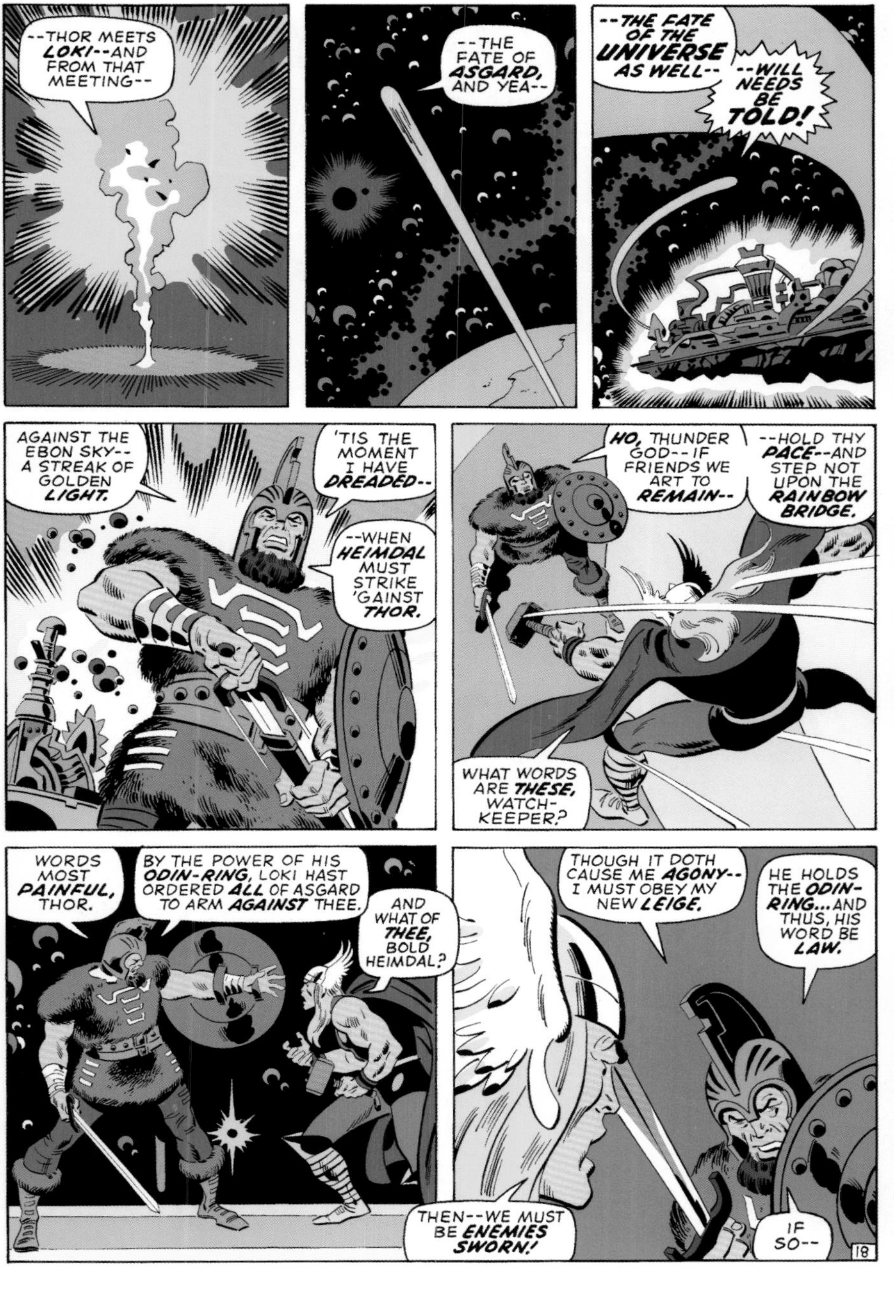
--THOR MEETS LOKI--AND FROM THAT MEETING--
--THE FATE OF ASGARD, AND YEA--
--THE FATE OF THE UNIVERSE AS WELL--
--WILL NEEDS BE TOLD!
AGAINST THE EBON SKY--A STREAK OF GOLDEN LIGHT.
'TIS THE MOMENT I HAVE DREADED--
--WHEN HEIMDAL MUST STRIKE 'GAINST THOR.
HO, THUNDER GOD--IF FRIENDS WE ART TO REMAIN--
--HOLD THY PACE--AND STEP NOT UPON THE RAINBOW BRIDGE.
WHAT WORDS ARE THESE, WATCH-KEEPER?
WORDS MOST PAINFUL, THOR.
BY THE POWER OF HIS ODIN-RING, LOKI HAST ORDERED ALL OF ASGARD TO ARM AGAINST THEE.
AND WHAT OF THEE, BOLD HEIMDAL?
THOUGH IT DOTH CAUSE ME AGONY--I MUST OBEY MY NEW LEIGE.
HE HOLDS THE ODIN-RING...AND THUS, HIS WORD BE LAW.
IF SO--
THEN--WE MUST BE ENEMIES SWORN!
18

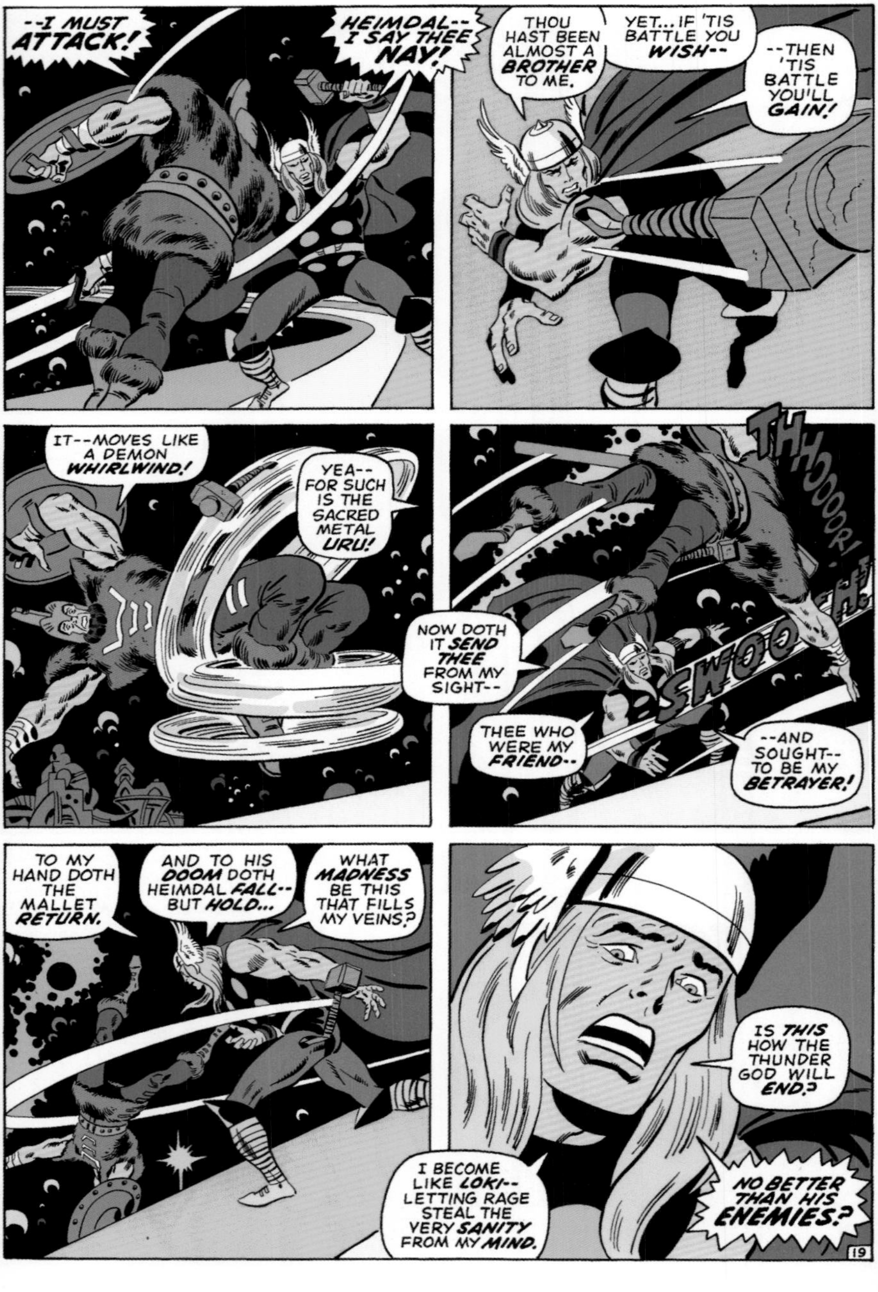
--I MUST ATTACK!
HEIMDAL-- I SAY THEE NAY!
THOU HAST BEEN ALMOST A BROTHER TO ME.
YET... IF 'TIS BATTLE YOU WISH--
--THEN 'TIS BATTLE YOU'LL GAIN!
IT--MOVES LIKE A DEMON WHIRLWIND!
YEA-- FOR SUCH IS THE SACRED METAL URU!
THHOOOOR!
NOW DOTH IT SEND THEE FROM MY SIGHT--
SWOOOSH!
THEE WHO WERE MY FRIEND--
--AND SOUGHT-- TO BE MY BETRAYER!
TO MY HAND DOTH THE MALLET RETURN.
AND TO HIS DOOM DOTH HEIMDAL FALL-- BUT HOLD...
WHAT MADNESS BE THIS THAT FILLS MY VEINS?
IS THIS HOW THE THUNDER GOD WILL END?
I BECOME LIKE LOKI-- LETTING RAGE STEAL THE VERY SANITY FROM MY MIND.
NO BETTER THAN HIS ENEMIES?
19

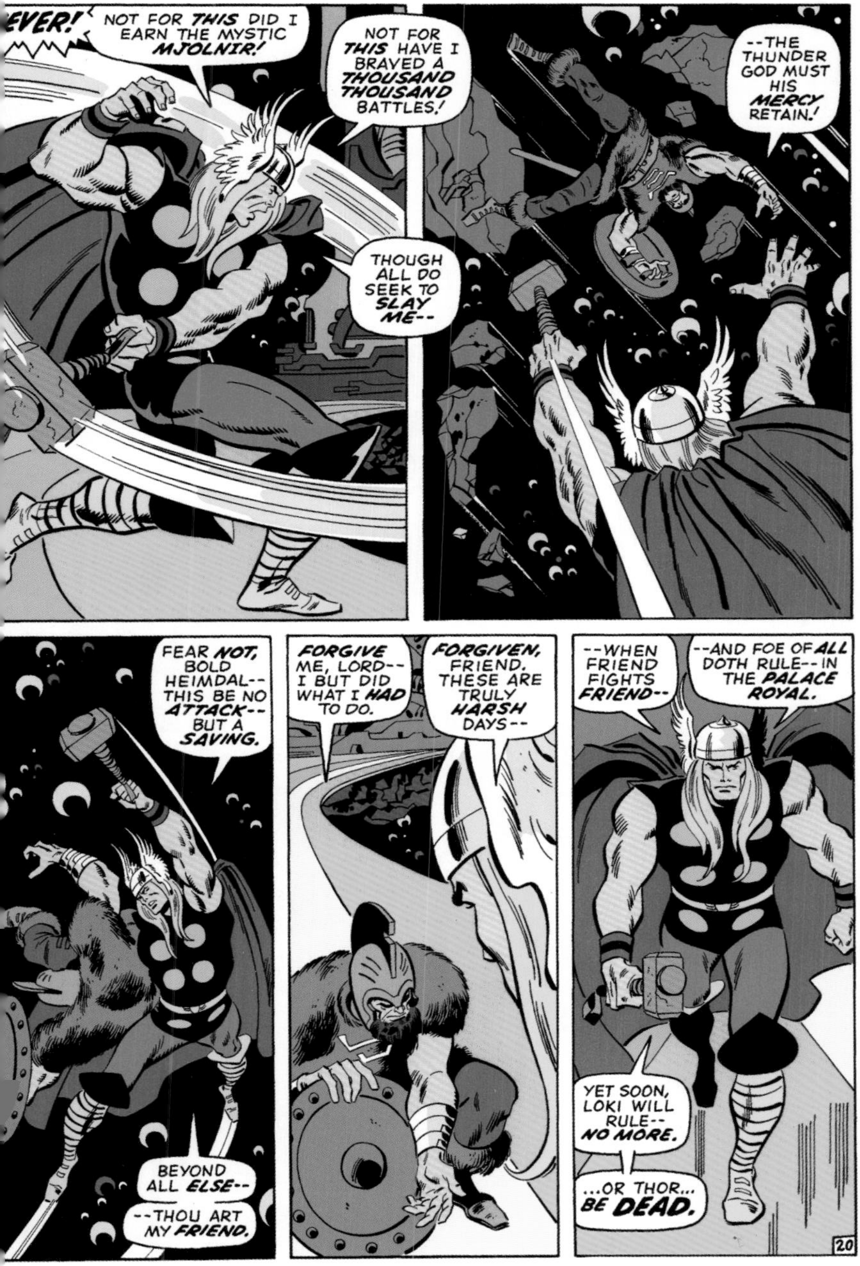
EVER!
NOT FOR THIS DID I EARN THE MYSTIC MJOLNIR!
NOT FOR THIS HAVE I BRAVED A THOUSAND THOUSAND BATTLES!
THOUGH ALL DO SEEK TO SLAY ME--
--THE THUNDER GOD MUST HIS MERCY RETAIN!
FEAR NOT, BOLD HEIMDAL-- THIS BE NO ATTACK-- BUT A SAVING.
BEYOND ALL ELSE--
--THOU ART MY FRIEND.
FORGIVE ME, LORD-- I BUT DID WHAT I HAD TO DO.
FORGIVEN, FRIEND. THESE ARE TRULY HARSH DAYS--
--WHEN FRIEND FIGHTS FRIEND--
--AND FOE OF ALL DOTH RULE--IN THE PALACE ROYAL.
YET SOON, LOKI WILL RULE-- NO MORE.
...OR THOR... BE DEAD.
20

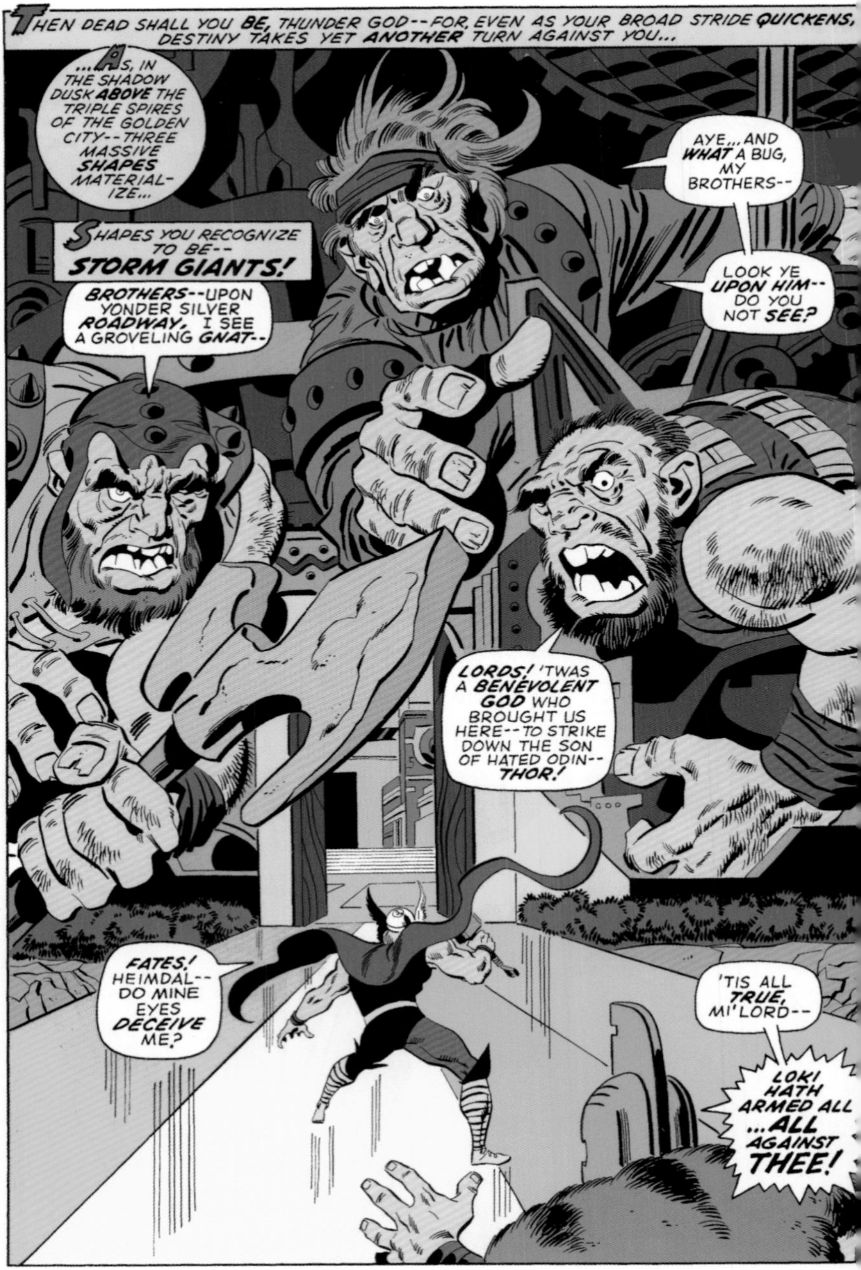
THEN DEAD SHALL YOU BE, THUNDER GOD--FOR, EVEN AS YOUR BROAD STRIDE QUICKENS, DESTINY TAKES YET ANOTHER TURN AGAINST YOU...
...AS, IN THE SHADOW DUSK ABOVE THE TRIPLE SPIRES OF THE GOLDEN CITY--THREE MASSIVE SHAPES MATERIAL-IZE...
SHAPES YOU RECOGNIZE TO BE--STORM GIANTS!
BROTHERS--UPON YONDER SILVER ROADWAY, I SEE A GROVELING GNAT--
AYE,...AND WHAT A BUG, MY BROTHERS--
LOOK YE UPON HIM--DO YOU NOT SEE?
LORDS! 'TWAS A BENEVOLENT GOD WHO BROUGHT US HERE--TO STRIKE DOWN THE SON OF HATED ODIN--THOR!
FATES! HEIMDAL--DO MINE EYES DECEIVE ME?
'TIS ALL TRUE, MI' LORD--
LOKI HATH ARMED ALL ...ALL AGAINST THEE!

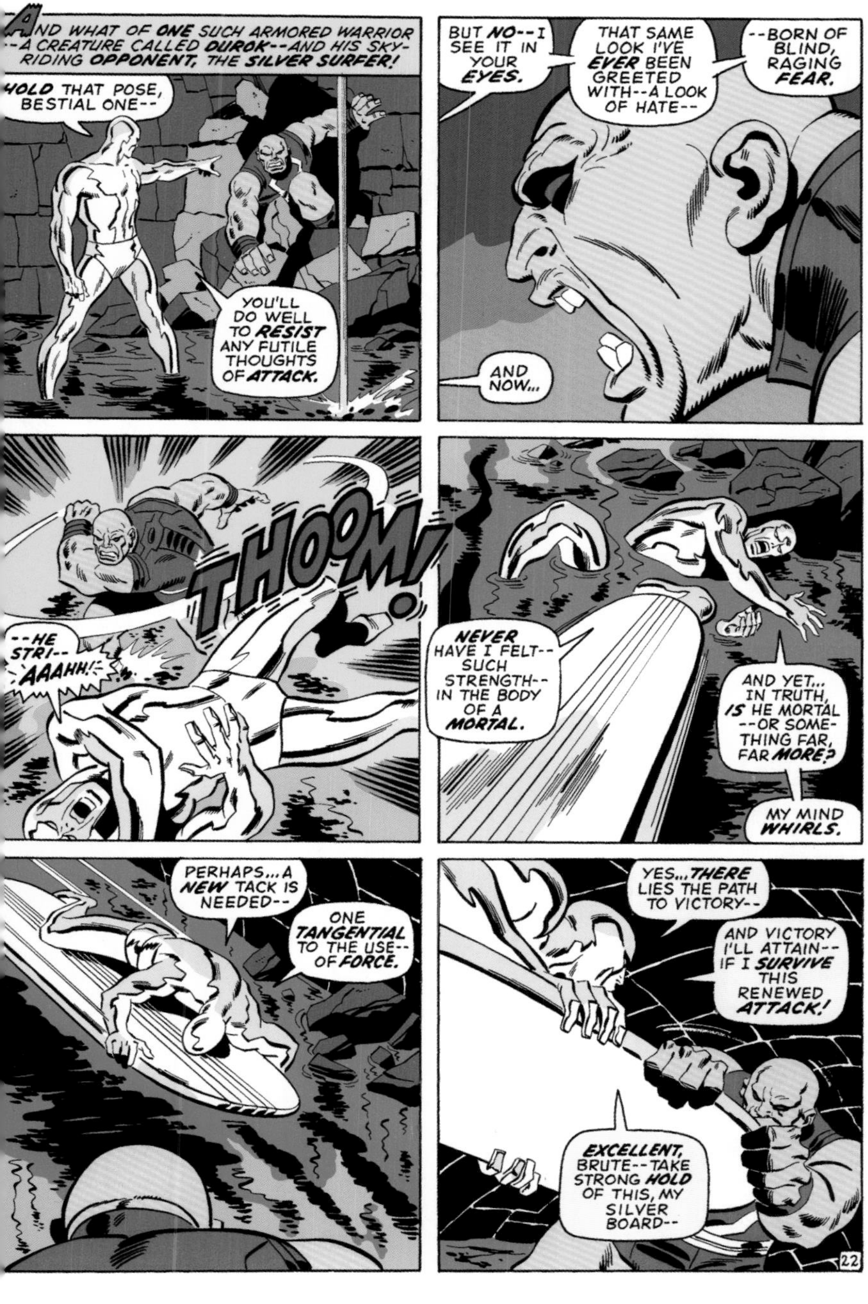

AND WHAT OF ONE SUCH ARMORED WARRIOR--A CREATURE CALLED DUROK--AND HIS SKY-RIDING OPPONENT, THE SILVER SURFER!
HOLD THAT POSE, BESTIAL ONE--
YOU'LL DO WELL TO RESIST ANY FUTILE THOUGHTS OF ATTACK.
BUT NO--I SEE IT IN YOUR EYES.
THAT SAME LOOK I'VE EVER BEEN GREETED WITH--A LOOK OF HATE--
--BORN OF BLIND, RAGING FEAR.
AND NOW...
THOOM!
--HE STRI--
AAAHH!
NEVER HAVE I FELT--SUCH STRENGTH--IN THE BODY OF A MORTAL.
AND YET... IN TRUTH, IS HE MORTAL--OR SOMETHING FAR, FAR MORE?
MY MIND WHIRLS.
PERHAPS... A NEW TACK IS NEEDED--
ONE TANGENTIAL TO THE USE--OF FORCE.
YES... THERE LIES THE PATH TO VICTORY--
AND VICTORY I'LL ATTAIN--IF I SURVIVE THIS RENEWED ATTACK!
EXCELLENT, BRUTE--TAKE STRONG HOLD OF THIS, MY SILVER BOARD--
22

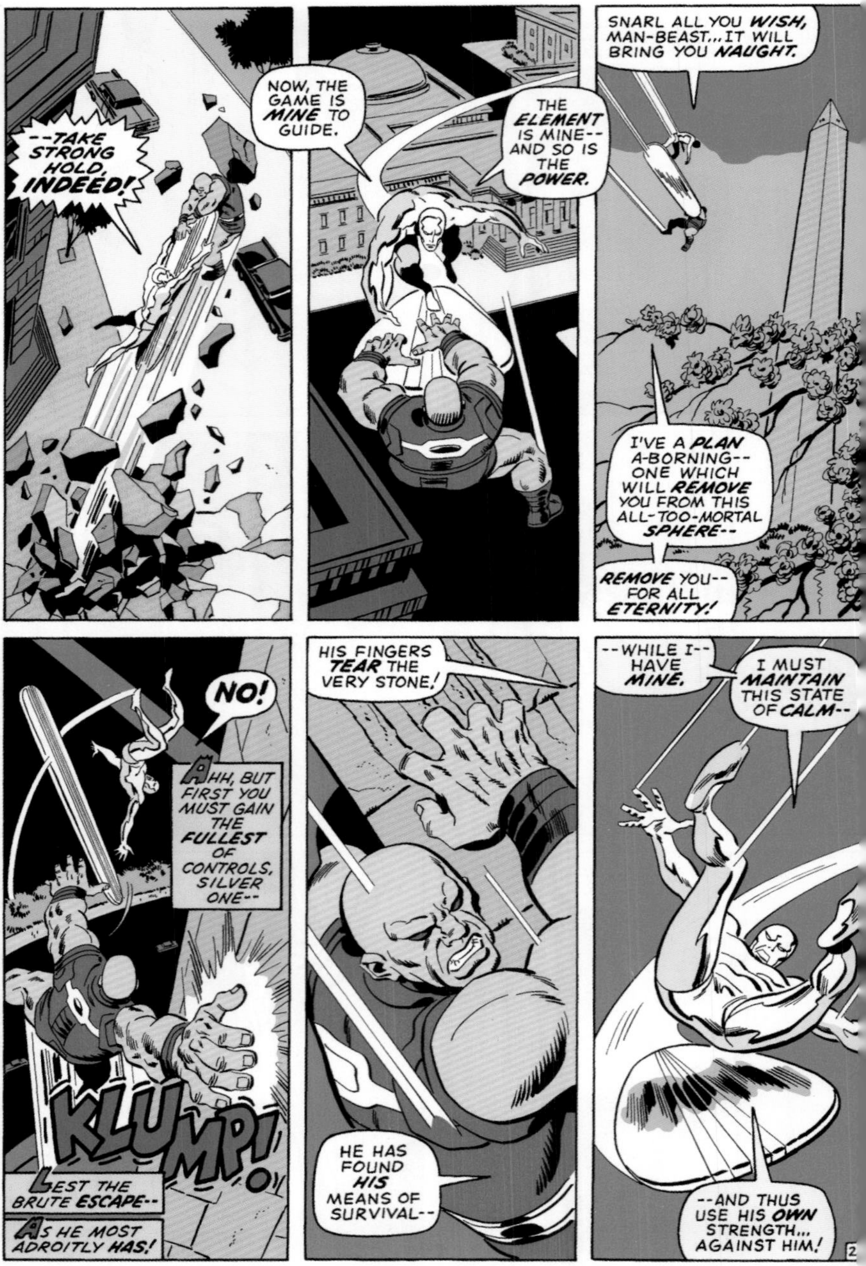
--TAKE STRONG HOLD, INDEED!
NOW, THE GAME IS MINE TO GUIDE.
THE ELEMENT IS MINE-- AND SO IS THE POWER.
SNARL ALL YOU WISH, MAN-BEAST... IT WILL BRING YOU NAUGHT.
I'VE A PLAN A-BORNING-- ONE WHICH WILL REMOVE YOU FROM THIS ALL-TOO-MORTAL SPHERE--
REMOVE YOU-- FOR ALL ETERNITY!
NO!
AHH, BUT FIRST YOU MUST GAIN THE FULLEST OF CONTROLS, SILVER ONE--
KLUMP!
LEST THE BRUTE ESCAPE--
AS HE MOST ADROITLY HAS!
HIS FINGERS TEAR THE VERY STONE!
HE HAS FOUND HIS MEANS OF SURVIVAL--
--WHILE I-- HAVE MINE.
I MUST MAINTAIN THIS STATE OF CALM--
--AND THUS USE HIS OWN STRENGTH... AGAINST HIM!
2

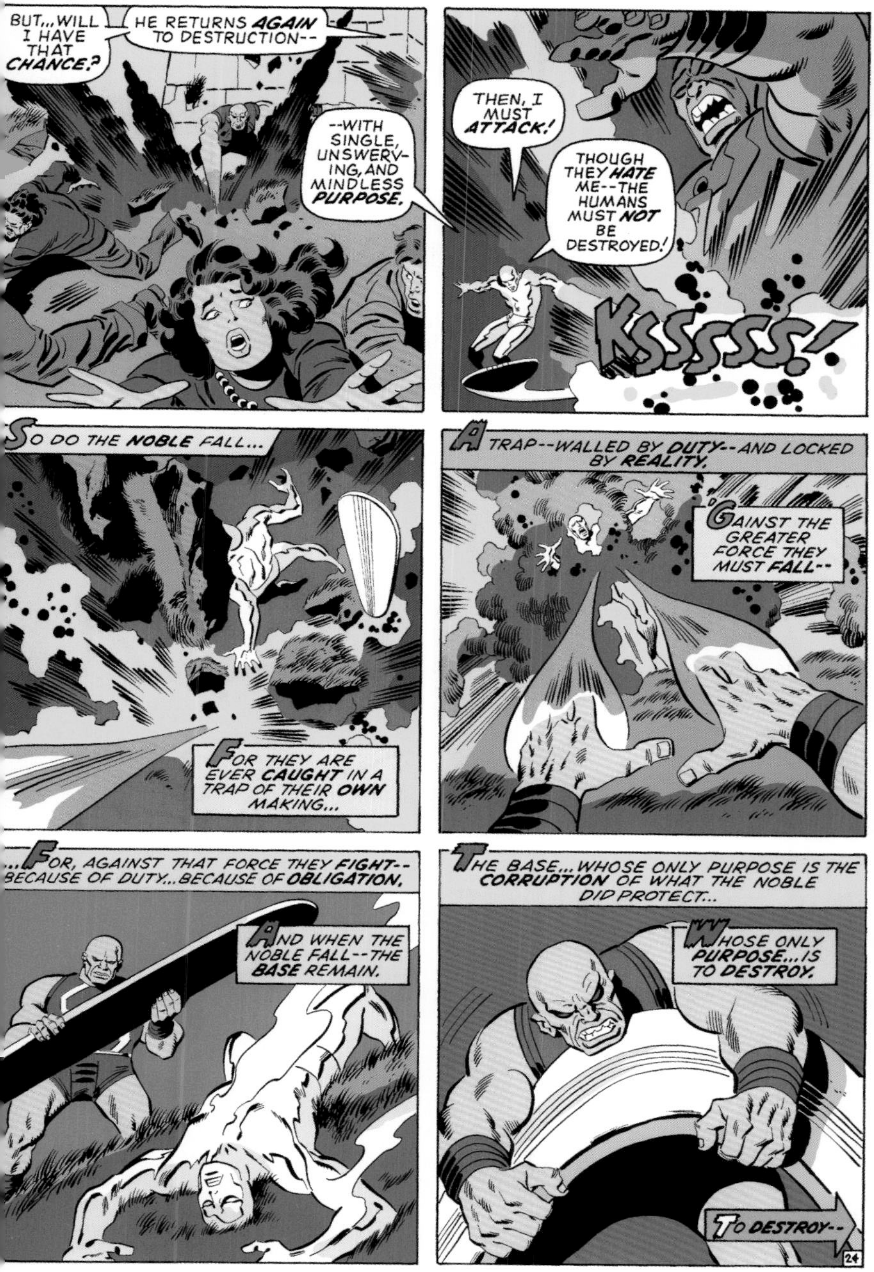
BUT... WILL I HAVE THAT CHANCE?
HE RETURNS AGAIN TO DESTRUCTION--
--WITH SINGLE, UNSWERVING, AND MINDLESS PURPOSE.
THEN, I MUST ATTACK!
THOUGH THEY HATE ME--THE HUMANS MUST NOT BE DESTROYED!
KSSSSS!
SO DO THE NOBLE FALL...
FOR THEY ARE EVER CAUGHT IN A TRAP OF THEIR OWN MAKING...
A TRAP--WALLED BY DUTY--AND LOCKED BY REALITY.
'GAINST THE GREATER FORCE THEY MUST FALL--
...FOR, AGAINST THAT FORCE THEY FIGHT--BECAUSE OF DUTY...BECAUSE OF OBLIGATION.
AND WHEN THE NOBLE FALL--THE BASE REMAIN.
THE BASE...WHOSE ONLY PURPOSE IS THE CORRUPTION OF WHAT THE NOBLE DID PROTECT...
WHOSE ONLY PURPOSE...IS TO DESTROY.
TO DESTROY--
24

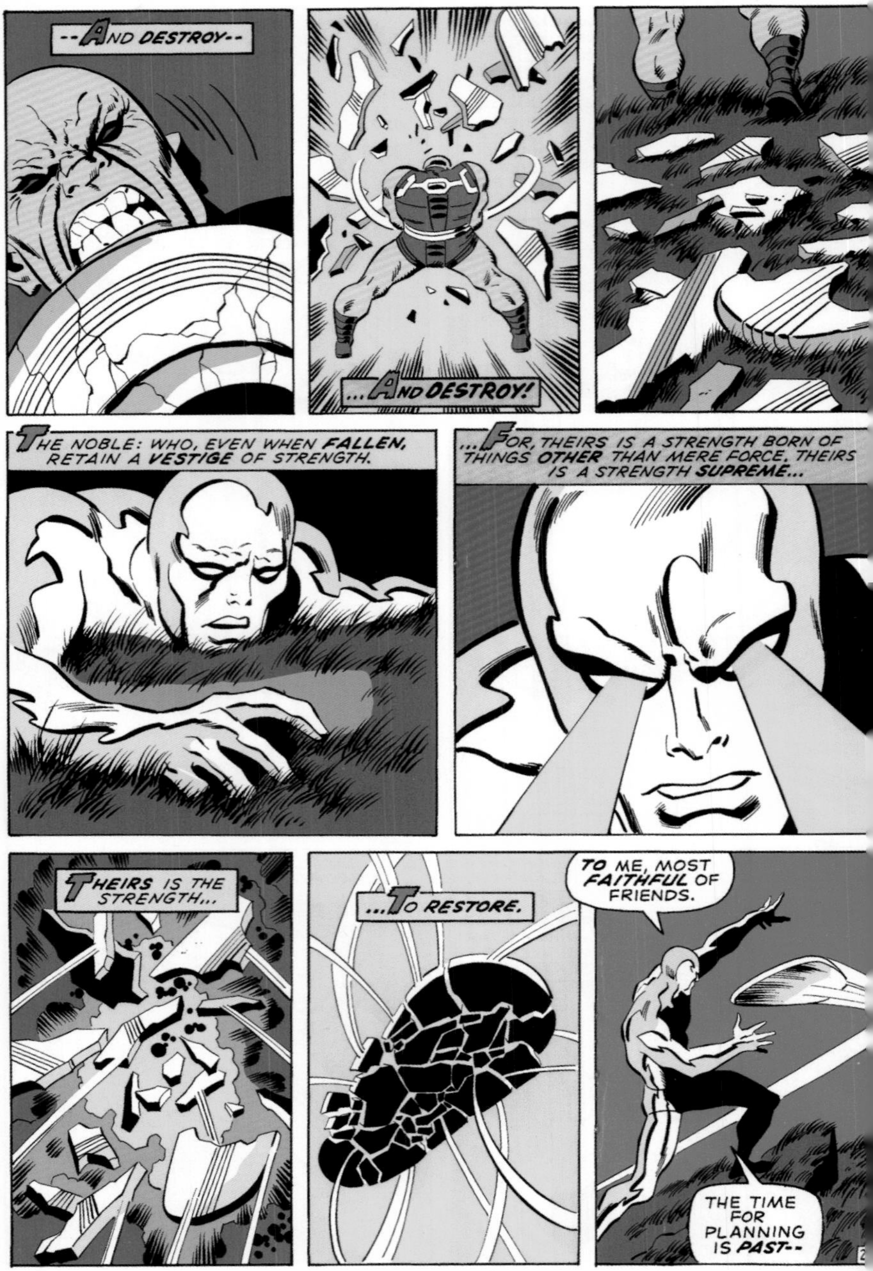
--AND DESTROY--
...AND DESTROY!
THE NOBLE: WHO, EVEN WHEN FALLEN, RETAIN A VESTIGE OF STRENGTH.
...FOR, THEIRS IS A STRENGTH BORN OF THINGS OTHER THAN MERE FORCE. THEIRS IS A STRENGTH SUPREME...
THEIRS IS THE STRENGTH...
...TO RESTORE.
TO ME, MOST FAITHFUL OF FRIENDS.
THE TIME FOR PLANNING IS PAST--

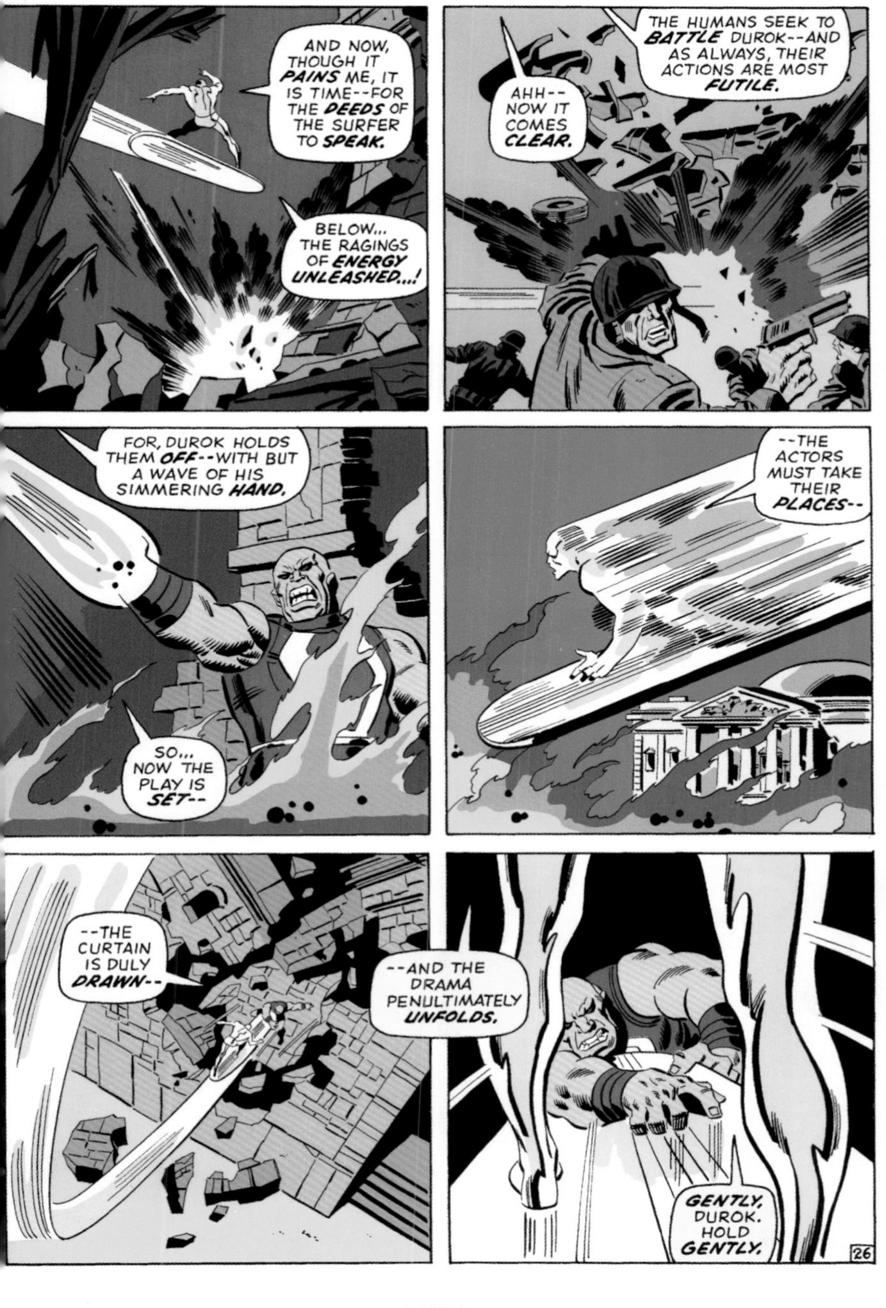
AND NOW, THOUGH IT PAINS ME, IT IS TIME--FOR THE DEEDS OF THE SURFER TO SPEAK.
BELOW... THE RAGINGS OF ENERGY UNLEASHED...!
THE HUMANS SEEK TO BATTLE DUROK--AND AS ALWAYS, THEIR ACTIONS ARE MOST FUTILE.
AHH--NOW IT COMES CLEAR.
FOR, DUROK HOLDS THEM OFF--WITH BUT A WAVE OF HIS SIMMERING HAND.
SO... NOW THE PLAY IS SET--
--THE ACTORS MUST TAKE THEIR PLACES--
--THE CURTAIN IS DULY DRAWN--
--AND THE DRAMA PENULTIMATELY UNFOLDS.
GENTLY, DUROK. HOLD GENTLY.
26

HIS SILENCE...IS UNSETTLING. ALMOST, I FEEL AS THOUGH I BATTLE A ROCK--
--AND NOT A BREATHING, LIVING THING.
BUT...WHAT MATTER SUCH ESOTERIC CONCERNS?
THOUGH WE STRUGGLE EACH FOR MASTERY-- SOON IT WILL ALL CEASE TO HAVE MEANING.
SOON... THERE WILL ONLY BE ONE ANSWER--
--ONLY ONE SURVIVOR.
EVEN NOW, MY BOARD MOVES EVER FASTER AT MY MENTAL COMMAND--
FASTER, 'TILL WE BREAK FROM THE VERY BOND OF GRAVITY.
NOW-- WE ORBIT YON MUDBALL GLOBE--
ORBIT--
--UNTIL THE VERY FABRIC--
--OF ETHER AND SPACE--
--IS TORN!
TORN!
27

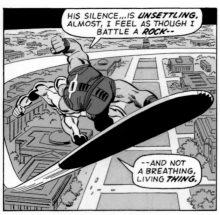

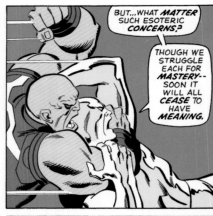

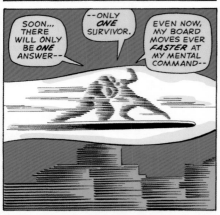

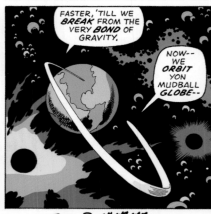

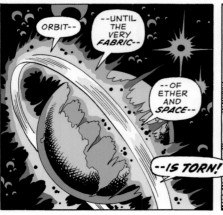

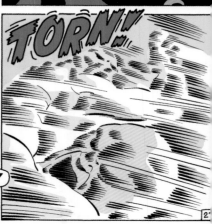

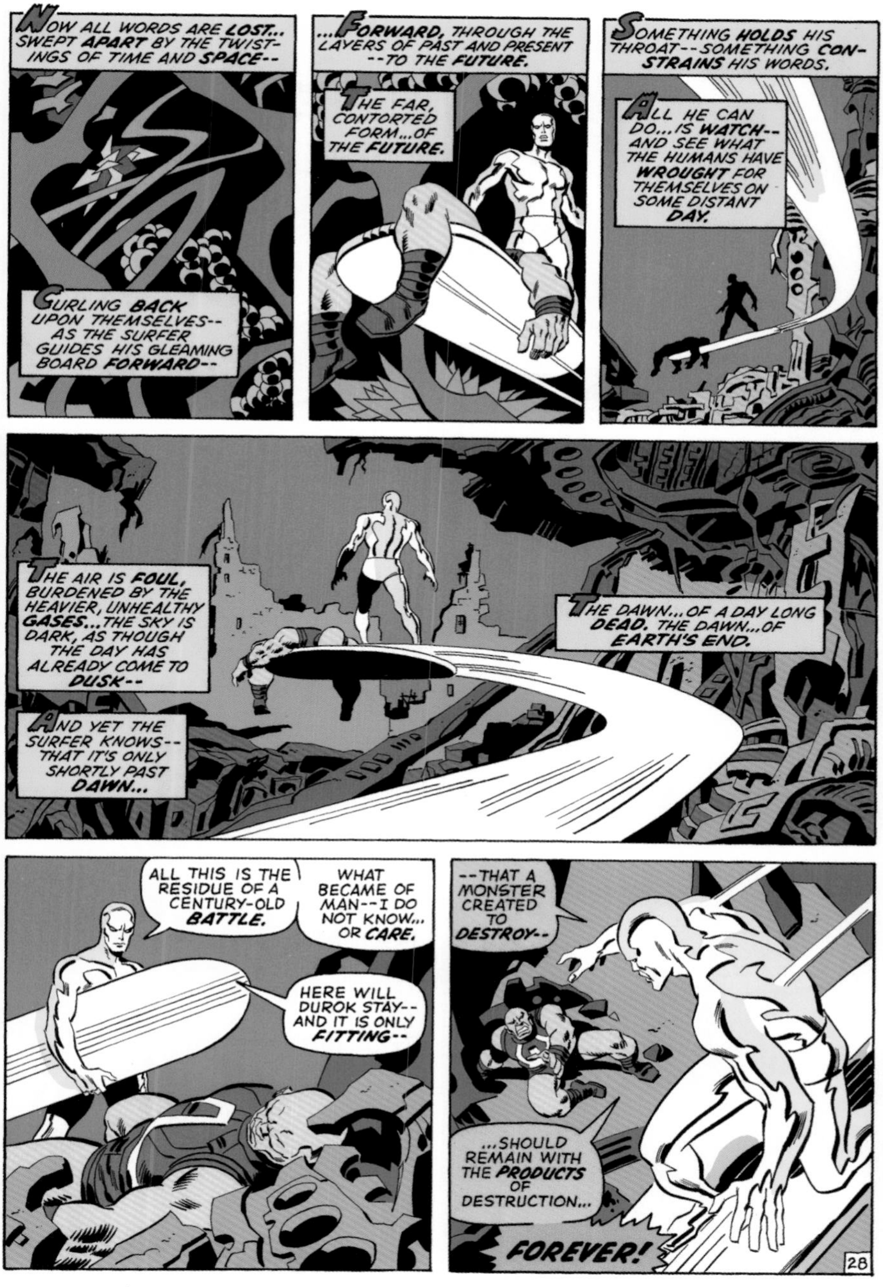
NOW ALL WORDS ARE LOST... SWEPT APART BY THE TWISTINGS OF TIME AND SPACE--
CURLING BACK UPON THEMSELVES--AS THE SURFER GUIDES HIS GLEAMING BOARD FORWARD--
...FORWARD, THROUGH THE LAYERS OF PAST AND PRESENT--TO THE FUTURE.
THE FAR, CONTORTED FORM...OF THE FUTURE.
SOMETHING HOLDS HIS THROAT--SOMETHING CONSTRAINS HIS WORDS.
ALL HE CAN DO...IS WATCH--AND SEE WHAT THE HUMANS HAVE WROUGHT FOR THEMSELVES ON SOME DISTANT DAY.
THE AIR IS FOUL, BURDENED BY THE HEAVIER, UNHEALTHY GASES...THE SKY IS DARK, AS THOUGH THE DAY HAS ALREADY COME TO DUSK--
AND YET THE SURFER KNOWS--THAT IT'S ONLY SHORTLY PAST DAWN...
THE DAWN...OF A DAY LONG DEAD. THE DAWN...OF EARTH'S END.
ALL THIS IS THE RESIDUE OF A CENTURY-OLD BATTLE.
WHAT BECAME OF MAN--I DO NOT KNOW... OR CARE.
HERE WILL DUROK STAY--AND IT IS ONLY FITTING--
--THAT A MONSTER CREATED TO DESTROY--
...SHOULD REMAIN WITH THE PRODUCTS OF DESTRUCTION...
FOREVER!
28

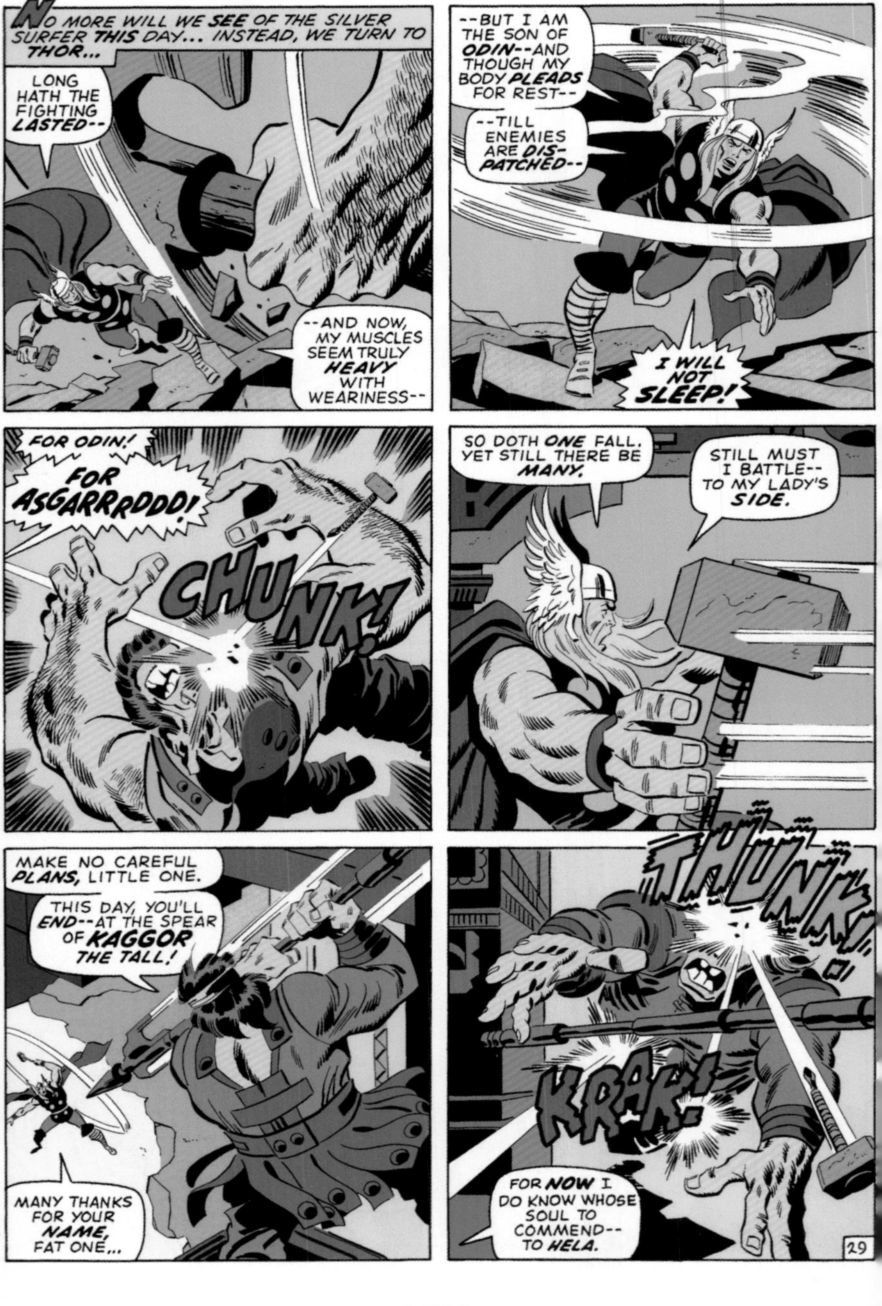
NO MORE WILL WE SEE OF THE SILVER SURFER THIS DAY... INSTEAD, WE TURN TO THOR...
LONG HATH THE FIGHTING LASTED--
--AND NOW, MY MUSCLES SEEM TRULY HEAVY WITH WEARINESS--
--BUT I AM THE SON OF ODIN--AND THOUGH MY BODY PLEADS FOR REST--
--TILL ENEMIES ARE DIS-PATCHED--
I WILL NOT SLEEP!
FOR ODIN!
FOR ASGARRRDDD!
CHUNK!
SO DOTH ONE FALL. YET STILL THERE BE MANY.
STILL MUST I BATTLE-- TO MY LADY'S SIDE.
MAKE NO CAREFUL PLANS, LITTLE ONE.
THIS DAY, YOU'LL END--AT THE SPEAR OF KAGGOR THE TALL!
MANY THANKS FOR YOUR NAME, FAT ONE...
THUNK!
KRAK!
FOR NOW I DO KNOW WHOSE SOUL TO COMMEND-- TO HELA.
29

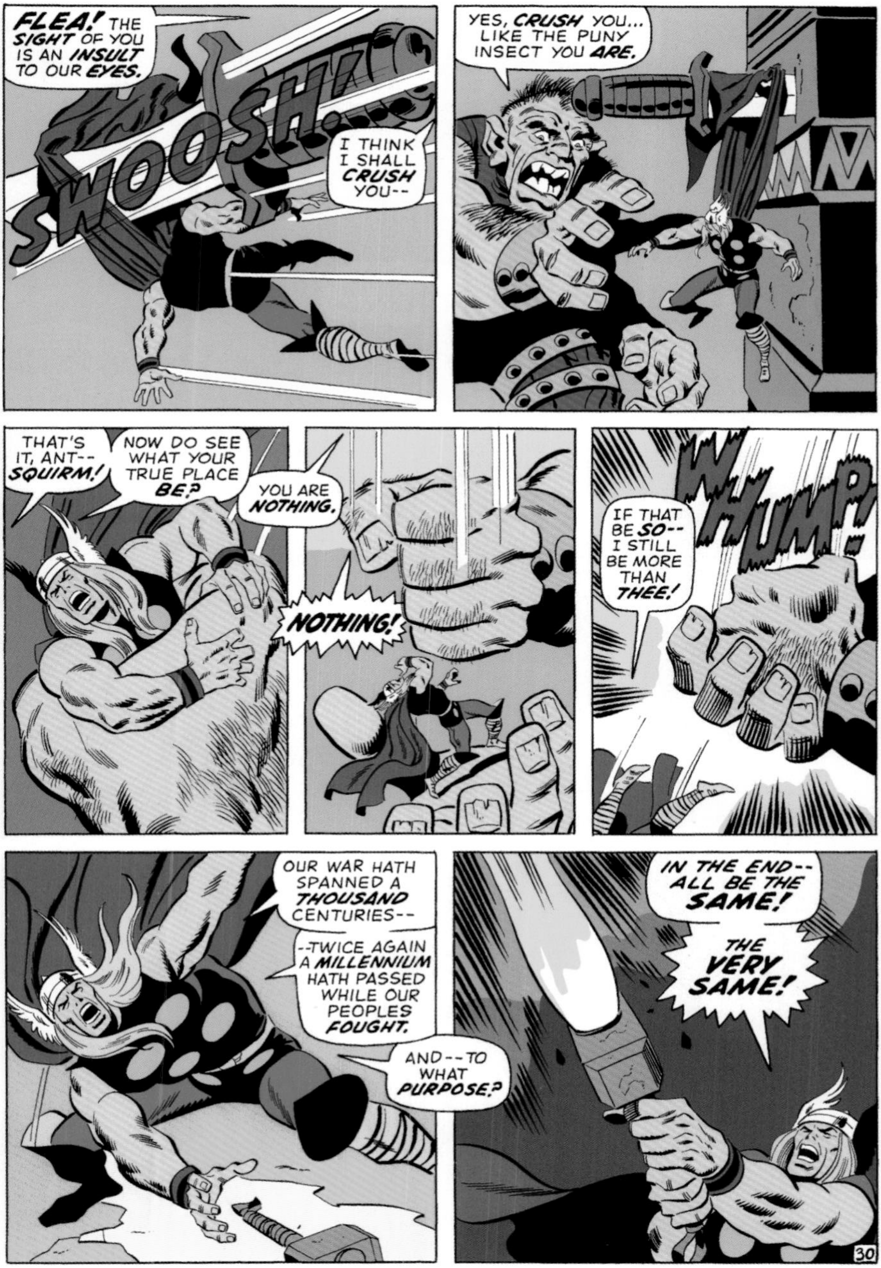
FLEA! THE SIGHT OF YOU IS AN INSULT TO OUR EYES.
SHOOSH!
I THINK I SHALL CRUSH YOU--
YES, CRUSH YOU... LIKE THE PUNY INSECT YOU ARE.
THAT'S IT, ANT-- SQUIRM!
NOW DO SEE WHAT YOUR TRUE PLACE BE?
YOU ARE NOTHING.
NOTHING!
WHUMP!
IF THAT BE SO-- I STILL BE MORE THAN THEE!
OUR WAR HATH SPANNED A THOUSAND CENTURIES--
--TWICE AGAIN A MILLENNIUM HATH PASSED WHILE OUR PEOPLES FOUGHT.
AND--TO WHAT PURPOSE?
IN THE END-- ALL BE THE SAME!
THE VERY SAME!
30

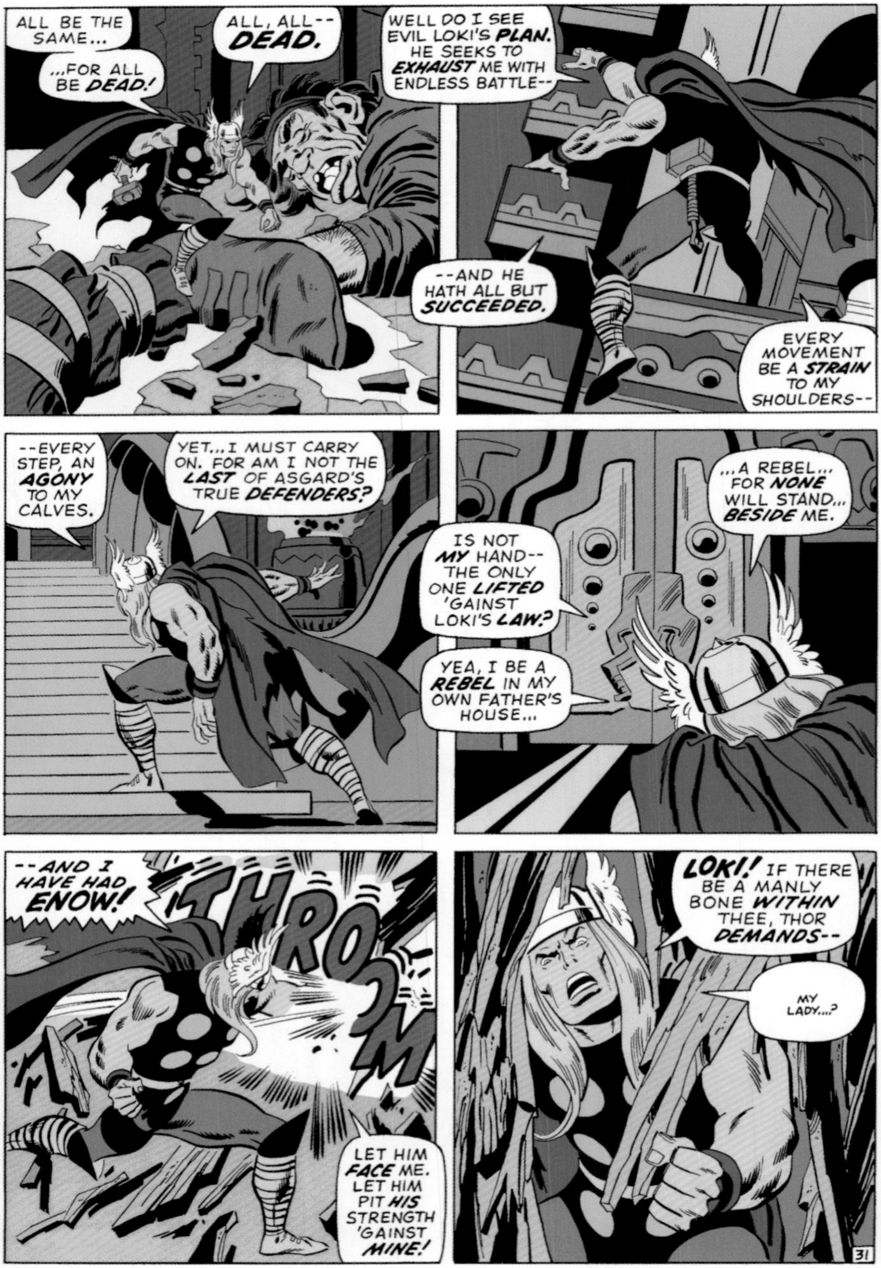
ALL BE THE SAME...
...FOR ALL BE DEAD!
ALL, ALL-- DEAD.
WELL DO I SEE EVIL LOKI'S PLAN. HE SEEKS TO EXHAUST ME WITH ENDLESS BATTLE--
--AND HE HATH ALL BUT SUCCEEDED.
EVERY MOVEMENT BE A STRAIN TO MY SHOULDERS--
--EVERY STEP, AN AGONY TO MY CALVES.
YET... I MUST CARRY ON. FOR AM I NOT THE LAST OF ASGARD'S TRUE DEFENDERS?
IS NOT MY HAND-- THE ONLY ONE LIFTED 'GAINST LOKI'S LAW?
YEA, I BE A REBEL IN MY OWN FATHER'S HOUSE...
...A REBEL... FOR NONE WILL STAND... BESIDE ME.
--AND I HAVE HAD ENOW!
THROOM
LET HIM FACE ME. LET HIM PIT HIS STRENGTH 'GAINST MINE!
LOKI! IF THERE BE A MANLY BONE WITHIN THEE, THOR DEMANDS--
MY LADY...?
31

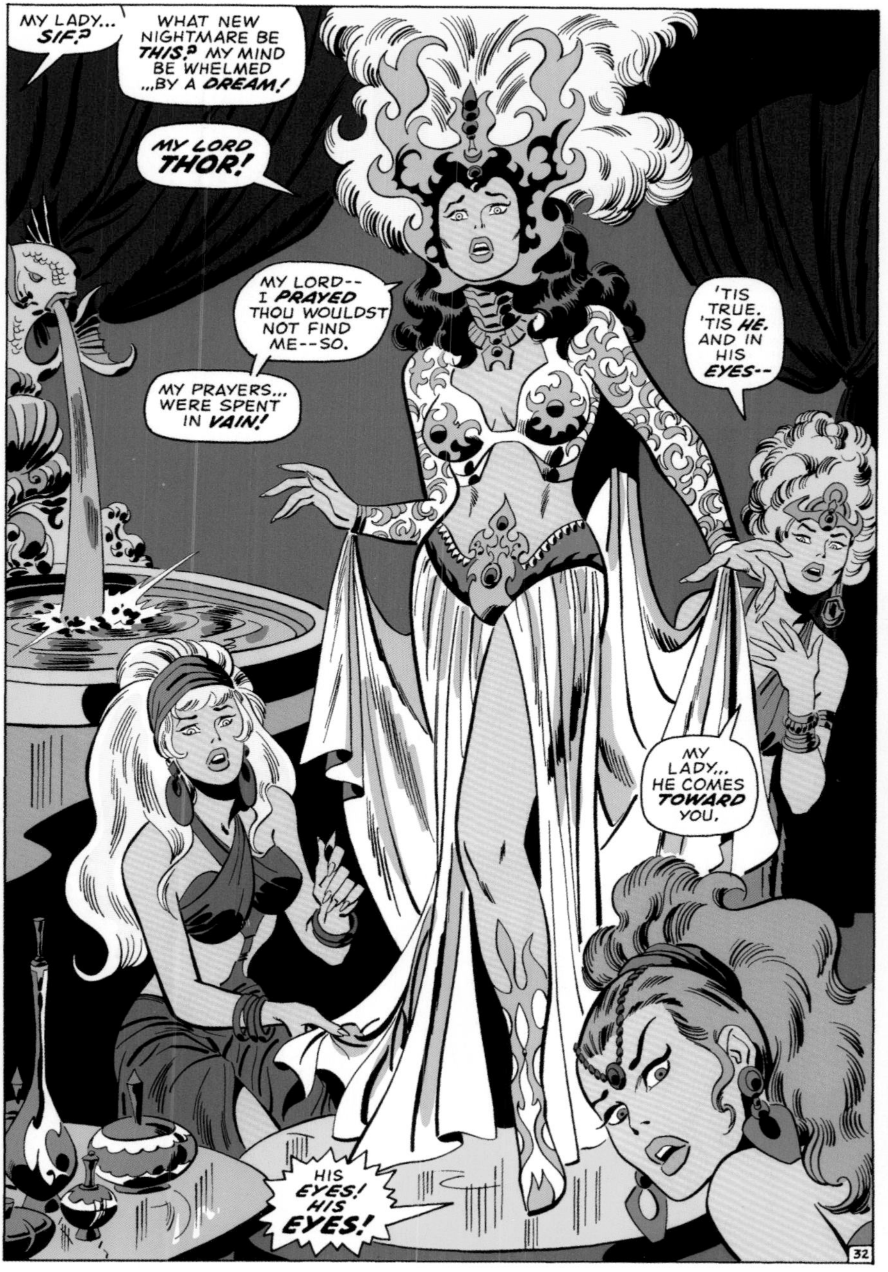
MY LADY... SIF?
WHAT NEW NIGHTMARE BE THIS? MY MIND BE WHELMED ...BY A DREAM!
MY LORD THOR!
MY LORD-- I PRAYED THOU WOULDST NOT FIND ME--SO.
MY PRAYERS... WERE SPENT IN VAIN!
'TIS TRUE. 'TIS HE. AND IN HIS EYES--
MY LADY... HE COMES TOWARD YOU.
HIS EYES! HIS EYES!
32

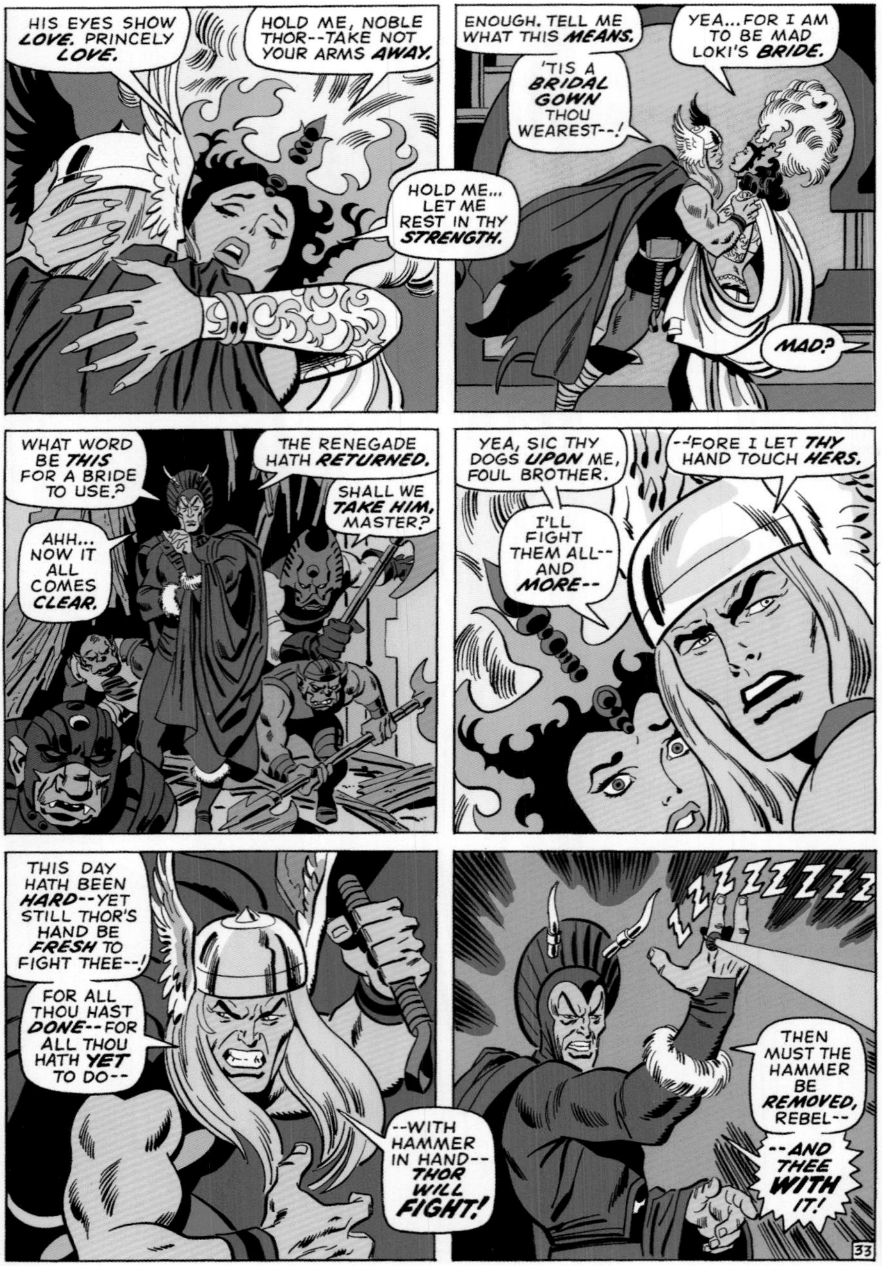
HIS EYES SHOW LOVE. PRINCELY LOVE.
HOLD ME, NOBLE THOR--TAKE NOT YOUR ARMS AWAY.
HOLD ME... LET ME REST IN THY STRENGTH.
ENOUGH. TELL ME WHAT THIS MEANS.
'TIS A BRIDAL GOWN THOU WEAREST--!
YEA...FOR I AM TO BE MAD LOKI'S BRIDE.
MAD?
WHAT WORD BE THIS FOR A BRIDE TO USE?
AHH... NOW IT ALL COMES CLEAR.
THE RENEGADE HATH RETURNED.
SHALL WE TAKE HIM, MASTER?
YEA, SIC THY DOGS UPON ME, FOUL BROTHER.
I'LL FIGHT THEM ALL--AND MORE--
--'FORE I LET THY HAND TOUCH HERS.
THIS DAY HATH BEEN HARD--YET STILL THOR'S HAND BE FRESH TO FIGHT THEE--!
FOR ALL THOU HAST DONE--FOR ALL THOU HATH YET TO DO--
--WITH HAMMER IN HAND--THOR WILL FIGHT!
ZZZZZZZZZ
THEN MUST THE HAMMER BE REMOVED, REBEL--
--AND THEE WITH IT!
33

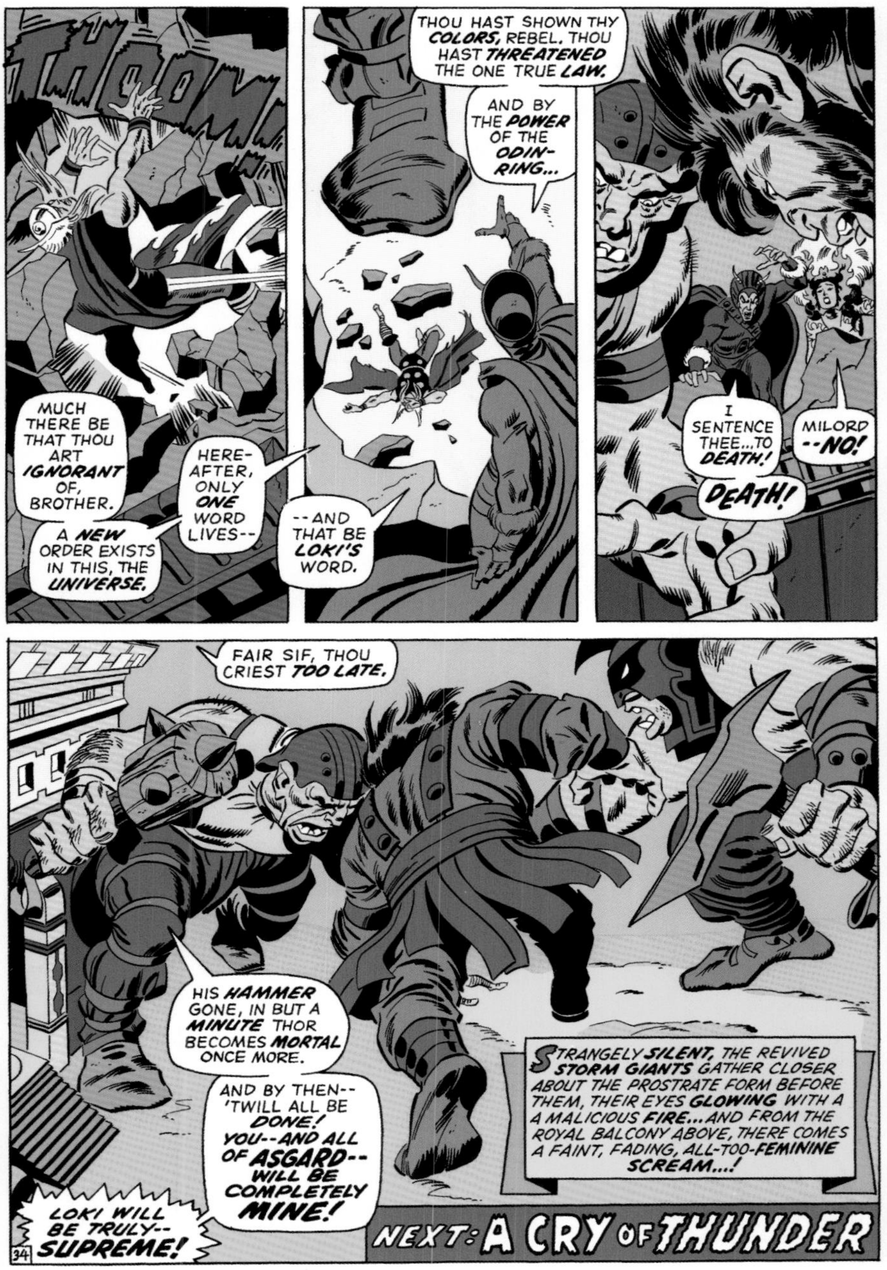
THOOM!
MUCH THERE BE THAT THOU ART IGNORANT OF, BROTHER.
A NEW ORDER EXISTS IN THIS, THE UNIVERSE.
HERE-AFTER, ONLY ONE WORD LIVES--
THOU HAST SHOWN THY COLORS, REBEL. THOU HAST THREATENED THE ONE TRUE LAW.
AND BY THE POWER OF THE ODIN-RING...
--AND THAT BE LOKI'S WORD.
I SENTENCE THEE...TO DEATH!
DEATH!
MILORD --NO!
FAIR SIF, THOU CRIEST TOO LATE.
HIS HAMMER GONE, IN BUT A MINUTE THOR BECOMES MORTAL ONCE MORE.
AND BY THEN-- 'TWILL ALL BE DONE! YOU--AND ALL OF ASGARD-- WILL BE COMPLETELY MINE!
LOKI WILL BE TRULY-- SUPREME!
STRANGELY SILENT, THE REVIVED STORM GIANTS GATHER CLOSER ABOUT THE PROSTRATE FORM BEFORE THEM, THEIR EYES GLOWING WITH A A MALICIOUS FIRE...AND FROM THE ROYAL BALCONY ABOVE, THERE COMES A FAINT, FADING, ALL-TOO-FEMININE SCREAM...!
NEXT: A CRY OF THUNDER
34

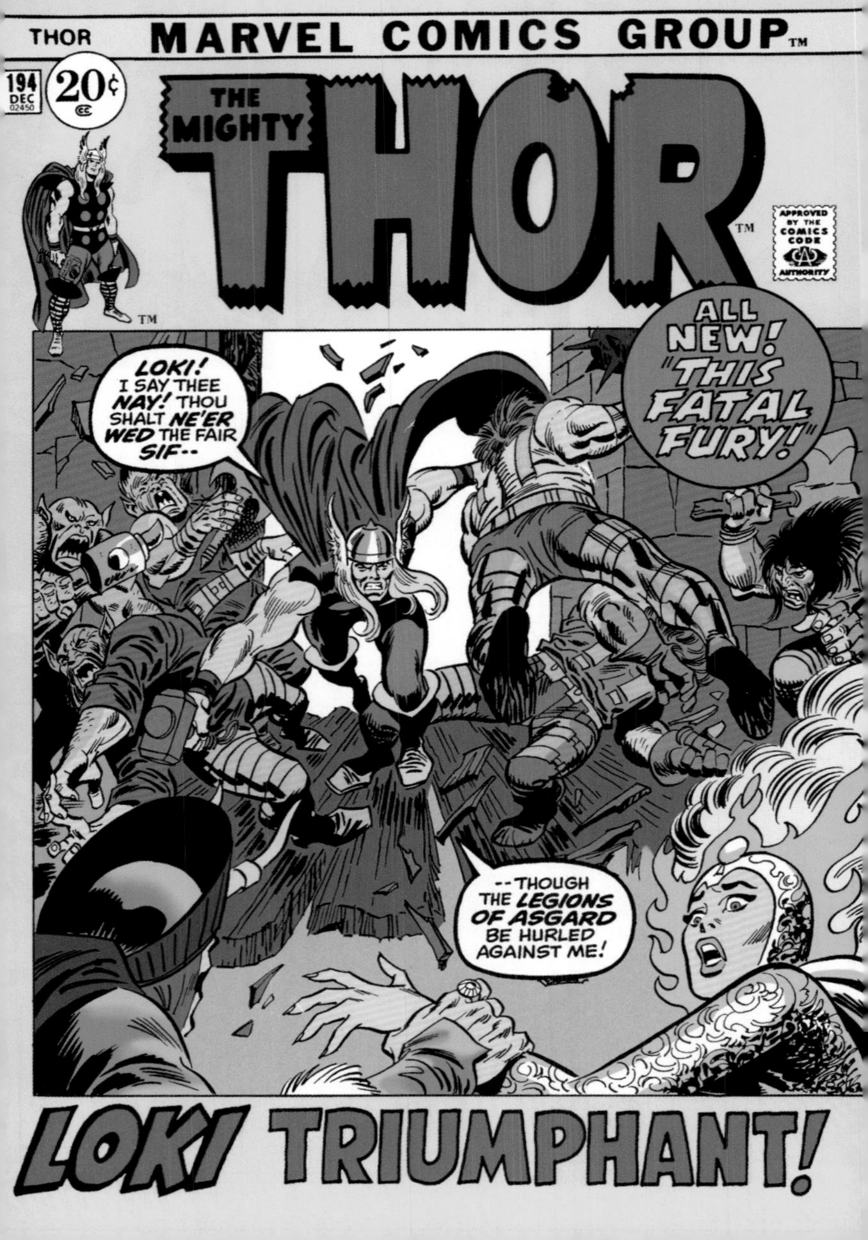
THOR
MARVEL COMICS GROUP™
194 DEC 02450
20¢
THE MIGHTY THOR™
APPROVED BY THE COMICS CODE AUTHORITY
ALL NEW! "THIS FATAL FURY!"
LOKI! I SAY THEE NAY! THOU SHALT NE'ER WED THE FAIR SIF--
--THOUGH THE LEGIONS OF ASGARD BE HURLED AGAINST ME!
LOKI TRIUMPHANT!

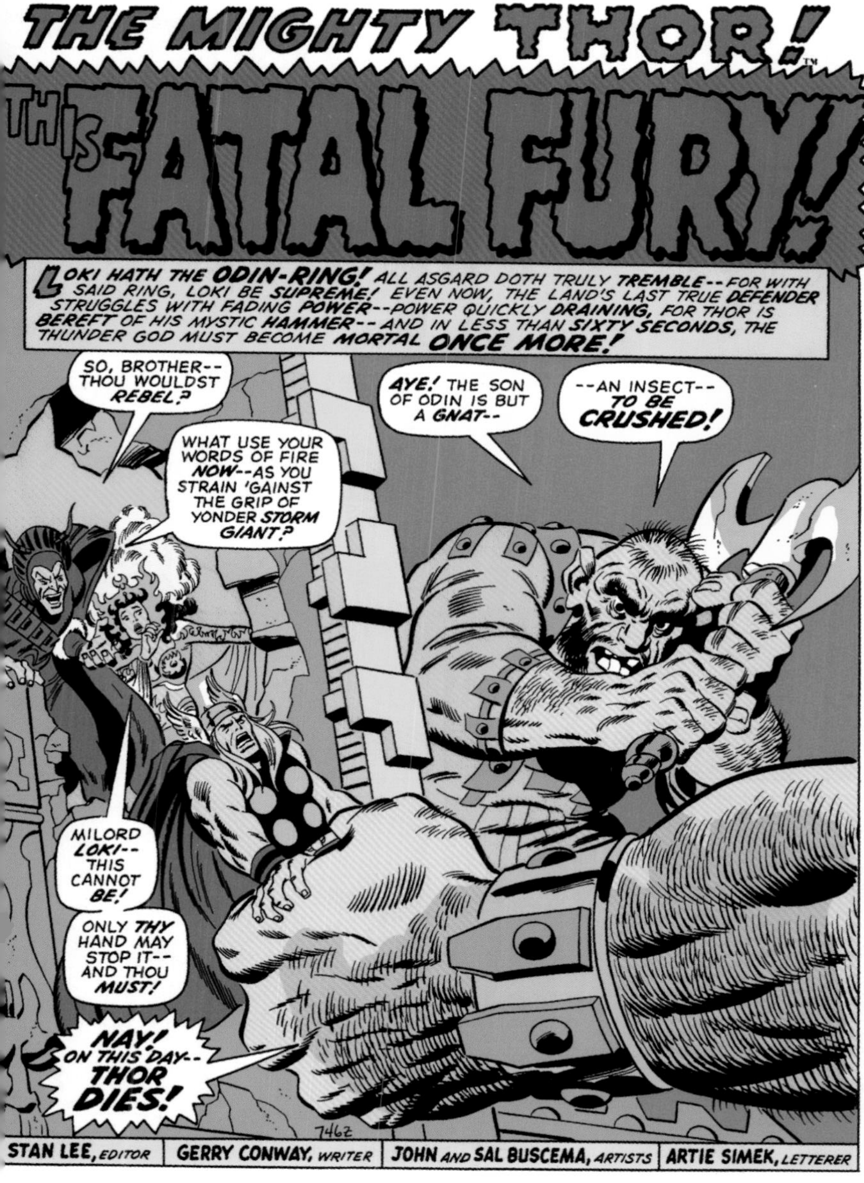
THE MIGHTY THOR!
THIS IS FATAL FURY!
LOKI HATH THE ODIN-RING! ALL ASGARD DOTH TRULY TREMBLE--FOR WITH SAID RING, LOKI BE SUPREME! EVEN NOW, THE LAND'S LAST TRUE DEFENDER STRUGGLES WITH FADING POWER--POWER QUICKLY DRAINING, FOR THOR IS BEREFT OF HIS MYSTIC HAMMER--AND IN LESS THAN SIXTY SECONDS, THE THUNDER GOD MUST BECOME MORTAL ONCE MORE!
SO, BROTHER--THOU WOULDST REBEL?
WHAT USE YOUR WORDS OF FIRE NOW--AS YOU STRAIN 'GAINST THE GRIP OF YONDER STORM GIANT?
AYE! THE SON OF ODIN IS BUT A GNAT--
--AN INSECT--TO BE CRUSHED!
MILORD LOKI--THIS CANNOT BE!
ONLY THY HAND MAY STOP IT--AND THOU MUST!
NAY! ON THIS DAY--THOR DIES!
STAN LEE, EDITOR | GERRY CONWAY, WRITER | JOHN AND SAL BUSCEMA, ARTISTS | ARTIE SIMEK, LETTERER

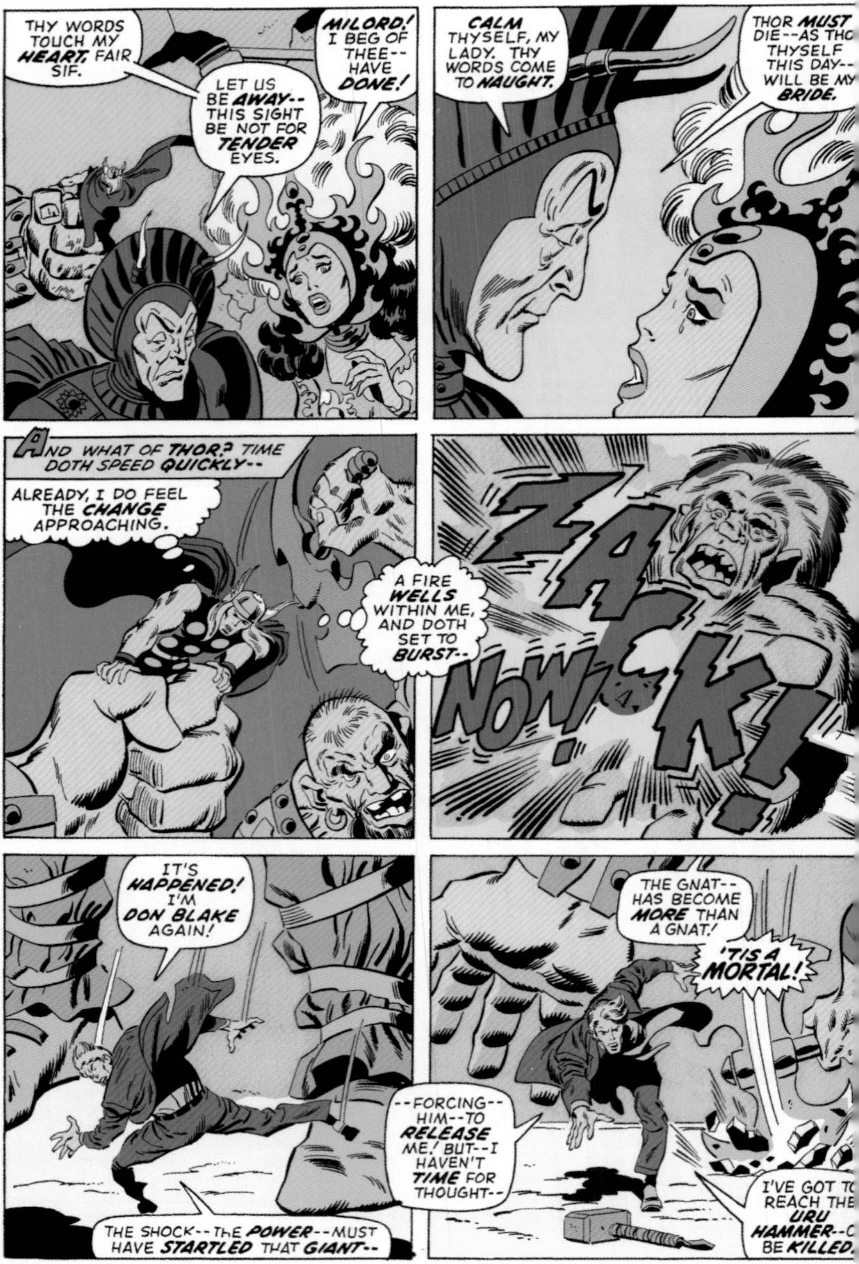
THY WORDS TOUCH MY HEART, FAIR SIF.
MILORD! I BEG OF THEE--HAVE DONE!
LET US BE AWAY--THIS SIGHT BE NOT FOR TENDER EYES.
CALM THYSELF, MY LADY. THY WORDS COME TO NAUGHT.
THOR MUST DIE--AS THO THYSELF THIS DAY--WILL BE MY BRIDE.
AND WHAT OF THOR? TIME DOTH SPEED QUICKLY--
ALREADY, I DO FEEL THE CHANGE APPROACHING.
A FIRE WELLS WITHIN ME, AND DOTH SET TO BURST--
ZAK!
NOW!
IT'S HAPPENED! I'M DON BLAKE AGAIN!
THE SHOCK--THE POWER--MUST HAVE STARTLED THAT GIANT--
--FORCING--HIM--TO RELEASE ME! BUT--I HAVEN'T TIME FOR THOUGHT--
THE GNAT--HAS BECOME MORE THAN A GNAT!
'TIS A MORTAL!
I'VE GOT TO REACH THE URU HAMMER--C BE KILLED.

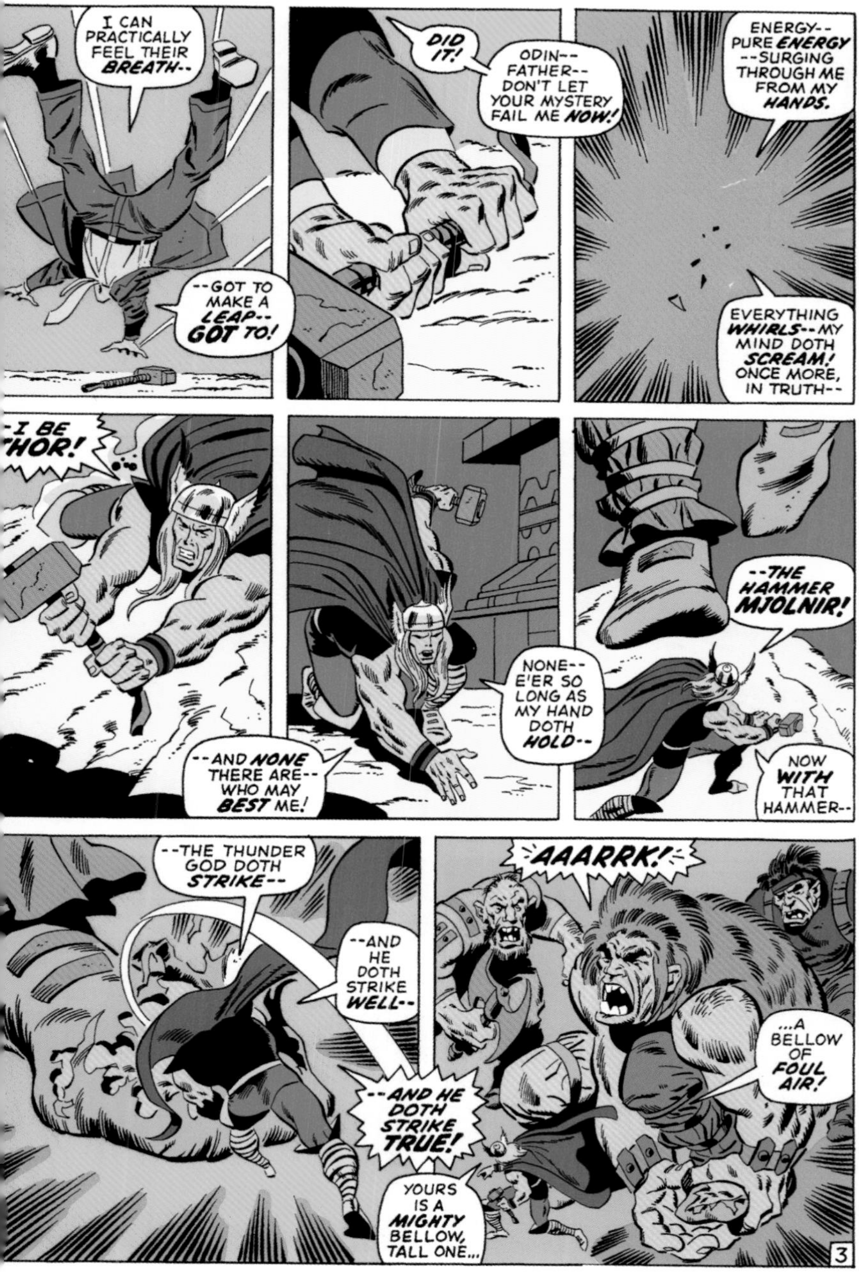
I CAN PRACTICALLY FEEL THEIR BREATH--
--GOT TO MAKE A LEAP--GOT TO!
DID IT!
ODIN--FATHER--DON'T LET YOUR MYSTERY FAIL ME NOW!
ENERGY--PURE ENERGY--SURGING THROUGH ME FROM MY HANDS.
EVERYTHING WHIRLS--MY MIND DOTH SCREAM! ONCE MORE, IN TRUTH--
--I BE THOR!
--AND NONE THERE ARE--WHO MAY BEST ME!
NONE--E'ER SO LONG AS MY HAND DOTH HOLD--
--THE HAMMER MJOLNIR!
NOW WITH THAT HAMMER--
--THE THUNDER GOD DOTH STRIKE--
--AND HE DOTH STRIKE WELL--
--AND HE DOTH STRIKE TRUE!
AAARRK!
...A BELLOW OF FOUL AIR!
YOURS IS A MIGHTY BELLOW, TALL ONE...
3

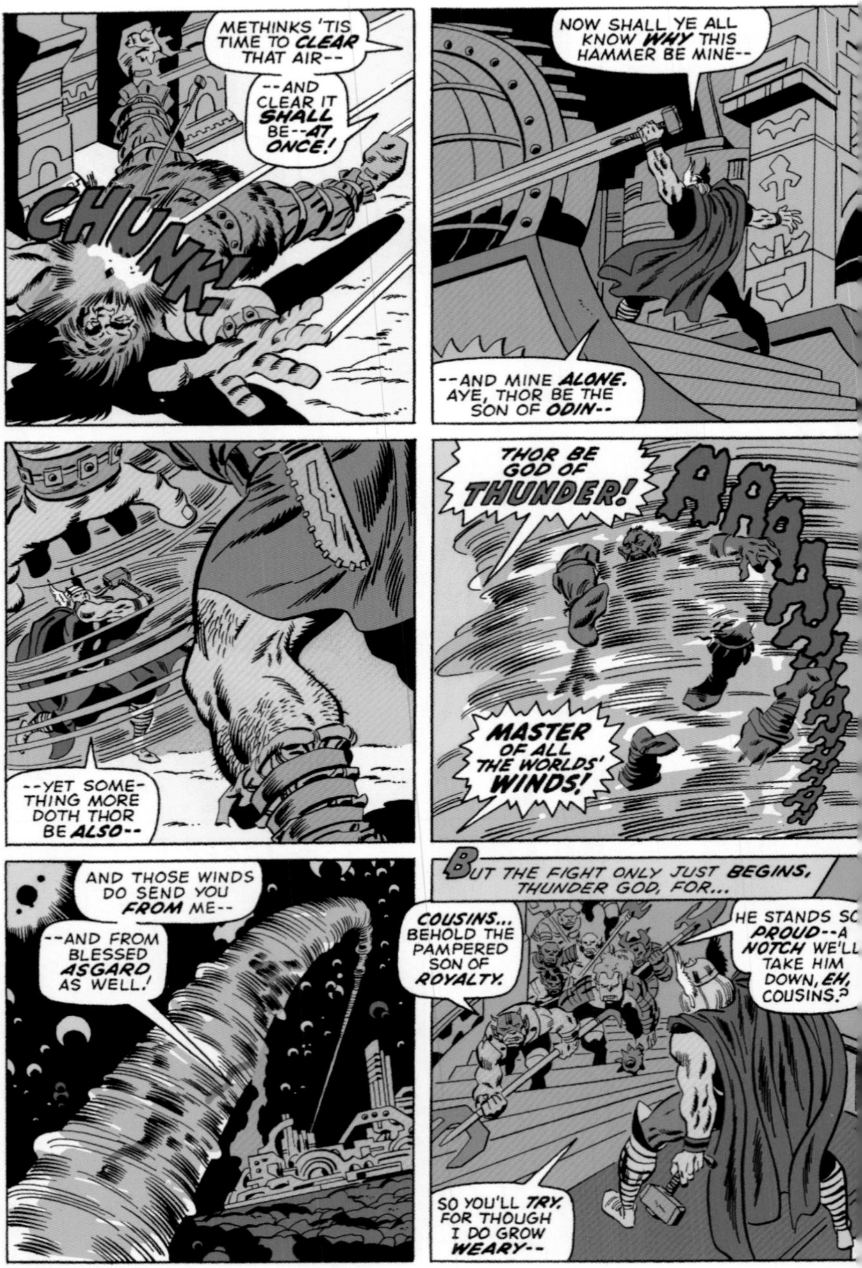
METHINKS 'TIS TIME TO CLEAR THAT AIR--
--AND CLEAR IT SHALL BE--AT ONCE!
CHUNK!
NOW SHALL YE ALL KNOW WHY THIS HAMMER BE MINE--
--AND MINE ALONE. AYE, THOR BE THE SON OF ODIN--
--YET SOMETHING MORE DOTH THOR BE ALSO--
THOR BE GOD OF THUNDER!
AAAHHHHHHHH
MASTER OF ALL THE WORLDS' WINDS!
AND THOSE WINDS DO SEND YOU FROM ME--
--AND FROM BLESSED ASGARD AS WELL!
BUT THE FIGHT ONLY JUST BEGINS, THUNDER GOD, FOR...
COUSINS... BEHOLD THE PAMPERED SON OF ROYALTY.
HE STANDS SO PROUD--A NOTCH WE'LL TAKE HIM DOWN, EH, COUSINS?
SO YOU'LL TRY. FOR THOUGH I DO GROW WEARY--

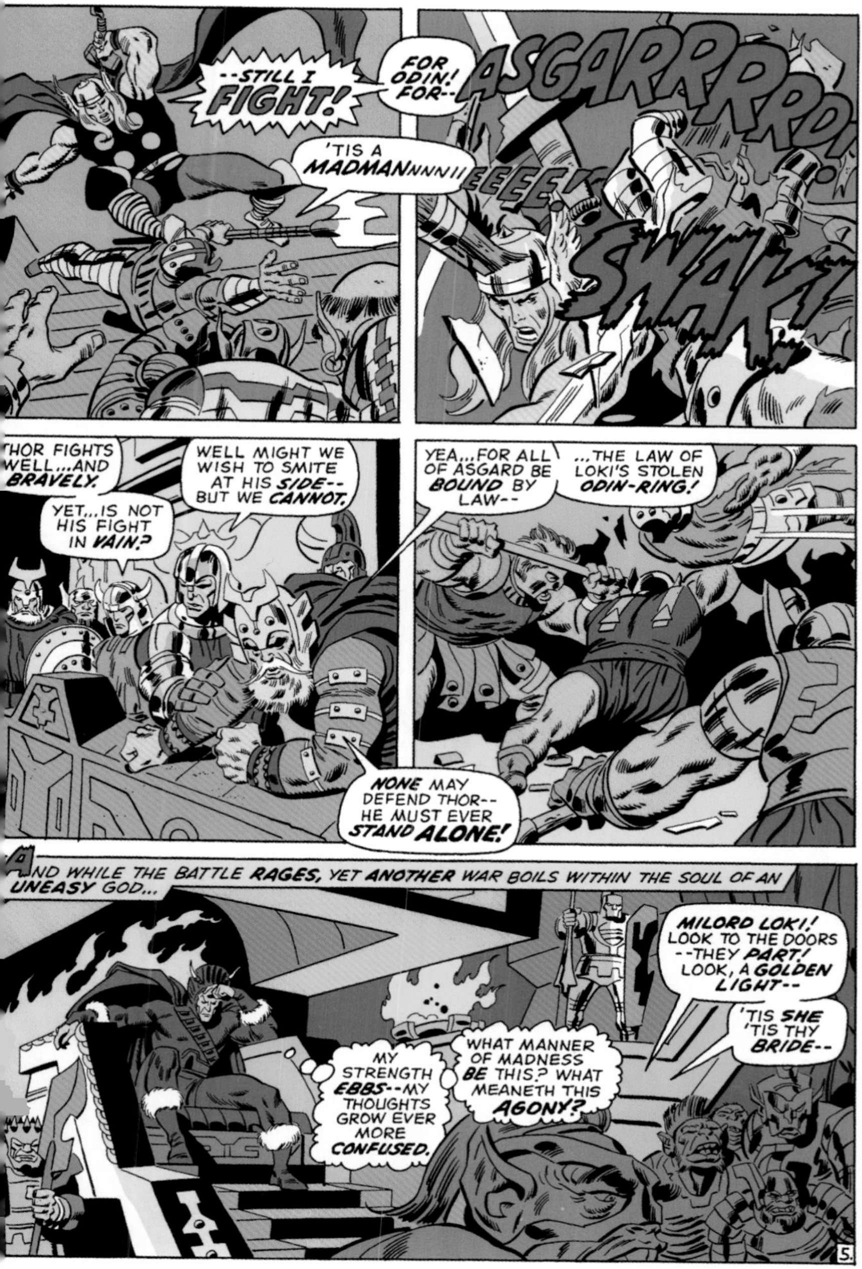
--STILL I FIGHT!
FOR ODIN! FOR--
ASGARRRRD!
'TIS A MADMANNNN!!
EEEEE!
SWAK!
THOR FIGHTS WELL...AND BRAVELY.
YET...IS NOT HIS FIGHT IN VAIN?
WELL MIGHT WE WISH TO SMITE AT HIS SIDE--BUT WE CANNOT.
NONE MAY DEFEND THOR--HE MUST EVER STAND ALONE!
YEA...FOR ALL OF ASGARD BE BOUND BY LAW--
...THE LAW OF LOKI'S STOLEN ODIN-RING!
AND WHILE THE BATTLE RAGES, YET ANOTHER WAR BOILS WITHIN THE SOUL OF AN UNEASY GOD...
MY STRENGTH EBBS--MY THOUGHTS GROW EVER MORE CONFUSED.
WHAT MANNER OF MADNESS BE THIS? WHAT MEANETH THIS AGONY?
MILORD LOKI! LOOK TO THE DOORS--THEY PART! LOOK, A GOLDEN LIGHT--
'TIS SHE 'TIS THY BRIDE--
5.

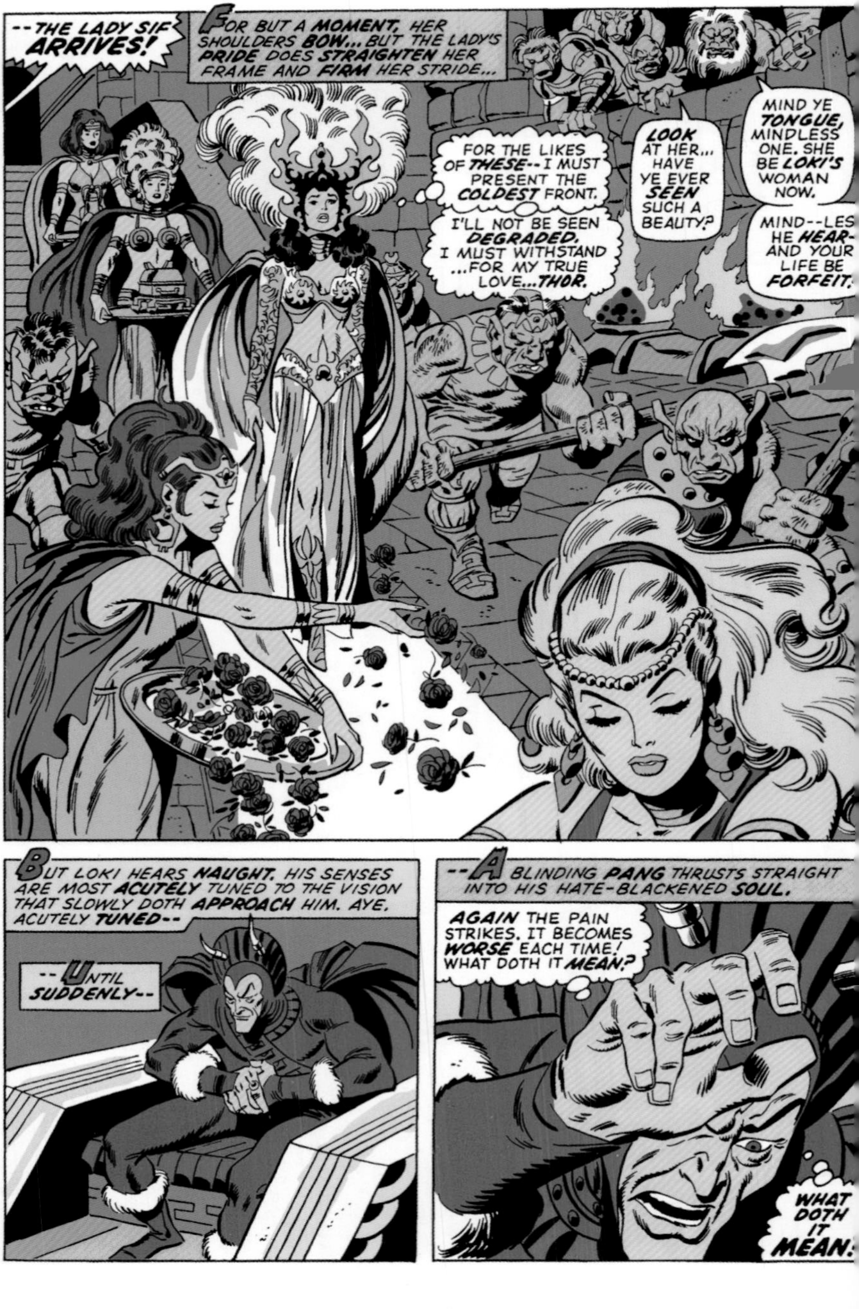
--THE LADY SIF ARRIVES!
FOR BUT A MOMENT, HER SHOULDERS BOW... BUT THE LADY'S PRIDE DOES STRAIGHTEN HER FRAME AND FIRM HER STRIDE...
FOR THE LIKES OF THESE--I MUST PRESENT THE COLDEST FRONT.
I'LL NOT BE SEEN DEGRADED. I MUST WITHSTAND ...FOR MY TRUE LOVE...THOR.
LOOK AT HER... HAVE YE EVER SEEN SUCH A BEAUTY?
MIND YE TONGUE, MINDLESS ONE. SHE BE LOKI'S WOMAN NOW.
MIND--LES HE HEAR- AND YOUR LIFE BE FORFEIT.
BUT LOKI HEARS NAUGHT. HIS SENSES ARE MOST ACUTELY TUNED TO THE VISION THAT SLOWLY DOTH APPROACH HIM. AYE, ACUTELY TUNED--
--UNTIL SUDDENLY--
--A BLINDING PANG THRUSTS STRAIGHT INTO HIS HATE-BLACKENED SOUL.
AGAIN THE PAIN STRIKES. IT BECOMES WORSE EACH TIME! WHAT DOTH IT MEAN?
WHAT DOTH IT MEAN?

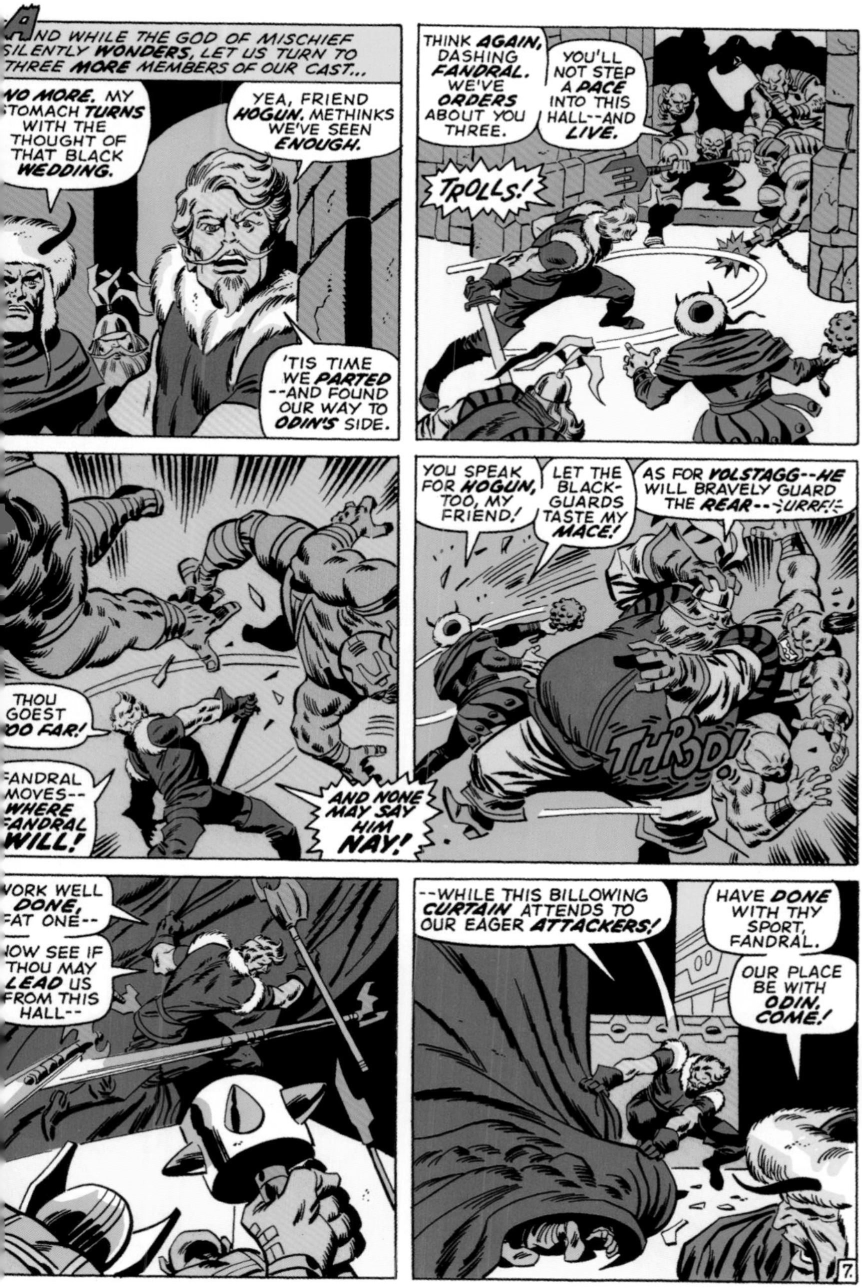
AND WHILE THE GOD OF MISCHIEF SILENTLY WONDERS, LET US TURN TO THREE MORE MEMBERS OF OUR CAST...
NO MORE. MY STOMACH TURNS WITH THE THOUGHT OF THAT BLACK WEDDING.
YEA, FRIEND HOGUN. METHINKS WE'VE SEEN ENOUGH.
'TIS TIME WE PARTED --AND FOUND OUR WAY TO ODIN'S SIDE.
THINK AGAIN, DASHING FANDRAL. WE'VE ORDERS ABOUT YOU THREE.
YOU'LL NOT STEP A PACE INTO THIS HALL--AND LIVE.
TROLLS!
THOU GOEST TOO FAR!
FANDRAL MOVES--WHERE FANDRAL WILL!
AND NONE MAY SAY HIM NAY!
YOU SPEAK FOR HOGUN, TOO, MY FRIEND!
LET THE BLACK-GUARDS TASTE MY MACE!
AS FOR VOLSTAGG--HE WILL BRAVELY GUARD THE REAR-- URRF!
THROOM!
WORK WELL DONE, FAT ONE--
NOW SEE IF THOU MAY LEAD US FROM THIS HALL--
--WHILE THIS BILLOWING CURTAIN ATTENDS TO OUR EAGER ATTACKERS!
HAVE DONE WITH THY SPORT, FANDRAL.
OUR PLACE BE WITH ODIN. COME!
7.

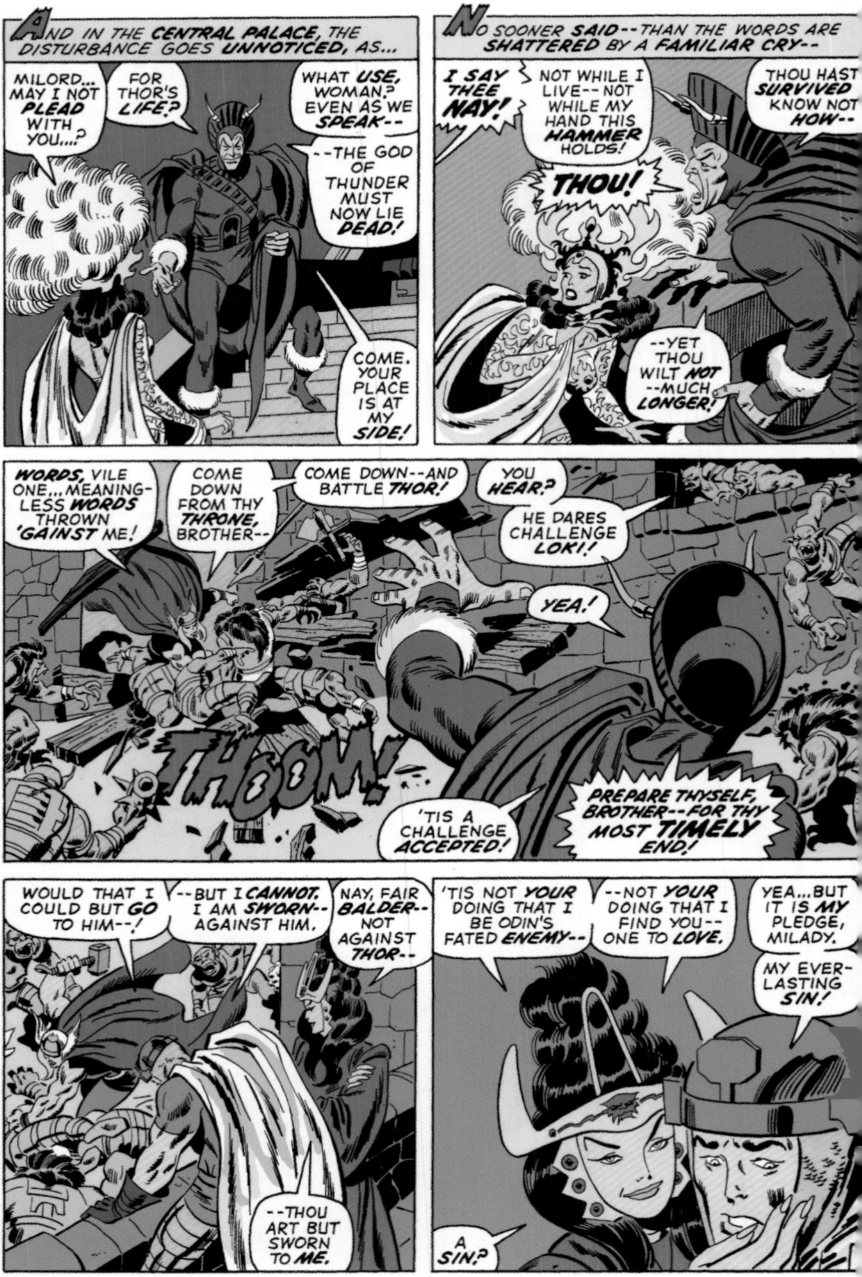
AND IN THE CENTRAL PALACE, THE DISTURBANCE GOES UNNOTICED, AS...
MILORD... MAY I NOT PLEAD WITH YOU...?
FOR THOR'S LIFE?
WHAT USE, WOMAN? EVEN AS WE SPEAK--
--THE GOD OF THUNDER MUST NOW LIE DEAD!
COME. YOUR PLACE IS AT MY SIDE!
NO SOONER SAID--THAN THE WORDS ARE SHATTERED BY A FAMILIAR CRY--
I SAY THEE NAY!
NOT WHILE I LIVE--NOT WHILE MY HAND THIS HAMMER HOLDS!
THOU!
THOU HAST SURVIVED KNOW NOT HOW--
--YET THOU WILT NOT --MUCH LONGER!
WORDS, VILE ONE...MEANINGLESS WORDS THROWN 'GAINST ME!
COME DOWN FROM THY THRONE, BROTHER--
COME DOWN--AND BATTLE THOR!
YOU HEAR?
HE DARES CHALLENGE LOKI!
YEA!
THOOM!
'TIS A CHALLENGE ACCEPTED!
PREPARE THYSELF, BROTHER--FOR THY MOST TIMELY END!
WOULD THAT I COULD BUT GO TO HIM--!
--BUT I CANNOT. I AM SWORN--AGAINST HIM.
NAY, FAIR BALDER--NOT AGAINST THOR--
--THOU ART BUT SWORN TO ME.
'TIS NOT YOUR DOING THAT I BE ODIN'S FATED ENEMY--
--NOT YOUR DOING THAT I FIND YOU--ONE TO LOVE.
YEA...BUT IT IS MY PLEDGE, MILADY.
MY EVERLASTING SIN!
A SIN?

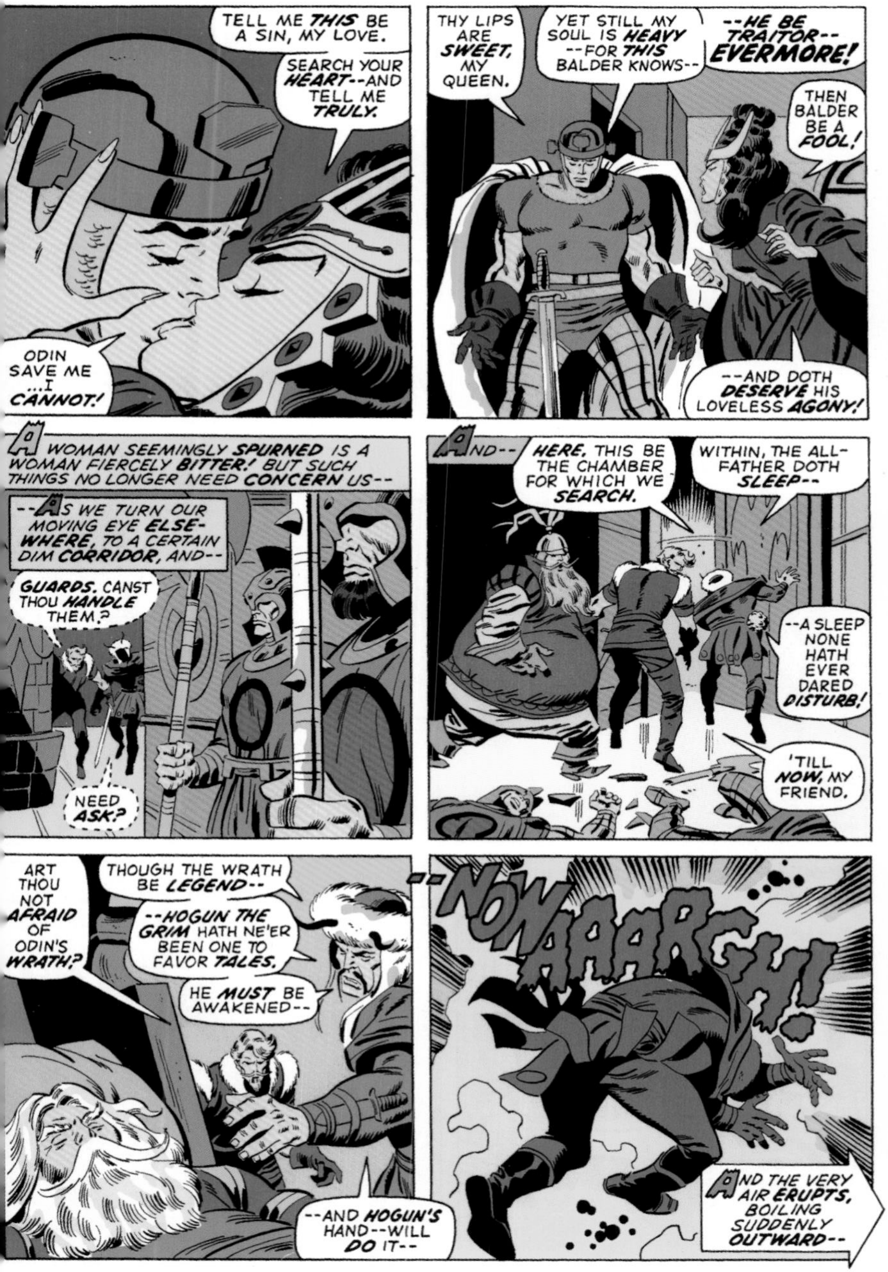
TELL ME THIS BE A SIN, MY LOVE.
SEARCH YOUR HEART--AND TELL ME TRULY.
ODIN SAVE ME ...I CANNOT!
THY LIPS ARE SWEET, MY QUEEN.
YET STILL MY SOUL IS HEAVY --FOR THIS BALDER KNOWS--
--HE BE TRAITOR-- EVERMORE!
THEN BALDER BE A FOOL!
--AND DOTH DESERVE HIS LOVELESS AGONY!
A WOMAN SEEMINGLY SPURNED IS A WOMAN FIERCELY BITTER! BUT SUCH THINGS NO LONGER NEED CONCERN US--
--AS WE TURN OUR MOVING EYE ELSE-WHERE, TO A CERTAIN DIM CORRIDOR, AND--
GUARDS. CANST THOU HANDLE THEM?
NEED ASK?
AND--
HERE. THIS BE THE CHAMBER FOR WHICH WE SEARCH.
WITHIN, THE ALL-FATHER DOTH SLEEP--
--A SLEEP NONE HATH EVER DARED DISTURB!
'TILL NOW, MY FRIEND.
ART THOU NOT AFRAID OF ODIN'S WRATH?
THOUGH THE WRATH BE LEGEND--
--HOGUN THE GRIM HATH NE'ER BEEN ONE TO FAVOR TALES.
HE MUST BE AWAKENED--
--AND HOGUN'S HAND--WILL DO IT--
--NOW
AAARGH!
AND THE VERY AIR ERUPTS, BOILING SUDDENLY OUTWARD--

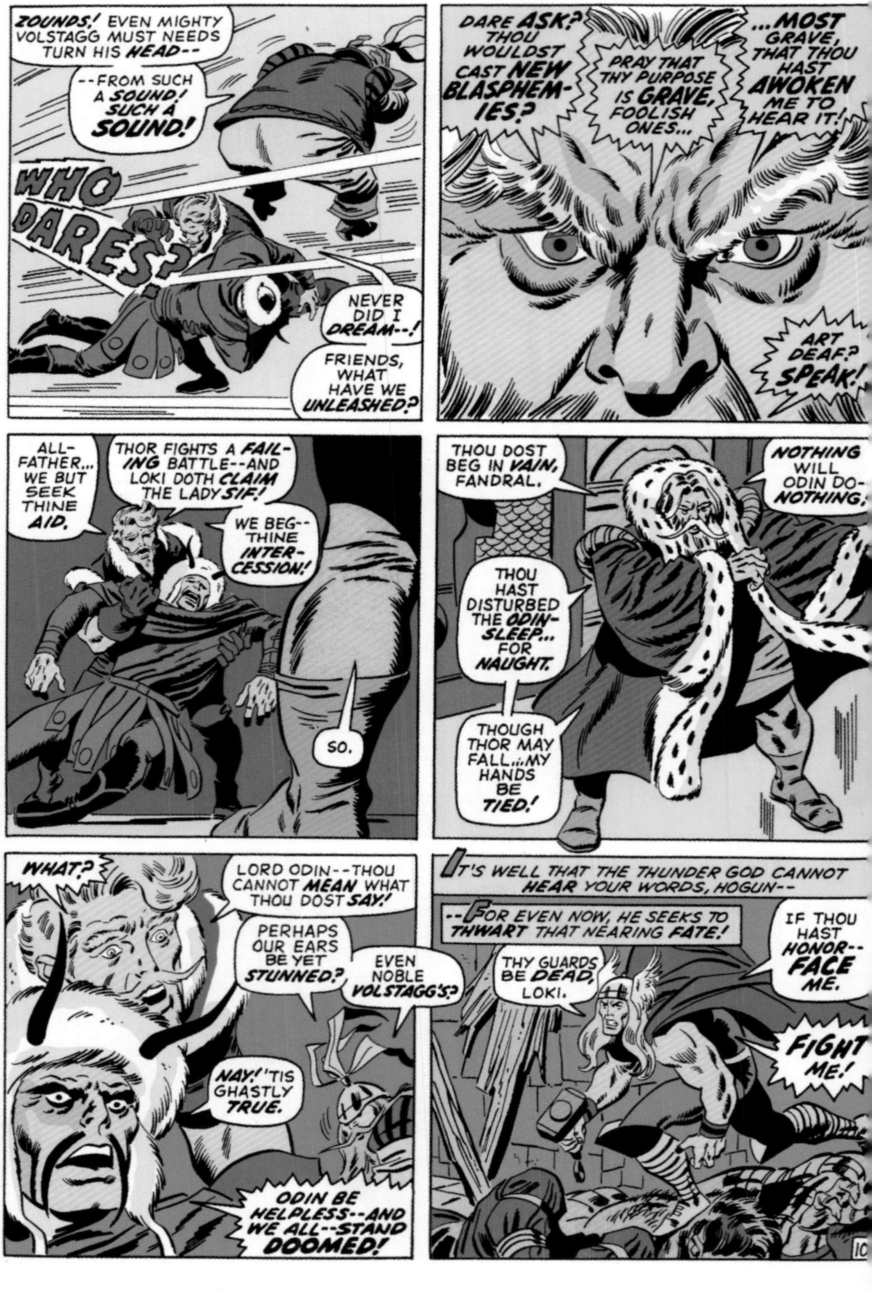
ZOUNDS! EVEN MIGHTY VOLSTAGG MUST NEEDS TURN HIS HEAD--
--FROM SUCH A SOUND! SUCH A SOUND!
WHO DARES?
NEVER DID I DREAM--!
FRIENDS, WHAT HAVE WE UNLEASHED?
DARE ASK? THOU WOULDST CAST NEW BLASPHEM-IES?
PRAY THAT THY PURPOSE IS GRAVE, FOOLISH ONES...
...MOST GRAVE, THAT THOU HAST AWOKEN ME TO HEAR IT!
ART DEAF? SPEAK!
ALL-FATHER... WE BUT SEEK THINE AID.
THOR FIGHTS A FAIL-ING BATTLE--AND LOKI DOTH CLAIM THE LADY SIF!
WE BEG--THINE INTER-CESSION!
SO.
THOU DOST BEG IN VAIN, FANDRAL.
NOTHING WILL ODIN DO--NOTHING!
THOU HAST DISTURBED THE ODIN-SLEEP... FOR NAUGHT.
THOUGH THOR MAY FALL... MY HANDS BE TIED!
WHAT?
LORD ODIN--THOU CANNOT MEAN WHAT THOU DOST SAY!
PERHAPS OUR EARS BE YET STUNNED?
EVEN NOBLE VOLSTAGG'S?
NAY! 'TIS GHASTLY TRUE.
ODIN BE HELPLESS--AND WE ALL--STAND DOOMED!
IT'S WELL THAT THE THUNDER GOD CANNOT HEAR YOUR WORDS, HOGUN--
--FOR EVEN NOW, HE SEEKS TO THWART THAT NEARING FATE!
THY GUARDS BE DEAD, LOKI.
IF THOU HAST HONOR--FACE ME.
FIGHT ME!
10

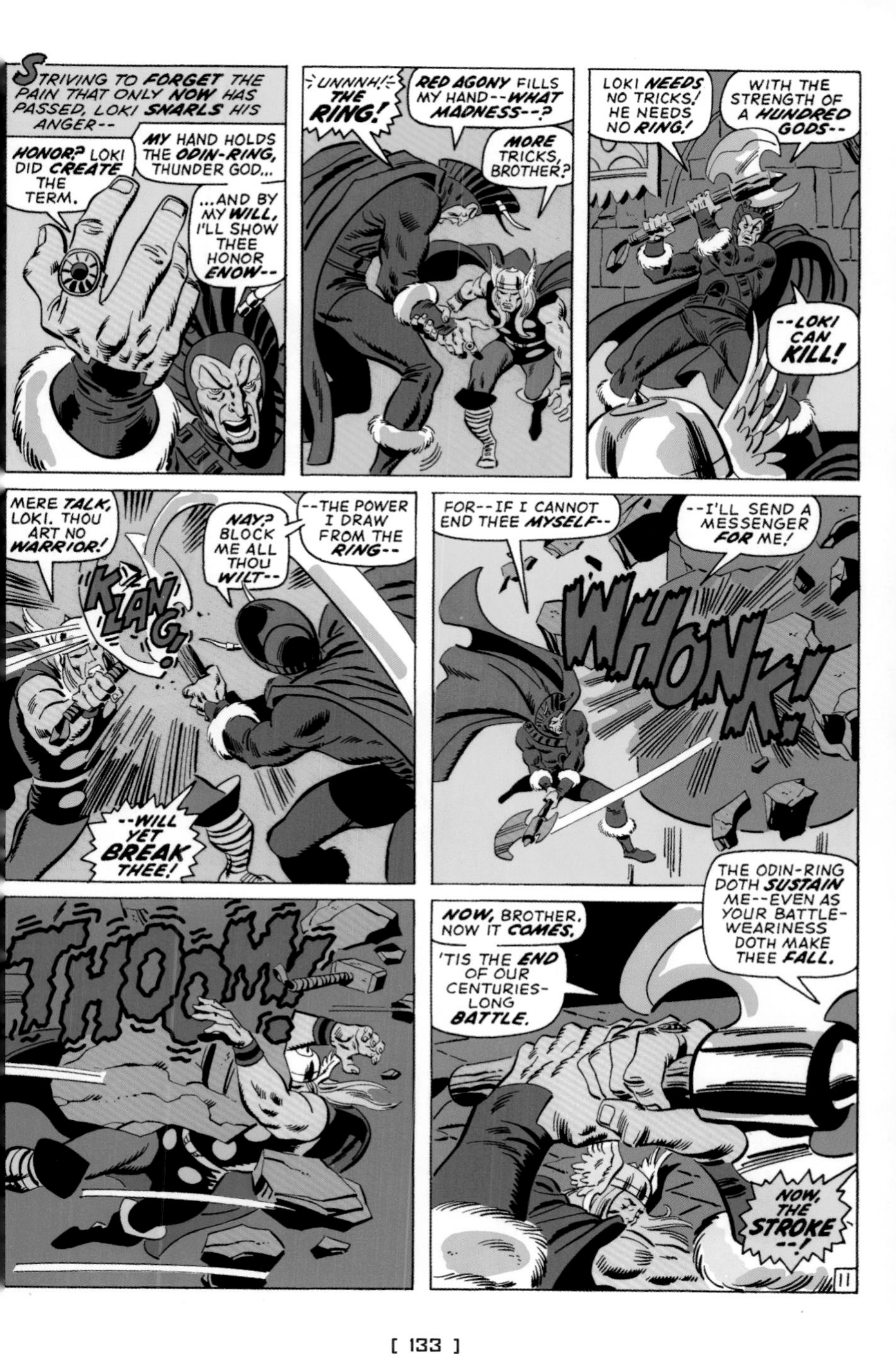
STRIVING TO FORGET THE PAIN THAT ONLY NOW HAS PASSED, LOKI SNARLS HIS ANGER--
HONOR? LOKI DID CREATE THE TERM.
MY HAND HOLDS THE ODIN-RING, THUNDER GOD...
...AND BY MY WILL, I'LL SHOW THEE HONOR ENOW--
UNNNH! THE RING!
RED AGONY FILLS MY HAND--WHAT MADNESS--?
MORE TRICKS, BROTHER?
LOKI NEEDS NO TRICKS! HE NEEDS NO RING!
WITH THE STRENGTH OF A HUNDRED GODS--
--LOKI CAN KILL!
MERE TALK, LOKI. THOU ART NO WARRIOR!
KLANG!
NAY? BLOCK ME ALL THOU WILT--
--THE POWER I DRAW FROM THE RING--
--WILL YET BREAK THEE!
FOR--IF I CANNOT END THEE MYSELF--
--I'LL SEND A MESSENGER FOR ME!
WHONK!
THOOM!
NOW, BROTHER. NOW IT COMES.
'TIS THE END OF OUR CENTURIES-LONG BATTLE.
THE ODIN-RING DOTH SUSTAIN ME--EVEN AS YOUR BATTLE-WEARINESS DOTH MAKE THEE FALL.
NOW, THE STROKE--!
11

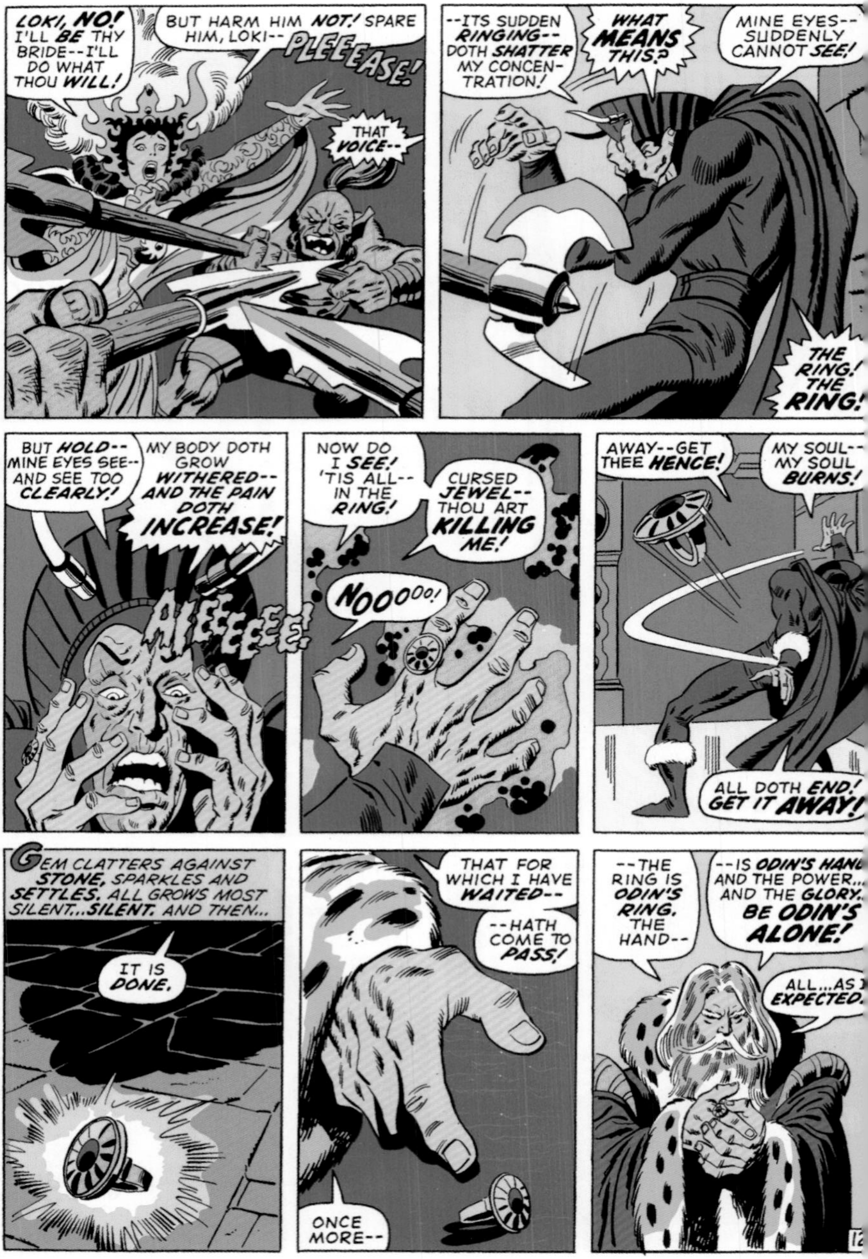
LOKI, NO! I'LL BE THY BRIDE--I'LL DO WHAT THOU WILL!
BUT HARM HIM NOT! SPARE HIM, LOKI--
PLEEEEASE!
THAT VOICE--
--ITS SUDDEN RINGING--DOTH SHATTER MY CONCENTRATION!
WHAT MEANS THIS?
MINE EYES--SUDDENLY CANNOT SEE!
THE RING! THE RING!
BUT HOLD--MINE EYES SEE--AND SEE TOO CLEARLY!
MY BODY DOTH GROW WITHERED--AND THE PAIN DOTH INCREASE!
AIEEEEEE!
NOW DO I SEE! 'TIS ALL--IN THE RING!
CURSED JEWEL--THOU ART KILLING ME!
NOOOOOO!
AWAY--GET THEE HENCE!
MY SOUL--MY SOUL BURNS!
ALL DOTH END! GET IT AWAY!
GEM CLATTERS AGAINST STONE, SPARKLES AND SETTLES. ALL GROWS MOST SILENT...SILENT. AND THEN...
IT IS DONE.
THAT FOR WHICH I HAVE WAITED--
--HATH COME TO PASS!
ONCE MORE--
--THE RING IS ODIN'S RING. THE HAND--
--IS ODIN'S HAND AND THE POWER... AND THE GLORY... BE ODIN'S ALONE!
ALL...AS I EXPECTED.
12

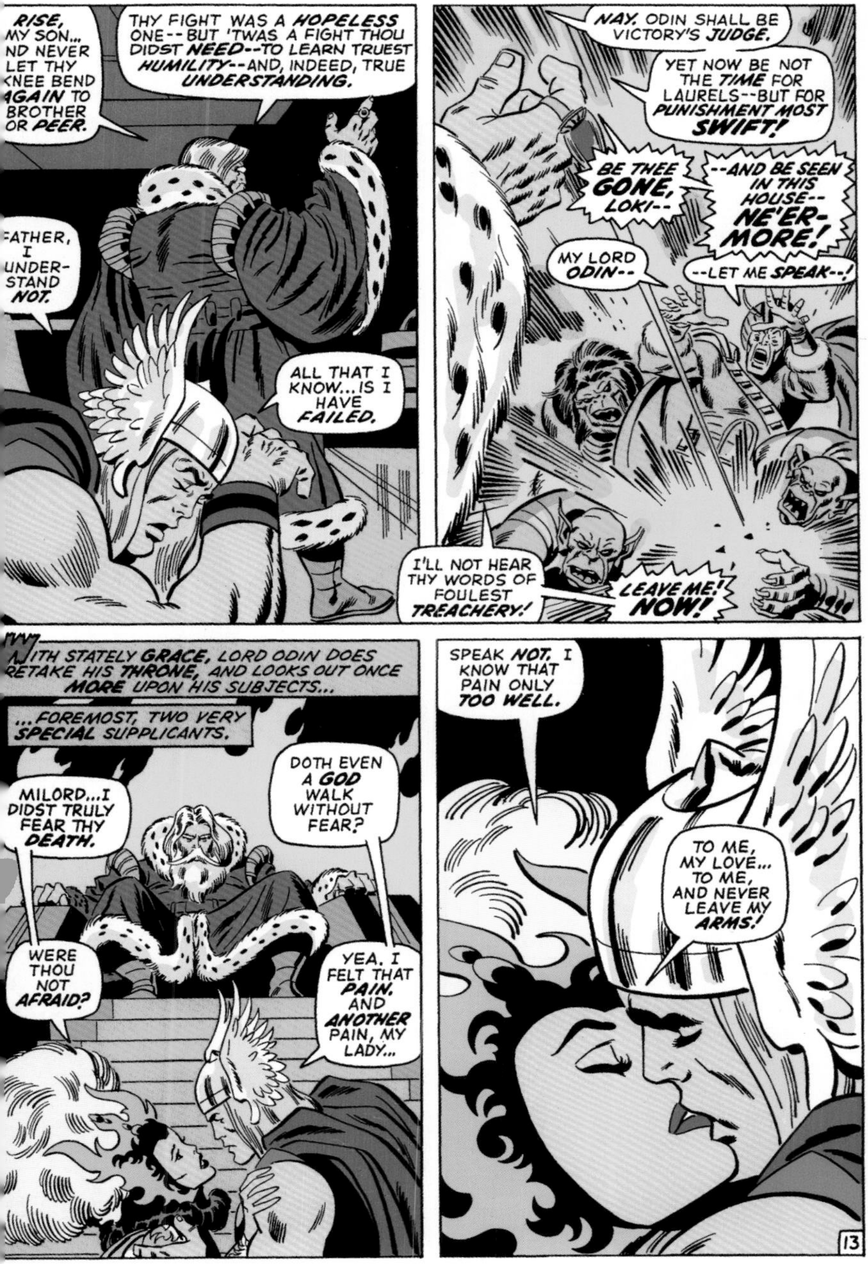
RISE, MY SON... ND NEVER LET THY KNEE BEND AGAIN TO BROTHER OR PEER.
THY FIGHT WAS A HOPELESS ONE--BUT 'TWAS A FIGHT THOU DIDST NEED--TO LEARN TRUEST HUMILITY--AND, INDEED, TRUE UNDERSTANDING.
FATHER, I UNDER-STAND NOT.
ALL THAT I KNOW...IS I HAVE FAILED.
NAY, ODIN SHALL BE VICTORY'S JUDGE.
YET NOW BE NOT THE TIME FOR LAURELS--BUT FOR PUNISHMENT MOST SWIFT!
BE THEE GONE, LOKI--
--AND BE SEEN IN THIS HOUSE--NE'ER-MORE!
MY LORD ODIN--
--LET ME SPEAK--!
I'LL NOT HEAR THY WORDS OF FOULEST TREACHERY!
LEAVE ME! NOW!
WITH STATELY GRACE, LORD ODIN DOES RETAKE HIS THRONE, AND LOOKS OUT ONCE MORE UPON HIS SUBJECTS...
...FOREMOST, TWO VERY SPECIAL SUPPLICANTS.
MILORD...I DIDST TRULY FEAR THY DEATH.
DOTH EVEN A GOD WALK WITHOUT FEAR?
WERE THOU NOT AFRAID?
YEA, I FELT THAT PAIN. AND ANOTHER PAIN, MY LADY...
SPEAK NOT. I KNOW THAT PAIN ONLY TOO WELL.
TO ME, MY LOVE... TO ME, AND NEVER LEAVE MY ARMS!
13

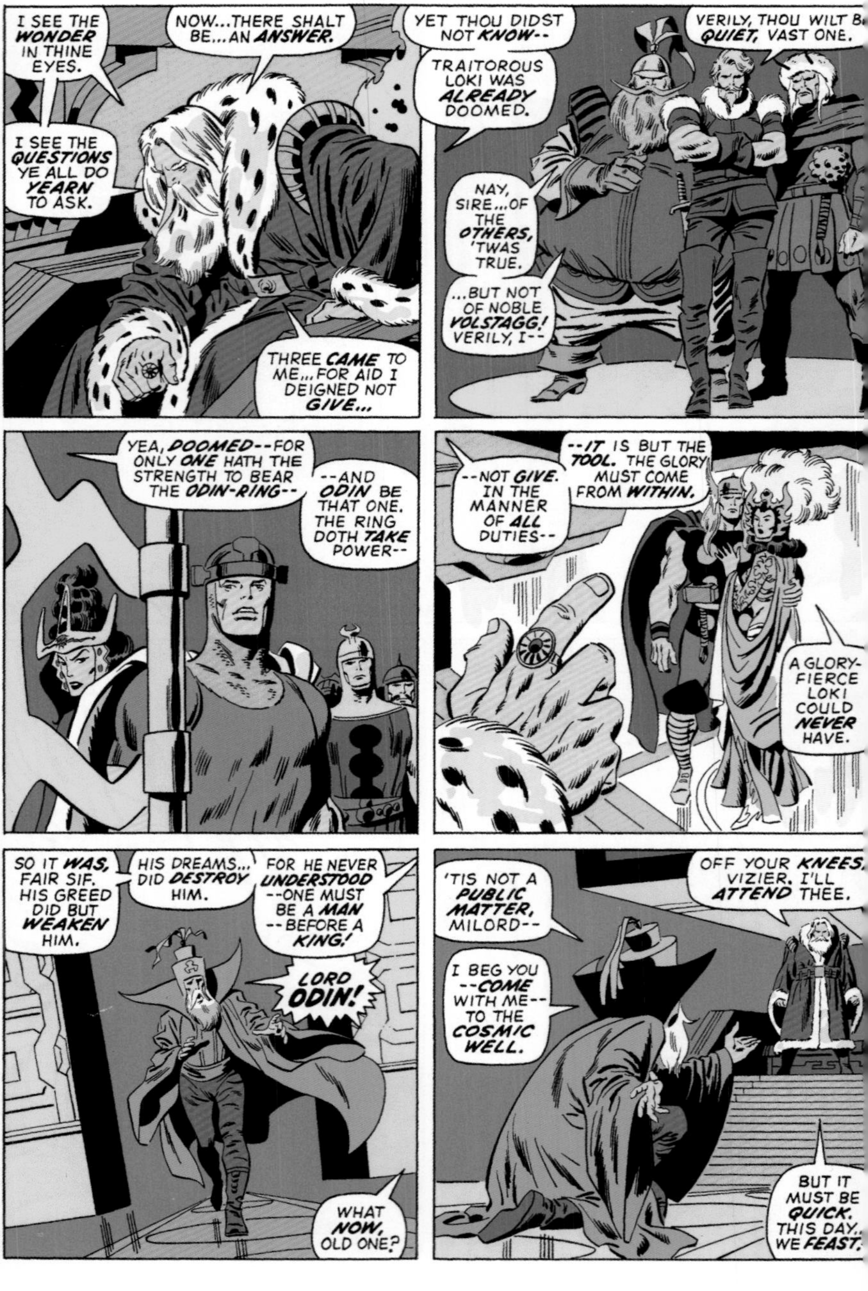
I SEE THE WONDER IN THINE EYES.
I SEE THE QUESTIONS YE ALL DO YEARN TO ASK.
NOW...THERE SHALT BE...AN ANSWER.
THREE CAME TO ME...FOR AID I DEIGNED NOT GIVE...
YET THOU DIDST NOT KNOW--
TRAITOROUS LOKI WAS ALREADY DOOMED.
NAY, SIRE...OF THE OTHERS, 'TWAS TRUE.
...BUT NOT OF NOBLE VOLSTAGG! VERILY, I--
VERILY, THOU WILT B QUIET, VAST ONE.
YEA, DOOMED--FOR ONLY ONE HATH THE STRENGTH TO BEAR THE ODIN-RING--
--AND ODIN BE THAT ONE. THE RING DOTH TAKE POWER--
--NOT GIVE. IN THE MANNER OF ALL DUTIES--
--IT IS BUT THE TOOL. THE GLORY MUST COME FROM WITHIN.
A GLORY-FIERCE LOKI COULD NEVER HAVE.
SO IT WAS, FAIR SIF. HIS GREED DID BUT WEAKEN HIM.
HIS DREAMS... DID DESTROY HIM.
FOR HE NEVER UNDERSTOOD --ONE MUST BE A MAN --BEFORE A KING!
LORD ODIN!
WHAT NOW, OLD ONE?
'TIS NOT A PUBLIC MATTER, MILORD--
I BEG YOU --COME WITH ME-- TO THE COSMIC WELL.
OFF YOUR KNEES, VIZIER. I'LL ATTEND THEE.
BUT IT MUST BE QUICK. THIS DAY, WE FEAST.

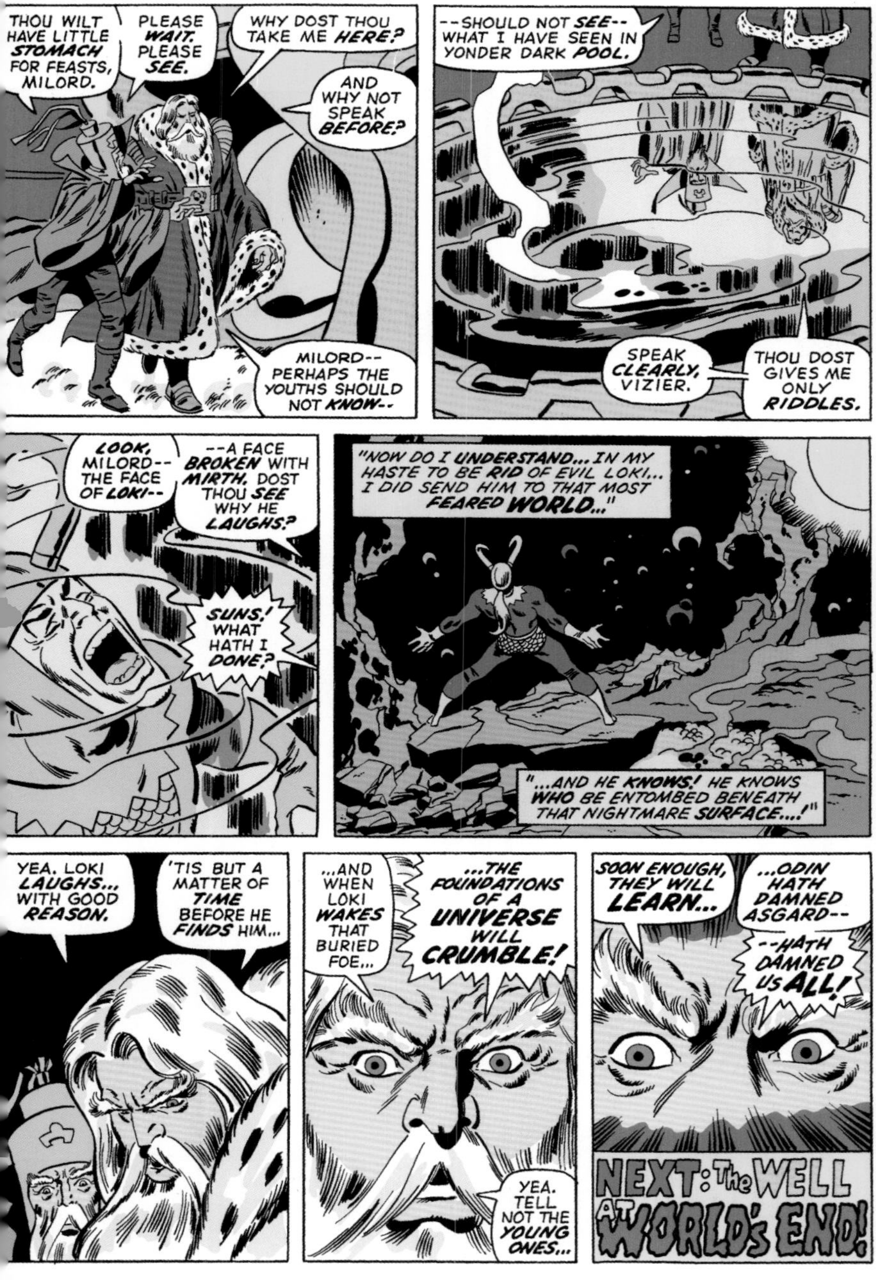
THOU WILT HAVE LITTLE STOMACH FOR FEASTS, MILORD.
PLEASE WAIT. PLEASE SEE.
WHY DOST THOU TAKE ME HERE?
AND WHY NOT SPEAK BEFORE?
MILORD-- PERHAPS THE YOUTHS SHOULD NOT KNOW--
--SHOULD NOT SEE-- WHAT I HAVE SEEN IN YONDER DARK POOL.
SPEAK CLEARLY, VIZIER.
THOU DOST GIVES ME ONLY RIDDLES.
LOOK, MILORD-- THE FACE OF LOKI--
--A FACE BROKEN WITH MIRTH. DOST THOU SEE WHY HE LAUGHS?
SUNS! WHAT HATH I DONE?
"NOW DO I UNDERSTAND... IN MY HASTE TO BE RID OF EVIL LOKI... I DID SEND HIM TO THAT MOST FEARED WORLD..."
"...AND HE KNOWS! HE KNOWS WHO BE ENTOMBED BENEATH THAT NIGHTMARE SURFACE...!"
YEA. LOKI LAUGHS... WITH GOOD REASON.
'TIS BUT A MATTER OF TIME BEFORE HE FINDS HIM...
...AND WHEN LOKI WAKES THAT BURIED FOE...
...THE FOUNDATIONS OF A UNIVERSE WILL CRUMBLE!
YEA. TELL NOT THE YOUNG ONES...
SOON ENOUGH, THEY WILL LEARN...
...ODIN HATH DAMNED ASGARD--
--HATH DAMNED US ALL!
NEXT: The WELL AT WORLD's END!

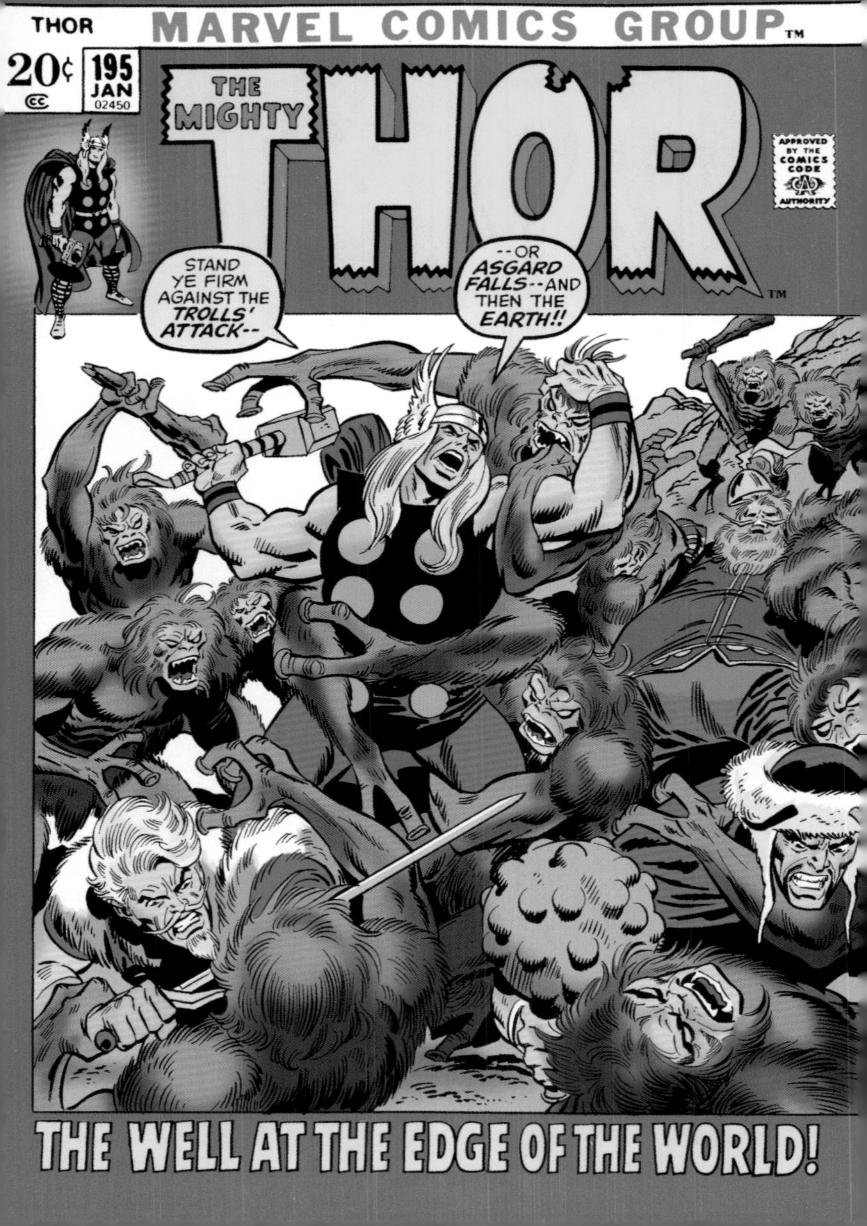
THOR
MARVEL COMICS GROUP™
20¢
CC
195
JAN
02450
THE MIGHTY
THOR™
APPROVED BY THE COMICS CODE AUTHORITY
STAND YE FIRM AGAINST THE TROLLS' ATTACK--
--OR ASGARD FALLS--AND THEN THE EARTH!!
THE WELL AT THE EDGE OF THE WORLD!

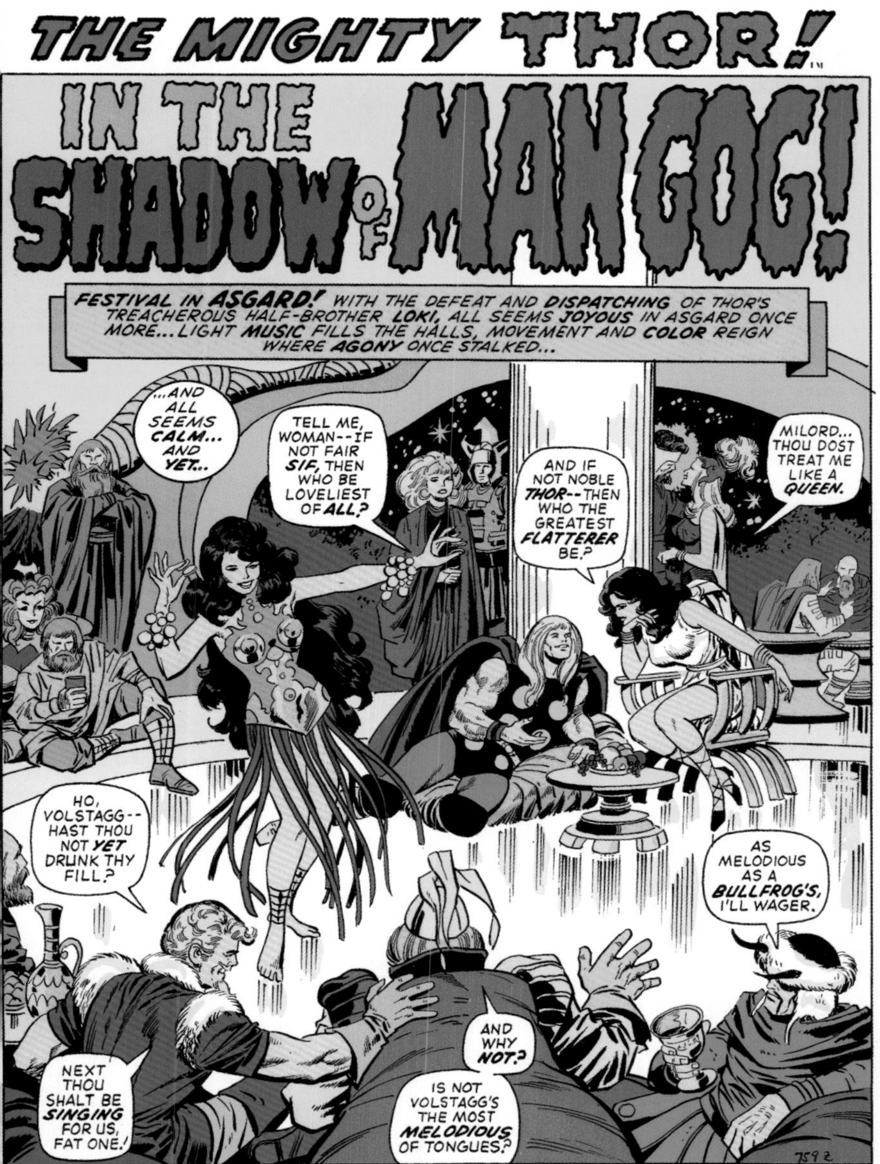
THE MIGHTY THOR!
IN THE SHADOW OF MANGOG!
FESTIVAL IN ASGARD! WITH THE DEFEAT AND DISPATCHING OF THOR'S TREACHEROUS HALF-BROTHER LOKI, ALL SEEMS JOYOUS IN ASGARD ONCE MORE... LIGHT MUSIC FILLS THE HALLS, MOVEMENT AND COLOR REIGN WHERE AGONY ONCE STALKED...
...AND ALL SEEMS CALM... AND YET...
TELL ME, WOMAN--IF NOT FAIR SIF, THEN WHO BE LOVELIEST OF ALL?
AND IF NOT NOBLE THOR--THEN WHO THE GREATEST FLATTERER BE?
MILORD... THOU DOST TREAT ME LIKE A QUEEN.
HO, VOLSTAGG--HAST THOU NOT YET DRUNK THY FILL?
AS MELODIOUS AS A BULLFROG'S, I'LL WAGER.
AND WHY NOT?
IS NOT VOLSTAGG'S THE MOST MELODIOUS OF TONGUES?
NEXT THOU SHALT BE SINGING FOR US, FAT ONE!
STAN LEE, EDITOR
GERRY CONWAY, WRITER
JOHN BUSCEMA, ARTIST
VINCE COLLETTA, INKER
ARTIE SIMEK, LETTERER

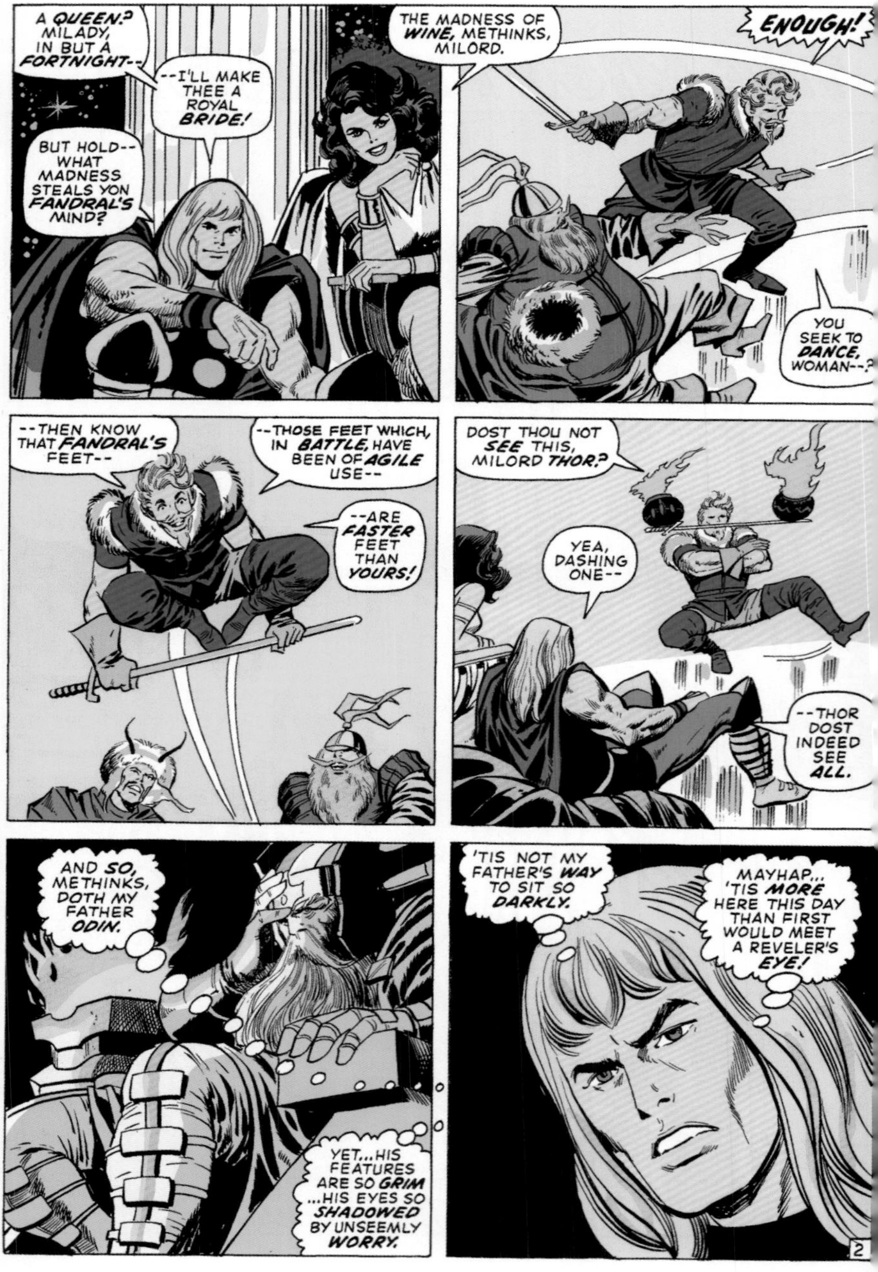
A QUEEN? MILADY, IN BUT A FORTNIGHT--
--I'LL MAKE THEE A ROYAL BRIDE!
BUT HOLD-- WHAT MADNESS STEALS YON FANDRAL'S MIND?
THE MADNESS OF WINE, METHINKS, MILORD.
ENOUGH!
YOU SEEK TO DANCE, WOMAN--?
--THEN KNOW THAT FANDRAL'S FEET--
--THOSE FEET WHICH, IN BATTLE, HAVE BEEN OF AGILE USE--
--ARE FASTER FEET THAN YOURS!
DOST THOU NOT SEE THIS, MILORD THOR?
YEA, DASHING ONE--
--THOR DOST INDEED SEE ALL.
AND SO, METHINKS, DOTH MY FATHER ODIN.
YET...HIS FEATURES ARE SO GRIM ...HIS EYES SO SHADOWED BY UNSEEMLY WORRY.
'TIS NOT MY FATHER'S WAY TO SIT SO DARKLY.
MAYHAP... 'TIS MORE HERE THIS DAY THAN FIRST WOULD MEET A REVELER'S EYE!
2

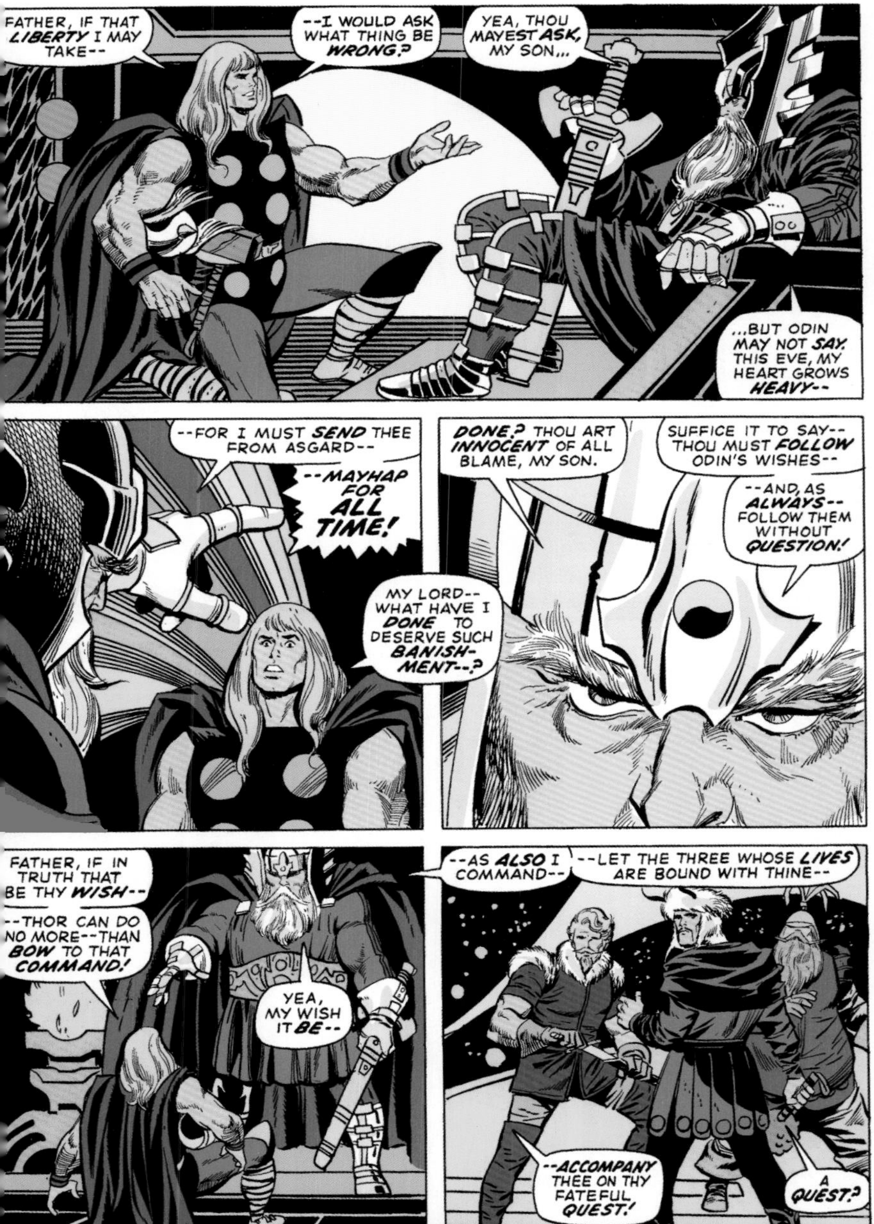
FATHER, IF THAT LIBERTY I MAY TAKE--
--I WOULD ASK WHAT THING BE WRONG?
YEA, THOU MAYEST ASK, MY SON...
...BUT ODIN MAY NOT SAY. THIS EVE, MY HEART GROWS HEAVY--
--FOR I MUST SEND THEE FROM ASGARD--
--MAYHAP FOR ALL TIME!
MY LORD-- WHAT HAVE I DONE TO DESERVE SUCH BANISH-MENT--?
DONE? THOU ART INNOCENT OF ALL BLAME, MY SON.
SUFFICE IT TO SAY-- THOU MUST FOLLOW ODIN'S WISHES--
--AND, AS ALWAYS-- FOLLOW THEM WITHOUT QUESTION!
FATHER, IF IN TRUTH THAT BE THY WISH--
--THOR CAN DO NO MORE--THAN BOW TO THAT COMMAND!
YEA, MY WISH IT BE--
--AS ALSO I COMMAND--
--LET THE THREE WHOSE LIVES ARE BOUND WITH THINE--
--ACCOMPANY THEE ON THY FATEFUL QUEST!
A QUEST?
3

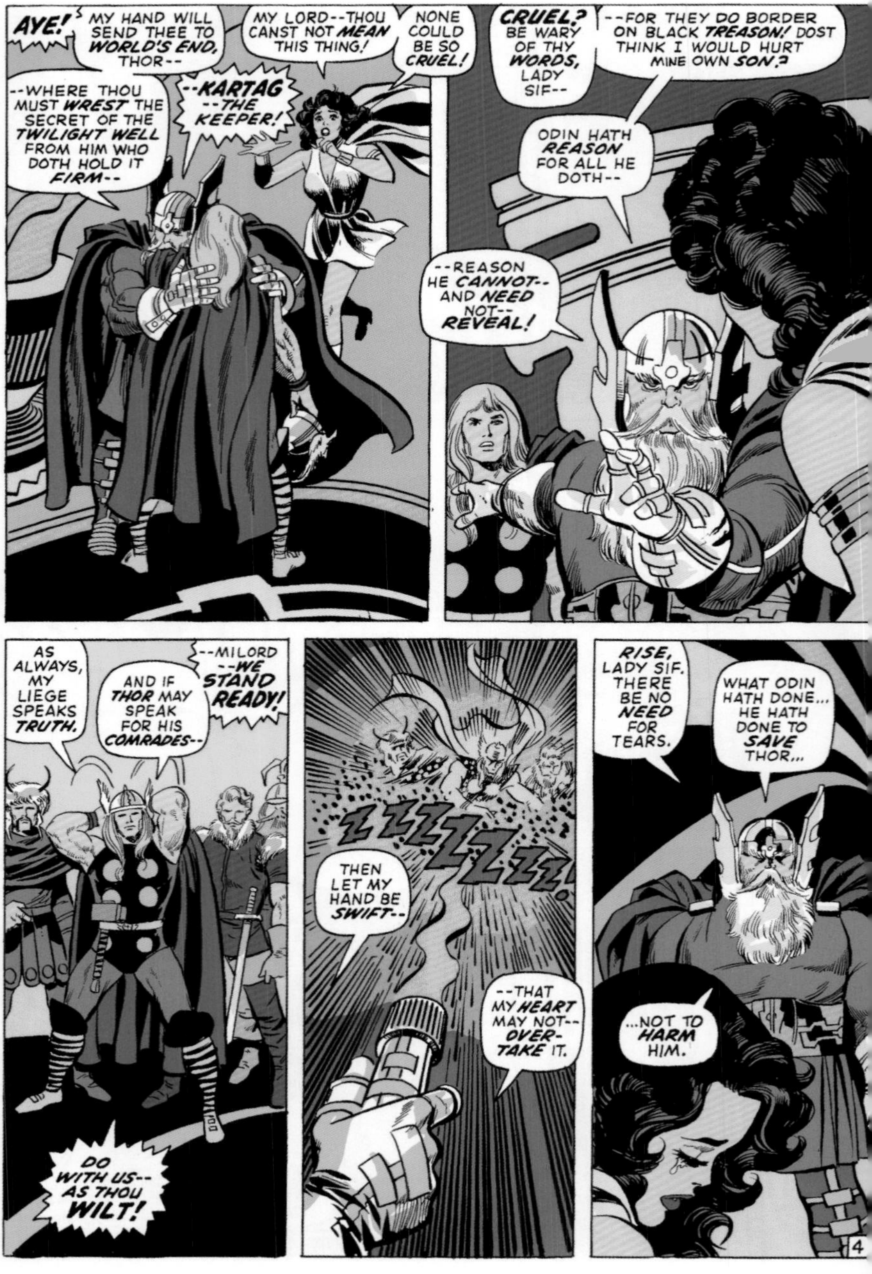
AYE!
MY HAND WILL SEND THEE TO WORLD'S END, THOR--
--WHERE THOU MUST WREST THE SECRET OF THE TWILIGHT WELL FROM HIM WHO DOTH HOLD IT FIRM--
--KARTAG --THE KEEPER!
MY LORD--THOU CANST NOT MEAN THIS THING!
NONE COULD BE SO CRUEL!
CRUEL? BE WARY OF THY WORDS, LADY SIF--
--FOR THEY DO BORDER ON BLACK TREASON! DOST THINK I WOULD HURT MINE OWN SON?
ODIN HATH REASON FOR ALL HE DOTH--
--REASON HE CANNOT--AND NEED NOT--REVEAL!
AS ALWAYS, MY LIEGE SPEAKS TRUTH.
AND IF THOR MAY SPEAK FOR HIS COMRADES--
--MILORD --WE STAND READY!
DO WITH US--AS THOU WILT!
ZZZZZZZZ
THEN LET MY HAND BE SWIFT--
--THAT MY HEART MAY NOT--OVERTAKE IT.
RISE, LADY SIF. THERE BE NO NEED FOR TEARS.
WHAT ODIN HATH DONE... HE HATH DONE TO SAVE THOR...
...NOT TO HARM HIM.
4

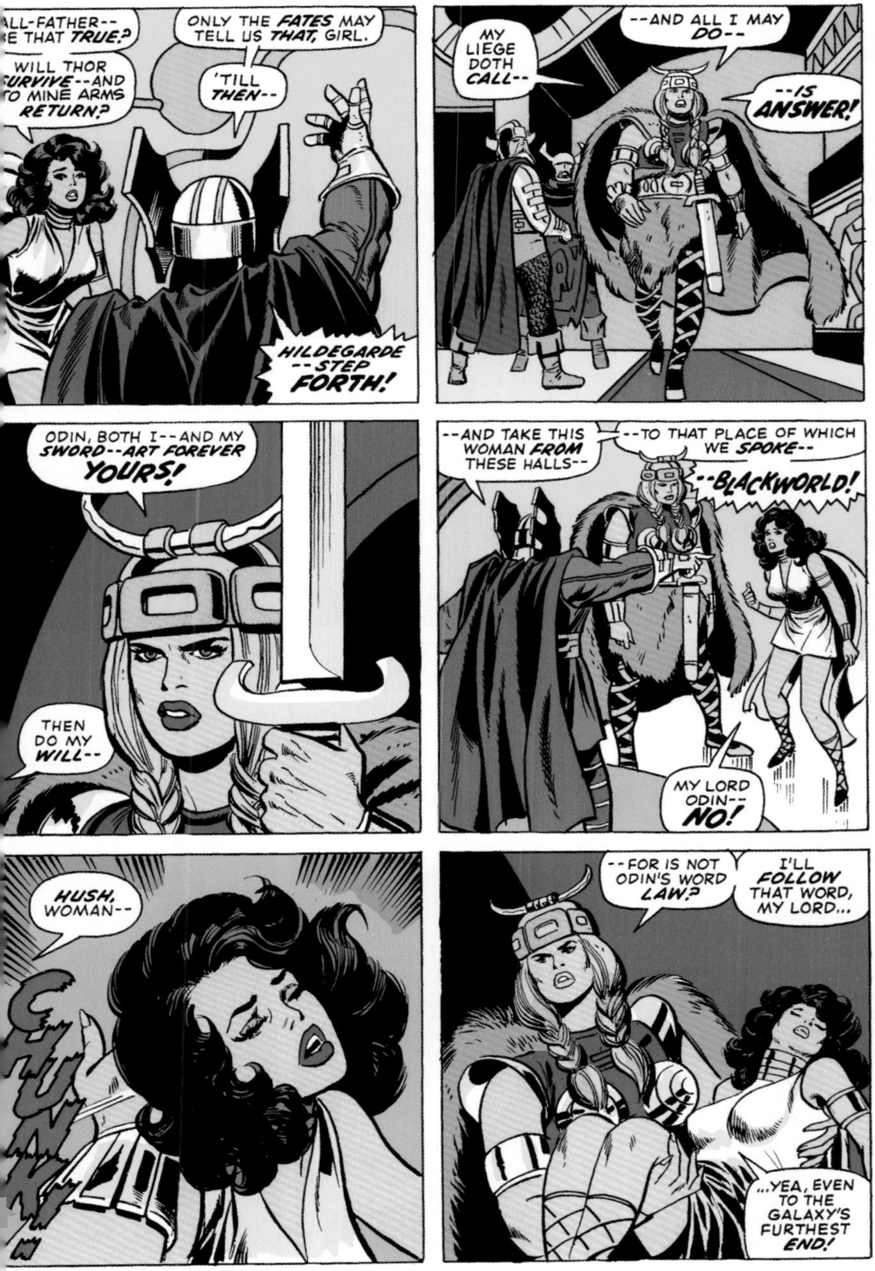
ALL-FATHER-- BE THAT TRUE?
WILL THOR SURVIVE--AND TO MINE ARMS RETURN?
ONLY THE FATES MAY TELL US THAT, GIRL.
'TILL THEN--
HILDEGARDE --STEP FORTH!
MY LIEGE DOTH CALL--
--AND ALL I MAY DO--
--IS ANSWER!
ODIN, BOTH I--AND MY SWORD--ART FOREVER YOURS!
THEN DO MY WILL--
--AND TAKE THIS WOMAN FROM THESE HALLS--
--TO THAT PLACE OF WHICH WE SPOKE--
--BLACKWORLD!
MY LORD ODIN-- NO!
HUSH, WOMAN--
CHUNK
--FOR IS NOT ODIN'S WORD LAW?
I'LL FOLLOW THAT WORD, MY LORD...
...YEA, EVEN TO THE GALAXY'S FURTHEST END!

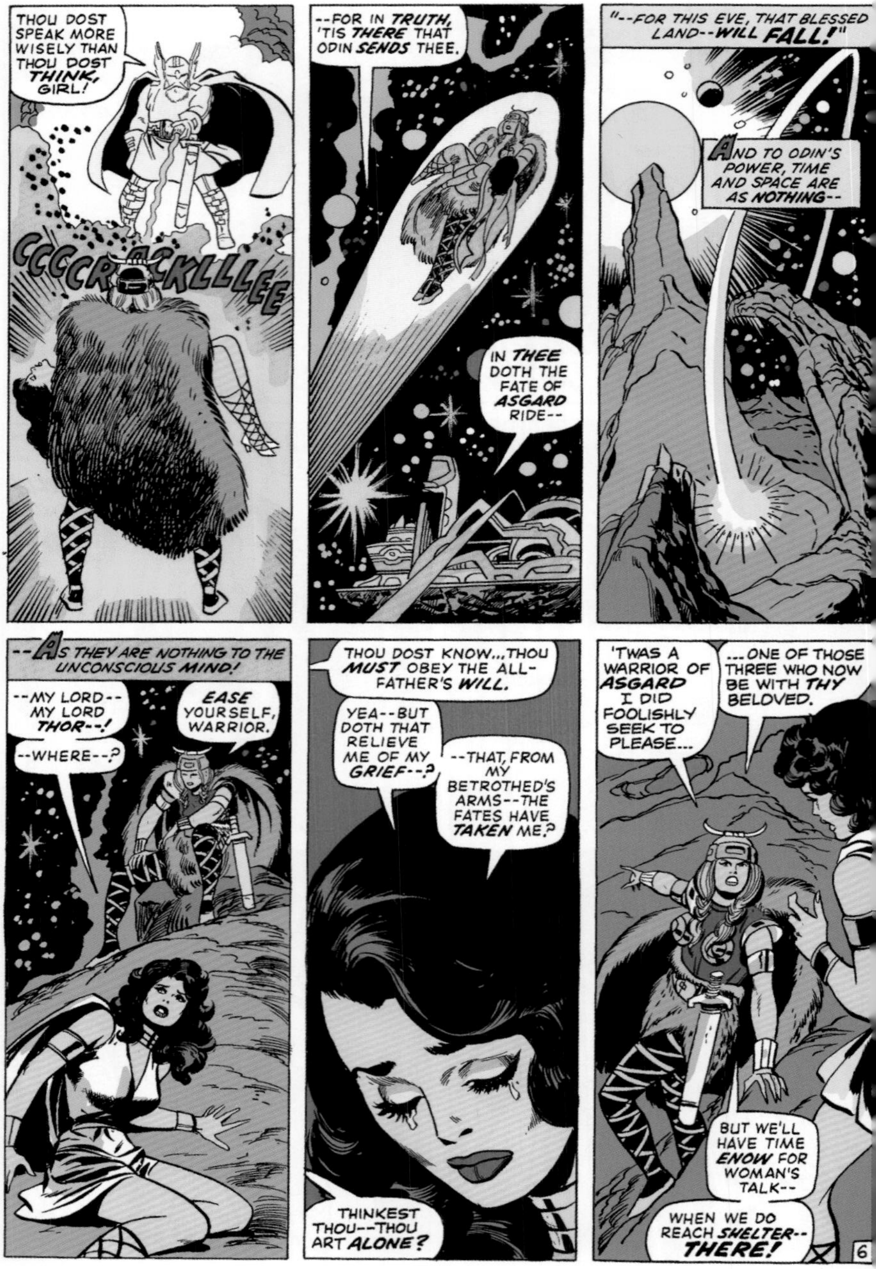
THOU DOST SPEAK MORE WISELY THAN THOU DOST THINK, GIRL!
CCCCRACKLLLLEE
--FOR IN TRUTH, 'TIS THERE THAT ODIN SENDS THEE.
IN THEE DOTH THE FATE OF ASGARD RIDE--
"--FOR THIS EVE, THAT BLESSED LAND--WILL FALL!"
AND TO ODIN'S POWER, TIME AND SPACE ARE AS NOTHING--
--AS THEY ARE NOTHING TO THE UNCONSCIOUS MIND!
--MY LORD-- MY LORD THOR--!
--WHERE--?
EASE YOURSELF, WARRIOR.
THOU DOST KNOW..., THOU MUST OBEY THE ALL-FATHER'S WILL.
YEA--BUT DOTH THAT RELIEVE ME OF MY GRIEF--?
--THAT, FROM MY BETROTHED'S ARMS--THE FATES HAVE TAKEN ME?
THINKEST THOU--THOU ART ALONE?
'TWAS A WARRIOR OF ASGARD I DID FOOLISHLY SEEK TO PLEASE...
...ONE OF THOSE THREE WHO NOW BE WITH THY BELOVED.
BUT WE'LL HAVE TIME ENOW FOR WOMAN'S TALK--
WHEN WE DO REACH SHELTER--THERE!
6

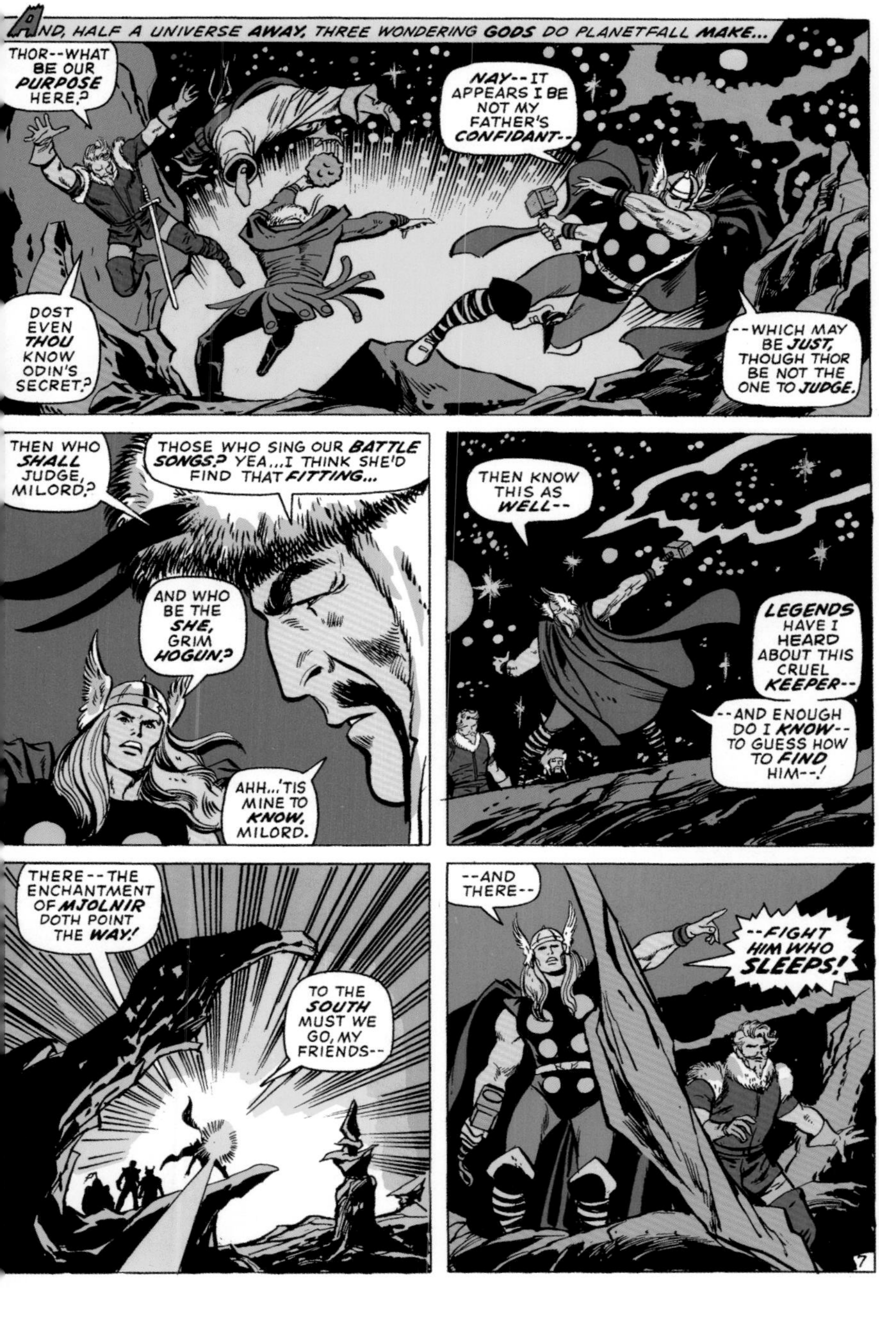
AND, HALF A UNIVERSE AWAY, THREE WONDERING GODS DO PLANETFALL MAKE...
THOR--WHAT BE OUR PURPOSE HERE?
NAY--IT APPEARS I BE NOT MY FATHER'S CONFIDANT--
DOST EVEN THOU KNOW ODIN'S SECRET?
--WHICH MAY BE JUST, THOUGH THOR BE NOT THE ONE TO JUDGE.
THEN WHO SHALL JUDGE, MILORD?
THOSE WHO SING OUR BATTLE SONGS? YEA...I THINK SHE'D FIND THAT FITTING...
AND WHO BE THE SHE, GRIM HOGUN?
AHH...'TIS MINE TO KNOW, MILORD.
THEN KNOW THIS AS WELL--
LEGENDS HAVE I HEARD ABOUT THIS CRUEL KEEPER--
--AND ENOUGH DO I KNOW--TO GUESS HOW TO FIND HIM--!
THERE--THE ENCHANTMENT OF MJOLNIR DOTH POINT THE WAY!
TO THE SOUTH MUST WE GO, MY FRIENDS--
--AND THERE--
--FIGHT HIM WHO SLEEPS!
7

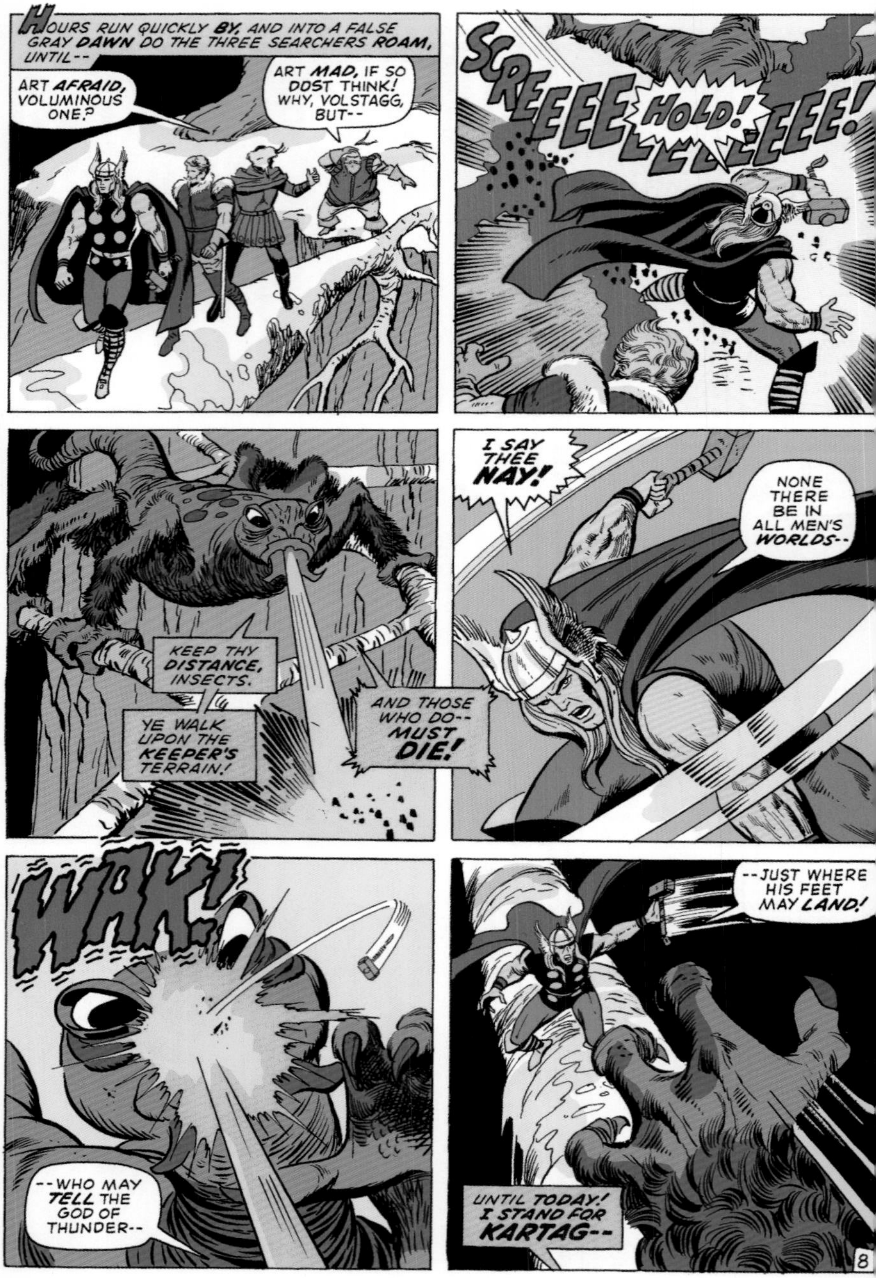
HOURS RUN QUICKLY BY, AND INTO A FALSE GRAY DAWN DO THE THREE SEARCHERS ROAM, UNTIL--
ART AFRAID, VOLUMINOUS ONE?
ART MAD, IF SO DOST THINK! WHY, VOLSTAGG, BUT--
SCREEEEEEEEEEE!
HOLD!
KEEP THY DISTANCE, INSECTS.
YE WALK UPON THE KEEPER'S TERRAIN!
AND THOSE WHO DO-- MUST DIE!
I SAY THEE NAY!
NONE THERE BE IN ALL MEN'S WORLDS--
WAK!
--WHO MAY TELL THE GOD OF THUNDER--
--JUST WHERE HIS FEET MAY LAND!
UNTIL TODAY! I STAND FOR KARTAG--
8

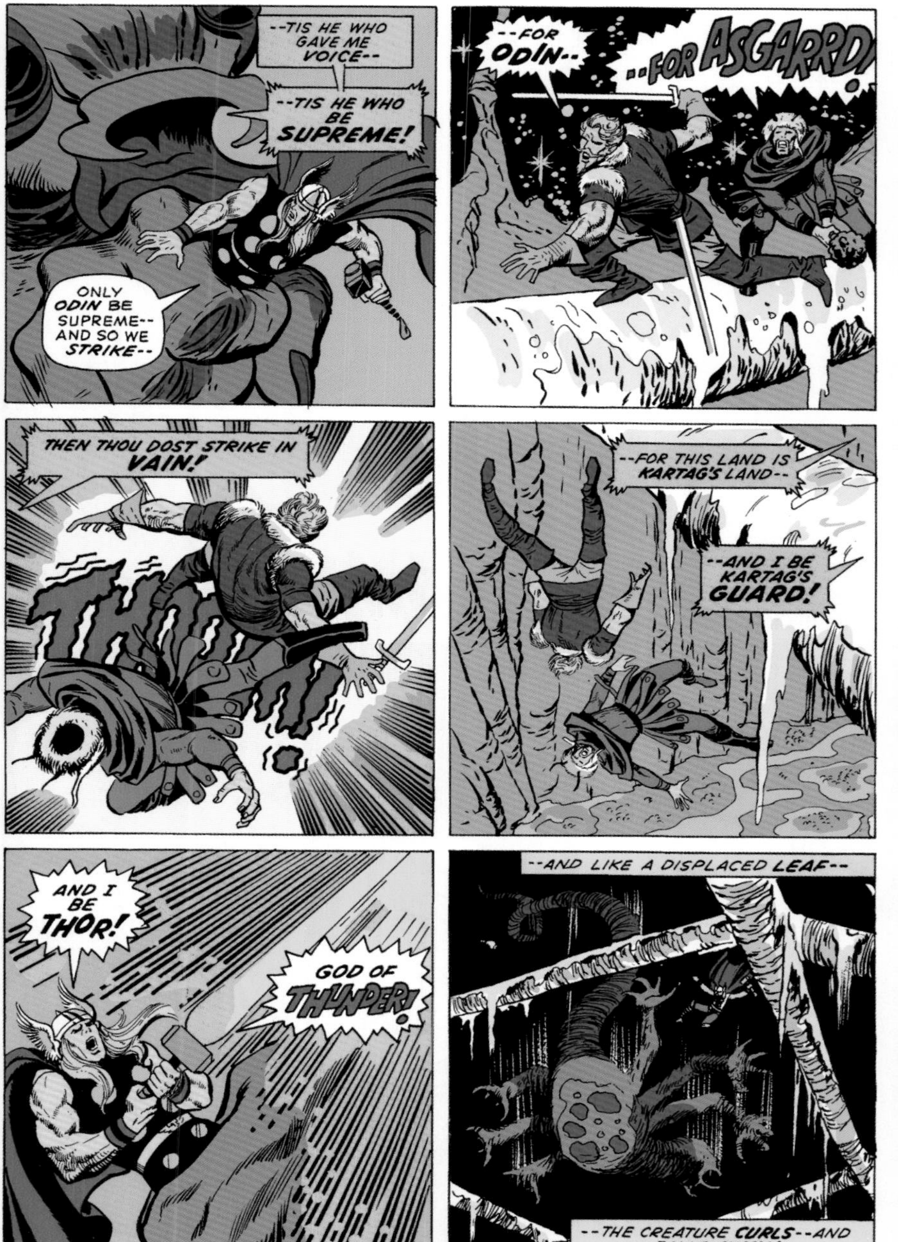
--TIS HE WHO GAVE ME VOICE--
--TIS HE WHO BE SUPREME!
ONLY ODIN BE SUPREME-- AND SO WE STRIKE--
--FOR ODIN--
--FOR ASGARRD!
THEN THOU DOST STRIKE IN VAIN!
THOOM
--FOR THIS LAND IS KARTAG'S LAND--
--AND I BE KARTAG'S GUARD!
AND I BE THOR!
GOD OF THUNDER!
--AND LIKE A DISPLACED LEAF--
--THE CREATURE CURLS--AND FALLS AWAY!

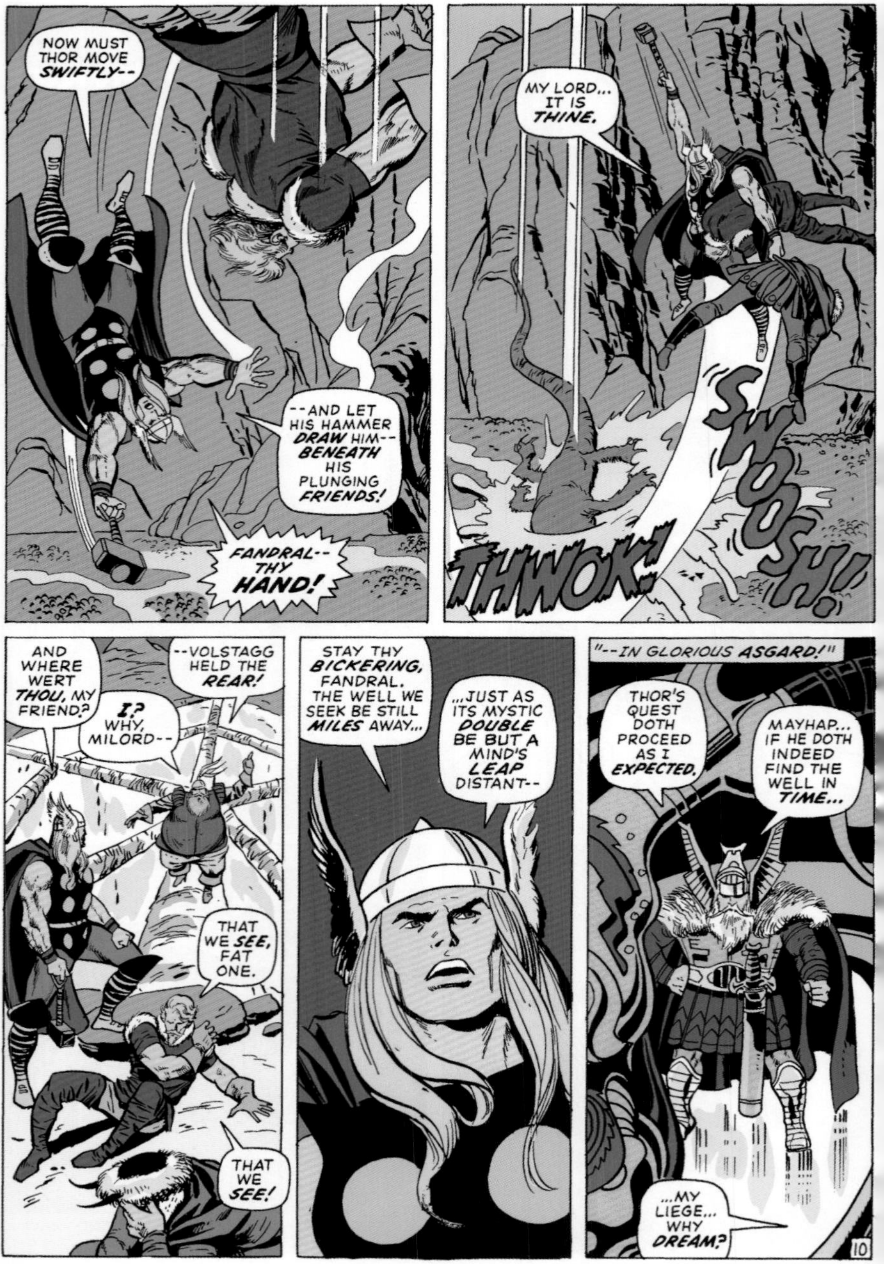

NOW MUST THOR MOVE SWIFTLY--
--AND LET HIS HAMMER DRAW HIM-- BENEATH HIS PLUNGING FRIENDS!
FANDRAL-- THY HAND!
MY LORD... IT IS THINE.
SWOOSH!!
THWOK!
AND WHERE WERT THOU, MY FRIEND?
--VOLSTAGG HELD THE REAR!
I? WHY, MILORD--
THAT WE SEE, FAT ONE.
THAT WE SEE!
STAY THY BICKERING, FANDRAL. THE WELL WE SEEK BE STILL MILES AWAY...
...JUST AS ITS MYSTIC DOUBLE BE BUT A MIND'S LEAP DISTANT--
"--IN GLORIOUS ASGARD!"
THOR'S QUEST DOTH PROCEED AS I EXPECTED.
MAYHAP... IF HE DOTH INDEED FIND THE WELL IN TIME...
...MY LIEGE... WHY DREAM?
10

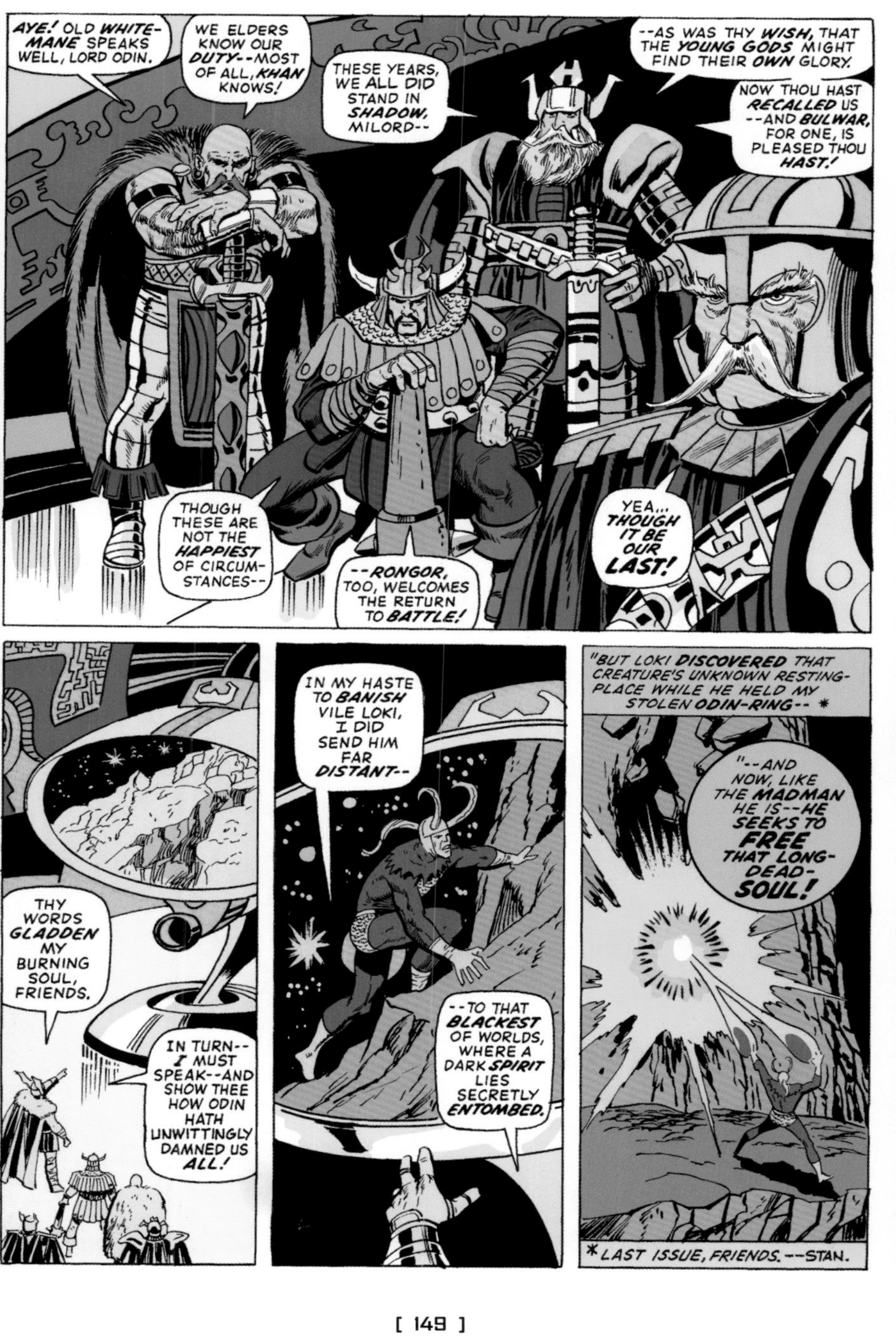
AYE! OLD WHITE-MANE SPEAKS WELL, LORD ODIN.
WE ELDERS KNOW OUR DUTY--MOST OF ALL, KHAN KNOWS!
THESE YEARS, WE ALL DID STAND IN SHADOW, MILORD--
--AS WAS THY WISH, THAT THE YOUNG GODS MIGHT FIND THEIR OWN GLORY.
NOW THOU HAST RECALLED US --AND BULWAR, FOR ONE, IS PLEASED THOU HAST.!
THOUGH THESE ARE NOT THE HAPPIEST OF CIRCUM-STANCES--
--RONGOR, TOO, WELCOMES THE RETURN TO BATTLE!
YEA... THOUGH IT BE OUR LAST!
THY WORDS GLADDEN MY BURNING SOUL, FRIENDS.
IN TURN-- I MUST SPEAK--AND SHOW THEE HOW ODIN HATH UNWITTINGLY DAMNED US ALL!
IN MY HASTE TO BANISH VILE LOKI, I DID SEND HIM FAR DISTANT--
--TO THAT BLACKEST OF WORLDS, WHERE A DARK SPIRIT LIES SECRETLY ENTOMBED.
"BUT LOKI DISCOVERED THAT CREATURE'S UNKNOWN RESTING-PLACE WHILE HE HELD MY STOLEN ODIN-RING-- *
"--AND NOW, LIKE THE MADMAN HE IS--HE SEEKS TO FREE THAT LONG-DEAD-SOUL!
* LAST ISSUE, FRIENDS.--STAN.

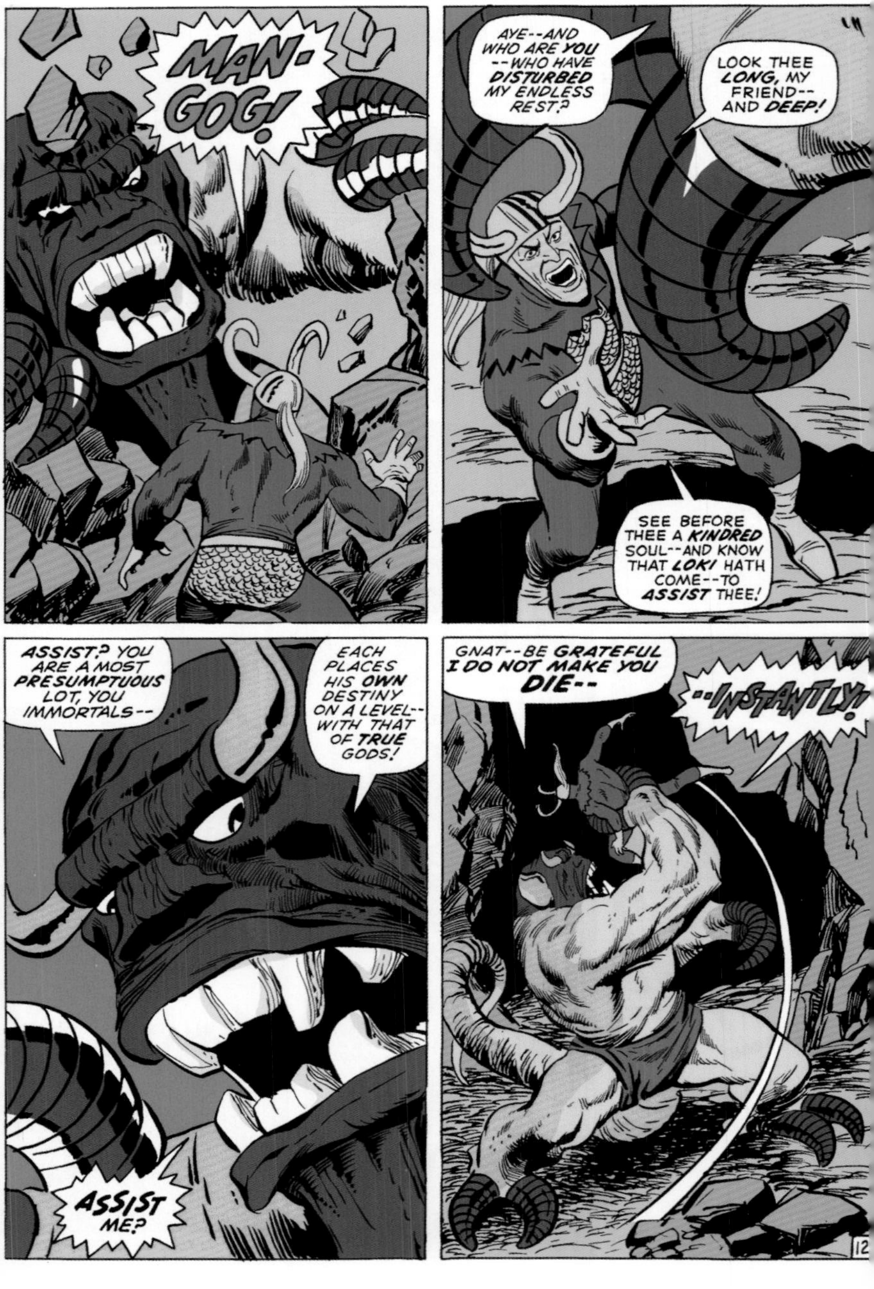
MAN-GOG!
AYE--AND WHO ARE YOU --WHO HAVE DISTURBED MY ENDLESS REST?
LOOK THEE LONG, MY FRIEND--AND DEEP!
SEE BEFORE THEE A KINDRED SOUL--AND KNOW THAT LOKI HATH COME--TO ASSIST THEE!
ASSIST? YOU ARE A MOST PRESUMPTUOUS LOT, YOU IMMORTALS--
EACH PLACES HIS OWN DESTINY ON A LEVEL--WITH THAT OF TRUE GODS!
ASSIST ME?
GNAT--BE GRATEFUL I DO NOT MAKE YOU DIE--
--INSTANTLY!
12

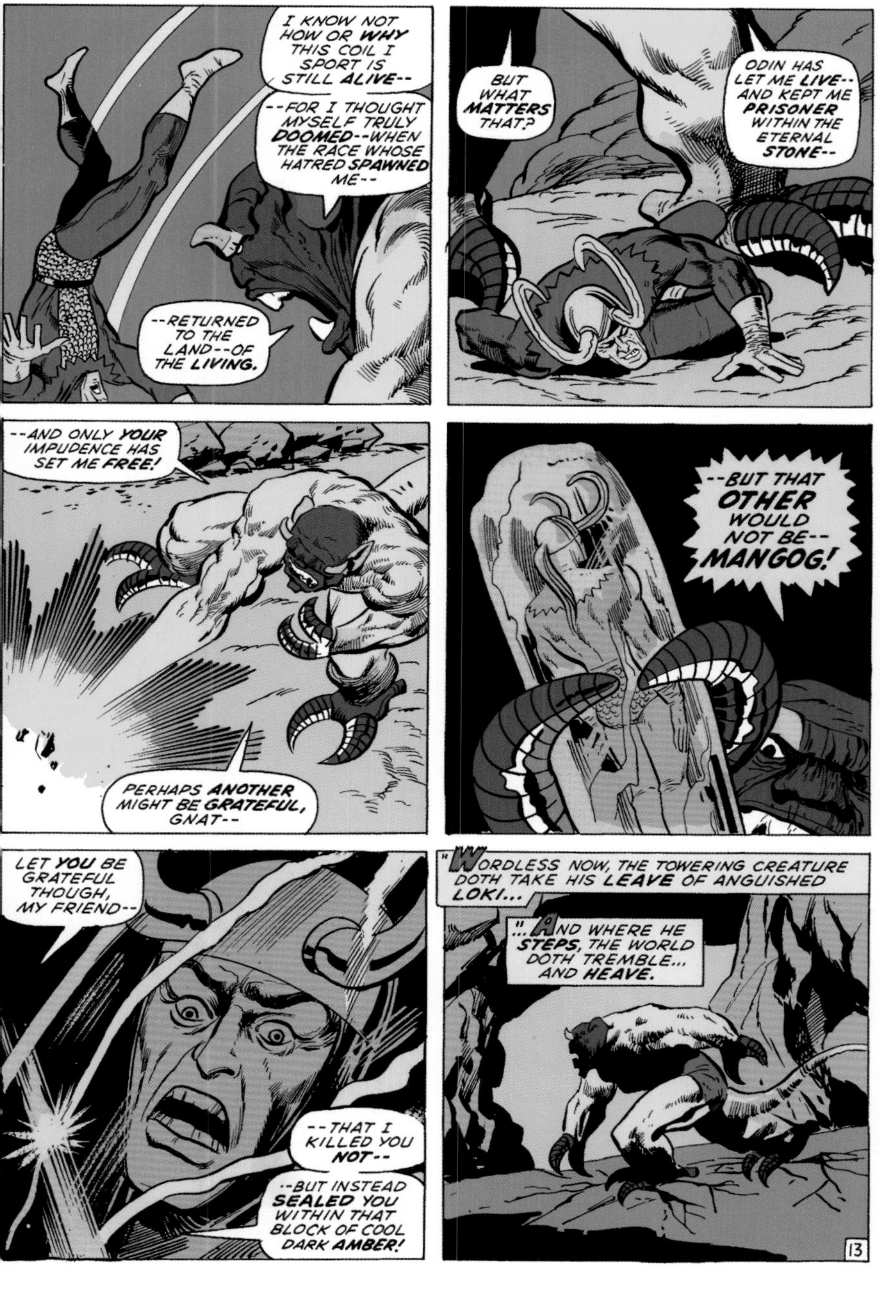
I KNOW NOT HOW OR WHY THIS COIL I SPORT IS STILL ALIVE--
--FOR I THOUGHT MYSELF TRULY DOOMED--WHEN THE RACE WHOSE HATRED SPAWNED ME--
--RETURNED TO THE LAND--OF THE LIVING.
BUT WHAT MATTERS THAT?
ODIN HAS LET ME LIVE--AND KEPT ME PRISONER WITHIN THE ETERNAL STONE--
--AND ONLY YOUR IMPUDENCE HAS SET ME FREE!
PERHAPS ANOTHER MIGHT BE GRATEFUL, GNAT--
--BUT THAT OTHER WOULD NOT BE--MANGOG!
LET YOU BE GRATEFUL THOUGH, MY FRIEND--
--THAT I KILLED YOU NOT--
--BUT INSTEAD SEALED YOU WITHIN THAT BLOCK OF COOL DARK AMBER!
"WORDLESS NOW, THE TOWERING CREATURE DOTH TAKE HIS LEAVE OF ANGUISHED LOKI...
"...AND WHERE HE STEPS, THE WORLD DOTH TREMBLE... AND HEAVE.
13

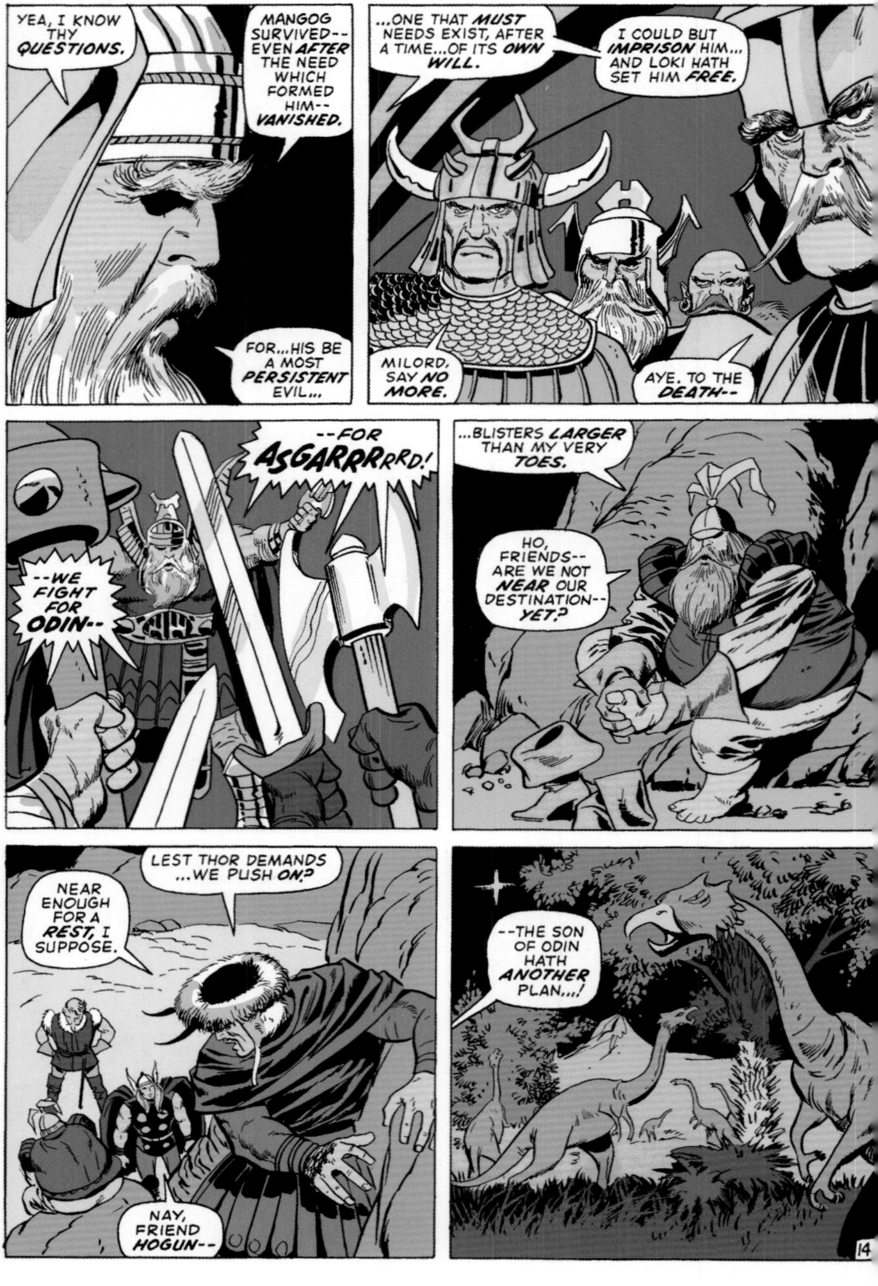

YEA, I KNOW THY QUESTIONS.
MANGOG SURVIVED-- EVEN AFTER THE NEED WHICH FORMED HIM-- VANISHED.
FOR...HIS BE A MOST PERSISTENT EVIL...
...ONE THAT MUST NEEDS EXIST, AFTER A TIME...OF ITS OWN WILL.
I COULD BUT IMPRISON HIM... AND LOKI HATH SET HIM FREE.
MILORD, SAY NO MORE.
AYE. TO THE DEATH--
--WE FIGHT FOR ODIN--
--FOR ASGARRRRRRD!
...BLISTERS LARGER THAN MY VERY TOES.
HO, FRIENDS-- ARE WE NOT NEAR OUR DESTINATION-- YET?
LEST THOR DEMANDS ...WE PUSH ON?
NEAR ENOUGH FOR A REST, I SUPPOSE.
NAY, FRIEND HOGUN--
--THE SON OF ODIN HATH ANOTHER PLAN...!
14

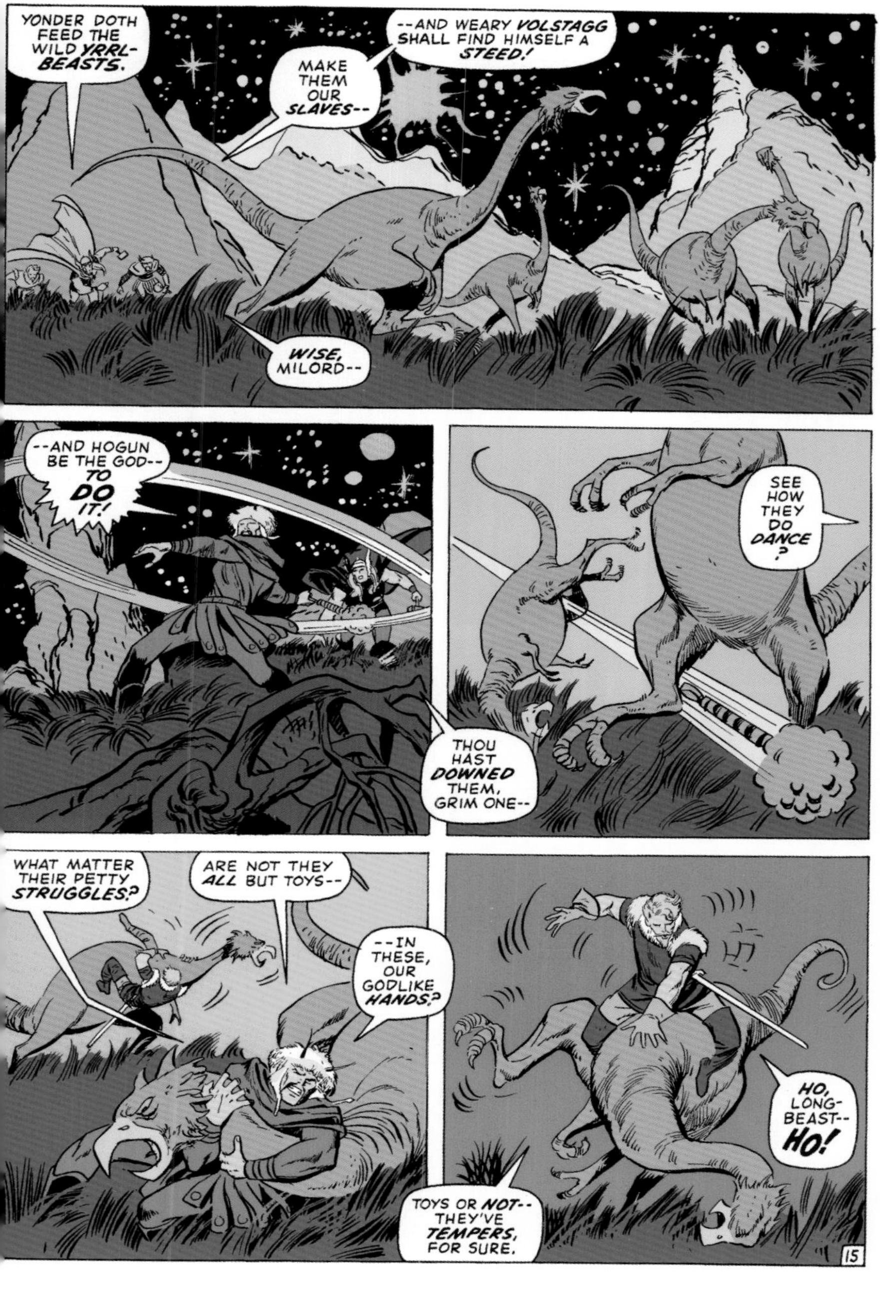

YONDER DOTH FEED THE WILD YRRL-BEASTS.
MAKE THEM OUR SLAVES--
--AND WEARY VOLSTAGG SHALL FIND HIMSELF A STEED!
WISE, MILORD--
--AND HOGUN BE THE GOD-- TO DO IT!
THOU HAST DOWNED THEM, GRIM ONE--
SEE HOW THEY DO DANCE?
WHAT MATTER THEIR PETTY STRUGGLES?
ARE NOT THEY ALL BUT TOYS--
--IN THESE, OUR GODLIKE HANDS?
TOYS OR NOT-- THEY'VE TEMPERS, FOR SURE.
HO, LONG-BEAST-- HO!
15

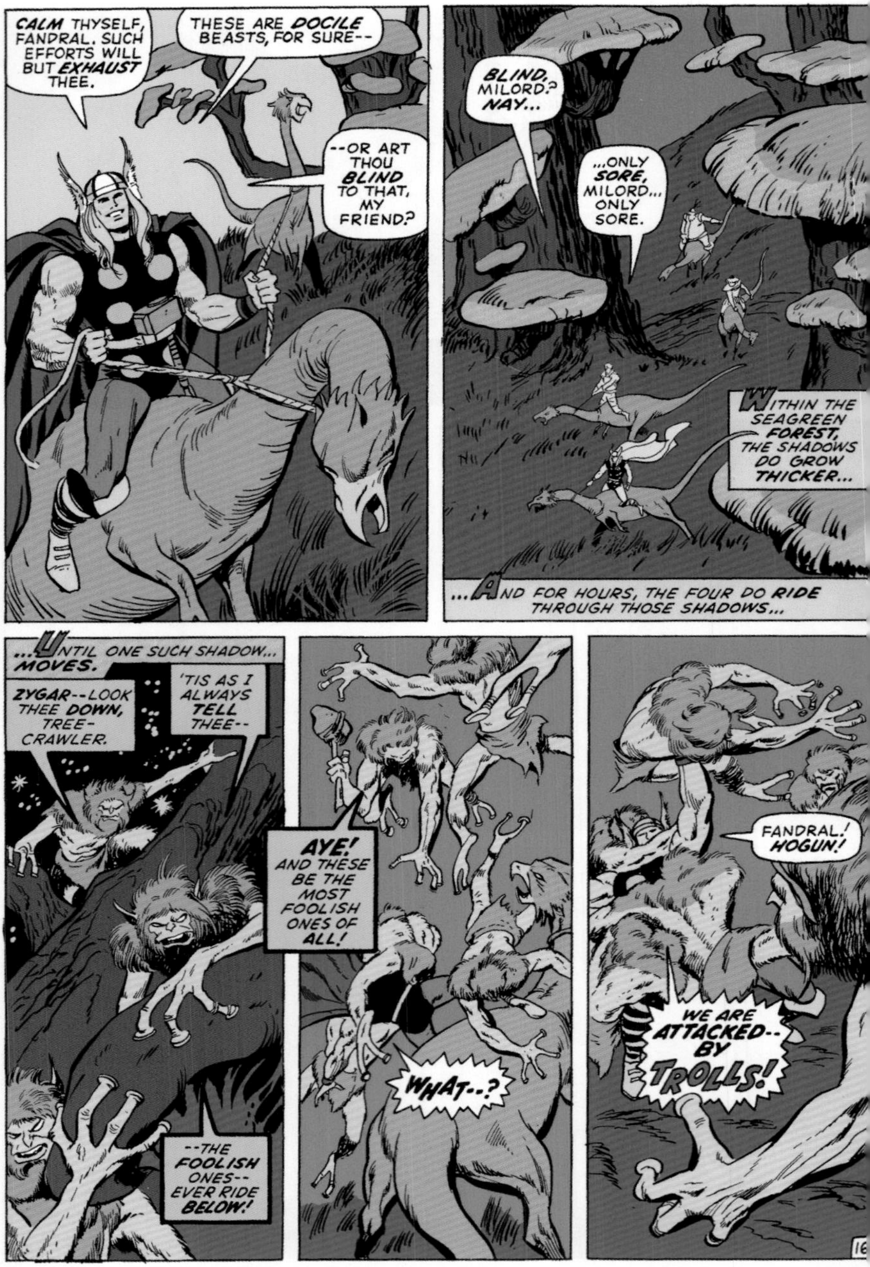
CALM THYSELF, FANDRAL. SUCH EFFORTS WILL BUT EXHAUST THEE.
THESE ARE DOCILE BEASTS, FOR SURE--
--OR ART THOU BLIND TO THAT, MY FRIEND?
BLIND, MILORD? NAY...
...ONLY SORE, MILORD... ONLY SORE.
WITHIN THE SEAGREEN FOREST, THE SHADOWS DO GROW THICKER...
...AND FOR HOURS, THE FOUR DO RIDE THROUGH THOSE SHADOWS...
...UNTIL ONE SUCH SHADOW... MOVES.
ZYGAR--LOOK THEE DOWN, TREE-CRAWLER.
'TIS AS I ALWAYS TELL THEE--
--THE FOOLISH ONES--EVER RIDE BELOW!
AYE! AND THESE BE THE MOST FOOLISH ONES OF ALL!
WHAT--?
FANDRAL! HOGUN!
WE ARE ATTACKED--BY TROLLS!
16

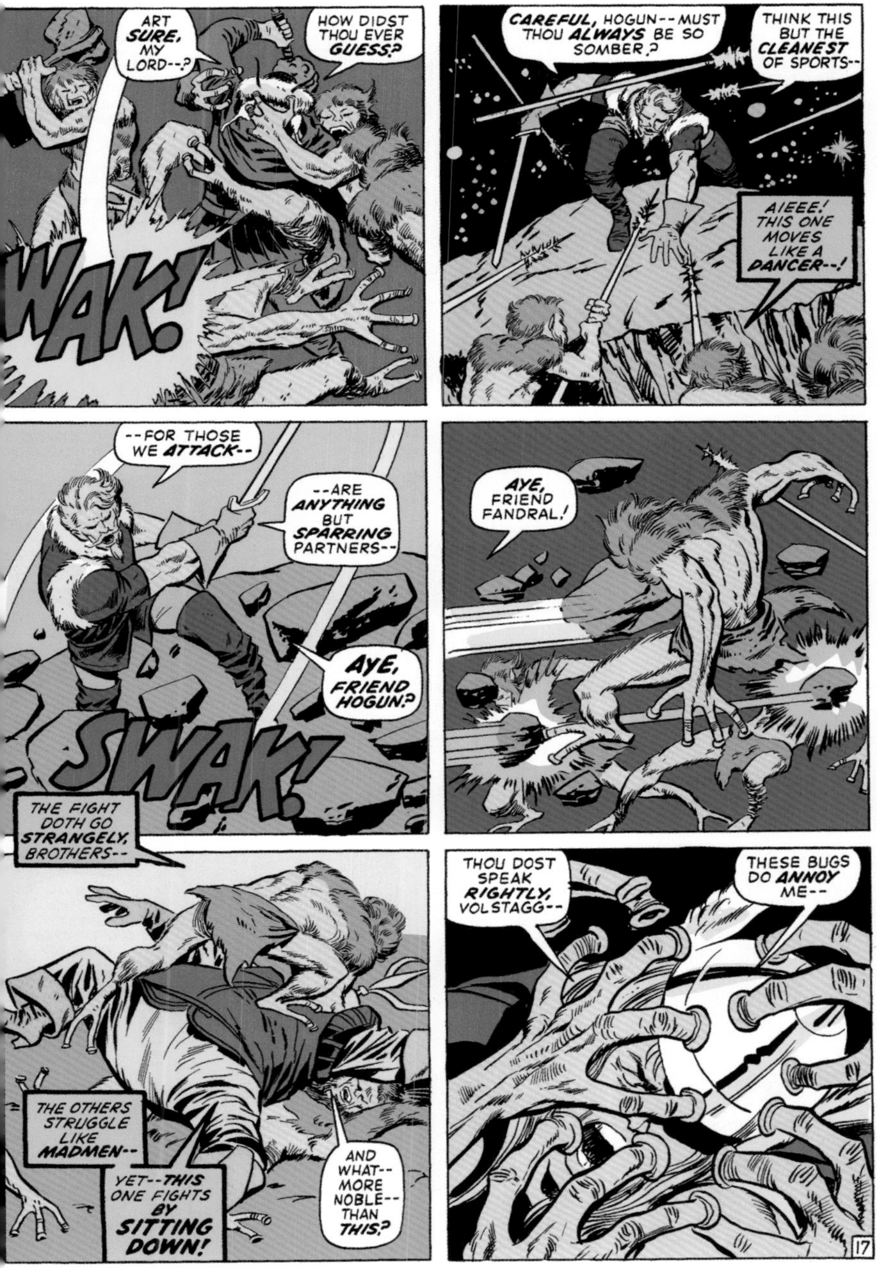

ART SURE, MY LORD--?
HOW DIDST THOU EVER GUESS?
WAK!
CAREFUL, HOGUN--MUST THOU ALWAYS BE SO SOMBER?
THINK THIS BUT THE CLEANEST OF SPORTS--
AIEEE! THIS ONE MOVES LIKE A DANCER--!
--FOR THOSE WE ATTACK--
--ARE ANYTHING BUT SPARRING PARTNERS--
AYE, FRIEND HOGUN?
SWAK!
AYE, FRIEND FANDRAL!
THE FIGHT DOTH GO STRANGELY, BROTHERS--
THE OTHERS STRUGGLE LIKE MADMEN--
YET--THIS ONE FIGHTS BY SITTING DOWN!
AND WHAT--MORE NOBLE--THAN THIS?
THOU DOST SPEAK RIGHTLY, VOLSTAGG--
THESE BUGS DO ANNOY ME--
17

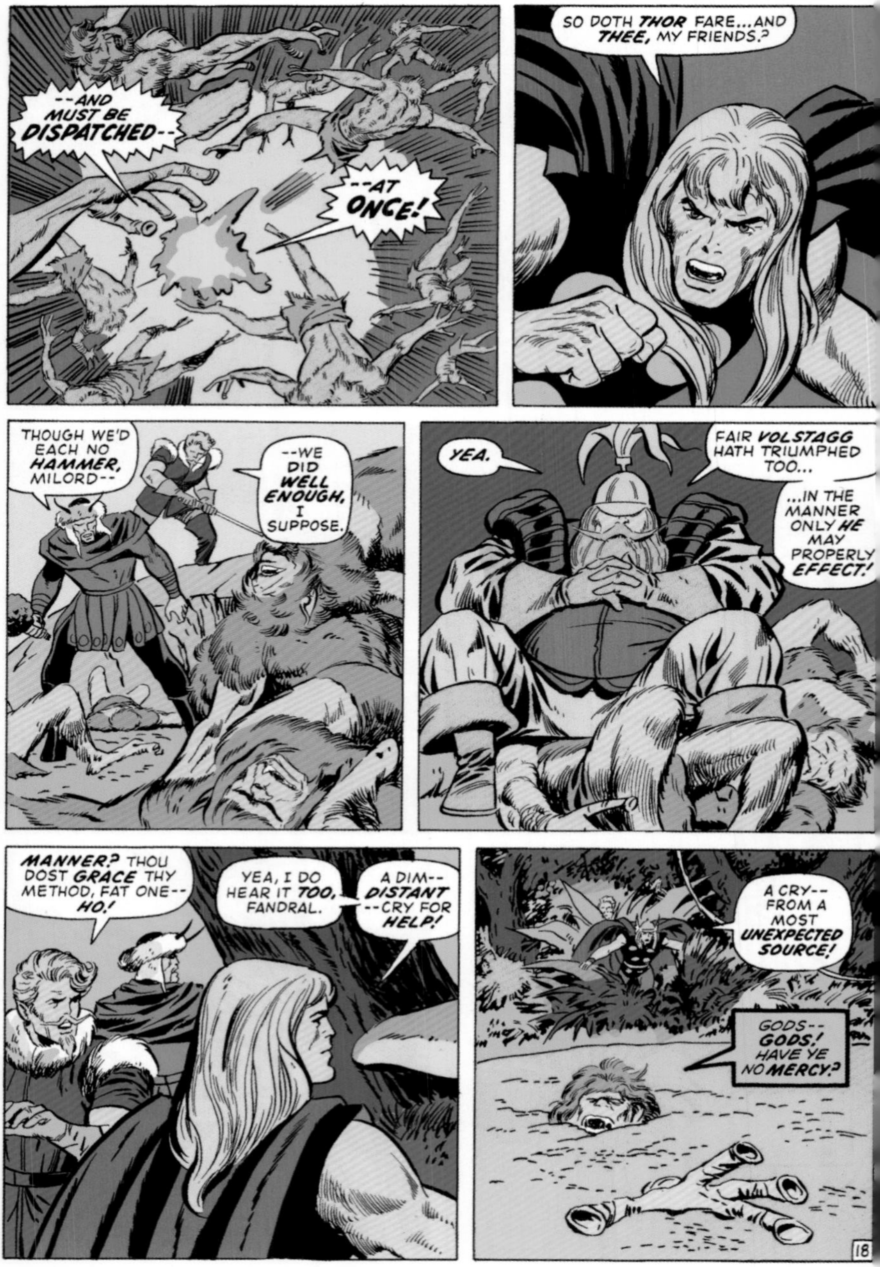
--AND MUST BE DISPATCHED--
--AT ONCE!
SO DOTH THOR FARE...AND THEE, MY FRIENDS?
THOUGH WE'D EACH NO HAMMER, MILORD--
--WE DID WELL ENOUGH, I SUPPOSE.
YEA.
FAIR VOLSTAGG HATH TRIUMPHED TOO...
...IN THE MANNER ONLY HE MAY PROPERLY EFFECT!
MANNER? THOU DOST GRACE THY METHOD, FAT ONE-- HO!
YEA, I DO HEAR IT TOO, FANDRAL.
A DIM-- DISTANT --CRY FOR HELP!
A CRY-- FROM A MOST UNEXPECTED SOURCE!
GODS-- GODS! HAVE YE NO MERCY?
18

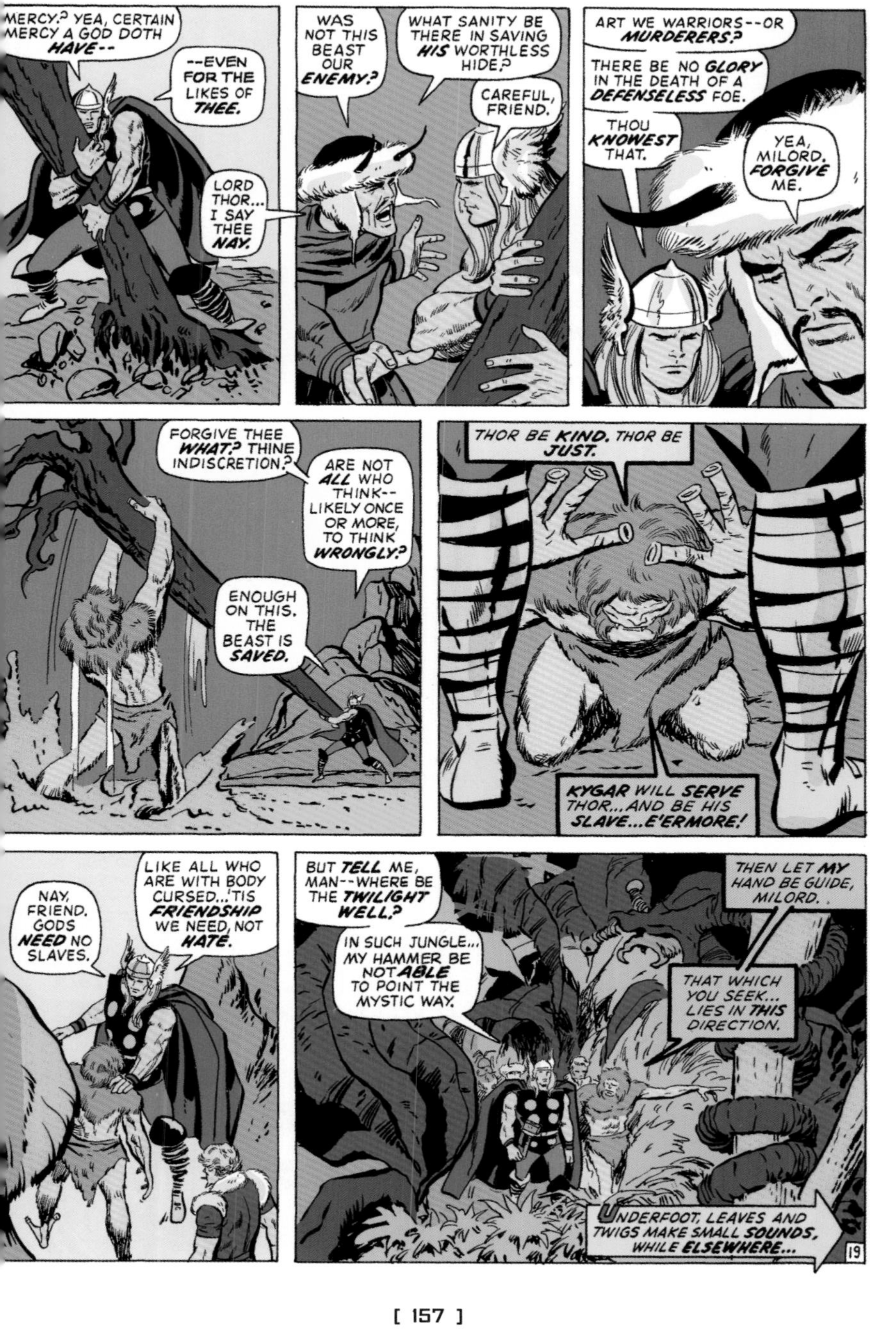
MERCY? YEA, CERTAIN MERCY A GOD DOTH HAVE--
--EVEN FOR THE LIKES OF THEE.
LORD THOR... I SAY THEE NAY.
WAS NOT THIS BEAST OUR ENEMY?
WHAT SANITY BE THERE IN SAVING HIS WORTHLESS HIDE?
CAREFUL, FRIEND.
ART WE WARRIORS--OR MURDERERS?
THERE BE NO GLORY IN THE DEATH OF A DEFENSELESS FOE.
THOU KNOWEST THAT.
YEA, MILORD. FORGIVE ME.
FORGIVE THEE WHAT? THINE INDISCRETION?
ARE NOT ALL WHO THINK--LIKELY ONCE OR MORE, TO THINK WRONGLY?
ENOUGH ON THIS. THE BEAST IS SAVED.
THOR BE KIND. THOR BE JUST.
KYGAR WILL SERVE THOR...AND BE HIS SLAVE...E'ERMORE!
NAY, FRIEND. GODS NEED NO SLAVES.
LIKE ALL WHO ARE WITH BODY CURSED...'TIS FRIENDSHIP WE NEED, NOT HATE.
BUT TELL ME, MAN--WHERE BE THE TWILIGHT WELL?
IN SUCH JUNGLE... MY HAMMER BE NOT ABLE TO POINT THE MYSTIC WAY.
THEN LET MY HAND BE GUIDE, MILORD.
THAT WHICH YOU SEEK... LIES IN THIS DIRECTION.
UNDERFOOT, LEAVES AND TWIGS MAKE SMALL SOUNDS, WHILE ELSEWHERE...
19

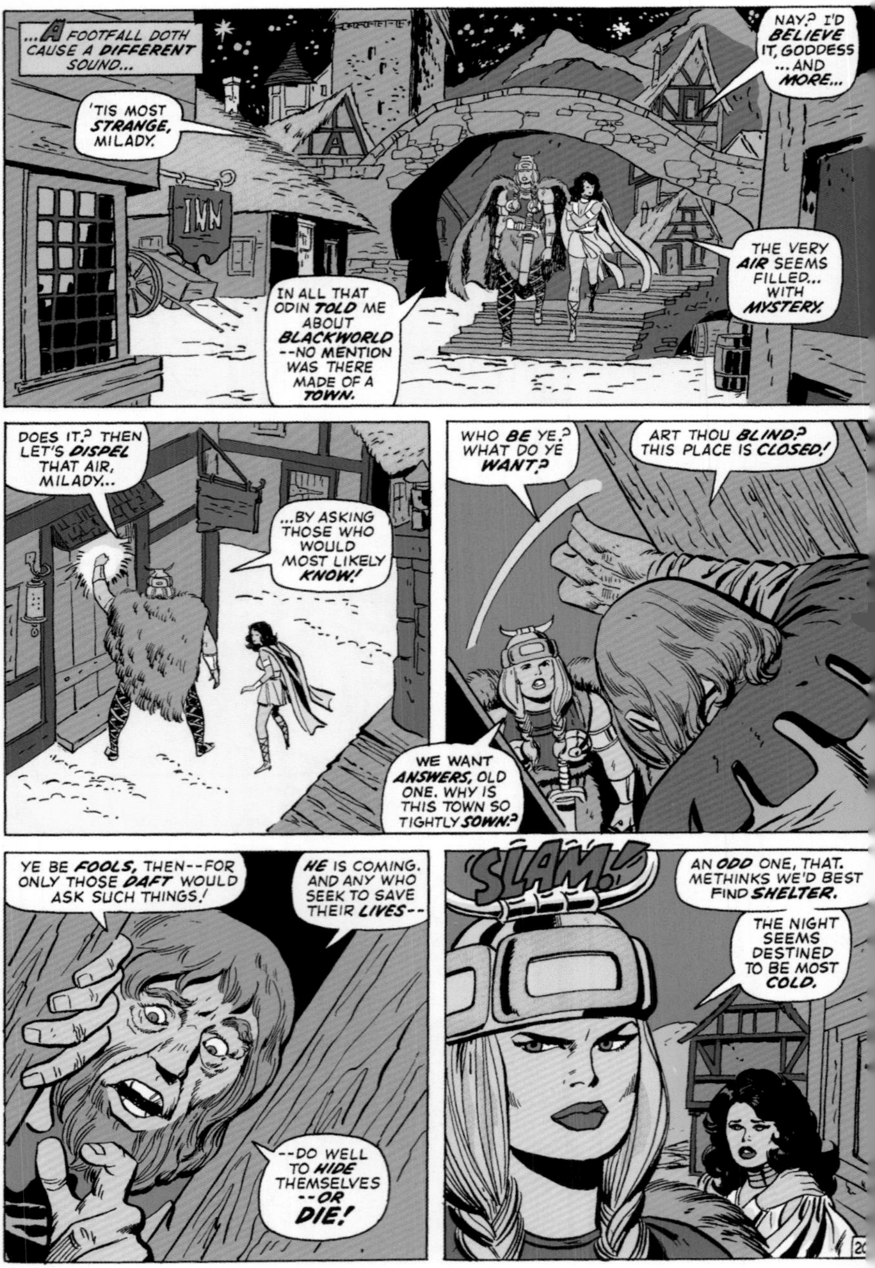
...A FOOTFALL DOTH CAUSE A DIFFERENT SOUND...
'TIS MOST STRANGE, MILADY.
NAY? I'D BELIEVE IT, GODDESS ...AND MORE...
IN ALL THAT ODIN TOLD ME ABOUT BLACKWORLD --NO MENTION WAS THERE MADE OF A TOWN.
THE VERY AIR SEEMS FILLED... WITH MYSTERY.
DOES IT? THEN LET'S DISPEL THAT AIR, MILADY...
...BY ASKING THOSE WHO WOULD MOST LIKELY KNOW!
WHO BE YE? WHAT DO YE WANT?
ART THOU BLIND? THIS PLACE IS CLOSED!
WE WANT ANSWERS, OLD ONE. WHY IS THIS TOWN SO TIGHTLY SOWN?
YE BE FOOLS, THEN--FOR ONLY THOSE DAFT WOULD ASK SUCH THINGS!
HE IS COMING. AND ANY WHO SEEK TO SAVE THEIR LIVES--
--DO WELL TO HIDE THEMSELVES --OR DIE!
SLAM!
AN ODD ONE, THAT. METHINKS WE'D BEST FIND SHELTER.
THE NIGHT SEEMS DESTINED TO BE MOST COLD.

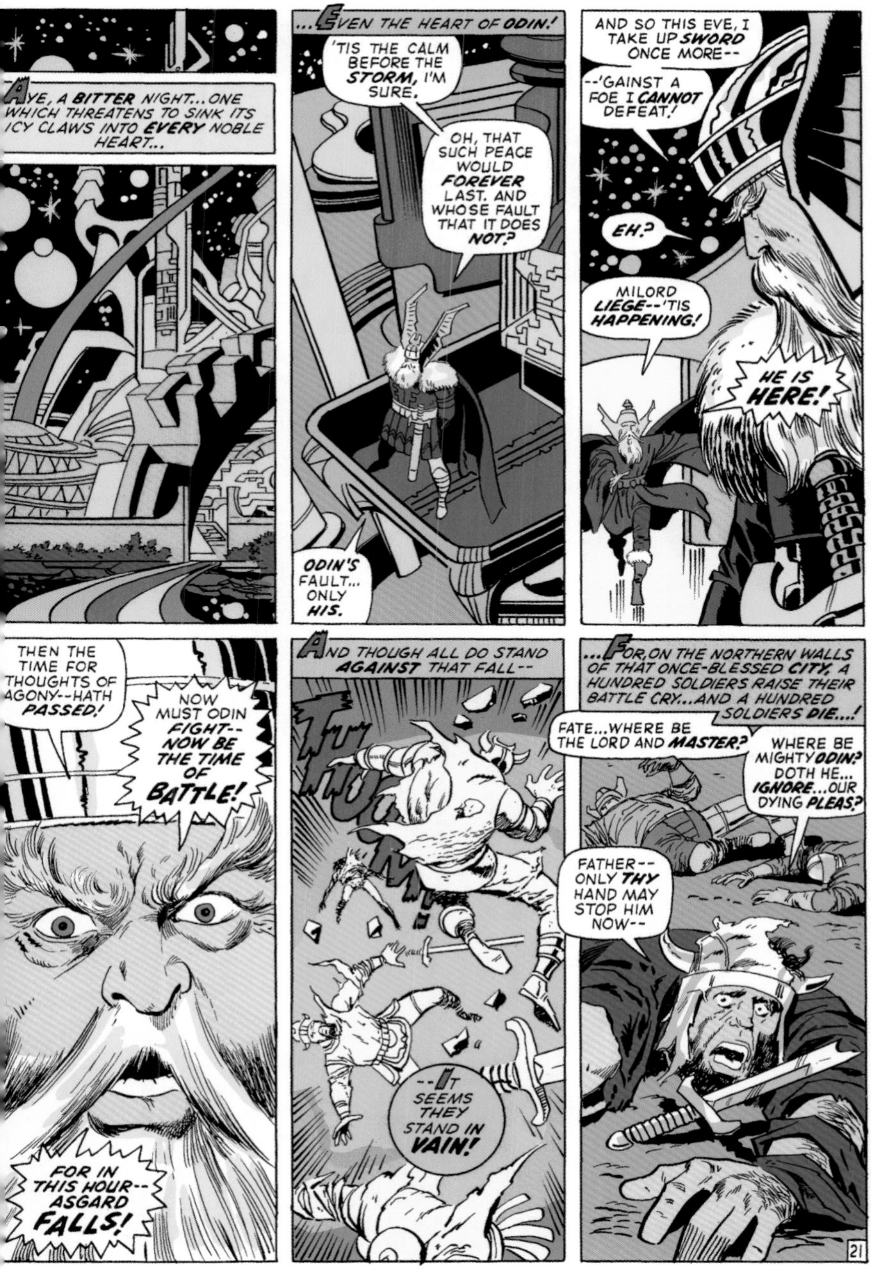
AYE, A BITTER NIGHT... ONE WHICH THREATENS TO SINK ITS ICY CLAWS INTO EVERY NOBLE HEART...
...EVEN THE HEART OF ODIN!
'TIS THE CALM BEFORE THE STORM, I'M SURE.
OH, THAT SUCH PEACE WOULD FOREVER LAST. AND WHOSE FAULT THAT IT DOES NOT?
ODIN'S FAULT... ONLY HIS.
AND SO THIS EVE, I TAKE UP SWORD ONCE MORE--
--'GAINST A FOE I CANNOT DEFEAT!
EH?
MILORD LIEGE--'TIS HAPPENING!
HE IS HERE!
THEN THE TIME FOR THOUGHTS OF AGONY--HATH PASSED!
NOW MUST ODIN FIGHT-- NOW BE THE TIME OF BATTLE!
FOR IN THIS HOUR-- ASGARD FALLS!
AND THOUGH ALL DO STAND AGAINST THAT FALL--
--IT SEEMS THEY STAND IN VAIN!
...FOR, ON THE NORTHERN WALLS OF THAT ONCE-BLESSED CITY, A HUNDRED SOLDIERS RAISE THEIR BATTLE CRY...AND A HUNDRED SOLDIERS DIE...!
FATE...WHERE BE THE LORD AND MASTER?
WHERE BE MIGHTY ODIN? DOTH HE... IGNORE...OUR DYING PLEAS?
FATHER-- ONLY THY HAND MAY STOP HIM NOW--
21

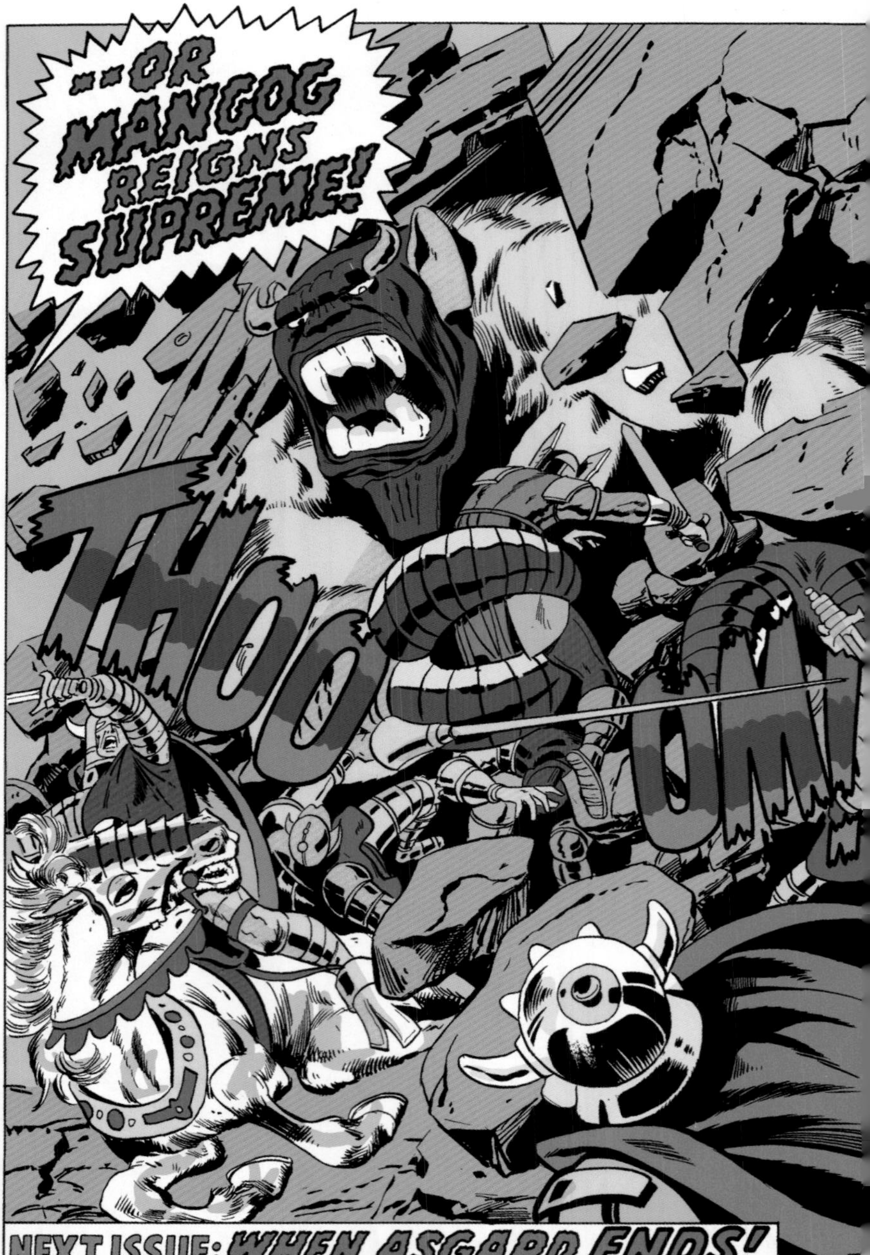
--OR MANGOG REIGNS SUPREME!
THOOOM!
NEXT ISSUE: WHEN ASGARD ENDS!
2

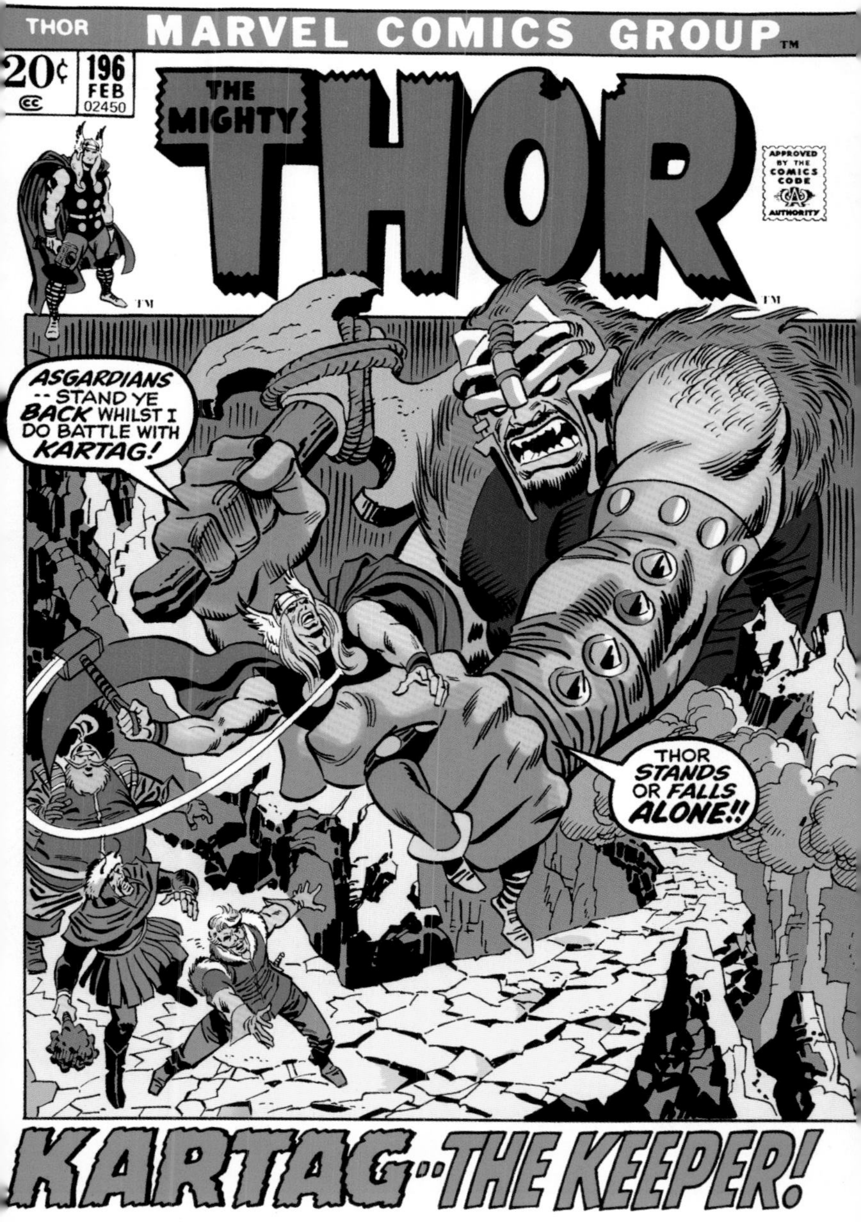
THOR
MARVEL COMICS GROUP
20¢
196
FEB
02450
THE MIGHTY
THOR
APPROVED BY THE COMICS CODE AUTHORITY
ASGARDIANS -- STAND YE BACK WHILST I DO BATTLE WITH KARTAG!
THOR STANDS OR FALLS ALONE!!
KARTAG -- THE KEEPER!

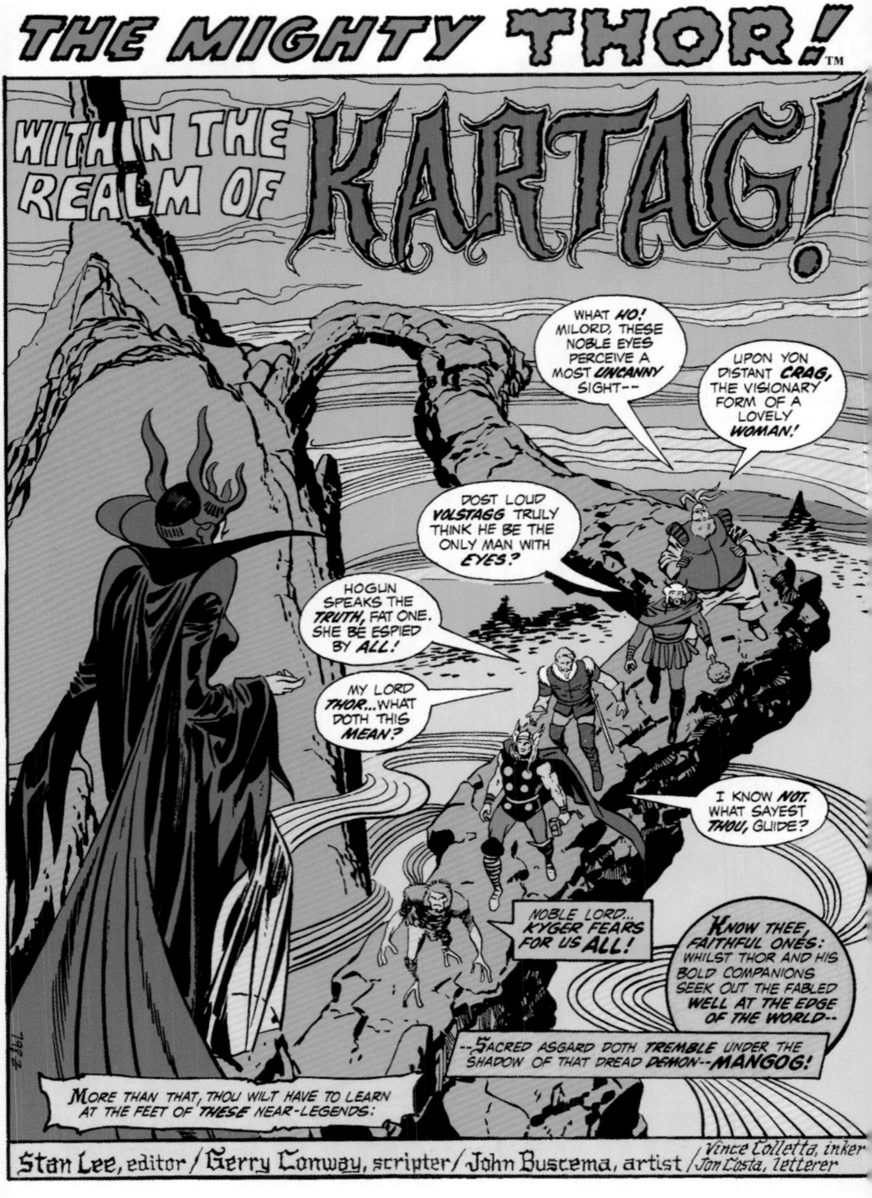
THE MIGHTY THOR!™
WITHIN THE REALM OF KARTAG!
WHAT HO! MILORD, THESE NOBLE EYES PERCEIVE A MOST UNCANNY SIGHT--
UPON YON DISTANT CRAG, THE VISIONARY FORM OF A LOVELY WOMAN!
DOST LOUD VOLSTAGG TRULY THINK HE BE THE ONLY MAN WITH EYES?
HOGUN SPEAKS THE TRUTH, FAT ONE. SHE BE ESPIED BY ALL!
MY LORD THOR... WHAT DOTH THIS MEAN?
I KNOW NOT. WHAT SAYEST THOU, GUIDE?
NOBLE LORD... KYGER FEARS FOR US ALL!
KNOW THEE, FAITHFUL ONES: WHILST THOR AND HIS BOLD COMPANIONS SEEK OUT THE FABLED WELL AT THE EDGE OF THE WORLD--
--SACRED ASGARD DOTH TREMBLE UNDER THE SHADOW OF THAT DREAD DEMON--MANGOG!
MORE THAN THAT, THOU WILT HAVE TO LEARN AT THE FEET OF THESE NEAR-LEGENDS:
Stan Lee, editor / Gerry Conway, scripter / John Buscema, artist / Vince Colletta, inker / Jon Costa, letterer

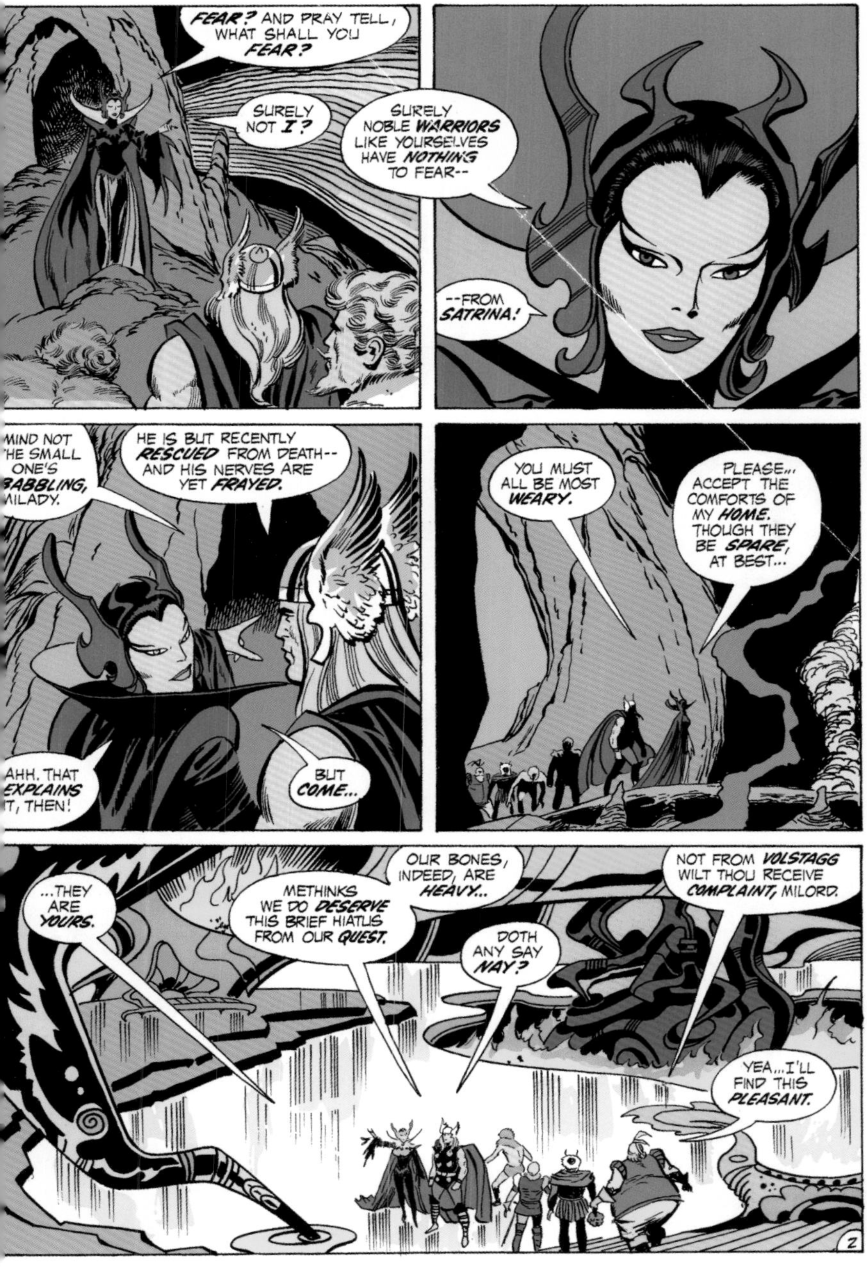
FEAR? AND PRAY TELL, WHAT SHALL YOU FEAR?
SURELY NOT I?
SURELY NOBLE WARRIORS LIKE YOURSELVES HAVE NOTHING TO FEAR--
--FROM SATRINA!
MIND NOT THE SMALL ONE'S BABBLING, MILADY.
HE IS BUT RECENTLY RESCUED FROM DEATH-- AND HIS NERVES ARE YET FRAYED.
AHH. THAT EXPLAINS IT, THEN!
BUT COME...
YOU MUST ALL BE MOST WEARY.
PLEASE... ACCEPT THE COMFORTS OF MY HOME. THOUGH THEY BE SPARE, AT BEST...
...THEY ARE YOURS.
METHINKS WE DO DESERVE THIS BRIEF HIATUS FROM OUR QUEST.
OUR BONES, INDEED, ARE HEAVY...
DOTH ANY SAY NAY?
NOT FROM VOLSTAGG WILT THOU RECEIVE COMPLAINT, MILORD.
YEA...I'LL FIND THIS PLEASANT.
2

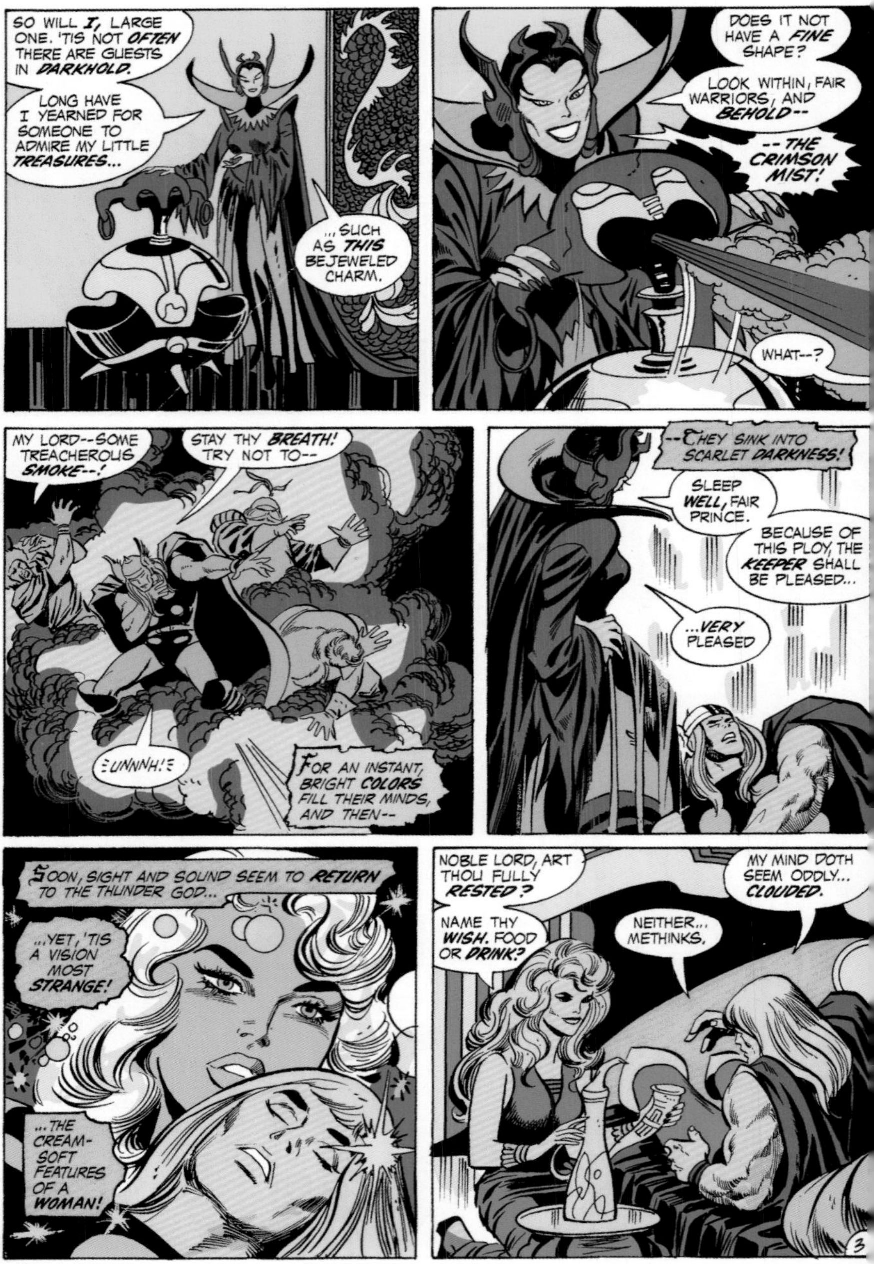

SO WILL I, LARGE ONE. 'TIS NOT OFTEN THERE ARE GUESTS IN DARKHOLD.
LONG HAVE I YEARNED FOR SOMEONE TO ADMIRE MY LITTLE TREASURES...
...SUCH AS THIS BEJEWELED CHARM.
DOES IT NOT HAVE A FINE SHAPE?
LOOK WITHIN, FAIR WARRIORS, AND BEHOLD--
--THE CRIMSON MIST!
WHAT--?
MY LORD--SOME TREACHEROUS SMOKE--!
STAY THY BREATH! TRY NOT TO--
UNNNH!
FOR AN INSTANT, BRIGHT COLORS FILL THEIR MINDS, AND THEN--
--THEY SINK INTO SCARLET DARKNESS!
SLEEP WELL, FAIR PRINCE.
BECAUSE OF THIS PLOY, THE KEEPER SHALL BE PLEASED...
...VERY PLEASED
SOON, SIGHT AND SOUND SEEM TO RETURN TO THE THUNDER GOD...
...YET, 'TIS A VISION MOST STRANGE!
...THE CREAM-SOFT FEATURES OF A WOMAN!
NOBLE LORD, ART THOU FULLY RESTED?
NAME THY WISH. FOOD OR DRINK?
NEITHER... METHINKS.
MY MIND DOTH SEEM ODDLY... CLOUDED.
3

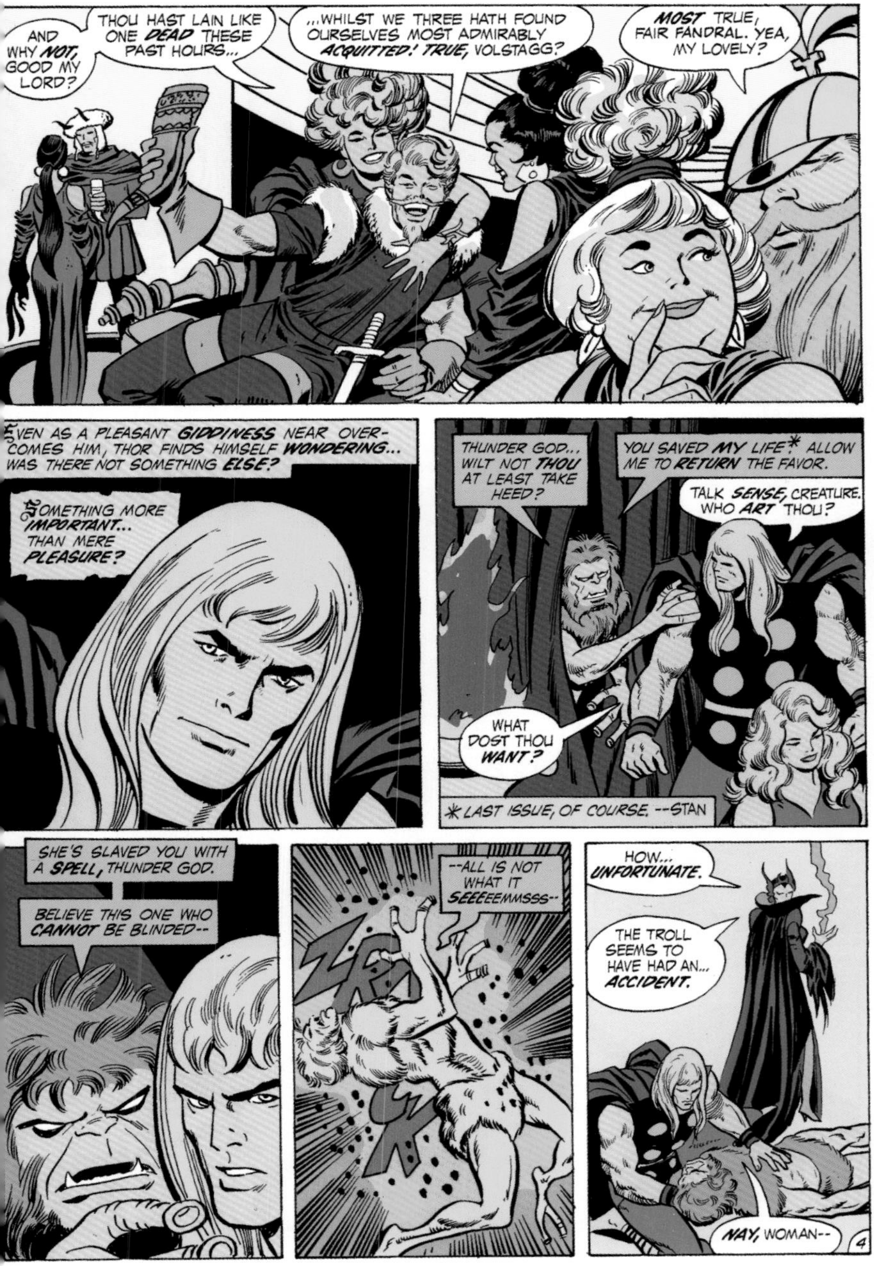
AND WHY NOT, GOOD MY LORD?
THOU HAST LAIN LIKE ONE DEAD THESE PAST HOURS...
...WHILST WE THREE HATH FOUND OURSELVES MOST ADMIRABLY ACQUITTED! TRUE, VOLSTAGG?
MOST TRUE, FAIR FANDRAL. YEA, MY LOVELY?
EVEN AS A PLEASANT GIDDINESS NEAR OVER-COMES HIM, THOR FINDS HIMSELF WONDERING... WAS THERE NOT SOMETHING ELSE?
SOMETHING MORE IMPORTANT... THAN MERE PLEASURE?
THUNDER GOD... WILT NOT THOU AT LEAST TAKE HEED?
YOU SAVED MY LIFE!* ALLOW ME TO RETURN THE FAVOR.
TALK SENSE, CREATURE. WHO ART THOU?
WHAT DOST THOU WANT?
*LAST ISSUE, OF COURSE. --STAN
SHE'S SLAVED YOU WITH A SPELL, THUNDER GOD.
BELIEVE THIS ONE WHO CANNOT BE BLINDED--
--ALL IS NOT WHAT IT SEEEEEMMSSS--
HOW... UNFORTUNATE.
THE TROLL SEEMS TO HAVE HAD AN... ACCIDENT.
NAY, WOMAN--
4

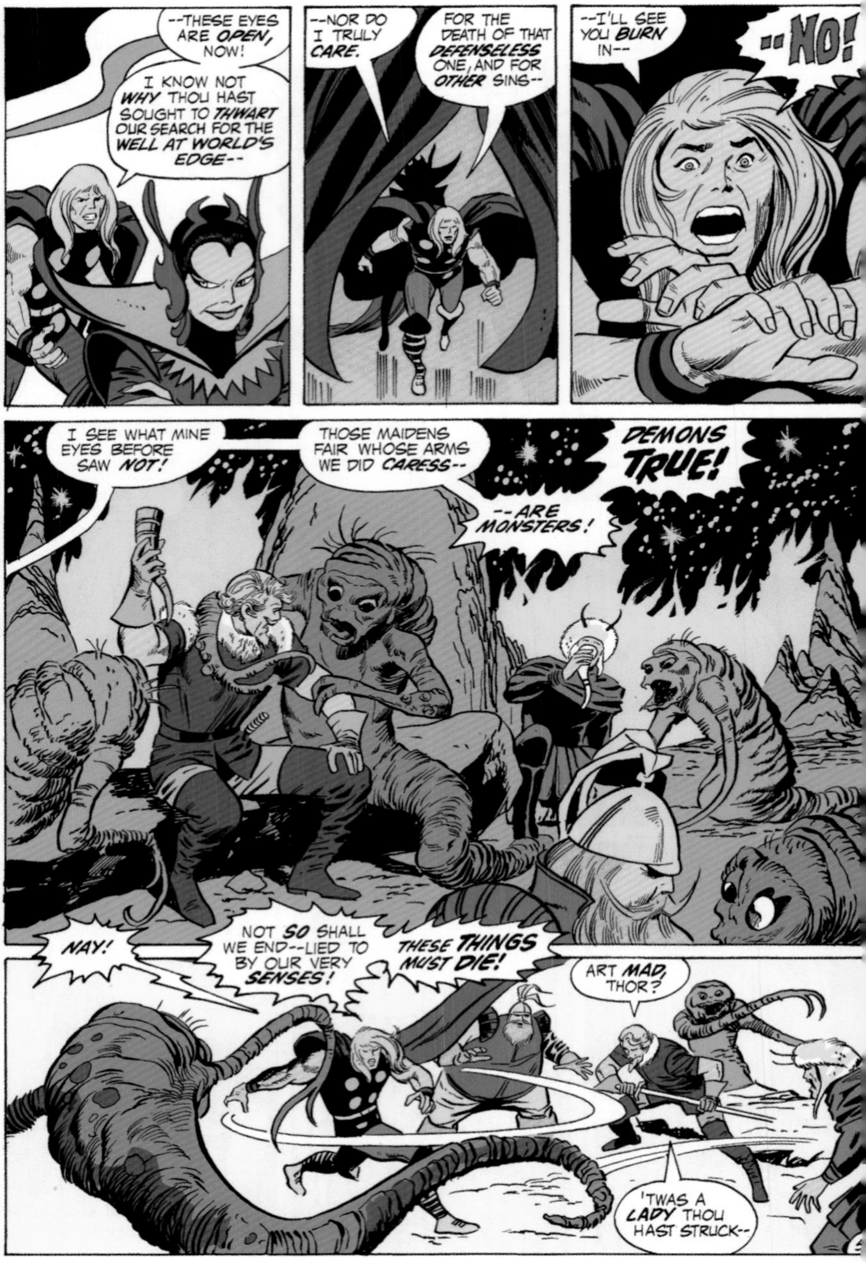
--THESE EYES ARE OPEN, NOW!
I KNOW NOT WHY THOU HAST SOUGHT TO THWART OUR SEARCH FOR THE WELL AT WORLD'S EDGE--
--NOR DO I TRULY CARE.
FOR THE DEATH OF THAT DEFENSELESS ONE, AND FOR OTHER SINS--
--I'LL SEE YOU BURN IN--
--NO!
I SEE WHAT MINE EYES BEFORE SAW NOT!
THOSE MAIDENS FAIR WHOSE ARMS WE DID CARESS--
--ARE MONSTERS!
DEMONS TRUE!
NAY!
NOT SO SHALL WE END--LIED TO BY OUR VERY SENSES!
THESE THINGS MUST DIE!
ART MAD, THOR?
'TWAS A LADY THOU HAST STRUCK--

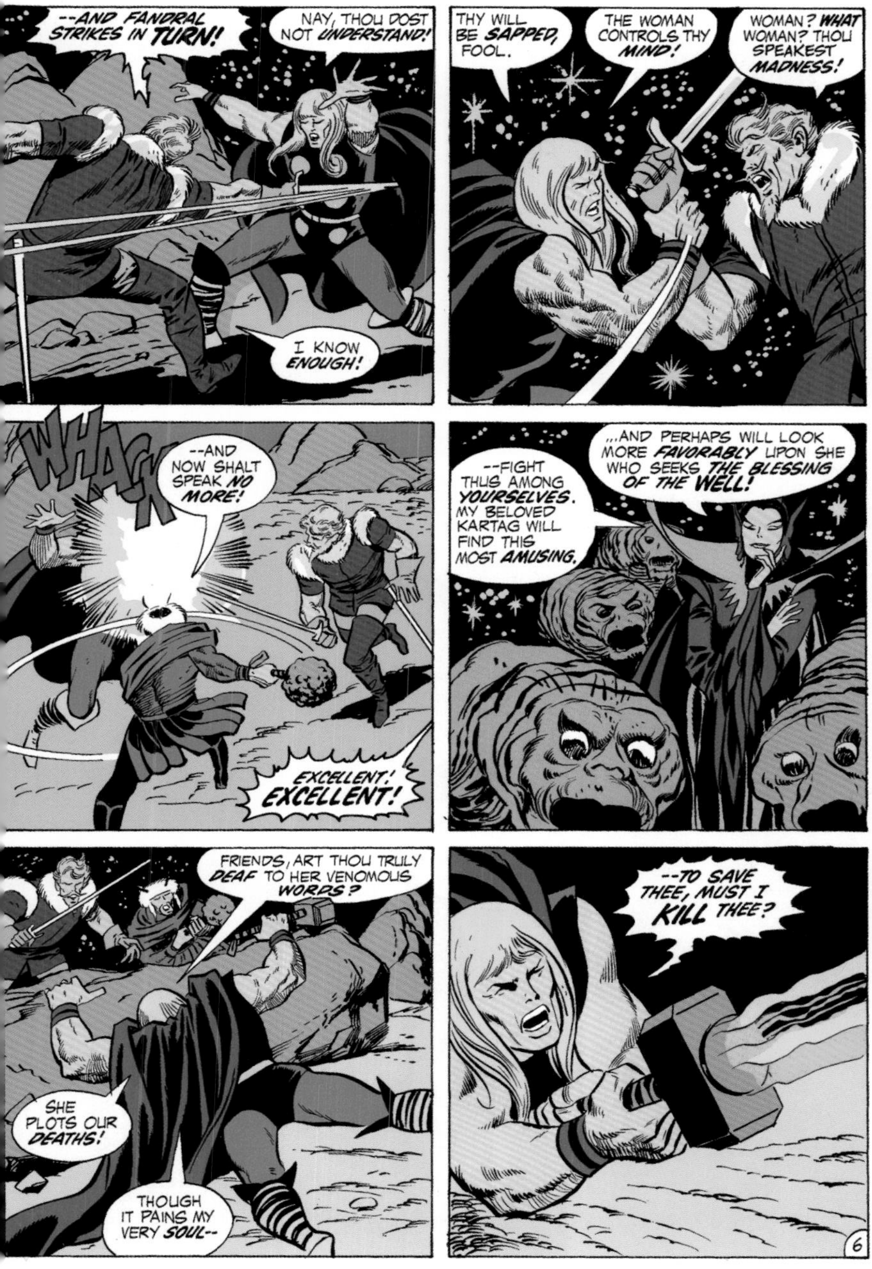
--AND FANDRAL STRIKES IN TURN!
NAY, THOU DOST NOT UNDERSTAND!
I KNOW ENOUGH!
THY WILL BE SAPPED, FOOL.
THE WOMAN CONTROLS THY MIND!
WOMAN? WHAT WOMAN? THOU SPEAKEST MADNESS!
WHACK
--AND NOW SHALT SPEAK NO MORE!
EXCELLENT! EXCELLENT!
--FIGHT THUS AMONG YOURSELVES. MY BELOVED KARTAG WILL FIND THIS MOST AMUSING.
...AND PERHAPS WILL LOOK MORE FAVORABLY UPON SHE WHO SEEKS THE BLESSING OF THE WELL!
FRIENDS, ART THOU TRULY DEAF TO HER VENOMOUS WORDS?
SHE PLOTS OUR DEATHS!
THOUGH IT PAINS MY VERY SOUL--
--TO SAVE THEE, MUST I KILL THEE?
6

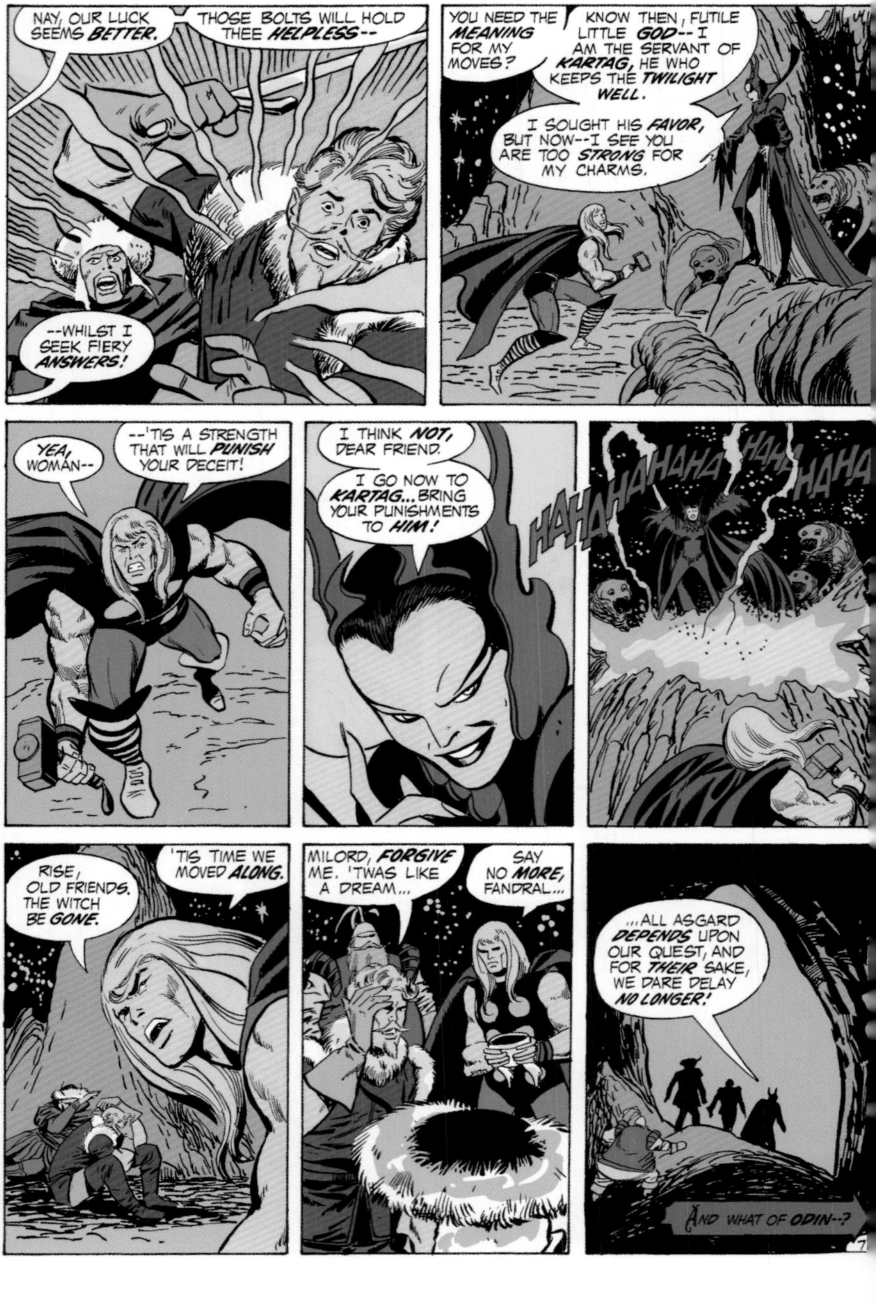
NAY, OUR LUCK SEEMS BETTER.
THOSE BOLTS WILL HOLD THEE HELPLESS--
--WHILST I SEEK FIERY ANSWERS!
YOU NEED THE MEANING FOR MY MOVES?
KNOW THEN, FUTILE LITTLE GOD-- I AM THE SERVANT OF KARTAG, HE WHO KEEPS THE TWILIGHT WELL.
I SOUGHT HIS FAVOR, BUT NOW--I SEE YOU ARE TOO STRONG FOR MY CHARMS.
YEA, WOMAN--
--'TIS A STRENGTH THAT WILL PUNISH YOUR DECEIT!
I THINK NOT, DEAR FRIEND.
I GO NOW TO KARTAG... BRING YOUR PUNISHMENTS TO HIM!
HAHAHAHAHA HAHA HAHA
RISE, OLD FRIENDS. THE WITCH BE GONE.
'TIS TIME WE MOVED ALONG.
MILORD, FORGIVE ME. 'TWAS LIKE A DREAM...
SAY NO MORE, FANDRAL...
...ALL ASGARD DEPENDS UPON OUR QUEST, AND FOR THEIR SAKE, WE DARE DELAY NO LONGER!
AND WHAT OF ODIN--?
7

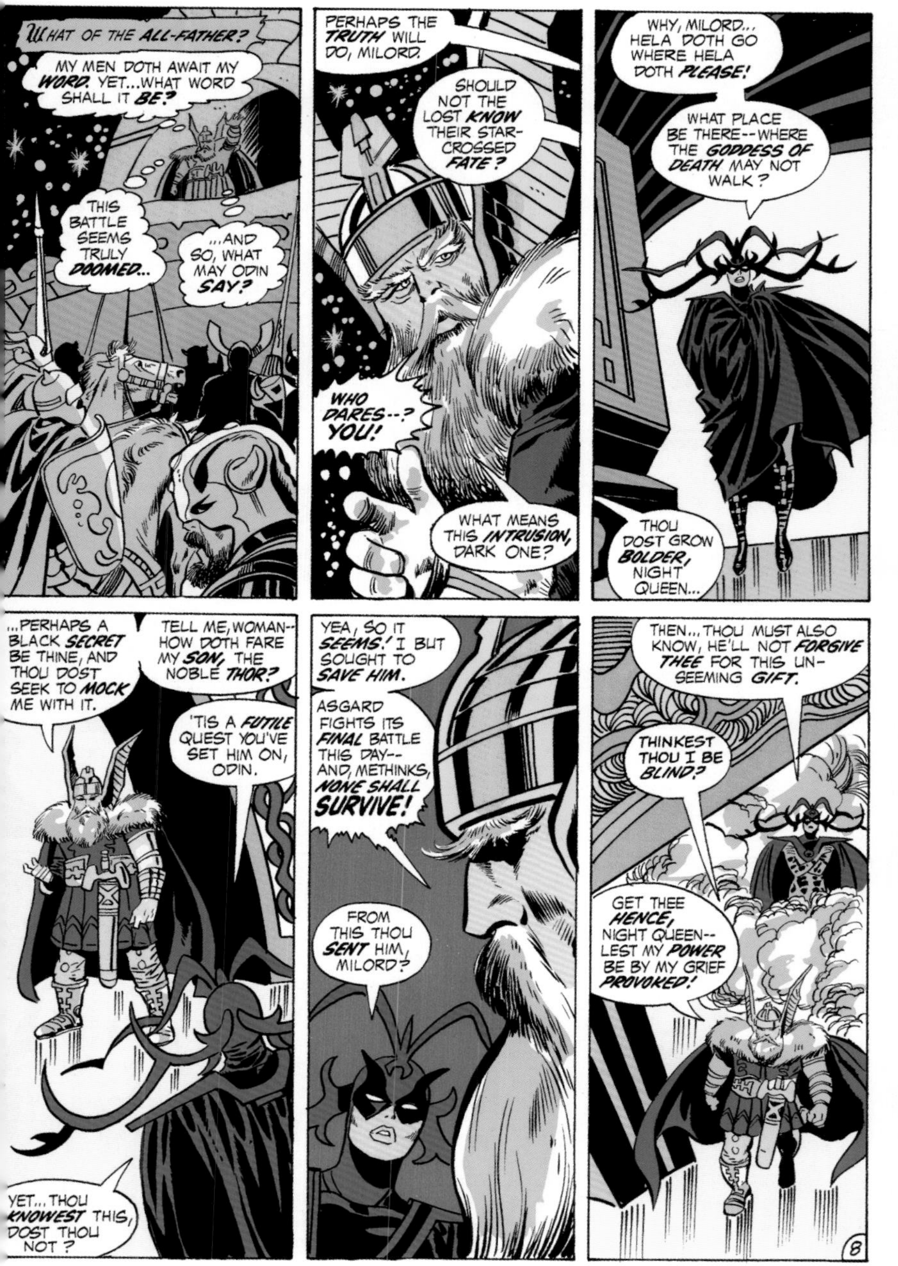
WHAT OF THE ALL-FATHER?
MY MEN DOTH AWAIT MY WORD. YET...WHAT WORD SHALL IT BE?
THIS BATTLE SEEMS TRULY DOOMED...
...AND SO, WHAT MAY ODIN SAY?
PERHAPS THE TRUTH WILL DO, MILORD.
SHOULD NOT THE LOST KNOW THEIR STAR-CROSSED FATE?
WHO DARES--? YOU!
WHAT MEANS THIS INTRUSION, DARK ONE?
WHY, MILORD... HELA DOTH GO WHERE HELA DOTH PLEASE!
WHAT PLACE BE THERE--WHERE THE GODDESS OF DEATH MAY NOT WALK?
THOU DOST GROW BOLDER, NIGHT QUEEN...
...PERHAPS A BLACK SECRET BE THINE, AND THOU DOST SEEK TO MOCK ME WITH IT.
TELL ME, WOMAN--HOW DOTH FARE MY SON, THE NOBLE THOR?
'TIS A FUTILE QUEST YOU'VE SET HIM ON, ODIN.
YET...THOU KNOWEST THIS, DOST THOU NOT?
YEA, SO IT SEEMS! I BUT SOUGHT TO SAVE HIM.
ASGARD FIGHTS ITS FINAL BATTLE THIS DAY--AND, METHINKS, NONE SHALL SURVIVE!
FROM THIS THOU SENT HIM, MILORD?
THEN...THOU MUST ALSO KNOW, HE'LL NOT FORGIVE THEE FOR THIS UN-SEEMING GIFT.
THINKEST THOU I BE BLIND?
GET THEE HENCE, NIGHT QUEEN--LEST MY POWER BE BY MY GRIEF PROVOKED!
8

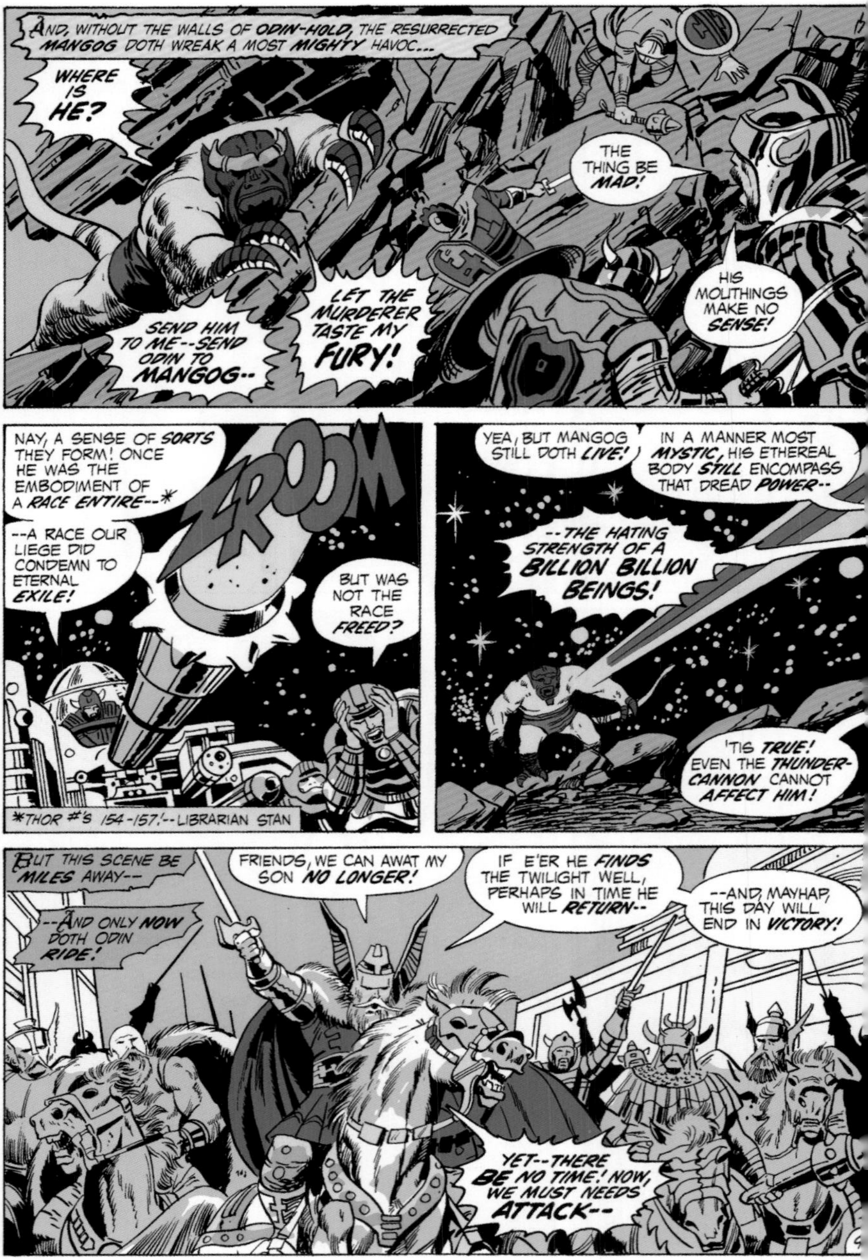
AND, WITHOUT THE WALLS OF ODIN-HOLD, THE RESURRECTED MANGOG DOTH WREAK A MOST MIGHTY HAVOC...
WHERE IS HE?
THE THING BE MAD!
HIS MOUTHINGS MAKE NO SENSE!
SEND HIM TO ME--SEND ODIN TO MANGOG--
LET THE MURDERER TASTE MY FURY!
NAY, A SENSE OF SORTS THEY FORM! ONCE HE WAS THE EMBODIMENT OF A RACE ENTIRE--*
ZROOOM
--A RACE OUR LIEGE DID CONDEMN TO ETERNAL EXILE!
BUT WAS NOT THE RACE FREED?
*THOR #'S 154-157!--LIBRARIAN STAN
YEA, BUT MANGOG STILL DOTH LIVE!
IN A MANNER MOST MYSTIC, HIS ETHEREAL BODY STILL ENCOMPASS THAT DREAD POWER--
--THE HATING STRENGTH OF A BILLION BILLION BEINGS!
'TIS TRUE! EVEN THE THUNDER-CANNON CANNOT AFFECT HIM!
BUT THIS SCENE BE MILES AWAY--
--AND ONLY NOW DOTH ODIN RIDE!
FRIENDS, WE CAN AWAT MY SON NO LONGER!
IF E'ER HE FINDS THE TWILIGHT WELL, PERHAPS IN TIME HE WILL RETURN--
--AND, MAYHAP, THIS DAY WILL END IN VICTORY!
YET--THERE BE NO TIME! NOW, WE MUST NEEDS ATTACK--

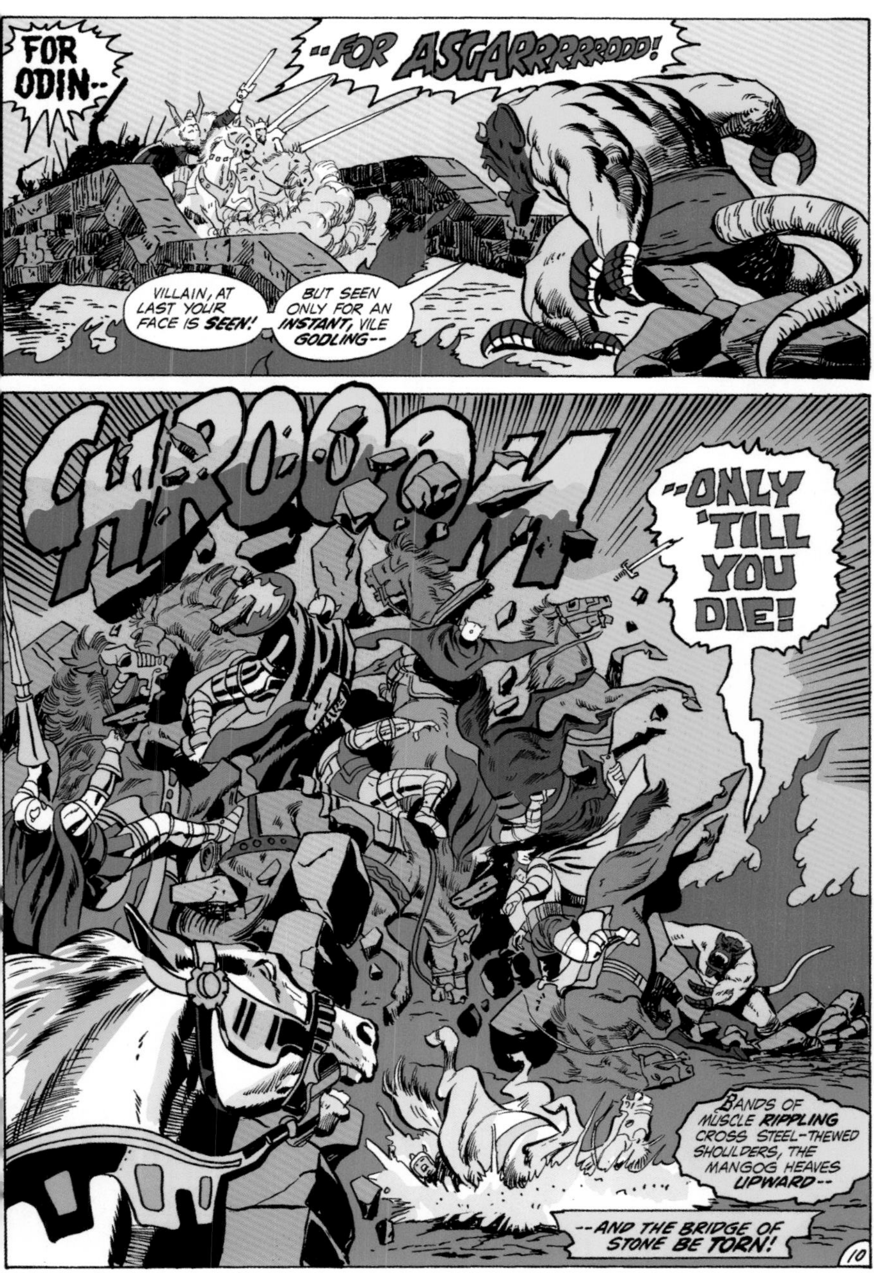
FOR ODIN--
--FOR ASGARRRRRODD!
VILLAIN, AT LAST YOUR FACE IS SEEN!
BUT SEEN ONLY FOR AN INSTANT, VILE GODLING--
CHROOOM
--ONLY 'TILL YOU DIE!
BANDS OF MUSCLE RIPPLING CROSS STEEL-THEWED SHOULDERS, THE MANGOG HEAVES UPWARD--
--AND THE BRIDGE OF STONE BE TORN!
10

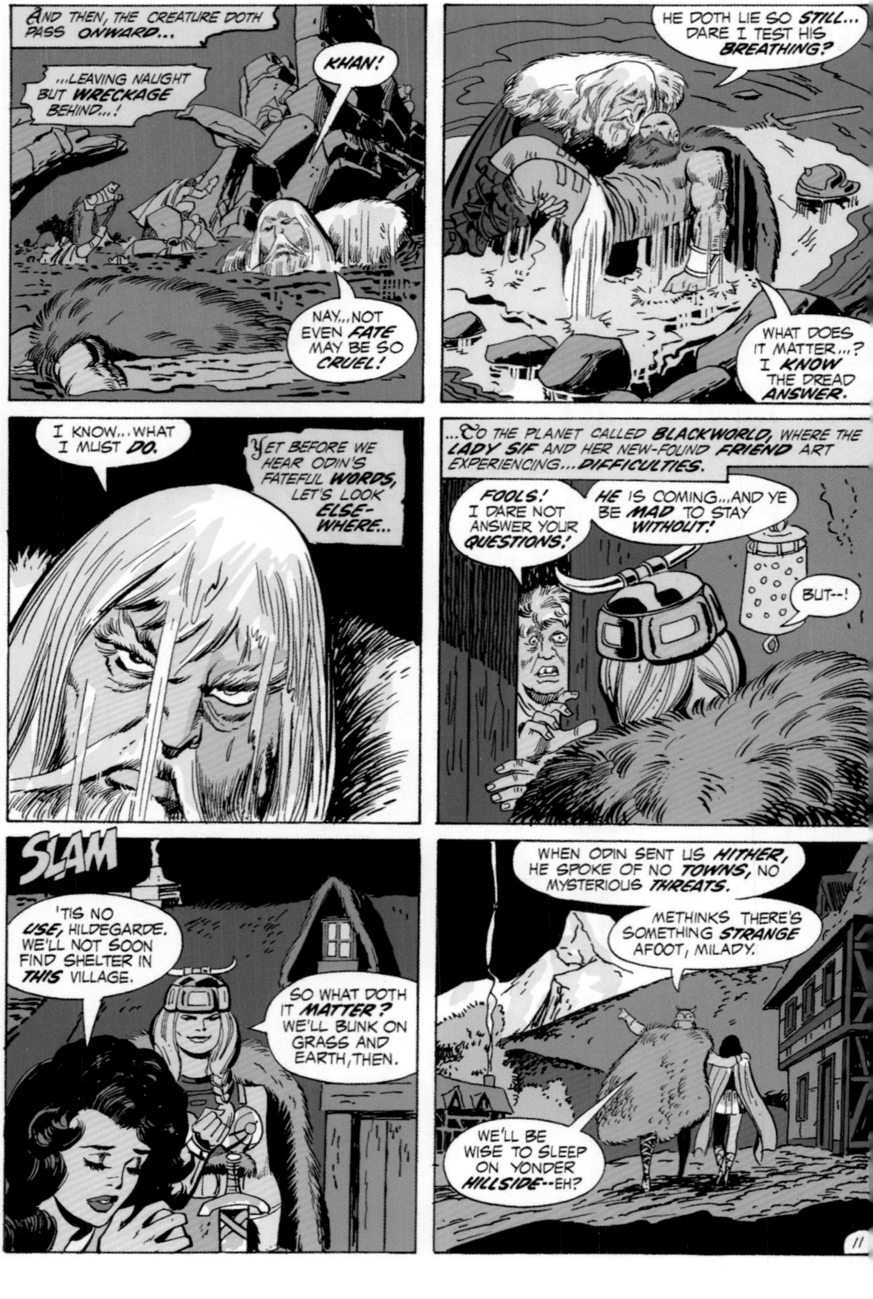
AND THEN, THE CREATURE DOTH PASS ONWARD...
...LEAVING NAUGHT BUT WRECKAGE BEHIND...!
KHAN!
NAY,..NOT EVEN FATE MAY BE SO CRUEL!
HE DOTH LIE SO STILL... DARE I TEST HIS BREATHING?
WHAT DOES IT MATTER...? I KNOW THE DREAD ANSWER.
I KNOW...WHAT I MUST DO.
YET BEFORE WE HEAR ODIN'S FATEFUL WORDS, LET'S LOOK ELSE-WHERE...
...TO THE PLANET CALLED BLACKWORLD, WHERE THE LADY SIF AND HER NEW-FOUND FRIEND ART EXPERIENCING...DIFFICULTIES.
FOOLS! I DARE NOT ANSWER YOUR QUESTIONS!
HE IS COMING...AND YE BE MAD TO STAY WITHOUT!
BUT--!
SLAM
'TIS NO USE, HILDEGARDE. WE'LL NOT SOON FIND SHELTER IN THIS VILLAGE.
SO WHAT DOTH IT MATTER? WE'LL BUNK ON GRASS AND EARTH, THEN.
WHEN ODIN SENT US HITHER, HE SPOKE OF NO TOWNS, NO MYSTERIOUS THREATS.
METHINKS THERE'S SOMETHING STRANGE AFOOT, MILADY.
WE'LL BE WISE TO SLEEP ON YONDER HILLSIDE--EH?
11

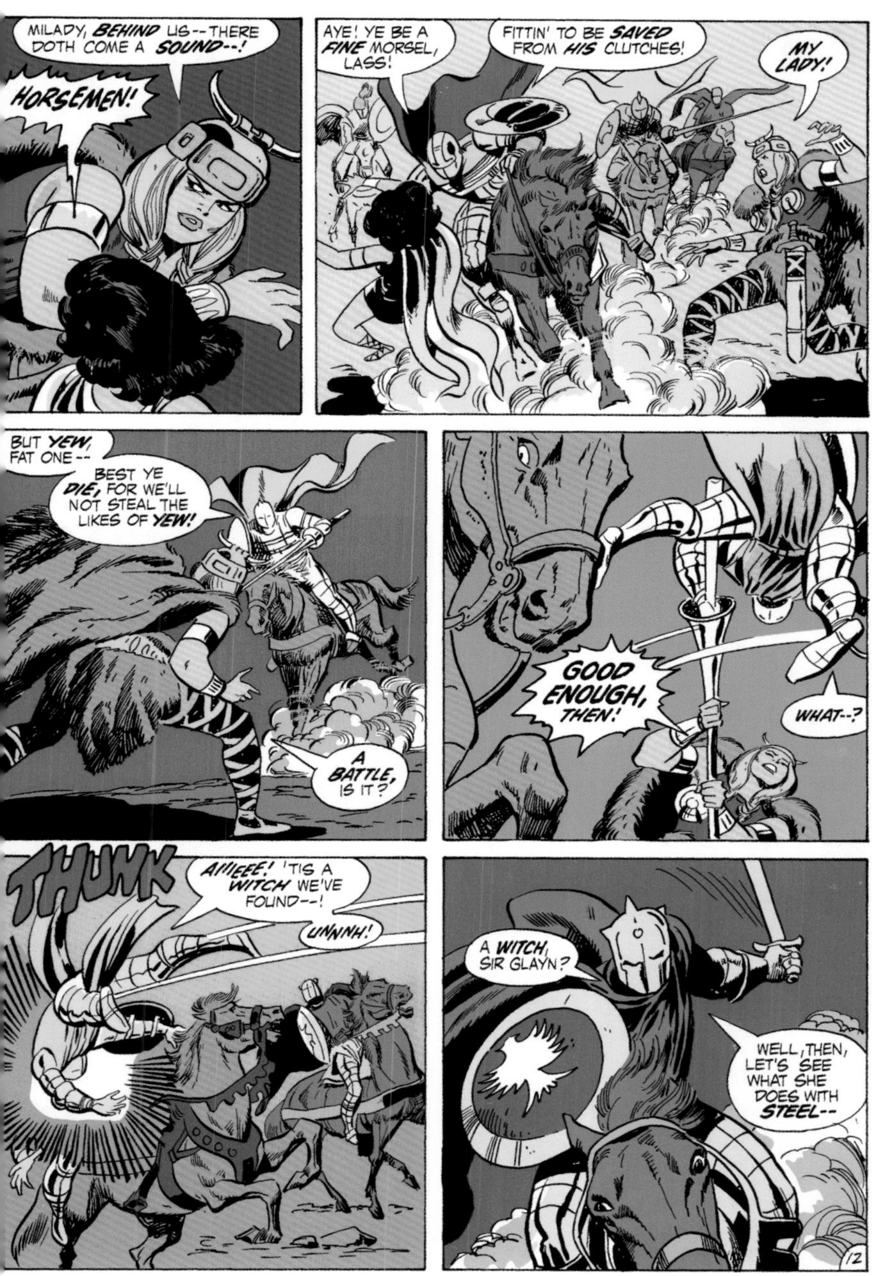
MILADY, BEHIND US--THERE DOTH COME A SOUND--!
HORSEMEN!
AYE! YE BE A FINE MORSEL, LASS!
FITTIN' TO BE SAVED FROM HIS CLUTCHES!
MY LADY!
BUT YEW, FAT ONE --
BEST YE DIE, FOR WE'LL NOT STEAL THE LIKES OF YEW!
A BATTLE, IS IT?
GOOD ENOUGH, THEN!
WHAT--?
THUNK
AIIIEEE! 'TIS A WITCH WE'VE FOUND--!
UNNNH!
A WITCH, SIR GLAYN?
WELL, THEN, LET'S SEE WHAT SHE DOES WITH STEEL--
12

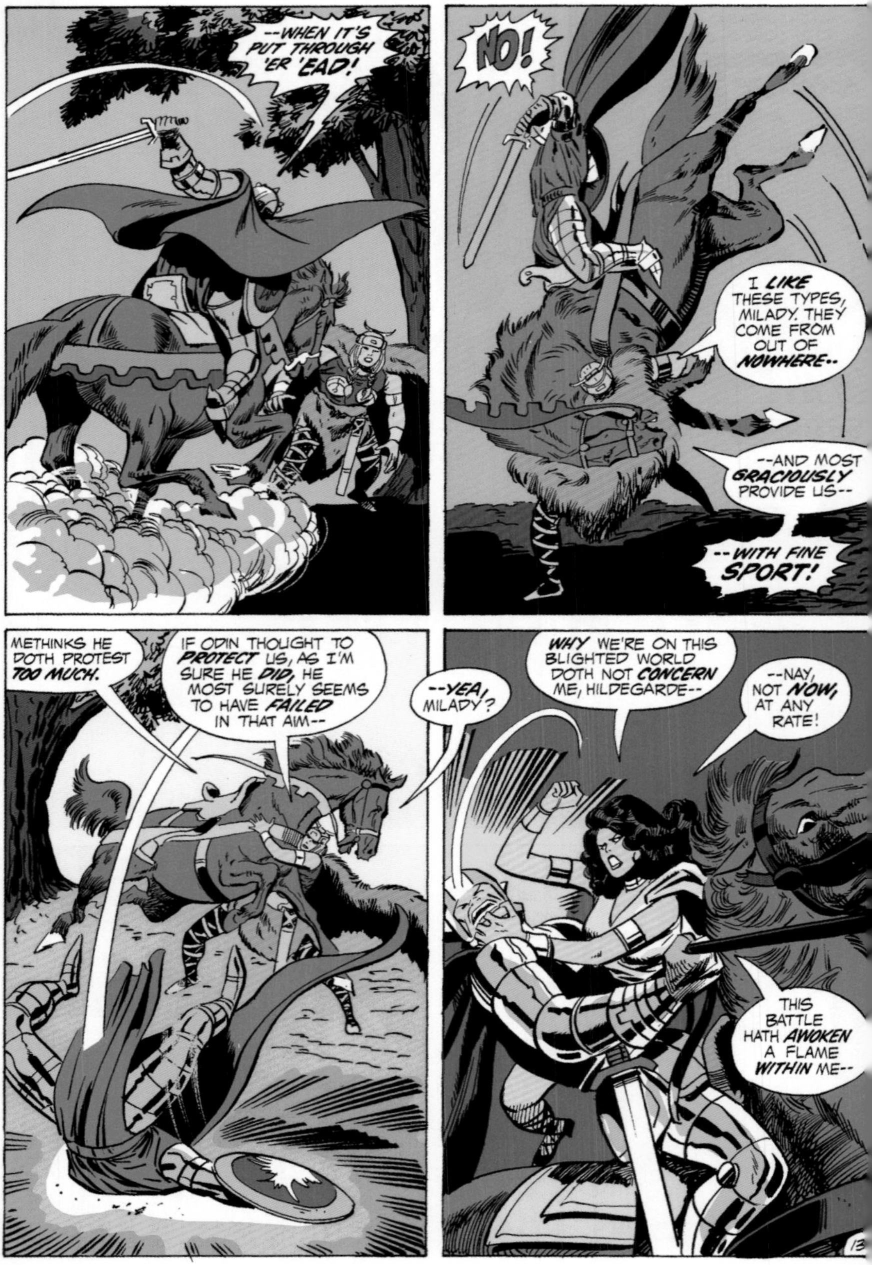
--WHEN IT'S PUT THROUGH 'ER 'EAD!
NO!
I LIKE THESE TYPES, MILADY. THEY COME FROM OUT OF NOWHERE--
--AND MOST GRACIOUSLY PROVIDE US--
--WITH FINE SPORT!
METHINKS HE DOTH PROTEST TOO MUCH.
IF ODIN THOUGHT TO PROTECT US, AS I'M SURE HE DID, HE MOST SURELY SEEMS TO HAVE FAILED IN THAT AIM--
--YEA, MILADY?
WHY WE'RE ON THIS BLIGHTED WORLD DOTH NOT CONCERN ME, HILDEGARDE--
--NAY, NOT NOW, AT ANY RATE!
THIS BATTLE HATH AWOKEN A FLAME WITHIN ME--
13

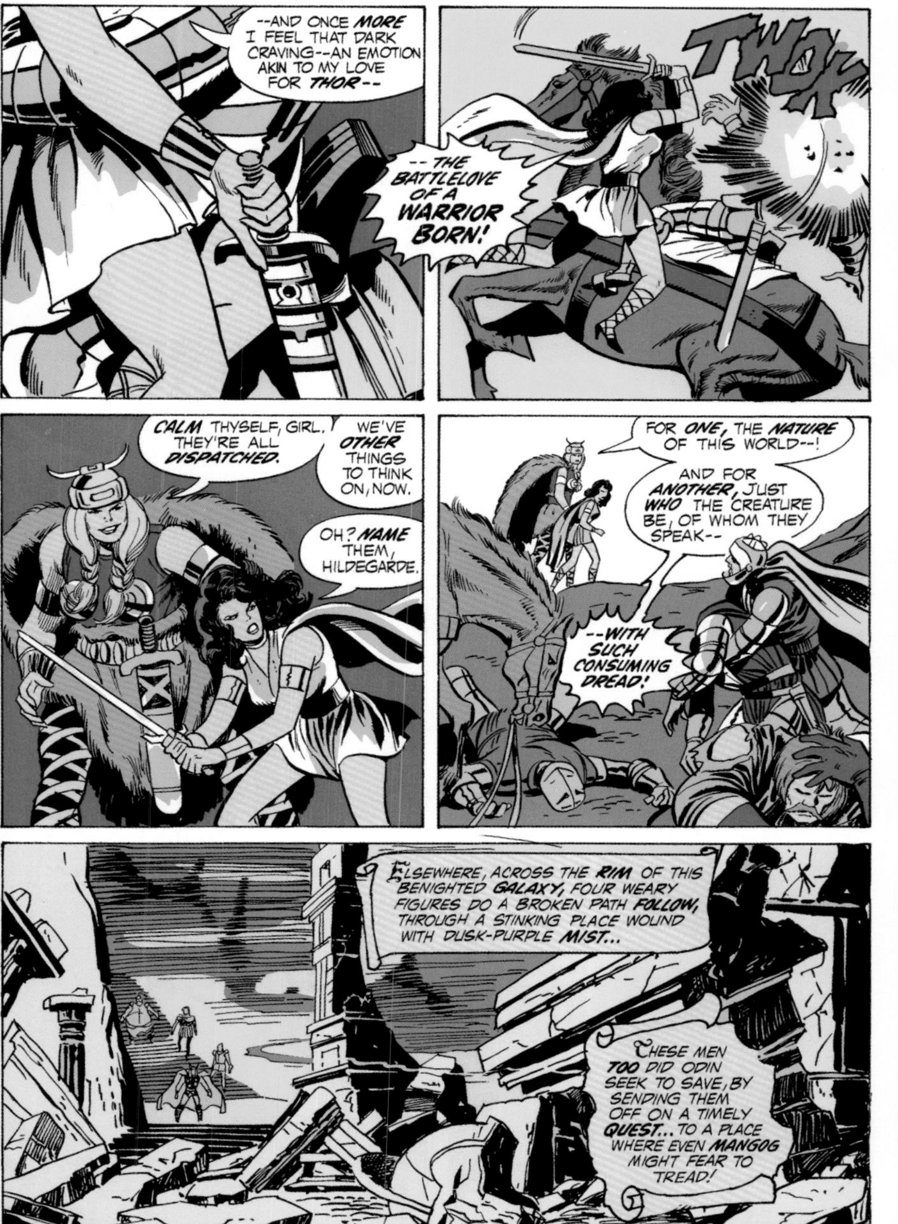
--AND ONCE MORE I FEEL THAT DARK CRAVING--AN EMOTION AKIN TO MY LOVE FOR THOR--
TWOK
--THE BATTLELOVE OF A WARRIOR BORN!
CALM THYSELF, GIRL. THEY'RE ALL DISPATCHED.
WE'VE OTHER THINGS TO THINK ON, NOW.
OH? NAME THEM, HILDEGARDE.
FOR ONE, THE NATURE OF THIS WORLD--!
AND FOR ANOTHER, JUST WHO THE CREATURE BE, OF WHOM THEY SPEAK--
--WITH SUCH CONSUMING DREAD!
ELSEWHERE, ACROSS THE RIM OF THIS BENIGHTED GALAXY, FOUR WEARY FIGURES DO A BROKEN PATH FOLLOW, THROUGH A STINKING PLACE WOUND WITH DUSK-PURPLE MIST...
THESE MEN TOO DID ODIN SEEK TO SAVE, BY SENDING THEM OFF ON A TIMELY QUEST... TO A PLACE WHERE EVEN MANGOG MIGHT FEAR TO TREAD!
14

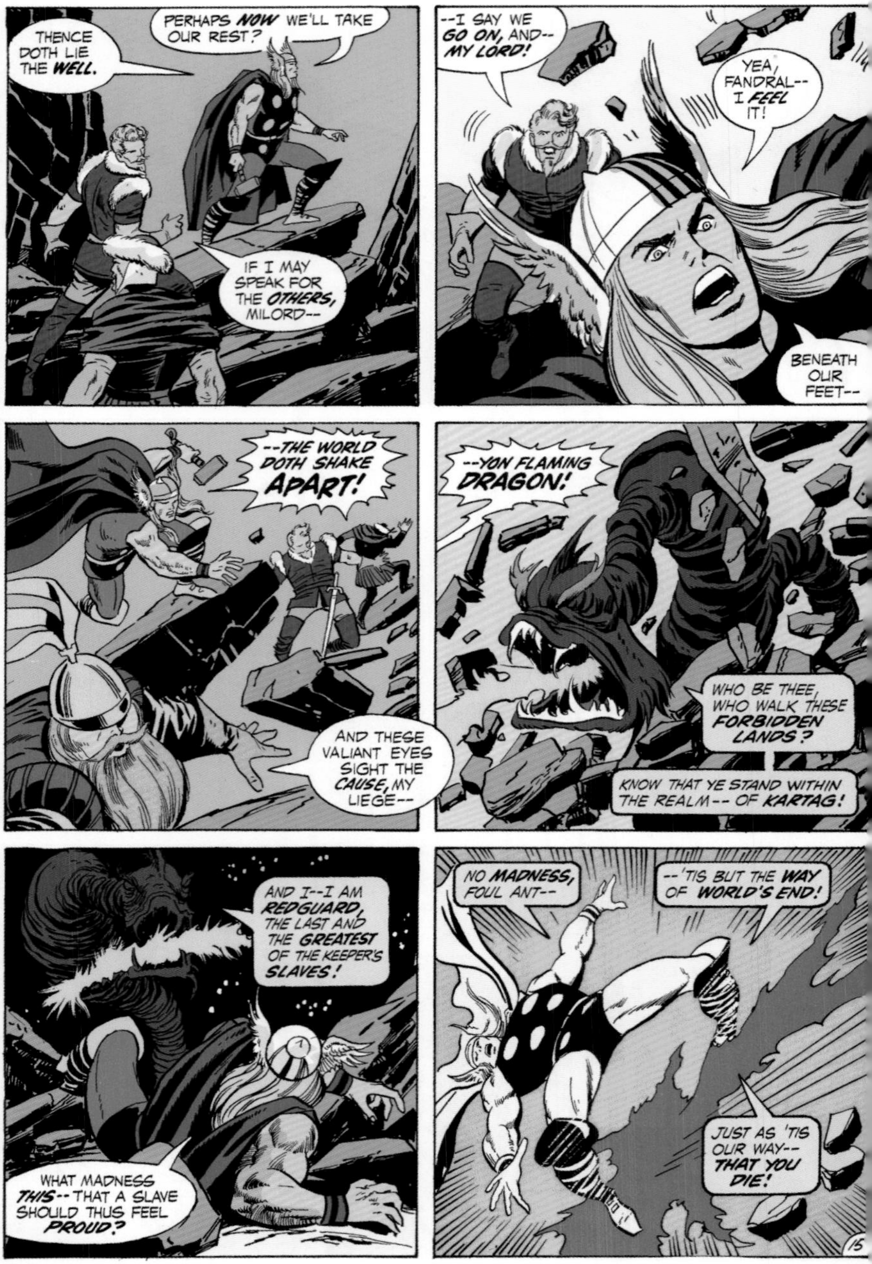
THENCE DOTH LIE THE WELL.
PERHAPS NOW WE'LL TAKE OUR REST?
IF I MAY SPEAK FOR THE OTHERS, MILORD--
--I SAY WE GO ON, AND-- MY LORD!
YEA, FANDRAL-- I FEEL IT!
BENEATH OUR FEET--
--THE WORLD DOTH SHAKE APART!
AND THESE VALIANT EYES SIGHT THE CAUSE, MY LIEGE--
--YON FLAMING DRAGON!
WHO BE THEE, WHO WALK THESE FORBIDDEN LANDS?
KNOW THAT YE STAND WITHIN THE REALM-- OF KARTAG!
AND I--I AM REDGUARD, THE LAST AND THE GREATEST OF THE KEEPER'S SLAVES!
WHAT MADNESS THIS-- THAT A SLAVE SHOULD THUS FEEL PROUD?
NO MADNESS, FOUL ANT--
--'TIS BUT THE WAY OF WORLD'S END!
JUST AS 'TIS OUR WAY-- THAT YOU DIE!
15

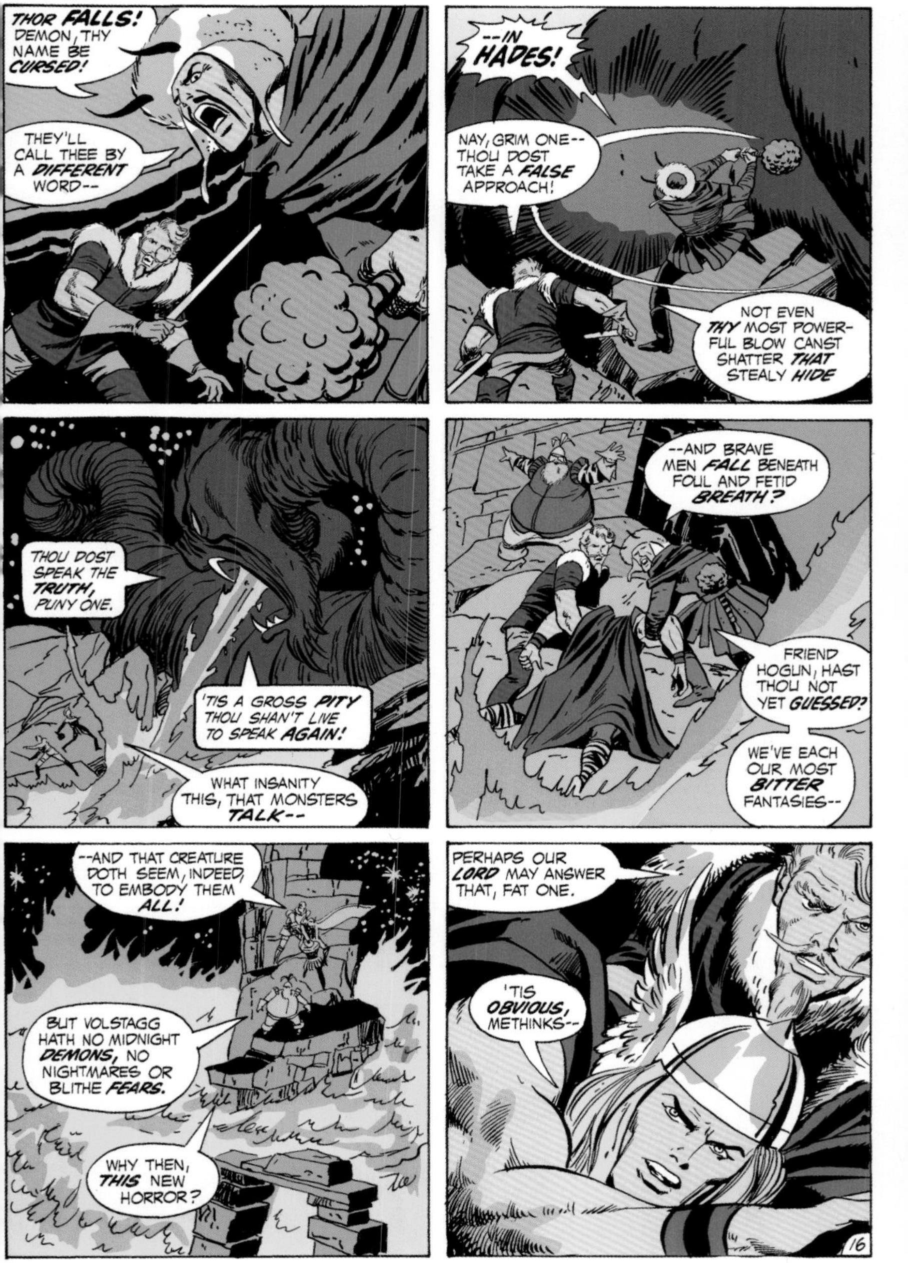
THOR FALLS! DEMON, THY NAME BE CURSED!
THEY'LL CALL THEE BY A DIFFERENT WORD--
--IN HADES!
NAY, GRIM ONE-- THOU DOST TAKE A FALSE APPROACH!
NOT EVEN THY MOST POWER-FUL BLOW CANST SHATTER THAT STEALY HIDE
THOU DOST SPEAK THE TRUTH, PUNY ONE.
'TIS A GROSS PITY THOU SHAN'T LIVE TO SPEAK AGAIN!
WHAT INSANITY THIS, THAT MONSTERS TALK--
--AND BRAVE MEN FALL BENEATH FOUL AND FETID BREATH?
FRIEND HOGUN, HAST THOU NOT YET GUESSED?
WE'VE EACH OUR MOST BITTER FANTASIES--
--AND THAT CREATURE DOTH SEEM, INDEED, TO EMBODY THEM ALL!
BUT VOLSTAGG HATH NO MIDNIGHT DEMONS, NO NIGHTMARES OR BLITHE FEARS.
WHY THEN, THIS NEW HORROR?
PERHAPS OUR LORD MAY ANSWER THAT, FAT ONE.
'TIS OBVIOUS, METHINKS--
16

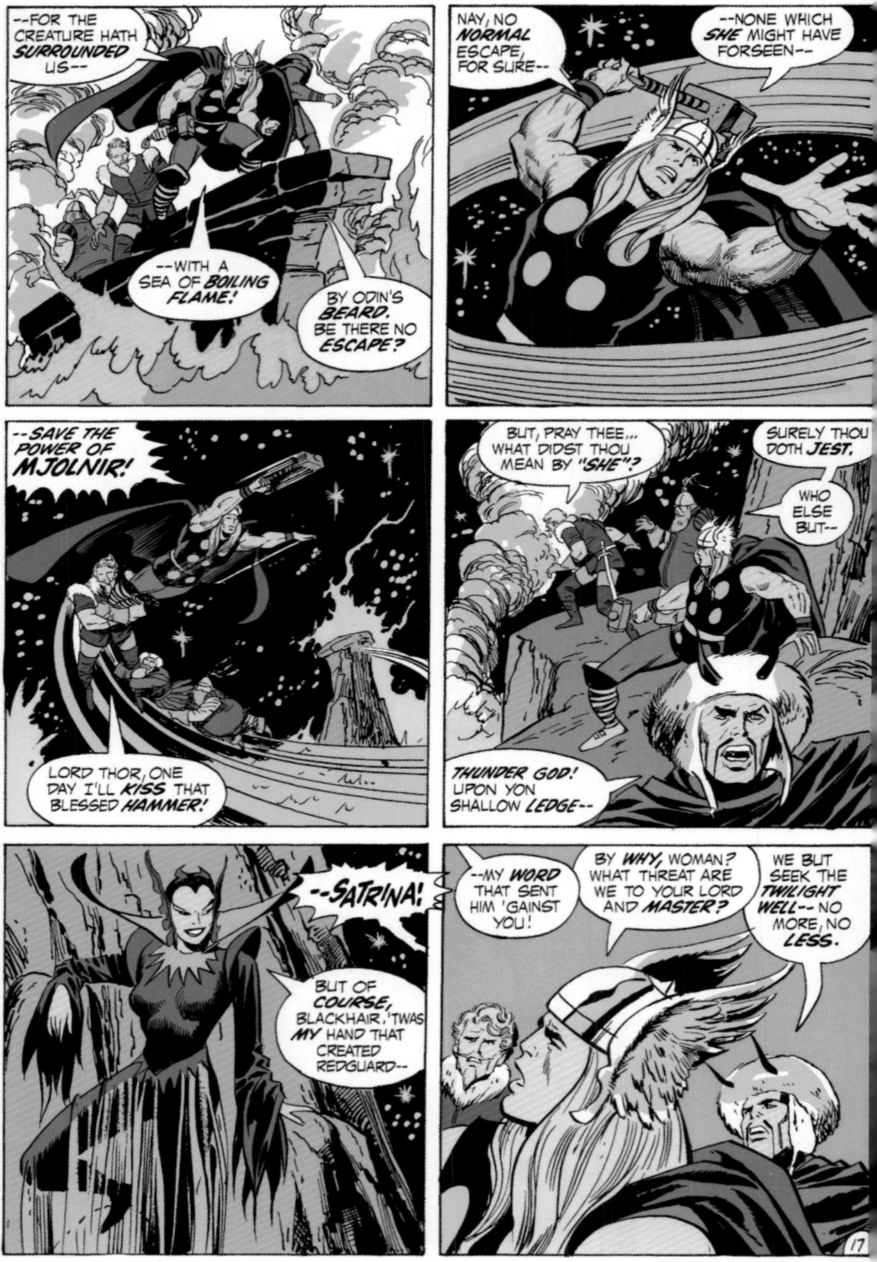
--FOR THE CREATURE HATH SURROUNDED US--
--WITH A SEA OF BOILING FLAME!
BY ODIN'S BEARD. BE THERE NO ESCAPE?
NAY, NO NORMAL ESCAPE, FOR SURE--
--NONE WHICH SHE MIGHT HAVE FORSEEN--
--SAVE THE POWER OF MJOLNIR!
LORD THOR, ONE DAY I'LL KISS THAT BLESSED HAMMER!
BUT, PRAY THEE... WHAT DIDST THOU MEAN BY "SHE"?
SURELY THOU DOTH JEST.
WHO ELSE BUT--
THUNDER GOD! UPON YON SHALLOW LEDGE--
--SATRINA!
BUT OF COURSE, BLACKHAIR, 'TWAS MY HAND THAT CREATED REDGUARD--
--MY WORD THAT SENT HIM 'GAINST YOU!
BY WHY, WOMAN? WHAT THREAT ARE WE TO YOUR LORD AND MASTER?
WE BUT SEEK THE TWILIGHT WELL-- NO MORE, NO LESS.
17

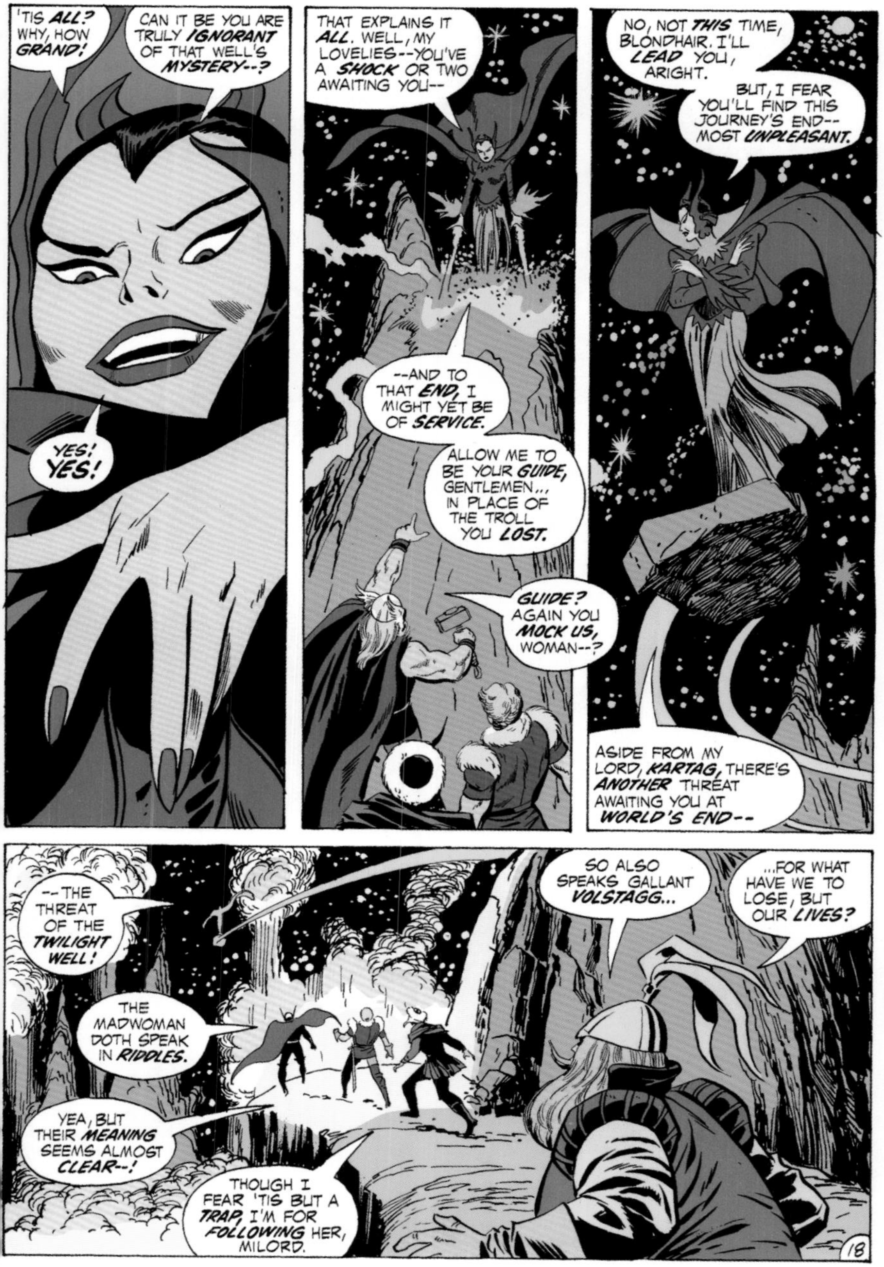
'TIS ALL? WHY, HOW GRAND!
CAN IT BE YOU ARE TRULY IGNORANT OF THAT WELL'S MYSTERY--?
YES! YES!
THAT EXPLAINS IT ALL. WELL, MY LOVELIES--YOU'VE A SHOCK OR TWO AWAITING YOU--
--AND TO THAT END, I MIGHT YET BE OF SERVICE.
ALLOW ME TO BE YOUR GUIDE, GENTLEMEN... IN PLACE OF THE TROLL YOU LOST.
GUIDE? AGAIN YOU MOCK US, WOMAN--?
NO, NOT THIS TIME, BLONDHAIR. I'LL LEAD YOU, ARIGHT.
BUT, I FEAR YOU'LL FIND THIS JOURNEY'S END--MOST UNPLEASANT.
ASIDE FROM MY LORD, KARTAG, THERE'S ANOTHER THREAT AWAITING YOU AT WORLD'S END--
--THE THREAT OF THE TWILIGHT WELL!
THE MADWOMAN DOTH SPEAK IN RIDDLES.
YEA, BUT THEIR MEANING SEEMS ALMOST CLEAR--!
THOUGH I FEAR 'TIS BUT A TRAP, I'M FOR FOLLOWING HER, MILORD.
SO ALSO SPEAKS GALLANT VOLSTAGG...
...FOR WHAT HAVE WE TO LOSE, BUT OUR LIVES?
18

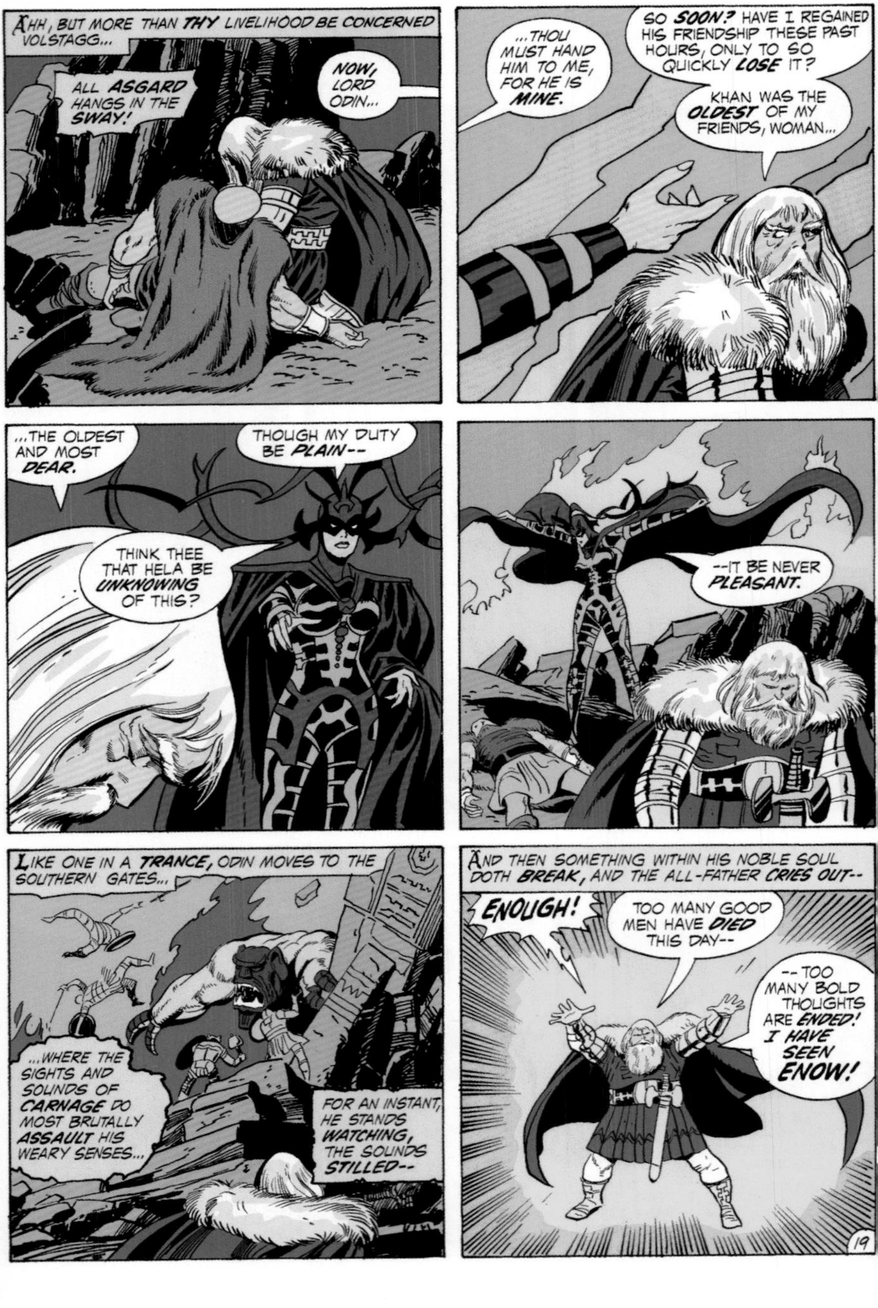
AHH, BUT MORE THAN THY LIVELIHOOD BE CONCERNED VOLSTAGG...
ALL ASGARD HANGS IN THE SWAY!
NOW, LORD ODIN...
...THOU MUST HAND HIM TO ME, FOR HE IS MINE.
SO SOON? HAVE I REGAINED HIS FRIENDSHIP THESE PAST HOURS, ONLY TO SO QUICKLY LOSE IT?
KHAN WAS THE OLDEST OF MY FRIENDS, WOMAN...
...THE OLDEST AND MOST DEAR.
THOUGH MY DUTY BE PLAIN--
THINK THEE THAT HELA BE UNKNOWING OF THIS?
--IT BE NEVER PLEASANT.
LIKE ONE IN A TRANCE, ODIN MOVES TO THE SOUTHERN GATES...
...WHERE THE SIGHTS AND SOUNDS OF CARNAGE DO MOST BRUTALLY ASSAULT HIS WEARY SENSES...
FOR AN INSTANT, HE STANDS WATCHING, THE SOUNDS STILLED--
AND THEN SOMETHING WITHIN HIS NOBLE SOUL DOTH BREAK, AND THE ALL-FATHER CRIES OUT--
ENOUGH!
TOO MANY GOOD MEN HAVE DIED THIS DAY--
--TOO MANY BOLD THOUGHTS ARE ENDED! I HAVE SEEN ENOW!
19

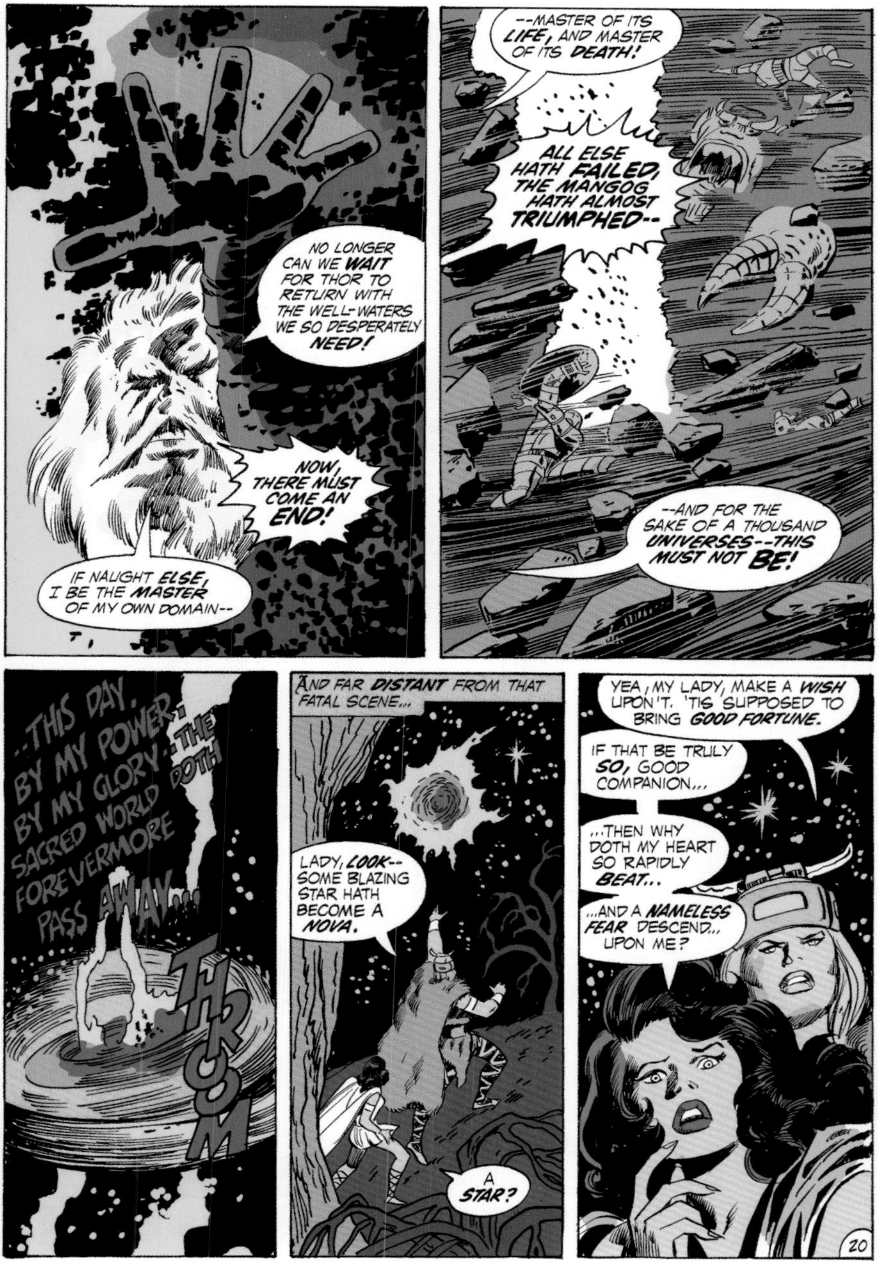
NO LONGER CAN WE WAIT FOR THOR TO RETURN WITH THE WELL-WATERS WE SO DESPERATELY NEED!
NOW, THERE MUST COME AN END!
IF NAUGHT ELSE, I BE THE MASTER OF MY OWN DOMAIN--
--MASTER OF ITS LIFE, AND MASTER OF ITS DEATH!
ALL ELSE HATH FAILED, THE MANGOG HATH ALMOST TRIUMPHED--
--AND FOR THE SAKE OF A THOUSAND UNIVERSES--THIS MUST NOT BE!
--THIS DAY, BY MY POWER, BY MY GLORY--THE SACRED WORLD DOTH FOREVERMORE PASS AWAY...
THROOM
AND FAR DISTANT FROM THAT FATAL SCENE...
LADY, LOOK-- SOME BLAZING STAR HATH BECOME A NOVA.
A STAR?
YEA, MY LADY, MAKE A WISH UPON'T. 'TIS SUPPOSED TO BRING GOOD FORTUNE.
IF THAT BE TRULY SO, GOOD COMPANION...
...THEN WHY DOTH MY HEART SO RAPIDLY BEAT...
...AND A NAMELESS FEAR DESCEND... UPON ME?
20

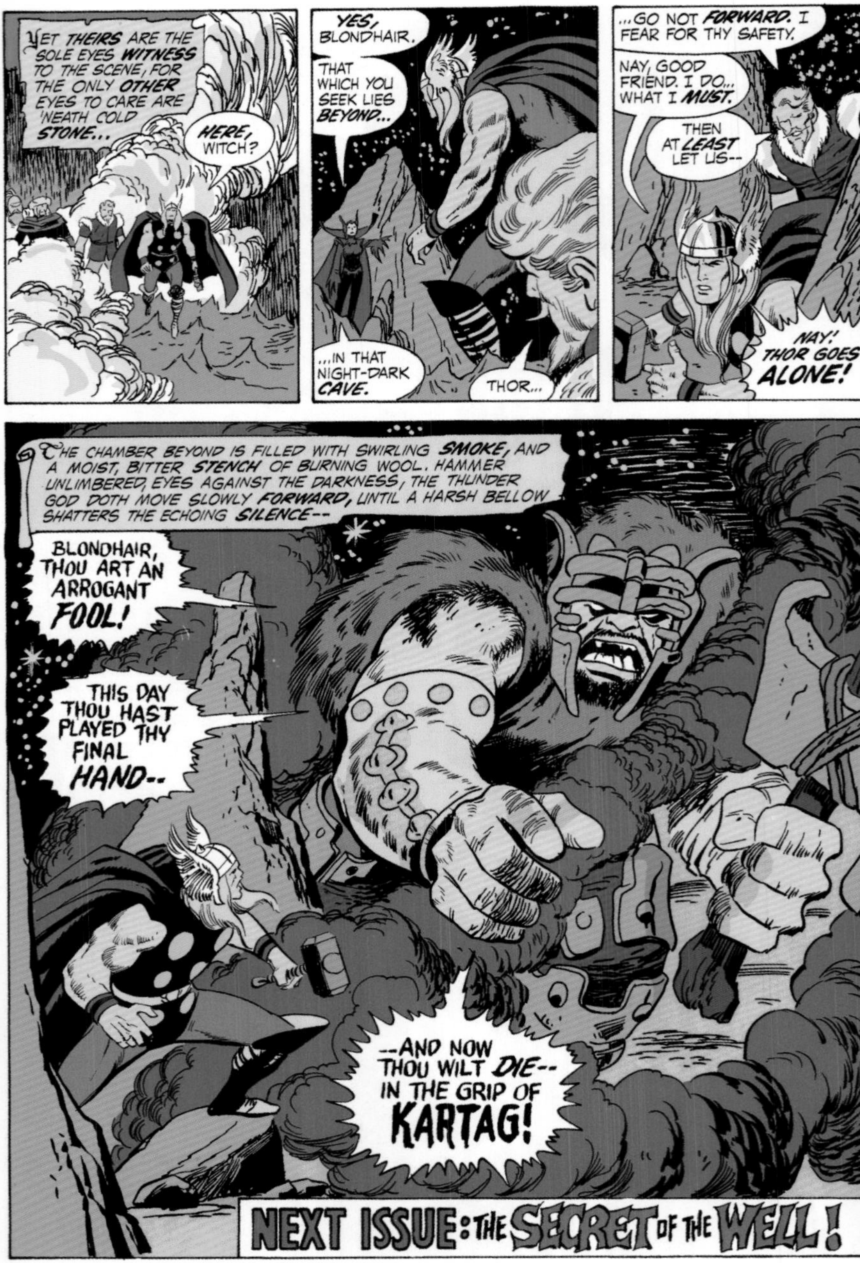
YET THEIRS ARE THE SOLE EYES WITNESS TO THE SCENE, FOR THE ONLY OTHER EYES TO CARE ARE 'NEATH COLD STONE...
HERE, WITCH?
YES, BLONDHAIR.
THAT WHICH YOU SEEK LIES BEYOND...
...IN THAT NIGHT-DARK CAVE.
THOR...
...GO NOT FORWARD. I FEAR FOR THY SAFETY.
NAY, GOOD FRIEND. I DO... WHAT I MUST.
THEN AT LEAST LET US--
NAY! THOR GOES ALONE!
THE CHAMBER BEYOND IS FILLED WITH SWIRLING SMOKE, AND A MOIST, BITTER STENCH OF BURNING WOOL. HAMMER UNLIMBERED, EYES AGAINST THE DARKNESS, THE THUNDER GOD DOTH MOVE SLOWLY FORWARD, UNTIL A HARSH BELLOW SHATTERS THE ECHOING SILENCE--
BLONDHAIR, THOU ART AN ARROGANT FOOL!
THIS DAY THOU HAST PLAYED THY FINAL HAND--
--AND NOW THOU WILT DIE-- IN THE GRIP OF KARTAG!
NEXT ISSUE: THE SECRET OF THE WELL!

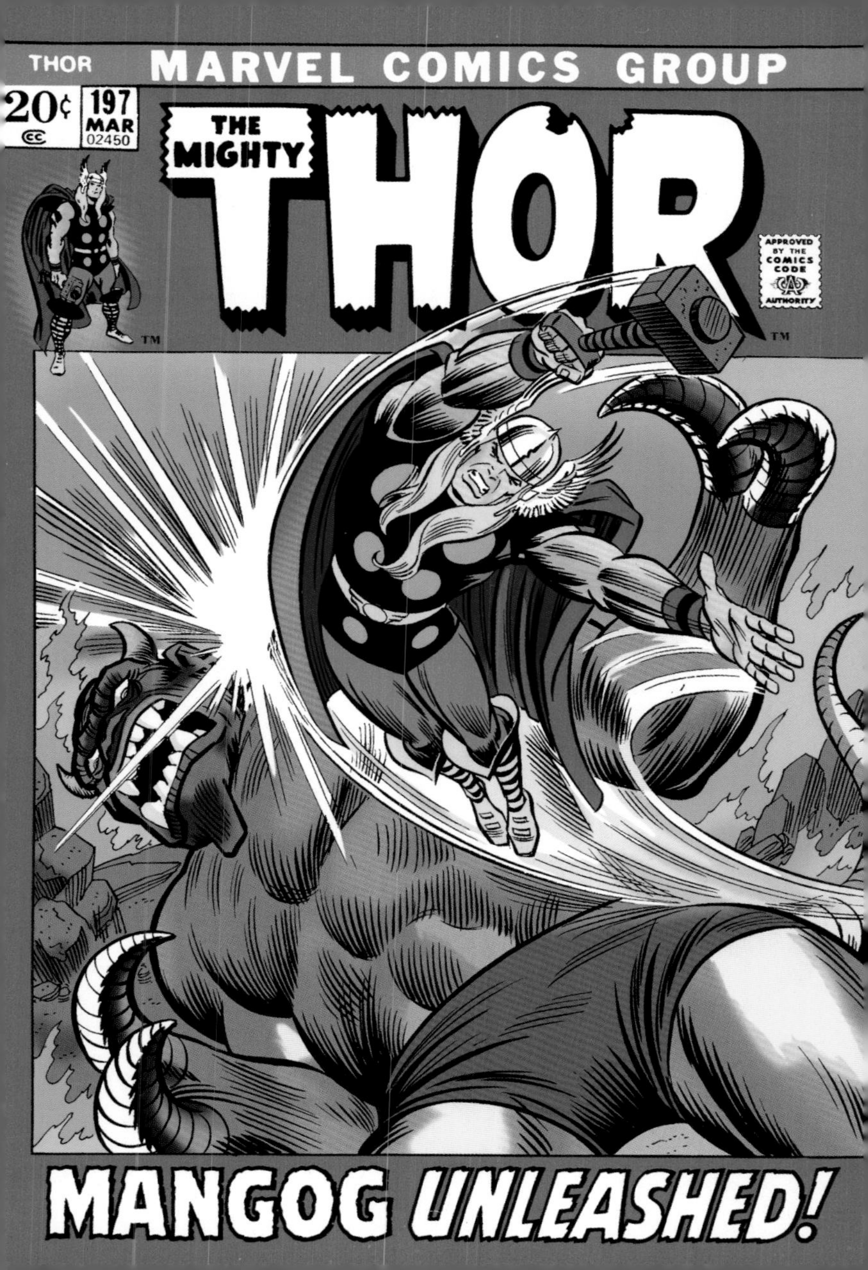
THOR
MARVEL COMICS GROUP
20¢
197
MAR
02450
THE MIGHTY
THOR
TM
APPROVED BY THE COMICS CODE AUTHORITY
TM
MANGOG UNLEASHED!

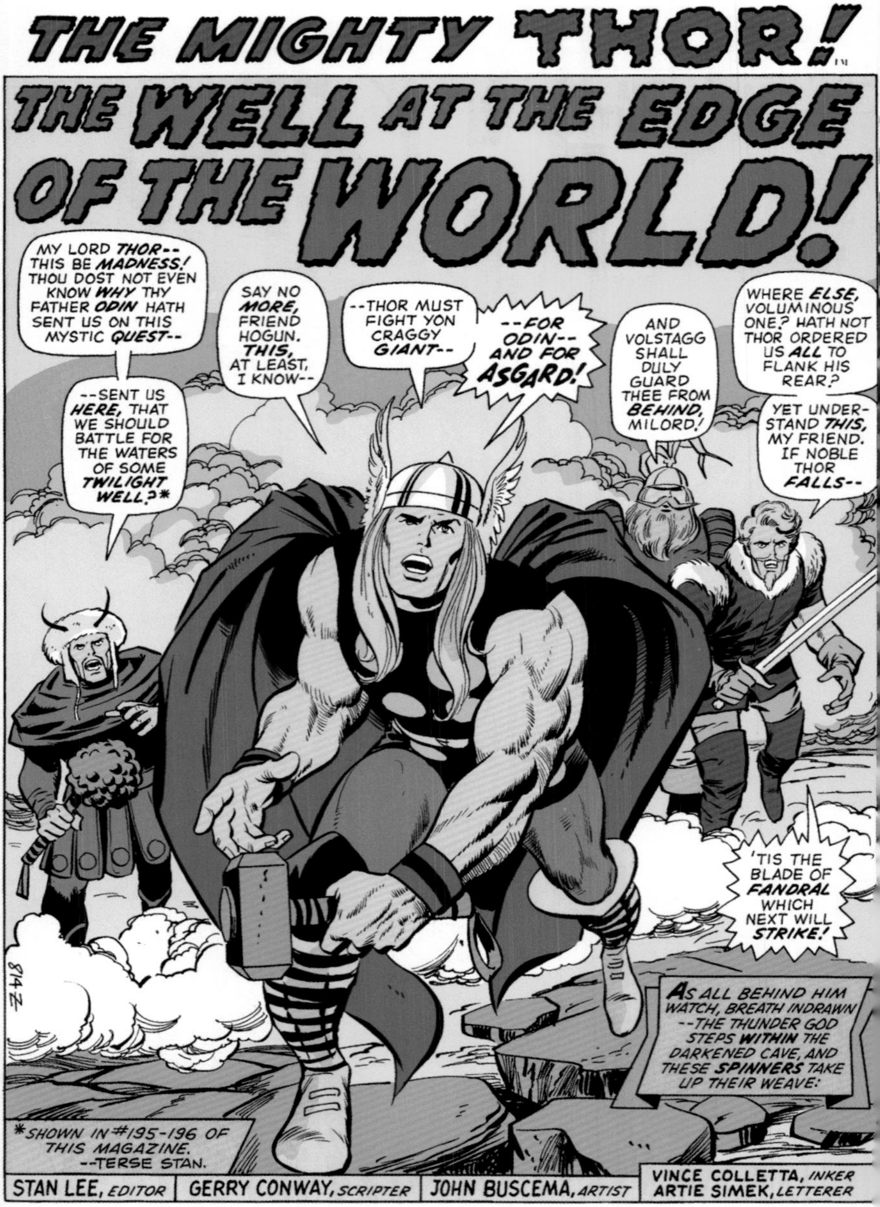

THE MIGHTY THOR!
THE WELL AT THE EDGE OF THE WORLD!
MY LORD THOR-- THIS BE MADNESS! THOU DOST NOT EVEN KNOW WHY THY FATHER ODIN HATH SENT US ON THIS MYSTIC QUEST--
--SENT US HERE, THAT WE SHOULD BATTLE FOR THE WATERS OF SOME TWILIGHT WELL?*
SAY NO MORE, FRIEND HOGUN. THIS, AT LEAST, I KNOW--
--THOR MUST FIGHT YON CRAGGY GIANT--
--FOR ODIN-- AND FOR ASGARD!
AND VOLSTAGG SHALL DULY GUARD THEE FROM BEHIND, MILORD!
WHERE ELSE, VOLUMINOUS ONE? HATH NOT THOR ORDERED US ALL TO FLANK HIS REAR?
YET UNDER-STAND THIS, MY FRIEND. IF NOBLE THOR FALLS--
'TIS THE BLADE OF FANDRAL WHICH NEXT WILL STRIKE!
AS ALL BEHIND HIM WATCH, BREATH INDRAWN --THE THUNDER GOD STEPS WITHIN THE DARKENED CAVE, AND THESE SPINNERS TAKE UP THEIR WEAVE:
*SHOWN IN #195-196 OF THIS MAGAZINE. --TERSE STAN.
814-Z
STAN LEE, EDITOR
GERRY CONWAY, SCRIPTER
JOHN BUSCEMA, ARTIST
VINCE COLLETTA, INKER
ARTIE SIMEK, LETTERER

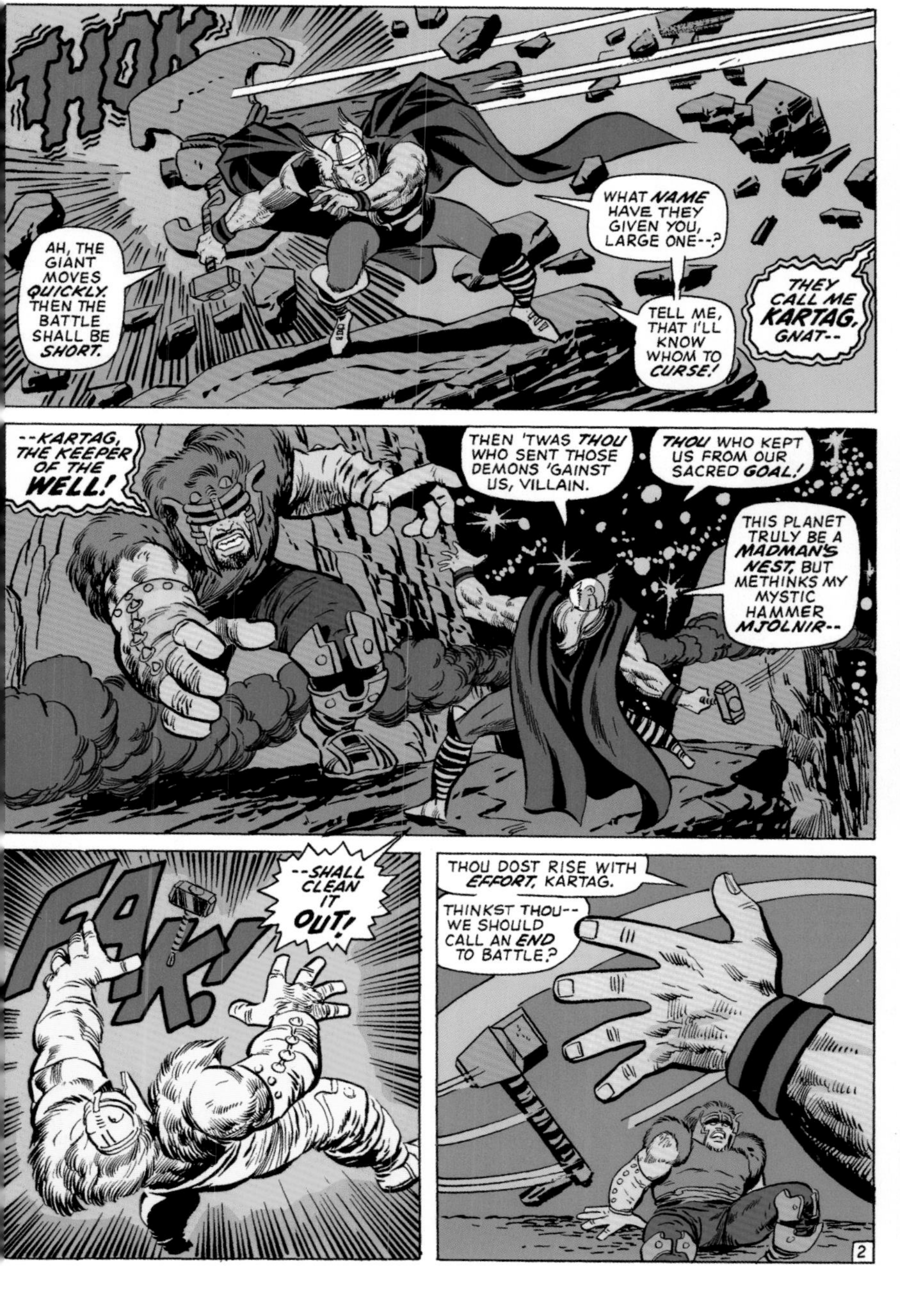
THOK
AH, THE GIANT MOVES QUICKLY. THEN THE BATTLE SHALL BE SHORT.
WHAT NAME HAVE THEY GIVEN YOU, LARGE ONE--?
TELL ME, THAT I'LL KNOW WHOM TO CURSE!
THEY CALL ME KARTAG, GNAT--
--KARTAG, THE KEEPER OF THE WELL!
THEN 'TWAS THOU WHO SENT THOSE DEMONS 'GAINST US, VILLAIN.
THOU WHO KEPT US FROM OUR SACRED GOAL!
THIS PLANET TRULY BE A MADMAN'S NEST, BUT METHINKS MY MYSTIC HAMMER MJOLNIR--
--SHALL CLEAN IT OUT!
THOU DOST RISE WITH EFFORT, KARTAG.
THINKST THOU-- WE SHOULD CALL AN END TO BATTLE?
2

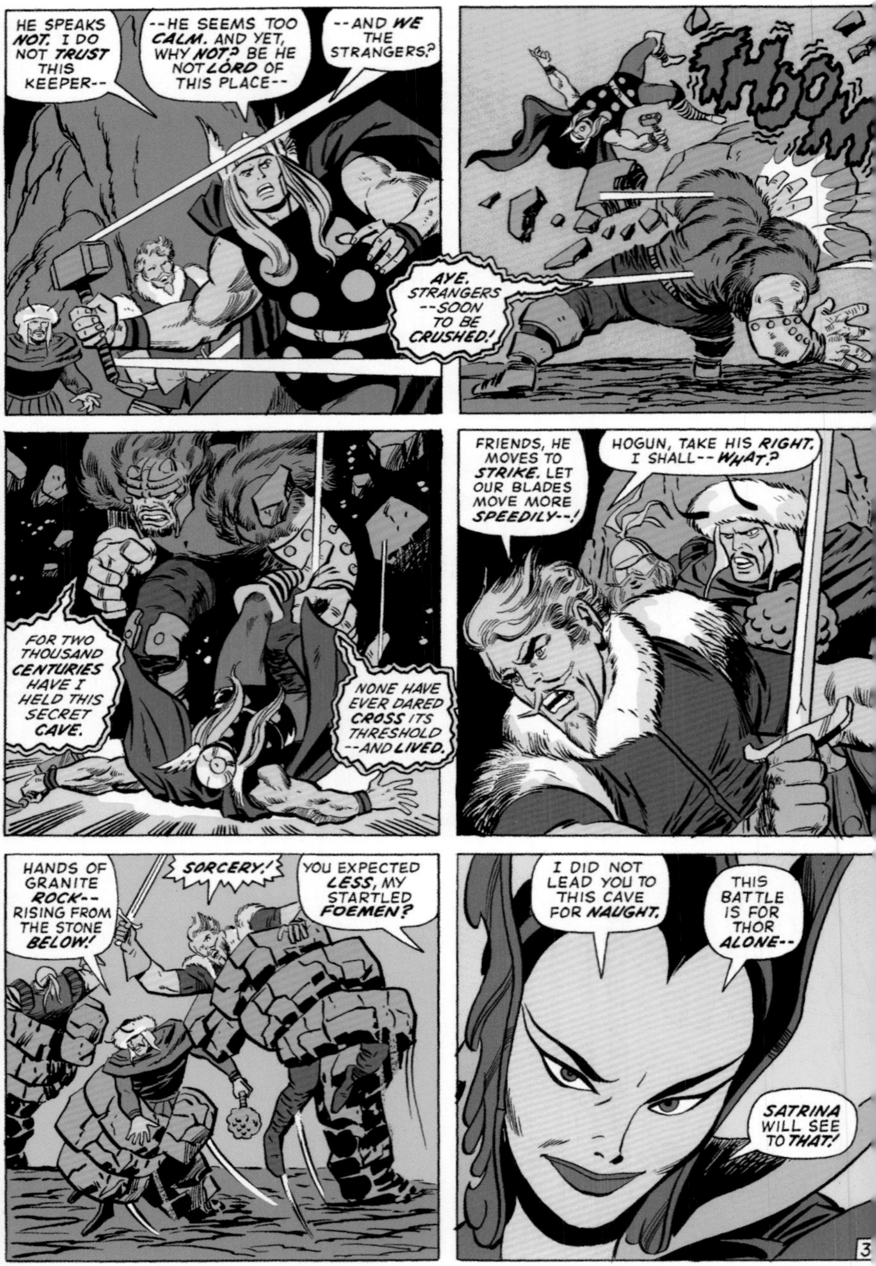
HE SPEAKS NOT. I DO NOT TRUST THIS KEEPER--
--HE SEEMS TOO CALM. AND YET, WHY NOT? BE HE NOT LORD OF THIS PLACE--
--AND WE THE STRANGERS?
AYE. STRANGERS --SOON TO BE CRUSHED!
THOOM
FOR TWO THOUSAND CENTURIES HAVE I HELD THIS SECRET CAVE.
NONE HAVE EVER DARED CROSS ITS THRESHOLD --AND LIVED.
FRIENDS, HE MOVES TO STRIKE. LET OUR BLADES MOVE MORE SPEEDILY--!
HOGUN, TAKE HIS RIGHT. I SHALL--WHAT?
HANDS OF GRANITE ROCK-- RISING FROM THE STONE BELOW!
SORCERY!
YOU EXPECTED LESS, MY STARTLED FOEMEN?
I DID NOT LEAD YOU TO THIS CAVE FOR NAUGHT.
THIS BATTLE IS FOR THOR ALONE--
SATRINA WILL SEE TO THAT!
3

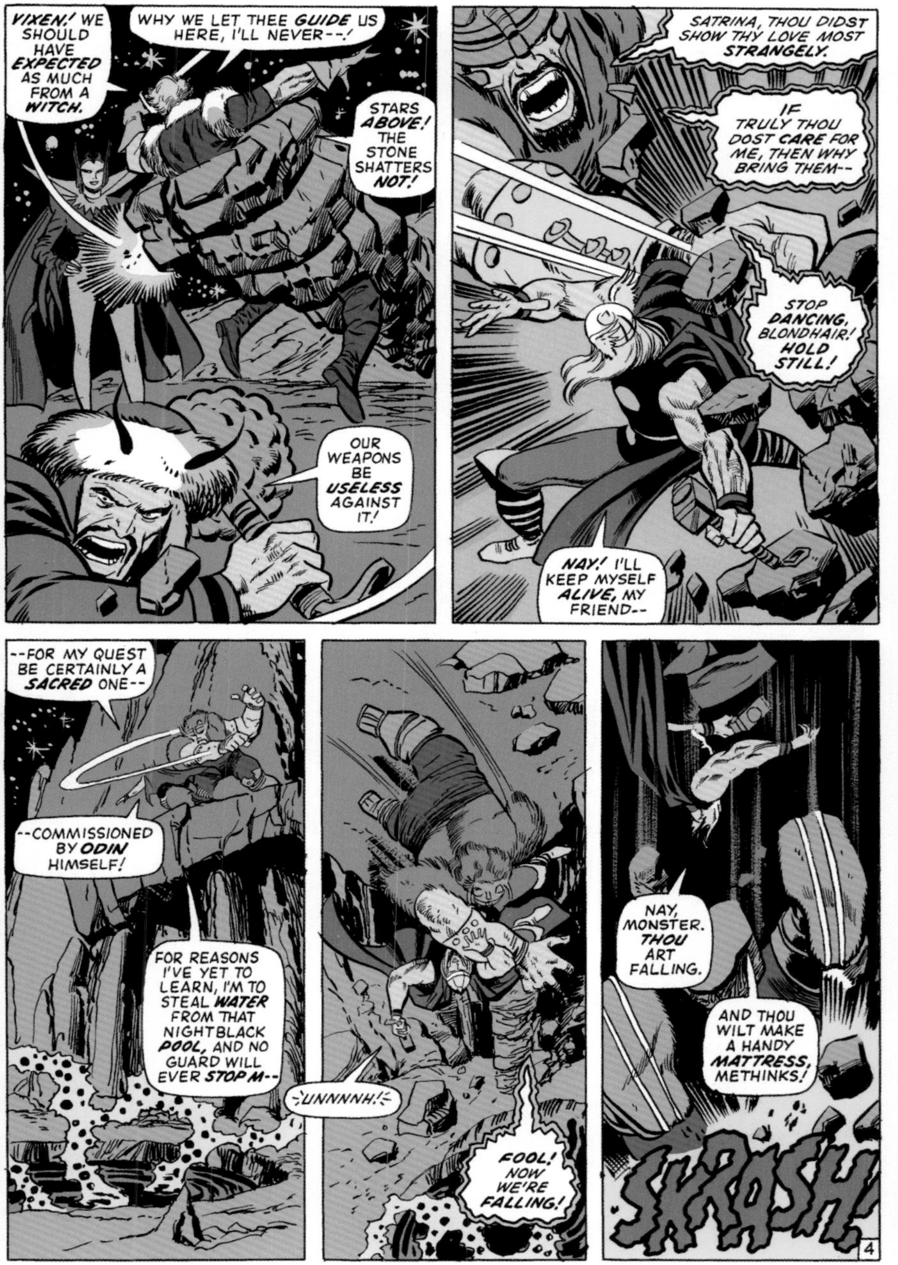
VIXEN! WE SHOULD HAVE EXPECTED AS MUCH FROM A WITCH.
WHY WE LET THEE GUIDE US HERE, I'LL NEVER--!
STARS ABOVE! THE STONE SHATTERS NOT!
OUR WEAPONS BE USELESS AGAINST IT!
SATRINA, THOU DIDST SHOW THY LOVE MOST STRANGELY.
IF TRULY THOU DOST CARE FOR ME, THEN WHY BRING THEM--
STOP DANCING, BLONDHAIR! HOLD STILL!
NAY! I'LL KEEP MYSELF ALIVE, MY FRIEND--
--FOR MY QUEST BE CERTAINLY A SACRED ONE--
--COMMISSIONED BY ODIN HIMSELF!
FOR REASONS I'VE YET TO LEARN, I'M TO STEAL WATER FROM THAT NIGHTBLACK POOL, AND NO GUARD WILL EVER STOP M--
UNNNNH!
FOOL! NOW WE'RE FALLING!
NAY, MONSTER. THOU ART FALLING.
AND THOU WILT MAKE A HANDY MATTRESS, METHINKS!
SKRASH!
4

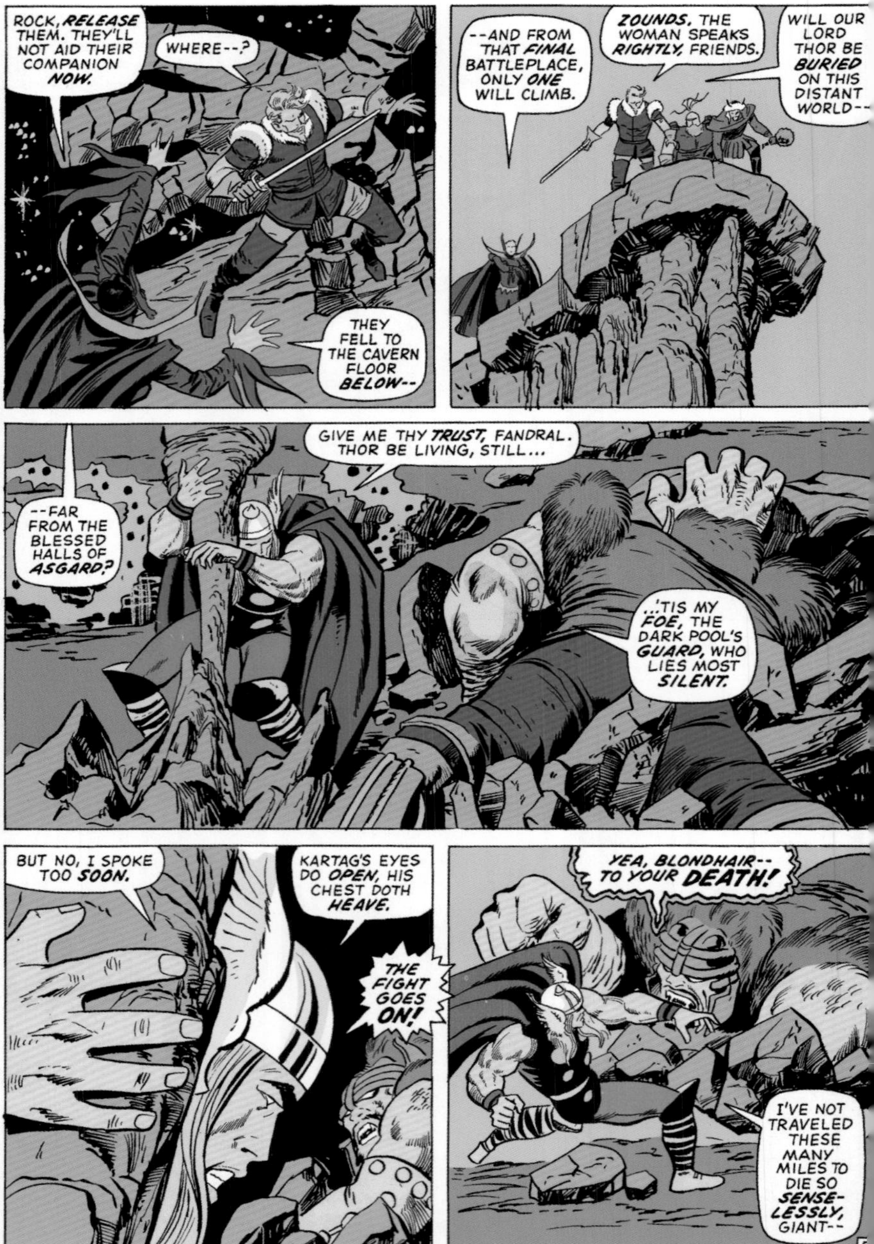
ROCK, RELEASE THEM. THEY'LL NOT AID THEIR COMPANION NOW.
WHERE--?
THEY FELL TO THE CAVERN FLOOR BELOW--
--AND FROM THAT FINAL BATTLEPLACE, ONLY ONE WILL CLIMB.
ZOUNDS, THE WOMAN SPEAKS RIGHTLY, FRIENDS.
WILL OUR LORD THOR BE BURIED ON THIS DISTANT WORLD--
--FAR FROM THE BLESSED HALLS OF ASGARD?
GIVE ME THY TRUST, FANDRAL. THOR BE LIVING, STILL...
...'TIS MY FOE, THE DARK POOL'S GUARD, WHO LIES MOST SILENT.
BUT NO, I SPOKE TOO SOON.
KARTAG'S EYES DO OPEN, HIS CHEST DOTH HEAVE.
THE FIGHT GOES ON!
YEA, BLONDHAIR-- TO YOUR DEATH!
I'VE NOT TRAVELED THESE MANY MILES TO DIE SO SENSE-LESSLY, GIANT--
5

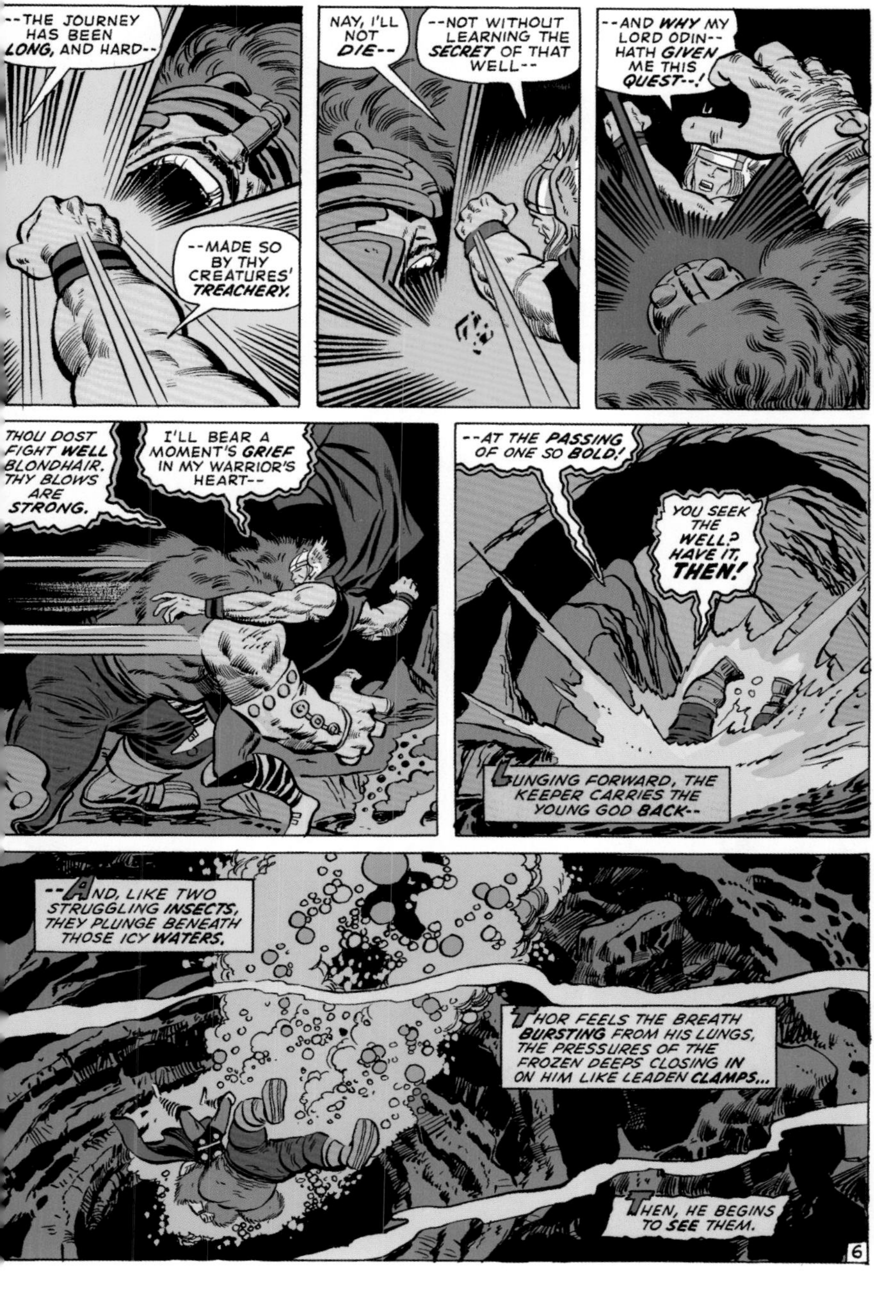
--THE JOURNEY HAS BEEN LONG, AND HARD--
--MADE SO BY THY CREATURES' TREACHERY.
NAY, I'LL NOT DIE--
--NOT WITHOUT LEARNING THE SECRET OF THAT WELL--
--AND WHY MY LORD ODIN-- HATH GIVEN ME THIS QUEST--!
THOU DOST FIGHT WELL BLONDHAIR. THY BLOWS ARE STRONG.
I'LL BEAR A MOMENT'S GRIEF IN MY WARRIOR'S HEART--
--AT THE PASSING OF ONE SO BOLD!
YOU SEEK THE WELL? HAVE IT, THEN!
LUNGING FORWARD, THE KEEPER CARRIES THE YOUNG GOD BACK--
--AND, LIKE TWO STRUGGLING INSECTS, THEY PLUNGE BENEATH THOSE ICY WATERS.
THOR FEELS THE BREATH BURSTING FROM HIS LUNGS, THE PRESSURES OF THE FROZEN DEEPS CLOSING IN ON HIM LIKE LEADEN CLAMPS...
THEN, HE BEGINS TO SEE THEM.
6

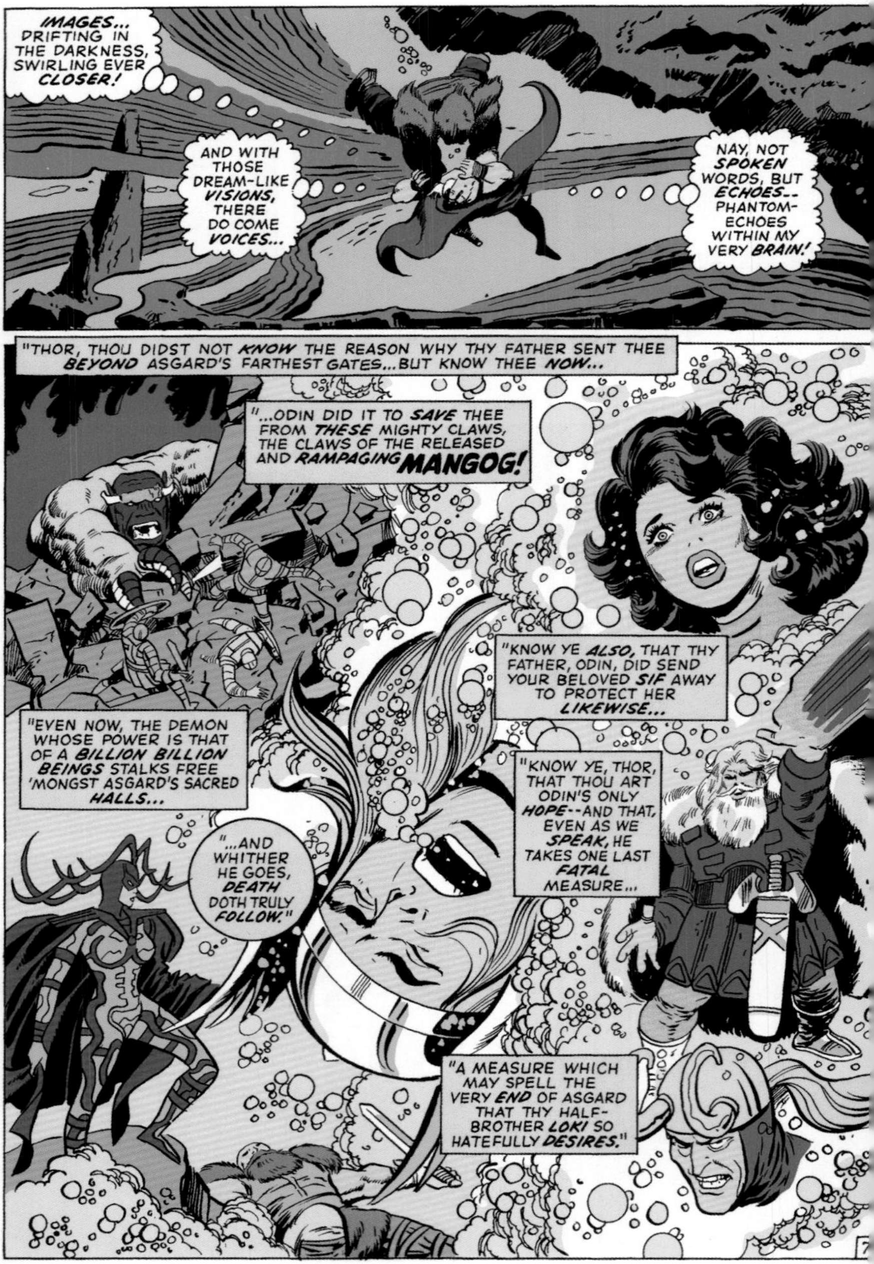
IMAGES... DRIFTING IN THE DARKNESS, SWIRLING EVER CLOSER!
AND WITH THOSE DREAM-LIKE VISIONS, THERE DO COME VOICES...
NAY, NOT SPOKEN WORDS, BUT ECHOES.. PHANTOM-ECHOES WITHIN MY VERY BRAIN!
"THOR, THOU DIDST NOT KNOW THE REASON WHY THY FATHER SENT THEE BEYOND ASGARD'S FARTHEST GATES... BUT KNOW THEE NOW...
"...ODIN DID IT TO SAVE THEE FROM THESE MIGHTY CLAWS, THE CLAWS OF THE RELEASED AND RAMPAGING MANGOG!
"KNOW YE ALSO, THAT THY FATHER, ODIN, DID SEND YOUR BELOVED SIF AWAY TO PROTECT HER LIKEWISE...
"EVEN NOW, THE DEMON WHOSE POWER IS THAT OF A BILLION BILLION BEINGS STALKS FREE 'MONGST ASGARD'S SACRED HALLS...
"...AND WHITHER HE GOES, DEATH DOTH TRULY FOLLOW."
"KNOW YE, THOR, THAT THOU ART ODIN'S ONLY HOPE--AND THAT, EVEN AS WE SPEAK, HE TAKES ONE LAST FATAL MEASURE...
"A MEASURE WHICH MAY SPELL THE VERY END OF ASGARD THAT THY HALF-BROTHER LOKI SO HATEFULLY DESIRES."
7

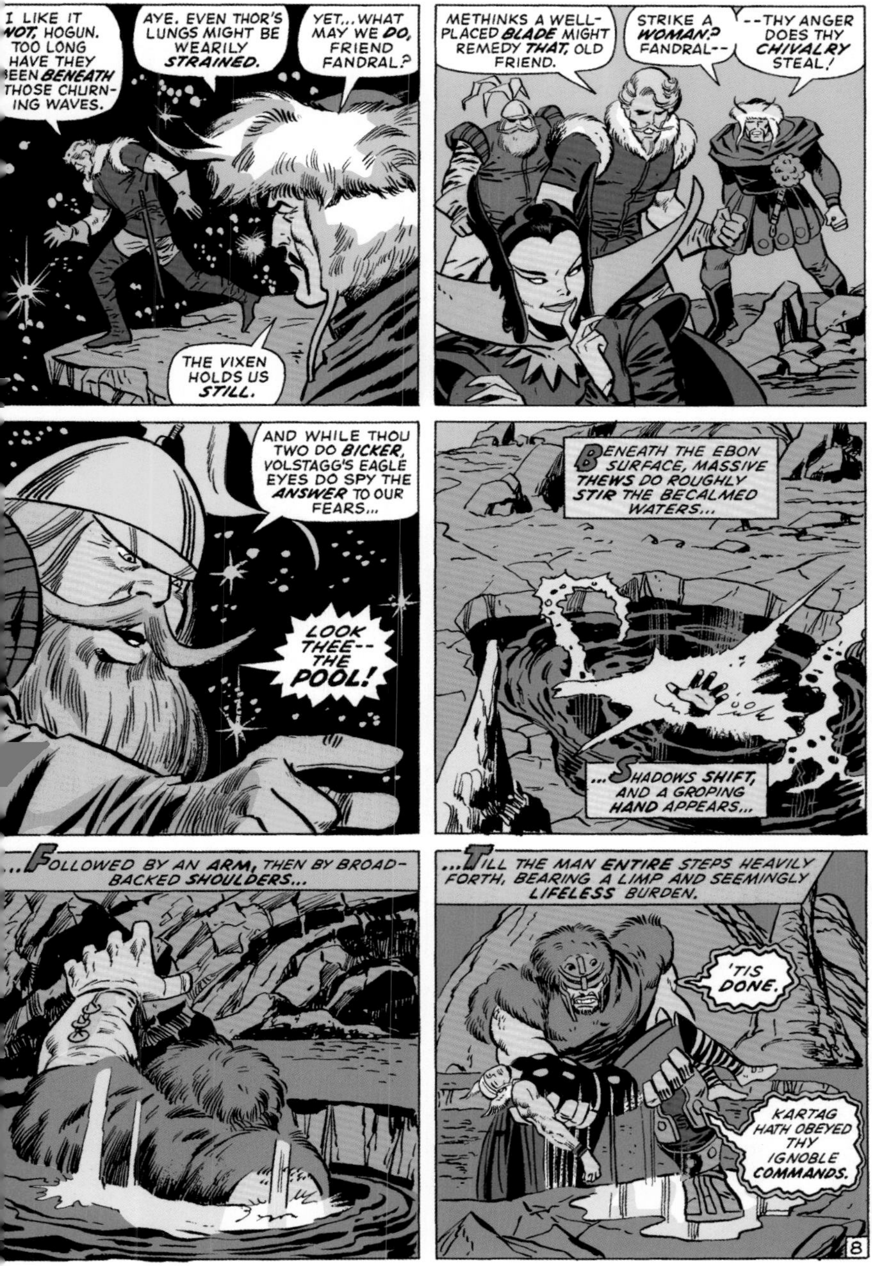

I LIKE IT NOT, HOGUN. TOO LONG HAVE THEY BEEN BENEATH THOSE CHURNING WAVES.
AYE. EVEN THOR'S LUNGS MIGHT BE WEARILY STRAINED.
YET... WHAT MAY WE DO, FRIEND FANDRAL?
THE VIXEN HOLDS US STILL.
METHINKS A WELL-PLACED BLADE MIGHT REMEDY THAT, OLD FRIEND.
STRIKE A WOMAN? FANDRAL--
--THY ANGER DOES THY CHIVALRY STEAL!
AND WHILE THOU TWO DO BICKER, VOLSTAGG'S EAGLE EYES DO SPY THE ANSWER TO OUR FEARS...
LOOK THEE-- THE POOL!
BENEATH THE EBON SURFACE, MASSIVE THEWS DO ROUGHLY STIR THE BECALMED WATERS...
...SHADOWS SHIFT, AND A GROPING HAND APPEARS...
...FOLLOWED BY AN ARM, THEN BY BROAD-BACKED SHOULDERS...
...TILL THE MAN ENTIRE STEPS HEAVILY FORTH, BEARING A LIMP AND SEEMINGLY LIFELESS BURDEN.
'TIS DONE.
KARTAG HATH OBEYED THY IGNOBLE COMMANDS.
8

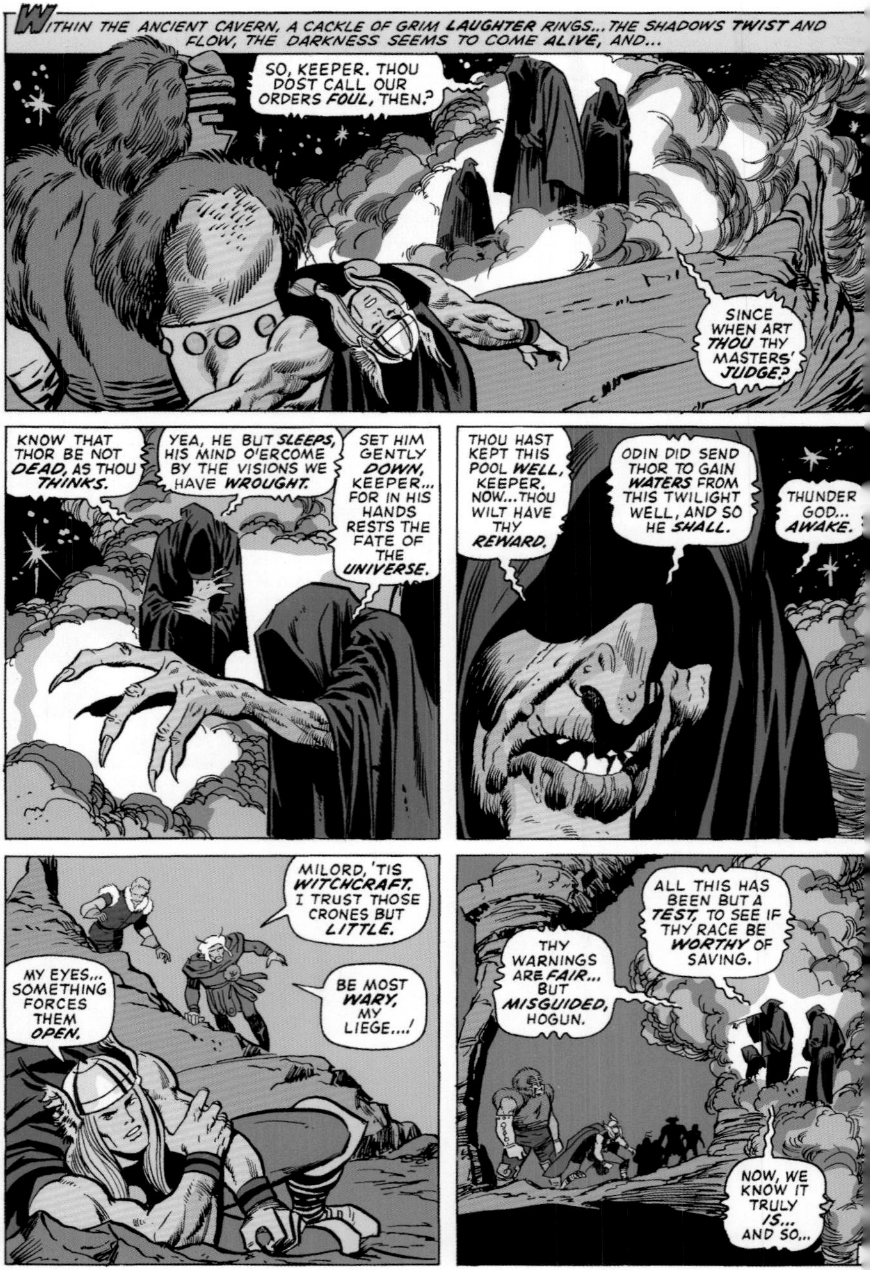
WITHIN THE ANCIENT CAVERN, A CACKLE OF GRIM LAUGHTER RINGS... THE SHADOWS TWIST AND FLOW, THE DARKNESS SEEMS TO COME ALIVE, AND...
SO, KEEPER. THOU DOST CALL OUR ORDERS FOUL, THEN?
SINCE WHEN ART THOU THY MASTERS' JUDGE?
KNOW THAT THOR BE NOT DEAD, AS THOU THINKS.
YEA, HE BUT SLEEPS, HIS MIND O'ERCOME BY THE VISIONS WE HAVE WROUGHT.
SET HIM GENTLY DOWN, KEEPER... FOR IN HIS HANDS RESTS THE FATE OF THE UNIVERSE.
THOU HAST KEPT THIS POOL WELL, KEEPER. NOW... THOU WILT HAVE THY REWARD.
ODIN DID SEND THOR TO GAIN WATERS FROM THIS TWILIGHT WELL, AND SO HE SHALL.
THUNDER GOD... AWAKE.
MILORD, 'TIS WITCHCRAFT. I TRUST THOSE CRONES BUT LITTLE.
MY EYES... SOMETHING FORCES THEM OPEN.
BE MOST WARY, MY LIEGE...!
ALL THIS HAS BEEN BUT A TEST, TO SEE IF THY RACE BE WORTHY OF SAVING.
THY WARNINGS ARE FAIR... BUT MISGUIDED, HOGUN.
NOW, WE KNOW IT TRULY IS... AND SO...

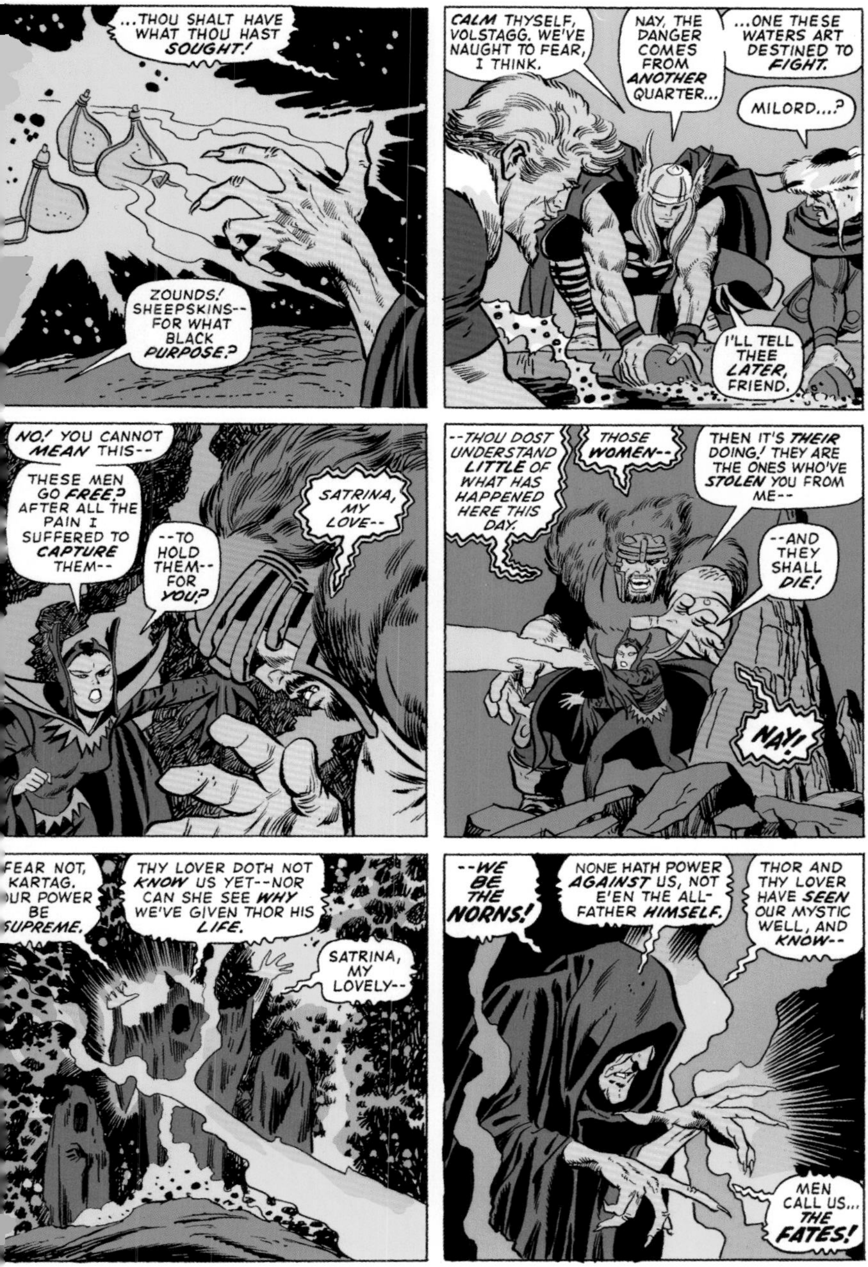
...THOU SHALT HAVE WHAT THOU HAST SOUGHT!
ZOUNDS! SHEEPSKINS-- FOR WHAT BLACK PURPOSE?
CALM THYSELF, VOLSTAGG. WE'VE NAUGHT TO FEAR, I THINK.
NAY, THE DANGER COMES FROM ANOTHER QUARTER...
...ONE THESE WATERS ART DESTINED TO FIGHT.
MILORD...?
I'LL TELL THEE LATER, FRIEND.
NO! YOU CANNOT MEAN THIS--
THESE MEN GO FREE? AFTER ALL THE PAIN I SUFFERED TO CAPTURE THEM--
--TO HOLD THEM-- FOR YOU?
SATRINA, MY LOVE--
--THOU DOST UNDERSTAND LITTLE OF WHAT HAS HAPPENED HERE THIS DAY.
THOSE WOMEN--
THEN IT'S THEIR DOING! THEY ARE THE ONES WHO'VE STOLEN YOU FROM ME--
--AND THEY SHALL DIE!
NAY!
FEAR NOT, KARTAG. OUR POWER BE SUPREME.
THY LOVER DOTH NOT KNOW US YET--NOR CAN SHE SEE WHY WE'VE GIVEN THOR HIS LIFE.
SATRINA, MY LOVELY--
--WE BE THE NORNS!
NONE HATH POWER AGAINST US, NOT E'EN THE ALL-FATHER HIMSELF.
THOR AND THY LOVER HAVE SEEN OUR MYSTIC WELL, AND KNOW--
MEN CALL US... THE FATES!

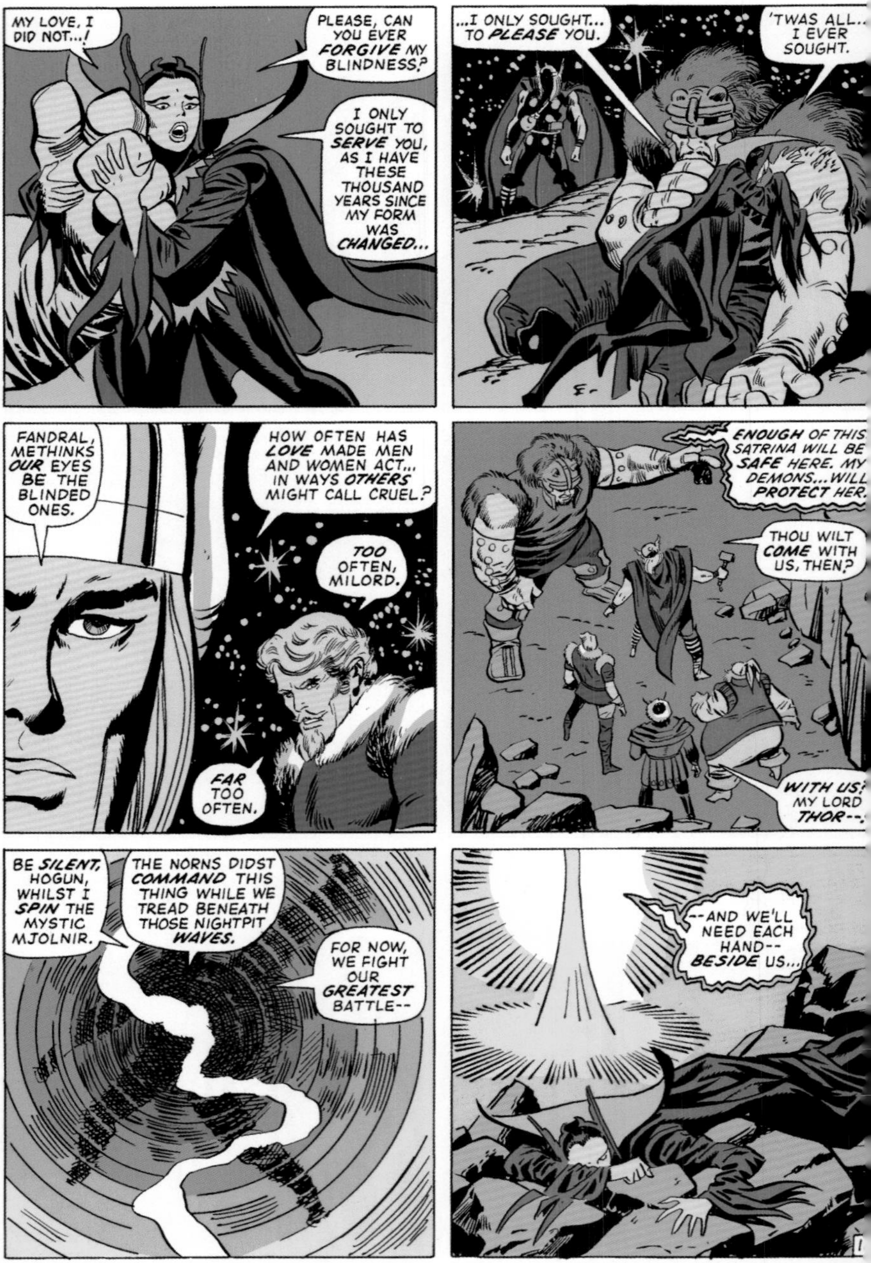
MY LOVE, I DID NOT...!
PLEASE, CAN YOU EVER FORGIVE MY BLINDNESS?
I ONLY SOUGHT TO SERVE YOU, AS I HAVE THESE THOUSAND YEARS SINCE MY FORM WAS CHANGED...
...I ONLY SOUGHT... TO PLEASE YOU.
'TWAS ALL... I EVER SOUGHT.
FANDRAL, METHINKS OUR EYES BE THE BLINDED ONES.
HOW OFTEN HAS LOVE MADE MEN AND WOMEN ACT... IN WAYS OTHERS MIGHT CALL CRUEL?
TOO OFTEN, MILORD.
FAR TOO OFTEN.
ENOUGH OF THIS SATRINA WILL BE SAFE HERE. MY DEMONS...WILL PROTECT HER.
THOU WILT COME WITH US, THEN?
WITH US! MY LORD THOR--.
BE SILENT, HOGUN, WHILST I SPIN THE MYSTIC MJOLNIR.
THE NORNS DIDST COMMAND THIS THING WHILE WE TREAD BENEATH THOSE NIGHTPIT WAVES.
FOR NOW, WE FIGHT OUR GREATEST BATTLE--
--AND WE'LL NEED EACH HAND-- BESIDE US...

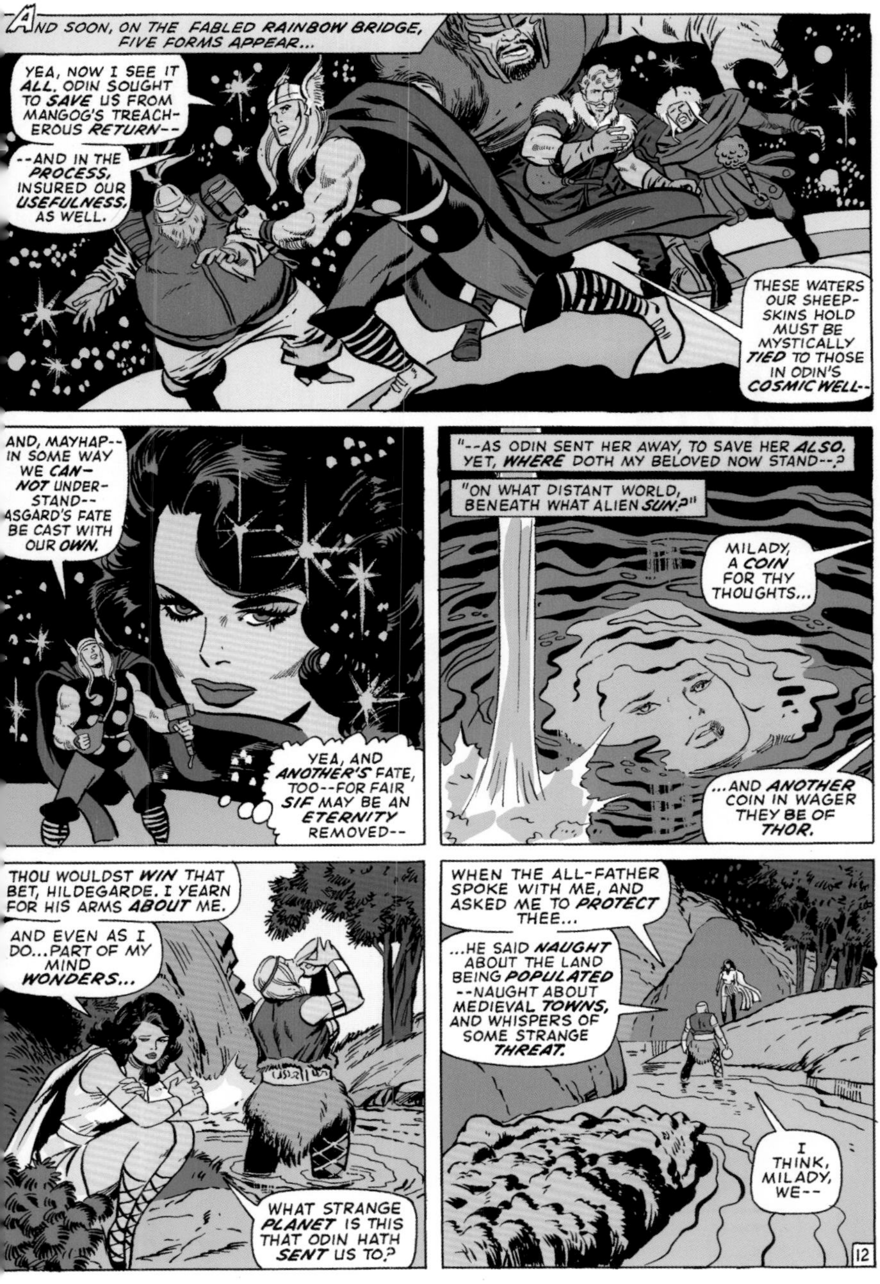
AND SOON, ON THE FABLED RAINBOW BRIDGE, FIVE FORMS APPEAR...
YEA, NOW I SEE IT ALL. ODIN SOUGHT TO SAVE US FROM MANGOG'S TREACHEROUS RETURN--
--AND IN THE PROCESS, INSURED OUR USEFULNESS, AS WELL.
THESE WATERS OUR SHEEPSKINS HOLD MUST BE MYSTICALLY TIED TO THOSE IN ODIN'S COSMIC WELL--
AND, MAYHAP-- IN SOME WAY WE CANNOT UNDERSTAND-- ASGARD'S FATE BE CAST WITH OUR OWN.
YEA, AND ANOTHER'S FATE, TOO--FOR FAIR SIF MAY BE AN ETERNITY REMOVED--
"--AS ODIN SENT HER AWAY, TO SAVE HER ALSO. YET, WHERE DOTH MY BELOVED NOW STAND--?
"ON WHAT DISTANT WORLD, BENEATH WHAT ALIEN SUN?"
MILADY, A COIN FOR THY THOUGHTS...
...AND ANOTHER COIN IN WAGER THEY BE OF THOR.
THOU WOULDST WIN THAT BET, HILDEGARDE. I YEARN FOR HIS ARMS ABOUT ME.
AND EVEN AS I DO...PART OF MY MIND WONDERS...
WHAT STRANGE PLANET IS THIS THAT ODIN HATH SENT US TO?
WHEN THE ALL-FATHER SPOKE WITH ME, AND ASKED ME TO PROTECT THEE...
...HE SAID NAUGHT ABOUT THE LAND BEING POPULATED --NAUGHT ABOUT MEDIEVAL TOWNS, AND WHISPERS OF SOME STRANGE THREAT.
I THINK, MILADY, WE--
12

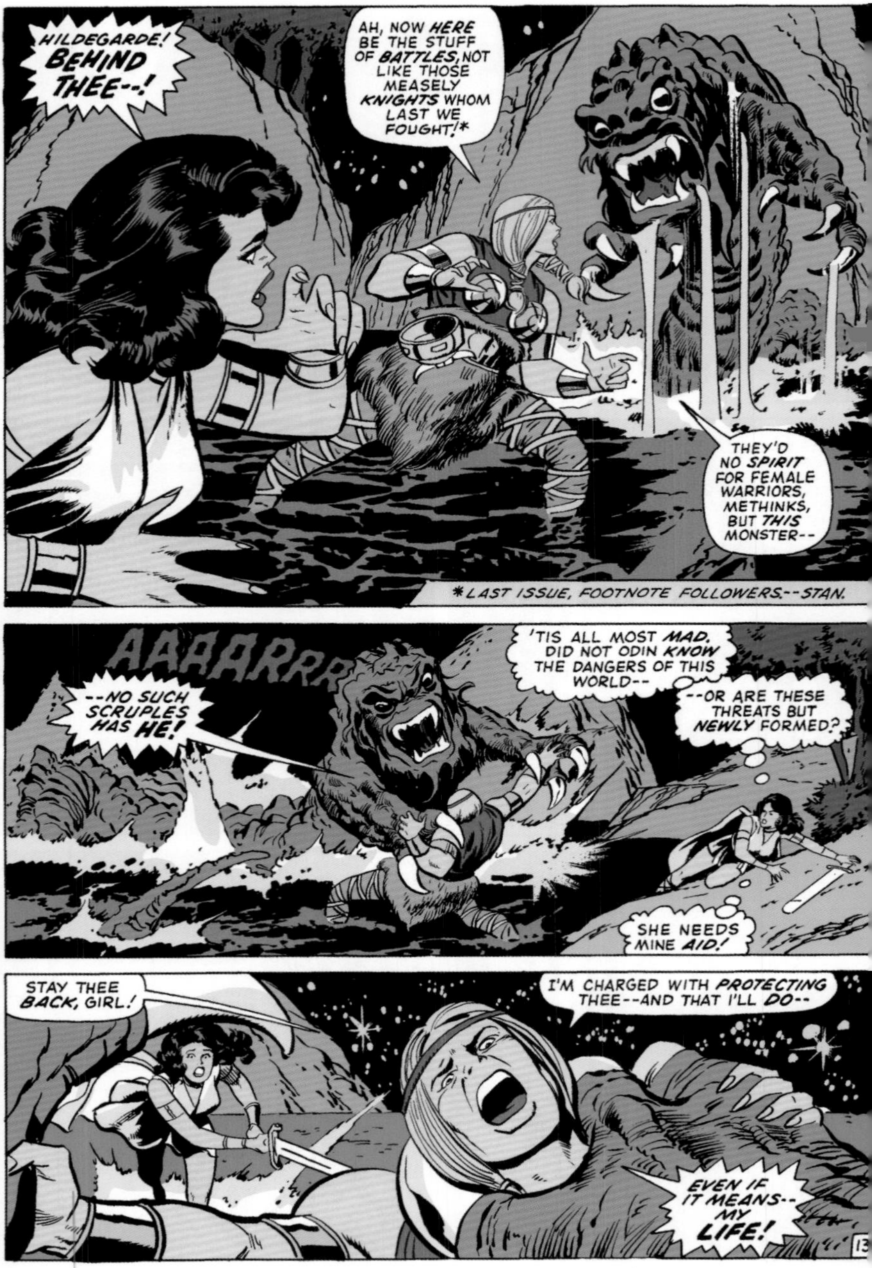
HILDEGARDE! BEHIND THEE--!
AH, NOW HERE BE THE STUFF OF BATTLES, NOT LIKE THOSE MEASELY KNIGHTS WHOM LAST WE FOUGHT!*
THEY'D NO SPIRIT FOR FEMALE WARRIORS, METHINKS, BUT THIS MONSTER--
*LAST ISSUE, FOOTNOTE FOLLOWERS.--STAN.
AAAAARRR
--NO SUCH SCRUPLES HAS HE!
'TIS ALL MOST MAD. DID NOT ODIN KNOW THE DANGERS OF THIS WORLD--
--OR ARE THESE THREATS BUT NEWLY FORMED?
SHE NEEDS MINE AID!
STAY THEE BACK, GIRL!
I'M CHARGED WITH PROTECTING THEE--AND THAT I'LL DO--
EVEN IF IT MEANS-- MY LIFE!
13

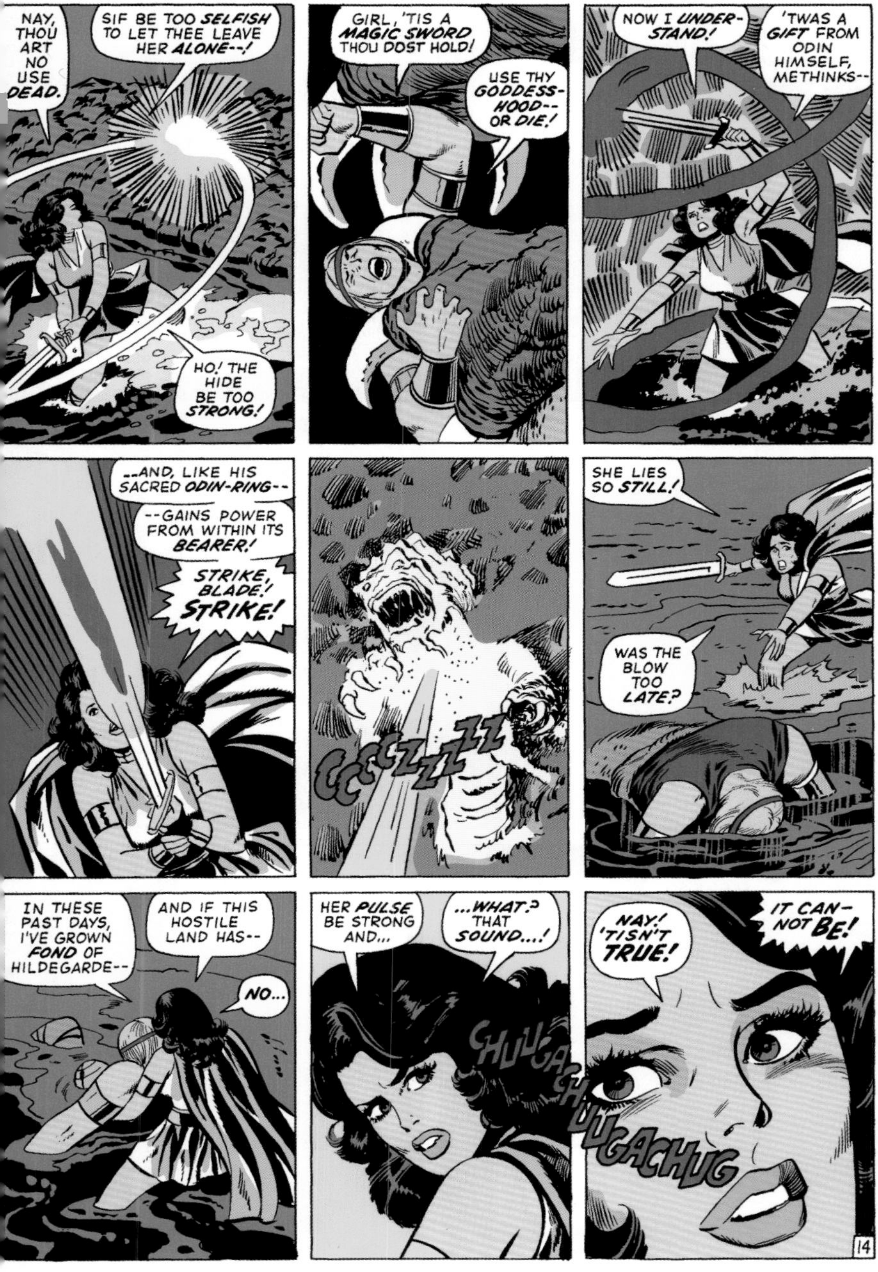
NAY, THOU ART NO USE DEAD.
SIF BE TOO SELFISH TO LET THEE LEAVE HER ALONE--!
HO! THE HIDE BE TOO STRONG!
GIRL, 'TIS A MAGIC SWORD THOU DOST HOLD!
USE THY GODDESS-HOOD--OR DIE!
NOW I UNDERSTAND!
'TWAS A GIFT FROM ODIN HIMSELF, METHINKS--
--AND, LIKE HIS SACRED ODIN-RING--
--GAINS POWER FROM WITHIN ITS BEARER!
STRIKE, BLADE! STRIKE!
CCCCZZZZZZ
SHE LIES SO STILL!
WAS THE BLOW TOO LATE?
IN THESE PAST DAYS, I'VE GROWN FOND OF HILDEGARDE--
AND IF THIS HOSTILE LAND HAS--
NO...
HER PULSE BE STRONG AND...
...WHAT? THAT SOUND....!
CHUGACHUGACHUGACHUG
NAY! 'TISN'T TRUE!
IT CANNOT BE!
14

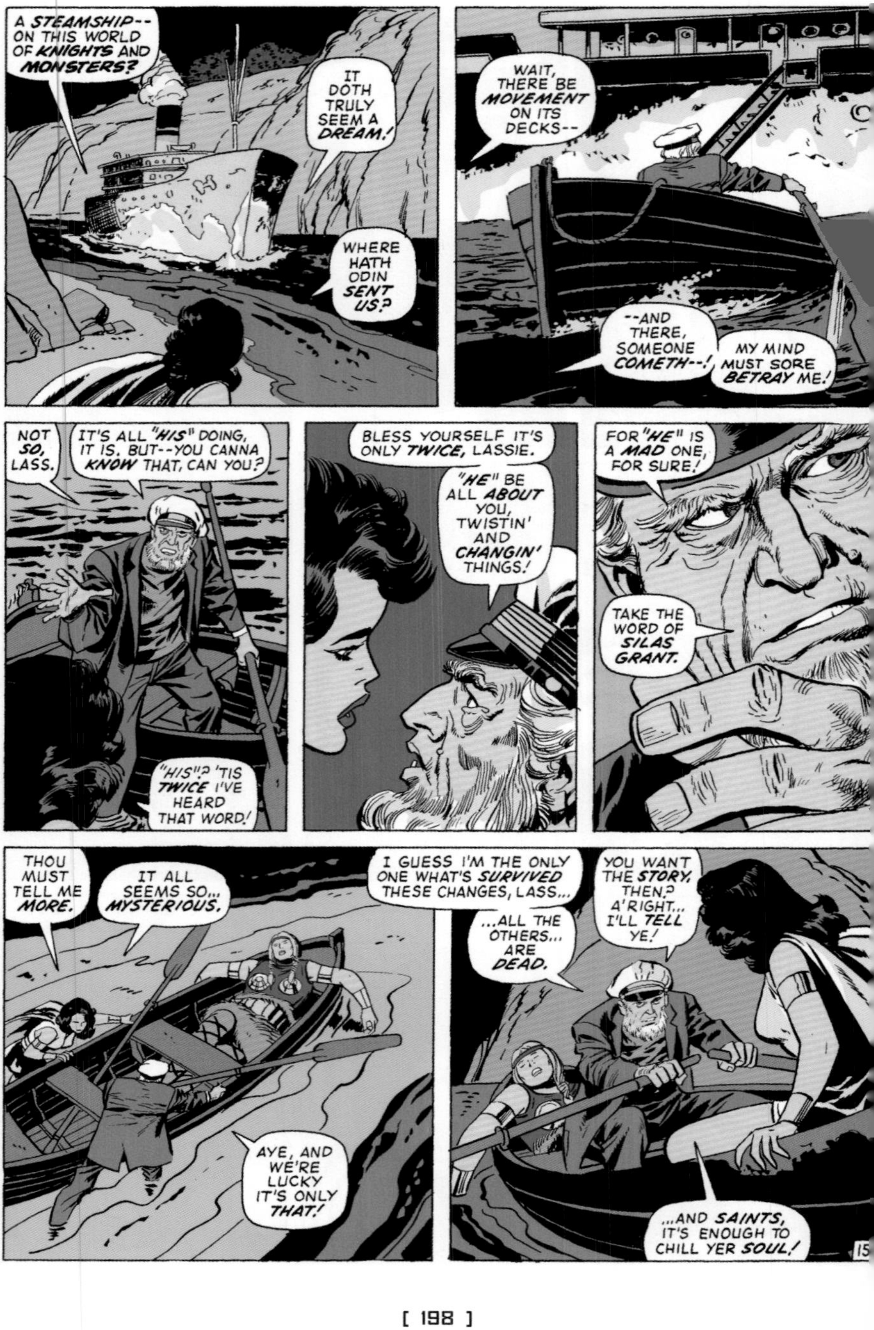
A STEAMSHIP-- ON THIS WORLD OF KNIGHTS AND MONSTERS?
IT DOTH TRULY SEEM A DREAM!
WHERE HATH ODIN SENT US?
WAIT, THERE BE MOVEMENT ON ITS DECKS--
--AND THERE, SOMEONE COMETH--!
MY MIND MUST SORE BETRAY ME!
NOT SO, LASS.
IT'S ALL "HIS" DOING, IT IS. BUT--YOU CANNA KNOW THAT, CAN YOU?
"HIS"? 'TIS TWICE I'VE HEARD THAT WORD!
BLESS YOURSELF IT'S ONLY TWICE, LASSIE.
"HE" BE ALL ABOUT YOU, TWISTIN' AND CHANGIN' THINGS!
FOR "HE" IS A MAD ONE, FOR SURE!
TAKE THE WORD OF SILAS GRANT.
THOU MUST TELL ME MORE.
IT ALL SEEMS SO... MYSTERIOUS.
AYE, AND WE'RE LUCKY IT'S ONLY THAT!
I GUESS I'M THE ONLY ONE WHAT'S SURVIVED THESE CHANGES, LASS...
...ALL THE OTHERS... ARE DEAD.
YOU WANT THE STORY, THEN? A'RIGHT... I'LL TELL YE!
...AND SAINTS, IT'S ENOUGH TO CHILL YER SOUL!
15

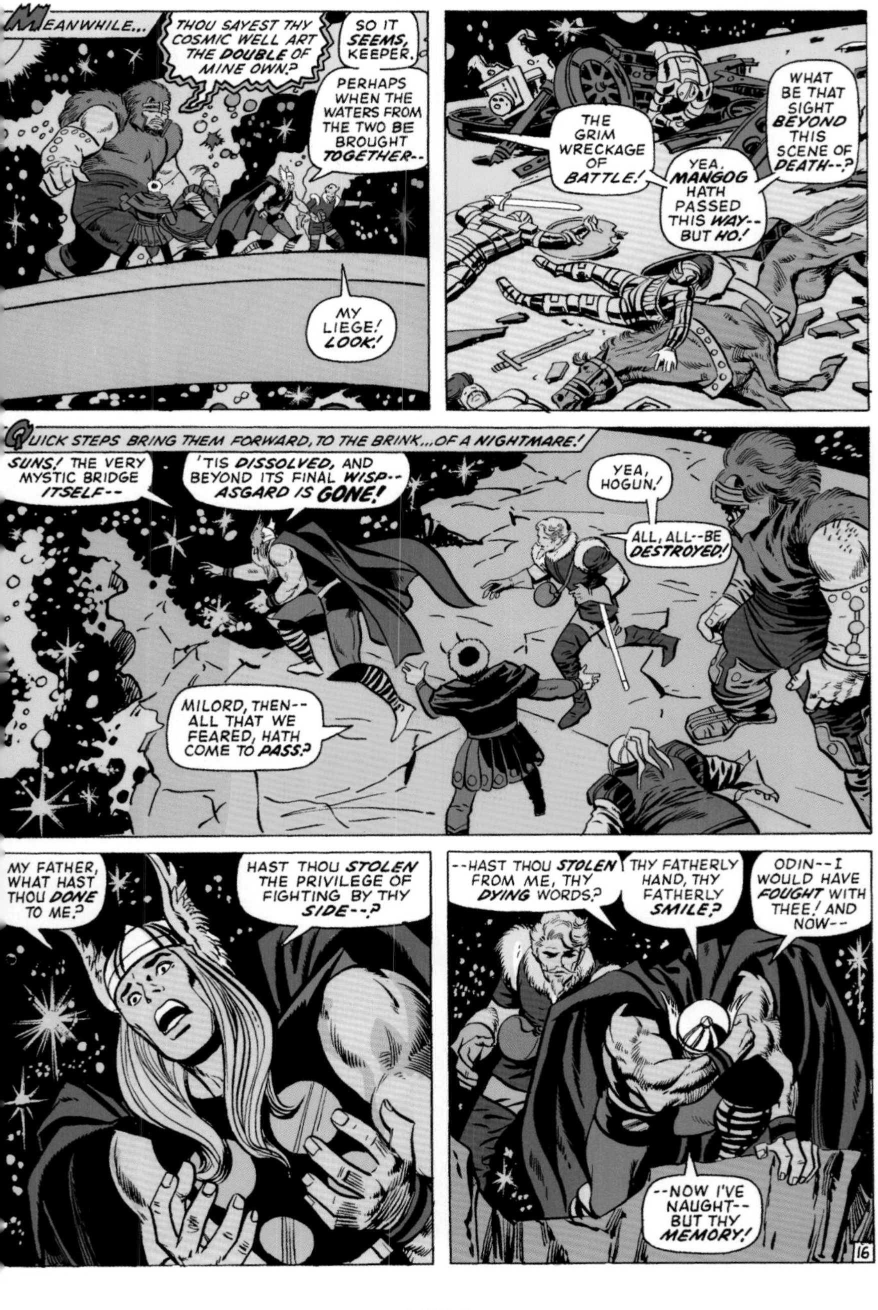
MEANWHILE...
THOU SAYEST THY COSMIC WELL ART THE DOUBLE OF MINE OWN?
SO IT SEEMS, KEEPER.
PERHAPS WHEN THE WATERS FROM THE TWO BE BROUGHT TOGETHER--
MY LIEGE! LOOK!
THE GRIM WRECKAGE OF BATTLE!
YEA. MANGOG HATH PASSED THIS WAY--BUT HO!
WHAT BE THAT SIGHT BEYOND THIS SCENE OF DEATH--?
QUICK STEPS BRING THEM FORWARD, TO THE BRINK...OF A NIGHTMARE!
SUNS! THE VERY MYSTIC BRIDGE ITSELF--
'TIS DISSOLVED, AND BEYOND ITS FINAL WISP--ASGARD IS GONE!
YEA, HOGUN!
ALL, ALL--BE DESTROYED!
MILORD, THEN--ALL THAT WE FEARED, HATH COME TO PASS?
MY FATHER, WHAT HAST THOU DONE TO ME?
HAST THOU STOLEN THE PRIVILEGE OF FIGHTING BY THY SIDE--?
--HAST THOU STOLEN FROM ME, THY DYING WORDS?
THY FATHERLY HAND, THY FATHERLY SMILE?
ODIN--I WOULD HAVE FOUGHT WITH THEE! AND NOW--
--NOW I'VE NAUGHT--BUT THY MEMORY!
16

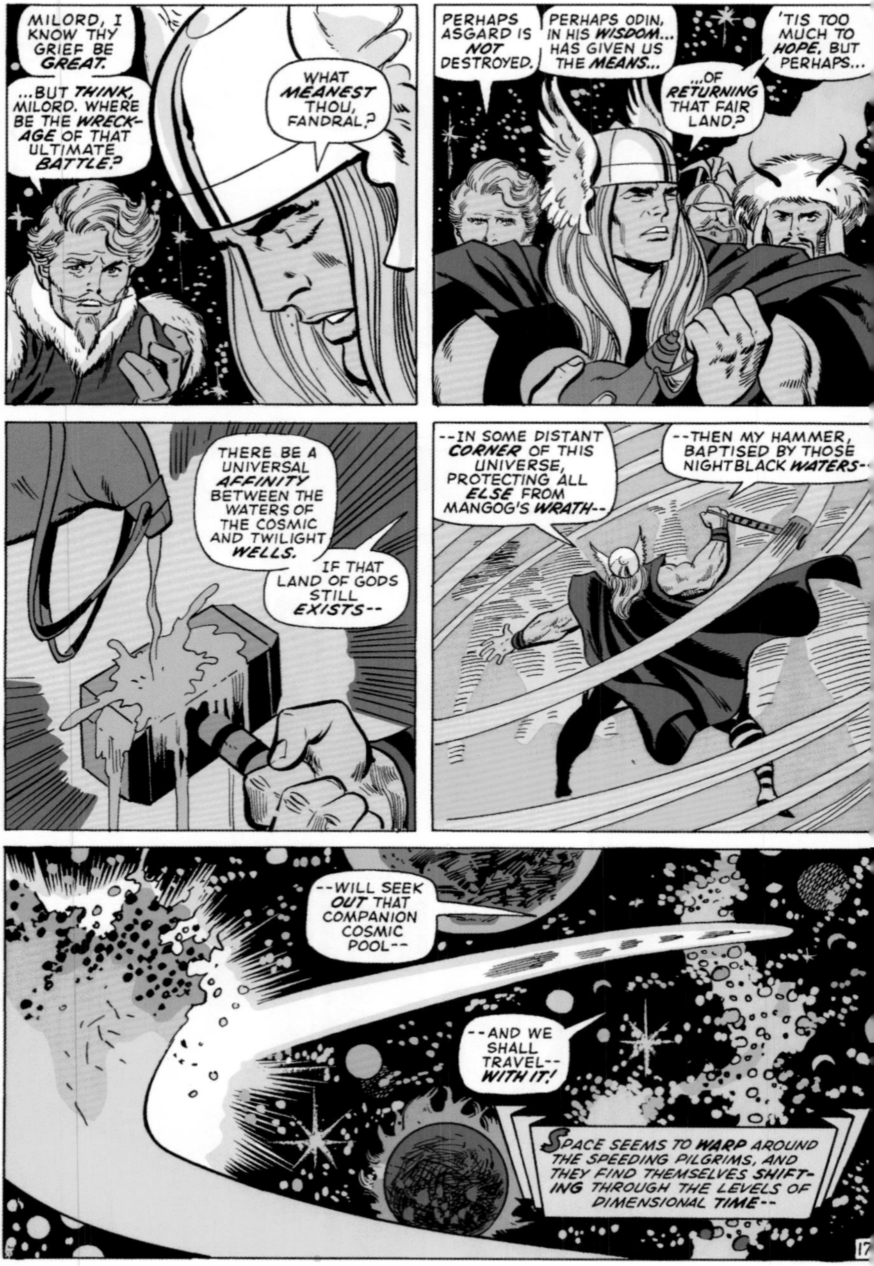
MILORD, I KNOW THY GRIEF BE GREAT.
...BUT THINK, MILORD. WHERE BE THE WRECKAGE OF THAT ULTIMATE BATTLE?
WHAT MEANEST THOU, FANDRAL?
PERHAPS ASGARD IS NOT DESTROYED.
PERHAPS ODIN, IN HIS WISDOM... HAS GIVEN US THE MEANS...
...OF RETURNING THAT FAIR LAND?
'TIS TOO MUCH TO HOPE, BUT PERHAPS...
THERE BE A UNIVERSAL AFFINITY BETWEEN THE WATERS OF THE COSMIC AND TWILIGHT WELLS.
IF THAT LAND OF GODS STILL EXISTS--
--IN SOME DISTANT CORNER OF THIS UNIVERSE, PROTECTING ALL ELSE FROM MANGOG'S WRATH--
--THEN MY HAMMER, BAPTISED BY THOSE NIGHTBLACK WATERS--
--WILL SEEK OUT THAT COMPANION COSMIC POOL--
--AND WE SHALL TRAVEL-- WITH IT!
SPACE SEEMS TO WARP AROUND THE SPEEDING PILGRIMS, AND THEY FIND THEMSELVES SHIFTING THROUGH THE LEVELS OF DIMENSIONAL TIME--
17

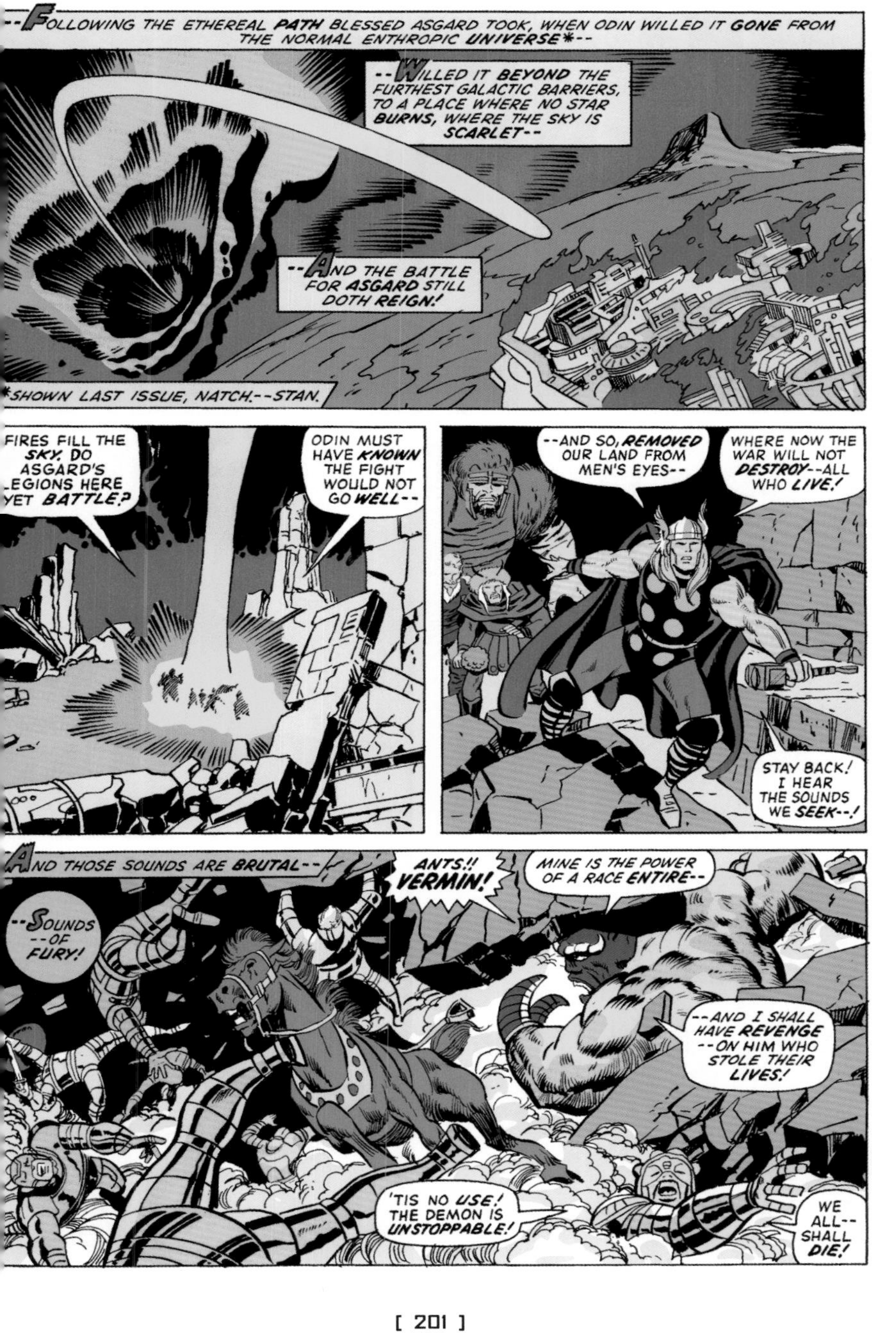
--FOLLOWING THE ETHEREAL PATH BLESSED ASGARD TOOK, WHEN ODIN WILLED IT GONE FROM THE NORMAL ENTHROPIC UNIVERSE*--
--WILLED IT BEYOND THE FURTHEST GALACTIC BARRIERS, TO A PLACE WHERE NO STAR BURNS, WHERE THE SKY IS SCARLET--
--AND THE BATTLE FOR ASGARD STILL DOTH REIGN!
*SHOWN LAST ISSUE, NATCH.--STAN.
FIRES FILL THE SKY. DO ASGARD'S LEGIONS HERE YET BATTLE?
ODIN MUST HAVE KNOWN THE FIGHT WOULD NOT GO WELL--
--AND SO, REMOVED OUR LAND FROM MEN'S EYES--
WHERE NOW THE WAR WILL NOT DESTROY--ALL WHO LIVE!
STAY BACK! I HEAR THE SOUNDS WE SEEK--!
AND THOSE SOUNDS ARE BRUTAL--
--SOUNDS --OF FURY!
ANTS!! VERMIN!
MINE IS THE POWER OF A RACE ENTIRE--
--AND I SHALL HAVE REVENGE --ON HIM WHO STOLE THEIR LIVES!
'TIS NO USE! THE DEMON IS UNSTOPPABLE!
WE ALL-- SHALL DIE!

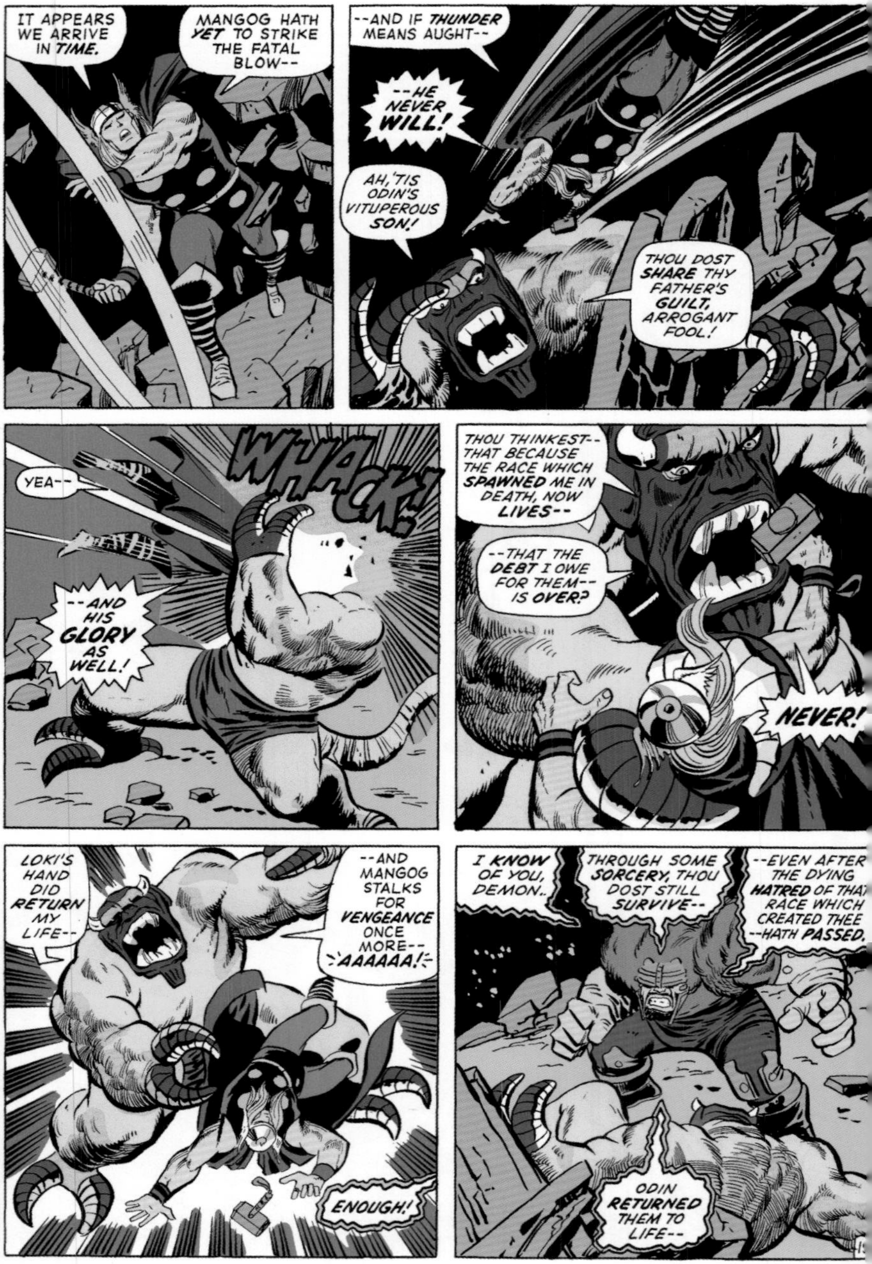

IT APPEARS WE ARRIVE IN TIME.
MANGOG HATH YET TO STRIKE THE FATAL BLOW--
--AND IF THUNDER MEANS AUGHT--
--HE NEVER WILL!
AH, 'TIS ODIN'S VITUPEROUS SON!
THOU DOST SHARE THY FATHER'S GUILT, ARROGANT FOOL!
YEA--
WHACK!
--AND HIS GLORY AS WELL!
THOU THINKEST--THAT BECAUSE THE RACE WHICH SPAWNED ME IN DEATH, NOW LIVES--
--THAT THE DEBT I OWE FOR THEM--IS OVER?
NEVER!
LOKI'S HAND DID RETURN MY LIFE--
--AND MANGOG STALKS FOR VENGEANCE ONCE MORE--
AAAAAA!
ENOUGH!
I KNOW OF YOU, DEMON..
THROUGH SOME SORCERY, THOU DOST STILL SURVIVE--
--EVEN AFTER THE DYING HATRED OF THAT RACE WHICH CREATED THEE --HATH PASSED.
ODIN RETURNED THEM TO LIFE--

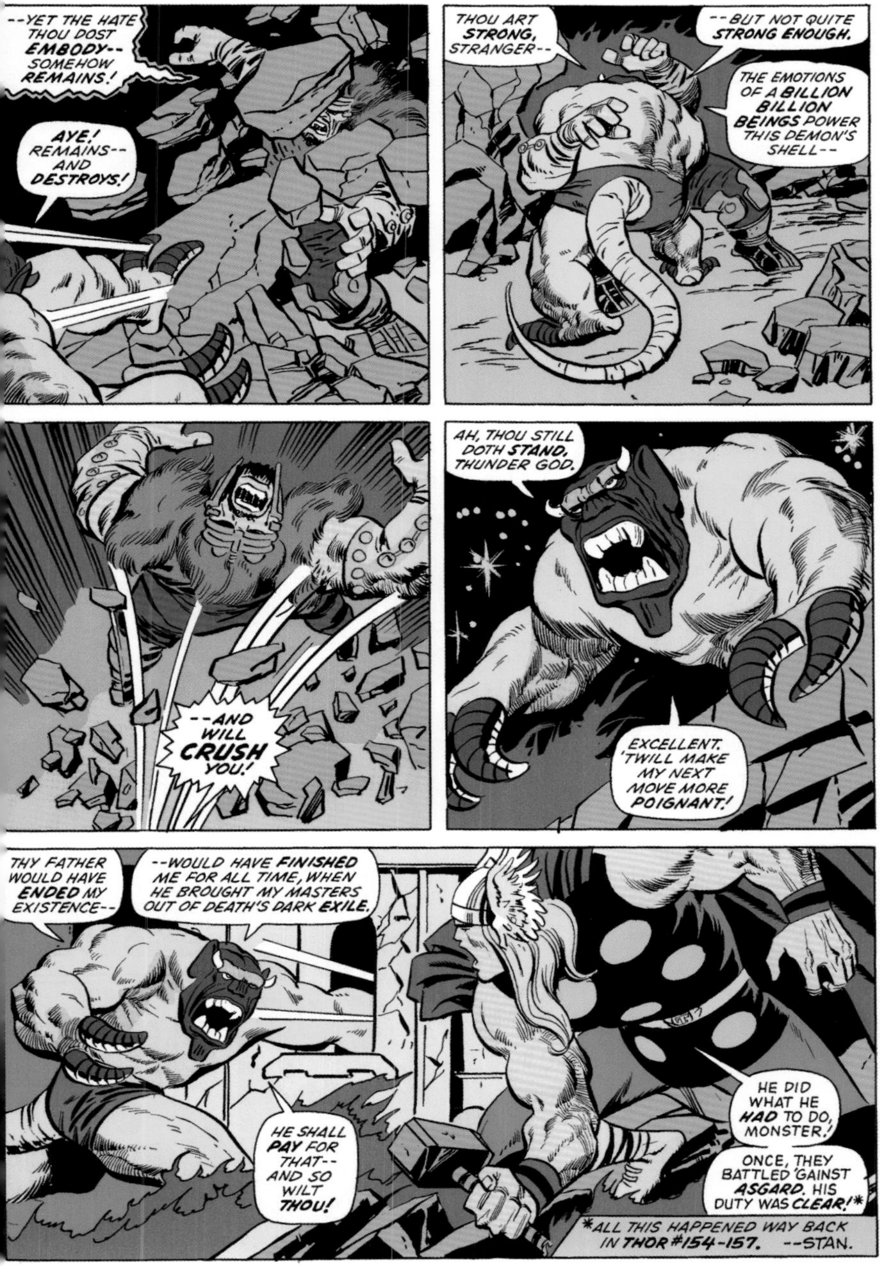
--YET THE HATE THOU DOST EMBODY-- SOMEHOW REMAINS!
AYE! REMAINS-- AND DESTROYS!
THOU ART STRONG, STRANGER--
--BUT NOT QUITE STRONG ENOUGH.
THE EMOTIONS OF A BILLION BILLION BEINGS POWER THIS DEMON'S SHELL--
--AND WILL CRUSH YOU!
AH, THOU STILL DOTH STAND, THUNDER GOD.
EXCELLENT. 'TWILL MAKE MY NEXT MOVE MORE POIGNANT!
THY FATHER WOULD HAVE ENDED MY EXISTENCE--
--WOULD HAVE FINISHED ME FOR ALL TIME, WHEN HE BROUGHT MY MASTERS OUT OF DEATH'S DARK EXILE.
HE SHALL PAY FOR THAT-- AND SO WILT THOU!
HE DID WHAT HE HAD TO DO, MONSTER!
ONCE, THEY BATTLED 'GAINST ASGARD. HIS DUTY WAS CLEAR!*
*ALL THIS HAPPENED WAY BACK IN THOR #154-157. --STAN.

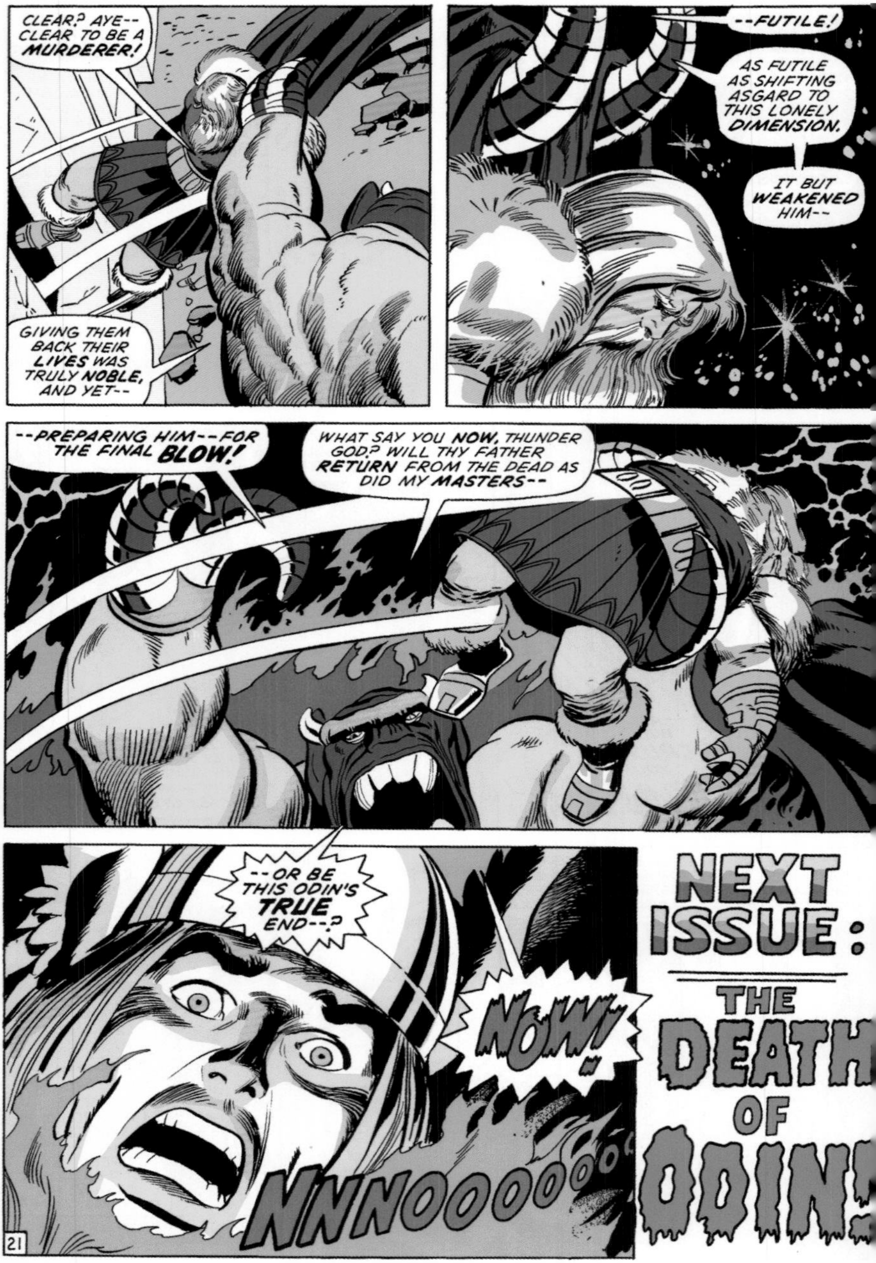
CLEAR? AYE-- CLEAR TO BE A MURDERER!
GIVING THEM BACK THEIR LIVES WAS TRULY NOBLE, AND YET--
--FUTILE!
AS FUTILE AS SHIFTING ASGARD TO THIS LONELY DIMENSION.
IT BUT WEAKENED HIM--
--PREPARING HIM--FOR THE FINAL BLOW!
WHAT SAY YOU NOW, THUNDER GOD? WILL THY FATHER RETURN FROM THE DEAD AS DID MY MASTERS--
--OR BE THIS ODIN'S TRUE END--?
NOW!
NNNOOOOOOOO
NEXT ISSUE:
THE DEATH OF ODIN!
21

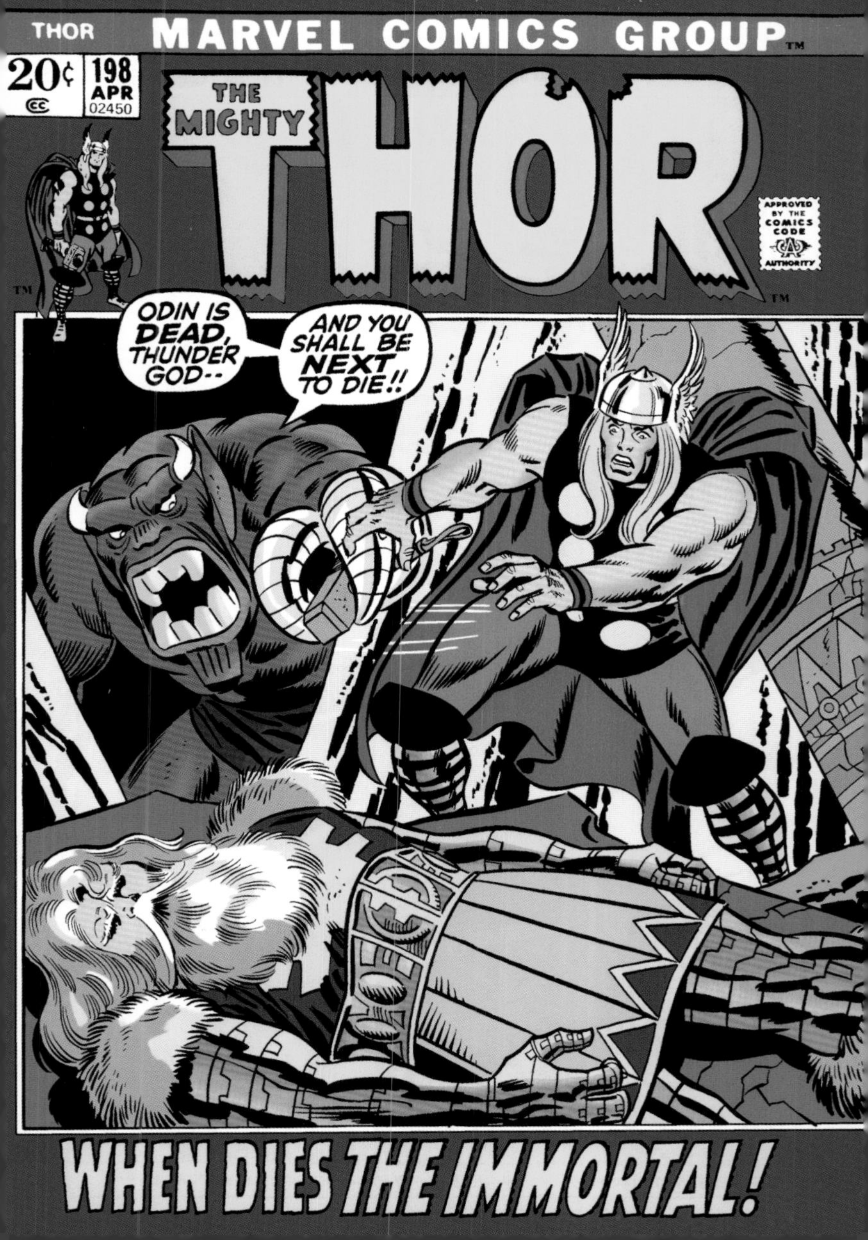
THOR
MARVEL COMICS GROUP
20¢
198
APR
02450
THE MIGHTY
THOR
APPROVED BY THE COMICS CODE AUTHORITY
ODIN IS DEAD, THUNDER GOD--
AND YOU SHALL BE NEXT TO DIE!!
WHEN DIES THE IMMORTAL!

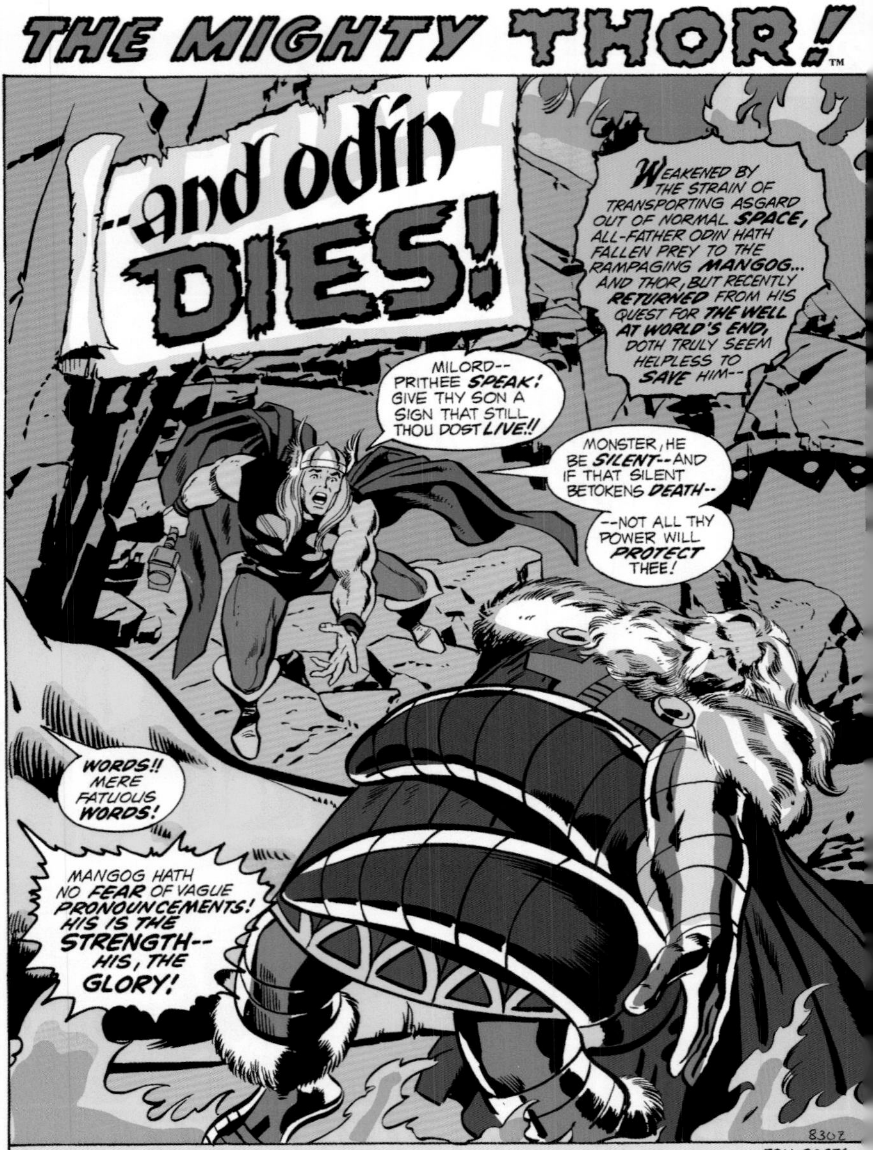
THE MIGHTY THOR!
--and odin DIES!
WEAKENED BY THE STRAIN OF TRANSPORTING ASGARD OUT OF NORMAL SPACE, ALL-FATHER ODIN HATH FALLEN PREY TO THE RAMPAGING MANGOG... AND THOR, BUT RECENTLY RETURNED FROM HIS QUEST FOR THE WELL AT WORLD'S END, DOTH TRULY SEEM HELPLESS TO SAVE HIM--
MILORD-- PRITHEE SPEAK! GIVE THY SON A SIGN THAT STILL THOU DOST LIVE!!
MONSTER, HE BE SILENT--AND IF THAT SILENT BETOKENS DEATH--
--NOT ALL THY POWER WILL PROTECT THEE!
WORDS!! MERE FATUOUS WORDS!
MANGOG HATH NO FEAR OF VAGUE PRONOUNCEMENTS! HIS IS THE STRENGTH-- HIS, THE GLORY!
STAN LEE, EDITOR/ GERRY CONWAY, SCRIPTER/ JOHN BUSCEMA, ARTIST/ VINCE COLLETTA, INKER/ JON COSTA, LETTERER

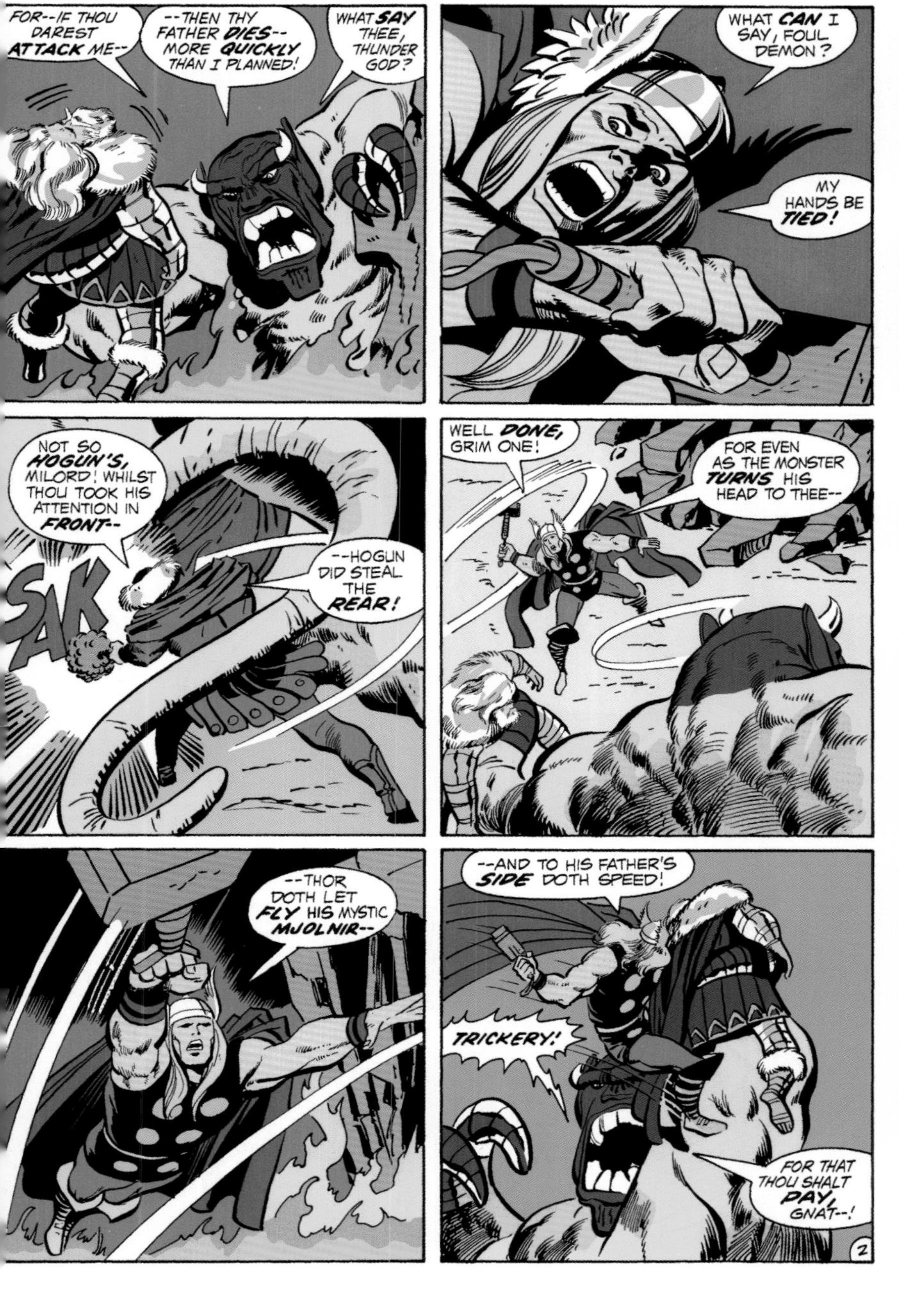
FOR--IF THOU DAREST ATTACK ME--
--THEN THY FATHER DIES-- MORE QUICKLY THAN I PLANNED!
WHAT SAY THEE, THUNDER GOD?
WHAT CAN I SAY, FOUL DEMON?
MY HANDS BE TIED!
NOT SO HOGUN'S, MILORD! WHILST THOU TOOK HIS ATTENTION IN FRONT--
SAK
--HOGUN DID STEAL THE REAR!
WELL DONE, GRIM ONE!
FOR EVEN AS THE MONSTER TURNS HIS HEAD TO THEE--
--THOR DOTH LET FLY HIS MYSTIC MJOLNIR--
--AND TO HIS FATHER'S SIDE DOTH SPEED!
TRICKERY!
FOR THAT THOU SHALT PAY, GNAT--!
2

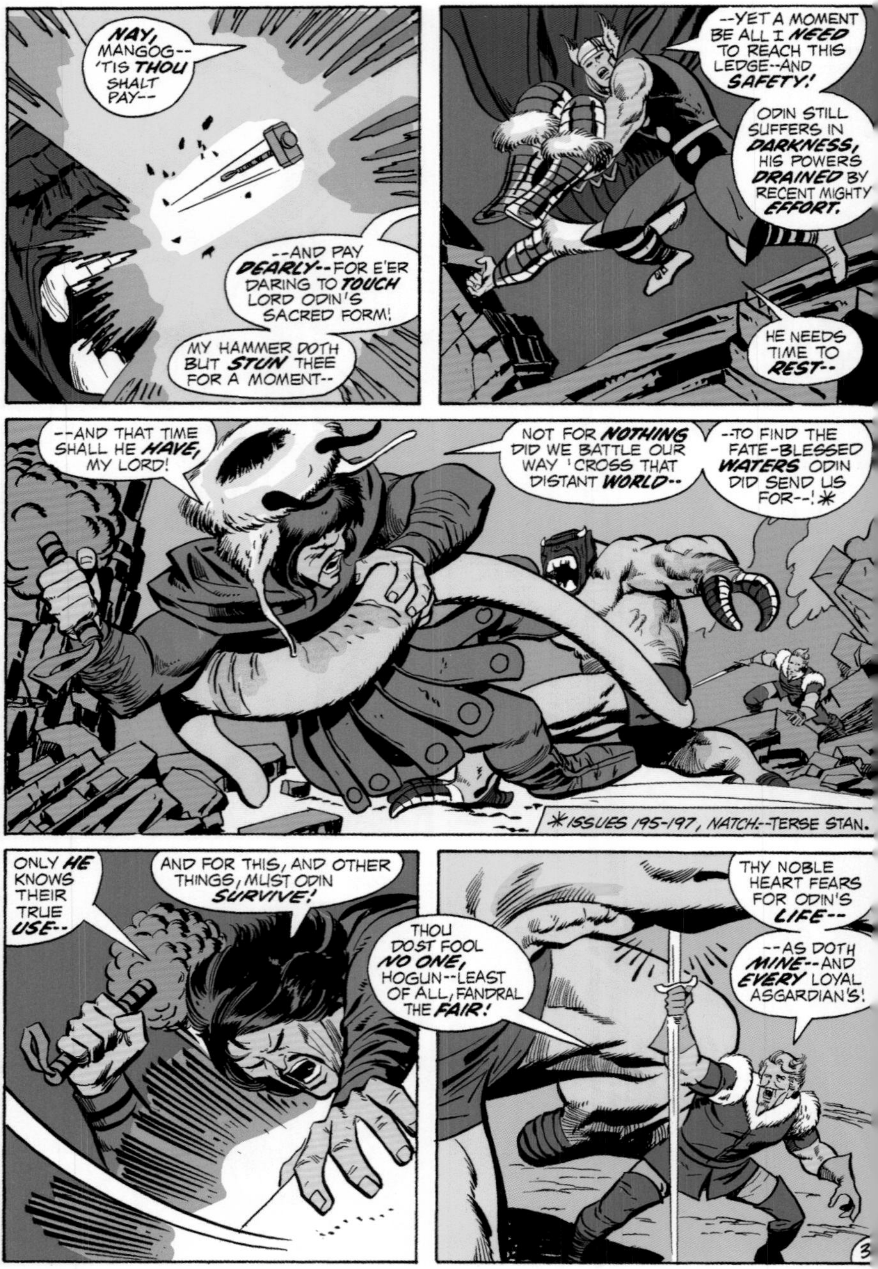
NAY, MANGOG--'TIS THOU SHALT PAY--
--AND PAY DEARLY--FOR E'ER DARING TO TOUCH LORD ODIN'S SACRED FORM!
MY HAMMER DOTH BUT STUN THEE FOR A MOMENT--
--YET A MOMENT BE ALL I NEED TO REACH THIS LEDGE--AND SAFETY!
ODIN STILL SUFFERS IN DARKNESS, HIS POWERS DRAINED BY RECENT MIGHTY EFFORT.
HE NEEDS TIME TO REST--
--AND THAT TIME SHALL HE HAVE, MY LORD!
NOT FOR NOTHING DID WE BATTLE OUR WAY 'CROSS THAT DISTANT WORLD--
--TO FIND THE FATE-BLESSED WATERS ODIN DID SEND US FOR--! *
* ISSUES 195-197, NATCH.--TERSE STAN.
ONLY HE KNOWS THEIR TRUE USE--
AND FOR THIS, AND OTHER THINGS, MUST ODIN SURVIVE!
THOU DOST FOOL NO ONE, HOGUN--LEAST OF ALL, FANDRAL THE FAIR!
THY NOBLE HEART FEARS FOR ODIN'S LIFE--
--AS DOTH MINE--AND EVERY LOYAL ASGARDIAN'S!
3

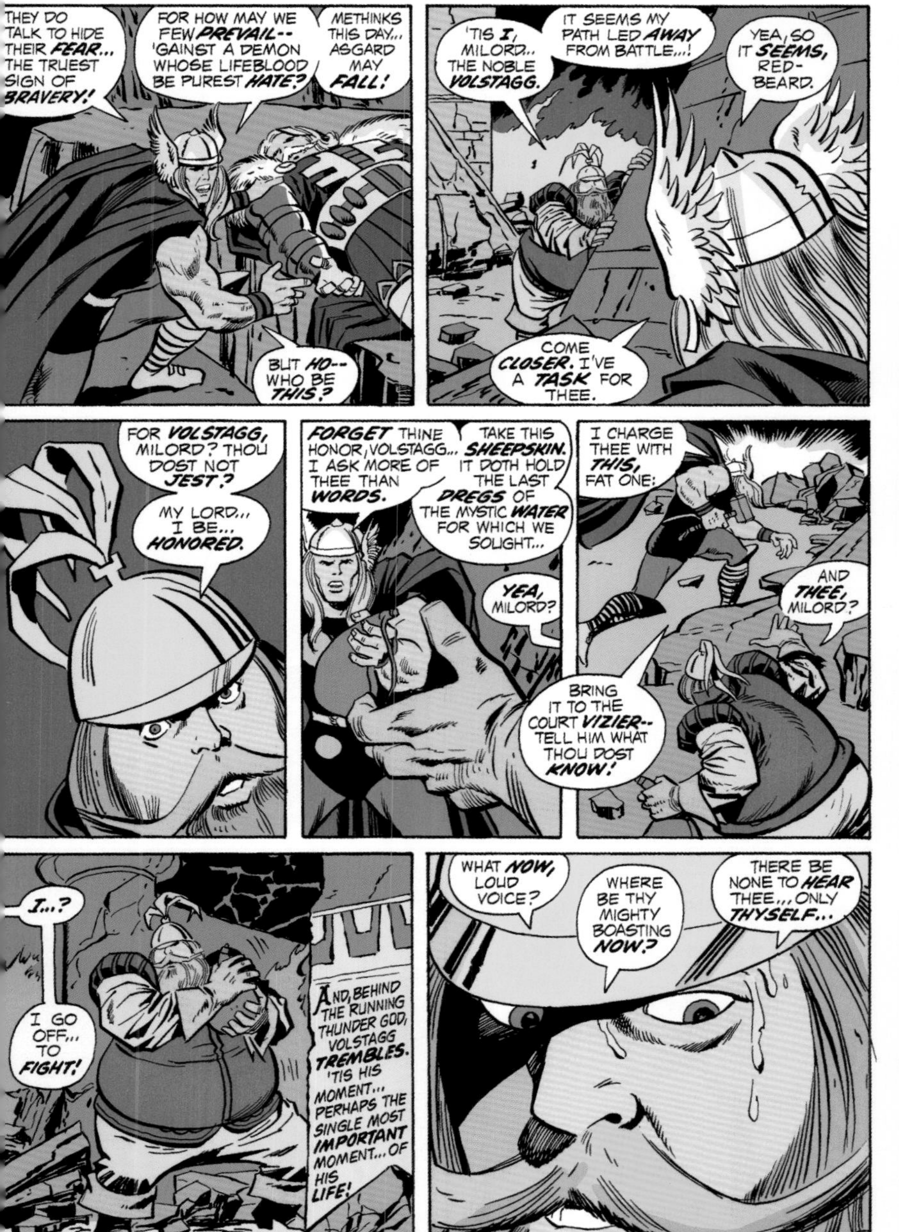
THEY DO TALK TO HIDE THEIR FEAR... THE TRUEST SIGN OF BRAVERY!
FOR HOW MAY WE FEW PREVAIL--'GAINST A DEMON WHOSE LIFEBLOOD BE PUREST HATE?
METHINKS THIS DAY... ASGARD MAY FALL!
BUT HO--WHO BE THIS?
'TIS I, MILORD.. THE NOBLE VOLSTAGG.
IT SEEMS MY PATH LED AWAY FROM BATTLE...!
YEA, SO IT SEEMS, RED-BEARD.
COME CLOSER. I'VE A TASK FOR THEE.
FOR VOLSTAGG, MILORD? THOU DOST NOT JEST?
MY LORD... I BE... HONORED.
FORGET THINE HONOR, VOLSTAGG... I ASK MORE OF THEE THAN WORDS.
TAKE THIS SHEEPSKIN. IT DOTH HOLD THE LAST DREGS OF THE MYSTIC WATER FOR WHICH WE SOUGHT...
YEA, MILORD?
I CHARGE THEE WITH THIS, FAT ONE:
BRING IT TO THE COURT VIZIER--TELL HIM WHAT THOU DOST KNOW!
AND THEE, MILORD?
I...?
I GO OFF... TO FIGHT!
AND, BEHIND THE RUNNING THUNDER GOD, VOLSTAGG TREMBLES. 'TIS HIS MOMENT... PERHAPS THE SINGLE MOST IMPORTANT MOMENT... OF HIS LIFE!
WHAT NOW, LOUD VOICE?
WHERE BE THY MIGHTY BOASTING NOW?
THERE BE NONE TO HEAR THEE... ONLY THYSELF...
4

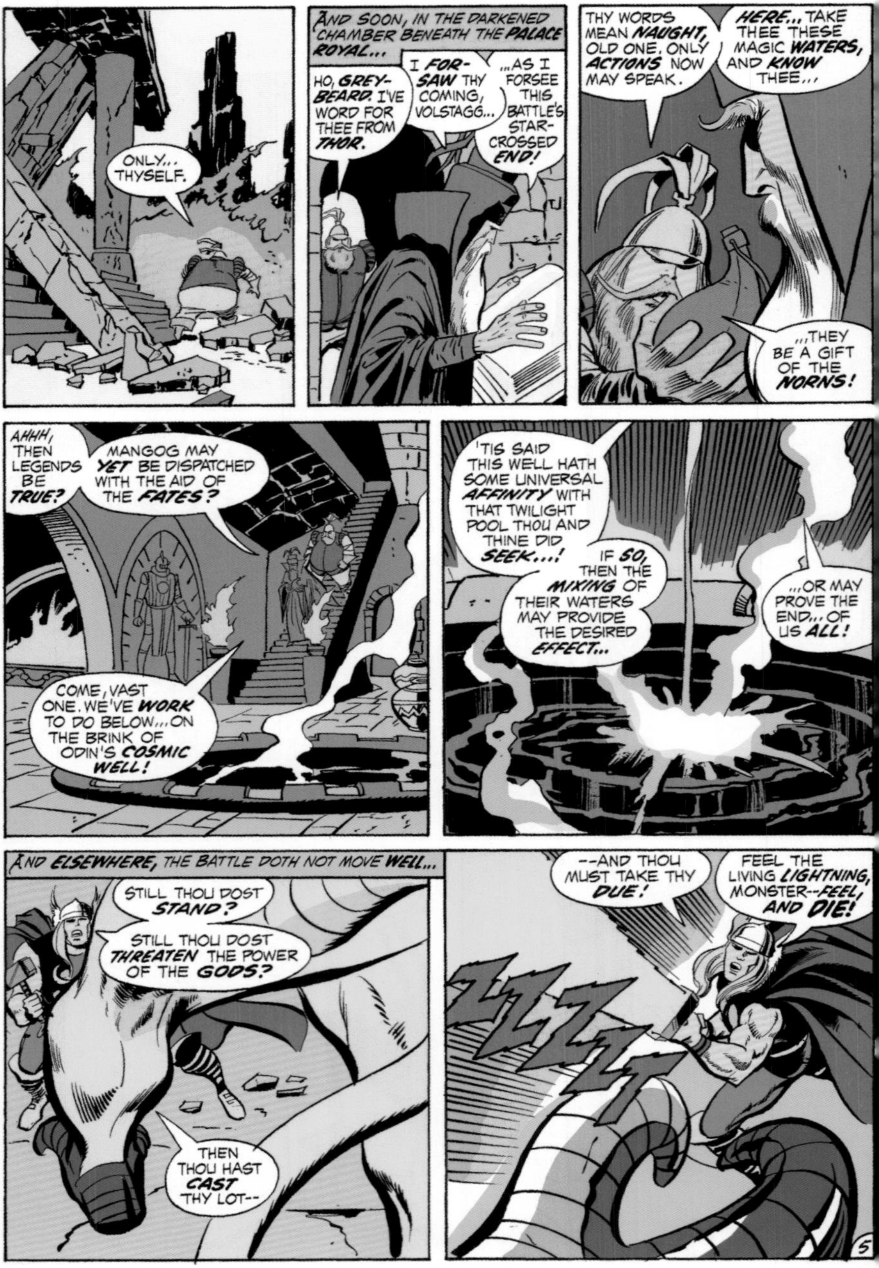
ONLY... THYSELF.
AND SOON, IN THE DARKENED CHAMBER BENEATH THE PALACE ROYAL...
HO, GREY-BEARD! I'VE WORD FOR THEE FROM THOR.
I FORSAW THY COMING, VOLSTAGG...
...AS I FORSEE THIS BATTLE'S STAR-CROSSED END!
THY WORDS MEAN NAUGHT, OLD ONE. ONLY ACTIONS NOW MAY SPEAK.
HERE... TAKE THEE THESE MAGIC WATERS, AND KNOW THEE...
...THEY BE A GIFT OF THE NORNS!
AHHH, THEN LEGENDS BE TRUE?
MANGOG MAY YET BE DISPATCHED WITH THE AID OF THE FATES?
COME, VAST ONE. WE'VE WORK TO DO BELOW... ON THE BRINK OF ODIN'S COSMIC WELL!
'TIS SAID THIS WELL HATH SOME UNIVERSAL AFFINITY WITH THAT TWILIGHT POOL THOU AND THINE DID SEEK...!
IF SO, THEN THE MIXING OF THEIR WATERS MAY PROVIDE THE DESIRED EFFECT...
...OR MAY PROVE THE END... OF US ALL!
AND ELSEWHERE, THE BATTLE DOTH NOT MOVE WELL...
STILL THOU DOST STAND?
STILL THOU DOST THREATEN THE POWER OF THE GODS?
THEN THOU HAST CAST THY LOT--
--AND THOU MUST TAKE THY DUE!
FEEL THE LIVING LIGHTNING, MONSTER--FEEL, AND DIE!
5

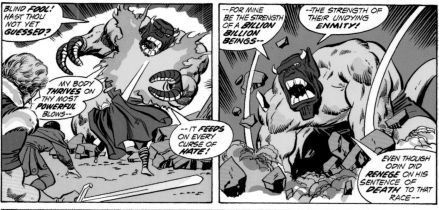

BLIND *FOOL!* HAST THOU NOT YET *GUESSED?*

MY BODY *THRIVES* ON THY MOST *POWERFUL* BLOWS--

--IT *FEEDS* ON EVERY CURSE OF *HATE!*

--FOR MINE BE THE STRENGTH OF A *BILLION BILLION* BEINGS--

--THE STRENGTH OF THEIR *UNDYING ENMITY!*

EVEN THOUGH ODIN DID *RENEGE* ON HIS SENTENCE OF *DEATH* TO THAT RACE--

--THEIR *HATE* LIVES ON--

--THEIR *HATE* GIVES ME *CAUSE!*

HE LIFTS THE VERY *ROADWAY* ITSELF!

HIS STRENGTH BUILDS BY THE *MOMENT!*

MILORD-- ARE WE *DOOMED?*

WHAT HOPE HAVE OUR *SWORDS*--'GAINST SUCH AS HE?

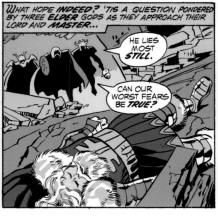

WHAT HOPE INDEED? 'TIS A QUESTION PONDERED BY THREE *ELDER* GODS AS THEY APPROACH THEIR LORD AND *MASTER...*

HE LIES MOST *STILL.*

CAN OUR WORST FEARS BE *TRUE?*

DOTH ODIN LIE... *DEAD?*

NAY, HOLD THY *TONGUE,* RONGOR, HE *STIRS!*

FATES BE *PRAISED,* WHITEMANE! OUR LIEGE DOTH *LIVE!*

6

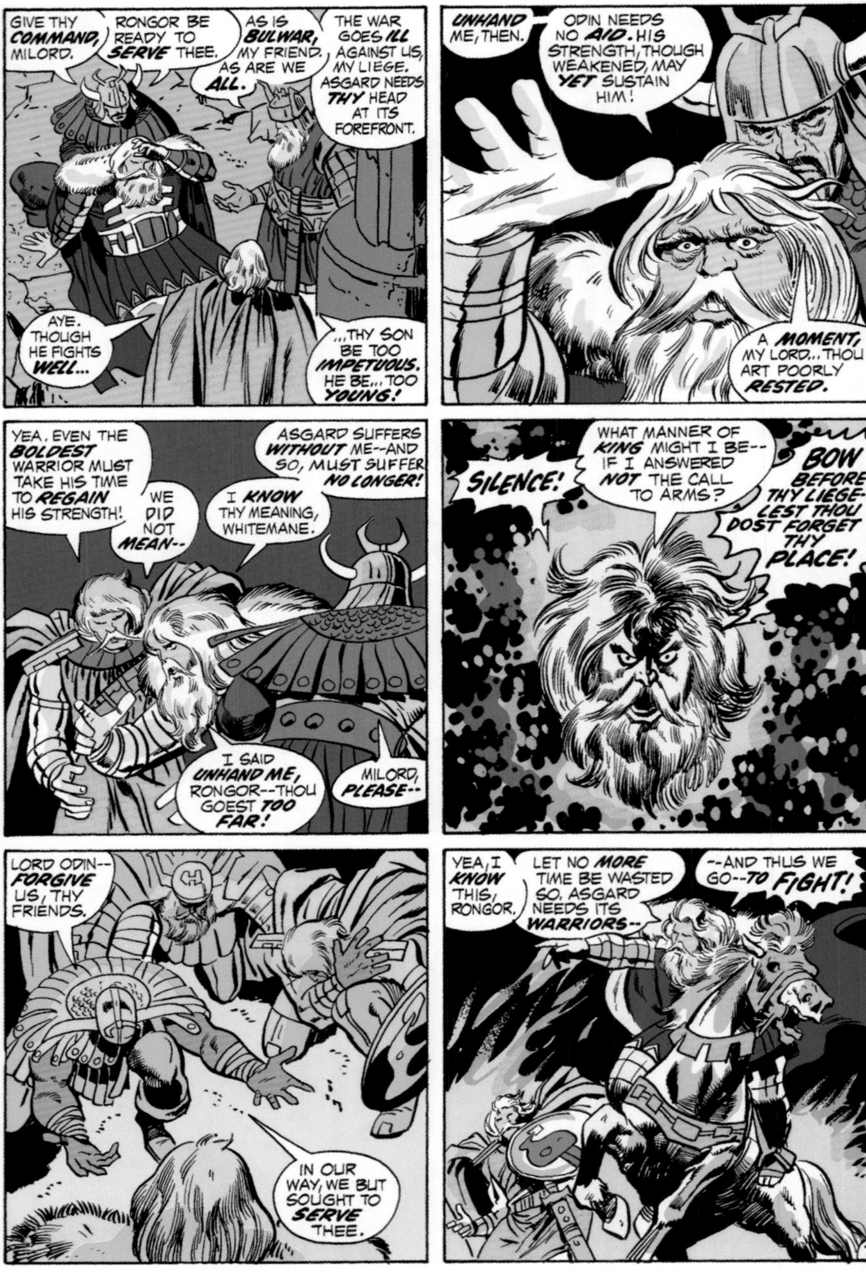
GIVE THY COMMAND, MILORD.
RONGOR BE READY TO SERVE THEE.
AS IS BULWAR, MY FRIEND. AS ARE WE ALL.
THE WAR GOES ILL AGAINST US, MY LIEGE. ASGARD NEEDS THY HEAD AT ITS FOREFRONT.
AYE. THOUGH HE FIGHTS WELL...
...THY SON BE TOO IMPETUOUS. HE BE... TOO YOUNG!
UNHAND ME, THEN.
ODIN NEEDS NO AID. HIS STRENGTH, THOUGH WEAKENED, MAY YET SUSTAIN HIM!
A MOMENT, MY LORD... THOU ART POORLY RESTED.
YEA, EVEN THE BOLDEST WARRIOR MUST TAKE HIS TIME TO REGAIN HIS STRENGTH!
WE DID NOT MEAN--
ASGARD SUFFERS WITHOUT ME--AND SO, MUST SUFFER NO LONGER!
I KNOW THY MEANING, WHITEMANE.
I SAID UNHAND ME, RONGOR--THOU GOEST TOO FAR!
MILORD, PLEASE--
SILENCE!
WHAT MANNER OF KING MIGHT I BE-- IF I ANSWERED NOT THE CALL TO ARMS?
BOW BEFORE THY LIEGE-- LEST THOU DOST FORGET THY PLACE!
LORD ODIN-- FORGIVE US, THY FRIENDS.
IN OUR WAY, WE BUT SOUGHT TO SERVE THEE.
YEA, I KNOW THIS, RONGOR.
LET NO MORE TIME BE WASTED SO. ASGARD NEEDS ITS WARRIORS--
--AND THUS WE GO--TO FIGHT!
7

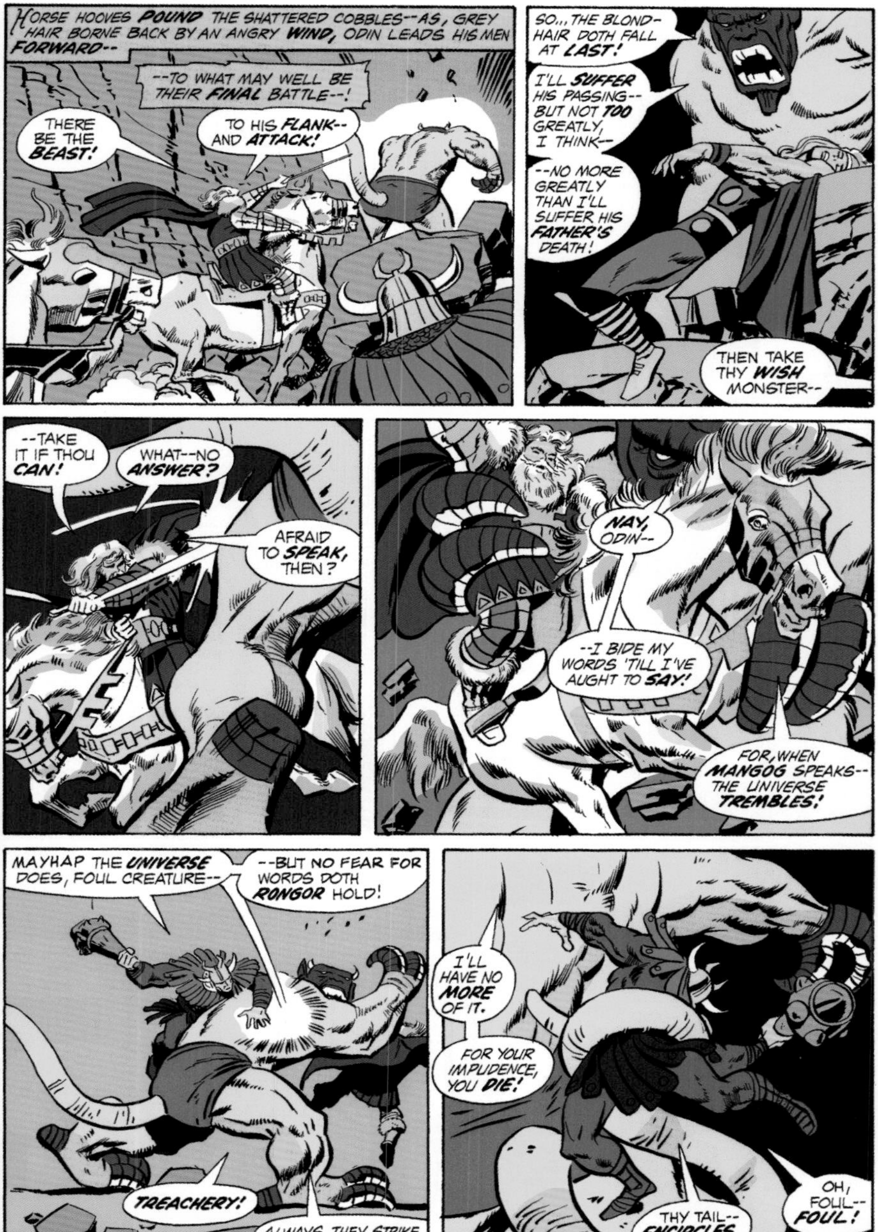
HORSE HOOVES POUND THE SHATTERED COBBLES--AS, GREY HAIR BORNE BACK BY AN ANGRY WIND, ODIN LEADS HIS MEN FORWARD--
--TO WHAT MAY WELL BE THEIR FINAL BATTLE--!
THERE BE THE BEAST!
TO HIS FLANK--AND ATTACK!
SO... THE BLOND-HAIR DOTH FALL AT LAST!
I'LL SUFFER HIS PASSING--BUT NOT TOO GREATLY, I THINK--
--NO MORE GREATLY THAN I'LL SUFFER HIS FATHER'S DEATH!
THEN TAKE THY WISH MONSTER--
--TAKE IT IF THOU CAN!
WHAT--NO ANSWER?
AFRAID TO SPEAK, THEN?
NAY, ODIN--
--I BIDE MY WORDS 'TILL I'VE AUGHT TO SAY!
FOR, WHEN MANGOG SPEAKS--THE UNIVERSE TREMBLES!
MAYHAP THE UNIVERSE DOES, FOUL CREATURE--
--BUT NO FEAR FOR WORDS DOTH RONGOR HOLD!
TREACHERY!
ALWAYS THEY STRIKE FROM BEHIND!
I'LL HAVE NO MORE OF IT.
FOR YOUR IMPUDENCE, YOU DIE!
THY TAIL--ENCIRCLES ME!
OH, FOUL--FOUL!
8

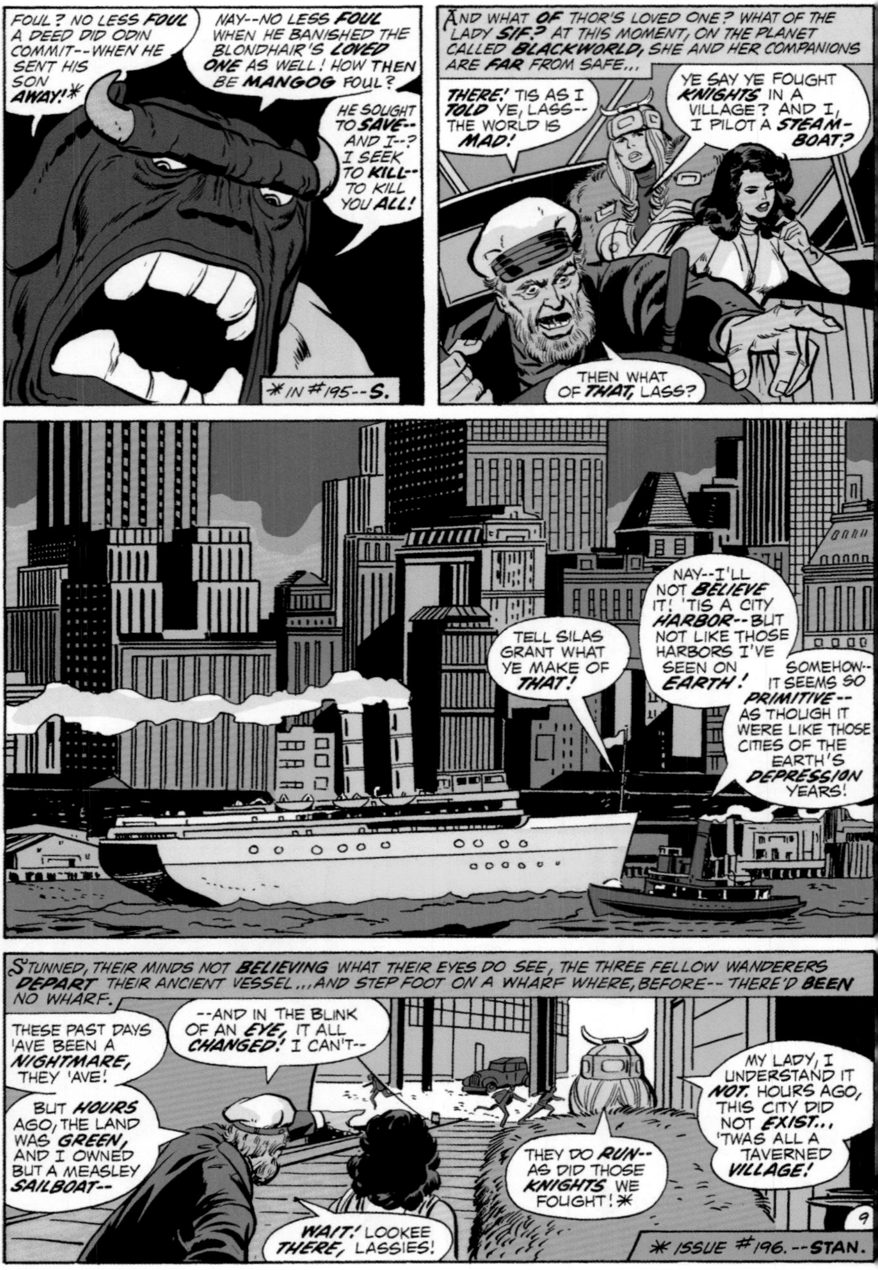
FOUL? NO LESS FOUL A DEED DID ODIN COMMIT--WHEN HE SENT HIS SON AWAY!*
NAY--NO LESS FOUL WHEN HE BANISHED THE BLONDHAIR'S LOVED ONE AS WELL! HOW THEN BE MANGOG FOUL?
HE SOUGHT TO SAVE-- AND I--? I SEEK TO KILL-- TO KILL YOU ALL!
*IN #195--S.
AND WHAT OF THOR'S LOVED ONE? WHAT OF THE LADY SIF? AT THIS MOMENT, ON THE PLANET CALLED BLACKWORLD, SHE AND HER COMPANIONS ARE FAR FROM SAFE...
THERE! TIS AS I TOLD YE, LASS-- THE WORLD IS MAD!
YE SAY YE FOUGHT KNIGHTS IN A VILLAGE? AND I, I PILOT A STEAM-BOAT?
THEN WHAT OF THAT, LASS?
TELL SILAS GRANT WHAT YE MAKE OF THAT!
NAY--I'LL NOT BELIEVE IT! 'TIS A CITY HARBOR--BUT NOT LIKE THOSE HARBORS I'VE SEEN ON EARTH!
SOMEHOW-- IT SEEMS SO PRIMITIVE-- AS THOUGH IT WERE LIKE THOSE CITIES OF THE EARTH'S DEPRESSION YEARS!
STUNNED, THEIR MINDS NOT BELIEVING WHAT THEIR EYES DO SEE, THE THREE FELLOW WANDERERS DEPART THEIR ANCIENT VESSEL...AND STEP FOOT ON A WHARF WHERE, BEFORE-- THERE'D BEEN NO WHARF.
THESE PAST DAYS 'AVE BEEN A NIGHTMARE, THEY 'AVE!
--AND IN THE BLINK OF AN EYE, IT ALL CHANGED! I CAN'T--
BUT HOURS AGO, THE LAND WAS GREEN, AND I OWNED BUT A MEASLEY SAILBOAT--
MY LADY, I UNDERSTAND IT NOT. HOURS AGO, THIS CITY DID NOT EXIST... 'TWAS ALL A TAVERNED VILLAGE!
THEY DO RUN-- AS DID THOSE KNIGHTS WE FOUGHT!*
WAIT! LOOKEE THERE, LASSIES!
9
*ISSUE #196.--STAN.

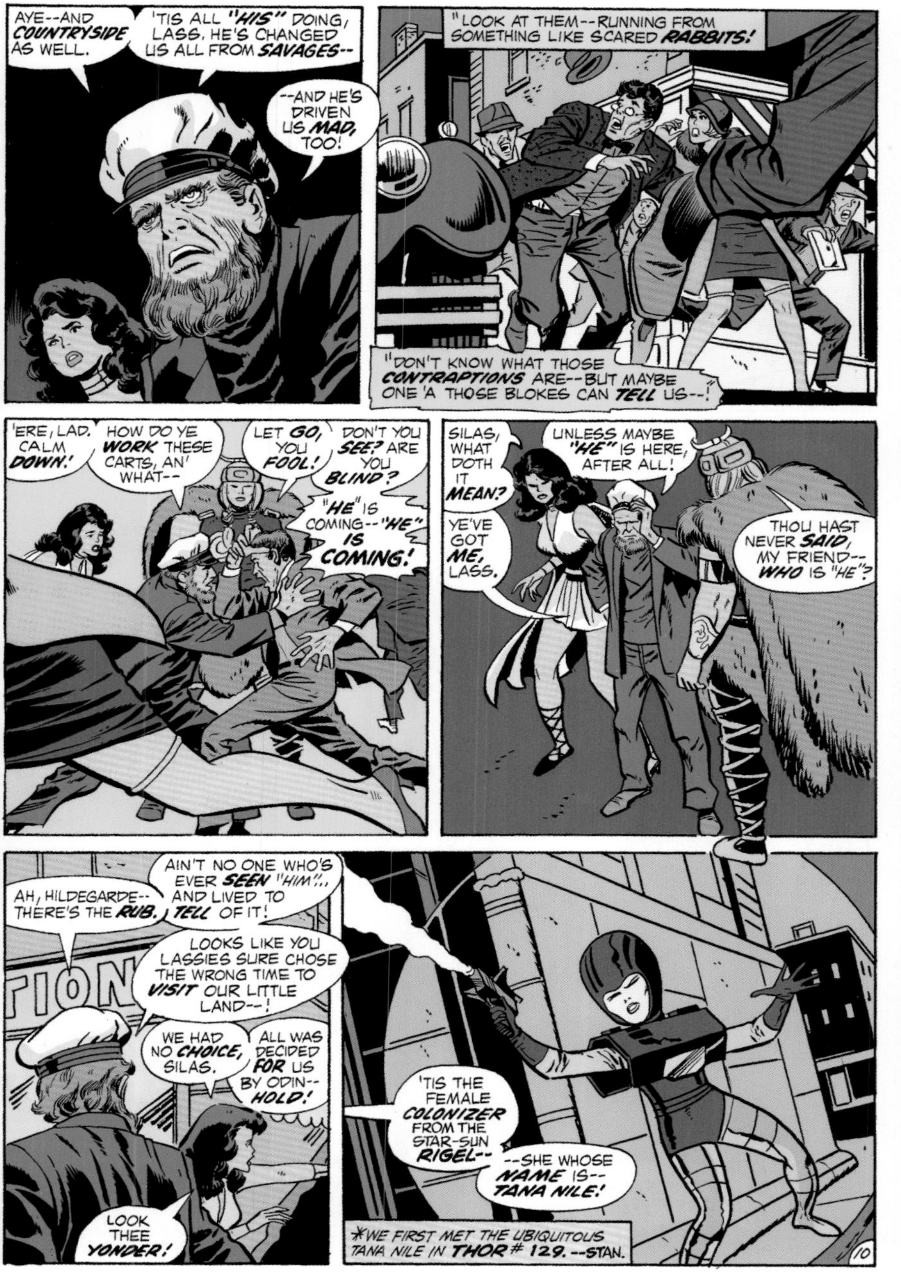
AYE--AND COUNTRYSIDE AS WELL.
'TIS ALL "HIS" DOING, LASS. HE'S CHANGED US ALL FROM SAVAGES--
--AND HE'S DRIVEN US MAD, TOO!
"LOOK AT THEM--RUNNING FROM SOMETHING LIKE SCARED RABBITS!
"DON'T KNOW WHAT THOSE CONTRAPTIONS ARE--BUT MAYBE ONE 'A THOSE BLOKES CAN TELL US--!
'ERE, LAD. CALM DOWN!
HOW DO YE WORK THESE CARTS, AN' WHAT--
LET GO, YOU FOOL!
DON'T YOU SEE? ARE YOU BLIND?
"HE" IS COMING--"HE" IS COMING!
SILAS, WHAT DOTH IT MEAN?
UNLESS MAYBE "HE" IS HERE, AFTER ALL!
YE'VE GOT ME, LASS.
THOU HAST NEVER SAID, MY FRIEND--WHO IS "HE"?
AH, HILDEGARDE--THERE'S THE RUB.
AIN'T NO ONE WHO'S EVER SEEN "HIM"!, AND LIVED TO TELL OF IT!
LOOKS LIKE YOU LASSIES SURE CHOSE THE WRONG TIME TO VISIT OUR LITTLE LAND--!
WE HAD NO CHOICE, SILAS.
ALL WAS DECIDED FOR US BY ODIN--HOLD!
LOOK THEE YONDER!
'TIS THE FEMALE COLONIZER FROM THE STAR-SUN RIGEL--
--SHE WHOSE NAME IS--TANA NILE!
*WE FIRST MET THE UBIQUITOUS TANA NILE IN THOR #129. --STAN.
10

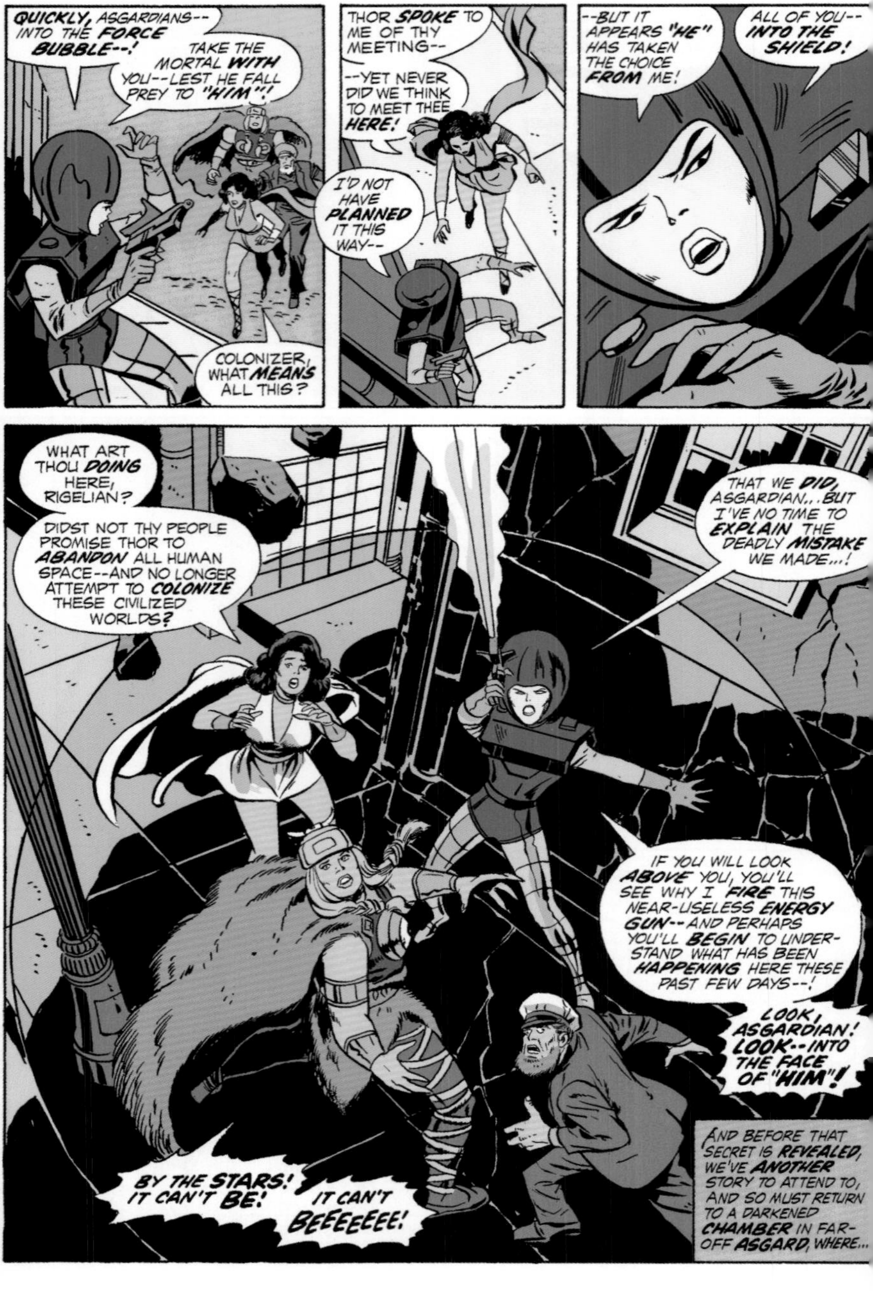
QUICKLY, ASGARDIANS-- INTO THE FORCE BUBBLE--!
TAKE THE MORTAL WITH YOU--LEST HE FALL PREY TO "HIM"!
COLONIZER, WHAT MEANS ALL THIS?
THOR SPOKE TO ME OF THY MEETING--
--YET NEVER DID WE THINK TO MEET THEE HERE!
I'D NOT HAVE PLANNED IT THIS WAY--
--BUT IT APPEARS "HE" HAS TAKEN THE CHOICE FROM ME!
ALL OF YOU-- INTO THE SHIELD!
WHAT ART THOU DOING HERE, RIGELIAN?
DIDST NOT THY PEOPLE PROMISE THOR TO ABANDON ALL HUMAN SPACE--AND NO LONGER ATTEMPT TO COLONIZE THESE CIVILIZED WORLDS?
THAT WE DID, ASGARDIAN...BUT I'VE NO TIME TO EXPLAIN THE DEADLY MISTAKE WE MADE...!
IF YOU WILL LOOK ABOVE YOU, YOU'LL SEE WHY I FIRE THIS NEAR-USELESS ENERGY GUN--AND PERHAPS YOU'LL BEGIN TO UNDERSTAND WHAT HAS BEEN HAPPENING HERE THESE PAST FEW DAYS--!
LOOK, ASGARDIAN! LOOK--INTO THE FACE OF "HIM"!
BY THE STARS! IT CAN'T BE!
IT CAN'T BEEEEEEE!
AND BEFORE THAT SECRET IS REVEALED, WE'VE ANOTHER STORY TO ATTEND TO, AND SO MUST RETURN TO A DARKENED CHAMBER IN FAR-OFF ASGARD, WHERE...

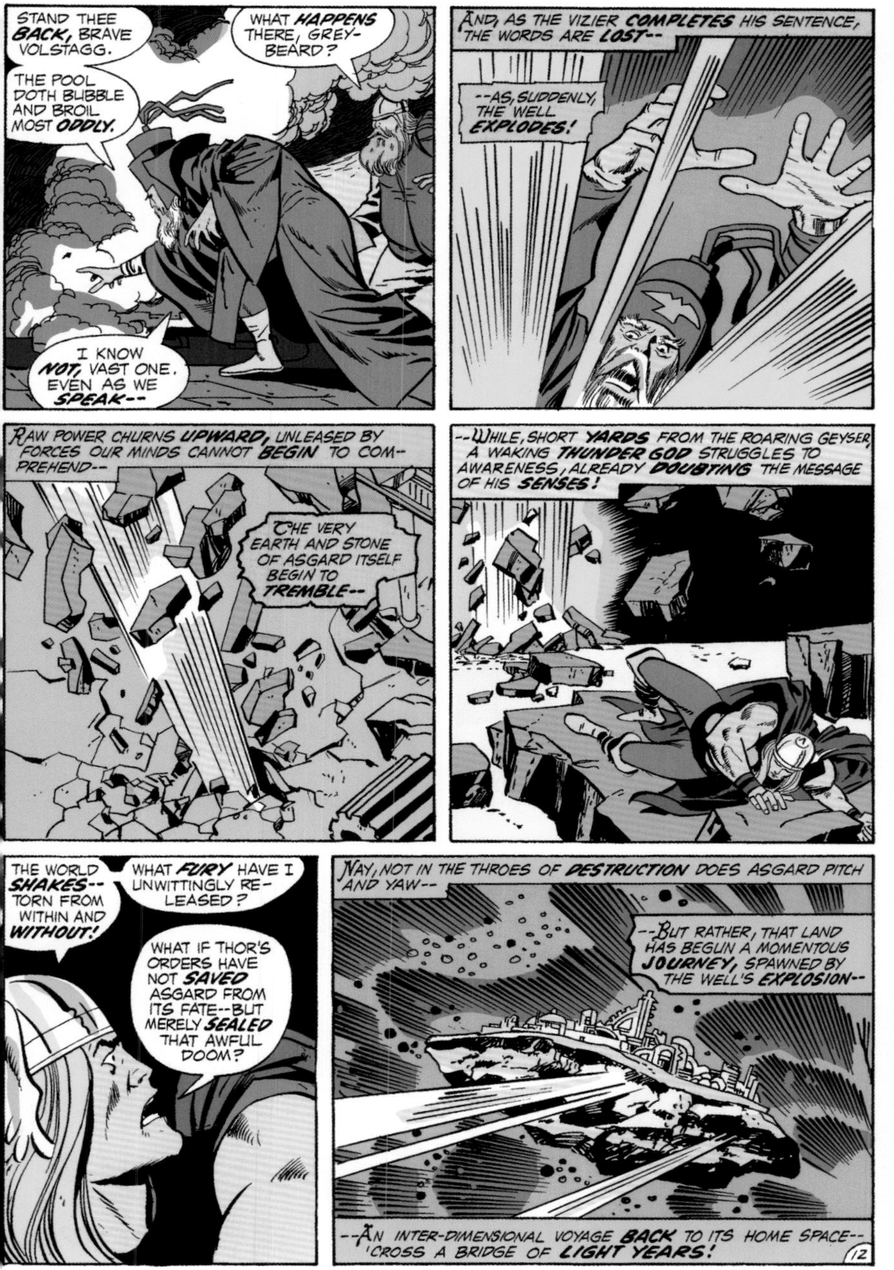
STAND THEE BACK, BRAVE VOLSTAGG.
THE POOL DOTH BUBBLE AND BROIL MOST ODDLY.
WHAT HAPPENS THERE, GREY-BEARD?
I KNOW NOT, VAST ONE. EVEN AS WE SPEAK--
AND, AS THE VIZIER COMPLETES HIS SENTENCE, THE WORDS ARE LOST--
--AS, SUDDENLY, THE WELL EXPLODES!
RAW POWER CHURNS UPWARD, UNLEASED BY FORCES OUR MINDS CANNOT BEGIN TO COM-PREHEND--
THE VERY EARTH AND STONE OF ASGARD ITSELF BEGIN TO TREMBLE--
--WHILE, SHORT YARDS FROM THE ROARING GEYSER, A WAKING THUNDER GOD STRUGGLES TO AWARENESS, ALREADY DOUBTING THE MESSAGE OF HIS SENSES!
THE WORLD SHAKES-- TORN FROM WITHIN AND WITHOUT!
WHAT FURY HAVE I UNWITTINGLY RE-LEASED?
WHAT IF THOR'S ORDERS HAVE NOT SAVED ASGARD FROM ITS FATE--BUT MERELY SEALED THAT AWFUL DOOM?
NAY, NOT IN THE THROES OF DESTRUCTION DOES ASGARD PITCH AND YAW--
--BUT RATHER, THAT LAND HAS BEGUN A MOMENTOUS JOURNEY, SPAWNED BY THE WELL'S EXPLOSION--
--AN INTER-DIMENSIONAL VOYAGE BACK TO ITS HOME SPACE-- 'CROSS A BRIDGE OF LIGHT YEARS!
12

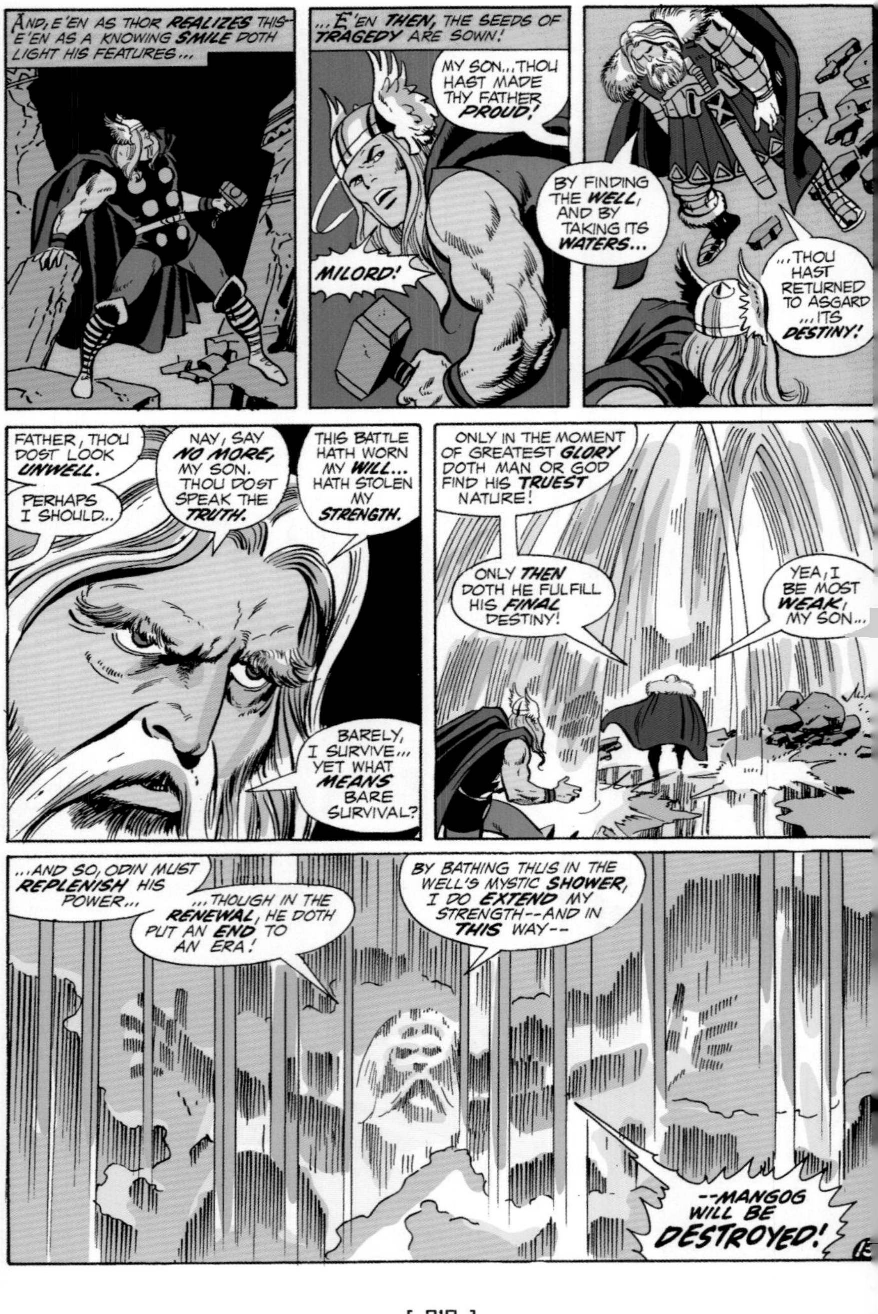
AND, E'EN AS THOR REALIZES THIS-- E'EN AS A KNOWING SMILE DOTH LIGHT HIS FEATURES...
...E'EN THEN, THE SEEDS OF TRAGEDY ARE SOWN!
MY SON...THOU HAST MADE THY FATHER PROUD!
MILORD!
BY FINDING THE WELL, AND BY TAKING ITS WATERS...
...THOU HAST RETURNED TO ASGARD ...ITS DESTINY!
FATHER, THOU DOST LOOK UNWELL.
PERHAPS I SHOULD...
NAY, SAY NO MORE, MY SON. THOU DOST SPEAK THE TRUTH.
THIS BATTLE HATH WORN MY WILL... HATH STOLEN MY STRENGTH.
BARELY, I SURVIVE... YET WHAT MEANS BARE SURVIVAL?
ONLY IN THE MOMENT OF GREATEST GLORY DOTH MAN OR GOD FIND HIS TRUEST NATURE!
ONLY THEN DOTH HE FULFILL HIS FINAL DESTINY!
YEA, I BE MOST WEAK, MY SON...
...AND SO, ODIN MUST REPLENISH HIS POWER...
...THOUGH IN THE RENEWAL, HE DOTH PUT AN END TO AN ERA!
BY BATHING THUS IN THE WELL'S MYSTIC SHOWER, I DO EXTEND MY STRENGTH--AND IN THIS WAY--
--MANGOG WILL BE DESTROYED!

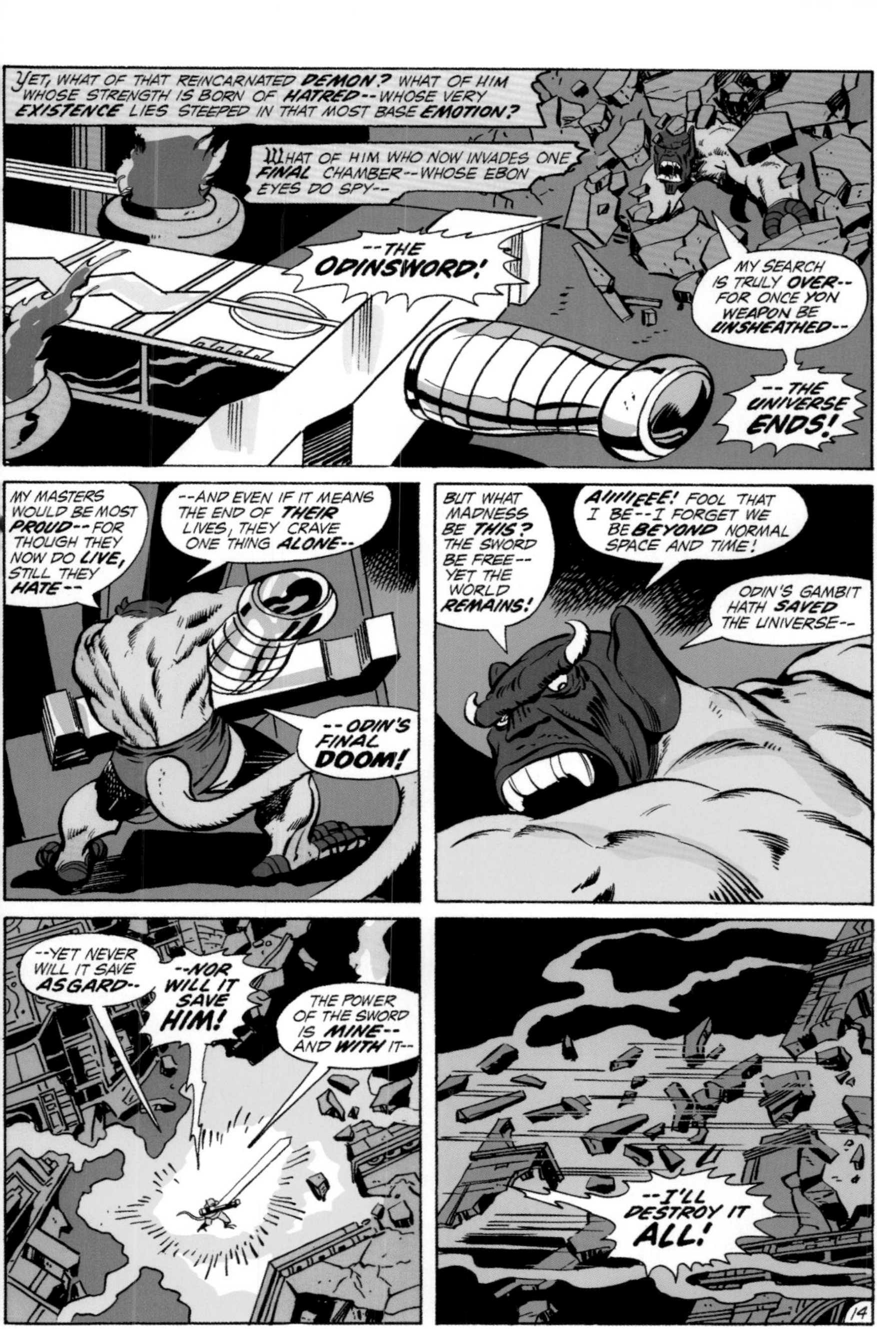
YET, WHAT OF THAT REINCARNATED DEMON? WHAT OF HIM WHOSE STRENGTH IS BORN OF HATRED--WHOSE VERY EXISTENCE LIES STEEPED IN THAT MOST BASE EMOTION?
WHAT OF HIM WHO NOW INVADES ONE FINAL CHAMBER--WHOSE EBON EYES DO SPY--
--THE ODINSWORD!
MY SEARCH IS TRULY OVER--FOR ONCE YON WEAPON BE UNSHEATHED--
--THE UNIVERSE ENDS!
MY MASTERS WOULD BE MOST PROUD--FOR THOUGH THEY NOW DO LIVE, STILL THEY HATE--
--AND EVEN IF IT MEANS THE END OF THEIR LIVES, THEY CRAVE ONE THING ALONE--
--ODIN'S FINAL DOOM!
BUT WHAT MADNESS BE THIS? THE SWORD BE FREE--YET THE WORLD REMAINS!
AIIIIEEE! FOOL THAT I BE--I FORGET WE BE BEYOND NORMAL SPACE AND TIME!
ODIN'S GAMBIT HATH SAVED THE UNIVERSE--
--YET NEVER WILL IT SAVE ASGARD--
--NOR WILL IT SAVE HIM!
THE POWER OF THE SWORD IS MINE--AND WITH IT--
--I'LL DESTROY IT ALL!
14

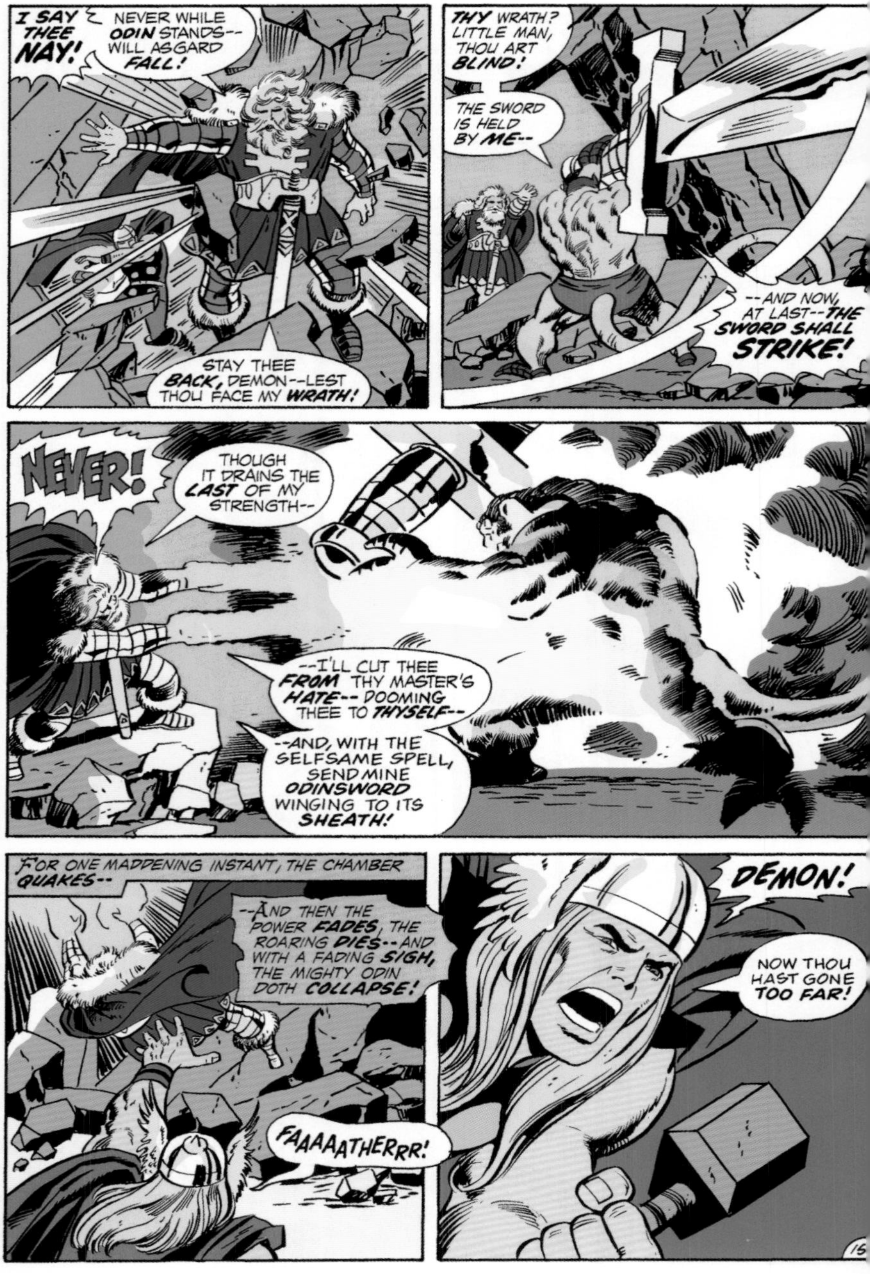
I SAY THEE NAY!
NEVER WHILE ODIN STANDS-- WILL ASGARD FALL!
STAY THEE BACK, DEMON--LEST THOU FACE MY WRATH!
THY WRATH? LITTLE MAN, THOU ART BLIND!
THE SWORD IS HELD BY ME--
--AND NOW, AT LAST--THE SWORD SHALL STRIKE!
NEVER!
THOUGH IT DRAINS THE LAST OF MY STRENGTH--
--I'LL CUT THEE FROM THY MASTER'S HATE-- DOOMING THEE TO THYSELF--
--AND, WITH THE SELFSAME SPELL, SEND MINE ODINSWORD WINGING TO ITS SHEATH!
FOR ONE MADDENING INSTANT, THE CHAMBER QUAKES--
--AND THEN THE POWER FADES, THE ROARING DIES--AND WITH A FADING SIGH, THE MIGHTY ODIN DOTH COLLAPSE!
FAAAAATHERRRR!
DEMON!
NOW THOU HAST GONE TOO FAR!
15

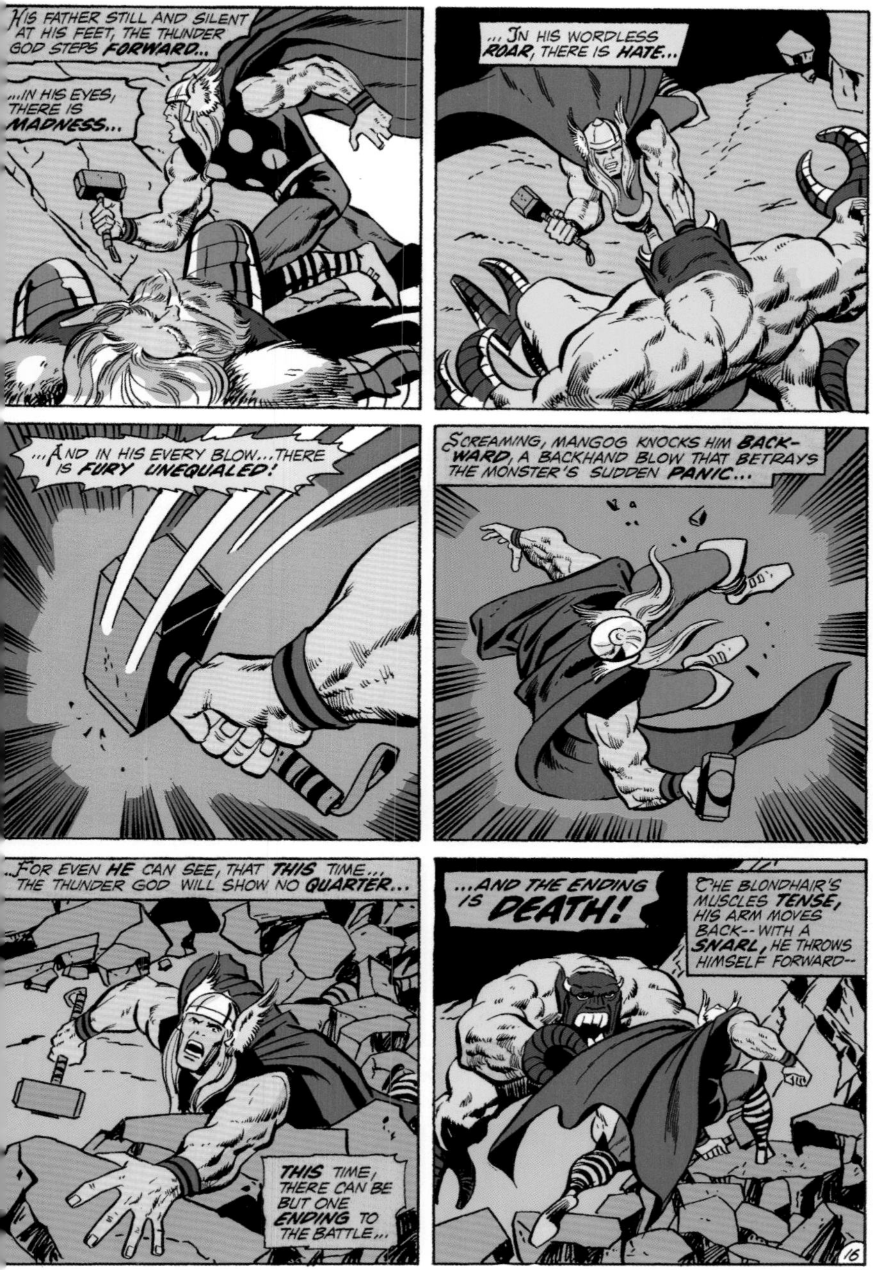
HIS FATHER STILL AND SILENT AT HIS FEET, THE THUNDER GOD STEPS FORWARD...
...IN HIS EYES, THERE IS MADNESS...
...IN HIS WORDLESS ROAR, THERE IS HATE...
...AND IN HIS EVERY BLOW...THERE IS FURY UNEQUALED!
SCREAMING, MANGOG KNOCKS HIM BACKWARD, A BACKHAND BLOW THAT BETRAYS THE MONSTER'S SUDDEN PANIC...
...FOR EVEN HE CAN SEE, THAT THIS TIME... THE THUNDER GOD WILL SHOW NO QUARTER...
THIS TIME, THERE CAN BE BUT ONE ENDING TO THE BATTLE...
...AND THE ENDING IS DEATH!
THE BLONDHAIR'S MUSCLES TENSE, HIS ARM MOVES BACK--WITH A SNARL, HE THROWS HIMSELF FORWARD--
16

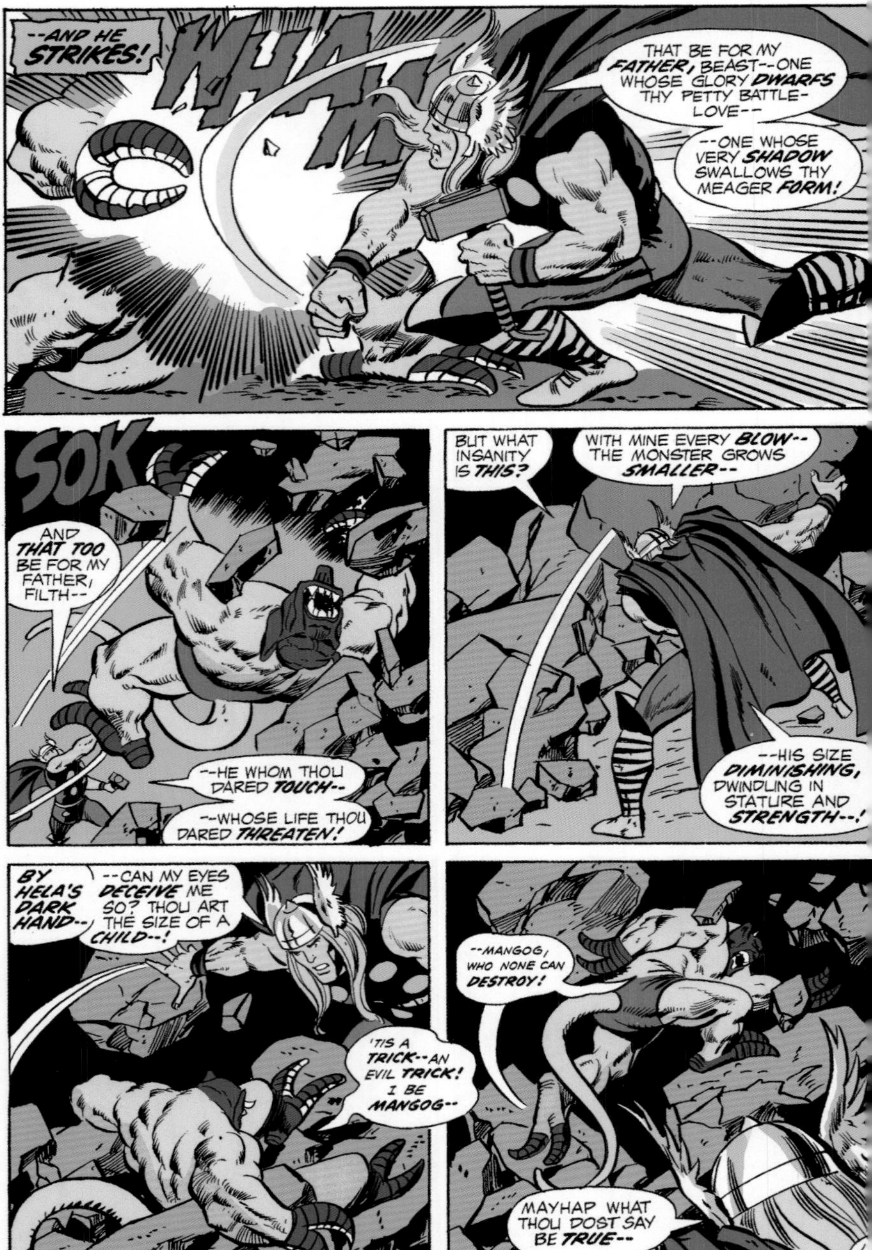
--AND HE STRIKES!
WHAM
THAT BE FOR MY FATHER, BEAST--ONE WHOSE GLORY DWARFS THY PETTY BATTLE-LOVE--
--ONE WHOSE VERY SHADOW SWALLOWS THY MEAGER FORM!
SOK
AND THAT TOO BE FOR MY FATHER, FILTH--
--HE WHOM THOU DARED TOUCH--
--WHOSE LIFE THOU DARED THREATEN!
BUT WHAT INSANITY IS THIS?
WITH MINE EVERY BLOW--THE MONSTER GROWS SMALLER--
--HIS SIZE DIMINISHING, DWINDLING IN STATURE AND STRENGTH--!
BY HELA'S DARK HAND--
--CAN MY EYES DECEIVE ME SO? THOU ART THE SIZE OF A CHILD--!
'TIS A TRICK--AN EVIL TRICK! I BE MANGOG--
--MANGOG, WHO NONE CAN DESTROY!
MAYHAP WHAT THOU DOST SAY BE TRUE--

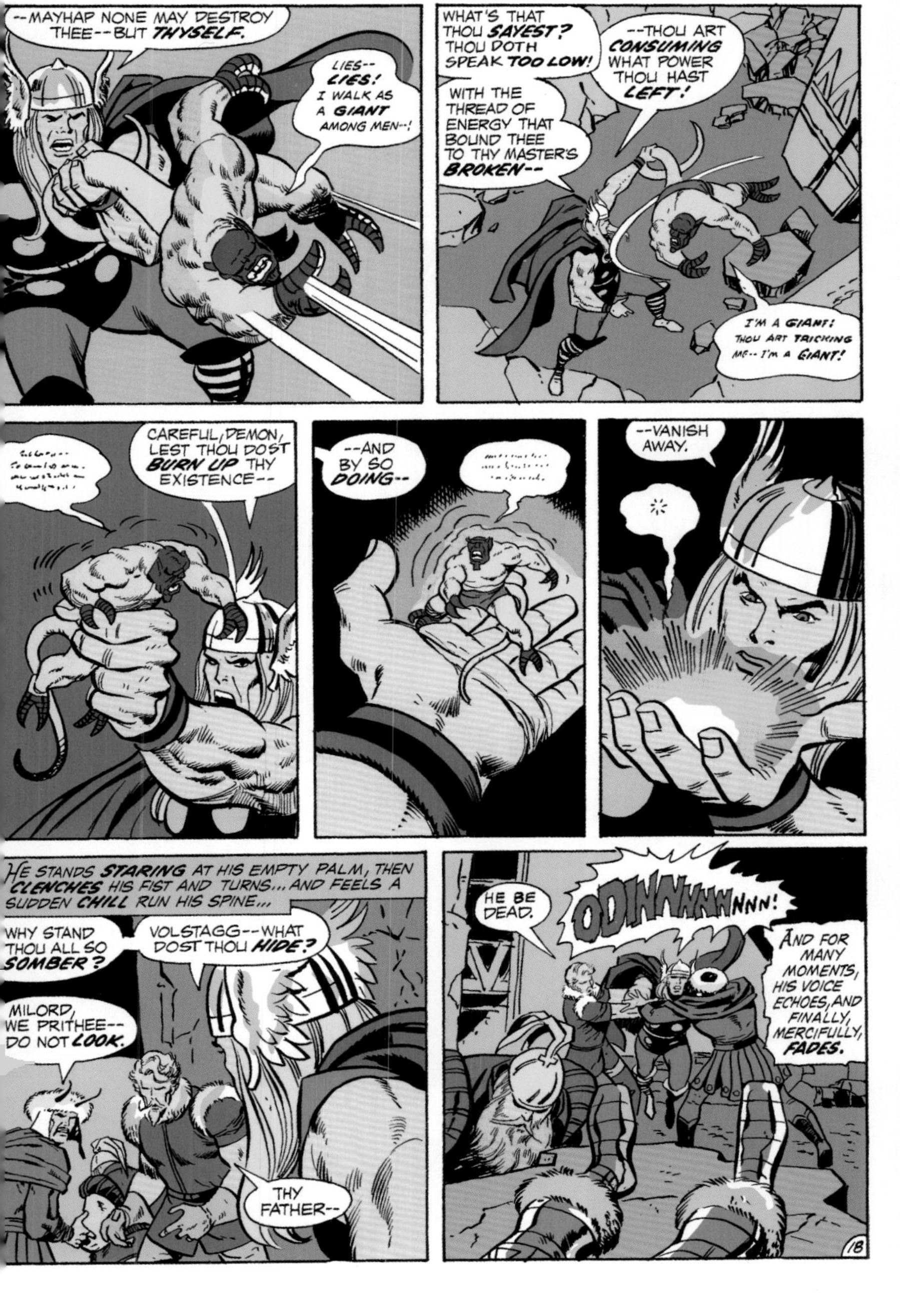

--MAYHAP NONE MAY DESTROY THEE--BUT THYSELF.
LIES--LIES! I WALK AS A GIANT AMONG MEN--!
WHAT'S THAT THOU SAYEST? THOU DOTH SPEAK TOO LOW!
--THOU ART CONSUMING WHAT POWER THOU HAST LEFT!
WITH THE THREAD OF ENERGY THAT BOUND THEE TO THY MASTER'S BROKEN--
I'M A GIANT! THOU ART TRICKING ME--I'M A GIANT!
CAREFUL, DEMON, LEST THOU DOST BURN UP THY EXISTENCE--
--AND BY SO DOING--
--VANISH AWAY.
HE STANDS STARING AT HIS EMPTY PALM, THEN CLENCHES HIS FIST AND TURNS... AND FEELS A SUDDEN CHILL RUN HIS SPINE...
WHY STAND THOU ALL SO SOMBER?
VOLSTAGG--WHAT DOST THOU HIDE?
MILORD, WE PRITHEE--DO NOT LOOK.
THY FATHER--
HE BE DEAD.
ODINNNNNNNNN!
AND FOR MANY MOMENTS, HIS VOICE ECHOES, AND FINALLY, MERCIFULLY, FADES.
18

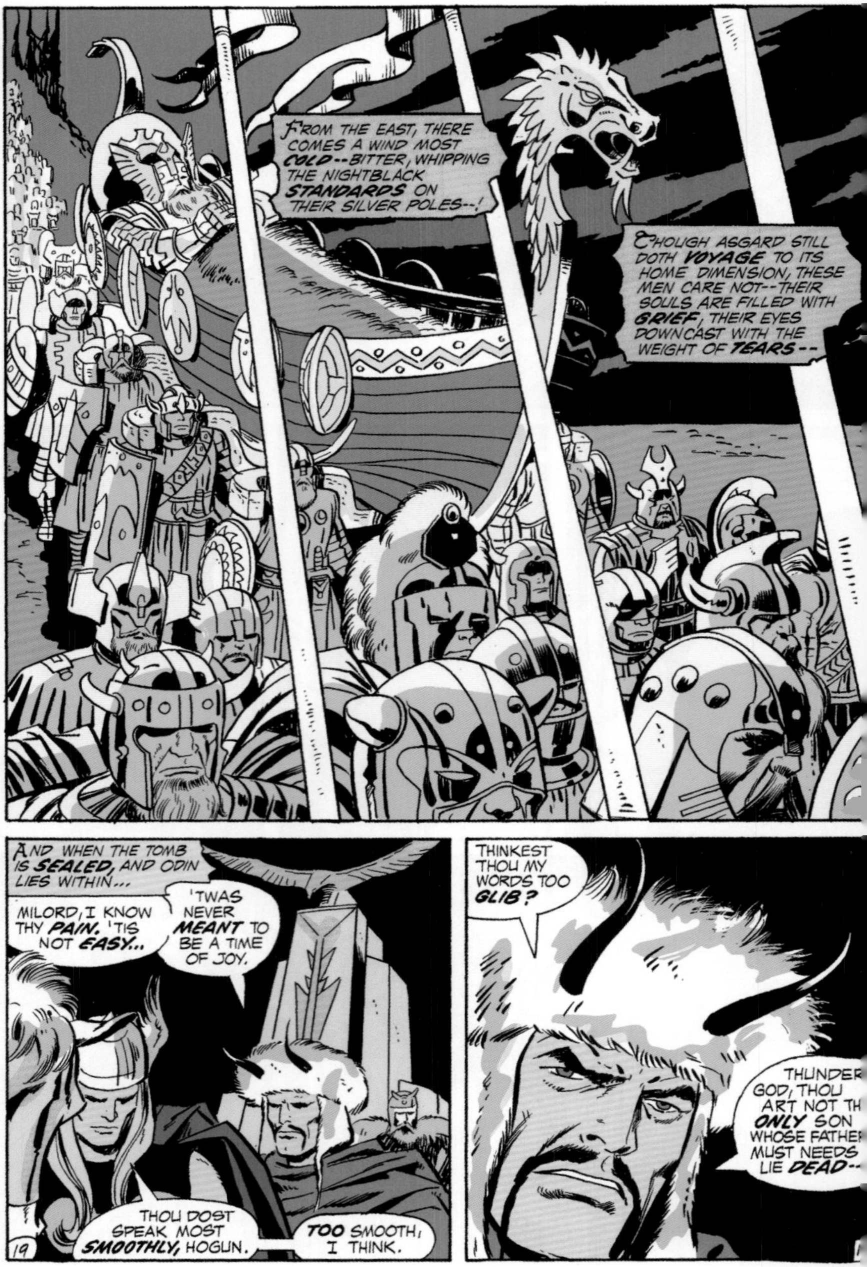

FROM THE EAST, THERE COMES A WIND MOST COLD--BITTER, WHIPPING THE NIGHTBLACK STANDARDS ON THEIR SILVER POLES--!
THOUGH ASGARD STILL DOTH VOYAGE TO ITS HOME DIMENSION, THESE MEN CARE NOT--THEIR SOULS ARE FILLED WITH GRIEF, THEIR EYES DOWNCAST WITH THE WEIGHT OF TEARS--
AND WHEN THE TOMB IS SEALED, AND ODIN LIES WITHIN...
MILORD, I KNOW THY PAIN. 'TIS NOT EASY...
'TWAS NEVER MEANT TO BE A TIME OF JOY.
THOU DOST SPEAK MOST SMOOTHLY, HOGUN.
TOO SMOOTH, I THINK.
19
THINKEST THOU MY WORDS TOO GLIB?
THUNDER GOD, THOU ART NOT TH ONLY SON WHOSE FATHER MUST NEEDS LIE DEAD--

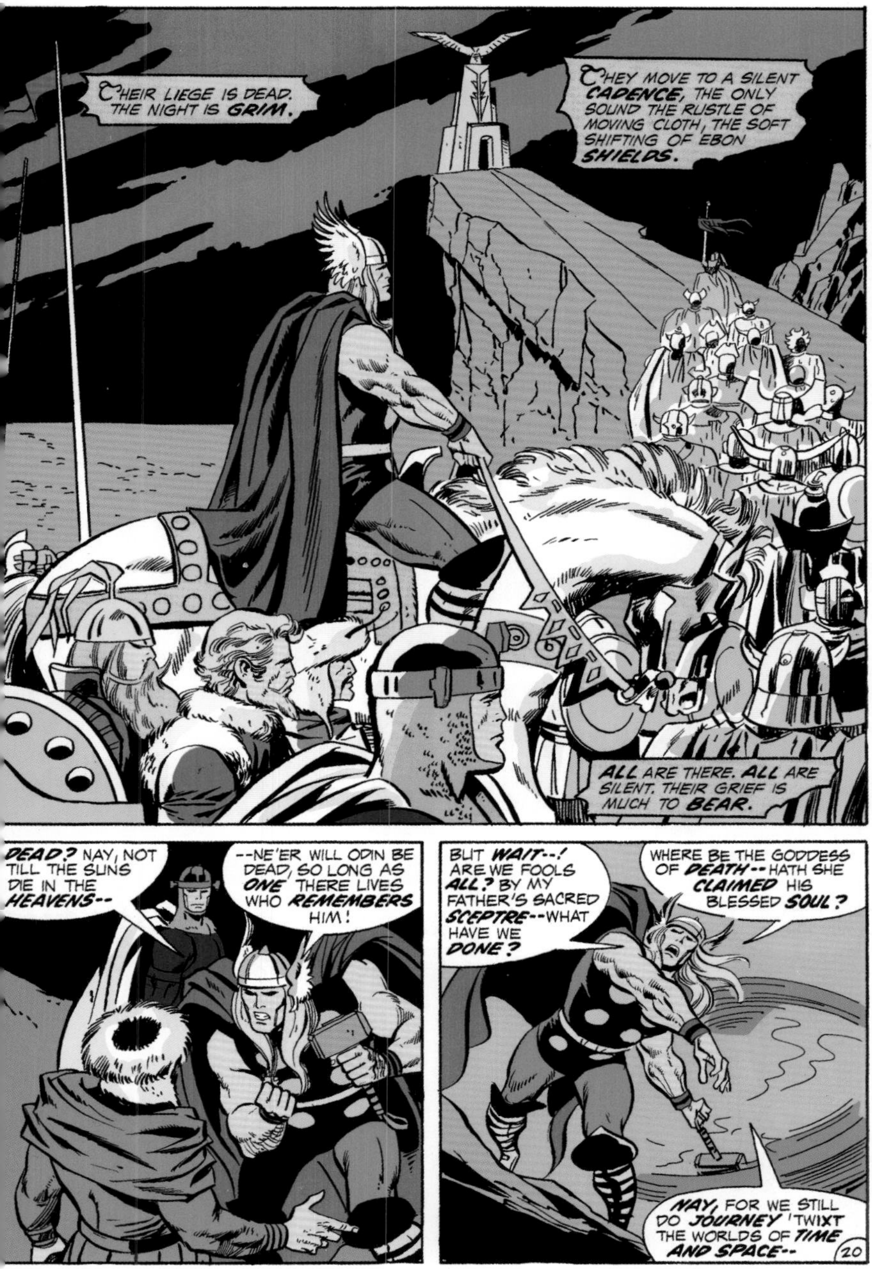
THEIR LIEGE IS DEAD. THE NIGHT IS GRIM.
THEY MOVE TO A SILENT CADENCE, THE ONLY SOUND THE RUSTLE OF MOVING CLOTH, THE SOFT SHIFTING OF EBON SHIELDS.
ALL ARE THERE. ALL ARE SILENT. THEIR GRIEF IS MUCH TO BEAR.
DEAD? NAY, NOT TILL THE SUNS DIE IN THE HEAVENS--
--NE'ER WILL ODIN BE DEAD, SO LONG AS ONE THERE LIVES WHO REMEMBERS HIM!
BUT WAIT--! ARE WE FOOLS ALL? BY MY FATHER'S SACRED SCEPTRE--WHAT HAVE WE DONE?
WHERE BE THE GODDESS OF DEATH--HATH SHE CLAIMED HIS BLESSED SOUL?
NAY, FOR WE STILL DO JOURNEY 'TWIXT THE WORLDS OF TIME AND SPACE--
20

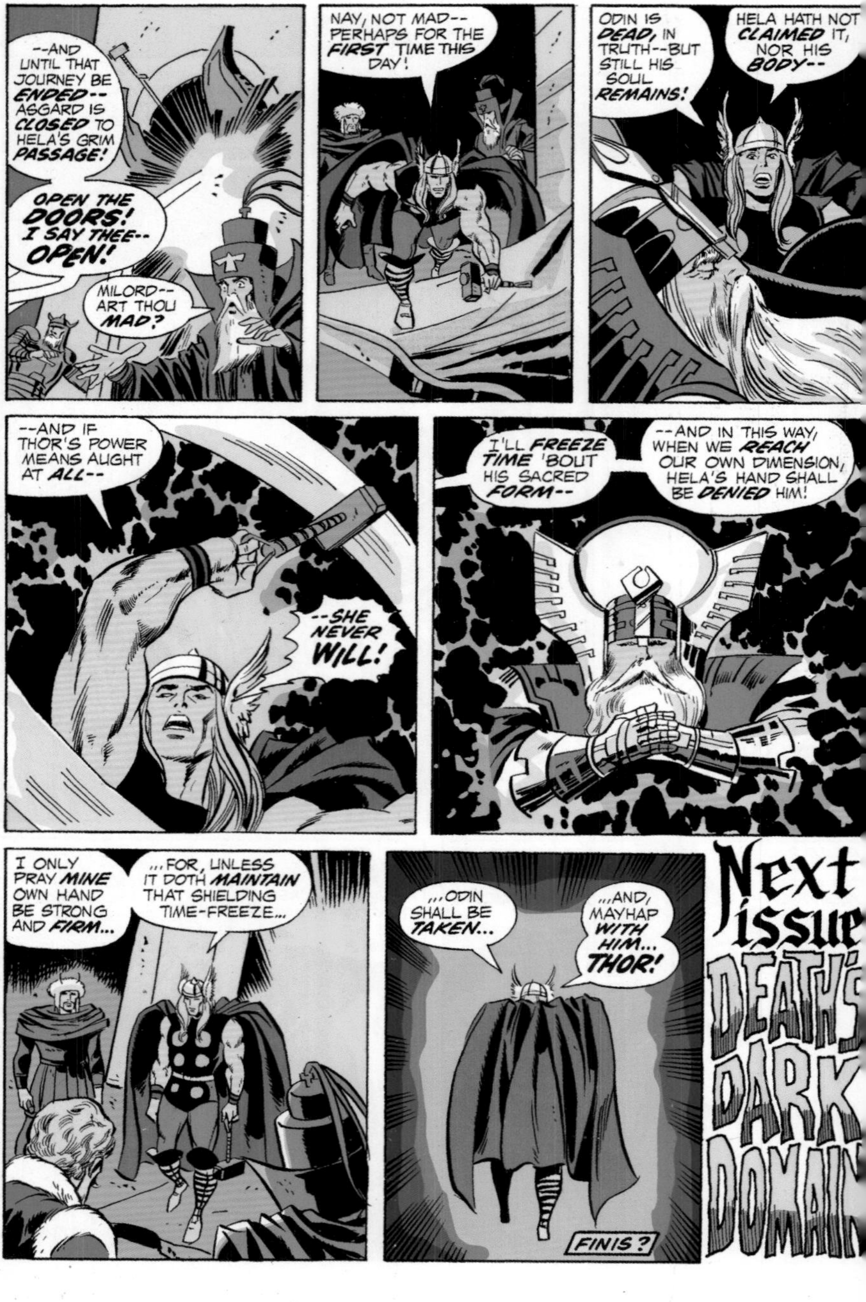
--AND UNTIL THAT JOURNEY BE ENDED-- ASGARD IS CLOSED TO HELA'S GRIM PASSAGE!
OPEN THE DOORS! I SAY THEE-- OPEN!
MILORD-- ART THOU MAD?
NAY, NOT MAD-- PERHAPS FOR THE FIRST TIME THIS DAY!
ODIN IS DEAD, IN TRUTH--BUT STILL HIS SOUL REMAINS!
HELA HATH NOT CLAIMED IT, NOR HIS BODY--
--AND IF THOR'S POWER MEANS AUGHT AT ALL--
--SHE NEVER WILL!
I'LL FREEZE TIME 'BOUT HIS SACRED FORM--
--AND IN THIS WAY, WHEN WE REACH OUR OWN DIMENSION, HELA'S HAND SHALL BE DENIED HIM!
I ONLY PRAY MINE OWN HAND BE STRONG AND FIRM...
...FOR, UNLESS IT DOTH MAINTAIN THAT SHIELDING TIME-FREEZE...
...ODIN SHALL BE TAKEN...
...AND, MAYHAP WITH HIM... THOR!
FINIS?
Next issue
DEATH'S DARK DOMAIN